C000143784

ISBN 978-1-331-39536-2
PIBN 10184231

This book is a reproduction of an important historical work. Forgotten Books uses
state-of-the-art technology to digitally reconstruct the work, preserving the original format
whilst repairing imperfections present in the aged copy. In rare cases, an imperfection in
the original, such as a blemish or missing page, may be replicated in our edition. We do,
however, repair the vast majority of imperfections successfully; any imperfections that
remain are intentionally left to preserve the state of such historical works.

1 MONTH OF
FREE
READING

at

www.ForgottenBooks.com

By purchasing this book you are eligible for one month membership to ForgottenBooks.com, giving you unlimited access to our entire collection of over 700,000 titles via our web site and mobile apps.

To claim your free month visit:

www.forgottenbooks.com/free184231

Similar Books Are Available from
www.forgottenbooks.com

HEARINGS

BEFORE THE

SUBCOMMITTEE ON OCEANOGRAPHY

OF THE

COMMITTEE ON MERCHANT MARINE AND FISHERIES

HOUSE OF REPRESENTATIVES

NINETY-FOURTH CONGRESS

ON

H.R. 1270, H.R. 6017, H.R. 11879

BILLS TO PROMOTE THE CONSERVATION AND ORDERLY DEVELOPMENT OF HARD MINERAL RESOURCES OF THE DEEP SEABED, PENDING ADOPTION OF AN INTERNATIONAL REGIME RELATING THERETO

MAY 16, 1975; FEBRUARY 23, 24, MARCH 8, AND 9, 1976

Serial No. 94–27

Printed for the use of the Committee on Merchant Marine and Fisheries

U.S. GOVERNMENT PRINTING OFFICE
73–794   WASHINGTON : 1976

COMMITTEE ON MERCHANT MARINE AND FISHERIES

LEONOR K. (MRS. JOHN B.) SULLIVAN, Missouri, *Chairman*

THOMAS L. ASHLEY, Ohio
JOHN D. DINGELL, Michigan
THOMAS N. DOWNING, Virginia
PAUL G. ROGERS, Florida
JOHN M. MURPHY, New York
WALTER B. JONES, North Carolina
ROBERT L. LEGGETT, California
MARIO BIAGGI, New York
GLENN M. ANDERSON, California
E (KIKA) DE LA GARZA, Texas
RALPH H. METCALFE, Illinois
JOHN B. BREAUX, Louisiana
FRED B. ROONEY, Pennsylvania
PAUL S. SARBANES, Maryland
BO GINN, Georgia
GERRY E. STUDDS, Massachusetts
DAVID R. BOWEN, Mississippi
JOSHUA EILBERG, Pennsylvania
RON DE LUGO, Virgin Islands
CARROLL HUBBARD, JR., Kentucky
DON BONKER, Washington
LES AUCOIN, Oregon
NORMAN E. D'AMOURS, New Hampshire
JERRY M. PATTERSON, California
LEO C. ZEFERETTI, New York
JAMES L. OBERSTAR, Minnesota

PHILIP E. RUPPE, Michigan
CHARLES A. MOSHER, Ohio
PAUL N. McCLOSKEY, JR., California
GENE SNYDER, Kentucky
EDWIN B. FORSYTHE, New Jersey
PIERRE S. (PETE) DU PONT, Delaware
DAVID C. TREEN, Louisiana
JOEL PRITCHARD, Washington
DON YOUNG, Alaska
ROBERT E. BAUMAN, Maryland
NORMAN F. LENT, New York
MATTHEW J. RINALDO, New Jersey
DAVID F. EMERY, Maine

ERNEST J. CORRADO, *Chief Counsel*
FRANCES STILL, *Chief Clerk*
RICHARD N. SHAROOD, *Chief Minority Counsel*

SUBCOMMITTEE ON OCEANOGRAPHY

JOHN M. MURPHY, New York, *Chairman*

THOMAS L. ASHLEY, Ohio
THOMAS N. DOWNING, Virginia
PAUL G. ROGERS, Florida
WALTER B. JONES, North Carolina
RALPH H. METCALFE, Illinois
JOHN B. BREAUX, Louisiana
LES AUCOIN, Oregon
GLENN M. ANDERSON, California
E (KIKA) DE LA GARZA, Texas
BO GINN, Georgia
GERRY E. STUDDS, Massachusetts
NORMAN E. D'AMOURS, New Hampshire
LEO C. ZEFERETTI, New York
JAMES L. OBERSTAR, Minnesota
LEONOR K. SULLIVAN, Missouri, *ex officio*

CHARLES A. MOSHER, Ohio
EDWIN B. FORSYTHE, New Jersey
PIERRE S. (PETE) DU PONT, Delaware
DAVID C. TREEN, Louisiana
ROBERT E. BAUMAN, Maryland
NORMAN F. LENT, New York
PHILIP E. RUPPE, Michigan, *ex officio*

CARL L. PERIAN, *Professional Staff Member*
JULIA P. PERIAN, *Professional Staff Member*
GRANT WAYNE SMITH, *Professional Staff, Minority*

(II)

CONTENTS

DEEP SEABED MINING

FRIDAY, MAY 16, 1975

U.S. House of Representatives,
Committee on Merchant Marine and Fisheries,
Subcommittee on Oceanography
Washington, D.C.

The subcommittee met, pursuant to call, at 9:25 a.m., in room 1334, Longworth Office Building, Hon. John M. Murphy [chairman of the subcommittee], presiding.

Mr. Murphy. The subcommittee will please come to order.

Today, we are meeting to discuss the recently concluded Geneva session of the Law of the Sea Conference.

We are going to concentrate on the negotiations in the first committee that deals with deep seabed mineral recovery.

I point out that the final working document that emerged on the last day of the conference that will supposedly form the basis of future Law of the Sea negotiations has been termed an unmitigated disaster for this country by members of the U.S. delegation.

United States' firms currently enjoy a technological lead in the deep seabed and are now working diligently to develop this infant industry into a viable, healthy part of the U.S. economy.

Two L.O.S. Delegates representing the American seabed mining industry will testify today. The future of these companies in the area of the retrieval of seabed resources is deeply intertwined with the L.O.S. Treaty which appears to be contrary to the interests of the United States and calculated to decimate the technology and skilled teams that several American firms have assembled to begin the exploration and exploitation of the ocean floor.

The United States needs the minerals that exist in the seabed not only to provide jobs for our workers but also to provide basic raw materials for our industrial plants.

The seabed promises the potential of lower prices for these minerals which we now must import from other countries. With lower prices for raw materials, we will have lower prices for the final products made from those raw materials. Clearly, this will lead to a higher standard of living for the United States. But, lower prices not only help Americans—they also help improve the lot of the rest of the world, especially the poorest nations.

However, this heritage of mankind will not be realized if a handful of land-based producers succeeds in restricting the production of minerals from the seabed, or worse, are able to organize mineral production into a worldwide cartel.

We have seen the results of the OPEC cartel: higher prices, infla-
tion, long lines at gasoline stations, and a recession in the United
States and other industrialized countries.

We have also seen severe economic hardship in the poorest of developing countries which has been caused by OPEC.

What we want to determine through the hearings beginning today
is whether the Law of the Sea Conference is on the road to economic
dislocation for the United States and the rest of the world.

We would also like to find out if United States policy is unwilling-
ly helping those countries who want to form cartels and otherwise
restrict the supply of minerals from the seabed.

We have with us today Jack Flipse, the president of Deepsea Ventures and Mr. Marne Dubs, director of Kennecott's Ocean Resources
Department.

Mr. Flipse and Mr. Dubs are two of a small group of pioneers who
are trying to bring an infant industry into being, in the face of great
difficulty.

We are interested in their detailing the potential importance of
seabed mineral recovery to the United States and also the difficulty
which the industry faces as a result of the Law of the Sea
Conference.

We also have with us Leigh S. Ratiner, the Ocean Mining Administrator for the Department of the Interior and the U.S. Representative on Committee One.

We would like to hear from him on the objectives of those coun
tries who oppose us in the deep seabed negotiations, the chances of
persuading them to take reasonable positions on the seabed mining
issue and the alternatives to the Law of the Sea negotiations if it
appears unlikely that we can get an agreement on the deep seabed
which our industry can live with.

This is the beginning of a series of hearings to determine the need
for and the type of unilateral legislation America needs to avoid the
kind of international economic strangulation which faces us if we
continue to attempt to achieve a binding treaty with countries, too
many of whom are obviously not dealing in good faith.

I ask unanimous consent that the informal single negotiating text
dated May 7, 1975, from Committee One be included at this point in
the record.

[The text referred to follows:]

UNITED NATIONS THIRD CONFERENCE ON THE LAW OF THE SEA

INFORMAL SINGLE NEGOTIATING TEXT PRESENTED BY THE CHAIRMAN
OF THE FIRST COMMITTEE

Note by the President of the Conference

At its 55th plenary meeting on Friday 18 April 1975 the Conference decided to
request the Chairman of its three Main Committees each to prepare a single
negotiating text covering the subjects entrusted to his Committee. In his concluding statement, before the Conference made this request, the President
stressed that the single text should take account of all the formal and informal
discussions held so far, would be informal in character and would not prejudice
the position of any delegation nor would it represent any negotiated text or
accepted compromise. It should, therefore, be quite clear that the single negotiating text will serve as a procedural device and only provide a basis for negoti-

ation. It must not in any way be regarded as affecting either the status of proposals already made by delegations or the right of delegations to submit amendments or new proposals.

CONVENTION ON THE SEA-BED AND THE OCEAN FLOOR AND THE SUB-SOIL THEREOF BEYOND THE LIMITS OF NATIONAL JURISDICTION

Part I

INTERPRETATION

Article 1

For the purposes of this Convention
(i) "States Parties" to this Convention means Contracting Parties.
(ii) "Activities in the Area" means all activities of exploration of the Area and of the exploitation of its resources, as well as other associated activities in the Area including scientific research.
(iii) "Resources" means resources *in situ.*
(iv) Mineral resources means any of the following categorisation:
(a) liquid or gaseous substances such as petroleum, gas, condensate, helium, nitrogen, carbon dioxide, water, steam, hot water, and also sulphur and salts extracted in liquid form in solution;
(b) useful minerals occurring on the surface of the sea-bed or at depths of less than three meters beneath the surface and also concretions of phosphorites and other minerals;
(c) solid minerals in the ocean floor at depths of more than three meters from the surface;
(d) ore-bearing silt and brine.

Part II: Principles

THE AREA AND ITS LIMITS

Article 2

1. This Convention shall apply to the sea-bed and ocean floor and subsoil thereof beyond the limits of national jurisdiction, hereinafter called the "Area".
2. States Parties to this Convention shall notify the International Seabed Authority established pursuant to Article 21 (hereinafter called the "Authority"), of the limits referred to in paragraph 1 of this article defined in this Convention and determined by co-ordinates of latitude and longitude and shall indicate the same on appropriate large scale charts officially recognised by that State.
3. The Authority shall register and publish such notification in accordance with rules adopted by it for the purpose.
4. Nothing in this article shall affect the validity of any agreement between States with respect to the establishment of limits between opposite or adjacent States.

COMMON HERITAGE OF MANKIND

Article 3

The Area and its resources are the common heritage of mankind.

NO CLAIM OR EXERCISE OF SOVEREIGNTY OR OTHER RIGHTS

Article 4

1. No State shal claim or exercise sovereignty or sovereign rights over any part of the Area or its resources, nor shall any State or person, natural or juridical, appropriate any part thereof. No such claim or exercise of sovereignty or sovereign rights, nor such appropriation shall be recognized.
2. States or persons, natural or juridical, shall claim, acquire or exercise rights with respect to the minerals in their raw or processed form derived from the Area only in accordance with the provisions of this Convention. Otherwise, no such claim, acquisition or exercise of rights shall be recognized.

GENERAL CONDUCT IN THE AREA AND IN RELATION TO THE AREA

Article 5

States shal act in, and in relation to, the Area in accordance with the provisions of this Convention and the United Nations Charter in the interests of maintaining international peace and security and promoting international co-operation and mutual understanding.

ACTIVITIES IN THE AREA

Article 6

Activities in the Area shall be governed by the provisions of this Convention and shall be subject to regulation and supervision by the Authority as provided herein. No such activities shall be carried out except in accordance with such regulations and the provisions of this Convention.

BENEFIT OF MANKIND AS A WHOLE

Article 7

Activities in the Area shall be carried out for the benefit of mankind as a whole, irrespective of the geographical location of States, whether coastal or land-locked, and taking into particular consideration the interests and needs of the developing countries.

RESERVATION AND USE OF THE AREA EXCLUSIVELY FOR PEACEFUL PURPOSES

Article 8

1. The Area shall be reserved exclusively for peaceful purposes.
2. The Area shall be open to use exclusively for peaceful purposes by all States Parties, whether coastal or land-locked, without discrimination, in accordance with the provisions of this Convention, and regulations made thereunder.

GENERAL PRINCIPLES REGARDING ACTIVITIES IN THE AREA

Article 9

1. The development and use of the Area shall be undertaken in such a manner as to:
   (a) foster the healthy development of the world economy and a balanced growth in international trade; and
   (b) avoid or minimize any adverse effects on the revenues and econo-mies of the developing countries, resulting from a substantial decline in their export earnings from minerals and other raw materials originating in their territory which are also derived from the Area.
2. Activities in the Area shall be carried out in an efficient manner to ensure:
   (a) orderly and safe development and rational management of the Area and its resources;
   (b) expanding opportunities in the use thereof;
   (c) conservation and utilization of the resources of the Area for optimum benefit of producers and consumers of raw materials and of products made from them;
   (d) equitable sharing in the benefits derived therefrom, taking into particular consideration the interests and needs of the developing countries, whether land-locked or coastal.

SCIENTIFIC RESEARCH

Article 10

1. Scientific research provided for in this Convention shall be carried out ex-clusively for peaceful purposes and for the benefit of mankind as a whole. The Authority shall be the centre for harmonizing and co-ordinating scientific research.
2. The Authority may itself conduct scientific research and may enter into agreements for that purpose.
3. States Parties shall promote international co-operation in scientific re-search in the Area exclusively for peaceful purposes by:
   (a) participation in international programmes and encouraging co-operation in scientific research by personnel of different countries and of the Authority;
   (b) ensuring that programmes are developed through the Authority for the benefit of developing countries and technologically less developed coun-tries with a view to
   (i) strengthening their research capabilities;

(ii) training their nationals and the personnel of the Authority in the techniques and applications of research;

(iii) fostering the employment of their qualified personnel in activities of research in the Area;

(c) effective publication of research programmes and dissemination of the results of research through the Authority.

TRANSFER OF TECHNOLOGY
Article 11

1. The Authority and through it States Parties to this Convention shall take necessary measures for promoting the transfer of technology and scientific knowledge relating to activities in the Area so that all States benefit therefrom. In particular, they shall promote:

(a) Programmes for the promotion of transfer of technology to developing countries with regard to activities in the Area, including, *inter alia* facilitating the access of developing countries to patented and non-patented technology, under just and reasonable conditions;

(b) Measures directed towards the acceleration of domestic technology of developing countries and the opening of opportunities to personnel from developing countries for training in marine science and technology and their full participation in activities in the Area.

PROTECTION OF THE MARINE ENVIRONMENT
Article 12

With respect to activities in the Area, appropriate measures shall be taken for the adoption and implementation of international rules, standards and procedures for, *inter alia:*

(a) The prevention of pollution and contamination, and other hazards to the marine environment, including the coastline, and of interference with the ecological balance of the marine environment, particular attention being paid to the need for protection from the consequences of such activities as drilling, dredging, excavation, disposal of waste, construction and operation or maintenance of installations, pipelines and other devices related to such activities;

(b) The protection and conservation of the natural resources in the Area and the prevention of damage to the flora and fauna of the marine environment.

PROTECTION OF HUMAN LIFE
Article 13

With respect to activities in the Area, the Authority and States shall take appropriate measures for the adoption and implementation of international rules, standards and procedures for the protection of human life to supplement existing international law and any specific treaties which may be applicable.

RIGHTS OF COASTAL STATES
Article 14

1. Activities in the Area, with respect to resources in the Area which lie across limits of national jurisdiction, shall be conducted with due regard to the rights and legitimate interests of any coastal State across whose jurisdiction such resources lie.

Consultations, including a system of prior notification, shall be maintained with the State concerned, with a view to avoiding infringement of such rights and interests.

2. Neither the provisions of this Convention nor any rights granted or exercised pursuant thereto shall affect the rights of coastal States to take such measures in accordance with applicable principles of international law as may be necessary to prevent, mitigate or eliminate grave and imminent danger to their coastlines or related interests from pollution or threat thereof or from other hazardous occurrences resulting from or caused by any activities in the Area.

LEGAL STATUS OF THE SUPERJACENT WATERS AND AIRSPACE
Article 15

Neither the provisions of this Convention nor any rights granted or exercised pursuant thereto shall affect the legal status of the waters superjacent to the Area or that of the airspace above those waters.

ACCOMMODATION OF ACTIVITIES IN THE AREA AND IN THE MARINE ENVIRONMENT

Article 16

1. Activities in the Area shall be carried out with reasonable regard for other activities in the marine environment.

2. Stationary and mobile installations relating to the conduct of activities in the Area shall be subject to the following conditions:

(i) Such installations shall be erected, emplaced and removed solely in accordance with the provisions of this Convention and subject to rules and regulations prescribed by the Authority. The erection, emplacement and removal of such installations shall be the subject of timely notification through Notices to Mariners or other generally recognized means of notification;

(ii) Such installations shall not be located in the Area where they may obstruct passage through sea lanes of vital importance for international shipping or in areas of intense fishing activity;

(iii) Safety zones shall be established around such installations with appropriate markings to ensure the safety both of the installations themselves and of shipping. The configuration and location of such safety zones shall not be such as to form a belt impeding the lawful access of shipping to particular maritime zones or navigation along international sea lanes;

(iv) Such installations shall be used exclusively for peaceful purposes;

(v) Such installations shall not possess the status of islands. They shall have no territorial sea, nor shall their presence affect the determination of territorial or jurisdictional limits of any kind.

3. Other activities in the marine environment shall be conducted with reasonable regard for activities in the Area.

RESPONSIBILITY TO ENSURE COMPLIANCE AND LIABILITY FOR DAMAGE

Article 17

1. Every State shall have the responsibility to ensure that activities in the Area, whether undertaken by governmental agencies, or non-governmental entities or persons under its jurisdiction, or acting on its behalf, shall be carried out in conformity with the provisions of this Convention. The same responsibility applies to international organizations and their members for activities in the Area undertaken by such organizations or on their behalf. Damage caused by such activities shall entail liability on the part of the State or international organization concerned, in respect of activities which it undertakes itself or authorizes.

2. A group of States or a group of international organizations, acting together shall be jointly and severally responsible under these articles.

3. Every State shall take appropriate measures to ensure that the responsibility provided for in paragraph 1 of this article shall apply *mutatis mutandis* to international organizations, of which it is a member.

PARTICIPATION OF DEVELOPING COUNTRIES, INCLUDING LAND-LOCKED AND OTHER GEOGRAPHICALLY DISADVANTAGED STATES

Article 18

Participation in the activities in the Area of developing countries, including the land-locked and other geographically disadvantaged States among them, shall be promoted, having due regard to their special needs and interests.

ARCHAELOGICAL AND HISTORICAL OBJECTS

Article 19

1. All objects of an archaelogical and historical nature found in the Area shall be preserved or disposed of by the Authority for the benefit of the international community as a whole, particular regard being paid to the preferential rights of the State of country of origin, or the State of cultural origin, or the State of historical and archaelogical origin.

2. The recovery and disposal of wrecks and their contents more than 50 years old found in the Area shall be subject to regulation by the Authority without prejudice to the rights of the owner thereof.

3. Any dispute with regard to a preferential right under paragraph 1 or a right of ownership under paragraph 2, shall, on the application of either party, be subject to the procedure for settlement of disputes provided for in this Convention.

Part II: The International Sea-Bed Authority

ESTABLISHMENT OF THE INTERNATIONAL SEA-BED AUTHORITY

Article 20

1. There is hereby established the International Sea-bed Authority which shall function in accordance with the provisions of this Convention.
2. All States Parties to this Convention are members of the Authority
3. The seat of the Authority shall be at Jamaica.
4. The Authority may establsh such regional centres or offices as it deems necessary for the performance of its functions.

NATURE AND FUNDAMENTAL PRINCIPLES OF THE FUNCTIONING OF THE AUTHORITY

Article 21

1. The Authority is the organization through which States Parties shall administer the Area, manage its resources and control the activities of the area in accordance with the provisions of this Convention.
2. The Authority is based on the principle of the sovereign equality of all of its Members.
3. All Members, in order to ensure to all of them the rights and benefits resulting from membership, shall fulfill in good faith the obligations assumed by them in accordance with this Convention.

FUNCTIONS OF THE AUTHORITY

Article 22

1. Activities in the Area shall be conducted directly by the Authority.
2. The Authority may, if it considers it appropriate, and within the limits it may determine, carry out activities in the Area or any stage thereof through States Parties to this Convention, or State enterprises, or persons natural or juridical which possess the nationality of such States or are effectively controlled by them or their nationals, or any group of the foregoing, by entering into service contracts, or joint ventures or any other such form of association which ensures this direct and effective control at all times over such activities.
3. Notwithstanding the provisions of paragraphs (1) and (2) of this article and in order to promote earliest possible commencement of activities in the area, the Authority, through the Council shall:
   (i) identify as early as practicable after coming into force of this Convention ten economically viable mining sites in the Area for exploration and exploitation of no more than . . . (size, etc.) ;
   (ii) enter into joint ventures in respect of these sites with States Parties to this Convention or State-enterprises or persons natural and juridical which possess the nationality of such States or are effectively controlled by them or their nationals or any group of the foregoing. Such joint ventures shall be subject to the conditions of exploration and exploitation established by and under this Convention and shall always ensure the direct and effective control of the Authority at all times.
4. In entering into such joint ventures as provided for in para. 3(ii) of this article, the Authority may decide on the basis of available data to reserve certain portions of the mining sites for its own further exploitation.

Article 23

1. In the exercise of its functions the Authority shall take measures pursuant to this Convention to promote and encourage activities in the Area and to secure the maximum financial and other benefit from them.
2. The Authority shall avoid discrimination in the granting of opportunities for such activities and shall, in the implementation of its powers, ensure that all rights granted pursuant to this Convention are fully safeguarded. Special consideration by the Authority under this Convention for the interests and needs of the developing countries, and particularly the land-locked among them, shall not be deemed to be discrimination.

3. The Authority shall ensure the equitable sharing by States in the benefits derived from activities in the Area, taking into particular consideration the interests and needs of the developing countries whether coastal or land-locked.

ORGANS OF THE AUTHORITY

Article 24

1. There are established as the principal organs of the Authority an Assembly, a Council, a Tribunal, an Enterprise and a Secretariat.

2. Such subsidiary organs as may be found necessary may be established in accordance with this Convention.

THE ASSEMBLY

Article 25

1. The Assembly shall consist of all the Members of the Authority.

° The Assembly shall meet in regular session every two years and in such special sessions as may be determined by the Assembly, or convened by the Secretary General at the request of the Council or of a majority of the Members of the Authority.

3. Sessions shall take place at the seat of the Authority unless otherwise determined by the Assembly. At such sessions, each member shall have one representative who may be accompanied by alternates and advisers.

4. The Assembly shall elect its President and such other officers as may be required at the beginning of each session. They shall hold office until the new President and other officers are elected at the next following session.

5. Each Member of the Assembly shall have one vote.

6. All decisions on questions of substance and the question whether a question is one of substance or procedure, shall be made by a two-thirds majority of the Members present and voting, provided that such majority shall include at least a majority of the Members of the Authority. Decisions on other questions shall be made by a majority of the Members present and voting.

7. A majority of the Members of the Assembly shall constitute a quorum.

8. Upon a written request to the President supported by not less than one-third of the Members of the Assembly, a vote on any matter before the Assembly shall be deferred pending reference to the Tribunal for an Advisory Opinion on any legal question connected therewith. Voting on such matter shall be stayed pending delivery of the Tribunal's Advisory Opinion, or for a period of six months from the receipt of the request, whichever is earlier.

POWERS AND FUNCTIONS OF THE ASSEMBLY

Article 26

1. The Assembly shall be the supreme policy-making organ of the Authority. It shall have the power to lay down general guidelines and issue general directions of a general character as to the policy to be pursued by the Council or other organs of the Authority on any questions or matters within the scope of this Convention. It may also discuss any questions or any matters within the scope of this Convention and make recommendations thereon.

2. In addition, the powers and functions of the Assembly shall include:

(i) Election of the members of the Council in accordance with article 28;

(ii) Appointment upon the recommendation of the Council, of the members of the Tribunal and of the Governing Board of the Enterprise;

(iii) Establishment, as appropriate, of such subsidiary organs as may be found necessary for the performance of its functions in accordance with the provisions of this Convention;

(iv) Assessment of the contributions of Parties to this Convention as necessary for meeting the administrative budget of the Authority;

(v) Adoption of the financial regulations of the Authority, including rules on borrowing;

(vi) Approval of the budget of the Authority on its submission by the Council;

(vii) Adoption of its rules of procedure;

(viii) Request and consideration of special reports from the Council and from the other organs of the Authority on any matter within the scope of this Convention;

(ix) Studies and recommendations for the purpose of promoting international co-operation concerning activities in the Area and encouraging the progressive development of international law relating thereto and its codification;

(x) Adoption of criteria, rules, regulations and procedures, for the equitable sharing of benefits derived from the Area and its resources, taking into special account the interests and needs of the developing countries, whether coastal or land-locked;

(xi) Consideration of problems arising from States in connection with activities in the Area, from the land-locked or otherwise geographically disadvantaged location of some of them and to recommend basic guidelines for appropriate action.

3. The powers and functions of the Authority not specifically entrusted to other organs of the Authority shall be vested in the Assembly.

THE COUNCIL

Article 27

1. The Council shall consist of 36 Members of the Authority elected by the Assembly; 24 to be elected in accordance with the principle of equitable geographical representation and 12 with a view to representation of special interests, taking into account the principle of equitable geographical representation, the election to take place in the following order:

(a) Six Members with substantial investment in, or possessing advanced technology which is being used for, the exploration of the Area and the exploitation of its resources, and Members which are major importers of landbased minerals which are also produced from the resources of the Area, provided only that at the first election at least one of these six members shall be from the Eastern (Socialist) European region.

(b) Six Members from among the developing countries, one being drawn from each of the following categories:

(i) States which are exporters of landbased minerals which may also be produced from the resources of the Area;

(ii) States which are importers of the minerals referred to in subparagraph (i);

(iii) States with large populations;

(iv) Land-locked States;

(v) Geographically disadvantaged States;

(vi) Least developed countries.

(c) Twenty-four Members in accordance with the principle of equitable geographical representation. For this purpose, the geographical regions shall be Africa, Asia, Eastern Europe, (Socialist), Latin America and "Western Europe and others".

2. Elections shall take place at regular sessions of the Assembly, and each member of the Council shall be elected for a term of 4 years. In the first election of members of the Council, however, eighteen members shall be chosen for a period of two years.

3. Members shall be eligible for re-election; but due regard should, as a rule, be paid to the desirability of rotating seats.

4. The Council shall function at the seat of the Authority, and shall meet as often as the business of the Authority may require, but not less than three times a year.

5. Each member of the Council shall have one vote.

6. Decisions on important questions shall be made by a two-thirds plus one majority of the members present and voting. The decision on an issue as to whether or not a matter is an important question shall be taken by a two-thirds majority. Decisions on other questions shall be decided by a majority of the members present and voting.

7. The Council shall establish a procedure whereby a Member of the Authority not represented on the Council may send a representative to attend a meeting of the Council when a request is made by such Member, or a matter particularly affecting it is under consideration. Such a representative shall be entitled to participate in the deliberations but not to vote.

POWERS AND FUNCTIONS OF THE COUNCIL

Article 28

The Council shall be the executive organ of the Authority. It shall exercise the powers and perform the functions entrusted to it by this Convention. In exercising such powers and performing such functions the Council shall act in a manner consistent with general guidelines and policy directions laid down by the Assembly.

The Council shall:

(i) Supervise and coordinate the implementation of the provisions of this Convention and, whenever it deems it appropriate, invite the attention of the Assemby to cases of non-compliance;

(ii) Recommend to the Assembly candidates for appointment to the Tribunal and to the Governing Board of the Enterprise;

(iii) Establish, as appropriate and with due regard to economy and efficiency, in addition to the Commissions provided for in article 30, such subsidiary organs as may be found necessary for the performance of its functions in accordance with the provisions of this Convention. In the composition of such subsidiary organs due regard shall be paid not only to the need for Members highly qualified and competent in the relevant technical matters which may arise in such organs but also to special interests and the principle of equitable geographical distribution;

(iv) Adopt its rules of procedure;

(v) Enter into agreements with the United Nations or other inter-governmental organisations on behalf of the Authority, subject to approval by the Assembly;

(vi) Transmit annually to the Assembly a schedule for apportionment of benefits derived from activities in the Area on the basis of criteria and rules adopted by the Assembly pursuant to sub-paragraph 1(x) of Article 26;

(vii) Transmit to the Assembly the reports of the Enterprise;

(viii) Transmit to the Assembly annual reports and such special reports as the Assembly may request;

(ix) Approve and supervise the carrying out of activities in the Area by the Enterprise;

(x) Approve on behalf of the Authority contracts for the conduct of activities in the Area and exercise direct and effective control over the activities in the Area;

(xi) Adopt, upon the recommendation of the Economic Planning Commission, programmes or measures to avoid or minimize adverse effects on the revenues of developing countries derived from the export of minerals and other products originating in their territories which are also derived from the resources of the Area. The Council shall ensure that developing countries importers of minerals or other products derived from the resources of the Area shall be given preferential access or favourable terms to such minerals and products;

(xii) Adopt, on the recommendation of the Technical Commission, rules, regulations and procedures and any amendments thereto concerning:

(a) technical, operational and financial matters relating to activities in the Area in accordance with the Basic Conditions annexed to this Convention;

(b) protection of human life and health;

(c) protection and preservation of the marine environment;

(d) discovery, identification, protection, acquisition and disposal of objects of archaeological and historical interest found in the Area:

(e) any other matters within the scope of the powers and functions of the Council.

(xiii) Arrange for and review the collection of all payments to be made by or to the Authority in connection with operations pursuant to this Convention;

(xiv) Make recommendations to the Assembly on the matters specified in sub-paragraph (ii) of paragraph 1 of Article 25 and Article 72, and, as appropriate, on any other matter within the scope of the functions of the Council;

(xv) Make recommendations to States concerning the policies and measures required to give effect to the principles of this Convention;

(xvi) Make recommendations to the Assembly concerning suspension of the privileges and rights of membership for gross and persistent violations of the provisions of this Convention.

ORGANS OF THE COUNCIL

Article 29

1. There are hereby established as organs of the Council an Economic Planning Commission, and a Technical Commission each of which shall be composed of fifteen members appointed by the Council with due regard to not only the need for Members highly qualified and competent in the technical matters which may arise in such organs but also to special interests and the principle of equitable geographical distribution.

2. The Council shall invite States Parties to this Convention to submit nominations for Appointment to each commission.

3. Appointment to each commission shall take place not less than sixty days before the end of a calendar year and the members of a commission shall hold office from the commencement of the next calendar year following their appointment until the end of the third calendar year thereafter. The first appointments to a commission, however, shall take place not less than thirty days after the entry into force of this Convention, and those so appointed shall hold office until the end of the calendar year next following the year of their appointment.

4. In the event of the death, incapacity or resignation of a member of a commission prior to the expiration of his term of office, the Council shall appoint a member from the same area or interest who shall hold office for the remainder of the previous member's term.

5. The Council shall appoint to the commission persons of high moral character who may be relied upon to exercise independent judgment. They shall serve in their individual capacity and shall receive such regular remuneration from the Authority as the Council shall from time to time determine. Members of a commission shall be eligible for re-appointment for one further term of office.

6. Each commission shall appoint its chairman and two vice-chairmen who shall hold office for one year.

7. The Council shall approve, on the recommendation of a commission, such rules and regulations as may be necessary for the efficient conduct of the functions of the commission.

8. Decisions shall be by a 2/3 majority of members of the Commission.

9. Each commission shall function at the seat of the Authority and shall meet as often as shall be required for the efficient performance of its functions.

THE ECONOMIC PLANNING COMMISSION

Article 30

1. Members of the Economic Planning Commission shall have appropriate qualifications and experience relevant to mining and the management of mineral resource activities, and international trade and finance.

2. The Economic Planning Commission, in consultation with the competent organs of the United Nations and the specialized agencies, shall review the trends of, and factors affecting, supply, demand and prices of raw materials which may be obtained from the Area and, bearing in mind the interests of both consuming and land-based mineral producing countries, and in particular the developing countries among them, make recommendations to the Council on programmes and measures with respect to the implementation of Article 22 of this Convention and in particular:

(a) Schedules of the extent of the Area or the volume of its resources which would be made availabe for exploitation; and

(b) Appropriate programmes or measures, including integrated commodity arrangements and buffer stock arrangements, to avoid or minimize adverse effects on developing countries whose economies substantially depend on the revenues derived from the export of minerals and other raw materials originating in their territories which are also derived from the resources of the Area under exploitation taking into account all sources of these minerals and raw materials.

3. The Commission shall advise the Council in the exercise of the Council's economic planning functions and make such special studies and reports on these functions as may be required by the Council from time to time.

4. Any State Party to this Convention whose *economy substantially depends on the export of minerals and other products originating in its territory which are also derived from minerals under exploitation in the Area* may bring to the

attention of the Economic Planning Commission a situation which is likely to lead to a substantial decline in its mineral export earnings. The Commission shall forthwith investigate this situation and shall make recommendations, in consultation with parties to this Convention and with the competent intergovernmental organizations to the Council in accordance with paragraph 2 of this article.

THE TECHNICAL COMMISSION

Article 31

1. Members of the Technical Commission shall have appropriate qualifications and experience in the management of sea-bed resources, ocean and marine engineering and mining and mineral processing technology ad practices, operating of related marine installations, equipment and devices, ocean and environmental sciences and maritime safety, accounting and actuarial techniques.

2. The Technical Commission shall:
(i) Formulate and submit to the Council the technical and operational rules, regulations and procedures referred to in paragraph (xiii) of Article 27;
(ii) Keep such rules, regulations and procedures under review and recommend to the Council from time to time such amendments thereto as it may deem necessary or desirable;
(iii) Make recommendations to the Council with regard to the carrying out of the Authority's functions with respect to scientific research and transfer of technology;
(iv) Prepare special studies and reports at the request of the Council;
(v) Prepare assessments of the environmental implications of activities in the area and consider and evaluate these implications before recommending the rules, regulations and procedures referred to in sub-paragraph (i) of this paragraph;
(vi) Supervise, on a regular basis, all operations with respect to activities in the Area, where appropriate in consultation and collaboration with any entity carrying out such activities or State or States concerned;
(vii) Notify the Council of any cases of failure to comply with the provisions of the present Convention, the rules, regulations and procedures prescribed thereunder and the terms and conditions of a contract, and make recommendations to the Council with respect to measures to be taken in that regard.

THE TRIBUNAL

Article 32

1. The Tribunal shall have jurisdiction with respect to:
(a) Any dispute relating to the interpretation or application of this Convention; and
(b) Any dispute connected with the subject matter of this Convention and submitted to it pursuant to a contract or arrangement entered into pursuant to this Convention.

2. The Tribunal shall exercise all powers and perform all functions referred to under articles 57, 58, 60, 61, 62 and 63.

3. The Tribunal shall be composed of a body of independent judges, elected regardless of their nationality from among persons of high moral character, who possess the qualifications required in their respective countries for appointment to the highest judicial offices, or are jurisconsults of recognized competence in law of the sea matters and other areas of international law.

4. The Tribunal shall consist of nine judges, five of whom shall constitute a quorum.

5. Members of the Tribunal shall be appointed by the Assembly on the recommendation of the Council from among candidates nominated by States Parties to this Convention. In appointing members of the Tribunal due regard shall be paid to the importance of assuring representation on the Tribunal of the principal legal systems of the world.

6. Members of the Tribunal hold office for five years and may be reappointed for one further term; provided that the terms of the four judges elected at the first election shall expire at the end of three years.

7. The Members of the Tribunal unless removed in accordance with paragraph 9 shall continue to discharge their duties until their places have been filled. Though replaced, they shall finish any cases which they may have begun.

8. Upon the occurrence of a vacancy in the Tribunal, the Council shall appoint a successor who shall hold office for the remainder of his predecessor's term, subject to the approval of the Assembly at its next regular session.

9. A member of the Tribunal may be removed from office by the Assembly, on the unanimous recommendation of the other members of the Tribunal and the approval of the Council.

10. The Tribunal shall establish its rules of procedure, elect its President annually, appoint a Registrar and such staff as may be necessary for the efficient discharge of its functions. The salaries and emoluments and terms of service of members of the Tribunal, and of its Registrar and staff, shall be determined by the Council.

Article 33

The Tribunal shall decide all disputes relating to the interpretation and application of this Part, the rules, regulations and procedures prescribed thereunder and the terms and conditions of any contracts entered into by the Authority which have been submitted to it, and shall render advisory opinions on the request of any organ of the Authority or as otherwise specifically provided in this Part.

Article 34

Nothing in the foregoing articles shall prevent Members of the Authority from settling their disputes by any other means prescribed by Article 57 of this Convention.

THE ENTERPRISE

Article 35

1. The Enterprise shall be the organ of the Authority which shall, subject to the general policy directions and supervision of the Council, undertake the preparation and execution of activities of the Authority in the Area, pursuant to Article 22. In the exercise of its functions, it may enter into appropriate agreements on behalf of the Authority.

2. The Enterprise shall have international legal personality and such legal capacity as may be necessary for the performance of its functions and the fulfillment of its purposes. The Enterprise shall function in accordance with the Statute set forth in Annex . . . to this Convention, and shall in all respects be governed by the provisions of this Convention. Appointment of the Members of the Governing Board under article 26(ii) of this Convention shall be made on the basis of equal representation of all geographical regions enumerated in artice 27(1)(c) and in accordance with the provisions of the Statute set forth in Annex II to this Convention.

3. Members of the Authority are *ipso facto* parties to the Statute of the Enterprise.

4. The Enterprise shall have its principal place of business at the seat of the Authority.

THE SECRETARIAT

Article 36

The Secretariat shall comprise a Secretary-General and such staff as the Authority may require. The Secretary-General shall be appointed by the Assembly upon the recommendation of the Council. He shall be the chief administrative officer of the Authority.

Article 37

The Secretary-General shall act in that capacity in all meetings of the Assembly and of the Council, and of any subsidiary organs established by them, and shall perform such other functions as are entrusted to him by any organ of the Authority. The Secretary-General shall make an annual report to the Assembly on the work of the organization.

Article 38

1. The staff of the Authority shall include such qualified scientific and technical and other personnel as may be required to fulfill the objective and functions of the Authority. The Authority shall be guided by the principle that its permanent staff shall be kept to a minimum.

2. The paramount consideration in the recruitment and employment of the staff and in the determination of their conditions of service shall be to secure

employees of the highest standards of efficiency, competence and integrity. Subject to this consideration, due regard shall be paid to the importance of recruiting staff on as wide a geographical basis as possible.

3 The staff shall be appointed by the Secretary-General. The terms and conditions on which the staff shall be appointed, remunerated and dismissed shall be in accordance with regulations made by the Council, and to general rules approved by the Assembly on the recommendation of the Council.

Article 39

In the performance of their duties, the Secretary-General and the staff shall not seek or receive instructions from any government or from any other source external to the Authority. They shall refrain from any action which might reflect on their position as international officials of the Authority responsible only to the Authority. They shall have no financial interest whatsoever in any activity relating to exploration and exploitation in the Area. Subject to their responsibilities to the Authority, they shall not disclose any industrial secret or data declared by the Authority to be proprietary or other confidential information coming to their knowledge by reason of their official duties for the Authority. Each Party to this Convention undertakes to respect the exclusively international character of the responsibilities of the Secretary-General and the staff and not to seek to influence them in the discharge of their responsibilities.

Article 40

1. The Authority shall, as necessary, establish a staff of inspectors. The staff of inspectors shall have the responsibility of examining all activitie in the Area to determine whether the provisions of this Convention, the rules, regulations and procedures prescribed thereunder, and the terms and conditions of any contract with the Authority pursuant to this Convention are being complied with.

2. The inspectors shall report any non-compliance to the Secretary-General. The Secretary-General shall immediately notify the Chairman of the Council and of the Technical Commission.

Article 41

1. The Secretary-General may send into the territory of a party to this Convention and into the Area and any installation established therein, inspectors after consultation with the parties concerned. The inspectors shall have access at all times to all places and data and to any person who deals with any activity in the Area pursuant to this Convention, and to any books of account and records kept with respect to such activity.

2. Inspectors shall, upon request made to the Secretary-General, be accompanied by representatives of any State Party to this Convention and any party involved, provided that the inspectors shall not thereby be delayed or otherwise impeded in the exercise of their functions.

Part III: Finance

Article 42

The Assembly shall establish the General Fund of the Authority.

All receipts of the Authority arising from activities in the Area, including any excess of revenues of the Enterprise over its expenses and costs in such proportion as the Council shall determine shall be paid into the General Fund.

Article 43

The Council shall submit to the Assembly annual budget estimates for the expenses of the Authority. To facilitate the work of the Council in this regard, the Secretary-General shall initially prepare the budget estimates. If the Assembly does not approve the estimates, it shall return them together with its recommendations, to the Council. The Council shall then submit further estimates to the Assembly for its approval.

Article 44

1. Expenses of the Authority comprise:

    (a) administrative expenses, which shall incude costs of the staff of the Authority, costs of meetings, and expenditure on account of the functioning of the organs of the Authority.

(b) expenses not incuded in the foregoing, incurred by the Authority in carrying out the functions entrusted to it under this Convention; and

(c) the expenditure of the Enterprise, to the extent that it cannot be met out of the Enterprise's own revenues and other receipts.

2. The expenses referred to in paragraph 1 of this article shall be met to an extent to be determined by the Assembly on the recommendation of the Council, out of the General Fund, the balance of such expenses to be met out of contributions by members of the Authority in accordance with a scale of assessment adopted by the Assembly pursuant to the sub-paragraph 1(iv) of Article 25.

Article 45

1. Any excess of revenues of the Authority over its expenses and costs to an extent determined by the Council, all payments received pursuant to Article 43 of this Convention and any voluntary contributions made by States Parties to this Convention shall be credited to a Special Fund.

2. Amounts in the Special Fund shall be apportioned and made available equitably in such manner and in such currencies, and otherwise in accordance with criteria, rules, regulations and procedures adopted by the Assembly pursuant to sub-paragraph 1(x) of Article 25.

Article 46

Subject to such limitations as may be approved by the Assembly in the financial regulations adopted by it pursuant to sub-paragraph 1(vi) of Article 25, the Council may exercise borrowing powers on behalf of the Authority without, however, imposing on members of the Authority any liability in respect of loans entered into pursuant to this paragraph, and accept voluntary contributions made to the Authority.

Article 47

The records, books and accounts of the Authority, including its annual financial statements, shall be subject to an annual audit by a recognized independent auditor.

STATUS, IMMUNITIES AND PRIVILEGES

Article 48

The Authority shall have full international legal personality, and such legal capacity as may be necessary for the exercise of its functions and the fulfillment of its purpose.

Article 49

To enable the Authority to fufill its functions it shall enjoy in the territory of each State Party to this Convention, the immunities and privileges set forth herein except as provided in annex   to this Convention with respect to operations of the Enterprise.

Article 50

The Authority, its property and assets, shall enjoy in the territory of each State Party to this Convention, immunity from legal process, except when the Authority waives its immunity.

Article 51

The property and assets of the Authority, wheresoever located and by whomsoever held, shall be immune from search, requisition, confiscation, expropriation or any other form of seizure by executive or legislative action.

Article 52

All property and assets of the Authority shall be free from restrictions, regulations, controls and moratoria of any nature.

Article 53

The President and members of the Assemby, the Chairman and members of the Council, members of any organ of the Assembly, or the Council, and members of the Tribunal, and the Secretary-General and staff of the Authority, shall enjoy in the territory of each member State:

(a) Immunity from legal process with respect to acts performed by them in the exercise of their functions, except when the Authority waives this immunity;

(b) Not being local nationals, the same immunities from immigration restrictions, alien registration requirements and national service obligations, the same facilities as regards exchange restrictions and the same treatment in respect of travelling facilities as are accorded by States Parties to this Convention to the representatives, officials and employees of comparable rank of other States Parties.

Article 54

The provisions of the preceding article shall apply to persons appearing in proceedings before the Tribunal as parties, agents, counsel, advocates, witnesses or experts; provided, however, that sub-paragraph (b) thereof shall apply only in connection with their travel to and from, and their stay at, the place where the proceedings are held.

Article 55

1. The archives of the Authority shall be inviolable, wherever they may be.
2. All proprietary data, industrial secrets or similar information and all personnel records shall not be placed in archives open to public inspection.
3. With regard to its official communications, the Authority shall be accorded by each State Party to this Convention treatment no less favourable than that accorded to other international organizations.

Article 56

1. The Authority, its assets, property and income, and its operations and transactions authorized by this Convention, shall be exempt from all taxation and customs duties. The Authority shall also be exempt from liability for the collection or payment of any taxes or customs duties.
2. Except in the case of local nationals, no tax shall be levied on or in respect of expense allowances paid by the Authority to the President or members of the Assembly, or in respect of salaries, expense allowances or other emoluments paid by the Authority to the Chairman and members of the Council, members of the Tribunal, members of any organ of the Assembly or of the Council and the Secretary-General and staff of the Authority.

SETTLEMENT OF DISPUTES

Article 57

When a dispute falling within article 32 of this Convention has arisen between States Parties to this Convention, or between such State Party and a national of another State Party, or between nationals of different States Parties, or between a State Party or a national of a State Party and the Authority or the Enterprise, the parties to the dispute shall first seek a solution through consultation, negotiation, conciliation or other such means of their own choice. If the dispute has not been resolved within one month of its commencement, any party to the dispute may institute proceedings before the Tribunal, unless the parties agree to submit the dispute to arbitration pursuant to article 63 of this Convention.

Article 58

1. Any State Party to this Convention which questions the legality of measures taken by the Council, or of any organ of the Council or the Assembly on grounds of a violation of this Convention, lack of jurisdiction, infringement of any fundamental rule of procedure or misuse of power, may bring the matter before the Tribunal.
2. The proceedings provided for in this article shall be instituted within one month of either the date of publication of the decision concerned of its notification to the complainant, or of the date on which he became aware of it.
3. If the Tribunal considers the complaint well-founded, it shall declare the decision concerned to be void, and shall determine what measures shall be taken to redress any damage caused.

Article 59

1. Judgements and orders of the Tribunal shall be final and binding. They shall be enforceable in the territories of Members of the Authority in the same way as judgments or orders of the highest court of that Member State.
2. If a Member of the Authority fails to perform its obligations under a judgment rendered by the Tribunal, the other party or parties to the dispute

may bring the matter before the Council which shall decide upon measures to be taken to give effect to the judgment.

Article 60

1. At any time after it is seized of the dispute, the Tribunal may, if it considers that the circumstances so require, order provisional measures for the purpose of preserving the respective rights of the parties, or preventing serious harm to the marine environment.

2. A party to the dispute directly affected by such provisional measures may request their immediate review. The Tribunal shall promptly undertake such review and confirm or suspend its order.

Article 61

1. The Tribunal may seek the opinion of any organ of the Council regarding an issue falling within its competence.

2. The Tribunal shall decide whether proceedings shall be suspended until the opinion sought has been made available.

Article 62

Any organ of the Authority may request the Tribunal to give an advisory opinion on any legal question connected with the subject matter of this Convention.

Article 63

1. If the parties to a dispute so agree, pursuant to Article 57, they shall submit the dispute to an Arbitration Commission. The Arbitration Commission shall be composed of three members. Each party to the dispute shall appoint one member to the Commission, while the third member, who shall be the Chairman, shall be chosen in common agreement between the parties. If the parties fail to agree on the designation of the third member within a period of one month, the third member shall be appointed by the President of the Tribunal. In case any of the parties fail to make an appointment within a period of one month the President of the Tribunal shall fill the remaining vacancy or vacancies.

2. The Arbitration Commission shall decide on matters placed before it by a simple majority.

3. The Arbitration Commission constituted pursuant to this article shall have such jurisdiction and shall exercise such powers and functions as the Tribunal constituted pursuant to Article 32. The provisions of Articles 58–61 shall apply *mutatis mutandis* to the Arbitration Commission.

Part IV: Final Provisions

AMENDMENT

Article 64

Amendments to this Convention may be proposed by any State Party to this Convention. Certified copies of the text of any amendment proposed shall be prepared by the Secretary-General and communicated by him to all parties, at least ninety days in advance of its consideration by the Assembly.

Article 65

Amendments shall come into force for all States Parties to this Convention when:

(i) Approved by the Assembly by a two-thirds majority of those present and voting after consideration of observations submitted by the Council on proposed amendments; and

(ii) Accepted by two-thirds of all the States Parties in accordance with their respective constitutional processes. Acceptance by a State Party shall be effected by the deposit of an instrument of acceptance with the Secretary-General of the United Nations.

GENERAL REVIEW

Article 66

At the third regular session of the Assembly following the coming into force of this Convention, the question of a general review of the provisions of this Convention shall be placed on the agenda of that session. On approval by a majority of the members present and voting, the review will take place at the following Assembly. Thereafter, proposals on the question of a general review of this Convention may be submitted for decisions by the Assembly under the same procedure.

SUSPENSION OF PRIVILEGES

Article 67

A State Party of the Authority which is in arrears in the payment of its financial contributions to the Authority shall have no vote in the Authority if the amount of its arrears equals or exceeds the amount of the contributions due from it for the preceding two years. The Assembly may permit such a State Party to vote if it is satisfied that the failure to pay is due to conditions beyond the control of the State Party.

Article 68

1. A member which has persistently violated the provisions of this Convention or of any agreement or contractual arrangement entered into by it pursuant to this Convention, may be suspended from the exercise of the privileges and the rights of membership by the Assembly acting on a two-thirds majority of the States Parties present and voting upon recommendations by the Council.

2. No action may be taken under this article until the dispute settlement procedures have been exhausted.

SIGNATURE

Article 69

The present Convention shall be open for signature by all States members of the United Nations or of any of the Specialized Agencies or of the International Atomic Energy Agency or parties to the Statute of the International Court of Justice, and by any other State invited to participate in the Third United Nations Conference on the Law of the Sea or invited by the Assembly of the Authority to become a party to the Convention, as follows: until 31 December 1976 at the Ministry of Foreign Affairs of the Republic of Venezuela, and subsequently, until 30 June 1977 at United Nations Headquarters, New York.

RATIFICATION

Article 70

The present Convention is subject to ratification. The instruments of ratification shall be deposited with the Secretary-General of the United Nations.

ACCESSION

Article 71

The present Convention shall remain open for accession by any State belonging to any of the categories mentioned in article 69. The instruments of accession shall be deposited with the Secretary-General of the United Nations.

ENTRY INTO FORCE

Article 72

1. The present Convention shall enter into force on the thirtieth day following the date of deposit of the thirty-sixth instrument of ratification or accession.

2. For each State ratifying or acceding to the Convention after the deposit of the thirty-sixth instrument of ratification or accession, the Convention shall enter into force on the thirtieth day after deposit by such State of its instrument of ratification or accession.

PROVISIONAL APPLICATION

Article 73

1. Pending the definitive entry into force of this Convention in accordance with the provisions of Article 72, a State may notify upon signing this Convention the Secretary-General of the United Nations that it will apply this Convention provisionally and that it will undertake to seek ratification or accession in accordance with constitutional procedures as rapidly as possible.

2. This Convention shall enter provisionally into force upon the thirty-sixth such notification to the Secretary-General of the United Nations.

3. Upon provisional entry into force of this Convention in accordance with paragraph 2, any State which has notified the Secretary-General of the United Nations of its intention to apply this Convention provisionally in accordance

with paragraph 1, shall be regarded as being Party for the purpose of provisional application of this Convention.

4. The provisional application of this Convention with respect to a State shall be terminated if that State notifies the other Parties to provisional application of the withdrawal of its notification under paragraph 1.

5. The provisional application of this Convention in accordance with this article shall be terminated:

(a) Upon the definitive entry into force of this Convention in accordance with Article 72;

(b) If, as a result of withdrawal of notification, in accordance with paragraph 4 above, the total number of Contracting Parties becomes less than that provided for in paragraph 2;

(c) At the end of a period of — years after the commencement of provisional application.

6. If, at the end of six months after the opening of the Convention for signature, provisional entry into force as provided for in Article 73 does not occur, an Interim Commission shall come into existence, as provided for in Annex III to this Convention.

DEPOSITORY

Article 74

The Secretary-General of the United Nations shall inform all States belonging to any of the categories mentioned in Article 69 of:

(a) Signature to the present Convention and of the deposit of instruments of ratification or accession in accordance with Articles 69, 70 and 71 respectively;

(b) Notification of provisional application in accordance with Article 73;

(c) The date on which the present Convention will enter into force in accordance with Article 72;

(d) Date on which the present Convention will provisionally enter into force in accordance with Article 73.

AUTHENTIC TEXTS

Article 75

The original of the present Convention, of which the Arabic, Chinese, English, French, Russian and Spanish texts are equally authentic, shall be deposited with the Secretary-General of the United Nations.

In witness whereof the undersigned Plenipotentiaries, being duly authorized thereto by their respective Governments, have signed the present Convention.

Done at Caracas, this _____ day of _____ one thousand nine hundred and seventy-six.

ANNEX I

BASIC CONDITIONS OF GENERAL SURVEY EXPLORATION AND EXPLOITATION

PART A

Rights in the area and its resources

1. The Area and its resources being the common heritage of mankind all rights in the resources are vested in the Authority on behalf of mankind as a whole. These resources are not subject to alienation.

Rights in minerals

2. Title to the minerals or processed substances derived from the Area shall pass from the Authority only in accordance with the provisions of this Convention, the rules and regulations prescribed by the Authority in accordance with this Convention, and the terms and conditions of the relevant contracts, joint ventures or other form of association entered into by it.

Access to the area and its resources

3. The Authority shall from time to time determine the part or parts of the Area in which the exploration of the Area and the exploitation of its resources and other associated activities may be conducted. In doing so the Authority shall be guided by the following principles:

(a) The Authority shall encourage the conduct of general survey operations, and to that end shall regularly, after consultation with all States Parties, open for general survey the sea-bed and ocean floor of such oceanic areas as are determined by it to be of interest for this purpose. General Survey may be carried out by any entity which meets the environmental protction regulations of the Authority and enters into a contract with it.

(b) The Authority may, upon the proposal of a State Party to this Convention or on its own initiative, open for evaluation and exploitation the sea-bed and ocean floor of oceanic areas determined by it on the basis of sufficient supporting data, to be of commercial interest. Such evaluation and exploitation shall be conducted directly by the Authority in accordance with part B and, within the limits it may determine in accordance with paragraph 8(f), through States Parties to this Convention, or State Enterprises, or persons natural or juridical which possess the nationality of such States, or are effectively controlled by them or their nationals, when sponsored by a State Party, by entering into contracts for associated operations in accordance with paragraphs 5 and 6.

(c) Provided, however, that the Authority may refuse to open any part or parts of the Area pursuant to this paragraph when the available data indicates the risk of irreparable harm to a unique environment or unjustifiable interference with other uses of the Area.

PART B

4. The Enterprise may at any time, in any part or parts of the Area determined by the Authority to be open for activities pursuant to paragraph 3 of these Basic Conditions, carry out directly scientific research or a general survey or exploration of the Area or operations relating to evaluation and exploitation of the resources of the Area, including feasibility studies, construction of facilities, processing, transportation and marketing pursuant to a Plan of Operations approved by the Council, subject to the following conditions:—

(a) The Enterprise shall submit to the Council in the form prescribed by it for the purpose such information, including a detailed financial analysis of costs and benefits, as would enable the Council to review the financial and technical aspects of the proposed Plan of Operations, as well as a Work Programme, which shall accommodate the objectives of the Authority as reflected in article 24 of this Part.

(b) If on the basis of such information and after taking into consideration all relevant factors, the Council determines that the proposed Plan of Operations offers optimum benefits to the Authority, the Council shall approve the Plan.

(c) Activities in the Area conducted directly by the Enterprise shall, *mutatis mutandis*, be subject to the relevant Basic Conditions set forth in Part C.

(d) To the extent that the Enterprise does not currently possess the personnel, equipment and services for its operations, it may employ them under its direction and management on a non-discriminatory basis if they meet the qualifications set forth in paragraph 5. The terms and conditions of such employment shall be in accordance with the relevant provisions of these Basic Conditions.

(e) Minerals and processed substances produced by the Enterprise shall be marketed in accordance with rules, regulations and procedures adopted by the Council in accordance with the folowing criteria

(i) The products of the Enterprise shall be made available to States Parties.

(ii) The Enterprise shall offer its products for sale at not less than international market prices. It may, however, sell its products at lower prices to developing countries, particularly the least developed among them.

(iii) Production and marketing of the resources of the Area by the Enterprise shall be maintained or expanded in accordance with the provisions of article 10 of this Part.

(iv) The Enterprise shall, except as specifically provided in this Part, market its products without discrimination.

PART C

Contracts for associated operations

5. On the application of any State Party to this Convention, or State enterprise, or person natural or juridical which possesses the nationality of a State Party or is effectively controlled by it or its nationals and is sponsored by a State Party or any group of the foregoing (hereinafter called the "applicant"),

the Authority may enter into a contract, joint venture or any other such form of association, for the conduct of scientific research, or for the carrying out of a general survey or exploration of the Area, or of operations relating to evaluation and exploitation of the Area including such stages as feasibility study, construction of facilities, processing, transportation and marketing (hereinafter called the "contract").

6. Every contract entered into by the Authority pursuant to paragraph 4 shall:

 (a) be in strict conformity with this Convention and the rules and regulations prescribed by the Authority in accordance with the Convention;

 (b) ensure direct and effective fiscal and administrative control by the Authority at all stages of operations through appropriate institutional arrangements entered into pursuant to this Part.

Qualification of applicants

7. (a) The Authority shall adopt appropriate administrative procedures and rules and regulations for making an application pursuant to paragraph 5, and the qualifications of any applicant referred to therein. Such qualifications shall include (1) financial standing, (2) technological capability, and (3) past performance and work experience.

(b) States Parties which apply to enter into contracts with the Authority shall be presumed to possess the qualifications specified in subparagraph (a). They shall be deemed to have waived their sovereign immunity with respect to financial and economic obligations covered by such contracts.

(c) Each applicant shall, in addition, submit to the Authority a work programme which shall accommodate the objectives of the Authority as reflected in this Part and the rules and regulations adopted thereunder.

(d) Each applicant shall undertake to comply with the provisions of this Convention and the rules and regulations adopted by the Authority, and to accept control by the Authority in accordance therewith.

Selection of applicants

8. (a) Upon receiving an application pursuant to paragraph 5 with respect to activities of evaluation and exploitation, the Authority shall first ascertain whether a competing application has been received for the area applied for. If no such competing application has been received, the Authority shall enter into negotiations with a view to concluding a contract with the applicant in respect of the area applied for, provided that the applicant has completed the procedures and possesses the qualifications prescribed pursuant to paragraph 6 and, after a consideration of all relevant factors is deemed to offer the Authority optimum benefits. The Enterprise may not refuse to enter into a contract if the criteria in paragraph 9(d) have been satisfied, and the contract in all other respects is in strict conformity with the provisions of this Part and of the rules, regulations and procedures adopted thereunder, subject to the stated resource policy established by the Authority.

(b) Applicants shall be required to comply with requirements of the Authority shall enter into negotiations with a view to concluding a contract with the

(c) If the Authority receives more than one application in respect of substantially the same area and category of minerals, selection from among the applicants shall be made on a competitive basis taking into account the extent to which each applicant satisfies the requirements of paragraph 6. The Authority shall enter into negotiatons with a view to concluding a contract with the applicant which, after a consideration of all relevant factors, is deemed to offer the Authority optimum benefits including financial arrangements in accordance with paragraph 9(d).

(d) The principles set forth in sub-paragraphs (a), (b) and (c) shall be applied *mutatis mutandis* in prescribing procedures, rules and regulations for the selection of applicants for contracts with respect to activities other than evaluation and exploitation.

(e) When a contractor that has entered into a contract with the Authority for one or some of the stages of operations referred to in paragraph 4 has completed performance under it, he shall have priority among applicants for a contract or contracts for one or more further stages of operations with regard to the same area and resources; provided, however, that where the contractor has not carried out his obligations satisfactorily, such priority may be withdrawn.

(f) The total number of contracts for evaluation and exploitation entered into by the Authority with a single State Party or with natural and juridical persons under the sponsorship of a single State Party shall not exceed — per cent of the total area open under paragraph 3, and shall be equal for all States Parties.

(g) Within the limits specified in sub-paragraph (f) the Council may every year determine the number of contracts to be entered into by the Authority with a single State Party or with natural and juridical persons under the sponsorship of a single State Party in order to give effect to the provisions of articles . . .

Rights and obligations under the contract

9. (a) Any State Party, or any State enterprise or person natural or juridical which possesses the nationality of a State Party or is effectively controlled by it or by its nationals, when sponsored by a State Party or any group of the foregoing which enters into a contract for activities relating to evaluation and exploitation with the Authority pursuant to paragraph 5 (hereinafter called the "Contractor") shall, except as otherwise agreed by the Authority, be required to use its own funds, materials, equipment, skills and know-how as necessary for the conduct of operations covered by the contract, and to post a bond by way of guarantee of satisfactory performance under the contract.

(b) The costs involved in the performance of the contract pursuant to paragraph (a) shall be recoverable by the respective parties out of the proceeds of operations. The Authority shall in its rules and regulations establish a schedule pursuant to which such costs will be recovered in the manner specified in sub-paragraph (d) of this paragraph.

(c) The proceeds of operations pursuant to the contract after deduction of costs, which shall be calculated according to accounting principles to be determined by the Authority and the terms of the contract, shall be apportioned between the Authority and the Contractor in the manner specified in the contract in accordance with sub-paragraph (d) of this paragraph

(d) [Financial arrangements]

10. The Contractor shall:

(a) Transfer in accordance with the rules and regulations and the terms and conditions of the contract to the Authority at time intervals determined by the Authority all data necessary and relevant to the effective implementation of the powers and functions of the organs of the Authority under this Convention in respect of the contract area. The Authority shall not disclose to third parties, without the prior consent of the Contractor, such of the transferred data as is deemed to be proprietary by the Contractor. Data which is necessary for the promulgation of rules and regulations concerning protection of the marine environment shall not be deemed to be proprietary. Except as otherwise agreed with the Authority the Contractor shall not be obliged to disclose proprietary equipment design data.

(b) Draw up programmes for the training of personnel, and take all such other action as may be necessary to fulfill its obligations pursuant to paragraph 8(b).

11. The Authority shall, pursuant to this Convention and the rules and regulations prescribed by the Authority, accord the Contractor the exclusive right to evaluate and/or exploit the contract area in respect of a specified category of minerals and shall ensure that no other entity operates in the same contract area for a different category of minerals in a manner which might interfere with the operations of the Contractor. The Contractor shall have security of tenure. Accordingly, the contract shall not be cancelled, modified, suspended or terminated, nor shall the exercise of any right under it be impaired, except for gross and persistent violations of the provisions of this Part and the rules and regulations adopted by the Authority thereunder, and after recourse to procedures provided under this Part for the settlement of any dispute that may have arisen. The Authority shall not, during the continuance of a contract, permit any entity to carry out activities in the same area for the same category of minerals.

Rules, regulations and procedures

12. The Authority shall adopt and uniformly apply rules, regulations and procedures consistent with the purposes and fundamental principles of the

functioning of the Authority and with these basic conditions in the following subjects.

(1) Applications to enter into contracts.

(2) Qualifications of applicants.

(3) Selection of applicants.

(4) Progress report.

(5) Submission of data.

(6) Application fees and bonds to secure satisfactory performance.

(7) Inspection and supervision of operations.

(8) Mining standards and practices including operational safety.

(9) Prevention of interference by the Contractor with other uses of the sea and of the marine environment.

(10) Apportionment of the proceeds of operations.

(11) Direct participation of personnel of developing countries, particularly the landlocked among them and of other countries lacking or less advanced in ocean mining and mineral processing technology, and the transfer of such technology to such countries.

(12) Passing of title to minerals and processed metals from the Area.

(13) Avoiding or minimizing adverse effects on the revenues of developing countries derived from exports of the minerals and products thereof from the Area.

(14) Transfer of rights by a Contractor.

(15) Activities in reserved areas.

(16) Financial and accounting rules.

In respect of rules, regulations and procedures for the following subjects the Authority shall uniformly apply the objective criteria set out below:

(17) *Protection of the marine environment.*—The Authority shall take into account in adopting rules and regulations for the protection of the marine environment the extent to which activities in the Area such as drilling, dredging, coring and excavation as well as disposal, dumping and discharge in the Area of sediment or wastes and other matters will have a harmful effect on the marine environment.

(18) *Size of area.*—The Authority shall determine the appropriate size of areas for evaluation which may be up to twice as large as those for exploitation in order to permit intensive continued survey and evaluation operations. Areas for exploitation shall be calculated to satisfy the production requirements agreed between the Authority and the Contractor over the term of the contract taking into account the state of the art of technology then available for ocean mining and the relevant physical characteristics of the area. Areas shall neither be smaller nor larger than are necessary to satisfy this objective. In cases where the Contractor has obtained a contract for exploitation, the area not covered by such contract shall be relinquished to the Authority

(19) *Duration of activities.*

(a) General survey shall be without time limit except in the case of violations of the Authority's regulations to protect the environment in which case the Authority may prohibit the violator from conducting general survey operations for a reasonable period of time.

(b) Evaluation should be of sufficient duration as to permit a thorough survey of the specific area, the design and construction of mining equipment for the area, the design and construction of small and medium-size processing plants for the purpose of testing mining and processing systems.

(c) The duration of exploitation should be related to the economic life of the mining project taking into consideration such factors as the depletion of the ore body, the useful life of mining equipment and processing facilities, and commercial viability. Exploitation should be of sufficient duration as to permit commercial extraction of the minerals of the area and should include a reasonable time period for construction of commercial scale mining and processing systems during which period commercial production should not be required. The total duration of exploitation, however, should also be short enough to permit the Authority an opportunity to amend the terms and conditions of the contract at the time it considers renewal in accordance with rules and regulations which it has issued subsequent to entering into the contract.

(20) *Performance requirements.*—The Authority shall require that during the evaluation stage, periodic expenditures be made by the Contractor which are reasonably related to the size of the contract area and the expenditures

which would be expected of a *bona fide* Contractor who intended to bring the area into full-scale commercial production within the time limits established by the Authority. Such required expenditures should not be established at a level which would discourage prospective operators with less costly technology than is prevalently in use. The Authority shall establish a maximum time interval after the evaluation stage is completed and the exploitation stage begins to achieve full-scale commercial production. To determine this interval, the Authority should take into consideration that construction of large-scale mining and processing systems cannot be initiated until after the termination of the evaluation stage and the commencement of the exploitation stage. Accordingly, the interval to bring an area into full-scale commercial production should take into account the time necessary for this construction after the completion of the evaluation stage and reasonable allowance should be made for unavoidable delays in the construction schedule.

Once full-scale commercial production is achieved in the exploitation stage, the Authority shall within reasonable limits and taking into consideration all relevant factors require the Contractor to maintain a reasonable level of commercial production throughout the period of the contract.

(21) *Categories of minerals.*—In determining the category of mineral in respect of which a contract may be entered into, the Authority shall give emphasis *inter alia* to the following characteristics:

(a) Resources which require the use of similar mining methods, and

(b) Resources which can be developed simultaneously without undue interference between Contractors in the same area developing different resources.

Nothing in this paragraph shall deter the Authority from granting a contract for more than one category of mineral in the same contract area to the same applicant.

(22) *Renunciation of areas.*—The contractor shall have the right at any time to renounce without penalty the whole or part of his rights in the contract area. In such cases the renounced area shall be deemed to be a reserved area and disposed of in accordance with paragraph 19.

13. The Authority shall have the right to take at any time any measures provided for under this Convention to ensure compliance with its terms, and in the performance of the control and regulatory functions assigned to it thereunder or under any contract. The Authority shall have the right to inspect all facilities in the Area used in connection with any activities in the Area.

Suspension or termination

14. A Contractor's rights in the contract area shall be suspended or terminated only if the Contractor has conducted his activities in such a way as to result in gross and persistent violations of this Part and rules and regulations and were not caused by circumstances beyond his control, if a Contractor has wilfully failed to comply with any decision of the [dispute settlement organ].

Revision of contract

15. [Circumstances under which terms and conditions (e.g. financial conditions) of contracts may be revised—to be drafted.]

Force majeure

16. Non-performance or delay in performance shall be excused if and to the extent that such non-performance or delay is caused by *force majeure*. The party invoking *force majeure* may take appropriate measures including revision, suspension or termination of the contract; provided, however, that in the event of a dispute the parties shall first have recourse to the procedures for the settlement of disputes provided for in this Part.

Transfer of rights

17. The rights and obligations arising out of a contract shall be transferred only with the consent of the Authority, and in accordance with the rules and regulations adopted by it. The Authority shall not withhold consent to the transfer if the proposed transferee is in all respects a qualified applicant, and assures all of the obligations of the transferor.

Applicable law

18. The law applicable to the contract shall be solely the provisions of this Convention, the rules and regulations prescribed by the Authority, and the terms

and conditions of the contract. The rights and obligations of the Authority and of the Contractor shall be valid and enforceable notwithstanding the law of any State, or any political subdivision thereof to the contrary. No contracting State may impose conditions on a Contractor that are inconsistent with the princi- -ples of this Convention.

Liability

19. Responsibility or liability for wrongful damage arising out of the conduct of operations by the Contractor or the Authority shall lie with the Contractor or the Authority as the case may be. It shall be a defence in any proceeding against a Contractor or the Authority that the damage was the result of an act or omission of the Authority. Similarly, any responsibility or liability for wrongful damage arising out of the exercise of the powers and functions of the Authority shall lie with the Authority. It shall be a defence in any proceeding against the Authority that the damage was a result of an act or omission of the Contractor. Liability in every case shall be for the actual amount of damage.

Settlement of disputes

20. Any dispute concerning the interpretation or application of this Convention, its rules and regulations or the terms and conditions of a contract and arising between the Authority and a Contracting State or any State enterprise or person natural or juridical which possesses the nationality of a Contracting State or is effectively controlled by it or its nationals, or any group of the foregoing shall on the application of either party be subject to the procedure for settlement of such disputes provided for in this Convention.

Arrangements following provisional entry into force of the convention

21. In the period immediately following provisional application of this Convention, the Authority shall, with respect to the first [. . .] such contracts, joint ventures or other such form of association, give priority to those covering integrated stages of operations.

Mr. MURPHY. We will hear first from Leigh Ratiner of the Interior Department.

Mr. Ratiner, take the witness stand and if there are any other members of your department or committee that you would like to have with you, they are also welcome.

Please proceed.

STATEMENT OF LEIGH S. RATINER, ADMINISTRATOR, OCEAN MINING ADMINISTRATION, DEPARTMENT OF INTERIOR

Mr. RATINER. Thank you, Mr. Chairman.

Mr. Chairman, I am pleased to be invited to appear before you today and to share some of my thoughts on developments at the recently concluded Geneva session of the Law of the Sea Conference.

As you are aware, my primary involvement in the conference is as our representative in committee one of the conference which deals with the deep seabed and ocean mining.

With your permission, I would like to restrict my remarks today to that subject. The NSC Interagency Task Force on the Law of the Sea is currently assessing the results of this session and reviewing what policy options should be pursued in the light of those results.

Accordingly, my remarks are only of the most preliminary and tentative nature.

The efforts of Committee One, which deals with the establishment of a new international regime and machinery for deep ocean mining for the seabed beyond the limits of national jurisdiction, were characterized by more serious negotiations at the Geneva session than have occurred in previous Committee One sessions of the Law of the Sea Conference.

However, these efforts were rewarded with only limited success. In my view, a major stumbling block in these negotiations is the desire on the part of most developing countries to use the deep seabed as a concrete opportunity to implement creation of a new economic order which involves increased use of the collective power and control over the sources, quantity, production and prices of raw materials, in contradistinction to the quest of the industrialized countries for new, secure sources of supplies of raw materials. For this reason, we have found progress in Committee One particularly difficult to achieve.

I believe the United States entered the Geneva session with a reasonable and forthcoming position on many of the issues that directly concern developing countries, particularly on the question of ensuring developing country participation in ocean mining.

Some developing countries also made an effort to be responsive to some of the basic concerns of the industrialized countries. Despite these attempts to reach an accommodation, little progress was made in bridging the gap among nations on the basic aspects of the system under which ocean mining will occur, although there were some significant signs of progress on issues involving the structure, powers and voting mechanisms of the proposed International Seabed Authority.

In summing up the differences among nations on the exploitation system, I believe the following comments by Ambassador John R. Stevenson in his final press statement in Geneva on May 9, 1975 are useful:

* * * in a world where we have all felt the effects not only of scarcity of vital raw materials, but of uncertainty of access to them, nations are not prepared in my judgment, to subject their access to seabed minerals to a system of exploration and exploitation and to a decision making process in which they do not have reasonable assurances of security of access, and may not be adequately represented. Moreover, I do not think it will be possible, seen against the background of today's developments in raw materials matters to agree to give ultimate powers of exclusive exploitation to a single new international entity. The United States has been willing to work with all nations of the world to ensure that a system of exploitation is devised that will permit both sharing in the benefits and future participation in the development of these resources. So far, however, basic compromises on this most difficult of issues have eluded all of us, although I am pleased to say that on some of the important issues progress has been made.

That is the end of the Ambassador's quote.

The most tangible result of the Geneva session in Committee One was the introduction by its chairman of an informal single negotiating text which you have just inserted in the record.

The single text was presented as a personal effort of the chairman at the request of the Conference. It is in no sense a consensus or an agreed negotiating text, but is intended to serve as a take off point for future negotiations.

In addition, this document included as an annex a set of basic conditions for general survey, exploration and exploitation. The Interagency Law of the Sea Task Force has not been able to review this text in detail, since it was introduced on the last day of the Conference.

It is important to emphasize, however, that these specific texts are intended to be the negotiating document for the next session of the Conference and were not discussed within Committee One. They are exclusively the personal work product of the individuals who prepared them.

With respect to the next session of the Conference, I am sure the committee is aware that the Conference decided to recommend to the General Assembly the convening of an 8-week session beginning March 29, 1976 in New York. It will also be possible to undertake additional work in 1976.

It is now clear that the General Assembly schedule which anticipated the conclusion of a Law of the Sea Convention by the end of 1975 has been proven to be overly optimistic.

During the next few weeks, the executive branch will be intensively studying what policies should now be adopted in light of this delay in the completion of the work of the Conference.

I am confident that this assessment will conclude that international cooperation in the deep seabed continues to be a worthwhile objective for the United States to pursue.

However, other available options will have to be given serious consideration. Following this review, executive branch representatives would be happy to consult with Congress and discuss with you their assessment.

Thank you, Mr. Chairman.

Mr. MURPHY. Thank you, Mr. Ratiner.

Was this statement cleared with the Department of the Interior or with other agencies?

Mr. RATINER. Yes, Mr. Chairman.

Mr. MURPHY. What agencies were they?

Mr. RATINER. Well, I am not certain which agencies actually participated in the clearance, but the normal procedure for clearance at this time is through the NSC Interagency Task Force on the Law of the Sea which contains representatives of the Department of State, Defense, Treasury, Commerce, Interior, and a number of other agencies.

Mr. MURPHY. You say the United States entered the Geneva session with a reasonable and forthcoming position on many of the issues that directly concern developing countries, particularly on the question of insuring developing country participation in ocean mining.

What was the United States' position in this respect?

Mr. RATINER. During the course of the negotiations in Geneva, Mr. Chairman, we introduced several ideas for discussion in various informal working groups of Committee One.

The principal ideas are basically that, first, profits from ocean mining could be shared with the International Seabed Authority and developing countries, those profits to be determined in accordance with a provision in the treaty; that provision has not been negotiated as yet.

Second, in view of the widespread insistence by developing countries that participation in the benefits of ocean mining should, in fact, include more than just a share of the profits but rather a true participation in both management of resources and a participation in understanding and learning technology, the United States tried to be as forthcoming as possible with respect to provisions on technology transfer in this treaty. Although I should say that we emphasized the teaching of knowledge concerning technology rather than the actual transfer of technology itself.

In addition, the developing countries have always seemed quite anxious to be able to directly exploit the area themselves through the International Seabed Authority.

The United States has rejected that approach but, nevertheless, did attempt to construct a proposal which would meet the developing countries halfway. That proposal was essentially that 50 percent of the area of the seabed might, through a mechanism which we came to call the "banking system," be reserved for joint venture contracts in which the international authority could negotiate freely the provisions on profits and technology transfer.

The other 50 percent of the area would not be open to negotiation, but rather those areas would be handed out on a relatively automatic basis to qualified applicants for joint venture contracts.

These are some of the proposals that we made in order to try to satisfy developing countries interests.

Mr. MURPHY. The U.S. position then was a 50 to 50 position on lease areas?

Mr. RATINER. I think that in fairness to characterizing the U.S. position it was that 50 percent of the area should go under relatively automatic terms and conditions to any qualified applicant and the other 50 percent of the area should go also to any qualified applicant, but on negotiated terms and conditions for profits and technology transfer rather than automatically.

Mr. MURPHY. Would the applicant have the option of picking which 50 percent of that area?

Mr. RATINER. No, he would not under the U.S. proposal.

Mr. MURPHY. In any instance would he be able to get the entire area?

Mr. RATINER. The system as put forward was that the applicant would select two mine sites based on his own prospecting work and that he would submit both of the mine sites, that is the coordinates of both mine sites to the International Authority.

In order to insure that they were roughly equivalent in commercial interest the Authority would then be entitled to choose—and we proposed a random selection—which of the areas would automatically be granted to the applicant and which would be held in reserve by the Authority for joint venture contracts that were fully negotiated.

Mr. MURPHY. Of the 50 percent that was awarded what percentage of product and profit would the Authority deed or give to the applicant?

Mr. RATINER. First of all, our proposal did not contain any ability to share in product. The proposal only related to profit sharing. We did not specify any figure for profit sharing, but rather chose to hold for a later time in the negotiations the precise formula pursuant to which the profit share would be arrived at.

Mr. MURPHY. What was the position of the developing countries as outlined in the Engo document?

Mr. RATINER. Mr. Chairman, I think the answer to that question requires a little bit of history in order to see the development of the Engo text, which does not necessarily reflect the views of developing countries, nor of the developed countries.

I should recall that 5 years ago in 1970 the United States and all other countries in the world agreed to a U.N. General Assembly Resolution declaring that area which is now under negotiation to be the common heritage of mankind.

In that declaration a series of principles were established, and those principles were supposed to guide the forthcoming negotiations which now occur in Committee One.

During a 5-year period, as you pointed out in your opening statement, Mr. Chairman, a great deal has happened in the world. Much has changed, and what we now face—and what I am sure will be seen by historians at a later time—is a very serious, almost historical struggle with the developing countries seeking to establish their primacy in world politics and particularly world economic affairs and seeking to correct what they view as the deficiencies of past world history.

Now, against that background, and against the background of the United States having learned I think in the last 5 years just how critical our dependence on raw materials is, the developing countries have gradually escalated the negotiations well beyond this Declaration of Principles which was supposed to have guided the negotiations.

The demands of developing countries as partially manifested in what is referred to as the Engo text are much greater now than they were when they agreed to the Declaration of Principles and when we agreed to it.

Indeed, a fair reading of the Declaration of Principles makes it clear that it was anticipated that States and their private companies would explore and exploit the resources of the deep seabed. That is no longer the view of the developing countries. Their view today, and this is reflected in the Engo text, is that the International Seabed Authority should be ultimately the sole exploiter of the resources of the deep seabed beyond the limits of national jurisdiction.

They are willing, however, to provide for a system in which, prior to the International Authority acquiring the capability to do this work itself, private companies and sovereign states may be engaged in contractual relationships for the purpose of exploring and exploiting the resources.

Their ultimate objective has not changed and that is to have the power in an International Authority to exclude exploitation by states and private companies.

Mr. MURPHY. I think at this point, because we are at the outset of this hearing, I would ask you to describe the different groups. We talk of developing countries and perhaps you might better articulate the developing countries and the other groups of countries that seem to have formed into blocs at this Conference.

Mr. RATINER. Well, I would like to confine my description of the politics of the Conference to Committee One, because the situation was markedly different in Committees Two and Three, where there is not quite so much solidarity among developing countries.

In Committee One, there are several significant groups of countries. First, there are what I might refer to as the highly industrialized countries whose views in most respects, although not in all, tend to coincide about what the future system of exploration and exploitation should be.

The second group of countries is those to whom many refer as the land-based producers, that is, those countries which produce substantial quantities of the minerals which will be found in manganese nodules. This group also includes those developing countries who are not presently land-based producers but who are in sympathy with the land-based producers because of developing country politics or solidarity, or because they fear that minerals will yet be discovered in the seabed of which they are, or may become, land-based producers.

The third group of countries, and I think this group is by far the largest in Committee One, are the developing countries without further characterizing them, that is, countries that regard themselves as now engaged in the historic struggle which I referred to earlier to right the wrongs of the past in respect of those areas where they have power. These developing countries have clearly identified the area of raw materials and sovereignty over resources as the area in which they have very substantial power, if they act collectively.

Combining the land-based producers and their sympathizers and the rest of the developing countries, you have a group of approximately 105 countries out of the 150 that are participating in the conference.

Mr. MURPHY. The developing countries number 105?

Mr. RATINER. Roughly 105 which more or less endorse with some reservations the positions that I have already outlined and which are found in more detail in what you have referred to as the Engo Text.

In addition, there are several developed countries that are not in this group of highly developed countries. These developed countries, which include countries such as Australia and Canada, are land-based producers. They tend to sympathize in certain key respects with the approach of the developing countries.

Mr. MURPHY. How many of those land-based producers and sympathizers would there be?

Mr. RATINER. Altogether, I think you would have to say that there are another 10 or 15. I am not being very precise now and I do not have tables in front of me, but there would be another 10 or 15 developed countries who would be sympathizers with the developing countries.

Mr. MURPHY. How many would constitute the highly industrialized countries?

Mr. RATINER. The highly industrialized countries are several members of the European Community, although not necessarily all of them. That community is somewhat divided on these issues.

Obviously, the chief industrialized countries are the Federal Republic of Germany, Japan, the United States, the Soviet Union, the United Kingdom, France, but there are, of course, others in the European Community who tend to think and behave like the highly industrialized countries that I have enumerated.

Altogether I think we are talking about perhaps 15 or 20 countries that would maintain solidarity along the lines of an industrialized country position, although I should point out that it became quite clear in the Geneva session and had become somewhat clear in the Caracas session, that even among the highly industrialized countries economic rivalry has caused certain fundamental splits.

As an example, certain of the industrialized countries, of the highly industrialized countries, favor a quota system pursuant to which the number of contracts that could be given to any one state or its nationals would be limited in number and also by year, so that there would be two limitations. This is within this very small group of 20 or so industrialized countries.

Mr. MURPHY. Then the so-called Group 77 actually runs to about 105?

Mr. RATINER. That is right.

Mr. MURPHY. And then about 20 of the highly industrialized, and 10 to 15 land-based countries.

Mr. RATINER. That is right.

Mr. MURPHY. You say the developing countries made a genuine effort to be responsive to some of the concerns of the industrialized countries.

In what respect was this so?

Mr. RATINER. During the course of the Geneva session, and a good deal of the negotiations and discussions were carried out in rather small groups and in private, it became apparent that the developing countries who exercised leadership in the Group of 77 were trying to find approaches to the negotiations which would give them total satisfaction on the system that would be used for exploration and exploitation, but which would provide ceretain guarantees for countries like the United States that the International Authority to be established could be trusted; that we could be assured that it would behave in a deliberative, careful, rational manner; that all of its decisions could be subject to dispute settlement in a separate tribunal.

In short, they were trying to provide what we Americans normally refer to as due process of law in the actual implementation of the system. In exchange for that, it is clear they expected us to agree, at least at this stage, to their concept of what the system of exploration and exploitation should be.

Mr. MURPHY. Was a major stumbling block in these negotiations the desire on the part of most developing countries to use the deep seabed as an opportunity to implement the so-called "new economic order" which calls for increasing the effective control of developing countries over needed raw materials and needs of the industrialized countries for new, secure sources of supplies of raw materials?

Mr. RATINER. Mr. Chairman, I think there can be no question that that is not only a major stumbling block but is a major stumbling

block for industrialized countries in many negotiations and in many
areas today around the world in multilateral conferences.

In the past, that issue—more or less the way you phrased it—has
tended to lie somewhat in the background in Committee One. It has
been raised to the level of a treaty article for the first time in the
Engo text which you referred to earlier. It is now found in paragraph
1 of article 9 of the Engo text, which establishes in rather clear
terms the rhetoric of the new economic order.

This is a new development, one we had not previously seen in
Committee One, although the problem was always there.

Mr. MURPHY. You point out that Ambassador John Stevenson
said:

I do not think it will be possible, seen against the background of today's
developments in raw materials matters, to agree to give ultimate powers of
exclusive exploitation to a single new international entity.

What impact does this statement have on the future of Committee
One?

Mr. RATINER. Well, I think Mr. Chairman, that that statement
which has been, and continues to be, a declaration of the administration's policy in these negotiations makes it impossible for the
United States to agree to a treaty which provides the system of exploration and exploitation that the developing countries have demanded right up until the very last day of Geneva.

Mr. MURPHY. You say also:

It is important to emphasize that these draft articles are intended to be the
negotiating documents for the next session of the Conference and were not discussed within Committee One. They are exclusively the personal work product
of the individuals who prepared them.

Are you referring to the Engo document?

Mr. RATINER. Yes, Mr. Chairman.

Mr. MURPHY. Can you give us a brief history of the development of
the so-called Pinto papers?

Mr. RATINER. Mr. Chairman, there are two kinds of Pinto papers
and I should distinguish clearly between them.

The first document to be called the, and I quote, "Pinto Paper"
was a draft attempt at compromise between the position of the industrialized countries in Caracas that there must be detailed rules
and regulations attached to the treaty itself for ocean mining and the
position of the developing countries that no such thing should be
attached to the treaty.

Thus, the first Pinto document sometimes known as "basic conditions," was an attempt to bridge the gap between those who wanted
rules and regulations and those who wanted nothing at all in the
treaty to guide the Authority in its ultimate rulemaking powers.

There is, however, another document which some have referred to
as the Pinto text, or the Pinto treaty. That document was an attempt
at what we might call staff work for Mr. Engo. That is, the conference had decided some 3 weeks prior to its conclusion in Geneva that
the chairmen of each of the three main committees should prepare
single negotiating texts and that those texts would then be presented
for the next session of the conference for the purpose of facilitating
negotiations.

In the normal course of events, a first draft of such a text would be done, perhaps by someone other than the chairman himself.

In this case, Chairman Engo turned to the vice chairmen of his committee of which there are three and to the Secretariat that serves him to prepare the first draft. That first draft was then prepared, in turn, by Mr. Pinto, who is the chairman of the working group of Committee One, the group that meets more informally and carries on the negotiations.

Mr. Pinto prepared a text, the first version of which was more or less similar to what you now see as the Engo text.

Mr. Pinto then showed the first version of his text to certain selected delegations to get their views, comments and attitudes and, on the basis of some consultation and some discussion, Mr. Pinto prepared a second text.

Unfortunately, his second text was not able to be submitted to Mr. Engo in time for the deadline which Mr. Engo had set for all staff input, so to speak, to his final and ultimate responsibility to draft the convention, or at least the draft of the convention.

Thus, the document which, in fact, emerged as the Engo text does not fully take into account many of the important features which were contained in the second version of the Pinto Text.

Mr. MURPHY. Why did not the Pinto paper II surface in time?

Mr. RATINER. I think, Mr. Chairman, as you, yourself, know from your experience in Congress that in order to put together a paper which may command reasonably wide spread support, very intensive consultations are required and, to my personal knowledge, Mr. Pinto was engaged in those very intensive consultations into the wee hours of the mornings preceding Mr. Engo's deadline.

Accordingly, he was not able to put the paper together and turned it in 24 hours late.

Mr. MURPHY. It seems strange that 24 hours would affect a Conference that is now in its third session and scheduled for another eight week session in New York in 1976 that they could not have extended the deadline for 24 hours.

You say:

In light of this unanticipated delay in the completion of the work of the Conference, other available options will have to be given serious consideration.

Could you outline the options open to the United States at this point in time?

Mr. RATINER. Mr. Chairman, I think in previous testimony given by Department of State witnesses, reference has been made to the need to consider alternative or complimentary legislative approaches in the event this Conference was neither timely nor successful.

I am sure that there are a variety of approaches through domestic legislation that will be considered by the executive branch, but it might be premature for me at this stage to try to elaborate what those optional approaches could be in view of the fact that the Administration has not yet had an opportunity to consider seriously the results of the Geneva Conference.

Mr. MURPHY. One of the options could be, though, that under international law as it exists today the United States can go ahead and develop seabed mineral mining in international waters.

Mr. RATINER. That is clearly an option that is available and has been from the very beginning.

The United States has made clear in all of our negotiating efforts and many times on the record in the Law of the Sea Conference that we regard the present state of international law to be such that there is no present bar to the development of these mineral resources by any American companies that choose to do so.

Mr. MURPHY. I have been informed that the Administration will soon be in a position to explain its position on what steps might be taken to promote ocean mining pending a new Law of the Sea Treaty.

Can you give us a firm date or a tentative date for when you will be prepared to announce this policy?

Mr. RATINER. Mr. Chairman, I would be most reluctant to do that, simply because the Administration's policy development process is totally beyond my own personal control and I would not want to be committed to a date I can have no control over.

I would hope it would be quite soon.

Mr. MURPHY. You are involved in that negotiation?

Mr. RATINER. In the discussions within the Administration, yes. I represent the Interior Department on the Law of the Sea Task Force.

Mr. MURPHY. Suppose the United States does not move unilaterally and we wait until the next session, what are the possibilities or real chances of successfully concluding a Treaty in 1976?

Mr. RATINER. I think, Mr. Chairman, that the answer to that question is somewhat complex and a variety of factors need to be taken into account.

First, the document that we have referred to today as the Engo text contains so many significant problems for the United States that it would be necessary to negotiate at some considerable length in any case to bring that document into a form that we could characterize as a negotiating document.

Right now, I personally could not characterize the Engo text as a negotiating document, and considerable work would have to be done to it before it would reach that level where it could be worked, on relatively easily. Thus, it is conceivable, but I am not speculating as to the probability, that in the next 8 weeks session of the conference beginning in New York, March 29 next year, the Engo text could become a negotiating document and, in part, a negotiated document. However, I have some reservations whether it would, in fact, be possible to firmly agree on a treaty in the next 8 weeks session. I think that would be difficult.

Mr. MURPHY. How would you characterize the Engo text as it exists today?

Mr. RATINER. As the personal work product of the Chairman of Committee One.

Mr. MURPHY. We should conclude a treaty in 1976, under that treaty or any reasonable language, when could deep seabed mining begin?

Mr. RATINER. In that respect, Mr. Chairman, we have had some good fortune in the negotiations.

There has been a general willingness on the part of the developing countries to try to accommodate what we regard as the urgency of getting the system set up, so that mining can commence in a proper way under the treaty system.

Accordingly, there seems to be reasonably wide spread sympathy for the idea that the treaty could be written so as to permit its provisional entry into force. There is also some support for the idea that at the final session of the conference rules and regulations might be developed to be used during that provisional period, so that we would not have to wait for the provisional authority to develop its own rules and regulations.

Now, this would then require a period after signature of the treaty in which a sufficient number of States would indicate their willingness to allow it to enter provisionally into force.

I think, to be realistic, that period of time would have to be roughly 6 months. I do not think that the Congress would want to agree to provisional entry into force of this treaty without a reasonable opportunity to study the implications of provisional entry into force.

Assuming a treaty on August 1, 1976, I think 6 months later the provisional machinery could be in place in what is apparently its new home, Kingston, Jamaica.

That provisional machinery would be faced immediately with applications for contracts and joint ventures, assuming the United States' position is successfully negotiated.

Those contracts, if the treaty read properly, that is, if we are successful in the negotiations, should be issued with very short delay. This should be a matter of only a few weeks because, under our concept, a relatively automatic system of issuing contracts would be developed. The authority would simply need to determine the technical and financial competence of the proposed applicant and satisfy itself that the work program of the applicant was in accordance with the treaty and the rules and regulations.

You could, therefore, under the best possible circumstances, have ocean mining contracts issued by a provisional international authority around March of 1977, but not before.

Mr. MURPHY. On the ratification of the treaty can you tell me whether the majority two-thirds is necessary to sign, and what the signing period is in order to ratify?

Mr. RATINER. Very little attention has been paid in terms of drafting treaty articles to those questions. There are competing factors which would influence that decision.

The shortest answer to your question is that it will depend on what the treaty says. Obviously, the factors that need to be taken into account on the one hand are the desires to have the treaty enter at the earliest possible date into force, assuming it is a satisfactory treaty, and on the other hand, the desire to assure that when it enters into force it has so many signatures and ratifications as to be clearly a widely accepted Convention on the Law of the Sea. So you might want to have a higher number of ratifications to insure that when it enters into force, it reflects the views of most of mankind.

Alternatively, in the interest of bringing it into force early, you might want to have a fewer number of signatures and ratifications.

This is a question that will need to be addressed by the administration prior to the drafting of the final clauses of the treaty, where these matters will be found.

Mr. MURPHY. In your view, what will be the effect of such a delay on our deep seabed resource interests, let us say a delay until March of 1977?

Mr. RATINER. Mr. Chairman, there is something unique about any pioneering industry, particularly in the hard minerals area, and that is that the skills, and particularly the management skills, the know how, in these early stages are fragile.

The putting together of an appropriate package for ocean mining is a delicate process and, in part, depends on the momentum which companies can sustain in continuing to develop this innovative technology.

Based on the information that is now available to the Department of Interior, and much of this information comes from industry sources, it would appear to us that if no further action were taken in respect of developing our ocean mining capabilities for 2 years, it is possible that this delicate and fragile development package could be dissipated, because of the lack of momentum that would result.

If that occurred, we would be set back in our early lead and in our ability to develop an independent capacity to exploit this vast resource of raw materials.

Mr. MURPHY. Then as a resource manager you do not think this delay is in the best interest of the United States?

Mr. RATINER. Mr. Chairman, I will not comment on the total best interest of the United States, which requires taking into consideration all of the other interests to be served by a law of the sea treaty.

As a resource manager, I would be quite disappointed if this 2 year delay caused American companies to slow down or abandon the work they have already done. I think that would be tragic.

Mr. MURPHY. We got to this question earlier, but I would like to clarify some differences.

I understand there are two different versions of the Committee One unified texts, one dated May 3 and the other dated May 7.

Could you explain the status of these two documents and why this duplication occurred?

Mr. RATINER. Yes. The May 3 document to which you refer is what I call the second "Pinto Text," the one that was developed after some consultation and intensive discussion with a variety of countries in Committee One.

The May 7 document is the "Engo Text," which was developed after consultation with interested delegates, but the actual document itself was prepared in secrecy.

In other words, the "Engo Text" did not take into account any give and take in the actual drafting of its provisions.

Mr. Engo did consult with delegations prior to going into seclusion to draft, but his actual drafting process did not reflect any consultation or give and take.

The May 3 Pinto document, on the other hand, was the product of private, personal consultations between Mr. Pinto and a variety of delegations in Committee One including, I think, a representative sampling of the developing countries from the most extreme to the most moderate.

Mr. MURPHY. You said the Law of the Sea Task Force has not reviewed the "Engo Text."

Which of the two texts in your opinion is in the best interest of the United States?

Mr. RATINER. Mr. Chairman, in my view neither of the two texts is in the best interest of the United States, but of the two, the "Pinto Text" is clearly a document which contains many, many fewer problems for the United States than the "Engo Text" does.

Mr. MURPHY. Is it possible to begin with the "Engo Text" next year and come out with any document that could be acceptable to the United States' interest?

Mr. RATINER. In a sense, Mr. Chairman, that depends on the political will of the committee and the will of the United States to communicate its views on the subject to the developing countries.

If the United States is firm, forthright and prepared to indicate that the "Engo Text" cannot serve as a basis for negotiation, and if the developing countries would prefer to see some international authority established with a reasonable degree of resource regulatory power, then I think it could be possible, but extremely difficult, to come out at the end of one more 8 weeks session with a treaty.

At the end of 16 weeks, assuming the two things I have just mentioned, I think it might be possible to have a treaty, yes.

Mr. MURPHY. To your knowledge, did the Cameroon delegation have technical assistance or advice from other countries or other sources in the formulation of the "Engo Text"?

Mr. RATINER. I have no personal knowledge whether Mr. Engo was assisted by any other delegation.

As is customary in any large convention, conference or meeting, rumors do fly and I will pass on to you what is purely a rumor. This rumor is that Mr. Engo may have had the assistance of three or four friends in the committee, who are also delegates.

Mr. MURPHY. From what countries?

Mr. RATINER. I really could not say with certainty, Mr. Chairman, from what countries they were.

Mr. MURPHY. Would they be from the three categorized industrialized countries? Would they be from the group of 77 countries or would they be from that third group that would be user countries?

Mr. RATINER. There is no evidence or rumor to the effect that they were from what I have characterized as the industrialized countries.

Taking only the rumors at their face value, it would appear that these were developing country representatives exclusively who participated in advising Mr. Engo on his text.

Mr. MURPHY. Are any of those nations in the so-called Eastern bloc countries?

Mr. RATINER. To my knowledge, no.

Mr. MURPHY. It would seem if the United States and a few other countries that urgently require completion of the treaty on the deep seabed that is in our interest, do the devloping countries in any way share in this sense of urgency?

Mr. RATINER. I think, Mr. Chairman, the only way to judge that is not by the subjective views that may be expressed by developing countries, but rather by their objective behavior. I would have to conclude, as one who has participated in these negotiations now for 8 years, that our sense of urgency is virtually unique in the negotiations. Not only do the developing countries not share our sense of urgency, but many developed countries are not quite as urgent as we are.

Mr. MURPHY. In other words, there are many undeveloped countries that today it would actually be in their interest and other developed nations that do not have the technical capability of the United States, it would also be in their interest not to conclude a treaty at the earliest possible time.

Mr. RATINER. Speaking purely as a professional negotiator Mr. Chairman, were I representing the other side I would favor very strongly a delay.

Mr. MURPHY. I have been advised that an analysis of relative bargaining strengths in the deep seabed negotiation can only lead to the conclusion that, if it is the United States that urgently needs a treaty, it will be the United States that will have to make more concessions.

Do you agree with that assessment?

Mr. RATINER. In Committee One, yes.

Mr. MURPHY. It seems to me that we could resolve our timing problem through domestic legislation.

If we were to adopt a different posture in the negotiation so that we could afford to take our time, is it possible that we might ultimately secure a treaty more favorable to our national interests in the deep seabed?

Mr. RATINER. I think, Mr. Chairman, there is no question that if we were prepared to take more time in the negotiations we could get a better result in Committee One. However, it must be borne in mind that, if we take more time, we may sacrifice other interests in the negotiation which are of considerable importance.

Mr. MURPHY. I am told that Committees Two and Three have made more progress than Committee One and that those documents are more acceptable to the U.S. perspective. Do you agree?

Mr. RATINER. Again, Mr. Chairman, the administration has not had an opportunity to study and review those documents.

I have, of course, with my long interest in the subject read the documents myself, and I think the Committee Two and Three documents do go further toward, at their present stage of development, meeting some of the objectives of the United States in this negotiation than the Committee One text produced by Chairman Engo.

On the other hand, I think it is important to note that the underlying strategy of the developing countries and others in this negotiation for the past many years has always been to recognize that many critical interest of the United States are found in Committee Two. Since it is in their interest to keep the United States actively interested in continued negotiations, it is possible that the Committee Two and Committee Three documents at this time are favorable to the United States for political as well as true negotiating reasons; that is, to keep us firmly interested in continued negotiations.

It is a very important factor to keep in mind that what is ultimately achieved in the conference depends on the approval of the Conference. That approval is measured by a vote, and it is not difficult to remove favorable provisions, if there is a collective will of the large majority of the countries to do so.

While I do think the Committee Two and Committee Three documents are good, I would have to confine that comment to "they are good right now."

Mr. MURPHY. Do you think it would be possible to conclude a treaty for Committee Two and Three while continuing the negotiation on the deep seabed and then go forward with a Committee One negotiation?

Mr. RATINER. Again, Mr. Chairman, this is a question where you really have to put yourself in the shoes of the other negotiators.

So far, there has been no evidence that they would be willing to break up the package.

Our position, our needs and our objectives in Committee Two and Three are quite clear and it is difficult, although not inconceivable, to imagine that the developing countries would sign a treaty which satisfied our basic objectives in Committees Two and Three but did not satisfy their basic objectives in Committee One.

Mr. MURPHY. With the progress the United States has made in Committees Two and Three and the interrelationship that you have just described to Committee One, would you say that our security interests or our economic interests in Committees Two and Three are in danger in any way because of the delay in Committee One.

Which of those two interests are the ones involved?

Mr. RATINER. Mr. Chairman, that is a difficult question to answer. I think all of our interests are in jeopardy as long as there is no treaty which satisfies those interests.

Now, in Committee Two and Committee Three I do not know whether the law of the sea task force and the administration as a whole will conclude that a truly successful negotiation at the next session is predictable.

If, on the basis of these single negotiating texts in Committees Two and Three, the administration concludes that satisfaction and accommodation of our basic objectives in those two committees is possible at the next session of the Conference, then obviously there would be a kind of pressure also to conclude work in Committee One.

Similarly, if Committee One were for some stretch of the imagination which right now eludes me, able to conclude a satisfactory treaty, then there might be pressure from the developing countries to wrap up the negotiation quickly and provide satisfaction in Committees Two and Three in order to preserve the gains they would have made in Committee One.

Right now, they have not made any gains in Committee One because of the Engo Text, which is a document we cannot view as a serious negotiating text.

Mr. MURPHY. On the last day of the Geneva Session of the Law of the Sea Conference, when the so-called single negotiating text emerged, it was touted as the new basis for negotiations.

In the accompanying statement by the chairman of the First Committee, Paul Engo of Cameroon, who allegedly authored the single negotiating text, he shid that his product was influenced by the "New International Economic Order" adopted by the United Nations General Assembly. That "New International Economic Order" called for cooperation among raw material producers of the Third World to raise prices paid for the commodities by the industrialized countries.

Did you see evidence of this in the negotiations and how important do you view this factor in reaching agreement on the deep seabed issues?

Mr. Ratiner. I think, Mr. Chairman, we would be foolish to ignore the fact that what Mr. Engo said is, in fact, the critical problem that confronts Committee One.

Committee One, in a sense, is not a part of the Law of the Sea Conference. It is a part of the developing country movement for control over raw materials generally, and it is much more akin to that movement than it is to a movement to simply obtain international cooperation in respect of the Law of the Sea.

That makes negotiations in Committee One particularly difficult. As I mentioned earlier, the new economic order was never before manifested in an overt and explicit manner in the Committee One negotiations. It was lingering behind the scenes. It was not necessarily widely endorsed.

Now, specific reference has been made to it by Mr. Engo in his statement and by Mr. Engo in his draft treaty text in article 9, paragraph 1. These references in a sense, may prove to be an escalation of the negotiations from which it will be extrmely difficult to recover.

Mr. Murphy. Engo said that there is a trend of thought in the committee that has pointed irresistably toward establishment of an international authority with wide powers.

He also said there appears to be a vast majority opinion that the Assembly should be the supreme policy making organ of the authority.

Does this mean that a bunch of United Nations politicians and bureaucrats are going to be telling our seabed miners what they can or cannot do in international waters?

Mr. Ratiner. Well, first it is true that a vast majority of the countries in the Committee One negotiations seeks sweeping, comprehensive policymaking for the one nation, on vote Assembly which would be established.

It is also true that developing countries recognize that, in order to have the participation of the industrialized countries, that kind of power in an assembly will have to be substantially modified and moderated.

In this respect, I would call your attention in particular to the May 3 "Pinto Text" where, despite the fact that the assembly was given supreme policymaking powers of the Authority, other provisions of that text provided for several protections against that policymaking power.

One of them was that each of the principal organs of the International Authority would not be able to interfere with the mandate of the other organs and that each was, in a sense, independent within its domain.

Then, that May 3 draft provided for an executive council which had the exclusive power to dictate the policy of the Authority in respect of exploration and exploitation and all activities connected with it.

That executive council, in the May 3 draft, took its decisions by a three-fourths vote and, in addition, was composed of three separate groups of countries, one of which would be the industrialized countries. With a three-fourths vote, a sufficient number of industrialized countries on that Council and with the Council being the sole organ that makes policy in respect of exploration and exploitation, the situation is markedly different than it is in the "Engo Text," which does not provide those same protections.

Mr. MURPHY. These protections then is where the document did not surface.

Mr. RATINER. That is right.

Mr. MURPHY. Engo also said that a vast majority now accepts that the Authority must be given power to exploit directly.

Here, we have this new super government that is going to regulate our miners and also engage in recovery operations itself.

How can we be sure that such an arrangement will not discriminate against our miners?

Mr. RATINER. Mr. Chairman, there is no absolute way to be sure that it will not discriminate.

The only way you can be comfortable with this international authority if it has the power to exploit directly—and I am now not referring to any exclusive power to exploit, but a parallel power to exploit—is through the establishment of what I referred to earlier as the many due process of law protections which we have been trying to build into the treaty. I am referring in particular to the voting in the council, the proper allocation of powers and functions to the different organs, the existence of a strong dispute settlement machinery. These types of things could provide, if drafted properly, reasonable protection, reasonable guarantees that the system would not be applied in a discriminatory manner. However, we do not have a text before us which provides those guarantees.

Mr. MURPHY. We do not have those protections?

Mr. RATINER. Not in the Engo Text, no, sir.

Mr. MURPHY. In your prepared statement, you indicate that "there were some significant signs of progress on issues involving the structure, powers and voting mechanisms of the proposed International Seabed Authority. However, the Engo single negotiating text offers little solace in that regard."

As I understand it, seabed producers will be a small minority in the Assembly and will have only 6 votes in the Council where it will take 12 just to block undesirable actions.

How can the United States be protected by an arrangement like that?

Mr. RATINER. The reference in my statement, Mr. Chairman, to progress in respect of the structure of the machinery is a reference to the 7 weeks of work which culminated, in a sense, in the Pinto May 3 document. It was not a reference to the Engo Text.

Mr. MURPHY. If there is one pervasive theme that reoccurs throughout the single negotiating text it is the direct and effective control of all the activities in the seabed by the International Authority.

It is my understanding that they are going to be into everything including the recovery operations, the processing plants, the books, the technology, the management and even into scientific research.

What legitimate reason could they have for this, or is it simply that they are after the miner's assets and technology without having to pay for them?

Mr. RATINER. Well, Mr. Chairman, again the views of the developing countries need to be understood in the context of their perspective on world economic affairs and world political affairs.

They feel that there has been a longtime injustice in the world; that they have not been adequately compensated for the resources which they own and which we have used to build a better country for ourselves. Accordingly, in their view, the deep seabed is an oppertunity to correct at the international and global level, if you will, some of this disequilibrium as they see it that has existed over the past several centuries in respect of the use of their raw materials.

Thus, I would not want to characterize their position as simply wanting to take our technology and our capital without paying for it. Rather, I think that in their view they feel they have paid for it for several hundreds of years, and that now it is time for the industrialized countries to try to equalize that imbalance.

I do not in any way want to suggest that those are my views, or the views of the administration, but in fairness to the developing countries I think you should know what they think.

Mr. MURPHY. The President of the Conference, Hamilton Shirley Amerasinghe of Sri Lanka reported at the end of the Geneva session that the so-called group of 77 Third World countries did not want anybody to begin recovery operations from the seabed. The reason they gave was that no member of the group of 77 now had the tech nology to engage in recovery operations.

Must we, the United States, wait until our firms lose their tech nological lead before the other side gets serious about reaching agree ment on a treaty?

Mr. RATINER. I think if one thing was clear in private discussions in Committee One, it was that the whole world expects and looks toward the United States to be the first developer of the bottom of the ocean. Even under the rather extreme proposals of the Group of 77, it is still anticipated that the principal exploiters for the foreseeable future—that is in resource terms, the forseeable future is 10 or 15 years—will be the United States. Thus, I do not think that the developing countries wish to hold off ocean mining until such time as they themselves acquire technology independently. Rather, I think their view is that we should get ocean mining started as soon as there is a treaty satisfactory to them. Over a period of time, once ocean mining begins, they believe that through various provisions of the treaty, they will transfer technology among them and acquire the capability to conduct ocean mining. However, I think they all recognize that without our participation and support they may not be able to acquire that ability.

Mr. MURPHY. Would current producers, that is countries that produce cobalt, manganese, nickel, copper, and related metals to seabed mining have an interest in delaying or in accelerating this treaty?

Mr. RATINER. They would have an interest in delaying the treaty.

Mr. MURPHY. This "single negotiating text" would exempt any income of the International Authority from national taxation and there would be governmental assessments to support the operations of the Authority.

As I understand, the plan also includes the maintenance of buffer stocks to keep mineral prices high.

Why is it necessary for the U.S. taxpayers to underwrite an effort that results in higher mineral prices for them and the rest of the world?

Mr. RATINER. It is neither necessary nor desirable, Mr. Chairman, and we do not have in our negotiating position any policy objective which would serve that interest.

Mr. MURPHY. There is detailed reference in the "single negotiating text" to a planning commission that is tasked with making specific recommendations to protect the export earnings of land-based producers including "commodity agerements and buffer arrangements." These are provisions that are commonly found in international cartel arrangements.

The text also says that "the Council shall adopt, on the recommendations of the Economic Planning Commission, programs or measures to avoid or minimize adverse effects on the revenues derived from the export of minerals."

This would appear that the Planning Commission has considerable power to build an OPEC-like cartel.

Is the United States going to let them do this?

Mr. RATINER. I agree with your statement, Mr. Chairman. I would again call your attention to the May 3 draft on the same subject, the Economic Planning Commission, where you will find that the Planning Commission would have to be composed of an equal balance between consumers and producers, and that in order to take decisions which, according to the May 3 draft, could only be recommendations a simple majority of both the consumer and producer groups would be necessary, followed by a two-thirds majority of the whole of the Planning Commission.

This is the kind of due process type protection that I was referring to earlier. Unfortunately, that approach to the Planning Commission is missing from the May 7 text.

Mr. MURPHY. Mr. De la Garza?

Mr. DE LA GARZA. Thank you, Mr. Chairman.

I have some questions that follow up, or even may be duplicative of the chairman's questions.

In the formulation of the Pinto papers, what was your individual participation, if any?

Mr. RATINER. Mr. De la Garza, I really would prefer to answer that question in executive session.

Mr. MURPHY. If you will yield for a moment, the witness is prepared to return for an executive session?

Mr. RATINER. Yes, sir.

Mr. MURPHY. And there will be no restrictions by any of the departments on his appearance?

Mr. RATINER. I know of no restrictions, Mr. Chairman, and I would be happy to come before you in executive session.

Mr. DE LA GARZA. Then I would defer, Mr. Chairman, questions along that line.

Let me jump over. In future negotiations next March or in the future beyond that, what agreement do you feel we could negotiate from our position relative to the votes within the Conference?

Mr. RATINER. The strength of our negotiation position is not in our votes. Clearly, we can be easily outvoted on any issue.

I think the strength of our negotiating position is first that we do, in fact, possess almost exclusively the technology and the know how to get this job done and the developing countries are well aware of that. There is a second strength in that most countries, particularly outside Committee One, seem to sincerely believe that if the Law of the Sea is to be, in a sense, rewritten and reorganized along the lines of the present negotiations the treaty will work only with universal acceptance. Therefore, the United States must be viewed, and is veiwed by most countries, as an indispensable ingredient in a satisfactory settlement of these issues by treaty.

Mr. DE LA GARZA. From your statement prior and your answer here, the fact is they look to the United States to be the first developers. They know we are the ones who have the technology, but the rules will be formulated apparently 100 percent to the wishes and desires and benefit of all the other countries.

Mr. RATINER. That would only be true under the May 7 Treaty that emerged from Committee One.

Under any satisfactory treaty, and I do not mean to imply that the May 3 Treaty is satisfactory because definitely it is not satisfactory, we would have a reasonable and substantial influence in the decision making process of the international organization. This is more the case in the May 3 Treaty.

Mr. DE LA GARZA. For the record and for information only and for no other reason where is Mr. Engo from?

Mr. RATINER. Cameroon.

Mr. DE LA GARZA. Where is Mr. Pinto from?

Mr. RATINER. Sri Lanka, formerly Ceylon.

Mr. DE LA GARZA. This is a general question beyond the scope of your testimony in the committee but in your opinion was there anything achieved at the conference that was favorable to the U.S.?

Mr. RATINER. Again, I would be very reluctant to answer before a detailed study of the treaty text, but I think certain things emerged rather clearly at this session.

I guess one of them, and one that is indispensable to any attempt to negotiate a global treaty, is the mere putting together of a single negotiating text. That is a major accomplishment and it should be borne in mind, particularly in respect of Committees Two and Three, that those negotiating texts are not simply the pure invention of a chairman, but rather are an attempt to capture what that chairman feels is the compromise on each and every issue—or the near compromise on each and every issue—consistent with what he has heard and seen in his committee over a period of several years.

This negotiating has been going on, at least in respect of Committees Two and Three, for 4 or 5 years. In respect of Committee One, in one form or another it began 8 years ago when Ambassador Pardo first made his speech in the U. N. General Assembly.

Mr. DE LA GARZA. With all due respect to your position in government, Mr. Ratiner, you, yourself, said you were a professional negotiator. I think you have truly become that if by your answer success is having arrived at a text, regardless of what is in it.

Mr. RATINER. I did not mean to say anything that would make me sound foolish.

Mr. DE LA GARZA. I do not mean to imply anything except you said success in a conference is arriving at a text and everyone cheers and applauds and we will get to what is in the thing later.

Mr. RATINER. Prior to entering the final phases of negotiation, it is extremely useful to have before you a single document that everybody can use.

Up until now, particularly in Committees Two and Three but also in Committee One, no such document existed, and it was extremely difficult to put one together. Thus, in a mehcanical sense, the Geneva session took an important stride forward, but I would not characterize it as a negotiating success.

Mr. DE LA GARZA. You mention in your testimony that the thrust or the intent or the desire for a provisional authority or a provisional arrangement of some sort within Committee One, and I did not get the thrust of your testimony. You mentioned it in a favorable light.

Do you mean to tell me now that the United States position is to work for a provisional authority and continue with further sessions of the conference?

Mr. RATINER. Not precisely, Mr. De la Garza.

What we hope for is to achieve a final treaty which is satisfactory to the United States and then, rather than wait for what could be a very lengthy period of ratifications, provide for the provisional entry into force of that final treaty. However, under our approach there would not be any further Sessions of the Law of the Sea Conference. The treaty would be reached, decided upon and signed, and then would enter into provisional force pending its permanent entry into force, which might take 6 or 7 years for the necessary ratifications to occur.

Mr. DE LA GARZA. Then I misunderstood you because your statement was that the final treaty should provide for a provisional application pending ratification, is that it?

Mr. RATINER. Yes, sir.

Mr. DE LA GARZA. Was there any attempt for any provisional authority pending a final treaty or a final ratification?

Mr. RATINER. No, sir.

Mr. MURPHY. I know this is beyond the scope of your testimony, but the provisional authority that you mentioned concerns the Committee One on the deep seabed but do you know if any attempt was made or the feelings is the same on the other committees that related, for example, to fisheries?

Mr. RATINER. Our position, sir, is that we favor the provisional entry into force of the Law of the Sea Convention and the establishment in accordance with that chapter that deals with the seabed, of a provisional authority.

We, in particular, favor the provisional entry into force of the treaty in respect of fisheries and the deep seabed. Now, it is in a sense a happenstance that the provisions of the draft treaty text on provisional entry into force comes out in the Committee One document, since it has always been a major effort of ours in Committee One to have the idea of provisional entry into force accepted by other countries.

In a sense, that issue has been negotiated in Committee One, but it is very much our intention to remove that provision from where it is now found and have it cover the whole of the convention if that is possible, including fisheries.

Mr. DE LA GARZA. To your knowledge from your participation was there any arrangement or agreement made for dissemination of the final Pinto or Engo text, the one that finally did not surface or surfaced but not quite clearly.

Mr. RATINER. As I understand it, Mr. De la Garza, the Pinto Text of May 7 has been informally passed along to most delegations, but does not have any official status and has not been reproduced as a document of the conference.

Mr. DE LA GARZA. Was there any decision made at Committee One to continue discussions sanctioned by the committee or was everyone left to their own resources?

Mr. RATINER. Well, sir, arrangements have been made by the United Nations Secretariat to provide facilities, funds, and interpretation accommodations in New York, in this year, perhaps during the summer. It is up to the members of each of the committees to try to arrange informal consultations on these matters in this intersessional period, if they are able to do so. However, there was no official sanction of any intersessional work nor was there any official decision that I am aware of in any committee to have intersessional work, with the exception of the quasi-official group known as the Evenson Group, which deals with the economic zone. As I understand it, that group has scheduled a meeting for possibly late summer and another one for the winter in New York.

Mr. DE LA GARZA. Mr. Chairman, the other questions I have would probably be on the borderline as to whether we could ask them here or in executive session.

In that case I would defer any futher questions.

Thank you.

Mr. MURPHY. Thank you.

Mr. Sharood?

Mr. SHAROOD. Mr. Chairman, is it your intention to seek an excutive session of this subcommittee where the witness will appear again?

Mr. MURPHY. Yes, with Mr. Ratiner and other witnesses.

Mr. SHAROOD. Then I will not pursue any of these matters at this time.

Mr. MURPHY. Mr. Perian?

Mr. PERIAN. There seems to be some confusion over precisely how much was given up of the oceans' seabeds in the so-called Pinto document of April 9, 1975.

I think in response to the chairman you said that there were two areas that would be selected; the authority would go to the bank and the developer would take the other area.

It is also outlined in the Pinto paper that the contractor gets one-half of the second area and the other half goes into the bank which in effect, means the authority gets 75 percent of the explored areas?

Mr. RATINER. I think that should be clarified, Mr. Perian. For the record, it should be clear that this is not the May 3 text we have been talking about, but rather the Pinto draft on basic conditions, the attempt to compromise on the rules and regulations. The explanation is that, in that document, Mr. Pinto, again exercising the personal powers of the chairman, attempted to put together a compromise paper. He did not accurately reflect the United States' position.

The United States' position which should have been reflected in paragraph 19 of that document to which you just referred was that at no time could the authority hold more than 50 percent of the area in the bank.

Chairman Pinto simply elected in presenting this document to drop that provision of the United States' proposal in his effort to lead the way to what he conceived of as a compromise in the committee.

Thus, in his document, our proposal is not reflected, and he made this quite clear himself in Committee One when he introduced that document. Under his document, there is a provision for relinquishment of areas; hence, if the developer gave one area to the bank and kept one for himself, he would then relinquish 50 percent of his area when he had identified the actual discreet ore deposit he wanted to mine.

This is a normal thing, relinquishment occurring in most resource management systems, including our own, but when he left out the provision in paragraph 19 that required the authority never to hold more than 50 percent, he made it possible for all of the relinquished areas to go into the bank. Thus, the authority would end up with 75 percent, but that is not the United States' position.

Mr. PERIAN. Well then, the U.S. delegation did not support the document of April 9, 1975.

Mr. RATINER. That is right. We made a statement in the working group of Committee One when Pinto finally put forward his last version of the basic conditions totally disassociating ourselves from that document.

Mr. PERIAN. But you did support the 50 percent?

Mr. RATINER. Yes, that was the United States' position, 50 percent.

Mr. PERIAN. Thank you.

Mr. MURPHY. Mr. Ratiner, when we talk of seabed minerals would you describe the surface areas in relation to the areas known as the Continental Shelf as to what areas we are speaking of and what relationship Committee One's work has to do with Continental Shelf?

Mr. RATINER. This, Mr. Chairman, is in part a political definition and in part, a geological definition.

The deep seabed, the area that is considered to be the primary focus of Committee One's work is generally speaking, that area which is beyond the Continental margins of coastal states; that is the shelf, the slope and the rise. The deep seabed is the abyssal ocean floor.

Now, one of the issues in Committee Two is where the coastal state's jurisdiction stops, and this is what I mean by a legal and political definition.

It is obviously agreed that 200 miles will be the boundary of coastal state purisdiction in the economic zone but it has not yet been agreed whether, in those cases where the Continental Shelf extends beyond 200 miles, that portion of the shelf that extends beyond 200 miles will be under the jurisdiction of the coastal state or under the jurisdiction of the International Seabed Authority.

Accordingly, depending on how that boundary issue is finally resolved, there may be two kinds of geology in the international area.

One kind would be the abyssal ocean floor and the other kind would be that portion of the Continental margin which extends beyond 200 miles. However, I think there probably will be a recognition in the treaty ultmiately that the coastal state has jurisdiction beyond 200 miles, if its Continental Shelf goes beyond 200 miles, but that is still subject to considerable negotiation.

Mr. MURPHY. What committee will make that determination?

Mr. RATINER. In the first instance, it would be made in Committee Two.

It has always been understood that Committee One would give recommendations to Committee Two on that subject, but Committee One shows no disposition to get into that issue. I would say it will be exclusively negotiated within Committee Two and ultimately, they will adopt the treaty article which will be sent to the plenary conference.

Mr. MURPHY. What percentage of the United States' Continental Shelf extends beyond 200 miles?

Mr. RATINER. I am not certain. I think the last figure I have heard was 7 percent, but I am not sure that is right, Mr. Chairman.

Mr. MURPHY. I have heard 5 to 7 percent from various witnesses we have had in the last month.

Mr. DE LA GARZA. Mr. Chairman, if I may—Mr. Ratiner, you may not be prepared to answer for the record the document of May 7 which is entitled A/Conf.72/WP.9/Part 1. You have seen the Engo Text and the Pinto Text. Which one would this be?

Mr. RATINER. The document of May 7 is the Engo Text. However, attached to it is an annex, what we sometimes call the other Pinto Text, which includes the basic conditions of general survey, exploration and exploitation.

Mr. Engo attached as an annex that particular work of Mr. Pinto. What is not in this document is the other Pinto Text, which we have referred to as the May 3 text. This was a draft of the Regime and Machinery Articles.

Mr. MURPHY. That is the 24-hour-late text?

Mr. RATINER. That is correct.

Mr. DE LA GARZA. So the May 7, 1975, is the second Engo Text with an annex No. 1 which would be the No. 1 Pinto Text, is that correct?

Mr. RATINER. No, sir, the 7 May text is the only Engo Text. There was only one, and it is the 7 May text. It attaches a document that Mr. Pinto had worked on separately in the working group of Committee One, which primarily deals with the criteria for developing rules and regulations for the system of exploration and exploitation.

The May 3 Pinto Text to which we refer did not include these basic conditions.

It is a text that would correspond to the May 7 Engo Text. The annex was treated separately and apart, so that the May 3 Pinto Text corresponds directly to the Engo Text minus the basic conditions.

The basic conditions are the product of Pinto's work.

Mr. DE LA GARZA. Thank you very much, Mr. Ratiner and thank you, Mr. Chairman.

Mr. MURPHY. Mr. Ratiner, we appreciate the forthright manner in which you have responded to all the questions and also Congressman De la Garza and myself have been observers at these conferences over the years and we also appreciate the expertise and dedication that you have exhibited in the performance of your duties on this very difficult international question.

We look forward to seeing you in executive session soon.

Mr. RATINER. Thank you, Mr. Chairman.

Mr. MURPHY. Our next witness is Mr. Jack Flipse, president of DeepSea Ventures.

Do you have any associates to accompany you?

STATEMENT OF JACK FLIPSE, PRESIDENT, DEEPSEA VENTURES, INC., GLOUCESTER POINT, VA.

Mr. FLIPSE. My name is John Flipse and I am president of Deep-Sea Ventures, Inc., of Gloucester Point, Va., the ocean mining subsidiary of Tenneco, Inc., of Houston, Tex.

I am a member of the Committee on Undersea Mineral Resources of the American Mining Congress and serve as an industry adviser on the State Department Advisory Committee on the Law of the Sea.

Mr. Chairman, it is a pleasure to report again to this committee and to express DeepSea Ventures' reaction to the recent Geneva session of the Third Law of the Sea Conference and the increasing need for the passage of domestic legislation such as the deep oceans mining bill, H.R. 1270.

The briefest and kindest statement one could make regarding the recent Geneva session is that it clearly indicates the need for domestic legislation on the subject of deep ocean mineral development, and constructive discussion with, and hopefully, collaboration of like-minded nations.

As an industrial technical adviser to the U.S. delegation for 2 weeks during April, I had the opportunity to attend regular morning U.S. delegation meetings and the infrequent sessions of the Deep Seabed Committee informal working group held in the Palace of Nations.

Except for one brief, private conversation with John Stevenson, chief of the U.S. delegation, I did not attend the interagency deliberations of the delegation nor any of the private and/or secret negotiating sessions between our delegation members and members of other delegations.

I did have the opportunity to address, in general terms, the progress of the Conference with certain members of the Conference Secreteariat and industrial advisers to other nation's delegations.

The opinions expressed herein are therefore entirely my own and not based upon confidential or private information.

Without a doubt, the efforts of the American participants in this session of the Conference were devoted, energetic, and entirely sincere. The extent and futility of the task makes such devotion a pitiful waste of American energy.

The sincerity and commitment of our State Department to obtain a treaty, however poor it might be, was not matched by their counterparts on other delegations

The obviousness of the successes of the delaying strategy of the Group of 77 was painfully apparent to those who arrived during the "progress" of the session.

Perhaps the most startling thing to an industrial observer was the apparent American strategy of making concession after concession without the concession being acknowledged or counteroffers made. This is not negotiation.

I believe that the other delegates were overwhelmed with our apparent generosity. As a sarcastic member of the 77 team pointed out, "our cup runneth over."

The Conference report addressing the work of the First Committee which is put forward as a negotiating text gives us no comfort.

Although the authors have removed a few of the odious terms and conditions which the Group of 77 wishes to be applied by the Authority to any ocean miner, there were no assurances or guarantees and the document is carefully structured to permit thsee terms to be reinstated under a very discretionary regulation promulgating authority.

The completeness of control over the American interests, including production and pricing, is an inherent obstacle to performance under this document or any feasible derivation therefrom.

I compliment our Committee One negotiator for the achievement of several drafting concessions including the insertion of some "weasel words" and the removal of repeated slaps in the face of the United States that characterized the Pinto document but regretfully state that the substitute only fails to mention these discriminatory controls and punishments and does not in any way limit their future application.

The proposed technique of overcoming impossible terms and conditions was to have the developed nations with effective control of the machinery of the Seabed Authority.

Following this, the second fallback position was to be an objective and fair tribunal where justice would be done.

Although there may be a possibility of negotiating some effective representation in the Council of the Authority, the intent is absolutely clear that the policy organization with the control is the assembly characterized by one nation, one vote.

The references to the tribunal may satisfy some lawyers, but give considerable pause to an industrialist when the standard of treatment is referred to as fair and reasonable.

The recent positions taken by the UN as a whole disregarding sanctity of contracts and actively promoting the right to expropriate to compensate for past injuries, real or imagined, suggest that what is fair to one may well fail to be fair to another.

The thrust of the foregoing should be apparent. I have little hope that the current negotiation will lead to a timely treaty under which our company could function as a profit oriented, competitive industrial operation.

To me, the logical and strikingly obvious next step is the passage of domestic legislation. H.R. 1270 represents the thoughtful consideration of a bill introduced some years ago by the American Mining Congress but now, through negotiation and deliberation, is con siderably modified from the original bill.

It appears also that there will be several additional pieces of legislation, of uncertain merit, which will indubitably be considered with the bill under discussion today.

It may be worthwhile to reintrodume the original bill so that the limits of the legislation are expanded.

I assure your committee that DeepSea Ventures is prepared to provide any but the most sensitive proprietary information to guide these deliberations and to provide state-of-the-art technical and business data so that the resultant laws of the United States can serve as a model for the like minded nations and permit development of these important alternate sources of key materials to the U.S. economy.

Thank you, Mr. Chairman.

Mr. MURPHY. Thank you; Mr. Flipse.

It is now clear that an LOS treaty on seabed mining will not be concluded in 1975, or even in 1976.

What will be the effect on you if the Congress does not act on interim ocean mining legislation?

Mr. FLIPSE. The political uncertainty has been a major factor affecting the level of funding which our parent corporation has been willing to advance.

It will undoubtedly affect the willingness to invest of the Joint Venture which DeepSea is now serving as a contractor. I think the uncertainty and the possible implications of a treaty on our business opportunities is a severe deterrent to availability of risk capital.

It is impossible to estimate how this factor will affect key individuals but their personal reactions to this risk is a most serious concern to us.

Mr. MURPHY. Any percent on the area of budget of equipment or personnel that you can provide us in this regard?

Mr. FLIPSE. The only accurate number is historic. Our budget was reduced to essentially one-third of its earlier level in 1972 when the first session of this Law of the Sea Conference was anticipated. When the group of 77 position became clearly known our funding in Deep-Sea Ventures was reduced from approximately $4.5 million to $1.5 million a year.

Mr. MURPHY. If a treaty is consummated, in what form do you see it taking shape, given the current posture of the U.S. negotiators?

Mr. FLIPSE. We have made the industry needs known through the Advisory Committee and I think that the U.S. Committee I negotiator fully understands our needs.

Our concern is that he will be unable to achieve a treaty that will meet these needs.

Let me just briefly point out what they are and the apparent lack of recognition of these in the current document that is serving as a negotiating text.

First, access to the area is essential in order to justify any investment. You cannot put together a mining venture without an ore body.

The second is freedom to manage your business. Discretionary controls by the authority, especially price and production controls, really make it impossible to run such an operation as a business.

Third, the need to limit exploration expenses. Banking and/or relinquishment concepts do serve a purpose and are provided for in H.R. 1270 in a realistic fashion. It appears that the group of 77 will be looking for both banking and relinquishment which would result in 75 percent of the area being under the authority.

Another concern is that of profit sharing. Certainly the lesser developed countries should not profit before there is a chance to get your investment back. As it is being discussed at the conference, profit sharing serves as a limit of incentive, or at best, as an excess profits tax. Without guarantees in the case you do not make your production or profit objectives you have the low side risk without the high side reward when you sell a project to a board of directors it is really the expectation of a reward that develops the interest. A reward that they cannot get by selling boxes, or pumping gas or some other very conventional low-risk operation.

It is the incentive on the top side that provides the risk capital in American industry.

The Authority, acting through the Enterprise, is supposed to be our competitor even while they act as judge, jury, and probably policemen. Both will be located comfortably in Kingston, Jamaica so they can carefully handle the business between the two bodies. Such an arrangement suggests an environment of conflict and stress for future relationships. I think human beings making business judgments tend to avoid these stressful situations.

I would also like to point out that the concept of provisional application of any treaty is a two-edged sword. If we did not like the treaty, if and when it is negotiated we would like to oppose it through the usual techniques of testimony to Congress and so forth.

If it is provisionally applied we find ourselves in the position of having to defend it because once you have started an activity under a given set of rules, the thing you can least afford is a change of those rules. Americans tend to live with bad deals rather than fight for a basically better deal if change is involved.

We are very much concerned with the connotation of provisional application. It has its risks.

Mr. MURPHY. Mr. Flipse, would you tell us who is on the advisory committee?

Mr. FLIPSE. It is a fair representation, I believe, of fishing, petroleum and mining industry people; certainly the academic community is well represented and the environmentalists are well represented. We would be happy to supply you with a list of the committee members.

Mr. MURPHY. How many members?

Mr. FLIPSE. Probably 40 or 45.

Mr. MURPHY. And do they have continuity throughout the negotiations?

Mr. FLIPSE. There have been some changes, Mr. Chairman, but basically it has been the same group of people over the last 6 or 7 years.

Mr. MURPHY. The committee would appreciate it if you would furnish that membership of the advisory committee.

Mr. FLIPSE. With pleasure.

[The information to be supplied follows:]

ADVISORY COMMITTEE ON THE LAW OF THE SEA

PUBLIC CHAIRMAN

Hon. Dean Rusk, the University of Georgia School of Law, Athens, Ga. 30601.

I. PETROLEUM SUBCOMMITTEE

Mr. Gordon L. Becker, Counsel, Exxon Corp., 1251 Avenue of the Americas, New York, N.Y. 10020.

Mr. George A. Birrell, General Counsel, Mobil Oil Corp., 150 East 42d Street, New York, N.Y. 10017.

Mr. Hollis Dole, General Manager, Colony Development Operation, Atlantic Richfield Corp., 15 Security Life Building, Denver, Colo. 80202.

Mr. John Norton Garrett, Gulf Oil Corp., P.O. Box 1166, Pittsburgh, Pa. 15230.

Mr. G. Winthrop Haight, Forsyth, Decker, Murray, 51 West 51st Street, New York, N.Y. 10091.

Mr. William J. Martin, Jr., Standard Oil Building, 22 Bust Street, San Francisco, Calif. 94104.

Mr. Bryon Milner, Vice President, Products Division, Atlantic Richfield Co., Box 2679—T.A. Los Angeles, Calif. 90051.

Mr. Maxwell McKnight, Senior Committee Coordinator, National Petroleum Council, 1625 K Street NW., Washington, D.C. 20006.

Mr. Cecil J. Olmstead, Vice President, Assistant to the Chairman of the Board, Texaco, 135 East 42d Street, New York, N.Y. 10071.

Mr. Richard Young, Attorney and Counsellor at Law, Van Hornesville, N.Y. 13475.

II. HARD MINERALS SUBCOMMITTEE

Mr. T. S. Ary, Vice President, Union Carbide Exploration Corp., 270 Park Avenue, New York, N. Y.

Mr. Paul S. Bilgore, Vice President, The Anaconda Co., 25 Broadway, New York, N. Y. 10004.

Mr. Charles F. Cook, Jr., 4012 North Stafford St., Arlington, Va. 22207.

Mr. Marne A. Dubs, Director, Ocean Resources Department, Kennecott Copper Corp., 161 East 42d Street, New York, N.Y. 10017.

Mr. John E. Flipse, President, Deepsea Ventures, Inc., Gloucester Point, Va. 23062.

Mr. John L. Shaw, International Nickel Co., Inc., 300 120th Avenue, N.W., Bellevue, Wash. 98005.

III. INTERNATIONAL FINANCE AND TAXATION SUBCOMMITTEE

Mr. Kenneth E. Hill, Eastman Dillon, Union Securities & Co., One Chase Manhattan Plaza, New York, N.Y. 10005.

Mr. John A. Redding, Continental Bank, 231 South LaSalle Street, Chicago, Ill. 60604.

Mr. John G. Winger, Vice President, The Chase Manhattan Bank, N.A., One Chase Manhattan Plaza, New York, N. Y. 10015.

IV. INTERNATIONAL LAW AND RELATIONS SUBCOMMITTEE

Mr. Lewis Alexander, University of Rhode Island, Law of the Sea Institute, 320 Washburn Hall, Department of Geography, Kingston, R. I. 02881.

Mr. R. R. Baxter, Harvard University, Law School, Cambridge, Mass. 02138.
Mr. Jose A. Cabranes, Office of Commonwealth of Puerto Rico, 1625 Massachusetts Avenue. NW., Washington. D.C. 20036.
Mr. Jonathan I. Charney. Assistant Professor of Law, School of Law, Vanderbilt University. Nashville, Tenn. 37420.
Mr. Aaron Danzig. Nemeroff, Jelline, Danzig Palsey & Kaufman, 350 Fifth Avenue, New York, N.Y. 10001.
Mr. Arthur H. Dean, 48 Wall Street, New York, N.Y. 10005.
Mr. Richard N. Gardner, Henry L. Moses, Professor of Law and International Organization, Columbia University School of Law, 435 West 116th Street, New York, N.Y. 10027.
Ms. Margaret L. Gerstle, Attorney-Consultant, 3016 O Street, NW., Washington, D.C. 20007.
Mr. Louis Henkin, Columbia University, School of Law, 435 West 116th Street, New York, N.Y. 10027.
Dr. Ann Hollick. Assistant Professor of Political Science, Johns Hopkins School of Advanced International Studies, 1740 Massachusetts Avenue, NW., Washington. D.C. 20036.
Mr. Philip C. Jessup, Pinefield Off Windrow Road, Norfolk. Conn. 06058.
Mr. H. Gary Knight, Louisiana State University, Law School, Baton Rouge, La. 70803.
Mr. Robert Krueger, Nossaman, Waters, Scott Krueger & Riordan, 445 South Figueroa Street, Los Angeles, Calif. 90017.
Mr. John G. Laylin, Covington and Burling, 888 16th Street, NW., Washington, D.C. 20006.
Mr. Myres McDougal, Yale Law School, New Haven, Conn. 06520.
Mr. Benjamin Read, President, German Marshall Fund, 11 Dupont Circle, Washington, D.C. 20036.
Mr. Charles S. Rhyne, World Peace Through Law Center, 400 Hill Building, Washington, D.C. 20006.
Mr. Louis B. Sohn, Bemis Professor of International Law, Law School of Harvard University, Cambridge. Mass. 02138.
Mr. John R. Stevenson, Sullivan & Cromwell, 48 Wall Street, New York, N.Y. 10005.
Mr. John Temple Swing, Council on Foreign Relations, 58 E 68th Street, New York, N.Y. 10021.

V. MARINE ENVIRONMENT SUBCOMMITTEE

Mr. Richard A. Frank, National Resource Defense Council, 1751 N Street, NW., Washington, D.C. 20036.
Mr. Eldon Greenburg, Center for Law and Social Policy, 1751 N Street, NW., Washington, D.C. 20036.
Mr. Bostwick H. Ketchum. Associate Director, Woods Hole Oceanographic Institution, Woods Hole, Mass. 02543.
Mr. Sam Levering, Save Our Seas, 245 Second Street, NE., Washington, D.C. 20002.
Mr. Anthony Wayne Smith, Attorney at Law, 1701 18th Street, NW., Washington, D.C. .20009.
Mr. George M. Woodwell, Marine Biological Laboratory, Woods Hole Oceanographic Institution, Woods Hole, Mass.

VI. FISHERIES SUBCOMMITTEE

Mr. Charles R. Carry, 215 Cannery Street, Tuna Research Foundation, Inc., Terminal Island, Calif.
Mr. J. Steele Culbertson, Director, National Fish Meal & Oil Association, 1730 Pennsylvania Avenue, Washington, D.C. 20006.
Mr. Jacob J. Dykstra, Pt. Judith Fishermen's Coop. Association, Point Judith, R.I. 02882.
Mr. Douglas B. Eaton, P.O. Box 2871, Kodiak, Alaska 99615.
Mr. August J. Felando, Tuna Boat Association, 1 Tuna Lane, San Diego, Calif. 92101.
Mr. Harold E. Lokken, 1921 N. 48th Street, Seattle, Wash. 98101.

Mr. Robert Mauermann, Executive Secretary, Texas Shrimp Association, 910 East Levee Street, Brownsville, Tex. 78520.

Mr. John J. Royal, Secretary/Treasurer, Fishermen and Allied Worker's Union, Local 33 I.L.W., 806 Palos Verdes Street, San Pedro, Calif. 90731.

Mr. Richard H. Stroud, Executive Vice President, Sport Fishing Institute, 608 13th Street, N.W., Washington, D.C. 20005.

Mr. William G. Saletic, Executive Manager, Seiners Association, P.O. Box 5106, 1111 NW. 45th Street, Seattle, Wash. 98107.

Mr. William Nelson Utz, Steele and Utz, 1225 19th Street, N.W., Washington, D.C. 20036.

Mr. Lowell Wakefield, Wakefield Seafoods, Inc., Port, Wakefield, Alaska 99550.

Mr. John Weddig, Executive Director, National Fisheries Institute, 1730 Pennsylvania Avenue, NW., Washington, D.C. 20006.

Mr. Walter V. Yonker, Executive Vice President, Association of Pacific Fisheries, 1600 South Jackson Street, Seattle, Wash. 98144.

VII. MARINE SCIENCE SUB-COMMITTEE

Mr. William T. Burke, Professor of Law, University of Washington School of Law (Condon Hall), Seattle. Wash. 98105.

Mr. John C. Calhoun, Jr., Vice President for Academic Affairs, Texas A. & M. University, College Station, Tex. 77843.

Dr. John P. Craven, University of Hawaii, Honolulu, Hawaii 96822.

Dr. L. Eugene Cronin, Associate Director for Research. Center for Environmental & Estuarine Studies, University of Maryland, Cambridge, Md. 21613.

Mr. Paul M. Fye, President, Woods Hole Oceanographic Institute, Woods Hole, Mass. 02543.

Mr. Bruce C. Heezen, Lamont-Doherty Geological Observatory, Columbia University. Palisades, N.Y. 10964.

Mr. John A. Knauss, Provost for Marine Affairs, University of Rhode Island, Kingston, R.I. 02881.

Mr. William Nierenberg, Scripps Institute of Oceanography, University of California, LaJolla, Calif. 92037.

Mr. Roger Revelle, Richard Saltonstall Professor of Population Policy, Director of the Center for Population Studies, 3 Bow Street, Cambridge, Mass. 02138.

Mr. Warren Wooster, Dean of Rosenstiel School of Marine and Atmospheric Science, 10 Rickenbacker Causeway, Miami, Fla. 33149.

VIII. MARITIME INDUSTRIES SUBCOMMITTEE

Capt. John W. Clark. President, Delta Steamship Lines, Inc., 1700 International Trade Mart, Box 50250, New Orleans. La. 70150.

Mr. William J. Coffey, American Institute of Merchant Shipping, 1625 K Street, NW., Washington, D.C. 20006.

Mr. Herman E. Denzler. Jr., International Association of Drilling Contractors, 101 Northland Avenue, New Orleans, La. 70114.

Mr. O. William Moody, Administrator. AFL–CIO Maritime Trades Department, 815 16th Street. NW., Washington, D.C. 20006.

Mr. Charles P. Murphy, Sea Land Services. Inc., Elizabeth, N.J.

Mr. Frank M. Tuttle. American Telephone & Telegraph Co., World Trade Center, New York, N.Y. 10048.

THE SENATE

Hon. James Buckley. U.S. Senate, Washington, D.C. 20515.

Hon. Clifford P. Case, U.S. Senate, Washington. D.C. 20515

Hon. Ernest F. Hollings. U.S. Senate, Washington, D.C. 20519

Hon. J. Bennett, Johnston, Jr.. U.S. Senate. Washington. D.C. 20515.

Hon. Warren G. Magnuson. U.S. Senate, Washington, D.C. 20515.

Hon. Thomas J. McIntyre, U.S. Senate, Washington. D.C. 20515.

Hon. Edmund S. Muskie, U.S. Senate, 115 Russell Office Building, Washington, D.C. 20515.

Hon. Claiborne Pell, U.S. Senate. 325 Russell Office Building, Washington, D.C. 20515.

Hon. Ted Stevens, U.S. Senate, Washington, D.C. 20512.
Hon. John G. Tower, U.S. Senate, Washington, D.C. 20515.

Hon. Charles E. Bennett, House of Representatives, Washington, D.C. 20510.
Hon. Thomas N. Downing, House of Representatives, Washington, D.C., 30510.
Hon. Joshua Eilberg, House of Representatives, Washington, D.C. 20510.
Hon. Donald M. Fraser, House of Representatives, Washington, D.C. 20510.
Hon. Benjamin A. Gilman, House of Representatives, Washington, D.C. 20510.
Hon. Gilbert Gude, House of Representatives, Washington, D.C. 20510.
Hon. Paul N. McCloskey, Jr., House of Representatives, Washington, D.C. 20510.
Hon. Philip E. Ruppe, House of Representatives, Washington, D.C. 20510.
Hon. Leonor K. Sullivan, House of Representatives, Washington, D.C. 20510.
Hon. Bob Wilson, House of Representatives, Washington, D.C. 20510.

GOVERNORS

Hon. Michael Dukakis, Governor of Massachusetts, State House, Boston, Mass.
Hon. Jay S. Hammond, Governor of Alaska, Juneau, Alaska.

Mr. MURPHY. What do you see as the ultimate goal of the group of 77 in terms of the treaty?

Mr. FLIPSE. I think it is perfectly clear they wish to limit and control this ultimate source of raw materials to protect their land producers and also to achieve the political and economic strength that Mr. Ratiner so capably defined for us.

Mr. MURPHY. Would you briefly characterize the Engo Text?

Mr. FLIPSE. Having been a merchant mariner myself, I suspect the proper word is not admissible in this forum.

It is a difficult document that gives us, as I said in my statement, no comfort as the basis for a treaty under which we could operate in an incentive stimulated competitive manner.

Mr. MURPHY. Engo said that "a vast majority now accepts that the authority must be given power to exploit directly."

This means the authority that is going to regulate our miners will also engage in recovery operations itself.

How can we be sure that such an arrangement will not discriminate against our miners?

Mr. FLIPSE. We feel certain it will discriminate against us.

Mr. MURPHY. What is the worst that can happen if you simply go forward with your activities under current international maritime law?

Mr. FLIPSE. We sincerely believe the realities of ocean mining and processing could progress rather normally.

I think the recent incident of the merchant ship in the Far Eastern waters gives us concern. I have stated before, publicly, that I did not think we needed gun boats to protect us, but I am not so certain now.

I would say the principal deterrent to operation under existing law is the fact that there is no way to calculate the cost of royalties, access to the material and so on. An estimate of the return on investment of the funding, and the total capital commitment is very difficult. This would be a serious deterrent to making such a commitment.

We do need, inou r opinion, legislation or a treaty, Mr. Chairman.

Mr. MURPHY. Mr. de la Garza?

Mr. DE LA GARZA [presiding]. The Chairman has several other questions that we will defer until his return.

Let me ask you a couple of questions of my own. How many American companies aside from yourself have the same level of technology in this field?

Mr. FLIPSE. The Kennecott Copper Corp. would be the only American company. One that is both American and Canadian is the International Nickel Company. I would say they are probably in the same technological position as DeepSea Ventures.

Mr. DE LA GARZA. Are there any foreign companies that advanced or at that same level of technology.

Mr. FLIPSE. Mr. de la Garza, there probably are no foreign programs as well advanced, but you should be aware that there are foregin participants in the joint venture of both the Kennecott program and our own.

Mr. DE LA GARZA. Therefore, when we speak of the authority sometime in the future doing its own mining where, if not from these few companies would they get their technology and operational expertise from?

Mr. FLIPSE. It is, in my opinion, highly unlikely that they could develop the technology through a normal research and development program as an industrialized country would tend to do it but if they would show some patience, in fact if the negotiations continue much longer, the patents that are the basis of our technology will become public property and except for the "know how" associated with them, much of this will become public domain in the not too distant future.

Mr. DE LA GARZA. Do you sense some interwoven interest to delaying the Conference associated with the statement just made?

Mr. FLIPSE. Yes, sir, I feel it and I have had members of the advisory groups to other nations express this very clearly. The Secretariat of the U.N. has felt this is one of their fundamental strategies.

Mr. DE LA GARZA. Do they seem to be succeeding in this effort?

Mr. FLIPSE. It is our sincere hope, Mr. Chairman, that this body will take the necessary steps to thwart their apparent success.

Mr. DE LA GARZA. Are you into any domestic operations and by that I mean within our jurisdictional zones—are you operating in the ocean to some degree now?

Mr. FLIPSE. Unfortunately, the higher quality deposits are all in waters that are clearly beyond the limits of the national territorial jurisdiction, or any of those that have been proposed, so the answer to your question is no, we are entirely in the waters now defined as international waters.

Mr. DE LA GARZA. Have you had any problem in that respect?

Mr. FLIPSE. None whatsoever. We see occasional ships of other nations and we are all obeying the rules of the road for international waters and we have no difficulty with any foreign vessels.

Mr. DE LA GARZA. Now this is without divulging any of your corporate decisions, but with relation to your operations if the "Authority" decides to promulgate certain rules and regulations that would not make it profitable for your operations as a private investor owned type operation would it be possible then that you could look toward the Government for an association with the Government and/or subsidy?

Mr. FLIPSE. It is possible and some 3 years ago, Mr. de la Garza, we investigated the possibility.

We were encouraged at that time, due to budget problems, to seek governmental aid. Such aid is certainly possible, but we would feel ocean mining could most effectively be done on an incentive basis via a competitive metal market.

I have my personal wish, of course, to maintain the viability of our ocean mining program and company. I cannot speak for our sponsors.

The tendency for oil companies is not to look toward the government for too much comfort, especially in matters legislatively.

Mr. DE LA GARZA. I trust when you say the government you mean other branches besides the legislative.

Mr. FLIPSE. The chief executive officer of our parent company was formerly the president of Tenneco Oil Co. The matter of depletion allowance is a very serious concern in the relations between our ocean hard mineral development, that has shown only costs to them, and their general long-range planning.

I would think they would like to do it on a profit basis rather than to try to do this as a subsidized operation.

Mr. DE LA GARZA. I can understand that. In all fairness, the legislative has not been quite fair to the oil industry in the depletion area. I say this coming from an oil producing state. Some of my colleagues see it in a different light.

Mr. Chairman, I see that you are back. I have taken perhaps too much time with the witness.

Mr. MURPHY [presiding]. Being from an oil consuming area I happen to support your conclusion on that patricular issue on depletion, but that is another issue.

Mr. Flipse, what percentage of the United States' requirements of the following minerals will be imported from the year 1980 on—cobalt, manganese, copper, and nickel?

Mr. FLIPSE. Mr. Chairman, we have done some estimates and I would be happy to give you an accurate number for the record.

Assuming there is no ocean mining the likelihood of finding economic domestic sources of either manganese or cobalt are very low and I would say our amount of imports would continue essentially at the same levels, that is in the high 90 percent figure.

In copper, we are a net importer now and Mr. Dubs of Kennecott, can speak with much more authority on this, but I think we will continue to have to import more and more copper while some 10 years ago we were a net exporter of copper.

The percentage is approaching 20 percent and I think certainly by 1980 that would be a fair number.

In the nickel business we are an importer and except for the use of scrap materials, we will import in the upper 80 percentile in 1980.

For three of the four key metals we are highly dependent on foreign imports and in copper we are becoming increasingly dependent.

Mr. MURPHY. Is there any chromium on the seabed?

Mr. FLIPSE. There is chrome. In fact, there are some 32 metals in these nodules but at present the concentrations and the processing technology are not suitable for getting many of them out profitably.

There are additional metals from the four you mentioned that we feel will be profitable including molybdenum and probably zinc. As research continues and development continues there are probably more metals that will be produced, however, not in very high quantities because of their low concentration in the ore bodies.

Mr. MURPHY. But for decades to come we will be net importers whether these metals come from the seabed or other foreign sources?

Mr. FLIPSE. Yes, sir; we will be net importers on all of these metals.

Mr. MURPHY. That is almost a total reliance.

Mr. FLIPSE. Yes, sir.

Mr. MURPHY. I indicated earlier that the President of the Conference, Mr. Amerasinghe of Sri Lanka, reported at the end of the Geneva session that the Group of 77 did not want anybody to begin recovery operations from the seabed.

The reason they gave was that no member of the Group of 77 now had the technology to engage in recovery operations.

When do you think one or more of these nations could achieve that capability?

Mr. FLIPSE. From a scientific or technical point of view they probably could develop the capability in a matter of 15 years if they would spend an amount of money on it that would be equivalent to one airplane in their national airline.

I am dead serious about this. They complain they do not have a technological basis to move ahead. My question always is: Is it not a matter of priority? If you would put $15 to $30 million into technical research you could do it.

Most of those countries would have a personnal-difficulty because they do not have many technical people of the type that are necessary, but they would find some very willing contractors and I am sure that they would also find that they do have the key scientists and technologies in many of the countries.

I would suggest that any country that seriously approached the problem would be technically prepared about the time that the first generation patents expire and where this technology would go into the public domain in certain parts of the world. That, plus a continning development effort on their part, would make them ocean miners in no longer time than it took ourselves.

By the time we will be in production, if things go well, it will be 20 years from the time the program started and I think this type of a time and dollar investment would do it for some of the lesser developed countries if they addressed the subject.

Mr. MURPHY. Do you agree with the Treasury Department that the "Engo Text" would create an international cartel?

Mr. FLIPSE. I have only had the "Engo Text" for a day and that is why I do not really feel prepared to address it in any depth.

In general, it is a totally unsatisfactory text and it does provide for discretionary control of price and production and yes, it has all the essential elements of a cartel.

Mr. MURPHY. Could you give the subcommittee a summary and time table for action you feel this Government should take in its exploitation of seabed mineral development?

Mr. Flipse. I think that any American operation, and certainly I can speak for your own, is going through a period of development and evaluation.

The work effort is to determine whether it is a good investment to commit major capital. This should be done in essentially 3 years. The end of 1978 will see the capital investment, the termination of the program, or the sale of the technology to some foreign country where they feel a nationally funded program is worthwhile.

Perhaps someone else can do it more rapidly, but I would guess that 3 years is the time it will take to test the feasibility and economics of the operation.

I feel it is essential that the political uncertainty be removed, let us say, a year from now, or at the most in 2 years from now because during that last year the economic studies will be well along.

It is always essential that the uncertainties be minimized in terms of the political risk. The domestication of the company will depend on the answer to the question: Will the legislation in the United States make it attractive for these joint ventures to domesticate in the United States?

We certainly hope they will, but they must consider domestication somewhere else if there is no constructive legislation here but there are tax and other restraints on the operation in the United States without an offsetting value. The real decisionmaking, the plantsiting, the economic calculations and so forth that make up a feasible report of the mining venture will be determined, I would say, within 1 year. Hence there is an urgency in getting ahead with our domestic legislation, certainly anticipating the impacts of an international treaty whenever it may come about so that the ground rules are established and so that the impact on the costs of the venture can be determined and so that the investment can be committed with some certainty.

Mr. Murphy. You mention two companies with the capability to exploit seabed minerals at the present time.

I was on the phone. What two companies are they?

Mr. Flipse. Two American companies. One was Kennecott Copper Corp., the other DeepSea Ventures. INCO is both a Canadian and American company. I think they are essentially at the same point in development as the other two.

Mr. Murphy. We have read a great deal lately about the GLOMAR. What capability does that company have?

Mr. Flipse. Well, Mr. Hughes does not confide in me regularly but we have watched the Summa Corp. technical program and felt that they were making considerable strides toward the mining side of ocean mining in the development of their ships which I believe they, indeed, were pursuing in the beginning years of that program.

However, now that we have the "submarine recovery" disclosures in the press it is quite easy to note that there was a change in their operations from research and development some years ago. I would suggest that a good deal of their marine operating technology be applicable to ocean mining but this would take them some time.

I do not think they have gone as far as either Kennecott or ourselves in exploration or in the metal processing.

We no longer consider them the leader in ocean mining although at a time some years ago I was willing to forecast they were getting ahead of us in terms of their at-sea work.

Mr. MURPHY. Mr. De la Garza?

Mr. DE LA GARZA. Mr. Flipse, I have a couple of questions. In your operation of the deep seabed mining is it restricted entirely to minerals or do you have any interest or expertise in food production, either as a supplement or as additives to food?

Mr. FLIPSE. We have been entirely in minerals. Our researchers have looked at some of the alternates.

We were hoping that by lifting enriched waters from the seabed up to the surface we might have a collateral fish farm with our mining operation. This does not look very likely now, but in any case, as my chairman said: "when you have some profits you can do some research in other fields. Right now concentrate on hard minerals development."

Mr. DE LA GARZA. If you feel you can answer do you know if any other companies feel the same way?

Mr. FLIPSE. I think they do.

Mr. DE LA GARZA. In relation to food?

Mr. FLIPSE. I think they do, but you could ask Mr. Dubs, who is your next witness, and he could answer for 50 percent of the remainder.

Mr. DE LA GARZA. Thank you very much, Mr. Chairman.

Mr. MURPHY. Mr. Flipse I would ask that while we get to our next witness Mr. Marne Dubs of the Kennecott Exploration, Inc., and representing the Under the Sea Mineral Resources of the American Mining Congress, I would ask that you stay because there may be questions appropriate to both of you.

At this point we will take a 5-minute recess.

[Brief recess.]

Mr. MURPHY. The subcommittee will come to order.

Our next witness is Mr. Marne Dubs.

Mr. Dubs, we are happy to have you and you may proceed in any fashion you choose.

STATEMENT OF MARNE DUBS, KENNECOTT EXPLORATION, INC NEW YORK, N.Y.

Mr. DUBS. My name is Marne A. Dubs and I am director of the ocean resources department of Kennecott Copper Corp.

I am also chairman of the Committee on Undersea Mineral Resources of the American Mining Congress, chairman of the Mining Panel of the Ocean Science and Technology Advisory Committee of NSIA, a member of the National Advisory Committee on Oceans and Atmosphere, a member of the Marine Minerals and Petroleum Advisory Committee to the Secretary of Commerce, and a member of the State Department's Advisory Committee on the Law of the Sea.

I serve as an expert on the U.S. delegation to the Law of the Sea Conference and in that capacity attended the Geneva session of the Law of the Sea Conference during a part of March, April, and May of this year for a total time of about 30 days.

In spite of all the credentials I have listed for you, I wish to testify this morning in a private capacity and my views may not necessarily coincide with those of the various organizations I serve.

I thank you, Mr. Chairman, for the opportunity to make a statement before your committee today. I congratulate you and your committee for launching your inquiry into the results of the Geneva session of the Third Law of the Sea Conference so promptly after the close of the session.

Your committee has always had a keen interest in the resources of the seabed and in the development of those resources for the benefit of the United States in particular.

I noted with pleasure your own interest in this issue as evidenced by your and Mr. Perian's visit to Geneva and by a recent statement made by you in a committee hearing on NACOA funding, and certainly the hearings today bespeak your continuing interest.

I believe that holding hearings on this subject before the Geneva ripples have died away has the undoubted merit of not only obtaining eyewitness accounts undimmed by time, but also of perhaps avoiding the rationalized histories which I am certain will magically but wrongly transform the obvious failures of Geneva into the penultimate negotiating stage, promising achievement of all our Nation's objectives at the next session of the Conference in New York in the spring of 1976.

Before discussing the Geneva session and its results, I would like to review the events leading up to Geneva and some of the expectations for that meeting.

Mr. Chairman, you will recall that the United Nations Seabed Committee deliberated many years on the question of the Law of the Sea.

This committee was, in its final stages, charged with doing the preparatory work for the Law of the Sea Conference. In 1973 its work was arbitrarily judged completed and the decision was taken to proceed with the Third Conference on the Law of the Sea.

In my view, the work was, in fact, far from complete and one need only examine the report of the committee to judge.

Volume II of the report deals with the deep seabed and contains complex alternative texts replete with bracketed words, phrases, sentences, and paragraphs that no one could agree on.

The texts did cover a complete seabed regime and machinery. However, I would defy anyone to pick out the United States position from this morass without tutelage from a studious participant in the work.

Nevertheless, of particular interest in this report are the alternative texts of article 9 of the regime for the deep seabed.

One alternative—the United States position—covered a licensing system which guaranteed access to the mineral resources under reasonable terms and conditions. This alternative read as follows:

All exploration and exploitation activities in the area shall be conducted by a Contracting Party or group of Contracting Parties or natural or juridical persons under its or their authority or sponsorship, subject to regulation by the Authority and in accordance with the rules regarding exploration and exploitation set out in these articles.

Another alternative—the group of 77 position—covered a system which put complete discretionary power into an all-powerful seabed authority with respect to when, how, or whether the seabed would be exploited. This alternative read as follows:

All activities of scientific research and exploration of the Area and exploitation of its resources and other related activities shall be conducted by the Authority directly or, if the Authority so determines, through service contracts or in association with persons natural or juridical.

Of equal interest as article 9 was the basic machinery for governing the seabed authority. The group of 77 advocated that all power should be lodged in a democratic assembly where the principle of sovereign equality would reign.

Put more bluntly, the vote of a poor tiny nation would have the same vote as the United States, and there are, of course, many such nations.

The United States proposal was somewhat equivalent to making the Assembly a political sounding board and lodging all power in a council structured so as to provide reasonable assurance of protecting the United States interests.

Mr. Chairman, although there are many complexities involved, the above issues were and are at the heart of the debate on the Law of the Sea with respect to the deep seabed.

Furthermore, positions with respect to these central issues have not appreciably changed, and the same issue of control was central in both Caracas and Geneva.

As you know, the Seabed Committee was disbanded and the Third Conference on the Law of the Sea was organized and initiated in late 1973.

However, substantive work did not begin until the 10-week session at Caracas in the summer of 1974. The Caracas session was most unproductive. There was a review of the proposed seabed regime articles with little change accomplished.

Of greater significance at Caracas was lengthy discussion on the economic implications of seabed mining for developing land-based producers.

It was alleged that seabed minerals would damage the economies of such countries and that there should be strict control over seabed mining.

The overtones of this debate indicated that its roots were probably in the new economic order being proclaimed by developing states and which had been strongly expressed in the Sixth General Assembly Special Session dealing with raw materials early in 1974.

With respect to article 9, there was a most protracted debate with no basic changes in the United States position and a slight hardening of the position of the group of 77. My written text quotes article 9 and you are all familiar with it and I will not restate it here.

At the strong iniative of the United States, the Caracas meeting did take up the question of the rules and regulations governing ocean mining.

Proposed rules were subsequently introduced by the United States, some Western European states including the United Kingdom, France, West Germany and others, and Japan, and Russia at Geneva.

After much pressure, the group of 77 responded by introducing so-called basic conditions of exploitation and a copy of this paper is herewith submitted for your record.

[The document referred to follows:]

ATTACHMENT

GROUP OF 77 POSITION—BASIC CONDITIONS

1. The area and its resources being the common heritage of mankind, the title to the Area and its resources and all other rights in the resources are vested in the Authority on behalf of mankind as a whole. These resources are not subject to alienation.

2. Title to the minerals and all other products derived from the resources shall not pass from the Authority except in accordance with the rules and regulations laid down by the Authority and the terms and conditions of the relevant contracts, joint ventures or any other such form of association entered into by it.

3. The Authority shall from time to time determine the part of parts of the Area in which activities relating to exploration and exploitation may be conducted.

4. All contracts, joint ventures or any other such form of association entered into by the Authority relating to the exploration of the Area and the exploitation of its resources and other related activities shall ensure the direct and effective control of the Authority at all times, through appropriate institutional arrangements.

5. The Authority may, if it considers it appropriate, enter into contracts relating to one or more stages of operations with any person, natural or juridical. These stages of operations may include the following: scientific research, general survey, exploration, evaluation, feasibility study and construction of facilities, exploitation, processing, transportation and marketing.

6. (a) The Authority shall establish appropriate procedures and prescribe qualifications on the basis of which persons natural or juridical may apply to the Authority for entering into contracts relating to one or more stages of operations.

(b) The selection from among applicants shall be made by the Authority on a competitive basis, taking into special account the need for the widest possible direct participation of developing countries, particularly the land-locked among them. The decision of the Authority in that regard shall be final and definitive.

7. Subject to the provisions of paragraph 6, a contractor who has fulfilled his contract regarding one or more stages of operations, as the case may be, to the satisfaction of the Authority shall have priority in the award of a contract for a further stage or stages of operations.

8. The rights and obligations arising out of a contract with the Authority shall not be transferred except with the consent of the Authority and in accordance with the rules and regulations laid down by it.

9. The Authority may, if it considers it appropriate, enter into a joint venture or any other such form of association with any person, natural or juridical, to undertake one or more stages of operations, provided, however, that the Authority shall have financial control through majority share and administrative control in such joint venture or other form of association.

10. The Authority shall ensure security of tenure to a contractor within the terms of the contract provided he does not violate the provisions of the Convention and the rules and regulations laid down by the Authority.

11. In case of a radical change in circumstances or "force majeure", the Authority may take appropriate measures, including revision, suspension or termination of the contract.

12. Any person, natural or juridical, entering into a contract, joint venture or any other such form of association with the Authority may be required to provide the funds, materials, equipment, skill and know-how necessary for the conduct of operations at any stage or stages, and to deposit a guarantee.

13. Any responsibility, liability or risk arising out of the conduct of operations shall lie only with the person, natural or juridical, entering into a contract with the Authority.

14. The share of the Authority in a contract, joint venture or any other such form of association may be, *inter alia*, in the form of the production or the proceeds from the resources.

15. (a) The Authority shall ensure that any person, natural or juridical, who enters into a contract, joint venture or any other such form of association with it undertakes to transfer to the Authority, on a continuous basis, technology, know-how and data relevant to the stage or stages of operations involved, during the life of such a contract, joint venture or any other such form of association.

(b) The Authority and any person, natural or juridical, who is a party to a contract, joint venture or any other such form of association, shall draw up a programme for the training of the personnel of the Authority.

(c) The Authority shall further ensure that any person, natural or juridical, who enters into a contract, joint venture or any other such form of association with it, undertakes to provide at all levels training for personnel from developing countries, particularly the land-locked among them, and employment, to the maximum extent possible, to qualified personnel from such countries.

16. The Authority shall have the right to take at any time the necessary measures in order to apply the provisions contained in this Convention, particularly those relating to regulation of production.

17. The applicable law shall be solely the provisions of this Convention, the rules and regulations laid down by the Authority, and the terms and conditions of the relevant contracts, joint ventures and any other such form of association entered into by the Authority.

Mr. Dubs. Examination of these "basic conditions" shows them to be merely an elaboration of the article 9 text quoted. Thus, the Caracas session ended with only infinitesimal progress on the development of new negotiating papers, strengthening of ideas on raw material control and the new economic order, and zero change in the basic positions on article 9, "Who May Exploit the Area."

With this legacy of the Seabed Committee and the poor results at Caracas, what could really be expected to be achievable at Geneva?

How might real progress be measured and judged?

It was crystal clear to almost all that there was no hope of achieving a treaty at Geneva, not only in the case of the deep seabeds, but also in respect of the issues being negotiated in other committees. However, sufficient progress in certain specific and significant issues could be accepted as indicating that a treaty acceptable to United States was achievable, that is post-Geneva.

Perhaps my list of issues and progress which would meet a sufficiency test would be of interest to the committee. My list follows:

One: Agreement on basic seabed authority machinery which would keep power out of the one-nation, one-vote Assembly and lodge real power in a Council so constituted as to clearly guard U.S. interests, with safeguards against the Assembly in any way usurping the Council's powers.

Two: Agreement on conditions of exploitation which would ensure access to seabed exploitation without discrimination and under reasonable terms and conditions.

Three: Agreement on elimination of price and production controls through either direct or indirect means.

Four: Agreement on protection of investiment through sanctity of contract.

Five: Agreement on a tribunal having binding powers with respect to disputes and to which private entities would have access.

Six: Agreement on a system of rule making, based on sound basic conditions in the treaty, that would be protected from undue political influence.

Seven: Agreement on a system for early provisional application of the treaty with prototype rules and regulations.

My own confidence in fulfilling this list was low prior to Geneva, and I have found that low confidence level fully justified by the final results of the Geneva session.

In fact, the final result, the single negotiating text developed in the last days of the Conference and provided on the very last day by Chairman Paul Engo of Committee One, is an unmitigated disaster.

I will discuss this unfortunate result in more detail later. However, it would be neither fair to the committee nor to our capable negotiator in Committee One, Mr. Leigh Ratiner of the Department of Interior, not to discuss some of the negotiations which preceded the final Engo paper and I will now do so.

The Geneva session was from the beginning a more promising affair than Caracas. While in Caracas the Group of 77 was willing to discuss only article 9; in Geneva they appeared to want to move, however slightly, a little more toward meeting the needs of developed states.

Thus, they were willing and in fact did discuss a broad range of issues relating to the basic conditions for, or more properly, the basic system of, exploitation of the mineral resources of the deep seabed.

In retrospect, this could well be a result of their appreciation that it would not be possible for the authority to carry out any exploitation unless the technology and capital resident in a few developed states could be attracted to the deep seabed.

Thus, they were somewhat willing to create at least marginally attractive conditions for the very beginning of seabed mining with the eventual objective of the authority taking over such exploitation in the futre when the authority had acquired both the technology and the capital.

This appears to me to be the basic motivating and guiding principle of their somewhat more forthcoming attitude.

The United States itself came to Geneva showing clearly a flexibility and willingness to discuss issues dear to the hearts of the 77 and, in fact, to compromise on some issues to n extent that, although the basic U.S. position would be protected, there would be little margin of safety.

At Caracas, the United States for example would discuss only definitive rules and regulations which would have to be included in the treaty.

At Geneva, the United States was agreeable to negotiating basic conditions which would define the content of and which would subsequently be elaborated into rules and regulations by the machinery of the treaty.

This, of course, was predicated on the existence of rulemaking machinery which could further protect U.S. interests.

It is noteworthy that the United States in fact, made a number of proposals to try to bridge the gap between us and the Group of 77.

I should add that all these proposals preserved the basic United States position and could have led to the fulfillment of the shopping list of results I gave above.

I believe our negotiator, Mr. Ratiner, used this flexibility capably and I believe made some notable strides toward bridging the gap, but unfortunately not sufficient.

As you know, Mr. Chairman, the Committee One negotiations at Geneva were carried out in small closed groups with regular general discussion in the working group of Committee One. Both activities were chaired by Mr. C. W. Pinto of Sri Lanka.

The focus of negotiation was on basic conditions of exploitation and the guidepost for discussion was the basic conditions of the Group of 77. It is well recognized that this was an impossible guidepost. Nevertheless, the discussions did lead to a better understanding of what basic conditions had to cover.

More importantly, the discussions did, in fact, dwell on the conditions of exploitation for entities other than the authority itself, and led to protracted consideration of the "joint venture" method of describing the relations between the authority and an entity carrying out exploitation.

Unfortunately, I believe there were probably 150 or more different ideas of what a joint venture is. Of course, I looked at it as another name for the contractual arrangements governing the relationship between an exploiter and the authority.

In its purest form, it could be exactly like a licensing system. In its most disastrous form, it could mean an equity venture with the authority owning 51 percent, but with the exploiter putting up all the capital, technology and management, and taking all the risks. It is easy to see how far apart we could be.

These discussions of basic conditions eventually led to a new paper by C.W. Pinto entitled "Basic Conditions of Exploration and Exploitation" which has already been discussed at this meeting, the paper of April 9, 1975.

A quick reading of this paper shows no abandonment of the group of 77 position in principle, but it is a far, far better document to negotiate from than the original Group of 77 paper.

In fact, it has a number of ideas incorporated into it which could have been developed into something satisfactory from my point of view, in particular its approach to rules and regulations.

Do not misunderstand me—this effort was not acceptable. It was also not well received by the Group of 77. At this point, negotiations became stalled and there was a general unwillingness to negotiate basic conditions any further.

During this stalled period there were apparently a number of initiatives taken to produce meaningful negotiations in small, secret sessions.

I was not there at that time, but I believe the United States may, in fact, have taken some initiatives which apparently came to naught.

At about this time two related ideas took hold of Committee One negotiations. The first was the conferencewide idea in the April 18 plenary meeting of having committee chairmen generate a so-called "Informal Single Negotiating Text."

The second was that Committee One should get down to the subject of the machinery section of the sought for treaty. It is noted that machinery had not been discussed for almost two years, yet it is the heart of the treaty and more than anything determines whether a treaty would be acceptable to the United States.

Accordingly, the full Committee One started a United Nations style debate on machinery on Friday, April 25, and completed it on Monday, April 28. During the next several days, every one was in private negotiations on machinery.

Two draft treaties resulted from this work. One is the work product of Mr. Engo which is now the official "Informal Single Negotiating Text" and which became available on May 9.

The other is the work product of Mr. Pinto which is also a complete draft treaty and which I believe was one of the inputs to the Single Text.

Unfortunately, the Pinto paper did not become available and it is possible that it is a better document to work with than the one we now have.

I say this with hope rather than conviction since the Engo paper appears to be an unmitigated disaster.

Although time does not permit a discussion of annex I to the Single Text, it is clear that this annex was prepared by C. W. Pinto and was destined to be attached to a different main treaty body. Its antecedents in the original Cab 12 are obvious. These basic conditions—although at first reading, and second one too, they are most unacceptable—do have some interesting concepts and ambiguities.

It is not perfectly clear, for example, that the authority can turn down a contract which meets basic financial conditions. However, the all important financial conditions are left blank.

There are also some better controls on the Enterprise and the possibility exists of the Enterprise being primarily a contracting agency.

It is another step down the road toward acceptability if one compares Caracas Basic Conditions, Pinto's Cab 12, and Annex I.

Of course, it is not a satisfactory document but the correct will and a little work might make it so, Mr. Chairman.

As the single visible product of Geneva, the Engo paper gives no hope for the early achievement of a seabed treaty acceptable to the United States. The defects of this paper are many and I will touch on only a few of the more important ones. I will start with article 22 entitled "Functions of the Authority." This, of course, is the famous article 9, "Who May Exploit the Area," in disguise.

Since this article is central, I quote it:

1. Activities in the Area shall be conducted directly by the Authority.

2. The Authority may, if it considers it appropriate, and within the limits it may determine, carry out activities in the Area or any stage thereof through States Parties to this Convention, or State enterprises or persons natural or juridical which possess the nationality of such States or are effectively controlled by them or their nationals, or any group of the foregoing, by entering into service contracts or joint ventures or any other such form of association which ensures this direct and effective control at all times over such activities.

3. Notwithstanding the provision of paragraphs (1) and (2) of this article and in order to promote earliest possible commencement of activities in the area, the Authority through the Council shall:

"(i) Identify as early as practicable after coming into force of this Convention ten economically viable mining sites in the Area for exploration and exploitation of no more than * * * (size, etc.) ;

"(ii) enter into joint ventures in respect of these sites with States Parties to this Convention or State enterprises or persons natural and juridical—which possess the nationality of such States or are effectively controlled by them or their nationals or any group of the foregoing. Such joint ventures shall be subject to the conditions of exploration and exploitation established by and under this Convention and shall always ensure the direct and effective control of the Authority at all times."

4. In entering into such joint ventures as provided for in paragraph 3(ii) of this Article, the Authority may decide on the basis of available data to reserve certain portions of the mining sites for its own further exploitation.

The meaning of article 22 is quite clear. The intent is for the Authority to carry out exploitation itself. However, it may contract portions out as it sees fit.

Since this system is patently unattractive to us and since the Authority would not have the immediate wherewithal to undertake operations, the 77 are trying to buy the developed countries off in my view, by offering ten sites under a joint venture scheme to get things started.

After that, they would presumably have acquired funds, technology and management from us so that we could be quickly and quietly removed from further seabed activity in the future. One hardly need do more to show the unacceptability of this negotiating text.

However, there is another difficulty of equivalent gravity. The text clearly makes the one-nation, one-vote Assembly the supreme policy making organ of the Authority.

The Assembly decides the policy of the Council and other organs on any matter within the convention. Obviously, this broad power provides no protection for the United States and we can be in no doubt that such broad power would be exercised to our detriment.

To continue, the Council, the powers of which are secondary to those of the Assembly, is so constituted that the influence of the United States and like-minded States is insufficient to protect our interests even within the framework of the powers it does have.

Thus, we could not expect to have reasonable protection in either the Assembly or the Council, Mr. Chairman.

Another major defect in this text is the absolute control of production granted to the Authority. The new article 9 requires that development and use of the seabed be undertaken so as to avoid or minimize any adverse effects on the revenues and economies of the developing countries, resulting from a substantial decline in their export earnings from minerals and other raw materials originating in their territory which are also derived from the area.

This is backed up in the machinery section with the Economic Planning Commission, article 20, which has broad powers with respect to the implementation of this noninjury requirement.

Mr. Chairman, I could go on and recite defects in specific article after article. There are many of them. There are problems in the dispute settlement machinery, rulemaking devices, the commissions and the secretariat.

This would not serve any useful purpose other than to drive more nails into the coffin of this corpse of a treaty text. However, I see a pattern in this draft treaty which although I am now certain you also have perceived, I would like to share with your committee.

The pattern I see, complete with its rhetoric, is that of the new economic order concept of the developing countries. Their new economic order concept requires several things of a seabed treaty, chief of which are the rapid transfer of money and technology from us to them and absolute control of seabed production. This Engo draft accomplishes this easily.

What is the evidence of this pattern? Some of the evidence can be seen as follows:

One: An all-powerful assembly affording complete control by the developing countries in article 26.

Two: Specific power in article 22 for the Authority to exploit or not to exploit and to choose its means of doing so.

Three: Power and direction of the Authority to avoid or minimize adverse effects on the revenues and economies of developing countries, implying production controls and that is in article 9, 28 (xi), 30.

Four: Power to undertake integrated commodity arrangements and buffer stock arrangements. This would indicate aspirations to integrate the seabed resources into a broad scheme of raw material control, perhaps even using seabed revenues as I know has been proposed, to finance the cartel aspirations of some land based producers.

Five: Provisions for the transfer of technology, article II, annex I, paragraph 10 (a) and (b).

I agree with Mr. Ratiner the particular articles that appeared in transfer of technology are not so bad as they could be, but the intent is still there.

Where does this leave us? What can we make of Geneva? The message is clear.

In the final analysis, the group of 77 was unwilling to negotiate or compromise. Our negotiators did their best and I know that none other worked so diligently toward success.

Thus, Geneva must be considered a failure because it produced no possibility of a treaty acceptable to the United States. In fact, I even doubt whether the Engo draft is acceptable to the 77.

As I compare the single text—unagreed to by anyone—to my list of the minimum which should have been accomplished I find a zero with, surprisingly, the one apparent exception of willigness to include early provisional application of the treaty.

This exception is marred by my analysis that it is motivated by a desire to buy us off and obtain seed funds and technology.

As terrible as the negotiating text appears to us, and I may be alone in this opinion, it could nevertheless be altered rather easily to being as completely satisfactory to U.S. interests as any such treaty could ever be.

However, that would require the Group of 77 to abandon their basic principle of complete sovereign control of the resources of the seabed through an authority ruled by a one-nation-one-vote assembly. Such abandonment is not likely.

My opinion is that the time is not ripe to obtain a successful, acceptable treaty. As long as we face the rhetoric and aspirations of the new economic order, real progress is not possible.

Thus, I predict no agreed upon treaty in 1976, one satisfactory to us, and probably not much of a possibility in 1977. The time has come for all to face these facts and to take the necessary alternative steps to foster the needs and well being of the United States.

Everyone must understand that an acceptable treaty cannot be obtained by our present nonnegotiating tactics of insisting that we must have a treaty. I speak for the deep seabeds.

Yes, a treaty is desirable; no, we do not need a treaty, Mr. Chairman.

It is my fervent hope that the executive branch will come to its senses and exercise its obligation to get going on the alternative solutions to the seabed resource issue.

I certainly have no objection to continuing negotiations at the Law of the Sea Conference and, in fact, would urge that we do so. However, it should be done in the spirit of seeking an eventual ideal international resolution but with no sense of pressure to obtain that solution today.

I know that many within the executive branch are sympathetic to this idea, but so far they have been neutralized by those who seem to want to get a treaty at almost any cost and as soon as possible.

There is, of course, before this committee legislation H.R. 1270, which is one potential answer to this problem. There is a draft bill being worked on in the Department of Interior to the same purpose.

There are rumors of other initiatives in the Congress and elsewhere. We in industry are in the process of reviewing the alternatives available.

The Committee on Undersea Mineral Resources of the American Mining Congress is taking the lead in this review and we plan to develop up to date recommendations. I would hope we would have the opportunity to present these views to this committee.

Finally, I would urge all of those with a keen interest and stake in the seabed issue to establish a joint venture, if I may use that overworked term, among the Congress, the administration, and industry to obtain an early and satisfactory solution to the problem of the early establishment of this new source of minerals necessary to our Nation's well being.

I believe further that if the United States leads the way, other like-minded nations will follow.

Thank you, Mr. Chairman.

Mr. MURPHY. Thank you, Mr. Dubs, for a very comprehensive statement.

You used the term "like-minded" twice. Is there another country like-minded to the United States in this regard in Committee One?

Mr. DUBS. I think it is possible that there are a few nations that are like-minded. When I say that, I mean in terms of they, too, being interested in the exploitation and exploration of the minerals of the seabed and it is my personal belief that they would, in fact, join us in such a venture.

At the same time I recognize that many of them are suspicious of the United States and are perhaps jealous of our deeds in this area. However, they are not so jealous as not to assist their companies who have joined in joint ventures with American companies.

For example Kennecott has a venture in manganese nodules in which two British companies are participating and the British Government has offered them monetary assistance in their participation in this program.

Possible like-minded nations, just to finish, would be France, the United Kingdom, West Germany and Japan.

I do not think they would take the lead, but if we took the lead I believe they might find it necessary to follow.

Mr. MURPHY. We are doing joint oceanographic research and projects with Germany and France?

Mr. DUBS. Yes. In fact, if I may, Mr. Chairman, if you look at ocean mining today you could consider it a venture that is dominated and controlled by U.S. companies. For the sake of argument I will call the INCO venture a U.S. effort as well since it is based in Seattle—but it is participated in by companies from the major developed nations of the world, Japan, France, the United Kingdom, West Germany and Canada—not France at this moment, but perhaps later on.

Mr. MURPHY. Well, you made it pretty clear that you do not expect a treaty in 1976 or even 1977.

What will be the effect on your company and other U.S. interests if the Congress does not act on interim ocean mining legislation?

Mr. DUBS. I think it will be very bad. We are planners and I guess I am a planner myself. As we have laid our plans for the bringing of these ocean minerals into commercial production, our own plans say that we need better security of investment than we have today and we say that we need it during this year, 1975.

Now, the absence of much security of investment and the continual threat, hanging over the head of industry, of a very adverse treaty decision, I think would cause us and others to slow down our activity. I believe as Mr. Ratiner said in his testimony that this new enterprise of mining the ocean is a pioneering enterprise which does not have a fragile existence and that we need to move ahead and to move ahead at a rapid pace without loss of momentum.

I know that the investments that are occurring today in this late engineering development stage are in themselves very high. One can easily see investment decisions in this year of 1975 of the $100 million order and this is prior to going into commercial production. So there is substantial money involved.

Mr. MURPHY. What is the worst that can happen if you or other American companies simply go forward with your activities under current international maritime law?

Mr. DUBS. Well, there are several problems in just going ahead. A very important problem and I will put it as bluntly as I can, is that we have this Law of the Sea Treaty and all its implications hanging over us. It is poised like the sword of Damocles and to make the huge investments that are involved with that sword hanging over us would not be an easy decision for any board of directors or a banker to make.

Another issue that troubles us is that in order to launch a project and be able to predict its outcome from a technical basis we have to be able to count on a supply of ore from a particular ore body for the length of the project so the lack of exclusive rights to a deposit along with the Law of the Sea Treaty hanging over our heads makes ocean mining a very difficult proposition.

Mr. MURPHY. Has the issue of grandfathering surfaced at all in any of these negotiations?

Mr. DUBS. No, it has not. Grandfathering has from time to time been discussed in some of the corridors, but it is not a concept which seems to have much credence at Geneva.

Mr. MURPHY. Mr. Ratiner, would you respond to that?

Mr. RATINER. Yes, Mr. Chairman, I think in all fairness Mr. Dubs is right since he has not been in the corridor conversations. However, in fact, the question of grandfathering has been discussed on a highly selected basis with some of the developing country leadership and it has met with some measure of sympathy from these countries.

The difficulty from their point of view with grandfathering is simply that it contains in it an implication that the United States would have begun mining prior to the conclusion of the treaty. Since they regard that as illegal, that is their view and not ours, it is hard for them to see how they could work the concept of grandfather rights into the treaty.

Mr. MURPHY. They would consider it illegal?

Mr. RATINER. Yes, sir.

Mr. MURPHY. That is an ipso facto consideration.

Mr. RATINER. The developing countries believe the "Declaration of Principles," to which I referred earlier, prohibits the mining of the seabed until a treaty is established for that purpose, and then mining could only occur pursuant to that treaty. This is their legal interpretation of the "Declaration of Principles."

Mr. MURPHY. Would you comment on that, Mr. Dubs?

Mr. DUBS. Well, I think first that this attitude of theirs with respect to the legal interpretation of the principals is as I have always heard it expressed. That attitude of course, resulted in a moratorium resolution being passed by the U.N. a couple of years ago.

With respect to acceptability of the grandfather clause, I think that to some extent the paragraph I quoted from article 22 with regard to 10 acceptable sites is somewhat in the nature of the kind of grandfather clause that they would consider.

In other words, their ultimate objective may be to exploit entirely themselves, but they might recognize that some limited initial exploration and exploitation could be done on a rather free basis.

I think that this is the kind of grandfather clause they might consider but with regard to a grandfather clause that would protect companies already in operation and turning out product, I am doubtful.

Mr. MURPHY. I asked this question of Mr. Flipse and the President of the Conference, Mr. Amerasinghe of Sri Lanka reported at the end of the Geneva session that the Group of 77 did not want anybody to begin recovery operations from the seabed. The reason they gave was that no member of the Group of 77 now had the technology to engage in recovery operations, and he responded with the answer that it was just a simple determination on the part of any one of these governments to devote $15 to $20 million to this area.

Would you comment on that?

Mr. DUBS. Well, I am afraid I must take issue with Mr. Flipse. I think that I would agree with him, with his analysis of the problem, if the country involved were West Germany, Japan or Italy, but I cannot agree that his analyses would apply to the developing countries at least as I know them.

The kind of technology we are dealing with is so new that there is simply no base in a developing country to supply that kind of technology. These resources are just so threadbare that it seems to me to be totally unlikely that they can apply it.

Now if, for example, Deep Sea Ventures or Kennecott entered into a contract to exploit the ocean under such a nation's aegis, that would be a kind of logical possibility but for them to marshal the management and technical and financial teams to carry this out, it just is not likely.

They have not really even succeeded in doing this in land based technology dealing with minerals and mining, as yet. So I do not think that the developing nations will, in fact, be nations that will, themselves, individually pick up and carry out ocean mining, not in the near future, not in the next 25 years.

Mr. MURPHY. Where is the expenditure great? Is it in the exploratory phase? Is it in the deep sea mining itself, or is it in the onshore refining operations where the capital expense is the greatest?

Mr. DUBS. The greatest? The way I look at the cost of carrying this out, the greatest capital costs and the greatest cash operating costs are on the short-based processing facilities.

If you look at a very rough division of costs and I mean this to be very rough, at least half of these costs are associated with the shore-based facility and half with the ocean side and of the ocean side, perhaps half of it might be associated with the mining and perhaps half with transport.

Now obviously, those are not accurate figures but just to give you a feel. Now, the amount of money invested in an area before one begins construction of production equipment at the present is very high and may amount to, and I speak very broadly, 25 percent of those total amounts of money because we are now in the initial development stage. However, if we look at the situation after the first seabed mining operation is under way, I think these costs would be more like the normal situation we find in land-based mining where say a $400 million project may only have $20 million in before you start your investment program.

Mr. MURPHY. Do you agree with the Treasury Department that the "Engo Text" would create an international cartel?

Mr. DUBS. Well, I am not an economist and I am not sure I really understand cartels, but if by that we mean that the "Engo Text" provides for complete control of the production of minerals from the seabed, of the rate of adding capacity and—the way I read it—also implies changing the production rates of capacity that is in service, then I would say yes it would create a cartel.

I would say further that the references to creating buffer stocks do, in fact, go down the road of a cartel.

Mr. MURPHY. Will you outline for us a time table on America's capability to develop a seabed minerals capability?

Mr. DUBS. Let me not speak for any other company other than my own and our time tables looks like this. We have at this particular time completed a very important piece of our basic development work, in fact, I flew in from California where I was reviewing this work last night for this hearing.

This results then in our being ready during the next several months to make a decision for committing very sizeable blocs of money toward the creation of an ocean mining machine.

The creation of this machine and its employment at sea, of course, takes a lot of time because you have to build very large complex equipment and it will take on the order of 3 years before such equipment is completely constructed and tested out.

Now we are talking about 1978 and at that time, sometime during the year 1978, I would expect, assuming our progress goes ahead as we plan, that we will have a working mining system that is capable of commercial production. We will then proceed, if the investment climate, the costs and all the other things that go into it work out properly, with the construction of the shore processing equipment and the other auxiliaries. Depending on, of course, the state of the economy, and how hard or how easy equipment is to get, we would then be talking about commercial production occurring about 1980–81. This then is the kind of time frame I see.

Mr. MURPHY. With the exploratory work already going on as to where to mine?

Mr. DUBS. We think we know exactly where we want to mine.

Mr. MURPHY. Has there been a substantial effect on your company's interest in investing as a result of the Law of the Sea Conferences and the United States attitude there?

Mr. DUBS. Well, I think the unsettled situation with respect to the Law of the Sea has resulted in a very obvious action by our company.

We see very large risks involved because of Law of the Sea activities. Therefore, we have taken steps to spread the risks.

First, there are the risks of a pioneering technology which one would be disposed to spread anyway. There is the usual risk of a very large project.

Then there are these ill-defined political risks. It is not accidental that we established an international consortium and not a purely U.S. consortium. Such a consortium does add to the political stability and reduces those ill-defined political risks. So this is a concrete example of a response to this situation.

Mr. MURPHY. Counsel?

Mr. PERIAN. I have no questions.

Mr. MURPHY. Mr. Dubs we certainly appreciate you, Mr. Flipse and Mr. Ratiner coming here today and I note that some of you came at considerable expense and great distance, but I felt it was necessary for us to proceed as quickly as possible after the termination of the latest phase of the Law of the Sea Conference.

Mr. Flipse?

Mr. FLIPSE. Mr. Chairman, I would like to correct an impression that I am afraid I left regarding the timing of the legislation.

I pointed out that in our program we will be making determinations on where to locate plants and these kind of decisions in a year and a half or at the latest, 2 years from now. I may have given the impression that 2 years from now would be an adequate time frame for the legislation.

We are aware that there will have to be an environmental impact statement done, that there will be trade-off studies that will factor in the environmental costs.

There will also be rules and regulations promulgated by the appropriate department of government. All of these which are time consuming and so I suggest I share fully Mr. Dubs' urgency in getting the bill on the books now so that the implementation of the bill can take place in time to meet our needs and help us to domesticate our activities in the United States under the laws of the United States.

I appreciate the opportunity, Mr. Chairman, to clarify that point.

Mr. MURPHY. Thank you very much, gentlemen.

The subcommittee will stand adjourned, subject to the call of the Chair.

[Whereupon, at 12:30 p.m., the subcommittee adjourned, subject to the call of the Chair.]

DEEP SEABED MINING

House of Representatives
Committee on Merchant Marine and Fisheries,
Subcommittee on Oceanography,
Washington, D.C.

The subcommittee met, pursuant to call, at 10:15 a.m., in room 1334 Longworth House Office Building, Hon. John M. Murphy (the Chairman), presiding.

Mr. Murphy. The subcommittee will come to order.

This morning the Subcommittee on Oceanography begins a series of hearings on the subject of deep ocean mining. This is not a subject which is new to the subcommittee. The previous Chairman has attempted to resolve the issues involved for several years and has introduced legislation to achieve the goal of promoting United States interests in this area.

We had a briefing last May from representatives of the Government and industry following the Geneva session of the Law of the Sea Conference. And before that we were briefed after Caracas. Now we are on the eve of yet another session of the Conference. This time in the great metropolis of New York.

At these hearings we will deal with three questions. First, we will review what has occurred since the last session of the Conference in Geneva, and will look forward to the prospects for the New York session. In doing so, we will finally decide within the next few weeks whether there is a need for interim domestic legislation to promote and regulate deep seabed mining. I, for one, am convinced there is.

The second question to deal with is part of the larger question of what form that legislation might take. We have some good bills to work from in this area and I am convinced that we can produce a product acceptable to the Congress and one that fills the needs of the United States. One of the issues to resolve between the various bills is whether regulatory authority should be vested in the Department of Commerce or the Department of the Interior.

The third aspect of our hearings will be to get the mining industry's viewpoint. We are interested in the state of the art of the mining industry and the form of the legislation which that industry would like to see emerge from this subcommittee.

I fully realize this issue was urgent last May—today it is critical for the industry.

Some may have the impression that I have already drawn conclusions on some of these questions.

For one, I was a congressional delegate to the Geneva session of the Conference, and since then I have not hid my feelings about the direction in which those negotiations are heading, or at least my impression in which direction they are heading.

In addition, I have introduced one of the bills which we will be considering at these hearings.

I cannot deny it. This whole subject is of grave concern to me, to me personally, and to most members of this subcommittee.

I intend to investigate the entire issue with due diligence, and take the required course of action without delay—there has been far too much of that already.

I had scheduled these hearings twice during the latter part of 1975 and each time I was asked by the administration to hold off—they would have an "interim solution" to the problem.

But none came forth, so we are going to proceed.

I cannot believe them any longer, this country cannot wait any longer, and I will not wait any longer.

In the opinion of experts at the Law of the Sea Conference, the value of the minerals contained in manganese nodules on the ocean floor is estimaed at $3 trillion. Experts also estimate that the nodules are so abundant that it would only take 1 percent of the ocean bottom to satisfy the world's needs for about 50 years. This will obviously be an important source of minerals in the future as the world's needs increase.

The ocean floor could be a particularly important source of minerals for the United States. For three of the four major metals contained in the nodules—manganese, nickel and cobalt—are imported by this country in great quantities. The Department of the Interior has estimated that we could be virtually independent of foreign sources of these metals by 1990 if we were to go ahead and begin recovery of the nodules today.

What is stopping the United States from beginning the development of these resources? It is certainly not the technology.

Representatives of many U.S. firms have been up here testifying before congressional committees for a year that the technology exists. Several companies have assembled highly sophisticated technical teams and spent over $100 million on the development of deep seabed mining technology.

They have tested pilot units at various depths and are satisfied that they can recover the nodules and process the minerals contained in them, in fact, they can even recover submarines and process them.

They report to us now that for the next stage of development they will have to invest hundreds of millions of dollars.

Unfortunately, the companies are just not prepared to make that investment today. Nor are banks prepared to make the necessary loans.

What is holding them back? Everyone agrees that the nodules are there. The firms themselves seem to be straining at the bit to begin commercial development. And yet we are now at a standstill.

There is no question that the only thing holding back this next stage of development is the lack of the proper investment climate.

The political picture is unclear. No one knows what international law will look like 1 year or 5 years from now.

The Law of the Sea Conference, which has been dragging on now for years, and seems to be no closer to an international agreement, is holding up American industry and has almost brought progress to a screeching halt. Everyone is waiting to see what kind, if any, of a so-called "international regime" will emerge from those talks.

I cannot blame industry for slowing down its pace to await some clearer sign of what sort of an international regime will be established. For the signs which seem to be emerging do not look promising for the American ocean mining enterprises.

The single negotiating text which resulted from the Geneva session is a disaster. It calls for three-fourths of the minerals discovered to be under the control of an Independent Seabed Resource Authority. That assembly would then have the authority to determine the rate of development and the price of these deep sea minerals. It would also reap the profits and determine how to distribute them.

The argument for this arrangement is that the resources of the deep seabed are the "common heritage of mankind," and should not be exploited for the sole benefit of the countries which have developed the high level of technology necessary for deep seabed mining.

This, on the surface, sounds like an honorable goal. But I think it is necessary to strike a more equitable balance between the developed and the underdeveloped countries. Otherwise, the Independent Seabed Resource Authority may find that no one is willing to develop the technology needed.

I have been very disappointed in the way the State Department has handled this issue. I do not think they have been forthright with the American people.

First of all, it seems to me that the State Department has embarked not on a course of negotiation, but on a course of preemptive concessions. They have repeatedly yielded to the Group of 77 in a headlong rush, an almost masochistic effort, to reach a settlement. Our industry has the talent, the technology, and the desire. This should give us a strong position. Yet the Department appears to be negotiating from a position of weakness—as if the rest of the world held all the chips.

The only inalienable right which the State Department is holding onto is the right of innocent passage for our military vessels and aircraft through international straits and coastal waters. All other rights, such as the right to develop these ocean resources, are being conceded.

I do not see any of the other countries making such concessions in an effort to reach an agreement. I think it is time we stood our ground and let someone else take a step toward settlement.

The National Security Council Interagency Task Force on the Law of the Sea promised us after the Geneva session last year that they were conducting a thorough reappraisal of their Law of the Sea policy. This reappraisal was to particularly emphasize interim measures for the protection of our own national ocean interests prior to the development of any treaty, assuming one would be forthcoming in the next decade.

Congress was promised a full briefing on the conclusions and recommendations for further action derived from this reappraisal.

We have seen nothing.

We have heard nothing.

We have received no briefing.

We are now being asked to sit through another 8-week act that may turn out to be one of the longest running plays in world history, and with only the slightest hope of any kind of breakthrough.

It is time for the Congress to act. While we have been waiting for some action by the State Department, and while the industry has slowed down its pace, foreign competitors are rushing to catch up with the United States.

Congress can no longer sit back and watch this erosion of our technological lead. We can no longer sit back and watch the State Department bargain away U.S. interests. We can no longer sit idly and watch as a secure source of minerals evaporates before our eyes.

It is time to act. We must enact legislation into law to enable the U.S. ocean mining industry to proceed with the development of their technology and the recovery of the manganese nodules.

That is wht we are here to do today and tomorrow and in the immediate weeks ahead. We will consider the various bills before this subcommittee which would authorize and license American industry to develop the hard minerals on the ocean floor.

Today we will hear from individuals involved in the Law of the Sea negotiations and will hear their assessment of the prospects for a settlement at the upcoming New York session.

Later on we will hear from the Department of the Interior and the Department of Commerce on the jurisdictional question of which agency should conduct the licensing program. And finally we will hear from industry on what they feel might be needed in the legislation to allow them to proceed.

We wanted to hear from Carlyle E. Maw, Under Secretary for Security Assistance today. I called him Friday, and he told me that Dr. Kissinger had asked him to leave the country on business. He appointed Robert Craft to read his statement, but I understand he has just found a replacement, and we are privileged this morning to have Otho E. Eskin, Staff Director of the National Security Council Interagency Task Force on the Law of the Sea.

I am going to ask Mr. Leigh S. Ratiner, Administrator, Ocean Mining Administration, U.S. Department of the Interior to join him at the witness stand, so that we can have both testimonies presented at this point.

Before they begin their testimony I am going to insert into the record my report dated May 2, 1975 in addition to the bills to be considered along with the agency reports received.

(The report, HR 1270, HR 6017, HR 11879, and agency reports follow herewith:)

U.S. HOUSE OF REPRESENTATIVES,
COMMITTEE ON MERCHANT MARINE AND FISHERIES,
Washington, D.C.

REPORT OF HON. JOHN M. MURPHY, CHAIRMAN, OCEANOGRAPHY SUBCOMMITTEE,
ON PARTICIPATION IN THE LAW OF THE SEA CONFERENCE

As Members know, one of the major issues before the Oceanography Subcommittee is the question of deep seabed minerals exploration and exploitation as embodied in H.R. 1270. The legislation outlines the procedures by which American technology can gather a part of the three trillion dollars worth of nickel manganese, copper and cobalt which is embedded in tomato-sized nodules in the deep ocean floor. Scientists at the Law of the Sea Conference estimate that these nodules contain twenty-seven other minerals and substances, some of value yet to be determined.

These resources are of vital importance to the United States which currently has the technology and the teams assembled to gather the nodules from the ocean floor. Because of the importance of these minerals, the question of who controls deep seabed mining on an international basis is one of the most contentious issues at the conference. The following chart is a Department of the Interior estimate that indicates with immediate unilateral planning and exploitation by the United States this country can become virtualy independent of foreign imports of manganese by 1990 and totally independent in terms of nickel, copper, and cobalt. (Chart #1) :

CHART #1

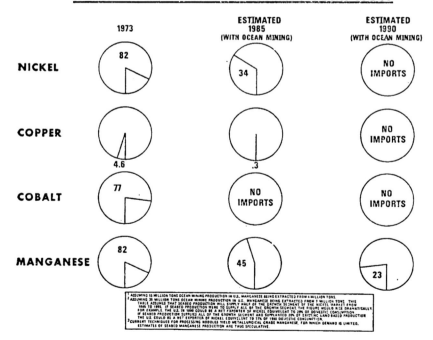

U.S. NET IMPORTS AS % OF CONSUMPTION

American companies have already invested approximately $150 million in ocean mining and by 1990 expect to invest $6 billion in deep sea bed mining operations at an average cost of one-half billion dollars per operation. Of immediate concern to the House of Representatives in terms of legislation is four million square miles of ocean floor between Hawaii and California which can and should be opened up to American exploration pending the apparent disaster which faces us if the Law of the Sea Conference should accept the envisioned plan. If the Law of the Sea Conference does not settle the issue as is now quite apparent we must still move in this area as the American companies involved have assembled the equipment and technological teams with the skills needed for these operations. Companies such as Kennecott Copper, Deep Sea Ventures (a subsidiary of Tenneco), and others needed a resolution of the treaty by early 1976 or unilateral legislation in the same time-frame because of the high cost of developing and maintaining equipment and holding together the highly skilled teams necessary for such operations.

As an opening position while I was in Geneva the United States was negotiating a treaty document that would give up our access to seventy-five percent of the deep sea bed mineral mines to an international authority of an undefined nature. Various concerned members of U.S. executive agencies told me that the land producers of copper and nickel in combination with the so-called group of seventy-seven (which is actually a group of one-hundred and four) emerging nations (or LDC's—Less Developed Countries) wanted to control deep sea bed mining through this authority and eliminate or severly circumscribe the industrial nations of the world through the treaty document. The so-called "regime" would set up the authority with machinery divided into three parts which are in effect legislative, executive, and judicial branches. The fear was expressed to me by members of the delegation, a fear which I shared, that the structure of such an authority was being developed that would lead to an international cartel not unlike the coalition of oil producing states that has all but wrecked the economics of the industrialized nations. These are the very nations I was informed the group of seventy-seven and their allies were attempting to "box-in".

I think it is a national disaster of tragic proportions that our opening position agreed to in the so-called Pinto document (named after C. W. Pinto the Committee I working group Chairman from Sri Lanka of 9 April 1975 stipulates that a country or an industrial entity must find two deep sea beds in its exploration phase and that both of these tracts be turned over to the international authority (see Appendix) The authority would then decide which of the two tracts it would keep in its own so-called bank and it would decide which of the two it would give back to the country or entity to mine. Even worse, it would only give back one-half of the second tract which in effect means seventy-five percent of the total deep sea bed tracts on which an American company, for example, has spent millions of dollars to locate would become a property of the authority for future disposition at its discretion. Certain members of the U.S. delegation were appalled at this proposition yet it was presented to Committee One of the Law of the Sea Conference and much to no one's surprise was subjected to severe criticism in fact, an outrageous diatribe by the Chinese delegation and others. When members of our delegation complained that we had given up too much, Carlyle E. Maw, Undersecretary for Security Assistance would considered by the State Department the ranking head of the Law of the Sea Conference, reprimanded one of our delegation stating that "If we are to get a treaty, we must give up more." I am still trying to determine how much more we can give up, why we should give it up in the first place and why the urgency on the part of the United States to achieve a treaty document. I did not detect the same sense of urgency on the part of other delegations at the Law of the Sea Conference.

I would point out to members of the Merchant Marine Committee that the very fact that the United States depends almost entirely on imports for nickel, cobalt, and manganese it is imperative that our own sources of supply be developed so that we do not become dependent upon some future OPEC-type situation where we could be subjected to arbitrary prices and even political blackmail.

I have attached for members of the Merchant Marine Committee a confidential document outlining the position of the various executive agencies on the questions relating to the establishment of ISRA (the International Seabed Resource Authority). The chart speaks for itself and as can be expected the State Department's position appears to be as in other cases inimical to the best interests of the United States of America. (Chart #2) :

FIG 2

	State Department	Treasury Department	Defense Department	Interior Department	Commerce Department	OMB	Council on International Econ Policy
(1) Joint ventures with ISRA	Yes	Must be limited		Limit on amount	Too general	Must be at arm's length	Must be at arm's length
(2) ISRA exploits in parallel	No	No		No	No	do if not discriminatory	No
(3) Decisionmaking protection (unspecified)	No	Nonnegotiable	Unrealistic to expect	Yes	Holds one st day	Action must app	Nonnegotiable
(4) Just fundamental conditions specified	No	No good		No	do	do	No good
(5) Commission to help LDC¹ producers	Yes	advisory only		Limit actions	Has misgivings	No	Role i advisory only
(6) Reservation of mining sites	Yes	No		Yes	No		No
(7) Training of LDC nationals	Yes	No		No	Reservations		Need sa eguards
(8) Joint ventures with ...	Yes	Less than 10 per-participation		Less than 10 pct part cipation	No		
(9) 3 pct royalty or 50 pct of profits	Somewhat limited	More study needed		Limited	Holds more study		
(10) U.S. tax credits or moratorium	No	No		Yes	No		No
(11) ISRA edits with firms	No				No		No
(12) Abandonment of 1st-in-time rights	Yes	No		Ambiguous	No	Acceptable if not discriminatory	

¹ Less developed countries.

I had several meetings with delegates to the conference who represent the American fishing industry including:
August Felando (Tuma Boat Owners)
Jake Dykstra (Coastal Fishermen, New England)
Charles Carry (Tuna Canners & Boat Owners)
Lowell Wakefield (State of Alaska, King Crab Industry)
William Utz (Distant Water Shrimp Industry)
Charles Meacham (State of Alaska)

As a result of private meetings with these gentlemen I can only describe their outlook for the future in reference to the Law of the Sea as desolate. They had concluded early on that the conference will not work especially in the area of the two hundred mile limit or economic zone and that the countries of the world would unilaterally go to a two-hundred mile limit or zone. (The tuna industry was, of course, the most disconsolate of all groups because the two-hundred mile zone will virtually eliminate their ability to function and despite State Department assurances they feel they are "on the chopping block" at Geneva.) They felt, to a man, that the State Department in order to obtain some kind of treaty document continually keeps giving their rights away.

These representatives are convinced that their only hope lies in solid domestic legislation from the United States Congress. Many in the fishing groups came to Geneva to participate and hopefully, contribute to the negotiations based on promised international protections by the State Department. For example, the representative from Alaska, felt they absolutely needed treaty protection for anadromous fish outside of the two-hundred mile limit. However, at that point in the conference, the group felt they had been "had" for purposes of bargaining positions by the State Department. Further, they were adamant in their judgment that the two-hundred mile fisheries legislation currently before the Merchant Marine and Fisheries Committee will not work for two reasons: (1) they felt it would hinder rather than help the domestic fisherman by overregulation and (2) they felt that it will still allow extensive foreign fishing in U.S. waters, perhaps even greater than in the past. They indicated that the longer the Law of the Sea Conference drags on the more numerous will become the countries that over-fish within our two-hundred mile zone. They pointed out that Poland and other Bloc countries had recently intruded on American waters and that once they are there any subsequent legislation will give them the right to fish in these waters in the future.

Another point of bitter debate was centered around the insistence of the emerging nations on not only unreasonable controls over the two-hundred mile economic zone but the insistence that actual *sovereignty be granted to the coastal states over that part of the ocean.* The Defense Department is adamantly against this type of arrangement and of course, the other major nuclear power, Russia is against this kind of treaty. This would pose many problems significant include our sensor equipment—or as they are referred to our "little sginificant include our sensor equipment—or as they are referred to our "little back boxes"—which are located at various points around the globe, sometimes within less than two-hundred miles off the coast of various countries. This would pose a serious military, legal, and ethical question for the United States were sovereignty to be granted 200 miles seaward to the coastal states.

Another serious result of such an arrangement to our defense capabilities would be in the various straits around the world where we could lose the capability to freely move our surface and undersea vessels. Defense Department negotiators considered it impossible for the United States to agree, for example, to a treaty that would require U.S. nuclear submarines to surface before moving through the Straits of Gibraltar, raise the American flag, and obtain permission from the appropriate nations to pass. This would also apply to overflights by American military aircraft; they would have to announce their intention of flying over the Straits, the flight times and obtain permission from the nations involved. In the event that such a provision were included in the LOS treaty, the Defense Department would recommend to President Ford that the treaty be rejected out of hand. In stressing the necessity for our sensor equipment, the DOD people pointed out to me that it was just such a "little black box" which detected the sunken Russian submarine off Hawaii, and it is Glomar type equipment which will be used in our deep seabed mining activities that raised a portion of the sunken Russian undersea boat. The Glomar revelations did have a definite impact on the Committee One deliberations. Pinto reportedly impressed on the Lesser Developed Countries the fact that the success of America's Glomar made it imperative that they control the proposed world seabed authority.

Subsequent to the world-wide publicity on the raising of the Russian sub, in a meeting between DOD-LOS officials and Russian-LOS representatives the interpretor for the USSR was changed and the gentleman who replaced him, was identified as a KGB agent. During the meeting the Russian agent sat with a black notebook containing news stories (and photographs) of the Glomar and its retrieval of the Russian sub and slowly turned the pages in an obvious manner so that the American negotiators could see what he was doing. It was the usual game of Russion one-upmanship, an attempt to embarras and put at a psychological disadvantage their American counterparts. Further, DOD felt the sudden presence of a KGB agent was to keep a watchful eye on the Russian delegation, members of which are not allowed to associate with or appear friendly to U.S. Representatives even though some of them have known our people since World War II.

Another complication in the treaty negotiations as regards the two-hundred mile economic zone is related to oil and gas development in the so-called "Outer Continental Margin" which is that part of the Outer Continental Shelf that lies beyond the proposed two-hundred mile economic zone of coastal nations.

A treaty provision—acceptable to the State Department—would require the coastal state that developed and exploited such natural resources beyond their two-hundred mile zone to turn over to a United Nations authority a percentage of the revenues derived from such activity. This area accounts for an estimated three percent of America's continental shelf. However, Treasury Department officials and other delegates estimated that the "giveaway" of a percentage of the potential oil and gas revenues from the U.S. shelf margin to a United Nations authority woud cost this nation one billion dollars a year at today's dollar. The most adamantly opposed to this proposal included the Canadians, the Australians, New Zealand, the United Kingdom and India among others who have a substantial outer continental shelf margin. When you consider the fact that Canada's margin accounts for perhaps 50 percent of its continental shelf one can understand the refusal of Canada and the others with extensive margins to give up their rights to major portions of the fifteen-hundred billion barrels of oil estimated to be under the ocean's floor.

DOD-LOS COMPUTER PREDICTION CAPABILITY UNDER WRAPS

One item that came to my attention during private briefings was the fact that the Center for Naval Analysis has spent in the neighborhood of $400,000 to reduce to a computerized information retrieval system every aspect of the Law of the Sea items being negotiated and the positions on these items of the various countries, groups of countries, committees, subcommittees, secret groups, and public groups.

The information is such that the computer can predict the votes of the other hundred and forty plus nations on any given issue in addition to being able to predict the actions of the various sub-groups outlined above. Members of the delegation complained to me that the Department of Defense has this information available and is keeping a close veil of secrecy around it and that it is being used only for defense purposes.

They charged that the Department of Defense refuses to fully share the information with other U.S. agencies so that they can advise their participants in the conference. This in spite of the fact that the Treasury Department, for example, could benefit greatly from the knowledge contained in this computer bank.

I was further informed that the Treasury Department has made efforts to contract for the information with the Navy but it was disallowed. Treasury officials feel most strongly about this especially in view of the fact that they lost out to the State Department in terms of giving items away that are of great national interest and importance. The previous confidential chart which shows the positions of the various federal agencies in addition to the one that I am now enclosing in the report indicates that the Treasury Department was at great variance with State. The charts portray the position prior to the LOS meeting in Geneva and from the final U.S. positions that were taken into the conference it is obvious that the Treasury Department has lost considerable ground in trying to protect the best interests of the United States since the earlier meetings in Caracas   #   .

CHART 3

	State Department	Treasury Department	Defense Department	Interior Department	Commerce Department	OMB	Control on International Economic Policy
(1) Seabed protection through voting system (specified). objection through ... conditions.	et... Yes.	Not acceptable, under present restrictions. do.	Unrealistic to expect ... No comment.	Yes ... Yes.	Needs more study ... do.	Washington must approve. do.	Negotiability questionable. In ed.
(2) Extent of continental margin...	and flexibility...	All.	do.	All.	All the continental margin.	All.	All.
(3) Revenue sharing in economic zone.	et.	No.	do.	Comments ambiguous.	et limited.	No.	et.
(4) Tax credit.	N.	No.	do.	Yes.	No.	No. Washington must approve.	No.
(5) Ad referendum authority for negotiations.	Yes.	No.	Very limited use	Yes.	No.		No.

Treasury officials described the position of the United States at the conference during the time that I was there as "disastrous", "an atrocity", and "a debacle".

Our current ambassador John R. Stevenson on Friday morning, April 18, 1975, appeared to be convinced that this particular Law of the Sea Conference was indeed coming apart at the seams. He had already had discussions with conference leaders over the next LOS meeting, had rejected a four week meeting in August of 1975 as premature, and had tentatively discussed with LOS leaders the next meeting possibly in January 1976, with New Delhi or Nairobi as potential conference sites.

I must say on behalf of the bulk of our negotiators that they worked long and hard, day and night, to obtain a treaty document that would set new standards for a hundred different intertwined issues including pollution protection, freedom of scientific research, national security protections and defense requirements. From my observations of the United States team I am convinced they were operating in good faith along with a host of other delegates to reach an acceptable and equitable treaty.

Unfortunately the coalition of nations many of them described as "the sharks of Geneva", whose only interest appears to be to delay the treaty in order to force increasingly greater concessions from the United States because of this country's intense desire for a treaty has at this point in time doomed our efforts. Until these international special interests and self-interest groups have a change of heart or are rendered powerless by the will of the majority I must with great reluctance conclude that the interests of the United States and the American people must be served in the months ahead and that these interests will best be served by immediate unilateral governmental actions. This action must be in the form of Congressional enactment of legislation in the areas I have discussed coupled with a firm insistence on adherence to that body of international law which already exists.

I spoke to members of the U.S. delegation by telephone on May 2, 1975, to confirm the essence of what is in this report. They informed me that the situation had deteriorated even further and that the U.S. had made yet more concessions in a new "Pinto paper" which my contacts refused to disclose on the telephone for security reasons. I was told the group of 77, however, was sitting back and waiting not responding to the State Department's latest "giveaway package" obviously trying to stall any treaty document until at least next year. Their judgment was that with U.S. prestige at an all time low because of Viet Nam and other diplomatic failures the best game to play is a waiting one.

[H.R. 1270, H.R. 6017, 94th Cong., 1st sess.]

BILLS To promote the conservation and orderly development of hard mineral resources of the deep seabed, pending adoption of an international regime relating thereto.

Be it enacted by the Senate and House of Representatives of the United States of America in Congress assembled, That this Act may be cited as the "Deep Seabed Hard Minerals Act".

DECLARATION OF POLICY

SEC. 2. (a) FINDINGS.—The Congress finds—

(1) that the Nation's hard mineral resource requirements will continue to expand in order to supply national industrial needs and that the demand for certain hard minerals will increasingly exceed available domestic sources of supply;

(2) that, in the case of some minerals, the Nation is totally dependent upon foreign sources of supply and that the acquisition of mineral resources from foreign sources is a substantial factor in the national balance-of-payments position;

(3) that the national security interests of the United States require for availability of mineral resources which are independent of the export policies of foreign nations;

(4) that there is an alternate source of supply of certain minerals which are significant in relation to national needs contained in the manganese nodules which exist in great abundance on the ocean floor;

(5) that, to the extent that such nodules are located outside the territorial limits and beyond the Continental Shelf of any nation, the nodules are avaible for utilization by any nation with the ability to develop them;

(6) that United States mining companies have developed the technology necessary for the development and processing of deep seabed nodules and, given the necessary security of tenure, are prepared to make the necessary capital investment for such development and processing; and

(7) that it is in the national interest of the United States to utilize technology and capabilities of United States mining companies by providing for interim legislation which will encourage further efforts to insure national access to available deep seabed hard minerals and to provide the means whereby the national program may be merged into an international program which evolves from negotiations on the Law of the Sea and is subsequently ratified by the United States.

(b) PURPOSES.—The Congress declares that the purposes of this Act are—

(1) to establish a national program to promote the orderly development of certain hard mineral resources of the deep seabed, pending the establishment of an international regime for that purpose; and

(2) to insure the establishment of all practicable requirements necessary to protect the quality of the marine environment to the extent that that environment may be affected by deep seabed hard mineral mining development.

DEFINITIONS

SEC. 3. For the purposes of this Act—

(a) "Secretary" means, except where its usage indicates otherwise, the Secretary of the Interior;

(b) "deep seabed" means the seabed, and the subsoil thereof, lying seaward and outside the Continental Shelf of any nation;

(c) "Continental Shelf" refers to the seabed and subsoil of the submarine areas adjacent to the coast of any nation (including the coasts of islands), but outside the area of the territorial sea, to a depth of two hundred meters or, beyond that limit, to where the depth of the superjacent waters admits of the exploitation of the natural resources of the said areas;

(d) "block" means an area of the deep seabed having four boundary lines which are lines of longitude and latitude, the width of which may not be less than one-sixth the length, comprising not more than forty thousand square kilometers, and extending downward from the seabed to a depth of ten meters;

(e) "hard mineral" or "hard mineral resources" refers to nodules or accretions containing, but not limited to, iron, manganese, nickel, cobalt, and copper;

(f) "development" means any operation of exploration and commercial recovery, other than prospecting, having the purpose of discovery, recovery, or delivery of hard minerals from the deep seabed;

(g) "prospecting" means any operation conducted for the purpose of making geophysical or geochemical measurements, bottom sampling, or comparable activities so long as such operation is carried on in a manner that does not significantly alter the surface or subsurface of the deep seabed;

(h) "person" includes private individuals associations, corporation, or other entities, and any officer, employee, agent, department, agency, or instrumentality of the Federal Government, of any State or local unit of government, or of any foreign government;

(i) "eligible applicant" means a citizen of the United States or a corporation or other juridical entity organized under the laws of the United States, or its States, territories, or possessions, and possessing such technical and financial capabilities as may be precribed by the Secretary in order to assure effective and orderly development of hard mineral resources pursuant to a license issued under this Act;

(j) "investment" means a commitment of funds, together with the interest costs thereof, commodities, services, patents, processes, and techniques, dedicated to the development of a licensed block or the processing of the recovered minerals;

(k) "exploration" means the onsite observation and evaluation activity following the location and selection by an eligible applicant of a hard mineral deposit of potential economic interest, which has, as its objective, the establishment and documentation of the nature, shape, concentration, and tenor of an ore deposit, and the nature of the environmental factors which will affect its susceptibility of being developed, including the sampling of the deposit necessary for the design, fabrication, installation, and testing of equipment;

(l) "commercial recovery" means recovery of hard minerals at a substantial rate of production (without regard to profit or loss), for the primary purpose of marketing or commercial use and does not include recovery for sampling, experimenting in recovery methods, or testing equipment or plant for recovery or treatment of hard minerals;

(m) "reciprocating state" means any foreign state, designated by the President as a state with requirements and procedures comparable to those of the United States under this Act, and which has undertaken to recognize licenses issued under this Act; and

(n) "international registry clearinghouse" means a recording agency or organization designated by the President in cooperation with reciprocating states.

ACTIVITIES PROHIBITED

SEC. 4. (a) Except (1) as authorized pursuant to the provisions of this Act, including subsection (b) hereof, (2) as authorized under a license issued by a reciprocating state, or (3 as may be authorized under a treaty, convention, or other international agreement, which is binding upon the United States, no person subject to the jurisdiction of the United States shall engage directly or indirectly in the development of hard mineral resources of the deep seabed. The prohibition of this subsection does not apply to equipment engineering development, prospecting, or scientific research, nor to the rendering of contractual engineering, construction, or other services, not amounting to actual exploration or commercial recovery, nor to the furnishing of machinery, products, supplies, or materials to any organization or person lawfully engaged in such development: *Provided*, That the development does not infringe upon a license recognized as exclusive under the provisions of section 5(b) hereof.

(b) In any case in which an eligible applicant is already engaged in the exploration of a block, on the date on which this Act takes effect, that eligible applicant may establish his priority of right by filing an application for a license to develop that block, without awaiting the issuance of applicable regulations under section 18. Thereafter, he may continue any exploration activities until such time as the Secretary acts upon the application, with any activity subsequent to the action of the Secretary to be determined by the decision of the Secretary under the provision of section 5 hereof.

LICENSE TO DEVELOP

SEC. 5. (a) GENERAL.—Pursuant to the provisions of this Act, the Secretary shall accept applications from, and issue licenses to eligible applicants for the development of hard mineral resources of the deep seabed. Any license issued pursuant to this section shall be issued to the first eligible applicant who makes written application thereof, and tenders a fee of $50,000 for the block specified in the application and available for licensing. Such fee shall be deposited into an appropriate fund to be established in the Department of the Treasury, which fund shall be utilized for administrative and other costs incurred in the processing of applications for licenses under this Act. The fund shall be available for such purposes only as appropriated to the Secretary annually therefor. Before he may issue a license, the Secretary must first determine, in the consideration of each license application—

(1) that the applicant is financially responsible and has demonstrated the ability to comply with applicable laws, regulations, and license conditions;

(2) that the operations under the license will not unreasonably interfere with other reasonable uses of the high seas, as defined by any operative treaty or convention to which the United States is signatory, or by customary international law;

(3) that the issuance of a license does not conflict with any obligations of the United States, established by treaty or other international agreement; and

(4) that operations under the license will not pose an unreasonable threat to the integrity of the marine environment and that all reasonable precautions will be taken to minmize any adverse impact on that environment.

(b) NATURE AND DURATION OF LICENSE.—(1) Subject to the provisions of section 12 hereof, any license issued pursuant to this Act shall be exclusive as against all persons subject to the jurisdiction of the United States or of any reciprocating state, and shall authorize development of the hard mineral resources of the deep seabed for specified blocks thereof: *Provided*, That in no event shall any license issued under this Act authorize the commercial recovery of such resources prior to January 1, 1976: *And provided further*, That, except to the extent that such licenses are authorized pursuant to the provisions of an international agreement establishing a regime for the development of mineral resources of the international seabed area beyond the limits of coastal state territorial or resource jurisdiction, no license shall be issued under this Act subsequent to the date on which such international agreement shall become binding upon the United States.

(2) Priority of right for the issuance of a license shall be created and maintained by receipt by the Secretary of a license application from an eligible applicant: *Provided*, That the application is submitted in conformity with the provisions of this Act and the regulations promulgated by the Secretary pursuant to section 18 hereof.

(3) An application, submitted in accordance with subsection (b) of section 4 hereof and prior to the effective date of the regulations promulgated pursuant to section 18 of this Act, shall be entitled to priority of right as established in paragraph (2) of this subsection: *Provided*, That the eligible applicant complies with the provisions of this Act, including, but not limited to, the tender of the fee required by section 5, the furnishing of information required by subsection (b) of section 6, and the minimum expenditures required by section 8: *Provided further*, That the eligible applicant brings his application and his other activities into compliance with all applicable regulations issued by the Secretary, as soon as such regulations become effective.

(4) Every license issued under this Act shall remain in force for fifteen years and, where commercial recovery of the hard mineral resources has begun from a licensed block within the fifteen-year period, such license shall remain in force for as long as commercial recovery from the block continues.

(c) TRANSFER OR SURRENDER OF LICENSE.—Any license issued under this Act may be surrendered at will or, upon written request of the licensee, may be transferred by the Secretary to any other eligible applicant. Such license, as issued or as transferred, may be revoked for willful, substantial failure to comply with the provisions of this Act, with any regulation promulgated thereunder, or with any license restriction or license condition: *Provided*, That the Secretary has first given the licensee written notice of such violation and the licensee has failed to remedy the violation within a reasonable period of time. Upon such failure, the Secretary shall notify the licensee in writing that he proposes to revoked such license and that the licensee has thirty-days in which to request a hearing in accordance with section 554 of title 5, United States Code, on the issues raised by the proposed revocation. The Secretary shall issue his decision regarding revocation within thirty days after the notice of proposed revocation, or after the completion of the hearings, if such hearings are requested by the licensee in accordance with this subsection. Any decision issued by the Secretary after hearings shall be subject to judicial review in accordance with the provisions of sections 701 through 706 of title 5, United States Code.

(d) LICENSE CONDITIONS.—The Secretary is authorized to include in any license issued, or transferred, under this Act, any reasonable conditions which he finds necessary to carry out the purposes of this Act. Such conditions shall be prescribed on the basis of rules and regulations promulgated pursuant to section 18 of this Act.

LICENSING PROCEDURES

SEC. 6. (a) GENERAL.—The Secretary is authorized to establish procedures governing the application for, and the issuance of, licenses pursuant to this

Act. Such procedures shall contain an adequate mechanism for full consultation with all other interested Federal agencies and departments, and for the full consideration of the views of any interested members of the general public.

(b) LICENSE APPLICATION.—Each application shall contain such financial, technical, and other information as is specified under rules and regulations promulgated pursuant to section 18 of this Act.

(c) PUBLIC ACCESS TO INFORMATION.—(1) Copies of any communications, documents, reports, or information received from any applicant shall be made available to the public upon identifiable request, and at reasonable cost, unless such information may not be publicly released under the provisions of this subsection.

(2) The Secretary shall not disclose information obtained by him under this section which concerns or relates to trade secrets or other confidential matter referred to in section 1905 of title 18, United States Code.

(3) Nothing contained in this subsection shall be construed to require the release to the public of any information described by subsection (b) of section 552 of title 5, United States Code, or which is otherwise protected by law from such release.

(4) Prior to the issuance of the license, the following specific information required to be furnished to the Secretary under this Act and which is not otherwise protected from disclosure under paragraphs (2) and (3) of this subsection may not be released outside the Government and may be disclosed within the Government only on a strictly need-to-know basis:

    (i) coordinates of licensed blocks;

    (ii) any other data which discloses directly or indirectly the coordinates of licensed blocks; and

    (iii) geological data related to the licensed block.

(d) NOTICE, DECISIONS, AND REVIEW.—(1) Within thirty days after receipt of an application, and prior to granting a license, the Secretary shall publish in the Federal Register a notice containing a summary of the application and Information as to where the application and the available supporting data may be examined allowing interested persons at least sixty days for the submission of written data, views, or arguments to the granting of the license. The Secretary shall utilize such additional methods as he deems reasonable to inform interested persons and groups about the application and to invite their comments thereon.

(2) The Secretary's decision granting or denying a license shall be in writing and shall be made within sixty days following receipt of all views. The Secretary shall grant the license applied for when he finds that the application, as submitted, or as modified, meets the requirements of this Act and the rules and regulations promulgated hereunder.

(3) Judicial review of the Secretary's decision shall be in accordance with sections 701 through 706 of title 5, United States Code.

(4) The Secretary shall maintain a registry in which is recorded the filing or withdrawal of an application for a license under this Act, the issuance, denial, expiration, surrender, transfer, or revocation of such license, or the relinquishment of any licensed portion of the deep seabed. Subject to the limitations of subsection (c) hereof, registry records shall be available for public inspection during the business hours of every working day.

(5) The Secretary shall, and the applicant or licensee may, notify the international registry clearinghouse within fourteen days of the filing or withdrawal of an application for a license under this Act, the issuance. denial, transfer, expiration, surrender, or revocation of such license, or the relinquishment of any licensed portion of the deep seabed.

(6) The function of the international registry clearinghouse shall consist solely of keeping records of notices, or applications for licenses, issuances, denials, transfers, or terminations of licenses, and the relinquishment of licensed portions of the deep seabed. Pending designation of such clearinghouse. notice to the Secretary shall constitute notice to the clearinghouse within the meaning of this Act.

ENVIRONMENTAL CRITERIA

SEC. 7. The Secretary shall consult with appropriate Federal agencies and departments regarding environmental criteria and shall establish objective environmental standards, based on tecshnical and scientific data, applied in a consistent manner under the rules and regulations of section 18, to which operations under a license issued under this Act shall adhere. The Secretary may, from time to time, propose revisions of the rules and regulations regarding environmental standards, as scientific data may warrant.

MINIMUM ANNUAL EXPENDITURES

Sec. 8. (a) Expenditures.—In connection with the development of hard mineral resources from each licensed block, the licensee shall make or cause to be made minimum expenditures in the following amounts per block until commercial recovery from such block is first initiated:

Year	Amount per year
1	$100,000
2-5	200,000
6-10	500,000
11-15	1,000,000

The minimum annual expenditures required under this section shall consist of expenditures for operations, facilities, and equipment as required or utilized for the evaluation of the block for which the development license is issued. Such expenditures in any year in excess of the required minimum may be credited to requirements for later years.

(b) Records.—Each recipient of a license under this Act shall keep such records as the Secretary shall prescribe, including records which fully disclose the expenditures for development required by this section, and such other records as will facilitate an effective audit of such expenditures.

(c) Audits.—The Secretary and the Comptroller General of the United States, or any of their duly authorized representatives, shall have access for the purpose of audit and examination to any books, documents, papers, and records of the licensees that are pertinent to the expenditures required under this section.

AUTHORIZATION TO BEGIN COMMERCIAL RECOVERY

Sec. 9. Upon completion of its exploration activities at any licensed block, the licensee shall so notify the Secretary and request from the Secretary an authorization to begin commercial recovery. Upon receipt of such request, and subject to the provisions of section 12, the Secretary shall grant such authorization: *Provided*, That the licensee is in compliance with all conditions of the license and has furnished the Secretary with copies of all raw data generated in the normal course of the applicant's work on the block and relating directly to the documentation of the nature, shape, concentration, and tenor of the ore deposit of the licensed block and the nature of the physical environmental factors which will affect such commercial recovery.

AREAS WITHDRAWN FROM LICENSING; DENSITY LIMITATIONS

Sec. 10. (a) No license shall be issued under this Act for any portion of the deep seabed—
(1) which has been relinquished by the applicant under a license issued under this Act within the prior three years;
(2) which is subject either to a prior application for a license, or an outstanding license, under this Act, or from a reciprocating state; and
(3) which, if licensed, would result in a holding by licensees under this Act of more than 30 per centum of an area of the deep seabed which is within a circle with a diameter of one thousand two hundred and fifty kilometers.
(b) No license shall be issued or transferred under this Act, and no person subject to the jurisdiction of the United States shall have a substantial interest in a license issued under this Act, which would result in any substantial interest or indirectly holding, controlling, or having a substantial interest in licenses for development of any portion of the deep seabed which that person could not hold directly under this Act in accordance with the limitations of this section.

RELINQUISHMENT OF LICENSED AREAS

SEC. 11. Within fifteen years of the license date for any block, and not later than the grant of authorization to exploit as provided for in section 9 hereof, the licensee shall, by written notice to the Secretary, relinquish 75 per centum of such block measured laterally. The relinquishment shall be such that the unrelinquished area or areas shall conform to the shape of a block as defined in section 3 hereof. The licensee shall select the area of the block to be relinquished and as many as four contiguous blocks of the same type held by the licensee may be treated as a single unit for selecting the area to be relinquished.

INTERNATIONAL REGIME

SEC. 12. At such time as an international agreement, providing for the establishment of an international regime for the development of the hard mineral resources of the deep seabed, shall become binding upon the United States, no additional licenses shall be issued pursuant to this Act, and licenses previously issued under this Act shall be made subject to the provisions of that agreement. To the extent that they are consistent with the provisions of the international regime, licenses previously issued shall continue in effect and, to the extent possible under the international agreement, the United States shall exercise its rights and responsibilities under the agreement to insure their continuation under the international regime.

INVESTMENT GUARANTY

SEC. 13. To the extent that an international agreement, binding upon the United States, shall differ from the requirements of this Act, the United States shall provide the licensee with compensation in an effectively realizable form representing the reduction in value of the investment resulting from the differing requirements: *Provided,* That the liability for compensation shall, until after an authorization for commercial recovery has been granted, be limited to compensation in relation to equipment and facilities utilized for exploration purposes: *Provided further,* That the Secretary of Commerce shall determine in the first instance the amount owing on the claims for compensation under this section: *And provided* further. That after an authorization for commercial recovery has been granted, the value of the investment shall be determined by subtracting from the value of the original investment any gross profits realized from development and processing operations: *And provided further,* That the liability under this section shall terminate ten years after commercial recovery has begun.

INVESTMENT INSURANCE

SEC. 14. (a) On annual payment by any licensee of a premium to be determined by the Secretary of Commerce, utilizing standard insurance practices and based upon the relative risks involved. the United States shall insure the licensee, in an amount not exceeding the value of the investment, for any damages suffered through the impairment of the insured investment, or through the removal of hard minerals from the licensed block, by any other person against whom a legal remedy either does not exist or is unavailable in any legal forum to which the licensee has access. The Secretary of Commerce shall determine the amount owing on any claim for reimbursement under this section.

(b) Insurance under this section shall be available solely upon the request of the licensee and after the Secretary of Commerce has determined that the insurance coverage requested is not readily available at a reasonable premium elsewhere.

INVESTMENT GUARANTY AND INSURANCE FUND

SEC. 15. There shall be established in the Treasury of the United States a Guaranty and Insurance Fund, which shall have separate accounts to be known as the Guaranty Reserve and the Insurance Reserve, which reserves shall be available for discharge of liabilities, as provided in sections 13 and 14 of this Act, until such time as all such liabilities have been discharged or have expired or until all such reserves shall have been expended in accordance with the provisions of this section. The Insurance Reserve shall be funded by the premiums received from licensees, as provided in section 14 of this Act, and the Guaranty Reserve shall be funded by such sums as shall be appropriated pursuant to section 22 of this Act.

NONDISCRIMINATORY TREATMENT

SEC. 16. For purposes of export controls, section 27 of the Act of June 5, 1920, customs laws, and tax laws of the United States, and the applicable implementing regulations thereof, all hard minerals recovered from the deep seabed under a license issued pursuant to this Act shall be deemed to have been recovered within the United States, and such laws, regulations, and controls shall be administered so that there will be no discrimination between hard minerals recovered from the deep seabed and similar hard minerals recovered within the United States.

CONSORTIA

SEC. 17. (a) In any case of agreement between entities of the United States and foreign entities, with the resulting combination of interests receiving a development license under the authority of this Act, the applicability of sections 13, 14, and 16, of this Act shall be limited to the proportion of interest owned by the United States entity or entities.

(b) In the case of an agreement between entities of the United States and foreign entities with the resulting combination of interests receiving a development license from a reciprocating State, the provisions of section 16 of this Act, other than the applicability of section 27 of the Act of June 5, 1920, shall be applied as if the proportion of interest owned by the United States entity or entities were licensed pursuant to this Act.

REGULATORY AUTHORITY

SEC. 18. (a) The Secretary is authorized to issue such reasonable rules and regulations as may be necessary to carry out the provisions of this Act, other than the provisions of sections 13, 14, and 15.

(b) The rules and regulations issued under subsection (a) shall include provisions covering:

    (1) eligibility standards and compliance;

    (2) licensing procedures, requirements, and compliance;

    (3) work requirements compliance;

    (4) environmental standards and compliance;

    (5) multiple use standards and compliance; and

    (6) other matters specifically delegated to the Secretary under the Act.

(c) The Secretary of Commerce is authorized to issue such reasonable rules and regulations as may be necessary to implement the provisions of sections 13, 14, and 15 of this Act.

(d) Rules and regulations issued under this section shall be promulgated in accordance with provisions of section 553 of title 5, United States Code.

JURISDICTION OF UNITED STATES DISTRICT COURTS

SEC. 19. United States district courts shall have original jurisdiction of cases and controversies arising out of, or in connection with, development activities conducted in any area of the deep seabed under the authority of this Act, and proceedings with respect to any such case or controversy may be instituted in the judicial district in which any defendant resides, or may be found, or in the judicial district nearest the place where the cause of action arose.

PENALTIES

SEC. 20. (a) CIVIL PENALTIES.—Any person subject to the jurisdiction of the United States who violates any provision of this Act, or any rule or regulation issued pursuant to section 18 hereof, shall be liable to a civil penalty of $10,000 for each day during which the violation continues. The penalty shall be assessed by the Secretary, who in determining the amount of the penalty, shall consider the gravity of the violation, any prior violation, and the demonstrated good faith of the person charged in attempting to achieve rapid compliance after notification of the violation. No penalty may be assessed until the person charged shall have been given notice of the violation involved, and an opportunity for a hearing. For good cause shown, the Secretary may remit or mitigate any penalty assessed. Upon failure of the person charged to pay an assessed penalty, the Secretary may request the Attorney General to commence an action in the appropriate district court of the United States for collection of the penalty without regard to the amount involved, together with such other relief as may be appropriate.

(b) CRIMINAL PENALITIES.—In addition to any other penalty, any person subject to the jurisdiction of the United States who willfully and knowingly violates any provision of this Act, or any rule or regulation issued pursuant to section 18 hereof, shall be punished by a fine of not more than $25,000 for each day during which such violation continues.

(c) LIABILITY OF VESSELS.—Any vessel, except a public vessel engaged in noncommercial activities, used in a violation of this Act, or of any rule or regulation issued pursuant to section 18 hereof, shall be liable in rem for any civil penalty assessed or criminal fine imposed and may be proceeded against in any district court of the United States having jurisdiction thereof; but, no vessel shall be liable unless it shall appear that one or more of the owners, or bareboat charterers was, at the time of the violation, a consenting party, or privy to such violation.

ANNUAL REPORT

SEC. 21. The Secretary of Commerce and the Secretary of the Interior shall each report to the Congress annually, on or before June 30, with the first report to be made on or before June 30, 1976, on his activities under this Act, including recommendations for additional legislation as deemed necessary.

AUTHORIZATION FOR APPROPRIATIONS

SEC. 22. (a) There are authorized to be appropriated for the current fiscal year and for each of the two succeeding fiscal years, such sums as may be necessary for the administration of this Act.

(b) There are authorized to be appropriated to the Secretary of Commerce, to remain available until expended, such sums as may be necessary from time to time to replenish or increase the Guaranty Reserve of the Insurance and Guaranty Fund, or to discharge the liabilities under section 12 of this Act.

EFFECTIVE DATE

SEC. 23. This Act shall take effect on the date of its enactment.

DEPARTMENT OF JUSTICE,
Washington, D.C., February 26, 1976.

Hon. LEONOR K. SULLIVAN,
Chairman, Committee on Merchant Marine and Fisheries, House of Representatives, Washington, D.C.

DEAR MADAM CHAIRMAN: This is in response to your request for comments on H.R. 1270, a bill "To promote the conservation and orderly development of hard mineral resources of the deep seabed, pending adoption of an international regime relating thereto."

The purpose of this bill is to establish a national program to promote the orderly development of the hard mineral resources of the seabed beyond the limits of national jurisdiction by American companies pending the coming into force of an international regime for that purpose. The bill would establish guarantees for the investments of American companies against certain risks resulting from the present uncertainty regarding rights to those resources.

As you are aware, the question of jurisdiction over the resources of the seabed beyond the limits of national jurisdiction is a subject of major concern at the continuing Third United Nations Conference on the Law of the Sea. Although no resolution of the problem has yet been reached, it is anticipated that the Conference will result in an international agreement. Pending final outcome of the Conference, the National Security Council's Law of the Sea Task Force is responsible for preparing coordinated replies of the Executive

Branch with the matters bearing on the negotiations of the Conference. The Department of Justice is represented on the Task Force and Justice's views are taken into account in the preparation of such coordinated replies. Accordingly, the Department of Justice defers to the Law of the Sea Task Force with regard to H.R. 1270.

The Office of Management and Budget has advised that there is no objection to the submission of this report from the standpoint of the Administration's program.

Sincerely,

MICHAEL M. UHLMANN,
Assistant Attorney General.

COMPTROLLER GENERAL OF THE UNITED STATES,
Washington, D.C., July 16, 1975.

Hon. LEONOR K. SULLIVAN.
Chairman, Committee on Merchant Marine and Fisheries, House of Representatives.

DEAR MADAM CHAIRMAN: Reference is made to your request for our comments on H.R. 1270, 94th Congress, which, if enacted, would be cited as the "Deep Seabed Hard Minerals Act."

H.R. 1270 would establish a national program to insure the orderly development of hard mineral resources of the deep seabed, pending the establishment of an international regime for that purpose. The program would be administered by the Secretary of the Interior through the issuance of licenses for the development of specific blocks of the seabed to eligible applicants in accordance with conditions specified in the bill and regulations to be promulgated by the Secretary.

Section 3(1) of the bill defines "commercial recovery" as "recovery of hard minerals at a substantial rate of production (without regard to profit or loss) * * * ." Section 5(b)(4) would provide for licenses issued under the proposed Act to remain in force for 15 years, or where commercial recovery has begun within 15 years, for as long as commercial recovery from the block continues. We suggest that the phrase "substantial rate of production" in section 3(1) be more clearly defined to insure that licenses remaining "in force" under section 5(b)(4) are not held by licensees for primarily speculative purposes for extended periods of time.

Section 5(a) of the bill would provide for a set fee of $50,000 to be charged for licenses. Section 8(a) would provide for specific minimum amounts to be expended for development of each block. We suggest that since monetary values change with inflationary pressures, these amounts be stated as minimums, subject to revision by the Secretary of the Interior as he deems necessary.

Section 5(b)(1) would provide that no license under the proposed Act be issued subsequent to the date that an international agreement establishing an international regime becomes binding upon the United States. In addition, section 12 would provide that at such time as the international agreement shall become binding upon the United States, no additional licenses may be issued under the proposed Act; that previous licenses must conform to the international agreement; and that to the extent possible under the agreement, the United States is required to sponsor the licensee for continuation of his license under the international regime. The United States, at the third United Nations Law of the Sea Conference during June-August 1974, proposed that treaty articles concerning deep seabed mining be applied on a provisional basis (that is, after signature but before ratification.) If these treaty articles are provisionally applied, and when and if a Comprehensive Oceans Law Treaty is signed, further licensing activity would be delayed until an international regime is established to regulate ocean mining, which would take an extensive period of time. Therefore, the Committee may wish to consider providing for a procedure under which leasing could continue under the provisions of the bill during the interim period after a treaty is signed and before organization and licensing procedures under the treaty are in place.

Licenses issued under the proposed Act would be made subject to any subsequent international agreement binding upon the United States. In this connection, section 13 provides that the United States shall compensate a licensee for the value of the investment made and subsequently taken or impaired as a result of requirements imposed by the international agreement that would differ from those imposed by the proposed Act. We recognize that there may be a need for a compensation provision of this nature to encourage development. We suggest, however, that it may be desirable to place a monetary limit on the Government's liability for the compensation of any one licensee or with respect to any one block licensed for development.

Suggestions of technical and editorial changes to H.R. 1270 are enclosed.

Sincerely yours,

PAUL G. DEMBLING,
(FOR THE COMPTROLLER GENERAL OF THE UNITED STATES).

Enclosure.

SUGGESTED TECHNICAL AND EDITORIAL CHANGES TO H.R. 1270

1. On page 16, line 11, the last word should be "such."
2. On page 26, line 5, the number "13" should be substituted for "12."

[H.R. 11879, 94th Cong., 2d sess.]

A BILL To promote the conservation and orderly development of hard mineral resources of the deep seabed, pending adoption of an international regime relating thereto.

Be it enacted by the Senate and House of Representatives of the United States of America in Congress assembled, That this Act may be cited as the "Deep Seabed Hard Minerals Act".

DECLARATION OF POLICY

SEC. 2. (a) FINDINGS.—The Congress finds—

(1) that the Nation's hard mineral resource requirements will continue to expand in order to supply national industrial needs and that the demand for certain hard minerals will increasingly exceed available domestic sources of supply;

(2) that, in the case of some minerals, the Nation is totally dependent upon foreign sources of supply and that the acquisition of mineral resources from foreign sources is a substantial factor in the national balance-of-payments position;

(3) that the national security interests of the United States require the availability of mineral resources which are independent of the export policies of foreign nations;

(4) that there is an alternate source of supply of certain minerals which are significant in relation to national needs contained in the manganese nodules which exist in great abundance on the ocean floor;

(5) that, to the extent that such nodules are located outside the territorial limits and beyond the Continental Shelf of any nation, the nodules are available for utilzation by any nation with the ability to develop them;

(6) that United States mining companies have developed the technology necessary for the development and processing of deep seabed nodules and, given the necessary security of tenure, are prepared to make the necessary capital investment for such development and processing; and

(7) that it is in the national interest of the United States to utilize existing technology and capabilities of United States mining companies by providing for interim legislation which will encourage further efforts to insure national access to available deep seabed hard minerals and to provide the means whereby the national program may be merged into an international program which evolves from the Third United Nations Conference on the Law of the Sea and is subsequently ratified by the United States.

(b) PURPOSES.—The Congress declares that the purposes of this Act are—

(1) to establish a national program to promote the orderly development of certain hard mineral resources of the deep seabed, pending the establishment of an international regime for that purpose; and

(2) to insure the establishment of all practicable requirements necessary to protect the quality of the marine environment to the extent that the environment may be affected by deep seabed hard mineral mining development.

DEFINITIONS

SEC. 3. For the purposes of this Act—

(1) The term "Secretary" means, except where its usage indicates otherwise, the Secretary of Commerce.

(2) The term "deep seabed" means the seabed, and the subsoil thereof, lying seaward and outside the Continental Shelf of any nation.

(3) The term "Continental Shelf" refers to the seabed and subsoil of the submarine areas adjacent to the coast of any nation (including the coasts of islands), but outside the area of the territorial sea, to a depth of two hundred meters or beyond that limit to where the depth of the superjacent waters admits of the exploitation of the natural resources of the said areas.

(4) The term "block" means an area of the deep seabed having four boundary lines which are lines of longitude and latitude, the width of which may not be less than one-sixth the length, comprising not more than forty thousand square kilometers, and extending downward from the seabed to a depth of ten meters.

(5) The term "hard mineral" or "hard mineral resources" refers to modules or accretions containing, but not limited to, iron, manganese, nickel, cobalt and copper.

(6) The term "development" means any operation of exploration and commercial recovery, other than prospecting, having the purpose of discovery, recovery, or delivery of hard minerals from the deep seabed.

(7) The term "prospecting" means any operation conducted for the purpose of making geophysical or geochemical measurements, bottom sampling, or comparable activities so long as such operation is carried on in a manner that does not significantly alter the surface or subsurface of the deep seabed.

(8) The term "person" includes private individuals, associations, corporations, or other entities, and any officer, employee, agent, department, agency, or instrumentality of the Federal Government, of any State or local unit of government, or of any foreign government.

(9) The term "eligible applicant" means a citizen of the United States or a corporation or other juridical entity organized under the laws of the United States, or its States, territories, or possessions, and possessing such technical and financial capabilities as may be prescribed by the Secretary in order to assure effective and orderly development of hard mineral resources pursuant to a license issued under this Act.

(10) The term "investment" means a commitment of funds, together with the interest costs thereof, commodities, services, patents, processes, and techniques, dedicated to the development of a licensed block or the processing of the recovered minerals.

(11) The term "exploration" means the onsite observation and evaluation activity following the location and selection by an eligible applicant of a hard mineral deposit of potential economic interest, which has, as its objective, the establishment and documentation of the nature, shape, concentration, and tenor of an ore deposit, and the nature of the environmental factors which will affect its susceptibility of being developed, including the sampling of the deposit necessary for the design, fabrication, installation, and testing of equipment.

(12) The term "commercial recovery" means recovery of hard minerals at a substantial rate of production (without regard to profit or loss), for the primary purpose of marketing or commercial use and does not include recovery for sampling, experimenting in recovery methods, or testing equipment or plant for recovery or treatment of hard minerals.

(13) The term "reciprocating state" means any foreign state, designated by the President as a state with requirements and procedures comparable to those of the United States under this Act, and which has undertaken to recognize licenses issued under this Act.

(14) The term "international registry clearinghouse" means a recording agency or organization designated by the President in cooperation with reciprocating states.

ACTIVITIES PROHIBITED

SEC. 4. (a) Except (1) as authorized pursuant to the provisions of this Act, including subsection (b) hereof, (2) as authorized under a license issued by a reciprocating state, or (3) as may be authorized under a treaty, convention, or other international agreement, which is binding upon the United States, no person subject to the jurisdiction of the United States shall engage directly or indirectly in the development of hard mineral resources of the deep seabed. The prohibition of this subsection does not apply to equipment engineering development, prospecting, or scientific research, nor to the rendering of contractual engineering, construction, or other services, not amounting to actual exploration or commercial recovery, nor to the furnishing of machinery, products, supplies, or materials to any organization or person lawfully engaged in such development: *Provided*, That the development does not infringe upon a license recognized as exclusive under the provisions of section 5(b) hereof.

(b) In any case in which an eligible applicant is already engaged in the exploration of a block, on the date on which this Act takes effect, that eligible applicant may establish his priority of right by filing an application for a license to develop that block, without awaiting the issuance of applicable regulations under section 19. Thereafter, he may continue any exploration activities until such time as the Secretary acts upon the application, with any activity subsequent to the action of the Secretary to be determined by the decision of the Secretary under the provisions of section 5 hereof.

LICENSE TO DEVELOP

SEC. 5. (a) GENERAL.—Pursuant to the provisions of this Act, the Secretary shall accept applications from, and issue licenses to, eligible applicants for the development of hard mineral resources of the deep seabed. Any license issued pursuant to this section shall be issued to the first eligible applicant who makes written application thereof, and tenders a fee of $50,000 for the block specified in the application and available for licensing. Such fee shall be deposited into an appropriate fund to be established in the Department of the Treasury, which fund shall be utilized for administrative and other costs incurred in the processing of applications for licenses under this Act. The fund shall be available for such purposes only as appropriated to the Secretary annually therefor. Before he may issue a license, the Secretary must first determine, in the consideration of each license application—

(1) that the applicant is financially responsible and has demonstrated the ability to comply with applicable laws, regulations, and license conditions;

(2) that the operations under the license will not unreasonably interfere with other reasonable uses of the high seas, as defined by any operative treaty or convention to which the United States is signatory, or by customary international law;

(3) that the operations under the license will be conducted in accordance with guidelines and standards which shall be established by the Administrator of the National Oceanic and Atmospheric Administration to assure that such operations will not unreasonably interfere with the replenishment and harvesting of the living resources of the sea;

(4) that the issuance of a license does not conflict with any obligations of the United States, established by treaty or other international agreement; and

(5) that operations under the license will not pose an unreasonable threat to the integrity of the marine environment and that all reasonable precautions will be taken to minimize any adverse impact on that environment.

(b) NATURE AND DURATION OF LICENSE.—(1) Subject to the provisions of section 12 hereof, any license issued pursuant to this Act shall be exclusive as against all persons subject to the jurisdiction of the United States or of any reciprocating state, and shall authorize development of the hard mineral resources of the deep seabed for specified blocks thereof: *Provided*, That in no event shall any license issued under this Act authorize the commercial recovery of such resources prior to January 1, 1977: *And provided further*, That, except to the extent that such licenses are authorized pursuant to the provisions of an international agreement establishing a regime for the development of mineral resources of the international seabed area beyond the limits of coastal state territorial or resource jurisdiction, no licenses shall be issued under this Act subsequent to the date on which such international agreement shall become binding upon the United States.

(2) Priority of right for the issuance of a license shall be created and maintained by receipt by the Secretary of a license application from an eligible applicant: *Provided*, That the application is submitted in conformity with the provisions of this Act and the regulations promulgated by the Secretary pursuant to section 19 hereof.

(3) An application, submitted in accordance with subsection (b) of section 4 hereof and prior to the effective date of the regulations promulgated pursuant to section 19 of this Act, shall be entitled to priority of right as established in paragraph (2) of this subsection: *Provided*, That the eligible applicant complies with the provisions of this Act, including, but not limited to, the tender of the fee required by section 5, the furnishing of information required by subsection (b) of section 6, and the minimum expenditures required by section 8: *Provided further*, That the eligible applicant brings his application and his other activities into compliance with all applicable regulations issued by the Secretary, as soon as such regulations become effective.

(4) Every license issued under this Act shall remain in force for fifteen years and, where commercial recovery of the hard mineral resources has begun from a licensed block within the fifteen-year period, such license shall remain in force for as long as commercial recovery from the block continues.

(c) Transfer or Surrender of License. Any license issued under this Act may be surrendered at will or, upon written request of the licensee, may be transferred by the Secretary to any other eligible applicant. Such license, as issued or as transferred, may be revoked for willful, substantial failure to comply with the provisions of this Act with any regulation promulgated thereunder, or with any license restriction or license condition: *Provided*, That the Secretary has first given the licensee written notice of such violation and the licensee has failed to remedy the violation within a reasonable period of time. Upon such failure, the Secretary shall notify the licensee in writing that he proposes to revoke such license and that the licensee has thirty days in which to request a hearing in accordance with section 554 of title 5, United States Code, on the issues raised by the proposed revocation. The Secretary shall issue his decision regarding revocation within thirty days after the notice of proposed revocation, or after the completion of the hearings, if such hearings are requested by the licensee in accordance with this subsection. Any decision issued by the Secretary after hearings shall be subject to judicial review in accordance with the provisions of sections 701 through 706 of title 5, United States Code.

(d) License Conditions.—The Secretary is authorized to include in any license issued, or transferred, under this Act, any reasonable conditions which he finds necessary to carry out the purposes of this Act. Such conditions shall be prescribed on the basis of rules and regulations promulgated pursuant to section 19 of this Act.

LICENSING PROCEDURES

Sec. 6. (a) General. The Secretary is authorized to establish procedures governing the application for, and the issuance of, licenses pursuant to this Act. Such procedures shall contain an adequate mechanism for full consultation with all other interested Federal agencies and departments, and for the full consideration of the views of any interested members of the general public.

(b) License Applications.—Each application shall contain such financial, technical, and other information as is specified under rules and regulations promulgated pursuant to section 19 of this Act.

(c) Public Access to Information.—(1) The Secretary is authorized to promulgate regulations requiring the submission of all data concerning ocean mineral resources and the seabed from which they are extracted from any person subject to the provisions of this Act upon receipt of a license by such person under this Act, if such data is necessary to carry out the responsibilities conferred on him by this Act.

(2) Copies of any communications, documents, reports, or information received from any applicant shall be made available to the public upon identifiable request, and at reasonable cost, unless such information may not be publicly released under the provisions of this subsection.

(3) The Secretary shall not disclose information obtained by him under this section which concerns or relates to trade secrets or other confidential matter referred to in section 1905 of title 18, United States Code.

(4) Nothing contained in this subsection shall be construed to require the release to the public of any information described by subsection (b) of section 552 of title 5, United States Code, or which is otherwise protected by law from such release.

(5) Prior to the issuance of the license, the following specific information required to be furnished to the Secretary under this Act and which is not otherwise protected from disclosure under paragraphs (2) and (3) of this subsection may not be released outside the Government and may be disclosed within the Government only on a strictly need-to-know basis:

(i) coordinates of licensed blocks;

(ii) any other data which discloses directly or indirectly the coordinates of licensed blocks; and

(iii) geological data related to the licensed block.

(d) NOTICE, DECISION, AND REVIEW.—(1) Within thirty days after receipt of an application, and prior to granting a license, the Secretary shall publish in the Federal Register a notice containing a summary of the application and information as to where the application and the available supporting data may be examined allowing interested persons at least sixty days for the submission of written data, views, or arguments to the granting of the license. The Secretary shall utilize such additional methods as he deems reasonable to inform interested persons and groups about the application and to invite their comments thereon.

(2) The Secretary's decision granting or denying a license shall be in writing and shall be made within sixty days following receipt of all views. The Secretary shall grant the license applied for when he finds that the application, as submitted, or as modified, meets the requirements of this Act and the rules and regulations promulgated hereunder.

(3) Judicial review of the Secretary's decision shall be in accordance with sections 701 through 706 of title 5, United States Code.

(4) The Secretary shall maintain a registry in which is recorded the filing or withdrawal of an application for a license under this Act, the issuance, denial, expiration, surrender, transfer, or revocation of such license, or the relinquishment of any licensed portion of the deep seabed. Subject to the limitations of subsection (c) hereof, registry records shall be available for public inspection during the business hours of every working day.

(5) The Secretary shall, and the applicant or licensee may, notify the international registry clearinghouse within fourteen days of the filing or withdrawal of an application for a license under this Act, the issuance, denial, transfer, expiration, surrender, or revocation of such license, or the relinquishment of any licensed portion of the deep seabed.

(6) The function of the international registry clearinghouse shall consist solely of keeping records of notices, or terminations of licenses, and the relinquishment of licensed portions of the deep seabed. Pending designation of such clearinghouse, notice to the Secretary shall constitute notice to the clearinghouse within the meaning of this Act.

ENVIRONMENTAL CRITERIA

SEC. 7. (a) The Secretary, acting through the Administrator of the National Oceanic and Atmospheric Administration, shall consult with appropriate Federal agencies and departments regarding environmental criteria and shall establish objective environmental standards, based on technical and scientific data, applied in a consistent manner under the rules and regulations of section 19, to which operations under a license issued under this Act shall adhere. The Secretary may, from time to time, propose revisions of the rules and regulations regarding environmental standards, as scientific data may warrant.

(b) In conducting any research required by this section, the Administrator of the National Oceanic and Atmospheric Administration shall, wherever possible, utilize existing Government-owned and Government-operated marine research laboratories and vessels.

MINIMUM ANNUAL EXPENDITURES

SEC. 8. (a) EXPENDITURES.—In connection with the development of hard mineral resources from each licensed block, the licensee shall make or cause to be made minimum expenditures in the following amounts per block until commercial recovery from such block is first initiated ·

Year:	Amount per yea
1	$100, 000
2 to 5	200, 000
6 to 10	500, 000
11 to 15	1, 000, 000

The minimum annual expenditures required under this section shall consist of expenditures for operations, facilities, and equipment as required or utilized for the evaluation of the block for which the development license is issued. Such expenditures in any year in excess of the required minimum may be credited to requirements for later years.

(b) RECORDS.—Each recipient of a license under this Act shall keep such records as the Secretary shall prescribe, including records which fully disclose the expenditures for development required by this section, and such other records as well facilitate an effective audit of such expenditures.

(c) AUDIT.—The Secretary and the Comptroller General of the United States, or any of their duly authorized representatives, shall have access for the purpose of audit and examination to any books, documents, papers, and records of the licensees that are pertinent to the expenditures required under this section.

AUTHORIZATION TO BEGIN COMMERCIAL RECOVERY

SEC. 9. Upon completion of its exploration activities at any licensed block, the licensee shall so notify the Secretary and request from the Secretary an authorization to begin commercial recovery. Upon receipt of such request, and subject to the provisions of section 12, the Secretary shall grant such authorization: *Provided*, That the licensee is in compliance with all conditions of the license and has furnished the Secretary with copies of all raw data generated in the normal course of the applicant's work on the block and relating directly to the documentation of the nature, shape, concentration, and tenor of the ore deposit of the licensed block and the nature of the physical environmental factors which will affect such commercial recovery.

AREAS WITHDRAWN FROM LICENSING; DENSITY LIMITATIONS

SEC. 10. (a) No license shall be issued under this Act for any portion of the deep seabed—

(1) which has been relinquished by the applicant under a license under this Act within the prior three years;

(2) which is subject either to a prior application for a license, or an outstanding license, under this Act, or from a reciprocating state; and

(3) which, if licensed, would result in a holding by licensees under this Act of more than 30 per centum of an area of the deep seabed which is within a circle with a diameter of one thousand two hundred and fifty kilometers.

(b) No license shall be issued or transferred under this Act, and no person subject to the jurisdiction of the United States shall have a substantial interest in a license issued under this Act, which would result in any person directly or indirectly holding, controlling, or having a substantial interest in licenses for development of any portion of the deep seabed which that person could not hold directly under this Act in accordance with the limitations of this section.

RELINQUISHMENT OF LICENSED AREAS

SEC. 11. Within fifteen yeas of the license date for any block, and not later than the grant of authorization to exploit as provided for in section 9 hereof, the licensee shall, by written notice to the Secretary, relinquish 75 per centum of such block measured laterally. The relinquishment shall be such that the unrelinquished area or areas shall conform to the shape of a block as defined in section 3 hereof. The licensee shall select the area of the block to be relinquished and as many as four contiguous blocks of the same type held by the licensee may be treated as a single unit for selecting the area to be relinquished.

Sec. 12. At such time as an international agreement providing for the establishment of an international regime for the development of the hard mineral resources of the deep seabed, shall become binding upon the United States, no additional licenses shall be issued pursuant to this Act, and licenses prevously issued under this Act shall be made subject to the provisions of that agreement. To the extent that they are consistent with the provisions of the international regime, licenses previously issued shall continue in effect, and, to the extent possible under the international agreement, the United States shall exercise its rights and responsibilities under the agreement to insure their continuation under the international regime.

INVESTMENT GUARANTEE

Sec. 13. To the extent that an international agreement, binding upon the United States, shall differ from the requirements of this Act, the United States shall provide the licensee with compensation in an effective realizable form representing the reduction in value of the investment resulting from the differing requirements: *Provided*, That the liability for compensation shall, until after an authorization for commercial recovery has been granted, be limited to compensation in relation to equipment and failities utilized for exploration purposes: *Provided further*, That the Secretary shall determine in the first instance the amount owing on the claims for compensation under this section: *Provided further*, That after an authorization for commercial recovery has been granted, the value of the investment shall be determined by subtracting from the value of the original investment any gross profits realized from development and processing operations: *And provided further*, That the liability under this section shall terminate ten years after commercial recovery has begun.

INVESTMENT INSURANCE

Sec. 14. (a) On annual payment by any licensee of a premium to be determined by the Secretary utilizing standard insurance practices and based upon the relative risks involved, the United States shall insure the licensee, in an amount not exceeding the value of the investment, for any damages suffered through the impairment of the insured investment, or through the removal of hard minerals from the licensed block, by any other person against whom a legal remedy either does not exist or is unavailable in any legal forum to which the licensee has access. The Secretary shall determine the amount owing on any claim for reimbursement under this section.

(b) Insurance under this section shall be available solely upon the request of the licensee and after the Secretary has determined that the insurance coverage requested is not readily available at a reasonable premium elsewhere.

INVESTMENT GUARANTY AND INSURANCE FUND

Sec. 15. There shall be established in the Treasury of the United States a Guarantee and Investment Fund, which shall have separate accounts to be known as the Guarantee Reserve and Insurance Reserve, which reserves shall be available for discharge of liabilities, as provided in sections 13 and 14 of this Act, until such time as all such liabilities have been discharged or have expired, or until all such reserves shall have been expended in accordance with the provisions of this section. The Insurance Reserve shall be funded by the premiums received from licenses, as provided in section 14 of this Act, and the Guaranty Reserve shall be funded by such sums as shall be appropriated pursuant to section 23 of this Act.

RECIPROCATING STATES

Sec. 16. (a) The Secretary shall, in promulgating regulations under this Act, attempt to harmonize his regulations with the laws, regulations, or other officials acts of any other State which has enacted legislation or regulations or taken, pursuant to its own laws and procedures, equivalent official acts for purposes and policies similar to those of this Act. When the Secretary finds, in consultation with the Secretary of State, that the laws and regulations of the United States and similar actions of another State are in essential harmony one with the other, such other State shall be deemed to be a reciprocating State for the purposes of this Act.

(b) Any license or similar legal entitlement issued by a reciprocating State shall be accorded equivalent legal status as though it were issued by the Secretary: *Provided*, That the reciprocating State accords the same legal status to licenses issued by the Secretary: *Provided further*, That sections 13 and 14 of this Act shall not apply to persons subject to the jurisdiction of the United States in respect to mining licenses or similar legal entitlements issued to them by a reciprocating State.

(c) The Secretary of State shall, in conultation with the Secretary, enter into international agreements with all reciprocating States for the purpose of harmonizing their laws and procedures and assuring that areas covered by licenses or similar legal entitlements issued by different States do not conflict with each other. Such agreements shall to the maximum extent possible apply the same principles for the issuance of mining licenses and operations conducted thereunder as are found in this Act. The Secretary of State shall encourage other reciprocating States to provide insurance similar to that provided under section 13 of this Act to persons to whom they issue licenses or similar legal entitlements.

NONDISCRIMINATORY TREATMENT

SEC. 17. For purposes of export controls, section 27 of the Act of June 5, 1920. customs laws, and tax laws of the United States, and the applicable implementing regulations thereof, all hard minerals recovered from the deep seabed under a license issued pursuant to this Act shall be deemed to have been recovered within the United States, and such laws, regulations, and controls shall be administered so that there will be no discrimination between hard minerals recovered from the deep seabed and similar hard minerals recovered within the United States.

CONSORTIA

SEC. 18. (a) In any case of agreement between entities of the United States and foreign entities, with the resulting combination of interests receiving a development license under the authority of this Act. the applicability of sections 13. 14, and 15 of this Act shall be limited to the proportion of interest owned by the United States entity or entities.

(b) In the case of an agreement between entities of the United States and foreign entities with the resulting from combination of interests receiving a development license from a reciprocating State, the provisions of section 15 of this Act. other than the applicability of section 27 of the Act of June 5, 1920, shall be applied as if the proportion of interest owned by the United States entity or entities were licensed pursuant to this Act.

REGULATORY AUTHORITY

SEC. 19. (a) The Secretary is authorized to issue such reasonable rules and regulations as may be necessary to carry out the provisions of this Act.

(b) The rules and regulations issued under subsection (a) shall include provisions covering:

(1) eligibility standards and compliance:
(2) licensing procedures, requirements, and compliance;
(3) work requirements compliance;
(4) environmental standards and compliance;
(5) multiple use standards and compliance; and
(6) other matters specifically delegated to the Secretary under the Act.

(c) Rules and regulations issued under this section shall be promulgated in accordance with provisions of section 553 of title 5, United States Code.

JURISDICTION OF UNITED STATES DISTRICT COURTS

SEC. 20. United States district courts shall have original jurisdiction of cases and controversies arising out of. or in connection with, development activities conducted in any area of the deep seabed under the authority of this Act, and proceedings with respect to any such case or controversy may be instituted in the judicial district in which any defendant resides, or may be found, or in the judicial district nearest the place where the cause of action arose.

PENALTIES

SEC. 21. (a) CIVIL PENALTIES.—Any person subject to the jurisdiction of the United States who violates any provision of this Act, or any rule or regulation issued pursuant to section 17 hereof, shall be liable to a civil penalty of $10,000 for each day during which the violation continues. The penalty shall be asserted by the Secretary, who, in determining the amount of the penalty, shall consider the gravity of the violation, any prior violation, and the demonstrated good faith of the person charged in attempting to achieve rapid compliance after notification of the violation. No penalty may be assessed until the person charged shall have been given notice of the violation involved, and an opportunity for a hearing. For good cause shown, the Secretary may remit or mitigate any penalty assessed. Upon failure of the person charged to pay an assessed penalty, the Secretary may request the Attorney General to commence an action in the appropriate district court of the United States for collection of the penalty without regard to the amount involved, together with such other relief as may be appropriate.

(b) CRIMINAL PENALTIES.—In addition to any other penalty, any person subject to the jurisdiction of the United States who willfully and knowingly violates any provision of this Act, or any rule or regulation issued pursuant to secton 17 hereof, shall be punished by a fine of not more than $25,000 for each day during which such violation continues.

(c) LIABILITY OF VESSELS.—Any vessel, except a public vessel engaged in noncommercial activities, used in a violation of this Act or of any rule or regulation issued pursuant to section 19 hereof, shall be liable in rem for any civil penalty assessed or criminal fine imposed and may be proceeded against in any district court of the United States having jurisdiction thereof; but, no vessel shall be liable unless it shall appear that one or more of the owners, or bareboat charterers was, at the time of the violation, a consenting party, or privy to such violation.

ANNUAL REPORT

SEC. 22. The Secretary shall report to the Congress annually, on or before October 31 with the first report to be made on or before October 31, 1977, on his activities under this Act, including recommendations for additional legislation as he deems necessary.

AUTHORIZATION FOR APPROPRIATIONS

SEC. 23. (a) There are authorized to be appropriated for the current fiscal year and for each of the two succeeding fiscal years, such as may be necessary for the administration of this Act.

(b) There are authorized to be appropriated such sums as may be necessary from time to time to replenish or increase the Guaranty Reserve of the Insurance and Guaranty Fund, or to discharge the liabilities under section 13 of this Act.

EFFECTIVE DATE

SEC. 24. This Act shall take effect on January 1, 1977. If any provision of this Act or any application thereof is held invalid, the validity of the remainder of the Act, or of any other application, shall not be affected thereby.

DEPARTMENT OF STATE,
Washington, D.C., March 4, 1976.

Hon. LEONOR K. SULLIVAN,
Chairman, Committee on Merchant Marine and Fisheries, House of Representatives, Washington, D.C.

DEAR MADAME CHAIRMAN : The Secretary has asked me to reply to your letter of February 17 concerning the views and recommendations of the Department of State on HR 11879, a bill to promote the conservation and early development of hard mineral resources of the deep seabed pending adoption of an international regime relating thereto.

On February 23, Departmental Officer Otho E. Eskin, on behalf of Under Secretary of State for Security Assistance Carlyle E. Maw and Leigh S. Ratiner, Administrator of the Ocean Mining Administration, Department of Interior, presented testimony before the Oceanography Subcommittee of the House Merchant Marine and Fisheries Committee to explain the views of the Administration on interim policy for deep seabed minerals developed pending conclusion of the Law of the Sea negotiations. This testimony is enclosed.

As Under Secretary Maw's statement indicated, the Administration has concluded that it should not support any ocean mining legislation at this time. This conclusion applies to HR 11879.

The Department of State does not believe that HR 11879 would involve authorization to expand funds or to incur administrative expenses by the Department beyond existing authorization attendant upon the conduct of U.S. foreign policy.

Sincerely,

ROBERT J. MCCLOSKEY,
Assistant Secretary for Congressional Relations.

Enclosures.

TESTIMONY OF LEIGH S. RATINER ADMINISTRATOR, OCEAN MINING
ADMINISTRATION DEPARTMENT OF THE INTERIOR

Mr. Chairman, It is always a pleasure to appear before this Committee, and I am appreciative of the opportunity you have provided today for the Administration to share with you its thinking on the desirability of interim ocean mining legislation.

We have not had adequate time to review in detail the new bill which you, Mr. Chairman, have recently introduced. On a variety of occasions, however, the Administration has provided comments on the technical aspects of H.R. 1270 and similar bills that have been before the Congress. I do not believe it is necessary at this time to summarize our objections to the approaches contained in these bills.

Last May, I testified before this Committee on the results of the Geneva session of the Conference in Committee I. At that time, the United States was greatly disappointed that the Single Negotiating Text introduced by the Chairman of Committee I at the end of the Geneva session did not reflect many of the results which had been reached in private negotiations on issues of importance to United States interests in the deep seabed. I described those areas where we believed progress had been made in private consultations, but indicated that serious dispute remained on several of the most fundamental issues in the Committee I negotiation. Because of the apparent intransigence of the developing countries on the basic questions of State access to deep seabed minerals, price and production controls and the structure and powers of the international machinery, we had grave reservations that a law of the sea treaty satisfactory to U.S. interests in the deep seabed could be concluded.

Following the Geneva session, the Interagency Task Force on the Law of the Sea conducted a comprehensive analysis of the Committee I Single Negotiating Text. We concluded that the draft text required extensive revision in order to protect basic U.S. requirements of guaranteed access for States and their nationals to deep seabed mineral resources, under reasonable terms and conditions and through an international organization with adequately circumscribed powers and decision-making procedures, In light of this review, we have also been carefully examining the need for and content of possible interim legislative measure for ocean mining.

Our assessment of the need for interim deep seabed legislation has been strongly affected by developments in the Committee I negotiation since the Geneva session of the LOS Conference. During the intersessional period, those delegations most active in Committee I expressed an interest in continuing negotiations with a view towards advancing the Committee's work prior to the commencement of the next session. Thus, in November, and again in the first two weeks of February, informal meetings of Committee I were held in New York. In addition, extensive private consultations on deep seabed issues have been held with key leaders in the Committee.

The results of these consultations are by no means dramatic, but they do offer some hope that the more inflexible positions of developing countries in

Committee I could conceivably be modified at the next session of the Conference. If this recent tendency to moderate developing country demands in the negotiation were accelerated during the March session, I believe it could alter our previous assessment that an early and acceptable resolution of the major deep seabed issues is not possible. The evidence which might be interpreted as signs of emerging flexibility on the part of the developing country leadership can be characterized in the following manner:

First, there was a new willingness to confront squarely many of the principal, most divisive issues in the Single Negotiating Text and to explore viable compromises acceptable to both the developing and developed countries. In the past, the developing countries had maintained unacceptable positions both privately and publicly on the basic access system, the question of economic implications and the powers and decision-making procedures of the Authority. Their readiness to show flexibility on certain aspects of these key obstacles to progress in the negotiation may indicate that they are prepared to work towards an early settlement in Committee I. As we have repeatedly stated, many of the important details of the Single Negotiating Text can be expeditiously resolved, if there is the will to seek political accommodation.

Second, there was a willingness to explore potential compromises in the context of formulating precise amendments to the Single Negotiating Text.

Third, the Chairman of Committee I, Paul Engo, has devised a procedure for preparing on a personal basis revised draft articles attempting to reflect the main trends in these informal discussions. This procedure sharply contrasts with the preparation of the Single Negotiating Text, which did not reflect consultations.

Thus, the New York meeting just concluded resulted in the formulation by the Chairman of new, revised articles for the Single Negotiating Text. With your permission, Mr. Chairman, I would like to submit these draft articles for the record.

What these draft articles appear to represent is an attempt by some, although by no means all, of the members of the Group of 77 to remove from the Single Negotiating Text some of the more extreme elements of previous developing country positions. Whereas the original versions of these articles in the Single Negotiating Text manifested a one-sided and essentially biased approach to the issues, these new draft articles at least embody a more realistic approach.

Mr. Chairman, it is necessary to emphasize clearly at this juncture that these texts have no official status whatsoever. They are only the attempt of the Chairman to reflect the main themes emerging in the discussion on basic issues. Moreover, I do not in any way intend to give the impression that the U.S. finds these draft articles acceptable as final treaty provisions. We do not believe they are, not only because of their content, but also because of their inevitable dependence on a host of other important amendments which were not discussed in the New York meetings.

Among other things, these articles include texts which now recognize the right of States and private parties to undertake directly exploration and exploitation under the same basic terms and conditions applied to the Authority's operational arm, the Enterprise. Further, these texts contain certain new approaches to protecting developing country producers from the economic effects of ocean mining and contain no reference to the Authority's right to exercise direct price aind production controls. Given the highly tentative and informal nature of these draft articles, it would not appear necessary to analyze them in detail today.

It would in all candor be very difficult to predict with any confidence whether the first glimmerings of moderation on the part of some of the Group of 77 leadership and a readiness to expedite the Committee I negotiation will be borne out in the upcoming March session. At virtually any time in the next few months, the situation could change radically and prospects for a successful settlement could vanish.

The Group of 77 convenes at the beginning of March to develop its position for the Conference and will most certainly review the Committee I intersessional work. A rejection of the results of the recent New York session which reflect an attempt by some to take into account the interests of the industrialized countries, as well as of the developing countries, would be a major set-back. It would be a signal that there is little hope for progress in the negotiation.

If the substantive negotiation is to be completed this year, significant progress in Committee I in resolving the chief obstacles impeding an overall settlement will have to be made early in the March session. Unless the basic political accommodation on the key outlines of the total package can be tied down rapidly to the satisfaction of both the developing and industrialized States, insufficient time would remain to negotiate the host of subsidiary issues in the Single Negotiating Text which will be determinative of the treaty's acceptability to the United States.

On the eve of the third substantive session of the Law of the Sea Conference, there appears to be a genuine recognition among many nations that 1976 is the final opportunity for serious negotiation. Whether a comprehensive law of the sea treaty is concluded will largely depend on the political will of the Conference participants.

The Administration will have to keep the question of the desirability of deep seabed mining legislation under constant review, particularly in light of what happens at the next sesson of the LOS Conference. As Secretary Maw pointed out in his statement, the Administration is continuing to explore the question of appropriate ocean mining legislation so that we will be ready to take any necessary action once we can project the result of the ongoing deep seabed negotiations in the Law of the Sea Conference. We would prefer to suspend the debate on whether or not there should be legislation if it is not possible to conclude an early and satisfactory resolution if the deep seabed negotiation. Instead, we intend to devote our efforts to pursuing the chances of success at the Conference in the next few months.

Thank you, Mr. Chairman.

———

COMPTROLLER GENERAL OF THE UNITED STATES,
Washington, D.C., March 9, 1976.

Hon. LEONOR K. SULLIVAN.
Chairman, Committee on Merchant Marine and Fisheries,
House of Representatives.

DEAR MADAM CHAIRMAN: Reference is made to your request for our comments on H.R. 11879, 94th Congress, which, if enacted, would be cited as the "Deep Seabed Hard Minerals Act."

The purposes of H.R. 11879 are to establish a national program to promote the orderly development of certain hard mineral resources of the deep seabed, pending establishment of an international regime for that purpose; and to insure the establishment of all practical requirements necessary to protect the quality of the marine environment to the extent that it may be affected by deep seabed hard mineral mining development.

Section 3(2) defines "deep seabed" as the seabed and subsoil lying seaward and outside the continental shelf of any nation. Section 3(3) defines the continental shelf as the "seabed and subsoil of the submarine areas adjacent to the coast of any nation (including the coasts of islands) but outside the area of the territorial sea, to a depth of two-hundred meters or, beyond that limit to where the depth of the superjacent waters admits of the exploitation of the natural resources of the said areas."

We recognize that this definition of the continental shelf is substantially identical with that given in Article I of the Geneva Convention on the Continental Shelf, April 29, 1958, TIAS 5578, UST 15.1.471 and, therefore, an accepted term of definition. However, we believe it should be recognized that under such a definition, the ability to exploit at a given depth determines, in effect, what is to be considered the continental shelf of any nation. The subject of what comprises the continental shelf of a nation continues to be a matter of considerable international debate and has been addressed at Law of the Sea Conferences.

Section 3(12) defines "commercial recovery," for the purpose of the Act, as recovery of hard minerals at a substantial rate of production (without regard to profit or loss). Section 5(b)(4) would provide that licenses issued under the Act shall remain in force for 15 years and, where commercial recovery of the hard mineral resources has begun from a licensed block within the 15 year period, such license shall remain in force for as long as commercial recovery from the block continues. We believe that "a substantial rate of production" should be clearly defined to insure that licenses remaining "in force" under section 5(b)(4) are not held by licensee's for primarily speculative purposes for extended periods of time.

Section 5(a) of this bill provides for a fee of $50,000 from the applicant for a license. Also, section 8(a) provides for specific amounts of money to be expended annually for development. Since monetary values change with inflationary pressures, it may be desirable to state these amounts as minimums, subject to revision by the Secretary of Commerce as he deems necessary.

Section 5(a)(4) provides that the Secretary of Commerce must determine that issuance of a license does not conflict with any obligations of the United States, established by treaty or other international agreement. However, the Secretary of State is considered to be the final authority on inerpretation of U.S. treaties and international agreements. The bill should provide for coordination with the Secretary of State to avoid possible conflicting interpretations.

Section 5(b)(1) provides that no license under this bill may be issued subsequent to the date that an international agreement establishing an international regime becomes binding upon the United States. Furthermore, section 12 provides that upon the establishment of an international regime binding upon the United States, no additional licenses may be issued under this bill; that previous licenses must conform to the international agreement, and that to the extent possible under the agreement, the United States is required to sponsor the licensee for continuation of his license under the international regime. The United States, at the third United Nations Law of the Sea Conference during June–August 1974, proposed that treaty articles concerning deep seabed mining be applied on a provisional basis (that is, after signature but before ratification.) If these treaty articles are provisionally applied, and when and if a Comprehensive Oceans Law Treaty is signed, further licensing activity would be delayed until an international regime is established to regulate ocean mining, which could take an extensive period of time.

Since licenses issued under the proposed Act would be made subject to any subsequent international agreement binding upon the United States, section 13 provides that the United States shall compensate a licensee for the value of the investment made and subsequently taken or impaired as a result of requirements imposed by the international agreement that would differ from those imposed by the proposed Act. We recognize that there may be a need for a compensation provision of this nature to encourage development. We suggest, however, that it may be desirable to place a monetary limit on the Government's liability for the compensation of any one licensee or with respect to any one block licensed for development.

Section 7(a) of the bill, subtitled "Environmental Criteria." calls for the Secretary of Commerce, acting through the Administrator of the National Oceanic and Atmospheric Administration (NOAA), "to * * * establish objective environmental standards based on technical and scientific data, * * * to which operations under a licence (sic) issued under this Act shall adhere."

NOAA is currently conducting Phase I of the Deep Ocean Mining Environmental Study (DOMES). Phase I is intended to collect baseline data on the composition of the deep seabed and water layers. Phase II of the program is to be conducted during prototype testing of the various mining techniques to determine the impact of mining operations on the seabed, water and surrounding marine life.

Consideration might be given to including language to the effect that licensees shall not be permitted to conduct deep ocean mining operations until the completion of the environmental impact study being done under the DOMES project.

Section 19 of the bill, subtitled "Regulary Authority," provides that the Secretary is authorized to issue such reasonable rules and regulations as may be necessary to carry out the provisions of this Act, including environmental standards and compliance. The development of sound standards is dependent upon the type of data being developed under the DOMES project.

Finally, we should point out that it is possible that the current Law of Sea negotiations may not be completed by January 1, 1977. It should be recognized that if this bill is passed, the law would then require the Secretary of State to conduct bilaterial negotiations which could create difficulties in the Law of the Sea Conference.

Suggestions of technical and editorial changes to H.R. 11879 are enclosed.

Sincerely yours,

R. F. KELLER,
Acting Comptroller General, of the United States.

Enclosure.

SUGGESTED TECHNICAL AND EDITORIAL CHANGES TO H.R. 11879

1. On page 11, at the end of line 17, insert a comma.
·2. On page 24, in lines 20 and 25, the reference to section 15 should be changed to section 17.
3. On page 26, line 10 and page 27, line 5, the reference to section 17 should be changed to section 19.

Mr. MURPHY. Gentlemen, you may proceed.

STATEMENT OF OTHO E. ESKIN, ON BEHALF OF CARLYLE E. MAW, UNDER SECRETARY FOR SECURITY ASSISTANCE, DEPARTMENT OF STATE

Mr. ESKIN. Thank you, Mr. Chairman.

I will, as you know, read the statement that Under Secretary Carlyle E. Maw was to have presented this morning.

Mr. Chairman, I am pleased to appear before this Committee today to explain the views of the Administration concerning interim policy for deep seabed minerals development.

Ambassador Learson has asked me to express his regrets that a previously scheduled commitment out of the country prevents him from being here today.

I am accompanied by Leigh S. Ratiner, Administrator, Ocean Mining Administration, Department of the Interior.

Mr. Chairman, the Administration has been carefully reviewing its interim policy with respect to ocean mining. At the conclusion of the Geneva session of the Law of the Sea Conference last May, it became evident that the issue of the deep seabed regime and machinery was a major obstacle to a successful conclusion of the Law of the Sea negotiations.

In most other areas we had made substantial progress toward a treaty which the United States and a majority of other countries would probably be able to agree upon. This progress is reflected to a large extent in the single negotiating text which was produced at the end of the Geneva session.

Although there were a number of problems remaining to be solved, we felt optimistic that the basic elements of a satisfactory, comprehensive Law of the Sea package could be agreed upon in the relatively near future, subject to arriving at an acceptacle solution with respect to deep seabed mining.

In addition to our consideration of the status of the deep seabed negotiation, in arriving at our interim policy, we also took into account the current stage of development of United States ocean mining companies.

We are advised that American ocean mining firms have largely completed the research and development phase of their work and will begin this year the expensive development work which precedes commercial recovery of resources. Uncertainty about the timing and contents of a future treaty may impede commitments for the substantial capital outlays necessary for this new level of activity.

In our policy review we explored whether we could reduce these investment uncertainties through some form of domestic legislation without damaging the Law of the Sea negotiations. The latter point is particularly important in light of our decided preference to the development of the resources of the seabed under a widely accepted international agreement.

The Law of the Sea Conference provides us with an opportunity—possibly our last—to develop a system which would subject deep seabed mining to widely acceptable international rules embodied in a treaty and related regulations. Such a solution can contribute to the rational and efficient use of resources and can set a precedent for new forms of cooperation between the developing and developed nations.

Mr. Chairman, the Administration is continuing to explore the question of appropriate ocean mining legislation so that we will be ready to take any necessary action once we can project the result of the ongoing deep seabed negotiations in the Law of the Sea Conference.

Some of us have despaired at the Committee I statement apparent in Geneva and have evinced doubts that an acceptable result could be achieved in these negotiations within a reasonable time.

However, recent developments in the intersessional work of Committee I give some hope that early and satisfactory accommodations can be found which will meet the basic objectives of all interested nations and groups of nations.

Informal meetings of Committee I representatives were held during the intersessional period which provided an opportunity for a useful exchange of views on the major issues in the deep seabed negotiations and on the single negotiating text.

In addition, our representatives have been consulting with a number of key figures in the negotiations. In these discussions we discovered a greater willingness on the part of some developing countries to explore reasonable solutions to the problems in Committee I. There was some recognition by developing countries that the single negotiating text does not reflect the interests of both industrialized and developing countries in the negotiations.

In his statement, Mr. Ratiner will elaborate for the Committee these new developments.

The next session of the Law of the Sea Conference begins in New York three weeks from today. The imminence of the next session and the preliminary indications that a new negotiating climate may emerge in Committee I leads us to the conclusion that we should not support any ocean mining legislation at this time.

I can assure you, Mr. Chairman, that in the event that this session fails to move towards satisfactory resolution of the major disputes in Committee I. the question of interim legislation has a high priority on our agenda. We will continue to give the matter our serious consideration and hope to consult with you and other members of Congress during the course of the negotiations to share our assessment of the likelihood of concluding a satisfactory treaty. Thank you, Mr. Chairman.

Mr. MURPHY. Next we will hear from Mr. Leigh Ratiner, who has been the chief of the committee number I negotiating team at the Law of the Sea Conference, and one of the acknowledged world experts on the problem of deep seabed mining.

Mr. Ratiner, you may proceed.

STATEMENT OF LEIGH S. RATINER, ADMINISTRATOR, OCEAN MINING ADMINISTRATION, U.S. DEPARTMENT OF THE INTERIOR

Mr. RATINER. Mr. Chairman, it is always a pleasure to appear before this committee, and I am appreciative of the opportunity you have provided today for the administration to share with you its thinking on the desirability of interim ocean mining legislation.

We have not had adequate time to review in detail the new bill which you, Mr. Chairman, have recently introduced. On a variety of occasions, however, the administration has provided comments on the technical aspects of H.R. 1270 and similar bills that have been before the Congress. I do not believe it is necessary at this time to summarize our objections to the approaches contained in these bills.

Last May, I testified before this committee on the results of the Geneva session of the conference in committee I. At that time, the United States was greatly disappointed that the single negotiating text introduced by the chairman of committee I at the end of the

Geneva session did not reflect many of the results which had been reached in private negotiations on issues of importance to United States interests in the deep seabed.

I described those areas where we believed progress had been made in private consultations, but indicated that serious dispute remained on several of the most fundamental issues in the committee I negotiation. Because of the apparent intransigence of the developing countries on the basic questions of state access to deep seabed minerals, price and production controls and the structure and powers of the international machinery, we had grave reservations that a Law of the Sea treaty satisfactory to U.S. interests in the deep seabed could be concluded.

Following the Geneva session, the Interagency Task Force on the Law of the Seat conducted a comprehensive analysis of the committee I single negotiating text. We concluded that the draft text required extensive revision in order to protect basic U.S. requirements of guaranteed access for states and their nationals to deep seabed mineral resources, under reasonable terms and conditions and through an international organization with adequately circumscribed powers and decision making procedures.

In light of this review, we have also been carefully examining the need for and content of possible interim legislative measures for ocean mining.

Our assessment of the need for interim deep seabed legislation has been strongly affected by developments in the committee I negotiation since the Geneva session of the Law of the Sea Conference.

During the intersessional period, those delegations most active in committee I expressed an interest in continuing negotiations with a view towards advancing the committee's work prior to the commencement of the next session.

Thus, in November, and again in the first 2 weeks of February, informal meetings of committee I were held in New York. In addition, extensive private consultations on deep seabed issues have been held with key leaders in the committee.

The results of these consultations are by no means dramatic, but they do offer some hope that the more inflexible positions of developing countries in committee I could conceivably be modified at the next session of the Conference.

If this recent tendency to moderate developing country demands in the negotiation were accelerated during the March session, I believe it could alter our previous assessment that an early and acceptable resolution of the major deep seabed issues is not possible.

The evidence which might be interpreted as signs of emerging flexibility on the part of the developing countery leadership can be characterized in the following manner:

First, there was a new willingness to confront squarely many of the principal, most divisive issues in the single negotiating text and to explore viable compromises acceptable to both the developing and developed countries.

In the past, the developing countries had maintained unacceptable positions both privately and publicly on the basic access system, the question of economic implications and the powers and decisionmaking procedures of the Authority. Their readiness to show flexibility on certain aspects of these key obstacles to progress in the negotiation may indicate that they are prepared to work towards an early settlement in committee I. As we have repeatedly stated, many of the important details of the single negotiating text can be expeditiously resolved, if there is the will to seek political accommodation.

Second, there was a willingness to explore potential compromises in the context of formulating precise amendments to the single negotiating text.

Third, the chairman of committee I, Paul Engo, has devised a procedure for preparing on a personal basis revised draft articles attempting to reflect the main trends in these informal discussions. This procedure sharply contrasts with the preparation of the single negotiating text, which did not reflect consultations.

Thus, the New York meeting just concluded resulted in the formulation by the chairman of new, revised articles for the single negotiating text.

With your permission, Mr. Chairman, I would like to submit these draft articles for the record.

[The document referred to follows:]

APPENDIX—THE SO-CALLED "PINTO PAPER"
(See "Reservation of Areas for the Authority," p. 3 and "(17) *Size of area.*", p. 7)

BASIC CONDITIONS OF EXPLORATION AND EXPLOITATION

The Authority shall take measures pursuant to this Convention, including the adoption of rules and regulations, to promote and encourage scientific research and the exploration of the Area and the exploitation of its resources and other related activities, and to secure maximum financial and other benefits in accordance with these Basic Conditions. To that end the Authority shall avoid discrimination in the granting of opportunities for such activities and in the implementation of its powers, and ensure that all rights granted pursuant to this Convention are fully safeguarded. Special consideration by the Authority under this Convention for the interests and needs of the developing countries, and particularly the land-locked among them, shall not be deemed to be discrimination.

Rights in the area and its resources

1. The Area and its resources being the common heritage of mankind all rights in the resources are vested in the Authority on behalf of mankind as a whole. These resources are not subject to alienation.

Rights in minerals

2. Rights in the minerals or processed metals derived from the Area shall pass from the Authority only in accordance with the provisions of this Convention, the rules and regulations prescribed by the Authority in accordance with this Convention, and the terms and conditions of the relevant contracts, joint ventures or other form of association entered into by it.

Access to the area and its resources

3. The Authority shall from time to time determine the part or parts of the Area in which the exploration of the Area and the exploitation of its resources and other related activities may be conducted. In doing so the Authority shall be guided by the following principles:

(a) The Authority shall encourage the widest possible conduct of general survey operations, and to that end shall each year, after consultation with all Contracting States, open for general survey such broad oceanic areas as are determined by it to be of interest for this purpose.

(b) The Authority may, upon the proposal of a Contracting State or on its own initiative, open for evaluation and exploitation broad oceanic areas determined by it on the basis of sufficient supporting data, to be of commercial interest;

(c) The Authority shall periodically determine the part or parts of the Area in which Contracting States or the Authority by itself or by other means it may determine may carry out activities in accordance with this Convention. The ratio of the part or parts of the Area to be open for activities by Contracting States to the part or parts of the Area open to activities by the Authority directly or by other means it may determine, shall be . . .;

(d) The Authority shall, in broad oceanic areas opened by it designated sectors for exploration and exploitation exclusively by Contracting States.

Provided, however, that the Authority may refuse to open any part of parts of the Area pursuant to this paragraph when the available data indicates the risk of irreparable harm to a unique environment or unjustifiable interference with other parts of the Area.

Contracts for associated operations

4. On the application of any Contracting State, or State enterprise, or person natural or juridical which possesses the nationality of a Contracting State or is effectively controlled by it or its nationals, or any group of the foregoing (hereinafter called the "applicant"), the Authority may enter into a contract, joint venture or any other such form of association, for the conduct of scientific research, or for the carrying out of a general survey or exploration of the Area, or of operations relating to evaluation and exploitation of the Area including such stages as feasibility study, construction of facilities, processing, transportation and marketing (hereinafter called the "contract").

5. Every contract entered into by the Authority pursuant to paragraph 4 shall :

(a) be in strict conformity with this Convention and the rules and regulations prescribed by the Authority in accordance with the Convention ;

(b) ensure direct and effectie fivnancial and administrative control by the Authority at all stages of operations through appropriate institutional arrangements entered into pursuant to this Convention.

Qualification of applicants

6. (a) The Authority shall prescribe appropriate administrative procedures and rules and regulations for making an application pursuant to paragraph 4, and the qualifications of any applicant referred to therein. Such qualifications shall include (1) financial standing, (2) technological capability, and (3) past performance and work experience.

(b) Contracting States which apply to enter into contracts with the Authority shall be presumed to possess the qualifications specified in subparagraph (a).

(c) Each applicant shall, in addition, submit to the Authority a work programme which shall accommodate the objectives of the Authority as reflected in this Convention and the rules and regulations prescribed thereunder.

(d) Each applicant shall indicate its willingness to comply with the provisions of this Convention and the rules and regulations prescribed by the Authority, and to accept control by the Authority in accordance therewith.

Reservation of areas for the authority

7. Each applicant with respect to activities of evaluation and exploitation shall be required to propose to the Authority two alternative areas of equivalent commercial interest for the conduct of operations under contract. The Authority shall determine one such area to be a reserved area in accordance with paragraph 8.

Selection of applicants

8. (a) Upon receiving an application pursuant to paragraph 4 with respect to activities of evaluation and exploitation, the Authority shall first ascertain whether any competing application has been received for either of the two areas referred to in paragraph 7. If no such competing application has been received, the Authority shall enter into a contract with the applicant in respect of one of the two proposed areas which the Authority shall designate for the purpose provided that the applicant has completed the procedures and possesses the qualifications prescribed pursuant to paragraph 6 and, after a consideration of all relevant factors is deemed to offer the Authority the minimum financial and other benefits. The other area shall be deemed a reserved area subject to disposition by the Authority in accordance with paragraph 19.

(b) Applicant shall be required, as a condition of continued operation under a contract, to comply with the requirements prescribed by the Authority for the training of personnel of and transfer of ocean mining and mineral processing technology to, the developing countries, particularly the land-locked among them, as well as to other countries lacking or less advanced in such technology.

(c) If the Authority receives more than one application in respect of substantially the same area and category of minerals, selection from among the applicants shall be made on a competitive basis taking into account the extent to which each applicant satisfies the requirements of paragraph 6. The Authority shall enter into a contract with the applicant which, after a consideration of all relevant factors, is deemed to offer the Authority the maximum financial and other benefits.

(d) The principles set forth in sub-paragraphs (a), (b) and (c) shall be applied *mutatis mutandis* in prescribing procedures, rules and regulations for the selection of applicants for contracts with respect to activities other than evaluation and exploitation, except that the provisions of paragraph 7 shall not apply thereto.

(e) When a contractor that has entered into a contract with the Authority for one or some of the stages of operations referred to in paragraph 4 has completed performance under it, he shall have priority among applicants for a contract or contracts for one or more further stages of operations with regard to the same area and resources; provided, however, that where the contactor has not carried out his obligations to the satisfaction of the Authority, such priority may be withdrawn.

(f) The number of contracts entered into by the Authority with a single Contracting State in respect of areas designated pursuant to paragraph 3(d) shall be limited in such a way that the total area open for exploration and exploitation by that State pursuant to paragraph 3(d) shall not exceed the the limit specified by the Authority for each category of minerals, and shall be equal for all Contracting States.

Rights and obligations under the contract

(a) Any Contracting State, or any State enterprise or person natural or juridical which possesses the nationality of a Contracting State or is effectively controlled by it or by its nationals, or any group of the foregoing which enters into a contract for activities relating to evaluation and exploitation with the Authority pursuant to paragraph 4 (hereinafter called the "Contractor") shall, except as otherwise agreed by the Authority, be required to use its own funds, materials, equipment, skills and knowhow as necessary for the conduct of operations covered by the contract, and to deposit a sum by way of guarantee of satisfactory performance under the contract.

(b) The investment and operating costs made in performance of the contract pursuant to paragraph (a) shall be determined in advance by prior agreement with the Authority and deemed to be a cost reimbursable to the Contractor out of the proceeds of operations. The Authority shall in its rules and regulations establish a schedule pursuant to which such costs will be reimbursed based on generally accepted accounting principles.

(c) The balance of the proceeds of operations pursuant to the contract after deduction of costs of the Authority and the Contractor, but without deduction on account of national taxation, shall be apportioned between the Authority and the Contractor in a manner [to be specified].

10. The Contractor shall:

(a) Transfer in accordance with the rules and regulations and the terms and conditions of the contract to the Authority at time intervals determined by the Authority all data necessary and relevant to the effective implementation of the Authority's powers and functions under this Convention in respect of the contract area. The Authority shall not disclose to third parties, without the prior consent of the Contractor, such of the transferred data as is deemed to be proprietary by the Contractor. Data which is necessary for the promulgation of rules and regulations concerning protection of the marine environment shall not be deemed to be proprietary. The Contractor shall not be obliged to disclose proprietary equipment design data to the Authority.

(b) Draw up programmes for the training of personnel, and take all such other action as may be necessary to fulfill its obligations pursuant to paragraph 8(b).

11. The Authority shall, pursuant to this Convention and the rules and regulations prescribed by the Authority, accord the Contractor the exclusive right to evaluate and/or exploit the contract area in respect of a specified category of minerals and shall ensure that subsequent Contractors in the same contract area but for a different category of minerals do not interfere with the operations of the first Contractor. The Contractor shall have security of tenure. Accordingly, the contract shall not be cancelled, modified, suspended or terminated, nor shall the exercise of any right under it be impaired, except for gross and persistent violations of the provisions of this Convention and the rules and regulations prescribed by the Authority thereunder, and after recourse to procedures provided under this Convention for the settlement of any dispute that may have arisen. The Authority shall not, during the continuance of a contract, enter into a contract for the same area and operations with another applicant.

Rules, regulations and procedures

12. The Authority shall prescribe and ensure compliance by the Contractor with rules, regulations and procedures consistent with the purposes and fundamental principles of the functioning of the Authority and with these basic conditions in the following subjects:

(1) Applications to enter into contracts.

(2) Qualification of applications.

(3) Selection of applicants.

(4) Progress report.

(5) Submission of data.

(6) Application fees and deposits to secure satisfactory performance.

(7) Inspection and supervision of operations.

(8) Mining standards and practices including operational safety.

(9) Prevention of interference by the Contractor with other uses of the sea and of the marine environment.

(10) Apportionment of the proceeds of operations.

(11) Direct participation of personnel of developing countries, particularly the landlocked among them and of other countries lacking or less advanced in ocean mining and mineral processing technology, and the transfer of such technology to such countries.

(12) Passing of title to minerals and processed metals from the Area.

(13) Avoiding or minimizing adverse effects on the revenues of developing countries derived from exports of the minerals and products thereof from the Area.

(14) Transfer of rights by a Contractor.

(15) Activities in reserved areas.

In respect of rules and regulations for the following subjects the Authority shall uniformly apply the objective criteria set out below:

(16) *Protection of the marine environment.*—The Authority shall take into account in establishing rules and regulations for the protection of the account marine environment the extent to which activities such as drilling, dredging, coring and excavation as well as disposal, dumping and discharge in the Area of sediment or wastes and other matters will have a substantial harmful effect on significant marine life.

(17) *Size of area.*—The Authority shall determine the appropriate size of areas for evaluation which shall be twice as large as those for exploitation in order to permit intensive continued survey and evaluation operations. Areas for exploitation shall be calculated to satisfy the stated production requirements of the Contractor over the term of the contract taking into account the state of the art of technology then available for ocean mining and the relevant physical characteristics of the area. Areas shall neither be smaller nor larger than are necessary to satisfy this objective. In cases where the Contractor has obtained evaluation and exploitation rights, the area shall be reduced by one-half if the Contractor proceeds to exploitation. This relinquished area may be reserved by the Authority pursuant to paragraph 19.

(18) *Duration.*

(a) General survey shall be without time limit except in the case of violations of the Authority's regulations to protect the environment in which case the Authority may prohibit the violator from conducting general survey operations for a reasonable period of time.

(b) Evaluation should be of sufficient duration as to permit a thorough survey of the specific area, the design and construction of mining equipment for the area, the design and construction of small and medium size processing plants for the purpose of testing mining and processing systems and a reasonable grace period to allow for sudden market fluctuations before commercial production must begin.

(c) Exploitation should be of sufficient duration as to permit extraction of the resources of the area for as long as it is possible to produce the resources profitably and should include a reasonable time period for construction of commercial scale mining and processing systems during which period commercial production should not be required. The total duration of exploitation, however, should also be short enough to permit the Authority a fair opportunity to amend the terms and conditions of the contract at the time of renewal in accordance with rules and regulations which it has issued subsequent to entering into the contract. Prior to the first renewal of the contract the duration of exploitation should be related to the economic life of the mining project taking into consideration such factors as the depletion of the ore body, the useful life of mining equipment and processing facilities, and profitability.

(19) *Performance requirements.*—The Authority shall require that during the evaluation stage, periodic expenditures be made by the Contractor which are reasonably related to the size of the contract area and the expenditures which would be expected of a *bona fide* Contractor who intended to bring the area into fullscale commercial production within the time limits established by the Authority. Such required expenditures should not be established at a level which would discourage prospective operators with less costly technology than is prevalently in use. The Authority shall establish a maximum interval after the evaluation stage is completed and the exploitation stage begins to achieve fullscale commercial production. To determine this interval, the Authority should take into consideration that construction of large-scale mining and processing systems cannot be initiated until after the termination of the evaluation stage and the commencement of the exploitation stage. Accordingly, the interval to bring an area into fullscale commercial production should take into account the time necessary for this construction after the completion of the evaluation stage and reasonable allowance should be made for unavoidable delays in the construction schedule.

Once full-scale commercial production is achieved in the exploitation stage, the Authority shall within reasonable limits and taking into consideration possible adverse market conditions for the Contractor require the Contractor to maintain a reasonable level of commercial production throughout the period of the contract.

(20) *Categories of minerals.*—In determining the category of mineral in which contracts should be awarded the Authority shall give primary emphasis to the following characteristics:

(a) Resources which require the use of similar mining methods, and

(b) Resources which can be developed simultaneously without undue interference between Contractors in the same area developing different resources.

Nothing in this paragraph shall deter the Authority from granting a contract for more than one category of mineral in the same contract area to the same applicant.

(21) *Renunciation of areas.*—The Contractor shall have the right at any time to renounce without penalty the whole or part of his rights in the contract area. In such cases the renounced area shall be deemed to be a reserved area and disposed of in accordance with paragraph 19.

13. The Authority shall have the right to take at any time any measures provided for under this Convention to ensure compliance with its terms, and in the performance of the control and regulatory functions assigned to it thereunder or under any contract. In particular the Authority shall have the right to inspect all facilities in the Area used in connection with any operations carried out under a contract with the Authority.

Suspension of termination

14. A Contractor's rights in the contract area shall be suspended or terminated only after a finding by the [dispute settlement organ] that the Contractor has conducted his activities in the contract area in such a way as to result in gross and persistent violations of this Convention and rules and regulations and were not caused by circumstances beyond his control, or a finding that a Contractor has wilfully failed to comply with any decision of the [dispute

settlement organ]. Lesser penalties in the violations which are not gross and persistent provided the penalties are proportionate to the violation.

Force majeure

15. Non-performance or delay in performance by the Contractor or by the Authority shall be excused if and to the extent that such non-performance or delay is caused by *force majeure*. The party invoking *force majeure* may take appropriate measures including revision, suspension or termination of the contract; provided, however, that in the event of a dispute the parties shall first have recourse to the procedures for the settlement of disputes provided for in this Convention.

Transfer of rights

16. The rights and obligations arising out of a contract with the Authority shall be transferred only with the consent of the Authority, and in accordance with the rules and regulations prescribed by it. The Authority shall not withhold consent to the transfer if the proposed transferee is in all respects a qualified applicant.

Applicable law

17. The law applicable to the contract shall be solely the provisions of this Convention, the rules and regulations prescribed by the Authority, and the terms and conditions of the contract. The rights and obligations of the Authority and of the Contractor shall be valid and enforceable notwithstanding the law of any State, or any political subdivision thereof to the contrary. No contracting State may impose conditions on a Contractor that are inconsistent with the principles of this Convention. Neither the Authority nor the Contractor shall be entitled in any proceeding to assert any claim that any rule or regulation prescribed by the Authority or provision of the contract is invalid or unenforceable because of any provision of this Convention or for any other reason.

Liability

18. Responsibility or liability for wrongful damage arising out of the conduct of operations by the Contractor shall lie with the Contractor. It shall be a defense in any proceeding against a Contractor that the damage was the result of an act or omission of the Authority. Similarly, any responsibility or liability for wrongful damage arising out of the exercise of the powers and functions of the Authority shall lie with the Authority. It shall be a defense in any proceeding against the Authority that the damage was a result of an act or omission of the Contractor. Liability in every case shall be for the actual amount of damage.

Reservation of areas

19. Areas reserved by the Authority in accordance with paragraphs 7, 8, 12(17) and 12(21) above shall be explored and exploited in any manner determined by the Authority pursuant to this Convention and the rules and regulations prescribed therein.

Settlement of disputes

20. Any dispute concerning the interpretation or application of this Convention. its rules and regulations or the terms and conditions of a contract and arising between the Authority and a Contracting State or any State enterprise or person natural or juridical which possesses the nationality of a Contracting State or is effectively controlled by it or its nationals, or any group of the foregoing shall on the application of either party be subject to the procedure for settlement of such disputes provided for in this Convention.

GENERAL PRINCIPLES REGARDING ECONOMIC ASPECTS OF ACTIVITIES IN THE AREA

Article 9

Activities in the Area shall be undertaken in such a manner as to:

1. Foster the healthy development of the world economy and a balanced growth in international trade, and to promote international co-operation for the overall development of all countries, especially of developing countries;

2. Expand opportunities for all States Parties in participating in the development of the resources of the Area;

3. Increase availability of resources to meet world demand;

4. Protect against the adverse economic effects of a substantial decline in the mineral export earnings of developing countries for whom export revenues from minerals or raw materials also under exploitation in the Area represent a significant share of their gross domestic product of foreign exchange earnings, when such decline is caused by activities in the Area, by:

(i) facilitating, through existing forums for such new arrangements as may be appropriate and in which all affected parties participate, the growth, efficiency and stability of markets for those classes of commodities produced from the Area, at prices remunerative to producers and fair to consumers;

(ii) assuring that during an interim period, total production from the Area shall not exceed an amount specified in accordance with Article . . . ;

(iii) a system of compensation in respect of the losses specified above.

5. Ensure their safe, orderly and efficient conduct and, in accordance with commonly used principles of conservation, the avoidance of unnecessary waste;

6. Ensure equitable sharing in and distribution of financial and other economic benefits among States Parties from the activities in the Area, taking into particular consideration the interests and needs of the developing countries, in accordance with Article . . . and consistent with Articles 11, 18 and 23.

NATURE AND FUNDAMENTAL PRINCIPLES OF THE FUNCTIONING OF THE AUTHORITY

Article 21

1. The Authority is the organization through which States Parties shall organize and control activities in the Area, particularly with the view towards the administration of the resources of the Area, in accordance with this Convention.

In so doing the Authority shall promote the objectives set forth in Articles 9, 23 and . . .

2. The Authority is based on the principle of the sovereign equality of all of its members.

3. All members, in order to ensure to all of them the rights and benefits resulting from membership, shall fulfill in good faith the obligations assumed by them in accordance with this Convention.

FUNCTIONS OF THE AUTHORITY

Article 22

1. Activities in the Area shall be conducted directly by the Authority, and on its behalf, by States Parties, or State Enterprises, or persons natural or juridical which possess the nationality of States Parties or are effectively controlled by them or their nationals, when sponsored by such States, or any group of the foregoing in accordance with the provisions of Annex I, the rules, regulations and procedures of the Authority adopted under Article 28(xi) and the Statute of the Enterprise.

2. All Activities in the Area shall be carried out in accordance with a formal written plan of work drawn in accordance with Annex I and approved by the Council after review by the Technical Commission. In the case of Activities in the Area conducted on behalf of the Authority such a plan of work shall be in the form of a contract of exploration and exploitation.

3. The Authority shall exercise effective control of a general and overall nature in respect of the conduct of all Activities in the Area in accordance with the provisions of this Convention, Annex I and the rules, regulations and procedures of the Authority adopted under Article 28(xi). States Parties who sponsor persons natural or juridical shall assist the Authority by taking all necessary measures to assure compliance by such persons with this Convention and any contracts they may have with the Authority.

ORGANS OF THE AUTHORITY

Article 24

1. There are hereby established as the principal governing, judicial and administrative organs of the Authority: an Assembly, a Council, a Tribunal and a Secretariat.

2. There is hereby established the Enterprise, the organ through which the Authority will directly carry out activities in the Area.

3. Such subsidiary organs as may be found necessary may be established in accordance with this Convention.

4. The principal organs shall each be responsible for exercising those powers and functions which have been provided to them and shall, except as otherwise specified in this Convention, avoid taking any actions which may impede the exercise of specific powers and functions entrusted to another organ.

THE ASSEMBLY

Article 25

1. The Assembly shall consist of all the members of the Authority.

2. The Assembly shall meet in regular session every two years and in such special sessions as may be determined by the Assembly, or convened by the Secretary-General at the request of the Council or of a majority of the members of the Authority.

3. Sessions shall take place at the seat of the Authority unless otherwise determined by the Assembly. At such sessions, each member shall have one representative who may be accompanied by alternates and advisers.

4. The Assembly shall elect its President and such other officers as may be required at the beginning of each session. They shall hold office until the new President and other officers are elected at the next following session.

5. Each member of the Assembly shall have one vote.

6. All decisions on questions of substance and the question whether a question is one of substance or procedure, shall be made by a two-thirds majority of the members of the Authority. Decisions on other questions shall be made by a majority of the members present and voting.

7. Any decision of the Assembly on an important question of substance shall come into effect 90 calendar days following the session in which it was adopted, provided that within that time period one-third of the members of the Authority plus one have not given notification of their objection in writing to the Secretary-General of the Authority. This procedure shall not apply to decisions on important questions of substance which have been taken by consensus.

8. When a matter of substance comes up for voting for the first time, the President may, and shall, if requested by at least 15 representatives, defer the question of taking a vote on such matter for a period not exceeding 5 calendar days. The provisions of this paragraph may be applied only once on the matter.

9. A majority of the members of the Assembly shall constitute a quorum.

10. Upon a request to the President supported by not less than one-fourth of the members of the Authority, a vote on any matter before the Assembly shall be deferred pending reference to the Tribunal for an advisory opinion on the legality of the proposed action. Voting on such matters shall be stayed pending delivery of the Tribunal's advisory opinion. If the advisory opinion is not received during the session in which it is requested, the Assembly shall decide when it will meet to vote upon the deferred question.

POWERS AND FUNCTIONS OF THE ASSEMBLY

Article 26

1. The Assembly shall have the power to lay down general guidelines as to the policies to be pursued by the Authority on any questions or matters within the competence of the Authority by adopting resolutions and making recommendations. In laying down guidelines with regard to any such questions or matters not specifically entrusted to a particular organ of the Authority, the Assembly shall indicate to which organ the guidelines are directed. It may also discuss any questions or any matters within the scope of this Convention and make recommendations thereon.

2. In addition, the powers and functions of the Assembly shall be:

(i) Election of the members of the Council in accordance with article 27;

(ii) Appointment, upon the recommendation of the Council, of the Secretary-General, and of the members of the Tribunal and the Governing Board of the Enterprise;

(iii) Establishment, as appropriate, of such subsidiary organs as may be found necessary for the performance of its functions in accordance with the provisions of this Convention. In the composition of such subsidiary organs due account shall be taken of the principle of equitable geographical distribution and special groups, and the need for members highly qualified and competent in the relevant technical matters dealt with by such organs;

(iv) Assessment of the contributions of States Parties to the administrative budget of the Authority in accordance with the general assessment scale used by the United Nations until the Authority shall have sufficient income for meeting its administrative expenses;

(v) Adoption of the financial regulations of the Authority upon the recommendations of the Council;

(vi) Approval of the budget of the Authority on its submission by the Council;

(vii) Adoption of its rules of procedure;

(viii) Request and consideration of special reports from the Council and from the other organs of the Authority on any matter within the scope of this Convention:

(ix) Studies and recommendations for the purpose of promoting international co-operation concerning activities in the Area and encouraging the progressive development of international law relating thereto and its codification;

(x) Adoption of criteria, rules, regulations and procedures for the equitable sharing among States Parties of financial and other economic benefits derived from activities in the Area, taking into particular consideration the interests and the needs of the developing countries;

(xi) Consideration of problems of a general nature arising for States in connection with activities in the Area resulting from their land-locked or otherwise geographically disadvantaged location.

(xii) Suspension of members pursuant to Article 68:

(xiii) Receipt of reports from the Enterprise.

3. In exercising its powers and functions, the Assembly shall have particular regard to Article 24.4.

Mr. RATINER. What these draft articles appear to represent is an attempt by some, although by no means all, of the members of the Group of 77 to remove from the Single Negotiating Text some of the more extreme elements of previous developing country positions.

Whereas the original versions of these articles in the Single Negotiating Text manifested a one-sided and essentially biased approach to the issues, these new draft articles at least embody a more realistic approach.

Mr. Chairman, it is necessary to emphasize clearly at this juncture that these texts have no official status whatsoever. They are only the attempt of the chairman to reflect the main theme emerging in the discussion on basic issues.

Moreover, I do not in any way intend to give the impression that the United States finds these draft articles acceptable as final treaty provisions. We do not believe they are, not only because of their content, but also because of their inevitable dependence on a host of other important amendments which were not discussed in the New York meetings.

Among other things, these articles include texts which now recognize the right of States and private parties to undertake directly exploration and exploitation under the same basic terms and conditions applied to the authority's operational arm, the Enterprise.

Further, these texts contain certain new approaches to protecting developing country producers from the economic effects of ocean mining and contain no reference to the authority's right to exercise direct price and production controls.

Given the highly tentative and informal nature of these draft articles, it would not appear necessary to analyze them in detail today.

It would in all candor be very difficult to predict with any confidence whether the first glimmerings of moderation on the part of the Group of 77 leadersip and a readiness to expedite the Committee One negotiation will be borne out in the upcoming March session. At virtually any time in the next few months, the situation could change radically and prospects for a successful settlement could vanish.

The Group of 77 convenes at the beginning of March to develop its position for the Conference and will most certainly review the Committee One intersessional work. A rejection of the results of the recent New York session which reflect an attempt by some to take into account the interests of the industrialized countries, as well as of the devolping countries, would be a major setback. It would be a signal that there is little hope for progress in the negotiation.

If the substantive negotiation is to be completed this year, significant progress in Committee One in resolving the chief obstacles impeding an overall settlement will have to be made early in the March session.

Unless the basic political accommodation on the key outlines of the total package can be tied down rapidly to the satisfaction of both the developing and industrialized States, insufficient time would remain to negotiate the host of subsidiary issues in the Single Negotiating Text which will be determinative of the treaty's acceptability to the United States.

On the eve of the third substantive session of the Law of the Sea Conference, there appears to be a genuine recognition among many nations that 1976 is the final opportunity for serious negotiation. Whether a comprehensive Law of the Sea treaty is concluded will largely depend on the political will of the Conference participants.

The administration will have to keep the question of the desirability of deep seabed mining legislation under constant review, particularly in light of what happens at the next session of the Law of the Sea Conference.

As Secretary Maw pointed out in his statement, the administration is continuing to explore the question of appropriate ocean mining legislation so that we will be ready to take any necessary action once we can project the result of the ongoing deep seabed negotiations in the Law of the Sea Conference.

We would prefer to suspend the debate on whether or not there should be legislation if it is not possible to conclude an early satisfactory resolution of the deep seabed negotiation. Instead, we intend to devote our efforts to pursuing the chances of success at the Conference in the next few months.

Thank you, Mr. Chairman.

Mr. MURPHY. Thank you, Mr. Ratiner.

Now, I am going to read Mr. Ratiner's testimony before the U.S. Senate about the attitudes of these less developed countries on the issues involved, and I ask him to contrast that testimony with statements he made today as far as the change in attitude of the Group of 77 countries is concerned, and I am quoting:

I must tell you what some of the areas are in which there was no progress and also no sign of progress in the future.

First, Mr. Chairman, the developing countries as a group presently hold intransigent views on the question of whether the international seabed authority should be empowered to exploit the whole of the area to the exclusion of desirous States and private companies, they have said the authority must have this power and we have said it may not have this power.

Second, they hold with almost equal vigor the view that ultimately decisions, policies and the actions of the authority must be subordinate and all organs of the authority must be subordinate to a one-nation, one-vote assembly. We do not agree to this approach. We cannot agree to it in the interest of preserving the objectives of the United States in the deep seabed.

Third, Mr. Chairman, they insist, and there is no sign of flexibility that even if the authority chooses to exploit the area through a contractual mode, that is, in cooperation with private companies and sovereign States, it must be almost entirely free to dictate the terms and conditions of contract particularly those relating to the transfer of technology and profits. They feel to insure a strong bargaining position in such contractual negotiations, the authority must have the right to keep the seabed area closed until the authority decides to open it.

They believe the three points I just made are the absolute minimum that they must achieve in Committee I in order to insure their control over the raw materials of the seabed. This is a foreign policy objective of many, if not all developing countries in the world today. This policy, as Ambassador Stevenson has pointed out, is pursued actively in every international forum to which they have access. And as you see, characterized as the creation of a new economic order.

Now, Mr. Ratiner has just testified there has been a change, not at the heads of Committee One, but in working groups since Geneva.

Perhaps you can elaborate on that, Mr. Ratiner.

Mr. RATINER. Yes, Mr. Chairman, the statement which you just read was, at the time it was delivered, entirely accurate.

Since then, developing countries have first had an opportunity following Geneva to review not only the Single Negotiating Text, which as you will recall emerged on the final day of the Conference, but also to review other materials, including, for example, the statement which you just read yourself.

They now have the ability to evaluate the impact which the Single Negotiating Text had on important parties to the Law of the Sea negotiation.

Second, Mr. Chairman, it is reasonably clear to me, based on my consultation with other delegations in the Conference, that the pendency of legislation in the Congress on deep sea mining, as well as the passage of legislation by the Congress on fishing has had some impact on the thinking of developing countries in this negotiation.

They seem now to better appreciate the amount of time that is left for the completion of the Law of the Sea negotiations.

Most of them, though not necessarily all, would like to see a treaty on the Law of the Sea and on all the subjects which we are addressing in that negotiation, rather than a patchwork quilt of claims by various nations.

I think that in the intervening period between Geneva and today developing countries have finally concluded that a treaty on the terms indicated in the Single Negotiating Text in Committee One is not possible, that a treaty is desirable, and that there is a risk that the United States and possibly other industrialized nations will lose confidence in the treaty negotiation process and, in fact, enact unilateral legislation on these matters.

Those factors combined to produce an awareness that, if the treaty is to be completed in substance in 1976, it would be extremely important to find basic compromises even before the March meeting.

This is what was attempted during the 2 weeks in February. I think concrete evidence emerged from those discussions that the developing countries with whom we negotiated at that session are seriously trying to find compromise in critical areas.

Mr. MURPHY. Mr. Mosher?

Mr. MOSHER. Thank you, Mr. Chairman.

How much assurance is there that the people you have been talking to most recently in the interim can speak with authority and responsibility for the larger group?

Mr. RATINER. Mr. Mosher, the people that we have been talking to in the early weeks of February, with one or two exceptions, are the principal leaders of the developing countries, and have been since 1968 when these negotiations began.

Mr. Mosher, they are the same people that produced the climate in which the Single Negotiating Text, which was unacceptable to us, emerged.

There were, however, certain of those key leaders who were not present in New York in February.

On the other hand, the chairman of the committee was present, and the new texts which emerged are his own work product, thus carrying considerable political weight.

Moreover, the Group of 77 will meet in the first 2 weeks of March to consider, among other things, these new texts. If the leadership in the Group of 77 with whom we negotiated in New York 2 weeks ago are forceful in defending the chairman's new text, then presumably they could have the same influence over the Group of 77 that they have always had in the past.

On the other hand, I am not sure that we can predict that they will be as forceful in their control of the Group of 77 looking toward moderation as they have been in the past when they were looking toward more extremist positions.

Mr. MOSHER. But you do feel that you have not been speaking to a dissident or political group, that they are responsible spokesmen?

Mr. RATINER. No sir, these were among the principal representatives of the developing country producers and also the spokesmen.

Mr. MOSHER. In your current testimony, that is today's testimony, where you used the phrase the more inflexible positions, or you referred to the principal most divisive issues, and so forth, are those still essentially the same list of issues that the chairman just mentioned more specifically in quoting your earlier testimony?

Mr. RATINER. Yes, they are, sir.

Mr. MOSHER. Those are still the views?

Mr. RATINER. The issues on which the chairman produced compromise texts in New York during this recent 2 week meeting are the same issues as the ones Congressman Murphy referred to.

Mr. MOSHER. Now, you just hinted that the unilateral action of Congress concerning the 200-mile fishing limit perhaps had some modifying impact here, mellowing, that is, and I am not quite sure what the word should be.

To what degree is there analogy here in these two situations?

If Congress triggered some movement on the part of the other group by its unilateral action on the 200-mile zone, would it not be reasonable to think that unilateral action on the deep sea legislation, perhaps establishing a date sometime in the future, that would allow time for the law of the sea people to catch up with us, is there not some reason to believe that would be a good thing for us to do here?

Mr. RATINER. Mr. Mosher. I think there is a significant difference between the 200-mile fisheries legislation and the deep sea mining legislation and their respective impact on the Conference.

While our action was premature and did not await the results of negotiations, the 200-mile bill was not perceived by most developing countries as depriving them of what they considered to be basic rights that they were trying to achieve through a treaty negotiation process.

The fact that the United States makes certain claims in that legislation impinges on a very few countries' interests in the negotiation, and generally speaking, not on the national interests of developing countries.

In Committee One, however, legislation by the United States would go directly to the heart of what developing countries are seeking to achieve in a treaty, and would jeopardize their chances for achieving reasonable amounts of what they have said they want.

For that reason, I suggest that deep sea mining legislation would have a somewhat different impact, if actually passed by the U.S. Congress. on the perceptions of developing countries about our willingness to negotiate in good faith.

Therefore, I would simply say that I think deep sea mining legislation might just go a little too far.

Mr. MOSHER. Well, then you are saying it is not a parallel situation, it not analogous.

Mr. RATINER. No, sir, it is not. I think deep seabed mining legislation passed by the U.S. Congress today would tend to destroy negotiations rather than expedite them.

Mr. MOSHER. You are saying it would be an abrasive element in negotiations, counterproductive. That is what you are saying?

Mr. RATINER. Yes; it is, at this time.

Mr. MOSHER. Thank you, Mr. Chairman.

Mr. MURPHY. Mr. Oberstar?

Mr. OBERSTAR. I will have some questions later.

Mr. MURPHY. Mr. Forsythe?

Mr. FORSYTHE. Thank you, Mr. Chairman.

This basic question which Mr. Mosher is discussing is the efficacy of movement, and you indicate a very short time in this March meeting that things should become rather clear.

I think it is apparent that the committee could not really be as far down the road on this issue as the Congress of course is on the 200-mile issue, but you also wind up if the debate should cease, putting it a little more bluntly than you did, but do you not think if we were to proceed with hearings and discussions of this it would help you up there, really?

Mr. RATINER. Well, sir, I do not see any risk to the negotiation of the Law of the Sea treaty if our Congress is attempting to pass

legislation and worrying about contingency plans in the event the
conference should fail. I see no risk whatever.

The only risk to the negotiation would be if both Houses were
today to pass ocean mining legislation.

Mr. FORSYTHE. I assure you it will not happen today.

Mr. RATINER. I know that, sir.

Mr. FORSYTHE. But it does seem to me, I take some pride, as a
matter of fact, to think that with the 200-mile legislation things are
seeming to fall into place because of that.

I would hope you could expand in his critical area. I certainly
fully support the idea of getting an International Convention on
Deep Sea Mining. I think it is critical in the history of the world.

Mr. MOSHER. Would the gentleman yield?

Mr. FORSYTHE. Yes.

Mr. MOSHER. You obviously are referring to the last paragraph
in Mr. Ratiner's testimony, where he says we would prefer to suspend
the debate on whether or not there should be legislation if at all
possible.

Are you talking about the debate between the Congress and the
administration there, or are you talking about the debate within
Congress?

Mr. RATINER. Mr. Mosher, we are talking about the debate between
Congress and the administration. In fact, all we are really saying
is that we cannot pay full attention in this critical period before
the negotiations to both testimony on his subject and preparing
ourselves for negotiations.

Mr. MOSHER. So you are not particularly objecting to our discussing it within the Congress; you just want to confine your efforts
to discussing it with the other nations, is that it?

Mr. RATINER. That is all we intended, sir.

Mr. FORSYTHE. Thank you.

Mr. MURPHY. Mr. Ratiner, on February 17, 1976, Secretary of
State Kissinger, in a speech in Caracas referred to "issues relating to
the sea which have complicated relations in the past," and how "in
the interim between now and the final Law of the Sea Conference
we will continue to attempt to find solutions."

Now, it is clear from the speech that he was talking about more
than fisheries.

What I would like to know is what additional concessions are you
cooking up as a solution to the deep seabed negotiations?

For example, are we going to commit our seabed miners to a
moratorium?

Mr. RATINER. Mr. Chairman, there is not any intention that I
am aware of in the administration to commit us to a moratorium.

We expect this conference essentially to end, and to have a
treaty for signature, within approximately 1 year from now.

I say "expect" because it is very difficult to predict the precise
procedures which will be used.

We are hoping that there will be an 8-week session in March,
which is now confirmed, followed by a session during the summer.
We are not sure how long a summer session would be. Presumably,
at some short period thereafter, we would hope for a session in
Caracas to sign the treaty on the Law of the Sea.

Mr. MURPHY. When?

Mr. RATINER. I think it is important to emphasize this is not just a perception that we in the U.S. executive branch bring to you.

When we talked about a timely and successful conference, it used to be from our own perception. However, most delegates we have seen between the Geneva session and today seem to share our view that we really do have just these two sessions left to determine whether it is going to be a bust or a success. No more time than that seems to be asked for by any delegation.

Mr. MURPHY. Does that include the delegate from Sri Lanka?

Mr. RATINER. As far as I know, it does. I have had conversations with him, and he seems to feel we should be ending this conference very shortly, indeed.

Mr. MURPHY. Is he a party to the compromises that you mention?

Mr. RATINER. No. The delegate from Sri Lanka was not present in the New York meeting that was just concluded, because he had been appointed as his country's ambassador to the Federal Republic of Germany and had a conflict in schedule. Otherwise, he would have been there.

Mr. MURPHY. Has he not been the whip of the Group of 77 countries?

Mr. RATINER. The whip of the Group of 77 in Committee I has been Peru.

Mr. MURPHY. You said 15 March for the next Law of the Sea Conference, and one in the summer of 1976, followed by a signing ceremony in Caracas.

Mr. RATINER. Yes, sir.

Mr. MURPHY. When?

Mr. RATINER. Well, the dates are usually set for these things just after, or at the end of, the preceding session.

I assume that at the end of the summer session, or toward the end of the summer session, the conference would begin to discuss the precise dates and place for the signing of the treaty, assuming there will be one to be signed.

Mr. MURPHY. We have taken this before.

Mr. RATINER. Yes, we have.

Mr. MURPHY. Is the United States going to propose, or agree to a moratorium?

Mr. RATINER. As far as I know, we are not going to propose or agree to a moratorium.

Mr. MURPHY. The Kissinger Caracas speech indicated that the State Department favors: (1) Producer-consumer cooperation in specific commodities and, he is; (2) prepared to take practical steps in the transfer of technology.

I would appreciate your telling me if there is a connection between these concessions, to the outrageous demands of the new international economic order, in the deep seabed negotiations.

Specifically, I want to know if you people are going to New York to negotiate a commodity agreement in the first committee, and offer our technology as an inducement to the Group of 77.

Mr. RATINER. The answer to both questions, Mr. Chairman, is, no. We are not going to negotiate a commodity agreement, and we are not going to offer technology to induce negotiations.

If I could elaborate slightly, the issue of commodity agreements, or put more broadly, commodity arrangements, has been raised in the Committee I negotiations by consuming-developing countries, not producer countries. The reason they have raised this question is because consuming-developing countries would like to find a way to avoid price and production controls imposed by the International Seabed Resource Authority.

They are trying to find a way of protecting the interest of land-based producers who are developing countries, without at the same time sacrificing the interest of consuming countries.

For that reason, the new article 9 on economic implications, which I have introduced for the record today, very clearly sets forth that the thrust of any protection for land based producers should come from commodity arrangements if, in fact, commodity arrangements come to exist in the future.

Our intention in this treaty is not to establish a commodity arrangement or agreement, nor to provide to the International Seabed Resource Authority the same powers which would normally be found in a commodity arrangement or agreement.

With respect to technology tranfer, we have always indicated in these negotiations our willingness to try to find ways of assisting the developing countries in obtaining better information, better technical capabilities, and presumably, better approaches to applying technology.

Obviously, we cannot, and we do not intend to promise the transfer of technology which the U.S. Government does not own.

Mr. Murphy. In your discussions since Geneva, and particularly in February, with representatives of these countries, were those discussions with undeveloped countries who are presently producer countries, and whether or not they had agreed to concessions that the United States had proposed?

Mr. Ratiner. Our consultations since Geneva have been with leading producer countries, leading consumer countries, and in-industrialized countries.

Mr. Murphy. Did any of the producer-undeveloped countries agree to the concessions in the February meeting?

Mr. Ratiner. Mr. Chairman, I think the answer to that question is that on the basis of discussions which were held in February, the chairman of the first committee produced new Single Negotiating Text articles, which he felt better reflected the state of progress on what he had heard in these discussions and negotiations.

I would not want to say that any nation agreed in any binding sense to these new texts.

The way in which this negotiation is being conducted is a very useful way, a very progressive way, and benefits from the chairman himself taking personal responsibility for the new text.

Mr. Murphy. It is not the question I have asked twice.

What I am trying to find out is whether undeveloped countries who have a vested interest in these minerals have obstructed, assisted, or not voiced an opinion on the concessions of the February meeting.

Mr. Ratiner. They assisted in producing the compromise texts which the chairman introduced. They did not obstruct it.

Mr. Murphy. I am aware that an observer of, and high ranking participant in the deep seabed negotiations from another country suggested to our delegation that if we were serious about manganese nodules then we should take two actions.

He said the United States should pass domestic legislation for the deep seabed and walkout of the first committee.

Could you tell me, first, if our delegation evaluated these options along with others, and No. 2, if you rejected it, why?

It sounds like good advice to me.

Mr. RATINER. I do recall the first of those comments.

I do not recall any representative, high level or otherwise, suggesting that we walk out of the First Committee. I think the answer to your question is yes, this statement was evaluated and considered very seriously, by us, and was factored into our policy review process during the past several months.

This statement was, however, made prior to the February meeting in New York, where progress seemed to occur.

Mr. MURPHY. But you rejected it?

Mr. RATINER. Rejected the advice.

Mr. MURPHY. To pass a domestic law and walkout.

Mr. RATINER. Again, the walking out was not part of the advice but we did for the moment reject the advice to pass domestic legislation.

I am not sure that we could, in fact, successfully have done so, even if we had wanted to.

You yourself, in your opening statement pointed out the issue of who should have jurisdiction over ocean mining, if domestic legislation is passed. In my view, it would not have been possible to resolve that issue between the time this statement was made and the February meeting. Therefore, it would not have been practical to pass domestic ocean mining legislation, nor did we think it desirable.

Prior to the New York meetings in February, we had had some glimmerings that what actually happened might, in fact, occur. We had had private conversations with various developing countries, delegates from producing countries, and had reason to believe several months earlier that the New York session might go better than we otherwise would have anticipated.

It simply would not be prudent for the administration to propose the actual pasage of legislation, if things are starting to turn around in the Committee One negotiations.

Mr. MURPHY. I will say to my colleagues on the Committee One have a series of questions, but the Chair will yield at any time if anyone wants to ask questions.

Mr. Oberstar?

Mr. OBERSTAR. Thank you, Mr. Chairman.

One of the considerations in the Law of the Sea Conference is whether the resources should be developed by the first who gets there, or whether they are the so-called common heritage of man kind.

What view does the State Department hold of that resource, and how are you advocating the State Department viewpoint in that discussion?

Mr. RATINER. The United States has agreed in principle that the resources of the deep seabed are the common heritage of mankind.

However, the meaning of that term, common heritage of mankind, was actually put before the United Nations General Assembly by the United States spokesman at that time, Ambassador John Stevenson. In essense, we defined our understanding of the term common heritage to mean whatever the collection of treaty articles ultimately means, that the term would have no indepent meaning.

Now, it is true that there are many countries who think that common heritage of mankind means common property of mankind, and therefore, something that we cannot use without their consent.

This debate is an old one, and it is one which we do not repeat often in the negotiations at this stage.

The question now is how to establish a system pursuant to which the resources will be disposed of on a bisis which gives reasonable guarantees to the United States of access and maintaining our rights once we have access.

Mr. OBERSTAR. In your judgment, how many other countries besides the United States are technically capable of developing the seabed resources in the way that we are able to do?

Mr. RATINER. At this time there is no other country that has the capability of the United States, to the best of our knowledge.

In a broader sense, there are roughly a half a dozen countries which could, with accelerated spending efforts, develop that tech nology reasonably quickly.

Mr. OBERSTAR. Such as?

Mr. RATINER. Japan, the Federal Republic of Germany, the United Kingdom, France, Belgium, and Canada.

Mr. OBERSTAR. The Russians are not actively developing this capability?

Mr. RATINER. We do not have good information as to whether the Soviet Union is actively developing deep seabed mining technology.

Mr. OBERSTAR. Essentially, we are now talking about an international treaty to regulate the activity of one country, the United States.

Mr. RATINER. That is a way of looking at the problem.

There are, of course, other ways of looking at it, which take into account the fact that the treaty has many parts to it, covers many issues, and indeed, would guide in a very broad sense all nations' activities, both within the oceans and in the deep seabed.

Mr. OBERSTAR. Getting back to this question of common heritage of mankind, are you working toward a definition in the treaty of that term?

Mr. RATINER. No, sir, we are not.

Mr. OBERSTAR. Why not?

Mr. RATINER. We think that the common heritage of mankind principles if I can be blunt, is a glittering generality. Therefore, we can leave the phrase alone, provided the rest of the treaty says the right things.

Mr. OBERSTAR. We will get to those "right things" in a minute.

On page 3 of your testimony you talk about the Law of the Sea Conference providing the United States with the "opportunity to develop a system which would subject the deep seabed mining to widely acceptable international rules."

What widely acceptable international rules do you have in mind?

Mr. RATINER. Well, first, sir, there would be rules which set forth the system pursuant to which access is obtained, that is how one would get a right. Is it a license, is it a contract?

Mr. OBERSTAR. You are saying we do not now have a right to undertake this?

Mr. RATINER. No, I did not say that. We do have the right now.

We are now speaking of what would happen when the treaty came into force.

Mr. OBERSTAR. I want to get your terminology clear.

You said under the terms and conditions a right would be granted. If we already have that right, then you must be talking about a limitation on that right.

Mr. RATINER. Yes, I am. I am talking about the United States agreeing.

Mr. OBERSTAR. The limitations we will agree upon are limitations on our inherent right to mining.

Go ahead.

Mr. RATINER. First of all, under present international law an ocean mining company of the United States could simply go out and begin mining.

The kind of limitation we are talking about is that under the new international law, as manifested in this treaty, should it be successfully negotiated, a United States company could not just go out and mine the resources.

First, it would have to demonstrate that it was financially competent to do so. It would have to demonstrate that it was technically competent to do so. Rules would be applied to it to insure that it made serious and bona fide investment efforts, one it had been granted rights to carry on and to insure that it conducted its mining activities in an environmentally sound manner, and so on ad so forth.

There is a long list of limitations that would be applied to what is now the absolute, free right to do as companies please, subject to a very vague principle of law in the Geneva Convention on the High Seas that requires them to have reasonable regard for the rights of other countries under the freedom of the high seas.

Under the new treaty, ocean mining would be a regulated activity.

Right now it is an unregulated one. The question, I think, is really to what degree will we accept regulation of deep sea mining in the treaty which we do not like or want to accept. That is an extremely difficult question to answer.

So far, we have not accepted anything in the deep sea mining portion of the treaty negotiations which we did not like.

Mr. OBERSTAR. Now, in your statement just a moment ago you postulated a right to mine, and the possibility of a company exercising that right.

Now, does the company have the right, or does the United States have the right?

Mr. RATINER. Of course, it is difficult to be definitive, because we do not have a final treaty yet, but the treaty negotiations at present would reveal reasonably widespread agreement that both States and private companies would acquire rights, and that private companies would acquire direct rights through the International Seabed Resource Authority.

Mr. OBERSTAR. Yet, most of the other countries with the notable exception of maybe Japan and Great Britain, and possibly France, would be State enterprises that would engage in undersea mining.

If we are going to put a State in competition with a single company in the United States I see some problems there.

Are you looking to a resolution of that difficulty in the course of these treaty negotiations?

Mr. RATINER. There could be certain problems. On the other hand, in practice, States which engage directly in State commercial activity tend to organize that activity in much the same way that American companies organize themselves.

For example, Mr. Oberstar, the Soviet Union flies a state airline, Aerofloat. Aerofloat is operated, I am not commenting on how it is funded, but it is operated in very much the same way that a private airline would be operated. So, in practice, we would be competing in the deep seabed with state trading corporations.

Mr. OBERSTAR. With the exception, of course, that a State enterprise is not necessarily a profitmaking venture.

Just as we have seen in our Merchant Marine Subcommittee hearings about the Soviet and Balt—Atlantic and Polish fleets that operate, you know, in a below cost basis, at noncompensatory rates, and make up the difference out of national funds, because they are in it fo the prestige, or some other purpose. You have the same thing here.

I think that that question of profitmaking venture versus a noncompensatory one ought to enjoy some further consideration.

Mr. MURPHY. Would the gentleman yield at that point?

Mr. OBERSTAR. Certainly.

Mr. MURPHY. Vietnam is currently trying to arrange an agreement with an American company, the Glomar Co., to do Continental Shelf drilling for them, or other Shelf or seabed work.

It would be simple for some State with no technology to get a concession, and then employ, or lease technology from the United States.

Mr. RATINER. Might I comment briefly?

Mr. OBERSTAR. Certainly.

Mr. RATINER. I do not think this treaty will change the reality of that question. That can easily be true today or tomorrow without a treaty.

This is a risk that we have every day in all of our commercial activities, that we will have to compete with a sovereign state, which may outcompete us by an excessive amount of funding, or by not requiring profits, and so on and so forth.

That is a fundamental issue of public policy which the United States has to deal with on many occasions. Obviously, it always raises the question whether, if something is important enough to the United States, and we are being outcompeted, we should subsidize the American industry in the same way that, say, a Soviet trading company is being subsidized by its government.

That question is not unique to this negotiation, nor will the treaty change that problem.

Mr. OBERSTAR. No; but we have a unique opportunity to provide for the future, and not hamstring ourselves by giving up something that we might not later be able to recapture.

The question of technology transfer was raised a moment ago. I would like to pursue that further.

The question was raised in the context of offering technology transfer as an inducement to other countries to negotiate.

Let's take that one step further: tell us about treaty commitments that the United States might be making to other countries to transfer technology, that is to train them, to give them information that the United States now has, or that private industry has developed, so that those countries then can be on an equal position to develop the seabed?

Mr. RATINER. Well, we have not agreed, nor can we agree to treaty articles which would require th transfer of technology from private companies to the International Seabed Resource Authority, or to developing countries individually.

We can make best efforts. We can endeavor to facilitate the transfer of technology. In some areas, such an undertaking makes good sense, since we are trying to establish a balanced and accommodating international law for various uses of the ocean.

Developing countries, for example, can use new technologies to better enable them to manage the resources off their coasts.

We do not necessarily, as a nation, suffer from improving the lot of developing countries and their ability to exploit resources near their coasts.

We are sympathetic to the developing countries' desire for technology transfer, but in the area of deep sea mining, we do not feel we are able to undertake any direct obligation to transfer such technology to them.

Mr. OBERSTAR. I would hope so. It is bad enough having private industry going over to Taiwan, or Austria, to get labor to produce goods, which our technology has developed here at home.

It is something else, and very objectionable, from my standpoint, for the United States to give that technology away to other countries.

Is there any consideration being given in your discussions to apportionment of profits on a formula basis under the authority of this independent Seabed Resource Authority?

I understand that it would have the authority to determine rate of development, and the price of minerals, and it would retain the profits and distribute them.

Is there a formula for distribution of those profits?

Mr. RATINER. Under the new compromise texts, which I described in very general terms today, there would be no power to establish the rate of development, nor would there be any power to fix prices.

On the question of profit sharing, there are, of course, various mechanisms for insuring that the International Seabed Resource Authority derives revenue from ocean mining.

One of the methods which we have discussed, but without commitment, and indeed, without the drafting of any treaty articles, is the sharing of profits. Under this approach, an American company would enter into a contract with the Authority for a right to explore and exploit the resources of the area, in exchange for which the profits of that company would be shared with the Authority which, pursuant to a formula included in the treaty.

Mr. OBERSTAR. Finally, I understand the ordinary and usual reluctance of the administration toward any action by Congress that might direct its hand in international negotiations, we would through this on the Law of the Sea Conference with respect to the 200-mile limit, and now we are back at it again on deep seabed mining, and you are telling us the same story, not you personally, but the administration, singing the same song that we heard a year ago.

I just wonder if it does not strengthen your hand if the Congress acts and does something a lot tougher, that goes a lot further than what you are negotiating in this Conference; if it does not strengthen your hand, to say to other countries, either you agree to something reasonable here, or the Congress is going to take us a lot further. What is your comment?

Mr. RATINER. I have no quarrel with your comment, Mr. Congressman.

I think that one's hand is strengthened by having a tough constituency to represent, and I have never quarreled with the idea that the pending legislation in Congress was a help to the United States.

We have only quarreled with Congress when Congress wanted to go ahead and pass it, which would remove its threat value.

Mr. OBERSTAR. The President still has the veto power.

Thank you, Mr. Chairman.

Mr. MURPHY. Mr. Forsythe?

Mr. FORSYTHE. The trend of your response, Mr. Ratiner, to my colleague from Minnesota, pretty well delineated that yes, we are giving up something in all of this process. It certainly would appear that way.

What do we get if we do finally come to a Law of the Sea Treaty on deep seabed mining?

I have some ideas, but I think you ought to be telling us.

Mr. RATINER. I think in respect to deep sea mining, and confining the quid pro quo, so to speak, to that subject, what we get is international acceptance of rights which we claim we now have, but which the rest of the world simply does not accept.

In short, we reduce the potential for conflict, for nonrecognition, for legal arguments, and for ships' cargoes being seized and brought into courts in foreign countries, all because they claim that we are holding illegally the common heritage of mankind.

We produce a more stable investment climate through a treaty than we would have if there were no treaty at all.

Now, I am not saying that the taking of unilateral action would produce a totally unstable investment climate. In fact, at this moment some legislation could create more stability than no legislation at all.

Ultimately, a treaty in which most, if not all, nations accept the rights of American companies will produce the greatest stability and the best investment climate.

It will, in short, be best for business if there is a good treaty, and I think that many of the ocean mining companies know that.

Their concern is whether the treaty itself will provide an investment climate that is better for them than would be provided if the rest of the world did not recognize our rights, and if we acted under unilateral legislation.

That is a question of fact. We can look at the treaty possibly within the next 6 months and determine whether it provides a stable and satisfactory investment climate.

If it does, then it is far better for the industry, in my view, to have that treaty than not to have it. I think many in industry would agree with that.

Mr. FORSYTHE. Is it not important, and on this record at this point in time, that this great phase "common heritage of mankind" means that anything that our nationals do out there can be challenged by any other nation, and at the same point, and in the same pot?

Mr. RATINER. I think it is important to have it clearly on the record that the principle of the common heritage has led to investment uncertainty.

Mr. FORSYTHE. A claim that is equal to everybody.

Mr. RATINER. Well, the rights that we claim right now under the high seas doctrine are equal to everybodys' rights, or rights which could be claimed by everybody else. However we are the only country that can exercise those rights in respect of ocean mining, and that creates a feeling of disequilibrium on the part of the rest of the world.

Nevertheless, they will challenge our rights if we exercise them in the absence of a treaty, and that is not a good situation for the United States to be in, if we can avoid it.

Mr. FORSYTHE. Thank you.

Thank you, Mr. Chairman.

Mr. MURPHY. Mr. Ratiner, how many States must ratify the proposed treaty to put it into effect?

Mr. RATINER. Mr. Chairman, there have been no serious negotiations undertaken yet on that question, to the best of my knowledge. Therefore, I cannot answer your question at this time.

I would hope that it would take a substantial number of States to bring this treaty into force.

Mr. MURPHY. Well, substantial can be pretty broad.

What number did it take at the recent IMCO Conference?

Mr. RATINER. I do not know.

Mr. MURPHY. How about on a percentage basis? Would it be 80 percent?

Mr. RATINER. I doubt that it would be that high, but it could be.

Mr. MURPHY. Two-thirds?

Mr. RATINER. I think there is someone here from the Coast Guard that might be able to answer that question.

Mr. MURPHY. Is there a Coast Guard representative here?

STATEMENT OF ENS. LUCILLE T. LALIBERTE, U.S. COAST GUARD RESERVE, LAW OF THE SEA STAFF OFFICER

Ensign LALIBERTE. We can supply that information for the record, Mr. Chairman.

Mr. MURPHY. We will submit it at this point in the record.

136

[The following was received for the record.]

The last five IMCO sponsored Conventions have had the following coming into force requirements:

1. International Conference on Revision of the International Regulations for Preventing Collisions at Sea, 1972, (a) 15 countries and 65% of the world's tonnage.

2. International Conference on Marine Pollution, 1973, (a) 15 countries and 50% of the world's tonnage.

. 3. International Convention for Safe Containers, 1974, (a) 10 countries.

4. International Legal Conference on the Carriage of Passengers and their Luggage on Board Ships, 1974, (a) 10 countries.

5. International Conference on Safety of Life at Sea, 1974, (a) 25 countries and 50% of the world's tonnage.

Mr. MURPHY. How long did it take to do this ratification process?

Mr. RATINER. The ratification process, Mr. Chairman, consumes a very unpredictable time period. Treaties can take a very short period to be ratified, or they can take as much as 10 years, and sometimes they might never come into force.

A lot will depend on the political realities that confront nations when they are trying to decide to sign and ratify a treaty.

For example, you have pending before you legislation which would precede the coming into force of a treaty, that is, it would establish certain legal rights and obligations for American companies.

Passage of that legislation after the treaty was opened for signature, but before it came permanently into force, could have one of two effects.

It could produce virtual overnight ratification and entry into force in order to prevent the United States from preempting the resources of the seabed. Or, it could produce an adverse reaction.

The latter would be an angry response, not necessarily a reasonable one, which would put off signing and ratification for a good many years.

There are also other interests in the negotiation. This treaty will be a single package. It will deal with such questions as fisheries, marine pollution, scientific research. Public pressures, both in our country and in many other countries, will determine whether the treaty comes into force quickly or after a long time.

Mr. MURPHY. It took 6 years to do the Shelf treaty.

Mr. OBERSTAR. Mr. Chairman, just at that point, a technical question.

How many countries are participating in the Law of the Sea Conference?

Mr. RATINER. Approximately 150.

Mr. OBERSTAR. One hundred and fifty?

Mr. RATINER. Yes, sir.

Mr. OBERSTAR. That is more than there are members of the United Nations.

Mr. RATINER. Approximately 150 are members of the United Nations that are participating in this Conference.

Mr. OBERSTAR. Thank you.

Mr. RATINER. The number does change fairly rapidly.

Mr. Chairman, I think your point about the Continental Shelf Convention bears directly on my earlier response. There was no real need for countries to ratify that convention.

Most nations believed, as a matter of customary international law, that they had rights to the Continental Shelf, which could not be disturbed by any other nation. Under the emerging customary law which began with the pronouncement by the United States, the Truman Proclamation, of our rights to the Continental Shelf, they believed their rights could extend as far out on the Shelf as exploitation permitted. Since the Continental Shelf Convention was a single treaty it had no other extraneous issues in it.

There was no particular motivation to ratify it.

Mr. MURPHY. It was remarkably quick for a noncontroversial issue, but how many years would it take for an issue that is controversial?

Mr. RATINER. It depends on whether nations believe they are going to lose more or gain more by not having the treaty ratified.

In this case, most countries, if they seriously want to participate in the management of deep seabed resources, would have a great deal to gain by ratifying quickly.

Mr. MURPHY. Spokesmen for the administration have repeatedly assured Congress that deep seabed mining by U.S. companies in the interval between the present time and the date when a treaty would become effective would receive U.S. diplomatic protection, and that the integrity of their investments during this period should be fully protected.

Is that still your position, and the U.S. position?

Mr. RATINER. Well, I am not sure what administration spokesmen you are quoting, Mr. Chairman. However, it is our contention that there should be integrity of investment in the interim period, and we have felt that the best way to deal with that problem would be for Congress to permit us to bring the treaty into force and effect on a provisional basis very early. Then, even if it took 5, 6, or 7 years to bring the treaty into permanent force and effect, a provisional regime and provisional machinery could be established shortly after the treaty was signed.

Mr. MURPHY. In the debate on the 200-mile fisheries bill there was a lot of talk about how the only issue standing in the way of a treaty on the law of the sea was the deep seabed.

You know, the deep seabed issues are rather distinct from the other issues, so why not try to separate the negotiations?

It seems to me that you could do this simply by not showing up at the First Committee. Since we alone have the technology, the know how, the capital and the intention to engage in seabed mining, they must reach accommodation with us.

If we are not there, they cannot reach an effective agreement, and the result is a separation of the deep seabed from the rest of the Law of the Sea Conference.

That seems sensible to me, and apparently to some delegates, some of our few friends from other countries.

What do you think of that idea?

Mr. RATINER. Not very much, Mr. Chairman.

Mr. Chairman, it is our common perception in the administration that the developing countries would probably not be willing to see emerge a treaty reflecting Committee II and Committee III issues, without including Committee I issues.

If our perception is correct, then by walking out of Committee I, or not negotiating in Committee I, we would, in essence, be making the decision to abandon the Law of the Sea Conference and the hope for a treaty on other issues, where it is extremely important that the United States have a treaty.

Mr. MURPHY. The 200-mile fisheries legislation was characterized as a unilateral extention of national jurisdiction that violates international law.

I am not sure that I am as convinced as you people are, but what I would like you to do is think through the comparison of the 200-mile bill and my deep seabed mining bill. The latter is simply legislation to regulate U.S. nationals in the exercise of a high sea freedom. It is not an extension of jurisdiction.

Further, its passage would be a healthy signal to the First Committee that we are serious about the U.S. interests in the deep seabed.

Mr. RATINER. Is that a question, Mr. Chairman?

Mr. MURPHY. Well, I would like a reaction to it.

What reason do you have for opposing such a course of action?

Mr. RATINER. Mr. Chairman, our principal reason for opposing that course of action is its political effect in the negotiating process.

I do not disagree with you that we have a legal right to pass legislation regulating the behavior of U.S. nationals on the deep seabed.

The only question which seems to me pertinent and relevant is what impact would the immediate passage of such legislation have on our ability to achieve a better approach, which is a treaty through which our rights are recognized and accepted.

Mr. MURPHY. Now, if you start to define this better approach, probably some of this better approach might have resulted from some of the February consultations.

What mechanism do you have for consulting with the Congress and the industry, that is American industry, that is on their reactions to a better approach as you move into a conclusion in the Law of the Sea?

Mr. RATINER. Well, one such mechanism in respect to Congress is this hearing today.

We have not dwelled on the new draft texts, perhaps because I furnished them only today and you have not had an opportunity to study them. However, I and others in the administration stand ready to discuss fully with Members of Congress, both publicly and privately, the impact of these new texts, what they mean and what direction they signal for the negotiations.

In respect to the industry, we have three methods for consultation. First, consulting the industry privately, which is usually the most effective method. And second, through the Public Advisory Committee on the Law of the Sea, which is an advisory committee to the Department of State.

The industry would receive copies in the normal course of events of all such new materials in the Conference and have ample opportunity to comment.

Finally, the industry will be present as advisors to the U.S. delegation in New York, consulted regularly and daily, and participate in much of the delegation's internal work.

Mr. MURPHY. Well, Mr. Ratiner, as a representative of the Department of the Interior, you have been particularly responsive to this committee and the Congress.

The State Department representatives are generally out of town every time we try to put a little sunshine on just what takes place in Geneva, Caracas, New York, and other places.

Now, this committee is prepared to take on a traveling road show, if necessary, to convince the State Department that we are serious about our responsibility in this issue, and we are not going to have them taking a walk every time we try to get down to a serious discussion as to what is going to take place.

Mr. RATINER. Mr. Chairman, the fact is that I travel more than most people in the State Department and, by some coincidence, you call your hearings when I am in town and they are not.

Mr. MURPHY. They are all around prior to the announcement of the dates of the hearing.

The last time you came here in May, following the Geneva session of the Conference, we discussed the so-called Engo document at length.

You told the subcommittee that the Interagency Task Force on the Law of the Sea had not yet had a chance to study that document but would be conducting a thorough reappraisal of our policy.

We were even promised a briefing on the reappraisal. We have postponed these hearings for several months as we awaited that briefing. What has happened to our briefing?

Mr. RATINER. Mr. Chairman, I was not aware of any request to postpone that briefing other than the initial request made immediately after the Geneva session which arose because we had not yet had time to study the Single Negotiating Text.

During the summer of 1975, we studied the Single Negotiating Text in detail. During that same time period we prepared an informal set of amendments to the Single Negotiating Text, which is now rather widely available. I would be happy to supply this document for the record of this committee.

These amendments are printed in such a fashion that they are parallel to the Engo text, and anyone reading them can see the two versions on a single page in front of him.

I will be happy at a subsequent time to go through the entire Single Negotiating Text and answer any questions.

I was not aware that we had asked for any postponement of that briefing.

Mr. MURPHY. We will have them submitted at this point for the record, and prior to the conclusion of these hearings, which is going to be very soon.

After we have had an opportunity to analyze that in parallel presentation, we will ask you to come back.

[The document referred to follows:]

PROPOSED AMENDMENTS TO THE

COMMITTEE I SINGLE NEGOTIATING TEXT

DECEMBER 1975

SINGLE NEGOTIATING TEXT	AMENDMENT	ARTICLE AS AMENDED
PART INTERPRETATION		PART INTERPRETATION

Article 1

| | Article 1 | Article |

For the purposes of this Convention:

Paragraph (i): Delete.

For the purposes of this Part

(i) "States Parties" to this Convention means Contracting Parties.

(i) [A thorough review of 'definitions' will need to be carried out at a later time.]

(ii) "Activities in the Area" means all activities of exploration of the Area and of the exploitation of its resources, as well as other associated activities in the Area including scientific research.

Paragraph (ii): Delete all after the word "exploration" and insert "for, and exploitation of, the resources of the Area".

(ii) "Activities in the Area" means all activities of exploration for, and exploitation of, the resources of the Area.

(iii) "Resources' means resources in situ.

Paragraph (iii): Insert the word "mineral" between "means" and "resources."

(iii) "Resources" means mineral resources in situ.

(iv) Mineral resources means any of the following categorisation:

Paragraph (iv): Delete.

(a) liquid or gaseous substances such as petroleum, gas, condensate, helium, nitrogen, carbon dioxide, water, steam hot water, and also sulphur and salts extracted in liquid form in solution;

(b) using mineral ores occurring on the surface of the sea-bed or at depths of less than three meters beneath the surface and also concretions of phosphorites and other minerals;

(c) solid minerals in the ocean floor at depths of more than three meters from the surface

d ore-bearing silt and brine.

SINGLE NEGOTIATING TEXT

PART II: PRINCIPLES

The Area and its Limits

Article 2

1. This Convention shall apply to the sea-bed and ocean floor and subsoil thereof beyond the limits of national jurisdiction, hereinafter called the Area."

2. States Parties to this Convention shall notify the International Seabed Authority established pursuant to Article 21 (hereinafter called the "Authority"), of the limits referred to in paragraph of this article defined in this Convention and determined by co-ordinates of latitude and longitude and shall indicate the same on appropriate large scale charts officially recognized by that State.

3. The Authority shall register and publish such notification in accordance with rules adopted by it for the purpose.

4. Nothing in this article shall affect the validity of any agreement between States with respect to the establishment of limits between opposite or adjacent States.

AMENDMENT

PART II

Article 2

Paragraph 2: Insert the word "Resource" between "Seabed" and "Authority."

ARTICLE 2 AS AMENDED

PART II: PRINCIPLES

The Area and its Limits

Article 2

1. This Part shall apply to the sea-bed and ocean floor and subsoil thereof beyond the limits of national jurisdiction, hereinafter called the Area.

2. States Parties to this Convention shall notify the International Seabed Resource Authority established pursuant to Article 21 (hereinafter called the "Authority"), of the limits referred to in paragraph 1 of this article defined in this Convention and determined by co-ordinates of latitude and longitude and shall indicate the same on appropriate large scale charts officially recognized by that State.

3. The Authority shall register and publish such notification in accordance with rules adopted by it for the purpose.

4. Nothing in this article shall affect the validity of any agreement between States with respect to the establishment of limits between opposite or adjacent States.

SINGLE NEGOT AT NG TEXT

AMENDMENT

ARTICLE 3 AS AMENDED

Comm n Heritage of Mankin

Article 3

Article 3

A icle 3

The Area and its resources are the common her tage f mankind.

No amendment proposed.

Article 4

S NGLE NEGOT AT NG TEXT	AMENDMENT	ART CLE 4 AS AMENDED
No Claim Or Exercise of Sov re gnty Or Other Rights		No Claim Or Exercise of Sov re gnty Or Other Righ ts
Article 4	*Article 4*	Article 4
1. No State shall claim or exercise sovereignty or sovereign rights over any part of the Area or its resources, nor shall any State or person, natural or juridical, appropriate any part thereof. No such claim or exercise of sov reignty or sov reign rights, nor such appropriation shall be recognized.		. No State shall claim or exercise sovereignty or sovereign rights over any part of th Area or its resources, nor shall any State or person, natural or juridical, appropriate any part thereof. No su th claim or exercise of sov reignty or sovereign rights, nor su th appropriation shall be recognized.
2. States or persons, natural or juridica shall claim, acquire or exercise rights with respect to the minerals in h itr raw or processed form derived from the Area only in accordance with the provisions of this Convention. Otherwise, no su th claim, acquisition or exercise of rights shall be recognized.	*Paragraph 2: Delete and substitute text at right.*	2. No State or person, natural or juridical, shall claim, acquire or exercise rig ts with respect to the resources of the Area except in accordance with the provisions of th s Part. Otherwise, no su th claim, a quis tion or exercise of such rights shall be recognized.

S GUE NEGOT AT NG TEXT	AMENDMENT	ART CLE 5 AS AMENDED
General C ndu t In The Area And In Re at on To The Area		General Conduct In The Area And In Relation To The Area
Article 5	*Article 6*	**Article 5**
States shall act in, and in rela i to, the Area in accordance with the provisions of this Convent on and the United Nations Charter in the interests of maintaining international peace and security and promoting international cooperation and mutual understanding.	*Delete all after enti d" and substitute the fo lowing:* *", the U ited Nations Charter and applicable princip es of international law in the interests of maintaining international peace and security and promoting international cooperation and mutual understanding."*	States shall act in, and in rela i to he Area in accordance with the provisions of th s Par t the United Nations Charter and applicable principles of international law in the interests of maintaining international peace and security and promoting international cooperation and mutual understanding.

S NGLE NEGOT AT NG TEXT	AMENDMENT	ART CLE 6 AS AMENDED
		Article 6
Activities In The Ar e		ctivities In The Area
Article '	Article 6	A icle 6
Activ ties n the Area shall be g v ened by the provisions of th s Convention and shall be subject to regulation and supervision by the Authority as provided herein. No such activities shall be carried out except in accordance with such regulat ns and the provisions of this Convention.	Delete the second sentence.	Activities in the Area shall be governed by the provisions of this Part and shall be subject to regulation and supervision by the Authority as provided herein.

S GLE NEGOTIATING TEXT	AMENDMENT	ART CLE 7 AS AMENDED
Benefit Of Mankind A A Whole		B n é t Of Mankind As A Whole
Article 7	Article 7	Article 7
Activit es in the Area shall be carried out for the benefit of mankind as a whole, irrespective of the geographica location of States, whether coasta or land-locked, and taking into particular eonsiderat on the interests and reeds of the developing countries.	*Delete the full stop and add "in accordance with the provisions of Article 23."*	Activit es in the Area shall be carried out for the benefit of mankind as a whole, irrespective of the geographical location of States, whether c as ɬ or land-locked, and taking into par i ul ɓ consideration the interests and needs of the developing countr es in accordance with the provisions of Article 23.

SINGLE NEGOTIATING TEXT

Reservation And Use Of The Area Exclusive For Peaceful Purposes

Article 8

1. The Area shall be reserved exclusively for peaceful purposes.

2: The Area shall be open to use exclusively for peaceful purposes by all States Parties, whether coastal or land-locked, without discrimination, in accordance with the provisions of this Convention, and regulations made thereunder.

AMENDMENT

Article 8

Paragraph 1: Delete.

Paragraph 2: Place a full stop after the word "discrimination" and delete the balance of the sentence.

ARTICLE 8 AS AMENDED

Reservation And Use Of The Area Exclusively For Peaceful Purposes

Article 8

The Area shall be open to use exclusively for peaceful purposes by all States Parties, whether coastal or land-locked, without discrimination.

SINGLE NEGOT AT NG TEXT

Genera Pr nciples Regarding Act vi es
In The Area

Article 9

The deve opment and use of the Area sha be
undertaken in such a manne r as to:

(a) foster the healthy development of the wor d
economy and a ba anced growth in international
trade; and

(b) avoid or minimize any adverse effects on the
revenues and economies of the developing
countries, resul ing from a substantial decline
in their export earnings from minerals and het-
raw ma rib s originating in h ib territory
which are a so derived from the Area.

2. Activities in b Area ha   be carried out in an
efficient manner to ensure

(a) rdee y and safe deve opment and rationa
management of the Area and its resources;

(b expanding opportunities in the use hereof;

(c) conservation and utilization of the resources
of the Area for optimum benefit of producers and
consumers of   ew materials and of products made
from them;

(d) equitable sharing in the benefits derived
therefrom, taking into particu ar c ne deration
b interests and needs of the deve op ng countries,
whether land-locked or coasta

AMENDMENT

Article 9

*Delete and substitute the text at
right.*

ARTICLE 9 AS AMENDED

Genera Principles Regard ng Activit es
n The Area

Article 9

1. Activ ies in the Area sha l be promoted and
encouraged and shall be carried out in such a manner
as o

(a) expand opportunities for a   States Par es
in participating in the development of the
resources of the Area;

(b) increase the availability of resources from
the Area; and

(c) ensure equitable sharing of revenues among
States Parties, taking into particular consideration the interests and needs of the
deve oping countries, whether land-locked or
coastal in accordance with Articles 18 and 23.

2. In car ying out their respective activities in the
Area, S ates Parties and the Authority shall take into
account through existing f rume or such new arrangements
as may be appropriate and in which all affected S ateb
Parties participate, the desirability of.

(a) ensuring that activities in the Area are unde ⊤
taken in a safe, rdeely and efficient manne r in
accordance with generally accepted principles of
conservation for avoiding unnecessary was te;

(b) offsetting the adverse economic effect of a
serious and harmful decline in the mineral export
earnings of developing countries for whom export
revenues from miner ls or raw materials also und e
exploitation in the Area represent a substantial
share of their gross domestic product and foreign
exchange earnings, when such decline is clearly
demonstrated to be d rectly a tributable to the
activities in the Area;

(c) advancing mankind's know edge of the deep seabed by promoting maximum exp rati e of he resources
of the Area;

(d) promoting prod cti e of resources from the
Area, and

(e) facilitating the growth, eff ciency and
stability of markets for those c asses of commodities produced from the Area, at prices
renumerative to pr ducers and fa r te consumers.

Article 0

| S NGLE NEGOT AT NG TEXT | AMENDMENT | ART CLE 0 AS AMENDED |

Sc ntifie Research

Article 0

1. Scientific research provid d for n this Convention sha l be carried out exclusive y for p ac fu purposes and for the benefit of mankind as a Wo e. The Authority sha l be the centre for harmon z ng and co-ordinating scientific research

2. The Authority may itself conduct scientific research and may enter into agreements for that purpose.

3. States Parties shall promote international co-operation in scientific research in the Area exc usively for peaceful purposes by:

(a) partic pa i n international programmes and encouraging co-operation in scientific research by personnel of different countries and of the Authority;

(b) ensur ng that programmes are developed through the Author ty for the benefit of developing countries and techno ogically ess developed countries with a v ew to

  (i) strengthening their research c pabilities;

  (ii) trainig their nationa s and the personne of the Authority in the techniques and applications of research;

  (iii) fostering the employment of the r qualified personnel in act vities of research in the Area;

(c) effective publ cation of research programmes and dissemination o the r se ts of research through the Auth re y.

Article 10

Paragraph 1: Delete 'provided for in this Convention" and the second sentence.

Paragraph 3: In subparagraph b delete the phrase "through the Authority" in the first sentence. In subparagraph (c) delete "the Authority" and substitute "appropriate i ternational channels." Also, delete in subparagraph (c) "publication of research programs and". The amended version of subparagraph (c should then read as shown at right.

Scientific Research

Article 0

1. Scientific research shall be carr ed out exc usively for peacefu purposes and for the benefit of mankind as a whole.

2. The Authority may itself conduct scientific research and may n t into agreements for that purpose.

3. States Parties shall promote international co-operation in scientific research in the Area exc usively for peaceful purposes by:

(a) participation in internationa programmes and encouraging co-operation in sci ne fic research by personnel of different countries and of the Authority;

(b ensuring that programmes are developed for the benefit of developing countries and techno logically less developed countries with a view to

  (i) strengthening their research papIlities

  (ii) training their nationals and the personnel of the Authority in the techniques and applications of research;

  (iii) fostering the employment of their qualified personnel n activities of research n the Area;

(c) effective diss mine ion of the resu ts of research through appropr ate nternational channe s.

A ticle 11

S NGLE NEGOT AT NG TEXT	AMENDMENT	ART CLE 11 AS AMENDED
Transfer of Techno ogy		Transfer of Techno ogy
Article 11	*Article 11*	Article 11
The Authority and through it States Par is to this Convention shall take necessary measures for promoting the transfer of technology and scientific know edge relating to activities in the Area so that all States benefit therefrom. In particular, they sha l promote:	*Paragraph 1: Delete through it. Insert "to cooperate in" after "measures" and delete "for."*	The Authority and States Part es to this Convention shall take necessary measures to cooperate in promoting the transfer of technology and scientific knowledge relating to activities in the Area so that all States benefit therefrom. In particular, they shall promote:
(a) Programmes for the promotion of transfer of technology to developing countries with regard to activities in the Area, including, inter alia, facilit ing the access of developing countries to patented and non-patented techno ogy, und e just and reasonable c ndi i ns;	*Paragraph 1(a): Delete 'patented and non-patented."*	(a) Programmes for the promotion of transfer of technology to developing countries w th regard to activities in the Area, including, inter alia, fe ilitating the access of developing countries to technology, und e just and reasonab e c nditions;
(b Measures directed towards the acceleration of domestic technol gy of developing countries and the p ening of opportunities to personnel from developing countries for training in marine science and techno ogy and their full participation in activi ties n the Area.	*Paragraph 1(b): Delete the first clause of the sentence and begin the sentence "The opening of . . ."*	(b The opening of opportunities to personnel from developing countries for training in marine science and techno ogy and their 6l participation in activities n the Area.

Article 2

| S NGLE NEGOTIAT NG TEXT | AMENDMENT | ART CLE 2 AS AMENDED |

Protect on Of The Mar ne Environment

Artic e 2

Protect on Of The Mar ne Environment

Article 2

W th respect to activities in the Area, appropriate measures shall be taken for the adoption and implementation of internationa rules, standards and procedures for, inter alia:

(a) The prevention of pollution and contaminat on, and other hazards to the marine environment, including the coastline, and of interference with the l gical balance of the marine environment, particular attention being paid to the n d for protection from the consequences of su b activities as drilling, dredging, excavation, disposal of was te construction and operation or maintenance of installations, pipelines and other devices related to su ch activities;

(b The protection and conservat on of the natura resources of the Area and the prevention of damage to the flora and fauna of the mar ne environment.

After the word "taken in the chapeau, insert "in accordance with article 28(xi) of this Part and paragraph 12 of Annex 1."

Article 12

With respect to activities n the Area, appropriate measures shall be taken in accordance with Ar i le 28(xi) of this Part and par graph 12 of Annex 1 for the adoption and implemen tion of international ru es, stardards and procedures for,
inter alia:

(a) The prevention of pollution and contamination, and other hazards to the marine environment, including the coastline, and of interference with the ecological balance of the marine environment, particular attention being paid to the n d for protection from the consequences of su ch activities as drilling, dredging, excavation, disposal of waste, construction and operation or maintenance of installations, pipelines and other d vic e related to su ch activities;

(b) The protection and conservation of the natural r sources of the Area and the prevention of damage to the flora and fauna of the marine environment.

S NGLE NEGOT AT NG TEXT

Protect.on Of Human L fe

Article '3

With respect to activ ties In the Area, the Authority and States shall take appropriate measures for the adoption and implementat on of international rules, standards and proc dur e for the protection of human life to suppl ement exis Img International and any specific treaties wh ch may be applicab e.

AMENDMENT

Article 13

After the word "procedures" insert "in accordance with Article 28(xi) of this Part and paragraph 12 of Annex I."

After the word "supplement" delete al after and substitute "applicab e international law."

ART CLE 13 AS AMENDED

Protect on Of Human L fe

Article '3

With respect to activitei s n the Area, the Authority and States shall take appropriate measures for the adoption and implementation of internationa rules, standards and procedures in accordance with Article 28(xi) of this P rt and paragraph 12 of Annex I for the protection of human life to supp ement applicable international law.

Article 3

SINGLE NEGOTIATING TEXT	AMENDMENT	ARTICLE 4 AS AMENDED
Rights Of Coastal States		Rights Of Coastal States
Article 14	*Article 14*	Article 4

SINGLE NEGOTIATING TEXT

Rights Of Coastal States

Article 14

1. Activities in the Area, with respect to resources in the Area which lie across limits of national jurisdiction, shall be conducted with due regard to the rights and legitimate interests of any coastal State across whose jurisdiction such resources lie.

Consultations, including a system of prior notification, shall be maintained with the State concerned, with a view to avoiding infringement of such rights and interests.

2. Neither the provisions of this Convention nor any rights granted or exercised pursuant thereto shall affect the rights of coastal States to take such measures in accordance with applicable principles of international law as may be necessary to prevent, mitigate or eliminate grave and imminent danger to their coastlines or related interests from pollution or threat thereof or from other hazardous occurrences resulting from or caused by any activities in the Area.

AMENDMENT

Article 14

In the first reference to "resources" change "resources to the singular and insert thereafter the word "deposits".

ARTICLE 4 AS AMENDED

Rights Of Coastal States

Article 4

1. Activities in the Area, with respect to resource deposits in the Area which lie across limits of national jurisdiction, shall be conducted with due regard to the rights and legitimate interests of any coastal State across whose jurisdiction such resources lie.

Consultations, including a system of prior notification, shall be maintained with the State concerned, with a view to avoiding infringement of such rights and interests.

2. Neither the provisions of this Part nor any rights granted or exercised pursuant thereto shall affect the rights of coastal States to take such measures in accordance with applicable principles of international law as may be necessary to prevent, mitigate or eliminate grave and imminent danger to their coastlines or related interests from pollution or threat thereof or from other hazardous occurrences resulting from or caused by any activities in the Area.

SINGLE NEGOTIATING TEXT

Legal Status Of The Superjacen
Waters and Air Space

Article 15

Neither the provisions of this Convention nor any rights granted or exercised pursuant thereto shall affet the legal status of the waters superjacent to the Area or that of the air space above those waters.

AMENDMENT

Article 15

No amendment proposed.

ARTICLE 5 A AMENDED

S NGLE NEGOT AT NG TEXT	AMENDMENT	ART CLE 6 AS AMENDED

Accommodat on Of Activ t es In The Area And In The Marine Environment

Article 6

Accommodation of Activ ies In The Area And In The Marine Environment

Article 16

1. Activities n the Area sha l be carried ot with reasonable r gard for other activ ties n the marine environment.

2. Stationary and mobile nsta lations relating to the conduct of activit es In the Area shall be subject to the fo lowing conditions:

(i) Such instal ations shall be erected, emplaced and removed solely in accordance with the provisi **ne** of this Convention and subject to rules and regulations prescr bed by the Authority. The erection, emplacement and r m vab of such instal- lations shall be the subject of timely notifi tion through **ttices** to Mariners or other generally recognized means of notification;

(ii) Such installations shall not be ocated in the Area wh re they may obstruct passage through sea lanes of vital importance for international shipping or in ar as of intense fishing activity;

(iii) Safety zones shall be established around such installations with appropriate markings to ensure the safety be h of the installations themselves and of shipping. The configuration and location of such safety zones shall not be su b as to form a belt impeding the lawful access of shipping to particular maritime zones or navigation al ng internat onal sea lanes;

Article 16

Paragraph 2 (i): Delete "prescribed" and substitute "applied."

. Act vities in the Area shall be carried out with reasonab e regard for other activities in the marine environment.

2. Stationary and mobile installations relating to the conduct of activities in the Area shall be subject to the foll wing conditions:

(i) Su b installations shall be erected, emplaced and removed solely in accordance with the provisions of this Convention and subject to ru es and regulations applied by the Authority. The erection, emplacement and r m v b of such installations shall be the subject of timely notification through Notices to Marin re or other generally recognized means of notification;

(ii Su b installations shall not be located in the Area where they may obstruct passage through sea lanes of vital importance for international shipping or in areas of intense fishing activ ty;

(iii Safety zones shall be established around such installations with appropriate markings to ensure the safety both of the installations themselves and of shipping. The configuration and lo ation of su h safety z n e shall not be such as to form a belt impeding the lawful access of shipping to particu ar maritime zones or navigation a ong nternationa sea anes;

SINGLE NEGOTIATING TEXT

(iv) Such installations shall be used exclusively for peaceful purposes;

(v) Such installations shall not possess the status of islands. They shall have no territorial sea, nor shall their presence affect the determination of territorial or jurisdictional limits of any kind.

3. Other activities in the marine environment shall be conducted with reasonable regard for activities in the Area.

Article 6
Para 2. (iv
Continued)
ARTICLE 6 AS AMENDED

AMENDMENT

(iv) Such installations shall be used exclusively for peaceful purposes;

(v) Such installations shall not possess the status of islands. They shall have no territorial sea, nor shall their presence affect the determination of territorial or jurisdiction on a limits of any kind.

3. Other activities in the marine environment shall be conducted with reasonable regard for activities in the Area.

Article 7

SINGLE NEGOTIATING TEXT	AMENDMENT	ARTICLE 7 AS AMENDED
Responsibility To Ensure Compliance And Liability For Damage		Responsibility To Ensure Compliance And Liability For Damage
Article 7	Article 17	Article 17

Paragraph 1: Insert the word "Parties" between the words "States" and "shall" in the first line. In the second sentence, delete "and their members" and "or on their behalf." In the third sentence, put a full stop after "liability" and delete all after.

1. Every State shall have the responsibility to ensure that activities in the Area, whether undertaken by governmental agencies, or non-governmental entities or persons under its jurisdiction, or acting on its behalf, shall be carried out in conformity with the provisions of this Convention. The same responsibility applies to international organizations and their members for activities in the Area undertaken by such organizations or on their behalf. Damage caused by such activities shall entail liability on the part of the State or international organization concerned, in respect of activities which it undertakes itself or authorizes.

2. A group of States or a group of international organizations, acting together shall be jointly and severally responsible under these articles.

3. Every State shall take appropriate measures to ensure that the responsibility provided for in paragraph 1 of this article shall apply mutatis mutandis to international organizations of which it is a member.

1. States Parties shall have the responsibility to ensure that activities in the Area, whether undertaken by governmental agencies, or non-governmental entities or persons under its jurisdiction, or acting on its behalf, shall be carried out in conformity with the provisions of this Part. The same responsibility applies to international organizations for activities in the Area undertaken by such organizations. Damage caused by such activities shall entail liability.

2. A group of States Parties or a group of international organizations, acting together shall be jointly and severally responsible under these articles.

3. States Parties shall take appropriate measures to ensure that the responsibility provided for in paragraph 1 of this article shall apply mutatis mutandis to international organizations.

S NGL NEGOT AT NG TEXT	AMENDMENT	ART CLE 8 AS AMENDED
		Article 8

Participation of Developing Countries, Including Land-locked And Other Geographically Disadvantaged States

Partic pation of D velop ng Countries, Inc udinq Land-locked And Other Geographically Disadvantaged States

Article 18

Article 8

Article 18

Delete and substitute text at right.

Participation in the ctɑvities in the Area of developing countries, ɪnc uding the and- ocked and other geographical y d sadvantaged States among them shall be promoted, hav ng due regard to their specia needs and nterests.

The fact that a country is land-locked or geo-graphically disadvantaged shall not constitute an obstacle to its participat on in activities of exploration for, and explo tɑion of, the resources of the Area. Special c ne deration for land-locked or geographical y disadvantaged countries shall be in accordance with Article 23.

S NGLE NEGOT AT NG TEXT	AMENDMENT	ART CLE 9 AS AMENDED

Archaelog ca And Histor ca Ob cte

Article 9

Article 19

Delete.

1. All objects of an archaelogical and histor ca nature found in the Area shall be preserved or disposed of by the Authority for the b n fit of the international community as a whole, parti a regard being paid to the preferential rights of the State or country of origin, or the State of cultural origin, or the State of historical and archaelogical origin.

2. The recovery and disposal of wrecks and their contents more than 50 y rs old found in the Area shall be subject to regulation by the Authority without prejudice to the rights of the owner thereof.

3. Any dispute with regard to a preferential right und e paragraph 1 or a right of ownership under paragraph 2, shall, on the application of either party, be subject to the procedure for settlement of d sputes provided for in this Convent on.

SINGLE NEGOTIATING TEXT

PART III: THE INTERNATIONAL SEA-BED AUTHORITY

Establishment of The International
Sea-Bed Authority

Article 20

1. There is hereby established the International
Sea-bed Authority which shall function in accordance
with the provisions of this Convention.

2. All States Parties to this Convention are members
of the Authority.

3. The seat of the Authority shall be at Jamaica.

4. The Authority may establish such regional centres
or offices as it deems necessary for the performance
of its functions.

AMENDMENT

Title: Insert "Resource"
between "Sea-bed" and "Authority".

Article 20

Paragraph 1: Insert "Resource"
between "Seabed" and "Authority".

Paragraph 2: Insert "ipso facto"
before "members."

ARTICLE 20 AS AMENDED

PART III: THE INTERNATIONAL SEA-BED AUTHORITY

Establishment Of The International Sea-bed
Resource Authority

Article 20

1. There is hereby established the International
Sea-bed Resource Authority which shall function in
accordance with the provisions of this Part.

2. All States Parties to this Convention are ipso facto
members of the Authority.

The seat of the Authority shall be at Jamaica.

4. The Authority may establish such regional centres or
offices as it deems necessary for the performance of
its functions.

SINGLE NEGOTIATING TEXT

Nature And Fundamental Principles
Of The Functioning Of The Authority

Article 2

1. The Authority is the organisation through which States Parties shall administer the Area, manage its resources and control the activities of the area in accordance with the provisions of this Convention.

2. The Authority is based on the principle of the sovereign equality of all of its Members.

3. All Members, in order to ensure to all of them the rights and benefits resulting from membership, shall fulfill in good faith the obligations assumed by them in accordance with this Convention.

AMENDMENT

Article 21

Paragraph 1: *Delete and substitute text at right.*

ARTICLE 2 AS AMENDED

Nature And Fundamental Principles
Of The Functioning Of The Authority

Article 2

1. The purpose of the Authority is to promote exploration for, and exploitation of the resources of the Area. The Authority shall to that end supervise activities in the Area in accordance with the provisions of this Part.

2. The Authority is based on the principle of the sovereign equality of all of its Members.

3. All Members, in order to ensure to all of them the rights and benefits resulting from membership, shall fulfilling good faith the obligations assumed by them in accordance with this Convention.

SINGLE NEGOTIATING TEXT	AMENDMENT	ARTICLE 22 AS AMENDED
Functions Of The Authority		Functions Of The Authority
Article 22	Article 22	Article 22

SINGLE NEGOTIATING TEXT

Activities in the Area shall be conducted direct y by the Authority.

2. Th Author ty may, if it c ne d re it appropriate, and within the limits it may determine, carry out activities in the Area or any stage thereof through States Parties to this C nv ne ion, or State enterpr es, or persons natur a or juridica which possess the nationality of such States or are effectively controlled by them or their nationals, or any group of the foregoing, by nt eing to service contracts, or jo nt ventures or any other ah form of association which ensures this direct and effective control at all times over such activities.

3. Notwithstanding the provisions of paragraphs (1) and (2) of this article and in rd e to promote earliest possible commencement of activ ties in the area, the Authority, thr ugh the Counci shall:

(i) dentify as early as practicab e after coming into force of this Convention ten economically viable mining sites in the Area for exploration and exploitation of no more than ...(size, etc.)

(ii) nt e into oint ventures in respect of these sites with States Parties to this Convention or State-enterprises or persons natural and juridical which possess the nationa ity of such States or are effectively ao led by them or their

AMENDMENT

Delete and substitute text at right.

ARTICLE 22 AS AMENDED

. Activities in the Area shall be conducted direct y by the Authority in accordance with Annex I and the rules, regulations and procedures adopted by the Authority under Article 28(xi) through the Enterprise estab ished pursuant to Article 35 by means of entering into contracts with the Authority.

2. Activities in the Area shall a so be conducted directly by States Parties, or State enterprises, or persons n tur a or juridica which possess the nationality of States Parties, or are ff ectively controlled by them or their nationals, when sponsored by such States, or any group of the foregoing, in accordance with Annex I and the rules, regulations and procedures adopted by the Author ity und e Article 28(xi), by means of entering to contracts with the Author ity.

3. All contracts entered into by the Authority pursuant to paragraphs and 2 of this article for activities in the Area shall ensure effective fisca and administrative supervision over such activities and shall be dr wn in accordance with Annex I. State Parties sponsoring persons natural or juridical und e paragraph 2 of this article shall be responsible for taking all appropriate measures to ensure that su b persons comply with the pvisions of this Part, Annex I, and the rules, r gelations and procedures adopted by the Author' ty und e Article 28(xi).

Article 22
Para 4,
(Continued)

SINGLE NEGOTIATING TEXT

nationals or any group of the foregoing. Such joint ventures shall be subject to the conditions of exploration and exploitation established by and under this Convention and shall always ensure the direct and effective control of the Authority at all times.

4. In entering into such joint ventures as provided for in para 3(ii) of this article, the Authority may decide on the basis of available data to reserve certain portions of the mining sites for its own further exploitation

AMENDMENT

ARTICLE 22 AS AMENDED

* (a) In order to promote the earliest possible commencement of activities in the Area and to safeguard the interests of entities who have made substantial investments in respect of such activities, the Authority shall enter into contracts for the conduct of activities in the Area with all qualified applicants, pursuant to paragraph 2 of this article, who give substantial evidence of prior work and investments made for the purpose of bringing parts of the Area into commercial production.

(b) The number of sites, the size of sites and the duration of the rights granted shall be sufficient to fully achieve the purpose of subparagraph (a) of this paragraph and paragraph 12 subparagraphs (14) and (15) of Annex I.

(c) Contracts entered into by the Authority under this paragraph shall be drawn with a view toward protecting prior investments. Any ambiguities in Annex I shall be resolved in favor of an applicant for a contract where necessary to achieve the purposes of this paragraph.

(d) Subsequent rules, regulations and procedures adopted by the Authority under Article 28 (xi) shall be applied to contracts entered into under this paragraph only to the extent they are consistent with the purposes of this paragraph and do not have the effect of a substantial impairment of investments made prior to or under such contracts.

---

* This amendment is included in Article 22 for convenience of reference. In the final drafting of the Convention, it may be desirable to place this amendment in another part of Part I or in Annex

SINGLE NEGOTIATING TEXT

AMENDMENT

Article 22
Para 4(e)
(Continued)

ARTICLE 22 AS AMENDED

(e) The Authority shall establish procedures for the award of contracts under this paragraph. Such procedures shall allow applicants for contracts not less than three months or more than one year to present the evidence called for in subparagraph (a) of this paragraph from the time this Convention enters into force on a provisional basis or permanently, whichever occurs first. Applications for contracts under this paragraph shall be approved and the contract awarded within 60 days of the submission of such evidence.

Article 23

S NGLE NEGOT AT NG TEXT

Article 23

1. In the exercise of its functions the Authority shall take measures pursuant to this Convention to promote and encourage activities in the Area and to secure the maximum financial and other benefit from them.

2. The Aority shall avoid discrimination n the granting of opportunities or such activities and shall, in the implementation of its powers, ensure that all rights granted pursuant to this Convention are fully safeguarded. Sp eiaᵀ c nsideration by the Authority under this Co v tion or the interests and needs of the developing countries, and particularly the land-locked among them, shall not be deemed to be discrimination.

3. Th Authority shall ensure the equitable sharing by States in the benefits derived from activities n the Area, taking into particular consideration the interests and needs of the d veloping countries whether coastal or land-locked.

AMENDMENT

Article 23

Delete and substitute the text a
 b.

ART CLE 2 AS AMENDED

Article 2

1. In the exercise o its functions, the Authority shall take measures pursuant to this Part to promote and encourage activities in the Area.

2. The Arity shall avoid discrimina ion in the granting of opportunities or such activ ties and in the exercise of ts powers and functions. No right granted pursuant to this Part shall be impaired by the Authori y and all such rights shall be fully safeguarded.

3. Special consideration by the Authority pursuant to Articles 10, 11, and 26, paragraph 2 (x), or the interests and ne ds of the developing coun ries, particularly the land- ocked and geographi ally dis-advantaged among them, shall not be deemed to be discrimination.

Artic e 24

S NGLE NEGOTIATING TEXT

AMENDMENT

ART CLE 24 AS AMENDED

Organs Of The Author ty

Article 24

Organs Of The Authority

Article 24

1. There are stab ished as the principa organs of the Authority an Assemb y, a Council, a Tribuna , an Enterprise and a Secretariat.

2 Such subsidiary orgáns as may be found necessary may be established n accordance with this Convention.

Article 24

Paragraph 1: Delete an Enterprise."

Add a new paragraph 3 as shown at right.

1. There are established as the principa organs of the Authority e Assembly, a Council, a Tribunal and a Secretariat.

2. Su b subsidiary organs as may be found necessar may be established in accordance w th this Part.

3. The principa organs shall ea e be responsib e for exercising those powers and fu ctions which have b een provided to them and shall avoid taking any actions which may impede the exercise of specific powers and functions entrusted to another organ.

Article 25

S NGLE NEGOT AT NG TEXT	AMENDMENT	ART CLE 25 AS AMENDED

The Assemb y

Art cle 2

Article 25

The Assemb y

Article 25

1. The Assembl y shall consist of all the Members of the Authority.

2. he Assembly shal et in regu ar session every two years and in such sp cial sessions as may be determined by he Assembly, or convened by the Secretary General at the request of the Council or of a majority of the Members of the Authority.

3. S sions sha l take place at the se t of the Authority un ess otherwise determined by the Assemb y. At such sess ons e e member shal have one represen-tative ho may be accompanied by a ternates and advisers.

4. The Assemb y shall elect ts President and su e other officers as may be required at the beginning of a b session. They shall hold office ntil the new President and other officers are elected at the next following session.

5. Ea h Member of the Assemb y shall have one vote.

6. All decisions on questions of substance and the question whether a question is one of substance or procedure, shall be mado by a wo-thirds majority of the Members present and voting, provided that such majority shall include at l ast a majority of the Members of the Authority. De isions on other questions sha l be mad by a majority of the Members present and et ng.

Paragraph 1: Add "(i) after 1. and new subparagraphs ii and (iii) as shown in text at righ

Paragraph 6: Delete all after "include" and substitute:

"a simple majority of four of the few categories specified in paragraph 1 of this Article. Before a matter of substance is put to the vote, a determination

. (i) The Assembly shall cons st of all the Members of the Authority.

(ii) The Asse b y shal be divi dd into the fol owing categor es: (industrialized countr es with substantial nvestments or advanced technology in relation to he resources of he Area; (b) pri cip l producers of minerals originating in heir territories which are also derived from the Area; (c) principal consumers of minerals derived from the Area; (d) countries ho are land-locked or geographically disadvantaged; (e) any other State Party not falling within n one of he foregoing categories.

(iii) In the event a State Party qua ifies for more than one category it shall e ect one of the categories. Such a State Party may, however, participate in the deliberations without vote in all categories for which it is qualified when be question relat s to the election of the Council

2. The Assembly shall meet in regular session every two years and in su h special sessions as may be determined by the Assembly, or convened by he Secretary General at the request of he Council or of a majority of he Members of the Authority.

3. Sessions shall take p ace at the seat of the Authority un ess otherwise determined by the Assemb y. At su sess ons, a member shall have one representa-tive who may be accompanied by a ternates and advisers.

Artic e 25
Para. 4
Cont nued

S NGLE NEGOT AT NG TEXT	AMENDMENT	ART CLE 25 AS AMENDED

S NGLE NEGOT AT NG TEXT

7. A major ty of the Members of he Assemb y shall const tute a quorum.

8. Upon a written request to he President supported by not less than one-third of the Members of he Assembly, a vote on any matter before he Assembly shall be deferred pending reference to the Tribunal for an Advisory Opi i on or any legal question connected therewith. Voting on such matter shall be stayed p di g delivery of the Tribunal's Advisory Opi i on or for a period of six months from he receipt of the request, wh chever is ear ier.

AMENDMENT

that all efforts he be m made to reach general agreement shall be made by the same majorities Decisions on other questions sha l be made by a majority of the Members present and ng.

Paragraph 8: Delete "on e ird" an substitute "one-fourth" and de n" before "request. Delete nt of oe after "Opinion" on line 7.

ART CLE 25 AS AMENDED

4. The Assemb y shall e ect its Pres dent and such other off cers as may be required at he beginning of each s ss on. They shall ho d off ce unti l he new President and other officers are e ected at he next following session.

Ea h Member of the Assemb y shall have one vote.

6. A l decisions on questions of substance and the quest on whether a questi n is one of substance or procedure, shall be made by a e-thirds majority of he Members present and eting, provided that such maj rity shall include a simple majority of four of he fivo categories specified in paragraph l of this Article. Before a matter of substance is put to he vote, a determination that all efforts have been made to reach g neral agreement shall be made by he same majorities. Decisio s on orthe qu stions sha l be made by a maj ity of he M mbers present and eting.

7. A majo ity of he Members of the Assemb y shall constitute a quorum.

8. Upon a request to he Pres dent supported by not less than one-fourth of the Members of the Assemb y, a vote on ny matter before the Asse bly shall be deferred pending reference to the Tribunal for an Advisory Opinion on any legal question connected there-wi h. Voting on such matter shall be stayed pe ding delivery of he Tribuna 's Advisory Opinion.

SINGLE NEGOTIATING TEXT

Powers And Functions of the Assembly

Article 26

1. The Assembly shall be the supreme policy-making organ of the Authority. It shall have the power to lay down general guidelines and issue directions of a general character as to the policy to be pursued by the Council or other organs of the Authority on any questions or matters within the scope of this Convention. It may also discuss any questions or any matters within the scope of this Convention and make recommendations thereon.

2. In addition, the powers and functions of the Assembly shall include:

(i) Election of the members of the Council in accordance with article 27;

(ii) Appointment upon the recommendation of the Council, of the members of the Tribunal and of the Governing Board of the Enterprise;

(iii) Establishment, as appropriate, of such subsidiary organs as may be found necessary for the performance of its functions in accordance with the provisions of this Convention;

(iv) Assessment of the contributions of Parties to this Convention as necessary for meeting the administrative budget of the Authority;

(v) Adoption of the financial regulations of the Authority, including rules on borrowing;

AMENDMENT

Article 26

Paragraph 1: Delete "policy-making" and add "plenary."

Paragraph 2 chapeau: Delete the words "in addition" and delete the word "be" for "include."

Paragraph 2 (iii): Add "on the basis of economy and efficiency" after the word "appropriate"; delete "Convention" and substitute "Part"; add a new sentence as follows:

"In the composition of such subsidiary organs due account shall be taken of the principle of equitable geographical distribution and special interest groups in accordance with Article 25, paragraph 1, and the need for members highly qualified and competent in the relevant technical matters dealt with by such organs."

Paragraph 2 (iv): Delete and substitute at at followed by:

ARTICLE 26 AS AMENDED

Powers And Functions of the Assembly

Article 26

The Assembly shall be plenary organ of the Authority.

The powers and functions of the Assembly shall be:

(i) Election of the members of the Council in accordance with Article 27;

(ii) Appointment on the recommendation of the Council, of the members of the Tribunal and of the Governing Board of the Enterprise;

(iii) Establishment, as appropriate, on the basis of economy and efficiency of such subsidiary organs as may be found necessary for the performance of its functions in accordance with the provisions of this Part. In the composition of such subsidiary organs due account shall be taken of the principle of equitable geographical distribution and special interest groups in accordance with Article 25(1) and the need for members highly qualified and competent in the relevant technical matters dealt with by such organs;

(iv) Assessment of the contributions of States Parties to the administrative Budget of the Authority in accordance with the general scale used by the United Nations until the Authority shall have sufficient income for meeting its administrative expenses;

SINGLE NEGOTIATING TEXT	AMENDMENT	ARTICLE 26 AS AMENDED
(vi) Approval of the budget of the Authority on its submission by the Council	*Paragraph 2 (v): Delete the comma and the following phrase: "including rules on borrowing" and substitute: "upon the recommendation of the Council."*	(v) Adoption of the financial regulations of the Authority upon the recommendation of the Council;
(vii) Adoption of its rules of procedure;		(vi) Approval of the budget of the Authority on its submission by the Council;
(viii) Request and consideration of special reports from the Council and from the other organs of the Authority on any matter within the scope of this Convention;	*Paragraph 2 (x): Delete "criteria, and the semicolon and add "in accordance with the criteria set forth in Annex ___ to this Part." Insert "by States Parties" before "of benefits" and "activities" before "the Area" and delete "and its resources." Delete "benefits" and insert "revenues".*	(vii) Adoption of its rules of procedure;
(ix) Studies and recommendations for the purpose of promoting international cooperation concerning activities in the Area and encouraging the progress development of international law relating thereto and its codification;		(viii) Request and consideration of special reports from the Council and from the other organs of the Authority on any matter within the scope of this Part;
(x) Adoption of criteria, rules, regulations and procedures for the equitable sharing of benefits derived from the Area and its resources, taking into special account the interests and needs of the developing countries, whether coastal or land-locked;	*Paragraph 2 (xi): Delete and substitute text at right.*	(ix) Studies and recommendations for the purpose of promoting international cooperation concerning activities in the Area and encouraging the progressive development of international law relating thereto and its codification;
(xi) Consideration of problems arising from States in connexion with activities in the Area, from the land-locked or otherwise geographically disadvantaged location of some of them and recommending basic guidelines for appropriate action.	*Paragraph 3: Delete.*	(x) Adoption of rules, regulations and procedures for the equitable sharing by States Parties of revenues derived from activities in the Area, taking into special account the interests and needs of the developing countries, whether coastal or land-locked in accordance with the criteria set forth in Annex ___ to this Part.
3. The powers and functions of the Authority not specifically entrusted to the organs of the Authority shall be vested in the Assembly.		(xi) Consideration of problems of a general nature arising for States in connection with activities in the Area resulting from their situation as land-locked or geographically disadvantaged States, and to make appropriate recommendations.

SINGLE NEGOTIATING TEXT	AMENDMENT	ARTICLE 27 AS AMENDED
The Council		The Council
Article 27	*Article 27*	Article 27

SINGLE NEGOTIATING TEXT

The Council

Article 27

1. The Council shall consist of 36 Members of the Authority elected by the Assembly; 24 to be elected in accordance with the principle of equitable geographical representation and 12 with a view to representation of specific interests, taking into account the principle of equitable geographical representation, the election to take place in the following order:

(a) Six ... with ... initial investment in, or pasing advanced technology which is being ... ed ..., be exploration of ... and be exploitation of ts ... ed minerals which ae major ... of ... , pvi dd only ... at be fi st election at ... ce of be six ... shall be ... be Eastern (Sociali s) European regi a.

(b) Six Members from among the developing countries oe being drawn ... eh of the following categories:

(i) ... ts which are exporters of landbased minerals which may also be ... pd ... the ... es of ... la;

(ii) States wh b ee importers of the mnerais referred to in subparagraph (i);

(iii) States with arge populations

'iv' ... N-ocked St ees;

AMENDMENT

Article 27

Delete and substitute the text at right.

ARTICLE 27 AS AMENDED

The Council

Article 27

The Council shall consist of 36 Members of the Authority elected by the Assembly, be election to take place in the following ode n:

(a) The six ... at in drali ed ... eries which have ... be ... ding and exploration of be ... and be exploi ation of its ... as ... de ed by ... tial investments or advanced technology n relation to be ... es of be ..., pvi dd ... at ... ce of be members shall be ... be Easte n (social ist) European egion;

(b) Six ... ts ... em eg be developing countries two being ... n from ... eh of be following categories: States with large populati e, land-locked States and geographi ally disadvantaged States, and the l ast developed ... eries;

(c) Six ... ts ... em eg the States ... wh are principa ... s of minerals originating in their territori es which ae also drived from the Area;

(d) Six Members ... em a ... eg the States which are principa consumers of minerals de ved from the Area

(e) Twelve Members with due regard to equitable representation on be Council as a whole of the geographic egi as specified bl e, so that the dcil shall at all ti es i olude in this teg or at l et wo ... em eh of be Areas: Africa, Asia, atin Ameri a, Eastern Europe (Socialist), Western Europe ad e.

Article 27
& 2
... ed

AMENDMENT

ARTICLE 27 AS AMENDED

SINGLE NEGOTIATING TEXT

(v   Geographically d sadvantaged   ...

vi   ... bt developed countries.

d) Twenty-four   ...ts in   ...de with ...e principle of equitable g ographicab ...ation. ...r this   ..., ...e geographical regions ...ll be Africa, Asia, ...a, ...a, (Socialist), Latin America ...ad   ...n ...e ...ad others".

2. Elections shall ...be place at ...gu ar sessions of ...e Assembly, ...ad ...eh ...ar of ...e Council shall be elected ...r a ...em of 4 ...r. ...n ...e first election of ...ts of ...e Council, however, eighteen ...ts ...ba l be ...en ...r a period of ...o ...r.

3. ...ts ...ba i be eligible ...r re-election; ...bt ...de regard ...bu d, as a rule, be paid to ...e desirability of rotating ...

4. ...e Council shall function at ...e ...et of ...e Authority, ...ad shail ...et as ...n as ...e business of ...e Authority may require, ...bt ...ot ...es ...n ...e ti es a ...r.

5. Each ...r of ...e ...Ci ...ball have ...e ...e.

6. Decisi ...os on i ...et ...ti os shall be ...de by ...two-th rd plus ...e majority of ...e ...ts ...pt ...ed voting The ...de cision on an i ...ee as to ...r or ...ot a ...r ...is an ...t ...ation shall be taken by a ...two-th ...ds majority. Decisions on ...r questions shall be dc ...dd by a majority of ...e ...ts ...pt ...ad voting.

7. ...e ...Ci l ...ball ...ab ...sh a ...de ...ty ...a ...em br of ...e ...Ci l ...ny ...ed a ...tive to ...ed a meeting ...of ...e ...Ci l ...n a ...t is ...de by ...eh ...th, or a ...r ...ticularly ...ting it is ...r ...osi ...ti a. ...on ...ti a. ...6h a ...ative shall be ...titl ed to participate in ...e deliberations ...bt ...ot to ...e.

2. Elections ...ba l ...be p ...ce at regu ar ...es ...os of ...e Assembly, ...ad ...eh ...ar of ...e ...6c l shall be elected ...r a ...em of 4 ...r. ...n ...e first e ection of ...ts of ...e Council, however, eighteen ...ts ...ball be ...en ...r a period of ...o ...r.

3.   ...ts ...ball be e ...gible ...r reelection.

4. ...e Council ...bl function at ...e ...et of ...e Authority, ...ad ...ba l ...et as ...n as ...e business of ...e Authority ...ay ...qu ...e, ...bt ...ot ...ds ...n ...e times a ...r.

5. Each ...r of ...e ...6i ...ball have ...e ...e.

6. A l dcisi ...os on ...ti os of ...e ...r ...de ...ad on ...br a ...tion is ...e of ...e or ...de ...ball be ...de by a three-fourths ...rity of ...e ...ts ...pt ...ad ...ti g, ...pvi dd ...ht ...eh majority ...l ...ds a simple majority of at l ...et ...be of ...e ...r ...ds specified in ...in l of this article.   ...de a ...r of ...e ...is ...pt to ...be ...e, a ...mination ...bt all efforts have ...n ...de to ...br a ...gt shall be ...de by ...be ...ae majoriti ...e. Bcisions on ...r ...ti os ...n ...be by a majority of ...e ...ts ...pt ...ad ...ti g.

7. ...e ...6cil ...all ...blish a ...de ...rity ...at ... de ...ad on ...e ...6ci ...ay ...ed a ...tive to ...ed a ...eting on ...e ...6ci ...l ...n a ...r ...it is ...de by ...eh Member, or a ...r ...ticularly ...ting it is ...r ...osi ...ti o. Such a representative ...bll be ...titled to ...ptici ...pe in ...be deliberati ...os ...bt ...ot to ...e.

S NGLE NEGOT AT NG TEXT	AMENDMENT	ART CL 28 AS AMENDED
Powers And Functions Of The Council		Powers And Functions Of The Counc
Article 28	*Article 28*	Article 28
The Council shal be the executive rg a of the Authority. It shall exercise the powers and perform the functions entrusted to it by this Convention. In exercising su b powers and performing su b functions the Council shall act in a manner consistent with general guidelines and policy directions laid down by the Assembly.	*Article 28, chapeau: Delete the second and third sentences.*	The Counc shall be the executive organ of the Authority.
The Council shall:		ⓐ Counci shall:
(i) Sup **wise** and coordinate the implementation of the provisions of this Convention and, whenever it d eme appropriate, invite the attention of the Assemb y to cases of non-compliance;	*Paragraph (i): Delete the semicolon and add "after appropriate action by the Tribuna*[*]*"*	(i) Supervise and coordinate the mp ementation of the provisions of this Part and, whenever it d eme appropriate, invite the attention of the Assemb y to cases of non-comp iance after appropriate a ti ⓐ by the Tribunal;
(ii) Recommend to the Assemb y candidates for appointment to the Tribuna and to the Governing Board of the Enterprise;		(ii) Recommend to the Assemb y candidates for appointm ⓐ to the Tribunal and to ⓑe Governing Board of the Enterprise;
(iii) Estab ish, as appropriate and with due regard to economy and efficiency, in addition to the ⓐmissi ⓐ provided for n article 29, su ch subsidiary organs as may be f u d necessary for the performance of its functions in accordance with the provisions of this Convention. In the composi- tion of su ch subsidiary organs due regard shall be paid not only to the need for Members highly qualified and competent in the relevant technical matters which may arise in such organs but also to specia interests and the principle of equitable geographical distribution;	*Paragraph (iii): Delete and substitute text at right.*	(iii) Establish, as appropriate, and on the basis of om and eff ciency, in addition to the Commissions provided for in Article 29(l), such subsidiary or gans as may be f und necessary for the performance of its fu ctions in accordance with the provisions of this Part. In the composition of su ⓑ subsidiary organs, primary emphasis shall be placed on the need for members hi hly qua ified and competent in the relevant t ⓐnical matters dealt with by su ⓑ organs and, having due regard for the principle of equitable geographical dis- tribution and sp ⓐia interest groups in accordance with Article 27(l);
		iv Adopts ts rules of procedure

SINGLE NEGOTIATING TEXT

iv Adopts its rules of procedure;

(v) Enter into agreements with the United Nations or other inter-governmental organisations on behalf of the Authority, subject to approval by the Assembly;

(vi) Transmit annually to the Assembly a schedule for apportionment of benefits derived from activities in the Area on the basis of criteria and rules adopted by the Assembly pursuant to sub-paragraph 2(x) of Article 26;

(vii) Transmit to the Assembly the reports of the Enterprise;

(viii) Transmit to the Assembly annual reports and such special reports as the Assembly may request;

(ix) Approve and supervise the carrying out of activities in the Area by the Enterprise;

(x) Approve on behalf of the Authority contracts for the conduct of activities in the Area and exercise direct and effective control over the activities in the Area;

(xii) Act upon the recommendation of the Economic Planning Commission programmes or measures to avoid or minimize adverse effects on the revenues of developing countries derived from the export of minerals and other products originating in their territories which are also derived from the resources of the Area. The Council shall ensure that developing countries importers of minerals or other products derived from the resources of the Area shall be given preferential access or favourable terms to such minerals and products

AMENDMENT

Paragraph (vi): Delete "criteria and " Insert "and regulations" after "rules" and "among States Parties" before "derived." Subparagraph "1(x)" should read "2(x)." Delete the semicolon and add "and Annex ___ to this Part;" Delete "benefits" and insert "revenues."

Paragraph (vii): Delete the semicolon and add "with its recommendations;"

Paragraph (ix): Delete.

Paragraph (x): Delete direct and before "effective"

ARTICLE 28 AS AMENDED

(v) Enter into agreements with the United Nations or other inter-governmental organisations on behalf of the Authority, subject to approval by the Assembly;

(vi) Transmit annually to the Assembly a schedule for apportionment of revenues among States Parties derived from Activities in the Area on the basis of rules and regulations adopted by the Assembly pursuant to sub-paragraph 2(x) of Article 26 and Annex ___ to this Partie;

(vii) Transmit to the Assembly the reports of the Enterprise with its recommendations;

(viii) Transmit to the Assembly annual reports and such special reports as the Assembly may request;

(ix) Approve on behalf of the Authority contracts proposed by the Technical Commission pursuant to paragraphs 1 and 2 of Article 22 for the conduct of activities in the Area and exercise effective fiscal and administrative supervision over the activities in the Area;

(x Receive reports from the Economic Planning Commission and make recommendations to States thereon;

(xi) Establish and administer a system for the adoption and application of rules, regulations and procedures recommended by the Rules and Regulations Commission and any amendments thereto. Rules, regulations and procedures shall be restricted to the subjects specifically provided for in the Basic Conditions set forth in Annex I to this Part. Upon their approval by the Council, they shall be submitted directly to all States Parties to this

Artic e 28
& (xii)
(Continued)

S NGLE NEGOT AT NG TEXT

(xii)   A, un be recommendation of   be   In cal
6mis ion, ru.ss, regulations and   ds and
any amendments t   bo concerning:

(a)   tcal,   pt el and financial   as
relating to activities n be Aa in   de
wth be Basic conditions annexed to this Convention

b protection of   An life ad   ol b;

(c)   ction and preservation of be marine
environment;

(d) discovery, dentification, protection, acquisi-
on and disposa of   ts of archaeological and
historical   t found in be   A;

e) any   tr   es within be pe of be
ps ad functi os of be Council.

(xiii) Arrange or and review be co lection of ll
payments to be   te by or to be   ly in
connection wh operations pursuant to ts
Convention;

(xiv)   Me mendations to the A embly on
be   es specified in subparagraph 2(ii)
of Article 26 and Article 72, d,   tr within be
as   , on by   tr   6cil;
pe of be functi os of be

(xv)   Me   me ds to ts ts
be po icies and   es required to give
to be principles of this Convention;

(xvi) Make   ds to be Assemb y
concerning suspension of be privileges and ls
of membership or   gs and persistent vio ations
of be provisions of this Convention.

AMENDMENT

Paragraph (xii): Renumber   Me
as "(xi)"; delete and
ext at rig t.

Paragraph (xiii): Renumber
as . t)" and   de
"Arrange for and."

Paragraph (xiv): Delete.

Paragraph (xv): Renumber   ti

Paragraph (xvi):   tr tv
Delete the full   ep and dd tn
a finding by be   il and a re-
   d in   t de tn be
be 68."

New Paragraph (xv):   t at t.

AT CLE 28 AS AMENDED

Conventio.. Su.. . e, egulations and
pocedures sha!:   be effective 90 days
r submission, unless in be meantime ae
n one-third of be States   ts to this
Convention   r their disapproval wh be
Authority. This   ne   pd ll be suspended
in   t of any rule,   gl   n or   de
be validity of   th ts en challenged in
be Tribunal, pending a Tribunal   n on
be .

(x)   Review be co   n of a l payments
to be te by or to be Authority n connection
wi h operations   pt to this .

xiii) Make recommendations to States concern-
ng be policies ad   as required to give
t to be princip es of this Part;

(xiv)   Make   ations to be Assembly
ri ts of   psion of be privileges ad
violati os of be provisions of this   t
n a fi   dg by be Tribunal and a recom-
tion   t   psion be i   pd in
erdance with Article 68.

(xv)   Determine be policies of be Authority
with   pt to be ivities n be .

SINGLE NEGOTIATING TEXT

AMENDMENT

ARTICLE 29 AS AMENDED

Art 29

Rules Of The Council

Art 29

Art 29

Rules Of The Council

Art 29

Paragraph 1: Insert after "Economic Planning Commission" "a Rules and Regulations"

Paragraph 3: In the first sentence, ... "five of" before ... until the end of the ...

Artic e 29
Para. 5
(Continued

S NGLE EGOT AT NG TEXT

5. The C ouncil shal appoint to t e commission persons of high mo.. character wo may be roiled upon to exercise ind pendent judgment. The shcl serve in their individual apacity and shall serve su b regular remuneration from the Authority as the Cou w shall from time to time determine. Members of a commission sha l be eligible for re appointme n for one further term of office.

6. Each c mmission shall appo nt ts chairman and two vice-cnairmen who shall ho d office for one year.

7. The Council shall approve, on the recommendation of a commission, su ch rules and regulations as may be necessary for the efficie n conduct of the functions of the commission.

8. Decisions shall be mado by a two-thi ds majority of members of the Gmmission

9. Each commission shall function at the seat of the Authority and sha l m e as ft e as shall be required for the eff cient performance of its functions.

AME DMENT

Paragraph 5: insert "Except, as provided in Article 30: a the beginning of the paragraph

Paragraph 8: Delete and substitute text at right.

ART CLE 29 AS AMENDED

5. Ex ep as provided i n Article 30, the C un e sha app iot co a t commission persons of high moral characte w.v de. relied upon o exercise independent judgment. They sha l serve in their individual capacity and shall recive no instructions either from their government or from the Authority. Members of a commission shall ue eligible for re appointment fo one further term of fficeo

6. Each commission shall appo c its chairman and two vice-cnairmen wo shall noid office for one year.

7. The Council shall approve, on the recommendation of a commission, such rules and regulations as may be necessary for the efficient conduct of the runctions of the commission.

8. Except as prov ded n Artic e 30, decisions of the other mmissions shal be by a two-thirds majority.

9. Ea commission sha l function at the seat of the Authority and shall meet as fte as shall be required for the efficient performance of ts functions.

SI GLE NEGOT AT NG TEXT

@ Economic Planning Commission

Article 0

1. Members of the Economic Planning Commissin to shall have appropriate qualifications and experience relevant to mining and the ma agement of mi eral resource activities, and international tr de and finance.

2. The Economic Planning Commission, in consultation with the competent organs of the U it d Nations and the specialized agencies, shall review the trends of, and factors affecting, supply, demand and pric e of raw materials which may be obtained from the Area and, bearing in mind the interests of b to consuming and land-based mineral producing countries, and in particu ar the developing countries among them, make recommenda ti on to the Council on programmes and measures with respect to the implementation of Article 22 of this Convention and in particular:

(a) Schedules of the extent of the Area or the volume of its resources which ou d be made avai able for exploitation; and

(b Appropriate programmes or measures, inc ud ing integrated commodity arrangements and buffer stock arrangements to avoid or minimize adverse effects on developing countries whose economies substantially depend on the revenues d riv d from the export of minerals and t e raw mat rials originating in their territories wh e are also derived from the resources of the Area unde r exploitation taking into account all sources of these minerals and raw materials.

3. The Commission shall advise the Council in the exercise of the Council's economic planning functions and make su b spe a te studies and reports on these functions as may be required by the Council from time to time.

A E DMENT

ARTICLE 30 AS AMENDED

Article 30

Paragraph 1: Add the following:

"They shall be elected by the Council and shall represent their Governments. The Council shall, in electing the members of the Economic Planning Commission, ensure a fair and equitable balance of net export- ers of minerals and other raw mate- rials originating in their territories which are also derived from the resources of the Area, net importers of such minerals and other raw mate- rials and producers of such minerals and other raw materials from the Ar ea Each member shall have one vote and the three categories shall vote separately. Decisions of the Economic Planning Commission shall be taken by a majority in a cti of the three categories and a o- third majority of the Commission as a whole.

Paragraph 2: Place a full stop after the words "among them" and delete the bala ce of paragraph 2. Delete also the wor "and" between "from the Area" and "bearing in mind." Delete the word "both" and substitute "seabed producing."

Paragraph 3: Delete "advise the Council in the exercise of the Council's economic planning functions and". Als delete "on these functions"

---

he Economic Planning mi s on

rticle 30

1. Members of the economic Planning Commission shal have appropriate qualifications and experience relevant to mining and the management of mineral resource activities, and international trade and finance. They shall be elected by the Council and shall repre- sent th ie governments. The Council shall, in electing the members of the Economic Planning Commission, ensure a fair and equitable balance of net exporters of minerals and other raw materials originating in their territories which are also derived from the resources of the Area, net importers of such minerals and other raw materials from the Area. Ea e memb er shal have one vote and the three categories shall vote separately. Decisions of the Economic Planning Com- mission shall be taken by a majority in ea e of the three categories and a two-third majority of the Commission as a whole.

2. The Economic Planning omis ion, i nconsultation with the competent organs of the United Nations, and the special zed agencies, shall review the trends of, and factors affecting, supply, demand and prices of raw mat oria s which may be bt ained from the Area, bear- ing in mind the interests of seabed producing, consuming and land-based mineral producing countries, and in particular the developing countries among them.

3. Th C mm ssion shall make su b specia studies and reports as may be required by the Counc from time to time.

Article 30 continued

S NGLE NEGOT AT NG TEXT

4. Any State Party to this Convention whose economy substantially depends on the export of minerals and other products originating in its territory which are also derived from minerals under exploitation in the Area may bring to the attention of the Economic Planning Commission a situation which is likely to lead to a substantial declino in its m neral export earnings. The Commission shall forthwith investigate this situ tion and shall make recommendations, in consultation with parties to this Convention and with the competent inter-governmental organizations to the C uncil in accordance with paragraph 2 of this artic e.

AMENDMENT

Paragraph 4: Delete and subst tute the text at right.

ART CLE O AS AMENDED

4. Any State Pa ty or who export revenues from minerals or iginating in its territory which are also derived from exploitation of resources in the Area represent a substantial share of its gross domestic product and foreign exchange earnings may bring to the attention of the Economic Planning Commission a situation whi b, based on substantial evidence is directly attributable to activities in the Area and is likely to lead to a substantial declino n its mineral export earnings. e declino n its mineral export earnings. e mission shall forthwith i v stigate this situation in consultation with States Parties to this Con-v ti n and s alh submit its findings to the Council which may transmit them to interested States Parties and appropriate international bodies.

S NGLE NEGOT AT NG TEXT	AMENDMENT	ART CLE 3 AS AMENDED

The Techn ca. Comm s on

Article 31

1. Members of the Technical Commission shall have appropriate qualifications and experience in the management of sea-bed resources, ocean and marine engineering and mining and mineral processing technology and practices, operation of relat d marine installations, equipment and devices, ocean and environmental sciences and maritime safety, accounting and actuarial techniques.

2. ⑨ Technica Commission shall:

(i) Formulate and submit to the Council the techn cal and operationa ru es, regulations and procedures referred to in subparagraph (xi) of ⓐle 28.

(ii) Ke p such rules, regulations and procedures un d ev iew and recommend to the Council from time to time such amendments thereto as it may deem necessary ơ desirable;

(iii) Make recommendations to the Council with regard to the carrying out of the Authority's functions with respect to scientific research and transfer of technology;

(iv Prepare special studies and reports at the request of the Council;

(v Prepare assessments of the environmental implications of activities n the sea and consider and evaluate these implications before recommending the rules, r guⓑations and procedures referred to in sub-paragraph (i);

(vi) Supervise, ⓞ a regular basis, al operations with r spe ❦ to activities in the Area where appropriate in consu tation and collaboration with any entity carrying out such activities or State or States concerned;

Article 31

Paragraph 2: Delete (i (ii), and (vii). In (v) place a full stop after "Area" and delete all after. Renumber the remaining subparagraphs and add the following new subparagraphs:

" v) Initiate proceedings before the Tribunal in cases of failure to comply;

"(vi) Upon a finding by the Tribunal in accordance with subparagraph (v) above, notify the Council and make recommendations with respect to measures to be taken;

"(vii) Inspect and audit all books, records and accounts related to financial obligations to the Authority concerning activities in the Area and collect all payments to the Authority prescribed thereunder, and the terms and conditions of any contract with the Authority are being complied with;

The Technical Commission

Article 3

1. Members of the Technica Commission shal have appropriate qualifications and experience in the management of sea-bed resources, ocean and marine engineering and mining and mineral processing technology and practices, operation of relat d marine installations, equipment and devices, ocean and environmental sciences and maritime safety, accounting and actuarial techniques.

2. The Technica Commission shall:

(i) Make recommendations to the Council with regard to the carrying out of the Authority's functions with respect to scientific research and transfer of technology.

(ii` Prepare special studies and reports at the request of the Council;

(iii) Prepare assessments of the environmental implications of activities in the Area;

(iv) Supervise, on a regular basis, all operat ons with respect to activities In the Area, where appropriate in consultation and collaboration with any entity carrying out su ⑧ activities or State or States concerned;

(v) Initiate proceedings before the Tribuna in cases of failure to comply;

(vi) Upon a finding by the Tribunal n accordance with subparagraph (v) ab ❧e, notify the Council and make recommendations with respect to measures to be taken;

(vii) Inspect and audit all books, records and accounts related to financial obligations in the Area and collect all payments to the Authority prescribed in Annex I;

SINGLE NEGOTIATING TEXT	AMENDMENT	ARTICLE 3 AS AMENDED
(v) Notify the Council of any case of failure to comply with the provisions of the present Convention the rules, regulations and procedures prescribed thereunder and the terms and conditions of a contract, and make recommendations to the Council with respect to measures to be taken in that regard.	(viii) Direct and supervise a staff of inspectors who shall inspect all activities in the Area to determine whether the provisions of this Part, the rules, regulations and procedures prescribed thereunder, and the terms and conditions of any contract are being complied with. (ix) Issue emergency orders to prevent serious harm to the marine environment arising out o any activity in the Area. (x) Take into at views on protection of the environment of recognized experts in the field before taking final decisions or making recommendations to the Council on the above matters as they relate to the protection of the marine environment.	(viii) Direct and supervise a staff of inspectors who shall inspect all activities in the Area to determine whether the provisions of this Part, the rules, regulations and procedures prescribed thereunder, and the terms and conditions of any contract with the Authority are being complied with. (ix) Issue emergency orders to prevent serious harm to the marine environment arising out of any activity in the Area. (x) Take into account views on protect on of the environment of recogn zed experts in the field before taking final decisions or making recommendations to the Co ncil on the above matters as they relate to the protection of the marine environment.

Article 3 bis

SINGLE NEGOTIATING TEXT

AMENDMENT

Article 31 bis

Add new Article 31 bis

ARTICLE 31 AS AMENDED

The Rules and Regulations Commission

Article 31 bis

Members of the Rules and Regulations Commission shall have high qualifications and substantial experience in the management of sea-bed resources, ocean and marine engineering and mining and minerals technology and practices, operation of related marine installations, equipment and devices, ocean and environmental sciences and maritime safety.

2. The Rules and Regulations Commission shall:

(i) Formulate and submit to the Council the rules, regulations and procedures referred to in paragraph (xi) of Article 28;

(ii) Keep under review and recommend to the Council from time to time such amendments thereto as it may deem necessary or desirable;

(iii) Assist the Technical Commission in preparing assessments of the environmental implications of activities in the Area and consider and evaluate these implications before recommending the rules, regulations and procedures referred to in sub-paragraph (i) of this paragraph;

(iv) Prepare special studies and reports at the request of the Council.

(v) Take into account views on protection of the environment of recognized experts in the field before recommending rules, regulations and procedures to the Council and report its views to the Council together with its recommendations.

The Tr bu a shall have jurisdiction with respe t to:

(a) Any dispute relating to the interpretation or app ication of this Convention; and

(b) Any dispute connected with the subject matter of this Convention and submitted to it pursuant to a contract or arrangement entered into pursuant to this Convention.

2 The Tribunal shall exercise all powers and perform a l functions referred to under artic es 57, 58, 60, 6 62 and 63.

3. The Tribunal shal be composed of a body of independent judges, el ct d regard ess of their nationality from among persons of high moral character, No possess the qualifica- tions required in the r respective countries for appointment to the hig s@ judicial offices, or are jurisconsults of recognized competence in law of the sea matters and other areas of international law.

4. The Tribunal shall consist of nine judges, five of m shall constitute a quorum.

5. Members of the Tribunal shall be appointed by the Assembly on the recommendation of the Council from among candidates nominated by States Parties to th is Con- ve ti on In appointing members of the Tribunal due regard shall be paid to the importance of assuring representation on the Tribunal of the principal lega systems of the world.

6. Members of the Tribu a shall hold office for five years and may be reappointed for one further term; provided that the terms of the four judges e ected at the first l cti e shall expire at the end of three years.

Article 32

Paragraph 1: Delete, substitute the text at right and renumber remaining paragraphs.

Paragraph 2: Insert "and" between "61" and "62" and delete "63".

Paragraph 3: Delete "juris- consultants of recognized competence" and substitute "lawyers of highest distinction.

The Tribuna shall have jurisdict on with respect t:

(a) Any dispute between States Parties to this Con- v ti e concern ng the interpretation or application of this Part re ating to activities in the Area, not falling with subparagraphs (b), (c) and (d) of this paragraph;

(b Any dispute concerning the conclusion of any contract, its interpretation or application or other activity in the Area which has arisen between States Parties to this Convention, or between su b State Party and a national of another b Party, or between nationals of different States Parties, or between a State Party or a national of a State Party and the Authority or the Enterprise;

(c Any dispute falling within article 58; and

d Any matter falling wit in article 39.

2. n a dispute falling within subparagraph (a) has ar sen, the parties to the dispute shall first seek a so ution through consultation negotiation, conciliat b or thes su ch means of their en choi e. If the dispute has not b e resolved within one month of its commencement, any party to the dispute may institute proceedings before the Tribuna , u l sa the parties agree to submit the dispute to arbitration.

3. The Tr bunal shal exercise a l powers and perform al functions referred to und o Articles 57, 58, 60, 61 and 62.

4. The Tribunal shall be composed of a body of independent judges, elected regardless of their nat ona ity from among persons of high mora character

Article 32 continued

AMENDMENT

ARTICLE 2 AS AMENDED

who possess the qualifications required in their respective countries for appointment to the highest judicial offices, or are lawyers of highest distinction in law of the sea matters and other areas of international law.

5. The Tribunal shall consist of nine judges, five of whom shall constitute a quorum.

6. Members of the Tribunal shall be appointed by the Assembly on the recommendation of the Council from among candidates nominated by States Parties to this Convention. In appointing members of the Tribunal due regard shall be paid to the importance of assuring representation on the Tribunal of the principal legal systems of the world.

7. Members of the Tribunal hold office for five years and may be reappointed for one further term; provided that the terms of the four judges elected at the first election shall expire at the end of three years.

8. The Members of the Tribunal will be removed in accordance with paragraph 9 shall continue to discharge their duties until their places have been filled. Though replaced they shall finish any cases which they may have begun.

9. Upon the occurrence of a vacancy in the Tribunal the Council shall appoint a successor who shall hold office for the remainder of his predecessor's term, subject to the approval of the Assembly at its next regular session.

0. A member of the Tribunal may be removed from office by the Assembly, on the unanimous recommendation of the other members of the Tribunal and the approval of the Council.

SINGLE NEGOTIATING TEXT

7. The Members of the Tribunal unless removed in accordance with paragraph 9 shall continue to discharge their duties until their place have been filled. Though replaced, they shall finish any as which they may have begun.

8. Upon the occurrence of a vacancy in the Tribunal the Council shall appoint a successor who shall hold office for the remainder of his predecessor's term, subject to the approval of the Assembly at its next regular session.

9. A member of the Tribunal may be removed from office by the Assembly, on the unanimous recommendation of the other members of the Tribunal and the approval of the Council.

10. The Tribunal shall establish its rules of procedure, elect its President annually, appoint a Registrar and sub staff as may be necessary for the efficient discharge of its functions. The salaries and emoluments and terms of service of members of the Tribunal, and of its Registrar and staff, shall be determined by the Council.

Article 33

SINGLE NEGOTIATING TEXT	AMENDMENT	ARTICLE 33 AS AMENDE

Article 3

Article 33

The Tribunal shall decide all disputes relating to the interpretation and application of this Part, the rules, regulations and procedures prescribed thereunder and the terms and conditions of any contracts entered into by the Authority which have been submitted to it, and shall render advisory opinions on the request of any organ of the Authority or as otherwise specifically provided in this Part.

Delete.

Article 4

ARTICLE 34 A AMENDE

AMENDMENT

Article 34

Delete.

S NGLE NEGOTIATING TEXT

Ar.icle 34

Nothing in the foregoing articles shall prevent
Members of the Authority from settling their disputes
by any othe means prescribed by Article 57 of this
Convention.

SINGLE NEGOTIATING TEXT	AMENDMENT	ARTICLE 35 AS AMENDED

The Enterprise

Article 35

1. The Enterprise shall be the organ of the Authority which shall, subject to the general policy directions and supervision of the Council, undertake the preparation and execution of activities of the Authority in the Area, pursuant to Article 22. In the exercise of its functions, it may ... into appropriate agreements on behalf of the Authority.

2. The Enterprise shall have international legal capacity and such legal capacity as may be necessary for the performance of its functions and the fulfilment of its purposes. The Enterprise shall function in accordance with the Statute set forth in Annex II to this Convention, and shall in all respects be governed by the provisions of this Convention. Appointment of the Members of the Governing Board under subparagraph 2(i) of article 26 of this Convention shall be made on the basis of equal representation of all geographical regions and in accordance with the provisions of the Statute set forth in Annex I to this Convention.

3. Members of the Authority are ipso facto parties to the Statute of the Enterprise.

4. The Enterprise shall have its principal place of business at the seat of the Authority.

Article 35

Delete and substitute the text at right.

The Enterprise

Article 35

The Enterprise established in accordance with the Statute set forth in Annex in Annex to this Part shall be the entity for implementing the provisions of Article 22, Paragraph 1.

2. The Enterprise shall have international legal personality and such legal capacity as may be necessary for the performance of its functions and the fulfilment of its purposes.

3. State Parties are ipso facto parties to the Statute of the Enterprise.

4. The Enterprise shall have its principal place of business at _____ . In order to ensure impartiality and non discrimination, the Enterprise should not be co-located with the Authority.

Article 6

SINGLE NEGOTIATING TEXT

AMENDMENT

ARTICLE 36 AS AMENDED

The Secretariat

Article 36

The Secretariat shall comprise a Secretary-General and such staff as the Authority may require. The Secretary-General shall be appointed by the Assembly upon the recommendation of the Council. He shall be the chief administrative officer of the Authority.

Article 36

No amendment proposed.

Article 37

ART CLE 7 AS AMENDED

AMENDMENT

Article 37

No amendment proposed.

S NGLE NEGOTIATING TEXT

Art cle 37

⑥ Secretary-General shall act in that capacity
in all meetings of the Assembly and of the Council,
and of any subsidiary organs established by them,
and shall perform su th o functions as are entrusted
to him by any organ of the Authority. The Secretary-
General shall make an annual report to the Assemb y
on the work of the organization.

Article 38

ARTICLE 38 AS AMENDED

AMENDMENT

Article 38

No amendment proposed.

SINGLE NEGOTIATING TEXT

Article 38

1. The staff of the Authority shall include such qualified scientific and technical and other personnel as may be required to fulfil the objectives and functions of the Authority. The Authority shall be guided by the principle that its permanent staff shall be kept to a minimum.

2. The paramount consideration in the recruitment and employment of the staff and in the determination of their conditions of service shall be to secure employees of the highest standards of efficiency, competence and integrity. Subject to this consideration, due regard shall be paid to the importance of recruiting staff on as wide a geographical basis as possible.

3. The staff shall be appointed by the Secretary-General. The terms and conditions on which the staff shall be appointed, remunerated and dismissed shall be in accordance with regulations made by the Council, and to general rules approved by the Assembly on the recommendation of the Council

SINGLE NEGOTIATING TEXT	AMENDMENT	ARTICLE 39 AS AMENDED

Article 39

In the performance of their duties, the Secretary-General and the staff shall not seek or receive instructions from any government or from any other source external to the Authority. They shall refrain from any action which might reflect on their position as international officials of the Authority responsible only to the Authority. They shall have no financial interest whatsoever in any activity relating to exploration and exploitation in the Area. Subject to their responsibilities to the Authority, they shall not disclose any industrial secret or data declared by the Authority to be proprietary or other confidential information coming to their knowledge by reason of their official duties for the Authority. Each Party to this Convention undertakes to respect the exclusively international character of the responsibilities of the Secretary-General and the staff and not to seek to influence them in the discharge of their responsibilities.

Article 39

Amend as follows: Delete "declared by the authority to be proprietary" and substitute "which is proprietary in accordance with paragraph 10 of Annex I."

Number the paragraph as "1" and add a new paragraph "2" as follows:

"2. Any violation of the responsibilities set forth in paragraph 1 of this article shall be considered a grave disciplinary offense and shall, in addition e tail persona liability for damages. Any State Party or natural or juridical person sponsored by a State Party may bring an alleged violation of this article before the Tribunal which may order monetary penalties or the assessment of damages. Upon an order, the Secretary-General shall dismiss the staff member concerned

Article 9

1. In the performance of their duties, the Secretary-General and the staff shall not seek or receive instructions from any government or from any other source external to the Authority. They shall refrain from any action which might reflect on their position as international officials of the Authority responsible only to the Authority. They shall have no financial interest whatsoever in any activity relating to exploration and exploitation in the Area. Subject to their responsibilities to the Authority, they shall not disclose any industrial secret or data which is proprietary in accordance with paragraph 10 of Annex I or other confidential information coming to their knowledge by reason of their official duties for the Authority. Each State Party to this Convention undertakes to respect the exclusively international character of the responsibilities of the Secretary-General and the staff and not to seek to influence them in the discharge of their responsibilities.

2. Any violation of the responsibilities set forth in paragraph 1 of this article shall be considered a grave disciplinary offense and shall, in addition tail personal liability for damages. Any State Party or natural or juridical person sponsored by a State Party may bring an alleged violation of this article before the Tribunal which may order monetary penalties or the assessment of damages. Upon such order, the Secretary-General shall dismiss the staff member concerned.

AMENDMENT

Article 40

Delet

SINGLE NEGOTIATING TEXT

Article 40

1. The Authority shall, as necessary, establish a staff of inspectors. The staff of inspectors shall have the responsibility of examining all activities in the Area to determine whether the provisions of this Convention, the rules, regulations and procedures prescribed thereunder, and the terms and conditions of any contract with the Authority pursuant to this Convention are being complied with.

2. The inspectors shall report any non-compliance to the Secretary-General. The Secretary-General shall immediately notify the Chairmen of the Council and of the Africa Commission.

ART CLE 4 AS AMENDED

S NGLE NEGOT AT NG TEXT

AMENDMENT

Art le 41

Article 41

Delete.

. The Secretary-General may send inspectors into be
territory of a party to this Convention ad into be Area
a d any installation established therein, aft e consultation with the parties concerned. The inspectors
shall have access at all times to all places and data
and to any person bo deals with any activity in be Area
pursuant to this Convention, and to any books of account
and records kept with respect to such activity.

2. Inspectors shall, upon request made to be Secretary-
General, be accompanied by representatives of any State
Party to this Convention and any party involved, provided
that be inspectors shall not thereby be delayed or
otherwise impeded in the exercise of heir functions.

*The question of inspection of da
is dealt with under Article 31 of
these amendments and its definition
is dealt with in paragraph 10 of
Annex I.*

Article 4 bis

SINGLE NEGOTIATING TEXT	AMENDMENT	ARTICLE 4 bis AS AMENDED

Article 41 bis

Article 41 bis

Ad new Article 41 bis

Nongovernmenta Organizations

Article 4 bis

1. The Secretary-General sha1, on matters within the competence of the Authority, make suitable arrangements with the approval of the Council, for consu tation and cooperation with nongovernmenta organ zations recognized by the Economic and Soc al Counc l of the United Nations.

2. Any organization which has en granted o- sultative status with the Authori y in accordance with paragraph 1 of this article may designate representati es to ed as observers meetings of the organs of the Authority in accordance with the rules of procedure of ny eh organ. Each concerned organ shall establish procedures for bai ning he vi ws of such organi ati as in appropri ae cases.

3. Wri en reports submi ed by these nongovern- mental organizations on subjects in which ey have special competence and which are related to the work of the Authority shall, upon the request of the organ concerned or its chairman, be distributed by the Secretary-Genera to S a es Parti e.

ART CLE 42 AS AMENDED

SINGLE EGOT AT NG TEXT

PART V

Finance

Article 42

The Assemb y hall blish be Genera Fund o be Authority.

All receipts of the Authority arising from activities in the Area, including ay ex as of evenues of be Enterprise ove Its ex ps and costs In ach proportion as be Council shall determine shal be paid into the General Fund

AMENDMENT

Article 2

No amendment proposed.

Article 43

Article 43

ARTICLE 43 AS AMENDED

AMENDMENT

Article 43

No amendmen pr d.

SINGLE NEGOTIATING TEXT

Article 43

The Council shall submit to the Assembly annual budget estimates for the expenses of the Authority. To facilitate the work of the Council in this regard, the Secretary-General shall initially prepare the draft estimates. If the Assembly does not approve the estimates, it shall return them, together with its recommendations, to the Council. The Council shall then submit further estimates to the Assembly for its approval.

198

SINGLE NEGOTIATING TEXT

Article 44

Expenses of the Authority comprise:

(a) administrative expenses, which shall include ... of the staff of the Authority, ... of meetings, and expenditure on ... of the functioning of the organs of the Authority;

(b) expenses ... included in the foregoing, incurred by the Authority in carrying out the functions entrusted to it under this Convention; and

(c) the expenditure of the Enterprise, to the extent that it ... be met out of the Enterprise's own revenues and other receipts.

2. The expenses referred to in paragraph 1 of this article shall be met to an extent to be determined by the Assembly on the recommendation of the Council, out of the General Fund, the balance of such expenses to be met out of contributions by members of the Authority in accordance with a scale of assessment pursuant to sub-paragraph 1(iv) of Article 26.

AMENDMENT

Article 44

Amend as follows:

Paragraph 1(a): add "and" after the semicolon.

Paragraph 1(b): Delete "and" *and substitute full* stop.

Paragraph 1(c): Delete.

Paragraph 2. ... to be determined by the Council, ... Fund, ... the paragraph ...

" ... its administrative ... as defined in paragraph 1(a) of this article, these ... Members of the ... by the Assembly in ... Article 26, ... 2 ... "

ARTICLE 44 AS AMENDED

Article 44

Expenses of the Authority comprise:

(a) administrative expenses, which shall include ... of the staff of the Authority, ... of meetings, and expenditure on ... of the functioning of the organs of the Authority;

(b) expenses ... included in the foregoing, incurred by the Authority in carrying out the functions entrusted to it under this Convention; and

2. The expenses referred to in paragraph 1 of this article shall be met out of the General Fund. Until the Authority has sufficient ... to receive ... under Article 42 for meeting its administrative expenses as defined in paragraph 1(a) of this article, the expenses shall be met out of contributions by Members of the Authority ... by the Assembly in accordance with Article 26, paragraph 2(iv).

SINGLE NEGOTIATING TEXT	AMENDMENT	ARTICLE 45 AS AMENDED
Article 45	Article 45	Article 45

SINGLE NEGOTIATING TEXT

Article 45

1. Any excess of revenues of the Auth o ty over its expenses and c sts to an extent determined by the Council, all payments rece ved pursuant to Art cle 42 of this Convention and any voluntary contribut ons made by States Parties to this convention shall be credited to a Special Fund.

2. Am u ts in the Special Fund shall be apporti d and made available quitably in su b man en and in su b currencies, and t rwise in accordance with criter a, rules, regu ations and procedures adopted by the Assemb y pursuant to sub-paragraph 2(v of Artic e 26.

AMENDMENT

Article 45

Amend as fo lows:

Paragraph 1: Delete "all payments r ceived pursuant to Article 43 of this Convention ad any voluntary contributions made by States Parties to this Convention." Add a new paragraph 3 as fo lows:

"3. The expenditure of the Enter- prise, to the extent that it be met out of the Enterprise's wn revenues and receipts shall be met [the sub- stance of this paragraph should be dealt with_in the Statute of the Enterprise_7."

ARTICLE 45 AS AMENDED

Article 45

1. Any excess revenues of the Authority over its expenses and c sts to an extent determined by the Council shall be cred ted to a Specia Fund.

2. Amounts n the Specia Fund shall be apporti ed and made ava lab e equitab y in su b manner and in such currenc es, and otherwise in accordance with criteria, ru es, regulations and procedures adopted by the Assembly pursuant to paragraph 2(x) of Article 26.

3. The expenditure of the Enterprise, to the extent that it cannot be met out of the Enterprise's own revenues and receipts sha l be met [the substance of this paragraph should be dea t with n the Statute of the Enterprise_7.

ART CLE 46 AS AMENDED

AMENDMENT

Article 46

S NGLE NEGOT AT NG TEXT

Article 46

Subject to ugh limitations as may be approved by the Assembly in the financial regulations adopted by it puant to sub-paragraph 2(v) of Article 26, the Council may exercise borrowing powers on behalf of the Authority wibh ut, however, imposing on members of the Authority any liability in respect of loans entered into pursuant to this paragraph, and accept voluntary contribut ons made to the Authority.

Dele e.

SINGLE NEGOTIATING TEXT

Article 47

The records, books and accounts of the Authority, including its annual financial statements, shall be subject to an annual audit by a recognized independent auditor.

AMENDMENT

Article 47

No amendment proposed.

ARTICLE 47 AS AMENDED

SINGLE NEGOTIATING TEXT

AMENDMENT

ARTICLE 48 AS AMENDED

Status, mmunities and Privileges

Article 48

Article 48

No amendment proposed.

The Auth oity shall have full internat eai lega
personality, and such legal capacity as may be
necessary for the exercise of its functions and the
fulfilment of its purp seo

S NGLE NEGOT AT NG TEXT | AMENDMENT | ART CLE 9 AS AMEND D

Article 49

To enable the Authority to fulfil its fun ctions it shall enjoy in the territory of each State Party to this Convention, the immunities and privileges set forth herein except as provided in annex... to this C nvention with respect to operations of the Enterprise..

Article 49

No amendment proposed.

204

ART CLE 0 A AMENDED

AM EM NT

Article 50

S NGLE NEGOTIATING TEXT

Article 50

The Authority, its property and assets, shall enjoy, in the territory of each State Party to this Convention, immunity from legal process, except when the Authority waives its immunity.

No amendment proposed.

Article 2

RTICLE 52 A AME DE

S NGLE NEGOTIATING TEXT	AMENDMENT
Ar tle 52	Article 52
Al property and assets of the Authority shall be free from restrictions, regulations, con trols and moratoria of any nature.	*No amendment proposed.*

S NGLE NEGOT AT NG TEXT

AMENDMENT

Article 53

Article 53

No amendment proposed.

The President and members of the Assemb y, the Chairman and members of the Council, members of a y organ of the Assembly, or the Council, and members of the Tribunal, and the Secretary-General and st ff of the Authority, shall enjoy in the territory of @ member St t a

(a) mmunity from lega process w th respect to acts performed by them n the exercise of thei r funct ons, except when the Auth orty waives this mmunity;

(b) Not being local nationals, the same immunit es from immigration restrictions, al en registration requirements and national service blig ions, the s me facilities as regards exchange restrictions and the same treatment in respect of travelling facilit es as are accorded by States Parties to this Convention to the representatives, officials and emp y es of comparable rank of other States Parties.

Article 54

ARTICLE 54 AS AMENDED

AMENDMENT

SINGLE NEGOTIATING TEXT

Article 54

Article 54

No amendment proposed.

The provisions of the preceding article shall apply to persons appearing in proceedings before the Tribunal as parties, agents, counsel, advocates, witnesses or experts; provided, however, that subparagraph (b) thereof shall apply only in connexion with their travel to and from, and their stay at, the place where the proceedings are held.

AMENDMENT

Article 55

No amendment proposed.

S NGLE NEGOLIATING TEXT

Article 55

1 The archives of the Authority shall be inviolab e, wh a ver they may be.

2. All proprietary d t a industrial secrets or sim ar information and all personnel records shall not be placed in archives p o to public inspection.

3. With regard to its official c mmunications, the Authority shall be accorded by ca State Party to this Convention treatment no less favourable than that accorded to other interrati naб organizations.

SINGLE NEGOT AT NG TEXT

AMENDMENT

Article 56

Article 56

No amendment proposed.

1. The Authority, its assets, property and income, and its operations and transactions authorized by this Convention, shall be exempt from all taxation and customs duties. The Aut ority shall also be exempt from iability for the collection or payment of any taxes or customs duties.

2. Except in the case of local nationals, no tax sha be levied on or in respect of expense allowances paid by the Authority to the President or members of the Assembly, or in respect of salaries, expense allowances or other lume ts paid by the Auth ority to the Chairman and members of tha Council, members of the Tribunal, members of any organ of the Assemb y or of the Council and the Secretary-General and staff of the Authority.

S NGLE NEGOT AT NG TEXT	AMENDMENT	ART CLE 57 AS AMENDED

Settlement of Disput s

Article 57

When a dispute fal ing within article 32 of this Con- v ti on has arisen between States Parties to this Convention, or between such Sta es Party and a nationa of another s Party, or between nationals of different States Parties, or between a Sta e Party or a national of a State Party and the Authority or the Enterprise, the p ties to the dispute shall first seek a solution through consult ation, negotiation, conciliation or other su ch means of their an choi e. If the disputa has not b n resolved wi th n one month of its commencement, a y pa ty to the disputa may institute proceedings before the Tribunal, unless the parties agree to subm t the dispute to arbitration pursuant to article 63 of this Convention.

Delete and substitute the text at right.

Settlement of Disputes

Article 57

Any party to any dispute falling within Article 32 paragraph I(b), (c) or (d) of this Part may institute proceedings before the Tribunal, provided, however, that when such a dispute is between a State Party and a natural or juridical person of another State Pa ty, the sponsoring state of the natural or juridical person shall be required to intervene.

Article 57

Article 58

SINGLE NEGOTIATING TEXT

Article 58

1. Any State Party to this Convention which questions the legality of measures taken by the Council, or by any organ of the Council or the Assembly on grounds of a violation of this Convention, lack of jurisdiction, infringement of any fundamental rule of procedure or misuse of power, may bring the matter before the Tribunal.

2. The proceedings provided for in this article shall be instituted within one month of the date of publication of the decision concerned or its notification to the complainant, or of the date on which he became aware of it.

3. If the Tribunal considers the complaint well-founded, it shall declare the decision concerned to be void, and shall determine what measures shall be taken to redress any damage caused.

AMENDMENT

Article 58

Delete and substitute the text at right.

ARTICLE 58 AS AMENDED

Article 58

1. Any State Party to this Convention which questions the legality of measures taken by any organ of the Council or of the Assembly on grounds of a violation of this Part, lack of jurisdiction, infringement of any fundamental rule of procedure or misuse of power, may bring the matter before the Tribunal.

2. Any national of a State Party may, subject to the same conditions, bring a complaint to the Tribunal with regard to a decision directed to that person, or in the case of a person conducting or seeking a contract to conduct activities in the Area, a decision which, although in form directed to another person, is of direct concern to that person.

3. The proceedings provided for in this article shall be instituted within one month of either the date of publication of the decision concerned or its notification to the complainant, or of the date on which he became aware of it.

4. If the Tribunal considers the complaint well-founded, it shall declare the decision concerned to be void, and shall determine what measures shall be taken to redress any damage caused.

S NGLE NEGOT AT NG TEXT	AMENDMENT	ART CLE 9 AS AMENDED
Article 59	Article 59	Article 59
1. Judgments and orders of tha Tribunal shall be fina and bind ng. They shall be enforceable In the territories of Members of the Authority in the same way as judgments or orders of the highest court of that Member State.	Paragraph 1: Delete the second sentence. Paragraph 2: Substitute State Party for "Member of the Authority."	1. Judgments and orders of the Tr bunal shall be final and binding.
2. If a Member of the Authority fails to perform its bligations under a judgment rendered by the Tribuna l, the other party or pa rties to the d spute may bring the matter before the Council which sha l d ide up on measures to be taken to give effect to the judgme t.		2. If a St te Party fails to perform ts obligations under a judgment rendered by the Tribunal, the other party or parties to the dispute may bring the matter before the C uncil which shall decide upon measures to be taken to give effect to the judgm nt.

Article 60

| S NGLE NEGOT AT NG TEXT | AMENDMENT | ART CLE 60 AS AMENDED |

S NGLE NEGOT AT NG TEXT

Article 60

1. At an y time after it is se zed of the disput e the Tr bunal may, if t considers t an the circumstances so require order provisional measures for the purpose of preserv ng the respective rights of the parties, or prevent ng ser ous harm to the marine environment.

2. A party to the dispute directly affected by such provisional measures may request their immediate review. The Tribunal shall promptly undertake such review and conform or suspend its order.

AMENDMENT

Article 60

Delete and substitute the text at right.

ART CLE 60 AS AMENDED

Article 60

. Upon the request of an y party to the dispute, the Tribunal may, if it considers that circumstances so require, after giving the party an opportunity to be heard, order provisional measures, which it c ns ders appropriate for preserving the respective rights of the parties, for minimizing d mag to an y party and for preventing serious harm to the marine environment, pending final adjudication.

2. Notice of any provisional measures ordered under this article shall be given forthwith to the parties to the dispute and to all States Parties. A party to the di spute directly affected by sucn pr visional measures may request their immediate review. The Tribunal shall promptly undertake such review and c nf rm or suspend the order.

3. Any provisional measures ordered under this article shall be bindi g upon the part es to the d spute.

Article 6

S NGLE NEGOTIATING TEXT

AMENDMENT

ARTICLE 6 AS AMENDED

Article 6.

Article 6

1. The Tribunal may seek the opinion of any o gan o the Council regarding an issue falling within its competence.

No amendment proposed.

2. The Tribunal shall decide whether proceedings shall be suspended until tho opinion s ught has been made available.

Article 6

SINGLE NEGOTIATING TEXT

Article 62

Any organ of the Authority may request the Tribunal to give an advisory opinion on any legal question connected with the subject matter of this Convention.

AMENDMENT

Article 62

No amendment proposed.

ARTICLE 62 AS AMENDED

SINGLE NEGOTIATING TEXT

AMENDMENT

Article 63

Article 63

Delete.

1. If the parties to a dispute so agree, pursuant to Article 57, they shall submit the dispute to an Arbitration Commission. The Arbitration Commission shall be composed of three members. Each party to the dispute shall appoint one member to the Commission, while the third member, who shall be the Chairman, shall be chosen in common agreement between the parties. If the parties fail to agree on the designation of the third member within a period of one month the third member shall be appointed by the President of the Tribunal. In case any of the parties fail to make an appointment within a period of one month the President of the Tribunal shall fill the remaining vacancy or vacancies.

2. The Arbitration Commission shall decide on matters put before it by a simple majority.

3. The Arbitration Commission constituted pursuant to this article shall have such jurisdiction and shall exercise such powers and functions as the Tribunal constituted pursuant to Article 32. The provisions of Articles 58-61 shall apply mutatis mutandis to the Arbitration Commission.

SINGLE NEGOTIATING TEXT

PART V: FINAL PROVISIONS

Amendments
Article 64

Amendments to this Convention may be proposed by any Sta e Party to this Convention. Certified copies of the tex. of any amendment proposed shall be pr pared by the Sec etary-General and c municated by him to all parties, at east ninety days in advance of its consideration by the Assembly.

AMENDMENT

Article 64

Delete.

ARTICLE 6 AS AMENDED

SINGLE NEGOTIATING TEXT	AMENDMENT	ARTICLE 65 AS AMENDED
Article 65	*Delete.*	*Article 65*
Amendments shall come into force for all States Parties to this Convention when:		
(i) Approved by the Assembly by a two-thirds majority of whoso present and voting after consideration of observations submitted by the Council on proposed amendments; and		
(ii) Accepted by two-thirds of all the States Parties in accordance with their respective constitutional processes. Acceptance by a State Party shall be effected by the deposit of an instrument of acceptance with the Secretary-General of the United Nations.		

SINGLE NEGOTIATING TEXT	AMENDMENT	ARTICLE 66 AS AMENDED
General Review		
Article 66	Article 66	

At the third regular session of the Assembly following the coming into force of this Convention, the question of a general review of the provisions of this Convention shall be placed on the agenda of that session. On approval by a majority of the members present and voting, the review will take place at the following Assembly. Thereafter, proposals on the question of a general review of this Convention may be submitted for decisions by the Assembly under the same procedure.

Delete.

S NGLE NEGOT AT NG TEXT

Susp ns on o Priv leqes

Artic e 67

A State Party of be Authority which is n arrears in the p ym nt of its financial contributions to the Aut ity shall have o vote in the Authority if the amount of its arrears equals or exceeds the m nt of the contributions due from it for the preceding two years. The Assembly may permit such a St a Party to vote if it is satisfied that the failure to pay is due to conditions b y d the control of the St a Party.

AMENDMENT

Article 67

No amendment proposed.

ARTICLE 67 AS AMENDED

S NGLE NEGOT AT NG TEXT	AMENDMENT	ART CLE 68 AS AMENDED

Article 68

1. A member which has persistently viol tea be provisl of this Convention or of a y agreement or contractual arrangement entered into by it pursuant to this Convention, may be suspended from the exercise of the privileges and the rights of membership by the Assembly acting on a tw -thirds majority of the States Parties present and voting up a recommendations by the Counc l.

2. No action may be taken under this artic e until the dispute settlement procedures have bn exhausted.

Article 68

Amend as follows:

Paragraph 1: Substitute "State Party" for "member." Insert "grossly and" before "persistently." Delete "acting on a two-thirds majority of the States Parties present and voting."

Paragraph 2: Delete all after the word "until" and substitute the following: "the Tribunal has found that a member has persistently violated the provisions of this Convention and has recommended suspension as the remedy for the violation."

Article 68

. A St te Party which has gross y and persistently violated the provisions of this Convention or of any agreement or contractual arrangement entered nto by it pursuant to this Part, may be suspended from he exercise of the privileges and the rights of membership by he Assembly on recommendatin by the Counci

2. No ct n may be taken u d or this artic e unti the Tribunal has found that a member has grossly and persistent y vio t al the prov si n of this Convention

SINGLE NEGOTIATING TEXT	AMENDMENT	ARTICLE 69 AS AMENDED
Signature		
Article 69	*Article 69*	
	Delete.	

The present Convention shall be open for signature by all States members of the United Nations or of any of the Specialized Agencies or of the International Atomic Energy Agency or parties to the Statute of the International Court of Justice, and by any other State invited to participate in the Third United Nations Conference on the Law of the Sea or invited by the Assembly of the Authority to become a party to the Convention, as follows: until 31 December 1976 at the Ministry of Foreign Affairs of the Republic of Venezuela, and subsequently, until 30 June 1977 at United Nations Headquarters, New York.

Article 70

SINGLE NEGOTIATING TEX

AMENDMENT

ARTICLE 70 AS AMENDED

Ratification

Article 70

Article 70

The present Convention is subject to ratification. The instruments of ratification shall be deposited with the Secretary-General of the United Nations.

Delete.

A ENDMENT

Article 71

SINGL NEGOTIATING EXT

Accession

Article 71

Delete.

The present Co v tion shall remain open for accession
by any State belonging to any of the categories m tioned
I narticle 69. The instr nts of accession shall be
posited with he Secretary-General of the United Nations.

rticle 72

ARTICLE 72 AS AMENDED

MENDMENT

Article 72

SINGLE NEGOTIATING TEXT

Entry into Force

Article 72

Dele e.

1. The present Convention shall enter into force othe thirtieth day following the date of deposit of the thirty-sixth instrument of ratification or accession.

2. For each State ratifying or acceding to the Convention after be deposit of the thirty-sixth instrument of ratification or accession, the Convention shall enter into force on be thirtieth day after de psit by such State of its instrument of ratification or accession.

SINGLE NEGOTIATING TEXT	AMENDMENT	ARTICLE 73 AS AMENDED

Provisional Application

Article 73

1. Pending the definitive entry into force of this Convention in accordance with the provisions of Article 72, a State may notify, upon signing this Convention, the Secretary-General of the United Nations that it will apply this Convention provisionally and that it will undertake to seek ratification or accession in accordance with constitutional procedures as rapidly as possible

2. This Convention shall enter provisionally into force upon the thirty-sixth such notification to the Secretary-General of the United Nations.

3. On provisional entry into force of this Convention in accordance with paragraph 2, any State which has notified the Secretary-General of the United Nations of its intention to apply this Convention provisionally in accordance with paragraph 1 shall be regarded as being Party for the purpose of provisional application of this Convention.

4. The provisional application of this Convention with respect to a State shall be terminated if that State notifies the other Parties to provisional application of the withdrawal of its notification or paragraph

5. The provisional application of this Convention in accordance with this article shall be terminated:

(a) Upon the definitive entry into force of this Convention in accordance with Article 72;

(b) If, as a result of withdrawal of notification in accordance with paragraph 4 above, the total number of Contracting Parties becomes less than that provided for in paragraph 2;

Article 73

No amendment proposed.

S NGLE NEGOTIATING TEXT

(c) At the end f a period of .....years after the
commencement of provisional application.

6. If, at he end of six months after the opening of the
Convent on for signature, provisional entry into force as
provided for in article 73 does not occur, an interim
Commission shall come into existence, as provided for in
annex III to this Convention.

SINGLE NEGOT AT NG TEXT	AMENDMENT	ART CLE 74 AS AMENDED

Depos tary

Article 74

Delete.

Article 74

The Secretary-Genera of be Un ed Nat ons shall Inform all St tes be ong ng to any of the categories mentioned in Article 69 of:

(a) Signature to the present Convent on and of be deposit of Instruments of ratification or accession in accordance with Artic es 69, 70 and 71 respect vely;

(b) Notification of provisional applicat on in accordance with Article 73;

(c) The date on which be present Convent on will e ten into force n accordance w th Article 72;

(d) Date on wh ch be present Convent on will prov siona ly e ten into force n accordance with Artic e 73.

Article 7

ARTICLE 7 AS AMENDED

AMENDME T

Article 75

SINGLE NEGOT AT.NG TEXT

Auth t[e Texts

Article 75

Delete.

The original of the present Convention, of which be Arabic, Chirese, English, French, Russian and Spanish texts are equally authentic, shall be deposi ed with be Secretary-General of the United Nations.

IN WITNESS WHEREOF the unde signed Pleni pentiaries, being duly authorized the eto by their respective Governments, have signed the present Conv ation.

DONE AT CARA 0,6, this .... ay of . one thousand nine hd and seventy-six.

SINGLE NEGOTIATING TEXT

AMENDMENT

ANNEX I*

BASIC CONDITIONS OF GENERAL SURVEY
EXPLORATION AND EXPLOITATION

PART A

Annex I, paragraph 1

RIGHTS IN THE AREA AND ITS RESOURCES

1. The Area and its resources being the common heritage of mankind all rights in the resources are vested in the Authority on behalf of mankind as a whole. These resources are not subject to alienation.

Delete.

No further annexes will be issued in the future, Annex II entitled "Statute of the Enterprise" and Annex III, "Statute of the Tribunal."

S NGLE NEGOT AT NG TEXT	AM NDME T	ANNEX PARAGRA H 2 S AMENDED

RIGHTS IN MINERALS

2. Title to the minerals or processed substances derived from the Area shall pass from be Authority only in accordance with be provisions of this Convention, the rules and regulations prescribed by be Authority in accordance with this Convention, and be terms and conditions of be relevant contracts, jo nt ventures or other form of association   :ed into by t.

Annex I, paragraph 2

Delete and *ustitute he*
at right.

2. Title to he resources shall vest in he Contractor at the moment   by are recovered from the Area pursuant to a contract with the Authority.

Annex
para.

SINGLE NEGOTIATING TEXT   AMENDMENT   ANNEX PARAGRAPH 3 AS AMENDED

ACCESS TO THE AREA AND ITS RESOURCES

3. The Authority shall from time to time determine the part or parts of the Area in which the exploration of the Area and the exploitation of its resources and other associated activities may be , in doing so associated activities shall be guided by the following principles

(a) The Authority shall encourage the dt of general survey operations, and to that end shall regularly, after consultation with all States Parties, open for general survey the e- and and ocean floor of such ocean c areas as are determined by it to be of interest for this purpose. General Survey may be carried at by any entity which as the environmental protection regulations of the Authority and enters into a contract with t.

(b) The Authority may, on the proposal of a State Party to this Convention or on its own initiative, on for evaluation and exploitation the e- and and on floor of oceanic areas determined by it on the basis of sufficient supporting data, to be of commerc a interest. Such evaluation and exploitation shall be and directly by the Authority in accordance with part B and within the limits it may determine in accordance with subparagraph 8(f), through States Parties to this Convention, or State Enterprises, or persons natural or juridical which as the nationality of on States, or are effectively controlled by them or their nationals, an sponsored by a State Party, by entering into contracts for associated operations as in accordance with paragraphs 5 and 6.

Provided, however, that the Authority may refuse to on any part or parts of the Area pursuant to this paragraph on be available dat indicates the risk of irreparable harm to a unique environment or unjustifiable interference with other es of the Area.

A az I, Paragraph 3

Amend as follows: All references to "general survey" should be deleted throughout Annex I and a new ph 2 as and as follows:

The as ball be on at al as to be dt of prospecting by any State or its nationals. The ty al as the a- dt of prospecting by any which meets the environmental on regu as of the ."

*Paragraph 3 chapeau:
substitute the fol
as shall be on at al as to
be dt of on at on ad
on in de th the
as of Annex I," de the sub-
paragraphs d) ad b, the
as the th the the
ad on the " e," er..."
to on" in dt the. for "re fise the.*

2 bis. The Area shall be on at all as to be dt of prospecting by any State or its nationals. The Authority shall encourage the . dt of prospecting by any entity which as the environmental protection regulations of the Authority.

3. The Area shall be on at all times to be dt of exploration and exploitation in accordance with the provisions of Annex I provided, however, that the Authority may close any part or parts of the Area pursuant to this paragraph on the available data indicates the risk of irreparable harm to a unique environment or unjustifiable interference with other es of the Area.

SINGLE NEGOTIATING TEXT

AMENDMENT

ANNEX   PARAGRAPH 4 AS AMENDED

Annex
para. 4

PART B

Annex I, Paragraph 4

Delete.

4. The Enterprise may at any t e, in any part or parts of the Area determined by the Authority to be open for activities pursuant to paragraph 3 of th se Basic Conditions, carry out directly scientific research or a general survey or exploration of the Area or operat ons relating to evaluatin and exploitation of the resources of the Area, including feasibility studies, construc- tion of facilities, processing, transportation and marketing pursuant to a Plan of Operations approved by the Council, subject to the following conditions:

(a) The Enterprise shall submit to the Counci in the form prescribed by it for the purpose such in- formation, including a detailed financial analysis of costs and benefits, as would enable the Council to review the financial and technical aspects of the proposed Plan of operations, as well as a Work Programme, wh ch shall accommodate the objectives of the Author ty as reflected in article 23 above.

(b) If on the basis of su b information and after taking nto consideration all relevant factors, the Council determines that the proposed Plan of Operations offers optimum benefits to the Authority the Council shall appr ve the Plan.

(c) Activities in the Area conducted directly by the Enterprise shall, mutatis mutandis, be subject to the relevant Basic Conditions set forth in Part C.

(d) To the extent that the Enterprise does not current y possess the personnel, equipment and services for its operations, it may employ them under its direction and management on a non-discriminatory bas s if they m e the qualifications set forth in paragraph 5. The t rms and conditions of su b employment shall be in accordance w th the re va e provis ons of th se Basic Condit ons.

/The substance of Part B of this An ex should be dealt with in the Statute of the Enterprise._/

AMENDMENT

S NGLE EGOT AT NG TXT

(e) Minerals and processed substances produced by
the Enterpr se sha l be marketed n accordance w th
rules, regu at ons and procedures adopted by the Council
In accordance with the fo lowing criteria

(i) The products of the Enterpr se shall be made
ava lab e to States Part es.

(ii) The Enterprise shall offer its products for sale
at not less t an nternational market pr ces. t
may, however, sel its products at lower pri es to
developing ounto es, particular y the least
developed among them.

(iii) Product on and marketing of the resources of the
Area by the Enterprise shall be mainta ned or
expanded in accordance with the provis ons of
article 9 above.

iv) The Enterprise shall, except as spec fica ly provided in this Part, market its products w t ou
discrimination.

SINGLE NEGOTIATING TEXT

AMENDMENT

ANNEX PARAGRAPH AS AMENDED

PART C

CONTRACTS FOR ASSOCIATED OPERATIONS

5. On the application of any State Party to this Convention or State enterprise, or personal natural or juridical which possesses the nationality of a State Party or is effectively controlled by it or its nationals and is sponsored by a State Party or any group of the foregoing (hereinafter called the "applicant"), the Authority may enter into a contract, joint venture or any other sub b form of association, for the conduct of scientific research, or for the carrying out of a general survey or exploration of the Area, or of operations relating to evaluation and exploitation of the Area including such stages as feasibility study, construction of facilities, processing, transportation and marketing (here nafter called the contract").

Annex I, Paragraph 5

Amend as follows: Delete "to this Convention" and date all after the first parenthetical phrase and substitute the following:

"the Authority shall ter: into a contract for the carrying at of exploration for, and exploitation of, the resources of the Area."

5. On the application of any State Party, or State enterprise, or persona natura or juridical which possesses the national ty of a State Party or is effectively controlled by it or its nationals and is sponsored by a ab Party, or any group of the foregoing (hereinafter called the "applicant"), the Authority shall t e nto a contract for the carrying out of exploration for, and exploitation of the resources of the area.

SINGLE NEGOTIATING TEXT

AMENDMENT

ANNEX PARAGRAPH 6 AS AMENDED

SINGLE NEGOTIATING TEXT

6. Every con_tract_ en_tered_ ed into by the __Author__ty pursuant to paragraph 4 _sh_all:

(a) be in _st_rict con_for_mity with th_is_ Convent_i_on and the rules and regulations pescri_bed_ by the __Authority__ in accordance with the Convention;

(b) ensure di_rect_ and _eff_ective f_i_scal _and_ _adm_in-strative control by _the_ Authority at all stages of operations thr_ough_ appropriate institutional arrange-me_nts_ entered into pursuant to this _A_.

AMENDMENT

Annex I, Paragraph 6

Amend as follows:

Paragraph 6, chapeau: Substitute "5" for "4".

Subparagraph (b): Delete the word _and_ _the_ 'supervision.' Place a full _st_op after the word "Authority' and _the_ the remainder of the sentence.

ANNEX PARAGRAPH 6 AS AMENDED

6. Every contract _enter_ed into by _the_ Authority pursuant to paragraph 5 shal_l_:

a) be in strict conform_it_y w_ith_ Part _I_ of th_is_ Convention and _the_ rules and regulat_i_ons pr_e_scr_ibed_ by _the_ Authority in accordance w_ith_ Part I of this Convention;

(b) ensure _direc_t and _effec_ti_ve f_isca_l and _adm_inistrative supervision by _the_ Authority.

AMENDMENT

S NGLE NEGOT AT NG TEXT

QUALIFICATION OF APPLICANTS

7. (a) The Authority ll t gl al os r making an application s d rules and t to h 5, d be qualifications of y applicant d to h qualifications shall incl de (1) financial standing, (2) technological capability, d (3) t d k experience.

(b) s Parties which apply to r into con- s with he Authority ba l be d to h (a). y he qualifications specified n shall be d to have waived their sovereign immunity with t to fi a cial d c obligations covered by h d.

(c) Each applicant ball, in addition, submit to he Authority a work ge h shall he objectives of he Authority as l ed in this t d he rules and gu ations d.

(d) Each pp icant shall e to p y w th he provisions of this Convention d he s d regulations d by he Authority, and to t l by he i ty ln he therewith.

Annex I, Paragraph 7

Amend as follows:

Paragraph 7(a): After "fi a al standing" insert he d "and". Place a full p after he d lity" and de be de of he t.

Paragraph 7b): Delete the second sentence.

Paragraph 7(c): Be d after he second "shall" and he following: "fully te into at he requirements of he ts d gu ts of he Authority."

Paragraph 7(d): he he d "control" and substitute h."

7. (a) The Authority ba l t app he adm t trative s and rules and gul s r g an application t to h 5, and be l fications of y ppli t rred to h qualifications shall i ol de (1) fi a cial g d (2) technological capability.

(b) s Parties which pp y to r into contracts with he Authority bl be d to s he qualifications ff ed n b h (a).

(c) Each pp cant bl n addition, submit to he Authority a k ge which ba l fully e do t he requirements of he rules d gl ds of he Authority.

(d) n pp on t bl ke to ply with he rules d regulati os d by he d to de pvision by he Authority in de bw h.

S BE NEGOT AT NG TEXT   AMENDMENT   ANNEX   PARAGRAPH 8 AS AMENDED

SELECTION OF ALLICANTS

8. a) On recieving an application t to
ad exploitation, he Authority shall first
tain r by competing application s n
received r be a applied . If no n
competing application s n received, he Authority
shall r o negotiations with a view to conclud-
ng a t with he applicant in t of he
a applied , provided t he qualifica-
completed e s he applicant s
tions prescribed t to   6 , ,
a consideration of all relevant s is d to
r he Authority optimum benefits. The Enterprise
ay at e to r o a t if he criteria
in all r s is in strict conformity with he
provisions of this t d of e rules, regulations
d e policy established by he Authority.

(b) Applicants shall be required to p y with
requirements of he Authority to achieve he objectives
t h in article 12 above.

(c) If the Aut ority receives more than a appl i-
tion in respect of substantially the same r and
category of minerals, selection from among the applicants
shall be made on a competitive basis taking into account
the extent to whi h each applicant satisfies the requirements of paragraph 6. The Authority shall enter into
negotiations with a view to concluding a contract with
the applicant wh h, after a c nsideration of all relevant factors, is d to offer the Authority optimum
b ne6its including fi a ial arrangements n accordance
with paragraph 9(d).

Annex I, Paragraph 8

d as follows:

Paragraph 8(a): and substitute *"exploration."*

Annex I. the following:

*"If no such competing applica-
tion has been received the Authority
shall conclude a contract with the
applicant in respect to the area
applied for, provided that the appli-
t has completed the procedures
d possesses the qualifications
pursuant to paragraphs 6 and 7."*

In the sentence and substitute
*"Authority." Delete l after
 ad t a fu 7*

Paragraph 8(b):

*Paragraph 8(c): At the end of e
first sentence delete the full
stop and add "and paragraph 7."
Delete the second sentence.*

8. a) On receiving an application t to
tion d exploitation, he Authority shall first
ascertain r y competing application s n
received r be a applied . If no n e-
peting application s n received he Authority
shall conclude a t with he applicant in
 t of e a applied , provided t e
applicant s completed e s d
 he qualifications prescribed t to r-
 s 6 and 7. he Authority ay t e to
 r o a t if he criteria in all
9(d) have n satisfied, d e t in all
 r s is in strict conformity with he
provisions of t I of this Convention d of
 he rules, regulations d s d

f) If the Auth ority receives more n oe
application in respect of substantially e e
 e and category of minerals, select n m
 g the applicants shall be made on a competitive
basis taking into account the extent to which h
applicant satisfies the requirements of r-
 h 6 and paragraph 7.

SINGLE NEGOTIATING TEXT

(d) The principles set forth in sub-paragraphs (a) (b) and (c) shall be applied mutatis mutandis in prescribing procedures, rules and regulations for the selection of applicants for contracts with respect to activities other than evaluation and exploitation.

(e) When a contractor that has entered into a contract with the Authority for all or some of the stages of operations referred to in paragraph 4 has completed performance under it, he shall have priority among applicants for a contract or contracts for the same area and resources; provided, however, that where the contractor has not carried out his obligations satisfactorily, such priority may be withdrawn.

(f) The total number of contracts for evaluation and exploitation entered into by the Authority with a single State Party or with natural and juridical persons under the sponsorship of a single State Party shall not exceed .. per cent of the total area open under paragraph 3, and shall be quale for all States Parties.

(g) Within the limits specified in sub-paragraph (f) the Council may every year determine the number of contracts to be entered into by the Authority with a single State Party or with natural and juridical persons under the sponsorship of a single State Party in order to give effect to the provisions of articles

AMENDMENT

Paragraph 8(d): Delete.

Paragraph 8(e): Transfer to the Statute of the Enterprise and make the following amendment" Insert after the words "shall have" "a preference and a." In the final clause insert after the word "such" "preference or." Delete the word "Authority" and substitute "Enterprise."

Paragraph 8(f) and (g): [This subject requires further discussion.]

RIGHTS AND OBLIGATIONS UNDER THE CONTRACT

9. (a) Any State P rty s or any State enterprise or person natural or juridical which possesses the nation- ality of a State Party or is effectively controlled by it or by its n ti al s when sponsored by a St ts Party or s y group of the foreg i g which enters into a contract for activities relating to evaluation s d exploitation with the Authority pursuant to paragraph 5 (hereinafter called the "Contractor") shall, except s otherwise agreed by the Authority, be required to us its wn funds, materials, equipment, skills s d know- bw s necessary r the conduct of operations covered by the contract s d to p s a bond by way of guarantee of satisfactory performance under the contract.

b) The costs involved in the performance of the t pursuant to subparagraph (a) sh ll be recoverable by the respective parties at of the proceeds of tions. The rity sh ll in its rules s d regulations establish a schedule pursuant to which such co st will be recovered in the r specified in sub-paragraph (d) of this paragraph.

(c) The proceeds of operations pursuant to the t r tion of co st , which sh l be calcul ed rding to ting principles to be mi ed by the rity ed the terms of the , sh ll be apporti ed n be rity ed the Contractor in the r specified in the t in de with subparagraph (d) of this paragraph.

d /F nancia arrangements/

Amend as follows:

Paragraph 9(a): Delete the phrase "except as otherwise agreed by the Authority, be required to use its " and substitute the following: "may available." Place a full stop after the word "contract" and delete the final clause relating to the posting of the d.

Paragraph 9(b): Delete the parties and subs the "contrac- th." Delete the full p after the " and dd "or by the t the s in the t the Authority s contributed to the s of performance." Delete the last

Paragraph 9(c): Delete "principles" ad t after "accounting" the s "rules ad procedures sh are in general se". Delete "to be determined by the Authority and the terms of the "

9. (a) Any St te Party, or s y State enterprise or person natural or juridi at which possesses the nationality of a State Party or is effectively controlled by it or by its nationals, when sponsored by a State Party or s y group of the foregoing which enters into a contract for activities relating to exploration s d exp oitation. with the Authority pursuant to paragraph 5 (here- inafter called the "Contractor") shall make avail- able all funds, materials, equipment, skil s s d know- bw s necessary r the conduct of operations covered by the contract.

(b) The co st invo ed in the performance of the recoverable by the r out of the proceeds of ations or by the respective parties in the event the rity h s r id to the co st of

(c) The proceeds of operations pursuant to the al ol ed r deduction of c tos which shall be ti ed n the Authority and the procedures which ee in general use shall be ti ed r in the r specified in the t in de with sub-paragraph (d) of this paragraph.

d /Financia arrangements/

Annex ,
paragraph 0

SINGLE NEGOTIATING TEXT

AMENDMENT

ANNEX PARAGRAPH 0 AS AMENDED

0. The Contractor shall:

(a) ... in ... de w th the rules ad regulations ad the es ad conditions of the et to the
Authority at time i terval determined by the Authority
all its necessary and relevant to the effective imple-
an of the ps ad functions of the organs of
the Authority at et this C vent on in at
to third parties, without the prior et of the e-
t, sh of the ed da as ae ad to be
proprietary by the ed da which ae necessary
for the promulgation of rules ad regulations concerning
protection of the marine environment sh ll not be ed
to be proprietary. Except s otherwise agreed with the
Authority the er sh l at be obliged to disc se
proprietary at design at

(b) Sw up es for the training of personne
ad the a l such or action as may be necessary to
fulfil its obligations pursuant to subparagraph 8 b).

Annex I, Paragraph 10

Amend as follows:

*Paragraph 10(a): Insert th is at
both after "all data." at
dd safe g" at the at
ment." Add a w ae at the
ad as fol t:*

"Any organ of the Authority
which comes into possession of da
submitted by a contractor pursuant
to Part I of this Convention and
these basic conditions shall at
under any circumstances disclose
such data or make such data available to any person connected with
the operations of the Enterprise
or employed by it."

*Paragraph b: Place full ep
after "pe a" ad de
ace of the b.*

0. The or ball:

(a) ... r in ... de with the rules ad
regulations and the es ad conditions of the
et to the y at time i terval t-
ad by the Authority all its which is h
necessary ad relevant to the effective implementa-
an of the powers ad es of the organs of
the Authority or this Part in at of the
et e. The Authority ll at disclose to
third parties, without the prior et of the e-
t, such of the ed da as is ad
to be proprietary by the ed da which is
necessary for the promulgation of es ad regulations concerning protection of the marine environment
ad dy shall not be ad to be proprietary.
Except as otherwi e agreed with the e
er sh ll at be obliged to discl es proprietary
equipment design d. Any organ of the Authority
which as into an of da submitted by a
at to Part I of its Convention
ad the basic conditions sh ll at or ey
circumstances di cl as such da or the such da
available to ay an ad w th the operations
of the Enterprise or employed by t.

b) Sw up programmes or the training of
pe

AN EX   PARAGRAPH 11 AS AMENDED

AMENDMENT

S NGLE NEGOT AT NG TEXT

Annex I, paragraph 11

No amendment proposed.

11. The Authority sha l, pursuant to this Convent on and the rules and r gu ations prescribed by the Authority, accord the Contractor the exclusive right to evaluate and/or exploit the contract area in respect of a specified category of minerals and shall ensure that no other entity operates in the same contract area for a different category of minera s in a manner which might interfere with the operations of the Contractor. The Contractor shall have security of tenure. Accordingly, the contract shall not be cancelled, modified, suspended or terminated, nor shall the exercise of any right under it be impaired, except for gross and persistent violations of the provisions of this part and the rules and regulations adopted by the Authority thereunder, and after recourse to procedures provided under this part for the settlement of any dispute that may have arisen. The Authority shall not, during the continuance of a contract, permit any entity to car y out activities in the same area for the same category of minerals.

Annex
para

SINGLE NEGOTIATING TEXT	AMENDMENT	ANNEX PARAGRAPH 2 AS AMENDED

RULES, REGULATIONS AND PROCEDURES

12. The Authority shall adopt and uniformly apply rules regulations and procedures consistent with the purposes and fundamental principles of the functioning of the Authority and with these basic conditions in the following subjects

(1) Application to enter into contracts

(2) Qualifications of applicants

(3) Selection of applicants

(4) Progress report

(5) Submission of data

(6) Application fees and bonds to secure satisfactory performance

(7) Inspection and supervision of operations

(8) Mining standards and practices including operational safety

(9) Prevention of interference by the Contractor with other uses of the sea and of the marine environment

(10) Apportionment of the proceeds of operations

(11) Direct participation of personnel of developing countries, particularly the landlocked among them and of other countries lacking or less advanced in ocean mining and mineral processing technology, and the transfer of such technology to such countries.

Annex I, Paragraph 12

Amend as follows:

Paragraph 12 chapeau or Delete "the purposes and fundamental principles of the functioning of the Authority and ith."

Paragraph 12(1): Insert "Procedures for" at the beginning of sentence.

Paragraph 12(2): Delete.

Paragraph 12(3): Insert "Procedures for" at the beginning of sentence.

Paragraph 12(5): Insert "Procedures for" at the beginning of sentence.

Paragraph 12(6): Delete and substitute the following: "Application f a designed to defray the administrative expenses of the Authority.

Paragraph 12(8): Delete and substitute the following: "Operational safety standards and practices."

Paragraph 12(10): Before the word "proceeds" insert "Authority's share of the."

Paragraph 12(11): Insert "Procedures for" at the beginning of sentence a Put a full stop after "ocean mining" and then delete the balance of the sentence.

12. The Authority shall adopt and uniformly apply rules, regulations and procedures consistent with these basic conditions in the following subjects:

(1) Procedures for applications to enter into contracts

(2) Procedures for selection of applicants

(3) Progress report

(4) Procedures for submission of data

(5) Application fees designed to defray the Administrative expenses of the Authority

(6) Inspection and supervision of operations

(7) Operational safety standards and practices

(8) Prevention of interference by the Contractor with other uses of the sea and of the marine environment

(9) Apportionment of the Authority's share of the proceeds of operations

(10) Procedures for direct participation of personnel of developing countries, particularly the landlocked among them and of other countries lacking or less advanced in ocean mining

(11) Procedures for transfer of rights by the Contractor

S NGLE NEGOT AT NG TEXT

(12) Passing of title to minerals and processed metals from he Area

(13) Avoiding or min mizing adverse effects on the reve uea of developing countries derived from exports of he minera s and products thereof from he Area

(14) Transfer of r ghts by he Contractor

(15) Activ t es In reserved are a

(16) F nancia and accounting ru es

In respect of oles, regulations and procedures for the following sub ects the Authority sha l un formly apply he objective criteria set out below

(17) Protection of the marine environment: The Authority shall take Into account In adopt-ing rules and regulations for he protection of the marine environment the extent to which activities In the Area such as drilling, dredging, coring and excavation as ll as disposal, dumping and discharge in th Area of sediment or wastes and othe r matters w ll have a harmful effect on he mar ne environment.

(11) Size of area. he Authority shall determine the appropriate size of areas or evaluation Wich may be up to twice as large as those or exploitation in or to permit int ns!ve conti ued survey and valuation operations. Areas for exploitation shall be calculated to satisfy the production requirements agreed between the Authority and th Contractor over the em of he contract taking into account he state of he art of technology then available for ocean mining and the relevant physical characteristics of the

AMENDMENT

Paragraph 12(12): Delete.

Paragraph 12(13): Delete.

Paragraph 12(14): Insert "Procedures for" at the beginning of sentence.

Paragraph 12(15): Delete.

Paragraph 12(16): Delete financia and.

Paragraph 12(17): Delete the chapeau before the number "17". [Note: The provisions of paragraph 12(17) may require revision at a later time in order to ensure consistency with other provisions in Part I of the Convention.]

Paragraph 12(18): In the second sentence delete "agreed between the Authority and the contractor" and substitute "of th contractor in his sole judgment." Delete the last sentence.

ANNEX PARAGRAPH 2 AS AMENDED

(1) Accounting rules

(13) Protection of he arine environment. The Authority shall take Into account In adopt-ing rules and regulations for he protection of the marine environment the extent to which activities In the Area such as drilling, dredging, coring and excavation as well as disposal, dumping and discharge in he Area of sediment or wastes and other matters will have a harmful effect on he marine environment.

(1.) Size of area. The Author ty shall determine th appropriate size of areas for exploration which may be up to twice as ge as those for exploitation in or to permit Intensive co tinued prospecting and exploration opera-tions. Areas for exploitation shall be calcula th to sa isfy the production require-ments of the contractor in his sole judgme th over the term of he contract taking Into account the state of the art of technology an available for ocean mi l g and th relevant physical characteristics of the area. Areas shall neither be smaller or larger than are necessary to satisfy this objective.

(1) Duration of activities.

(a) Prospecting shall be without time limit except in he ase of violations of he Authority's regulations to protect the environment in which ase the Authority may prohibit the violato r m conducting prospecting operations or a reasonable period of ti e.

b Exploration should be of sufficient d-tion as to permit a thorough survey of he spec fic area, the design and construction

SINGLE NEGOTIATING TEXT

AMENDMENT

ANNEX   PARAGRAPH   2   AS AMENDED

area. Areas shall ne   br be smaller nor
larger than are necessary to satisfy this
objective. In cases   be the Contractor
has obtained a   at   br expl   bt on,
the area not cov edr by such contract shall
be relinquished to be Authorty.

(1) Duration of activities.

(a) General survey shall be without time
limit except in be case of violations of
hte Authority's regulations to protect
be environment in which case th
Authority may prohibit the viola otr from
conducting general survey operations br
a reasonab e period of metl

b Eval ation   buld be of efficient duration as to pmit a thorough survey of
he plfic   e, he design and construction of mining equipment br be
ea, be   gh ed   etion of
all- ed medium-sized   eting mi i g
pl as br be   pe of   fling
ad   psing systems.

(c he   eh of exploitation bu d be
el ed to be emic life of the
mining project taking i no consideration
eh   bs as be depletion of be e
body, be   el life of mining eqi et
ad processing facilities, ed   ecial
viability. Exploi ation should be of
effici et   eh as tq permit e-
ecial extraction of be minerals of the
ea ed should i al de a   eble time
priod br   etion of   ecial
sale mining ed   psing systems dur ng
which priod d. he   et on of
be   eqi d. he   et on of
exploitation, however, should also be
bt gh to give be Authority an

Paragraph 12(19): Delete the tto
references to "general survey"
and substitute the word
"prospecting."

of mining equipment for the area, the
design and construction of small- and
m diumsize processing plants br be
purpose of   sti lp mining and processing systems.

(c The duration of exploitation should be
el ed to bh economic life of the mining
project taking into consideration such
factors as bh depletion of he ee body,
the useful life of mi i g equipment and
processing facilities, and commercial
viability. Exploitation should be of
sufficient dura iom as to pt commercia
extraction of be minerals of be area
and should include a reasonable time
period for construction of commercial
scale mi i g and processing systems dr ng
which period commercial production shou d
not be required. The to at duration of
exploitation, however, should also be short
gh to permit be Authority an opportu ty
to amend hte te msr and conditions of be
contract at bh time it considers renewal
in accordance with rules and regulations
which it has issued subsequent to entering
into bh contract.

(16) Erf ence requirements. he   arity ball
equire that during the expl etion stage, d-
priodic expendi ts be de by be   di-
dr which ee reasonably d ed to he size
of he   et   ea ed the expendi es
which would be expected of a ba fide d-
er ho   ed to bring he ea i to
full-scale   ecial   etion within he
time limits   ali ld by be Authority.
bh   eqi ed expendi es should at be
al ld at a level which ad discourage
prospective   es with less.costly
technology bn is prevalent y n a. The

S NGLE NEGOT AT NG TEXT

opportunity to amend the terms and conditions of the contract at the time it considers renewal n accordance with rules and regu a- tions wh ch it has issued subsequent to entering into the contract.

(O) Performance requirements. The Authority sha l require that during the evaluation stage, per- iodic expenditures be made by the Contractor which are reasonably related to the size of the contract area and the expenditures which would be expected of a bona fide Contractor who intended to bring the area into full-scale com- mercial production within the time limits established by the Authority. Such required expenditures should not be established at a level which would discourage prospective oper- ators with less costly technology than is prevalently in use. The Authority shall estab- lish a maximum time interval after the evalua- tion stage is completed and the exploitation stage begins to achieve full-scale commercia production. To determine this interval, the Authority should take into consideration that construction of large-scale mining and process- ing systems cannot be initiated until after the termination of the evaluation stage and the commencement of the exploitation stage. Accord- ingly, the interval to bring an area into fu l- scale commercial production should take into account the time necessary for this construction after the completion of the evaluation stage and reasonable allowance should be made for unavoid- able delays in the construction schedule.

Once full-scale commercial production is achieved in the exploitation stage, the Authority shall within reasonable limits and taking into consideration all relevant factors require the Contractor to maintain a reasonable level of commercial production throughout the period of the contract.

AMENDMENT

Paragraph 12(20): In the second paragraph delete "a reasonable level of."

ANNEX PARAGRAPH 2 AS AMENDED

Authority shall establ sh a maximum time interval after the exp oration stage is com- pleted and the exploitation stage begins to achieve full-scale commercial production. To determine this interval, the Authority should take into consideration that construction of large-scale mining and processing systems cannot be initiated until after the termination of the exploration stage and the commencement of the exploitation stage. Accordingly, the interval to bring an area into full-scale com- mercial production should take inco account the time necessary for this construction after the completion of the exploration stage and reasonable allowance should be made for unavoidable delays in the construct on schedu e.

Once full-scale commercia production is achieved in the exploitat on stage, the Authority shall within reasonable limits and taking into consideration all relevant factors require the Contractor to maintain commercial production throughout the period of the contract.

(17) Categories of minerals. In determining the category of mineral in respect of which a contract may be entered into, the Authority shall give emphasis inter alia to the fol ow- ing characteristics:

(a) Resources which require the use of similar mining methods, and

b Resources which can be developed simultaneously without undue interference between Contractors in the same area developing different resources.

Nothing in this paragraph shall deter the the Authority from granting a contract for more than one category of mineral in the same contract area to the same applicant.

SINGLE NEGOTIATING TEXT

(1) Categories of minerals. In determining the category of mineral in respect of which a contract may be entered into, the Authority shall give emphasis it er alla to the ollowing characteristics:

(a Resources which eu re the use of similar mining methods, and

(b) Resources which can be developed s mu taneously w thout undue nterference between Contractors in the same area developing different resources.

Nothing in th s paragraph shall deter the Authority from grant ng a contract for more than one category of mineral in the same contract area to the same applicant.

(22) Renunciation of areas. The contractor shall have the right at any time to renounce with ua penalty the whole or part of his rights in the contract area.

AMENDMENT

Paragraph 12(22): Delete the second sentence.

ANNEX I PARAGRAPH 2 AS AMENDED

(18) Renunciati on of areas. The contractor shall have the right at any time to renounce without penalty the whole or part of h's rights in the contract area.

2 bis. Commercia production for the purpose of paragraph 12 shall be deemed to have b gue lf for a period of several months a Contractor engages in activity of sustained large-scale recov y operations which yield a suffici quantity of materia as to clearly indicate that the principal purpose is large-scale production rather than production intended for nformation gathering analysis, equipment or plant testing.

S NGLE NEGOT AT NG EX

13. The Authority shall have the right to take at any time any measures provi d for u d m this Convention to ensure comp iance with its terms, and in the performance of the control and regulatory funct ons assigned to it thereunder or u dem any contract a l The Authority shall have the right to inspect a l facilities n the Area used in connexion with any activities n the Area.

AMENDMENT

Annex I, Paragraph 13

Ame nds follows: Delete the "control" and substitute "supervisory." In the second sentence delete "Authority" and substitute "technical Commission. d

ANNEX   PARAGRAPH 13 AS AMENDED

13. The Authority sha l have the r ght to take at any time any measures provided for under Part I of this Convention to ensure compliance with its terms, and in the performance of the supervisory and regulatory functions ass gned to it thereunder or u dem any contract. The Technical Commission shall have the right to inspect all facilities in the Area used in connexion with any act vit es in the Area.

An ex I,
para. 1

S NGLE NEGOT AT NG TEXT   AMENDMENT   ANNEX   PARAGRAPH   4 A   AMENDED

SUSPENSION OR TERMINATION

Annex I, Paragraph 14

14. A Contractor's rights in t e contract area shall be suspended or terminated only if the Contractor has conducted his activities in su b a way as to result in gross and persiste b violations of this Part and rules and regulations and were not caused by circumstances beyond his control, or if a Contractor has wilfully failed to comply with any decision of the _/d spute settlement organ_/.

Ame nds follows: Delete "/dispute e ttlement organ/" and substitute "Tribunal." Add a new sentence as follows: "Less e penalties in the nature of monetary penalties may be imposed by the Tribunal for violations which are not gross and persistent, provided the penalties are proportionate to the violation.

4. A Contractor's rights in the contract area shall be suspended or terminated only if the Contractor has conducted his activities in su b a way as to result in gross and persistent violations of Part I of this Convention and the rules and regulations adopted thereunder and were not caused by circumstances u d er his control, or if a Contractor has wilfully fail d to comply with any decision of the Tribunal. Lesser p e ties in the nature of monetary penalties may be imposed by the Tribunal for violations which are not gross and persistent, provided the penalties are pro-portionate to the v olati o

ANNEX   PARAGRAPH 15 AS AMENDED

AMENDMENT

Annex I, Paragraph 15

Delete.

S NGLE NEGOTIATI NG EX

REVISION OF CONTRACT

15. /Circumstances under which terms and conditions
(e.g. financial conditions) of contracts may be
rev sed - to be drafted.7

A NEX   PARAGRAPH 6 AS AMENDED

S NGLE NEGOTIATING TEXT

AMENDMENT

FORCE MAJEURE

16. Non-performance or de.ay in performance shal be excused if and to the extent that such non-performance or delay is caused by force majeure. The party invoking force majeure may take appropriate measures including revision, suspension or termination of the contract; provided, however, that in the ve b of a dispute the parties shall first have recourse to the procedures for the settlement of disputes provided for in this Part.

Annex I, Paragraph 16

Delete.

AMENDMENT

SINGLE NEGOTIATING TEXT

Annex I, paragraph 17

No amendment proposed.

TRANSFER OF RIGHTS

1. The right and obligations arising out of a contract shall be transferred only with the consent of the Authority, and in accordance with the rules and regulations adopted by it. The Authority shall not withhold consent to the transfer if the proposed transferee is in all respects a qualified applicant, and assumes all of the obligations of the transferor.

SINGLE NEGOTIATING TEXT	AMENDMENT	ANNEX PARAGRAPH 18 AS AMENDED

APPLICABLE LAW

18. The law applicable to the contract shall be solely the provisions of this Convention, the rules and regulations prescribed by the Authority, and the terms and conditions of the contract. The rights and obligations of the Authority and of the Contractor shall be valid and enforceable notwithstanding the law of any State, or any political subdivision thereof to the contrary. No contracting State may impose conditions on a Contractor that are inconsistent with the principles of this Convention.

Annex I, Paragraph 18

Amend as follows. Delete 'solely in the first sentence. Delete "and" then ' ; '"duty" and "the" in the first sentence. Delete the full stop and insert "and other applicable rules of law."

Delete sentences 2 and 3.

18. The law applicable to the contract shall be the provisions of Part I of this Convetion , the rules and regulations prescribed by the Authority, the terms and conditions of the contract and other applicable rules of law.

| SINGLE NEGOTIATING TEXT | AMENDMENT | ANNEX PARAGRAPH 9 AS AMENDED |

LIABILITY

19 Responsibility or liability for wrongful damage arising out of the conduct of operations by the Contractor or the Authority shall lie with the Contractor or the Authority as the case may be. It shall be a defence in any proceeding against a Contractor that the damage was the result of an act or omission of the Authority. Similarly, any responsibility or liability for wrongful damage arising out of the exercise of the powers and functions of the Authority shall lie with the Authority. It shall be a defence in any proceeding against the Authority that the damage was a result of an act or omission of the Contractor. Liability in every case shall be for the amount of damage.

Annex I, Paragraph 19

Amend as follows: _Delete the first second and third references to the "the Authority."_

19. Responsibility or liability for wrongful damage arising out of the conduct of operations by the Contractor shall lie with the Contractor. It shall be a defence in any proceeding against a Contractor that the damage was the result of an act or omission of the Authority. Similarly, any responsibility or liability for wrongful damage arising out of the exercise of the powers and functions of the Authority shall lie with the Authority. It shall be a defence in any proceeding against the Authority that the damage was a result of an act or omission of the Contractor. Liability in every case shall be for the amount of damage.

S NGLE NEGOTIATING TEXT

AMENDMENT

Annex I, Paragraph 20

Delete.

SETTLEMENT OF DISPUTES

20. Any dispute concerning the interpretation or application of this C ve tion, its rules nd regu a- ns or the terms nd conditions of a contract and arising n be Authority and a Contracting State or any State enterprise or person natural or ju idica which possesses he tionality of a Contracti g State or is ctive y controlled by it or its atio als, or any group of he foregoing shall on be pl ation of ei r party be subject to the procedure for ele- nt of h disputes provided for in this Convention.

S NGLE NEGOT AT NG TEX   AMENDMENT   ANNEX   PARAGRA H 2   AS AMENDED

Annex I, Paragraph 21

ARRANGEMENTS FOLLOWING PROVISIONAL ENTRY INTO FORCE OF THE CONVENTION

21. In the per dd immediately following provisional
plication of Ws Convention, be Authority ball,
with resp et to be first /...7 eh contra &, joint
ventures or other eh form of association, give
priority to those covering integrated stages of
operations.

Delete.

Mr. MURPHY. I also have notified the members of this committee that the subcommittee and full committee will markup this legislation on March 15 and 16.

I would like to ask the State Department representative if the Congress acts affirmatively in this legislative area, will the State Department recommend a veto or recommend signing of the legislation?

Mr. ESKIN. Mr. Chairman, I am not in a position to answer your question at this stage.

We will have to examine any legislation that come out of this committee carefully.

Mr. Ratiner outlined in his statement to you and his answers to your questions an accurate reflection of the Department of State's views on this legislation and those of the administration.

Mr. MURPHY. Well, I would like to refer you to a July 16, 1975, communication from the Comptroller General with their comments on H.R. 1270, and to take that question back and try to get me a better answer, a more definitive answer.

Mr. ESKIN. Yes, sir.

Mr. MURPHY. What will the voting procedure be at the Conference on the amendments we are talking about?

Mr. RATINER. Well, Mr. Chairman, there are two kinds of voting procedures. One is contained in the rules of procedure of the Conference, which essentially require a two-thirds majority of the members of the Conference present in voting, after all efforts have been made to achieve general agreement or consensus.

The second kind of voting procedure, which seems to me more germane, is the collective behavior of the delegates in respect of these treaty texts.

We have said to Congress for several years, and it still remains true, that there seems to be no willingness on the part of developing countries, indeed, to confront us with a vote on any critical issue.

There seems to be a very general understanding that this treaty, in order for it to be successful, must be accommodating. In order for it to be accommodating, key issues cannot be resolved by a vote in which critical industrialized countries are simply outvoted.

That tendency continues, and there is still no talk of adopting a treaty by general consensus.

Mr. MURPHY. That does not sound very realistic to me.

In the political sector, whether a local community or the United Nations or an international treaty, you are not going to get anything by consensus these days. You are going to have to call the roll, and you know how long that can take.

I can see it taking a decade, maybe two decades, before there is any atmosphere for that type of agreement.

Mr. RATINER. Mr. Chairman, I think the reason our negotiations have taken as long as they have is because we have been, in fact, following the procedure of seeking consensus.

If we were going to take votes, this treaty negotiation could have been completed a long time ago.

Mr. MURPHY. In other words, Committees Two and Three are ready to resolve all their issues and take the vote?

Mr. RATINER. No, they are not. I wish they were, Mr. Chairman, but Committee Two still has outstanding issues of importance to many countries, and so does Committee Three.

Mr. MURPHY. In reference to the Committee One negotiations and domestic legislation referring to Mr. Maw's statement on page 2, and I quote, "In our policy review, we explored whether we could reduce the investment uncertainties to some form of domestic legislation without damaging the Law of the Sea negotiations," what did he mean by damaging?

Mr. RATINER. He meant whether we could, in fact, develop domestic legislation which would be circumspect nature and avoid preempting what ultimately would be included in a treaty.

The fact of the matter is, Mr. Chairman, that we were not able, prior to the emergence of new developments in the Conference, to agree on any such form of legislation which would not be damaging to the Conference.

Mr. MURPHY. I derived from personal meetings in Geneva with the members of the U.S. negotiating team, most of them who stayed awake during those sessions with me, that the Engo document was and is an unmitigated disaster for this country.

Unilateral legislation is an attempt to undo the damage already perpetrated on the United States' ocean miners' invesment uncertainties.

Can you explain why they would have that attitude?

Mr. RATINER. I think they were quite correct.

The "Single Negotiating Text" produced by Mr. Engo was, in my view, and in the view of most members of the U.S. delegation, a disaster, a disaster not for its content, Mr. Chairman. That goes without saying. But it came at a point rather late in the negotiations, since a great deal more negotiations would have to occur before the text could be put back into a condition which the United States would accept.

It was because of our concern for a timely conclusion of the Conference that we considered the text a disaster.

It is substantively a disaster, but we had no intention of signing it so that is irrelevant.

The only question is, would a text like the Engo one enable us in a short period of time to move to a new text which was much, much better.

We thought, after Geneva, that this movement would be extremely difficult to achieve in 1976.

Now, there are indications that it may not be as difficult to achieve. However, it depends entirely on whether the group of 77, which will be meeting in New York between the 1st and 15th of March, is willing to accept the chairman's new compromise texts.

If they reject those new texts, then we are back in the same situation we were in immediately after the Geneva meeting.

If they accept those texts, we will quickly build on top of them and stand a reasonably good chance of concluding the negotiations in 1976.

Mr. MURPHY. And that will resolve the committee II and the committee III difficulties, too.

Mr. RATINER. Committees II and III will be resolved on their own merits, Mr. Chairman.

There are a variety of difficult issues in those committees that still require negotiation.

I have a feeling that when we first came back from Geneva, the United States delegation had a somewhat myoptic view of the state of negotiations. Because the Committee I text was as bad it was, the Committees II and III texts obviously appeared far better. And there was a tendency to oversimplify the true state of negotiations.

With the new compromise texts in committee I right now, it is entirely possible that, if the committee adopts useful and progressive procedures, the committee I text will be at least in as good shape by the end of the March meeting in New York as the committee II text was at the end of Geneva.

Mr. MURPHY. I am sorry to see on page 4 of Mr. Maw's statement that he does not support any ocean mining legislation at this time.

I would like to state that the Congress has heard this many times, but I think that the atmosphere is for the Congress to move forward at this time.

Mr. Ratiner, on page 3, you say extensive private consultations on deep seabed issues have been held with key leaders in the committee.

Will you elaborate a little more on that and let us know if you have discussed this with Mr. Engo and what he had to say?

Mr. RATINER. Yes, Mr. Chairman, I have met with Mr. Engo in New York, California and his capital in the Cameroon.

Most importantly, Mr. Engo chaired the 2-week meeting that took place in New York, and he produced the new compromise texts. Rather than elaborate on my conversations with him, I would simply refer to the concrete evidence of his change, which is manifest in his new texts.

Mr. MURPHY. On page 4, you said we have repeatedly stated many of the important details of the "Single Negotiating Text" can be expeditiously resolved if there is a will to seek political accommodation.

What do you mean by that?

Mr. RATINER. Simply that there are a handful of critical issues in Committee I, which include the questions of whether States will have access to the resources, price and production controls, a one nation, one vote assembly with dictatorial powers over the policies of the Authority. If there is evidence that there is a will to compromise on these critical issues, then most of the rest of the Single Negotiating Text will fairly rapidly fall into place.

Now, we have been the beginning of those compromises on those critical issues.

Mr. MURPHY. Did you feel that the unilateral action of the United States with the Congress taking or announcing a firm position had anything to do with that change in position, or was it strictly the persuasive powers of the United States' negotiator?

Mr. RATINER. Mr. Chairman, I take no credit at all for the change. I give it all to Congress.

Mr. MURPHY. You further say, on page 4, these new draft articles appear to represent an attempt by some, although by no means all of the members of the group of 77 to remove from the Single

Negotiating Text some of the more extreme elements of previous developing countries' positions.

How many countries do you say it represents and what are their relative positions in the power structure of the group of 77?

Mr. RATINER. It is a very difficult to say how many countries it represents.

First of all, when delegates speak in the Law of the Sea Conference, they can only bind their own countries.

Nevertheless, looking at the organization of Committee I and of the developing countries, the principal negotiators who were present during these New York meetings are the ones who have spoken in the past for the major interest groupings in the developing country world.

For example, present at these meetings was the representative of Singapore. Singapore has been one of the most active representatives of a large group of developing countries who are consumers of raw materials from the deep seabed.

Simultaneously present in these negotiations was the representative of Brazil, who has been one of the most active exponents of protecting land based producers.

The same is true in respect of Chile, which was also represented in these negotiations.

I think the fact that the chairman of Committee I, was also the author of these new texts and is a leading member of the African community in the Conference angers well for African support for these compromises that are emerging.

There are, of course, other developing country negotiators who were present, and these are only some examples.

These are some of the principal leading spokesmen for major interest or geographical groups in the negotiations.

Mr. MURPHY. The Group of 77 is almost a misnomer. I think it is more like the Group of 105, is it not?

Mr. RATINER. It is at least 105 and probably a few more by now.

Mr. MURPHY. What position does the Soviet Union take in Committee I?

Mr. RATINER. The Soviet Union's position in Committee I is quite similar to the United States' position in Committee I.

We have, to the best of our ability, tried to consult closely with the Soviet Union throughout this negotiation and, as much as possible, to coordinate our views on the matter.

Most of the amendments to the "Single Negotiating Text," which we have already included in the record and which were put out informally by the United States, are supported by the Soviet Union.

Mr. MURPHY. Mr. Ratiner, after giving us a glimmer of hope for four pages, on page 5 you say, "I do not in any way intend to give the impression that the United States finds these draft articles acceptable as final treaty provisions," and that you "do not believe they are, not only because of their content, but also because of their inevitable dependence on a host of other important amendments which were not discussed in the New York meetings."

In your own private opinion, given that statement, is not the guarded optimism you present here, and similar assessments made to me privately by Ambassador John Norton Moore, is not this in the realm of a faint glimmer of hope, and nothing more?

Mr. RATINER. I think that is a reasonable characterization.

Mr. MURPHY. I only use the term "glimmer" because it appears on page 6 in your testimony of today.

Mr. RATINER. This is a faint glimmer. It leads to greater hope than we have previously had concrete evidence to support in all of the years of this negotiation.

Still, there are difficult problems to be worked out. Most importantly, we cannot even think about working them out until we know whether these compromises are going to be accepted by the Group of 77.

If they are rejected, then there is no glimmer of hope whatsoever.

Mr. MURPHY. On page 6 you say at virtually any time in the next few months the situation could change radically, and prospects for a successful settlement could vanish.

Is that not a more realistic appraisal of what the situation is, based on your past experience?

Mr. RATINER. A statistical appraisal would bear out your statement, Mr. Chairman.

Committeee I has always been an extremely difficult negotiation, and there has never been much hope for its success.

But there is a new factor now, which is a general awareness and appreciation by developing countries that, if there is going to be a treaty on the law of the sea, it is probably going to be a treaty produced within the next 6 to 9 months.

If that is the case, then it would be reasonable at this time in the negotiation, notwithstanding years of no progress, that key compromise articles would have to begin to appear.

If that is a general view held by most developing countries, then I think we can expect to see compromises continue in Committee I with a view towards success.

If, on the other hand, that is simply the view of a few leaders in the Group of 77, not widely supported, then we will see these compromise texts vanish, and the hopes for a successful conference vanish with them.

Mr. MURPHY. On page 7, you say the administration will have to keep the question of the desirability of deep seabed mining legislation under constant review, particularly in light of what happens at the next session of the Law of the Sea Conference.

Does the administration have a position on legislation at this time?

Mr. RATINER. Well, the administration's position on legislation is stated in both Mr. Maw's testimony and mine. We are opposed to legislation at this time, and I cannot emphasize too strongly the words "at this time."

We mean, Mr. Chairman, at this moment, at this instant in time.

We will have a much better idea in 6 to 8 weeks as to whether we should have a positive position on legislation. You have heard this before, and I beg your indulgence.

Mr. MURPHY. I have a question.

Will you recommend a veto on legislation or not? You state there appears to be a genuine recognition that 1976 is the final opportunity for serious negotiation.

I wholeheartedly agree you should direct you efforts toward reaching agreement this time around.

However, you cannot rule out, and I am sure you have not ruled out the possibility that a settlement might not be reached, and might be out of reach.

If that is the case, then you can be sure the Congress will take some action on this domestic legislation before us today.

It seems to me you should be prepared for the eventuality and make some comments on the legislation before us.

I would therefore like to give you this opportunity, as well as state, to make some comments on the form the final legislation should take, and you can express yourself, not as a negotiator, but as the Administrator of the Ocean Mining Administration in the Department of the Interior, even though perhaps your verbal comments may not have beeen cleared with the Office of Management and Budget.

Mr. RATINER. That is quite a correct observation, Mr. Chairman. They have not.

First, let me say that we have, with a degree of care, presented comments to you and other committees of Congress on very similar legislation on past occasions.

Leaving aside the question of whether this is a politically sensible time to pass legislation, I might recall that we had certain objections to the legislation which is now pending before this committee.

For example, we objected to the establishment by law of block sizes, the duration of mining rights, a time period to come into commercial production, the minimum amount of investment dollars that would have to be expended in order to maintain rights, and the procedures to be used for obtaining rights.

We indicated in the past, and I reaffirm today, that we do not yet have in the U.S. Government the capability to assemble independently verifiable data needed to support the detailed provisions included in this legislation.

For example, in the legislation there is a provision for block sizes of 40,000 square kilometers.

Mr. Chairman, the information which supports a 40,000 square-kilometer block size to be reduced by 75 percent subsequent to the exploration period is largely obtained from the U.S. mining industry.

We have not been able to carry out programs in the executive branch which would produce sufficient data to verify that the data provided to us by industry to support these provisions is, in fact, accurate. In our view it would be wrong to pass legislation which set into concrete some of the most important provisions of any resource management scheme.

I might add, Mr. Chairman, that these bills that have been pending before Congress do not provide for the provisional application of the treaty. As far as the administration is concerned, this is one of the most important next steps, or preparatory steps, which the Congress will need to take in order to protect adequately American industry rights, if a treaty does come into force.

We have also objected to the provisions on insurance, which are contained in all of the legislation which has been pending before Congress for several years, including your new legislation.

We felt that the investment guarantee provision in all of these bills tends to provide absolute compensation to industry, in essence, to guarantee against the effects of U.S. treaty negotiation.

In fact, these provisions would guarantee against U.S. Government policy decision in a treaty negotiation when the treaty will ultimately be put before the Congress of the United States to determine whether it is a satisfactory resolution of the issues.

We do not think at the present time that the administration should be supporting legislation containing such investment guarantees against its own negotiation efforts.

I might also add, Mr. Chairman, that we have criticized in the past the absence from these bills of any meaningful provisions from which the United States would derive revenues for the benefit of its taxpayers.

As far as I can recall, these bills contain only a $50,000 license fee to be used to defray the cost of administering the system.

Finally, Mr. Chairman, as you well know, your new bill inserts a new issue concerning which department of the Government should have jurisdiction over ocean mining.

I understand that Under Secretary of the Interior Frizzell will testify before you tomorrow on that subject. Nevertheless, it should be clear that this aspect will cause new difficulties for the administration which have not heretofore been present in any legislation pending before Congress.

Mr. MURPHY. Kent Frizzell will be here tomorrow from the Department of Interior, and also a representative of Deep Sea Ventures, and we will try to get from him some response to your latest statement, just now, that the U.S. Government has no firm knowledge as to just what is on the seabed floor, although American industry does.

Are you prepared to accept provisions in a treaty less favorable to American interests than those proposed in H.R. 11879?

Mr. RATINER. Probably. The point of our treaty negotiation, Mr. Chairman, is to produce a treaty that establishes an attractive investment climate.

The provisions of pending legislation probably do establish an attractive investment climate, but those are not the only provisions which could establish one.

Mr. MURPHY. Are there other questions.

Mr. Forsythe?

Mr. FORSYTHE. No questions.

Mr. MURPHY. Mr. Oberstar?

Mr. OBERSTAR. No questions, Mr. Chairman.

Mr. MURPHY. I would like to thank the witnesses this morning, Mr. Ratiner and Mr. Eskin, for their comments.

The committee will now stand in recess until 10 o'clock tomorrow morning.

[Whereupon, at 12:05 p.m., the subcommittee recessed, to reconvene at 10 a.m., Tuesday, February 24, 1976.]

DEEP SEABED MINING

TUESDAY, FEBRUARY 24, 1976

HOUSE OF REPRESENTATIVES,
COMMITTEE ON MERCHANT MARINE AND FISHERIES
SUBCOMMITTEE ON OCEANOGRAPHY,
Washington, D.C.

The subcommittee met, pursuant to recess, at 10:16 a.m., in room 1334, Longworth House Office Building, Hon. John M. Murphy [chairman], presiding.

Mr. MURPHY. The subcommittee will come to order.

The Chair would like to apologize for the short delay, but Congress pased a railroad bill, but forgot the State of New York. We had to bring that slight oversight back into perspective this morning.

Our first witness today is the Under Secretary of Interior, Kent Frizzell.

Mr. Frizzell, introduce the other witnesses with you please.

STATEMENT OF HON. KENT FRIZZELL, UNDER SECRETARY OF THE INTERIOR, ACCOMPANIED BY W. L. FISHER, DEPUTY ASSISTANT SECRETARY FOR ENERGY AND MINERALS AND LEIGH S. RATINER, ADMINISTRATOR, OCEAN MINING ADMINISTRATION, DEPARTMENT OF THE INTERIOR

Mr. FRIZZELL. Certainly, Mr. Chairman.

The gentleman on my left is Dr. Wililam Fisher, Deputy Assistant Secretary for Energy and Minerals at the Department of the In terior.

The gentleman on my right is Mr. Leigh Ratiner, who is Administrator of the Ocean Mining Administration, as well as the U.S. negotiator in Committee One at the Law of the Sea Conference.

Mr. MURPHY. You may proceed.

Mr. FRIZZELL. Mr. Chairman and members of the subcommittee, I want to thank you for the opportunity to testify before you this morning on this important issue.

The Department of the Interior has not had an opportunity to analyze in any detail the technical aspects of the ocean mining legislation under consideration by this committee. But, regardless of whatever mineral resource management approach ultimately is established for deep ocean mining, we believe tht the objectives, policy and programs of Govrnment related to ocean mining during the

(265)

next few years will be an important factor in the establishment of a successful American-owned deep ocean mining capability.

The reasons given before this subcommittee just yesterday by Under Secretary Carlyle E. Maw of the State Department and by Mr. Leigh S. Ratiner of our Department, lead us to believe that we should not support any ocean mining legislation at this time.

However, I want to emphasize that, as Under Secretary Maw indicated in his statement of yesterday, the administration is continuing to explore the question of appropriate ocean mining legislation so that we will be ready to take any necessary action once we can project the results of the ongoing deep seabed negotiation in the Law of the Sea Conference.

Therefore, my remarks this morning will focus on Interior's past efforts to contribute to Government knowledge and expertise in this area. In addition, I will comment briefly on the kinds of work that should be initiated to support continued sound development of Government policy and programs in ocean mining.

Before turning attention to the activities of Government in ocean mining, some background on the status of the ocean mining industry might be useful.

In the past 12 months, ocean miners have reached the stages of research and development when they are nearly ready to embark on the capital-intensive commercial development process. Ocean mining companies estimate they may have to commit $300 to $600 million for each planned minesite in order to realize an annual commercial production of 1 to 3 million tons of nodules per mining operation early in the next decade. Decisions to make such substantial capital investments will have to be made within the next 18 months.

Through the Mining and Minerals Policy Act of 1970 the Department of the Interior is mandated to "foster and encourage--the development of economically sound and stable domestic mining, minerals and metals industries."

In the case of ocean mining, we have diligently sought to fulfill this responsibility. We have played a major role in Government efforts to achieve an internationally agreed stable legal regime for ocean mining.

We have actively participated in exploring executive branch policies and programs designed to stabilize the ocean mining investment climate prior to final resolution of a legal regime. And, we have begun to develop the requisite information base and in-house expertise to support comprehensive Government efforts in ocean mining.

For the past 6 years, the growth of the infant ocean mining industry, coupled with increasing international and domestic attention to ocean minerals has required Interior to call upon its long experience with mining and minerals industries to play an important role in Government ocean mining policy.

In order to assure adequate understanding within Government of the impact on domestic mineral supply of the deep ocean mining industry, the unique political/legal situation surrounding such an industry, and the implications of ocean mining technology and practices, we have conducted numerous technical and policy studies and have devoted staff resources from the Office of the Secretary exclusively to ocean mining.

Interior's ocean mining activities have included preparing the primary Government study of regulatory approaches to ocean mining, conducting periodic technology assessments to monitor progress of the industry, examining metallurgical processing techniques for winning metals from deep ocean nodules, conducting economic studies of ocean mining operations, undertaking resource assessment programs, developing and evaluating policy alternatives for the promotion of ocean mining, conducting a variety of economic studies on issues raised by the international negotiations and preparation in 1974 of a draft environmental impact statement for ocean mining.

Additionally, the Administrator of the Ocean Mining Administration, as I indicated earlier, Mr. Leigh S. Ratiner, has also served as the U.S. negotiator on the committee of the Law of the Sea Conference, dealing with ocean mining issues, and the Department has provided technical support for these negotiations.

Finally, because of the young, constantly growing nature of the ocean mining industry, we have maintained continuous close liaison with the industry so that we always have available the most up-to-date information, hopefully. In February 1975, the Ocean Mining Administration was created under the Assistant Secretary—Energy and Minerals, to provide increased coordination and guidance for technical work and to upgrade policy development activities.

Interior has been able to conduct this work without a large budget for ocean mining because it has been possible to draw upon existing expertise in the Department—primarily from the Bureau of Mines and Geological Survey.

Of course, if the Federal Government is to keep pace with the anticipated acceleration of ocean mining operations through the remainder of the decade we will need to allocate an increased share of our budget resources in order to acquire a more comprehensive data base and more detailed technical and policy studies in support of the continuing consideration of the best approach to follow in the new policy area. And I firmly believe that Interior's efforts in all aspects of ocean mining were helpful during the past years when ocean miners have sought to establish the viability of a new industry.

It is important to note that Interior's ocean mining activities are based on our overall experience in minerals development. Although domestic or international regulation of the industry has not commenced, policy-related studies were required frequently nonetheless.

To meet these ends, Interior sought to maintain the flexibility to draw on whatever Departmental resources are required, rather than to consolidate ocean mining programs in a single location within the Department.

I would note in this respect the outstanding contributions to our ocean mining effort from both the U.S. Geological Survey and the Bureau of Mines.

Furthermore, we feel that our contributions in this area are critical. Fundamental to an understanding of ocean minerals development is an understanding of basic principals of mineral resource management. Thus Interior has sought to provide certain kinds of expertise:

Geological capability to locate and define resource deposits;

In addition, analytic economic capability to determine potential deposit values;

So, too, capability to assess mining technologies as they relate to resource management goals;

An understanding of the relationship of ocean minerals potential to overall national resource needs;

Experience with mining regulatory techniques;

Experience with domestic and international mining laws;

And lastly, experience in international negotiations on mineral resource issues.

These capabilities are integral to our overall mineral resource responsibilities, and they can contribute greatly as Government prepares to address issues raised by full scale ocean mining.

Since the creation of the Ocean Mining Administration, questions have been raised by some members of the Congress and within the executive branch regarding the roles of the Department of the Interior and the Department of Commerce.

I am pleased to report that in view of these questions, the Department of the Interior and the Department of Commerce have been reviewing their respective roles in ocean mining. Former Secretary Morton and Secretary Kleppe met last December to discuss ocean mining jurisdiction.

Subsequently, I have worked with Dr. White of NOAA to more carefully define the roles of and relationship between our agencies. Secretary Kleppe, for his part, is anxious to establish a close working relationship between Interior's and NOAA's activities related to ocean mining and we have made substantial progress toward that end.

We believe the goal of each agency should be to establish cooperative and complementary ocean mining activities that will provide the Government policymakers with timely and complete information.

This committee will be kept fully informed of the progress of discussions between the two agencies.

In closing, I would like to briefly mention the kinds of work that we, in Interior, would emphasize in the near term with respect to ocean mining. Such things are:

Continued efforts to achieve an acceptable and timely international legal regime for ocean mining.

Studies of regulatory approaches for ocean mining should be revised and updated in light of more precise information about ocean mineral recovery operations.

Careful evaluation of measures to stabilize the investment climate for ocean mining, and refinement of economic studies of ocean mining operations.

Government must monitor and investigate the state of the art of nodule reovery technologies to understand their efficiency, their safety, and to learn techniques for proper conservation of the resource.

More precise information is required on the location and magnitude of manganese nodule deposits to determine reserve potentials and to make judgments as to appropriate management techniques.

So, too, additional research should be conducted on metallurgical processing techniques and waste disposal or utilization of tailings from nodule processing.

Assessments of the environmental impacts of ocean mining utilizing comprehensive baseline data should be completed and a revised draft environmental impact statement prepared.

Mr. Chairman, the Department of the Interior attaches great importance to the need to foster and encourage the promising new deep ocean mining capability in the Uitned States. I can assure you that we will maintain vigorous efforts to assure adequate and timely Government information about ocean mining, and to seek constructive policies to advance U.S. interests in access to ocean minerals and development of a domestic ocean mining base.

Mr. Chairman, that completes my prepared remarks.

Mr. MURPHY. Thank you, Mr. Frizzell.

Do the other witnesses have any statements at this time?

Mr. FISHER. No, sir.

Mr. MURPHY. Mr. Ratiner?

Mr. RATINER. No, sir.

Mr. MURPHY. Through yesterday's testimony I had the impression from Mr. Ratiner that the knowledge and expertise, as far as ocean minerals are concerned, was not centered in the Department of the Interior, but it was more or less an expertise that private industry had.

Yet, as I listened to your statement, particularly on pages 3 and 5, you express the great qualifications of the Department of the Interior in its assessment, knowledge, geology, technology as far as ocean minerals are concerned.

Will you comment on why you are so positive about the abilities of the Department of the Interior in this area, where as Mr. Ratiner was not yesterday?

Mr. FRIZZELL. Mr. Chairman, I think my personal answer to your question is this.

That knowledge which we have is shared between private industry and Government. Within the Department of the Interior our ocean mining capabilities are in the Geological Survey, the Bureau of Mines, and the Ocean Mining Administration.

Now, it may well be that we in Government do not have sufficient information, but so far as a department within Government, I think whatever ocean mining expertise there is resides primary within the Department of the Interior.

Mr. MURPHY. On page 1 you say the administration is continuing to explore the question of appropriate ocean mining legislation so we will be ready to take any necessary actions once we can to project the results of the on going deep seabed negotiation in the Law of the Sea Conference.

What do you mean by "project the results?"

Does this mean someone is going to finally make a hard decision on moving forward in the Government to save our ocean mining industry from the predictable fruitless efforts of Committee I at the Law of the Sea?

Mr. FRIZZELL. Mr. Chairman, I would hope that what you suggest would be true: that in the near term and the near future we will make that hard decision.

I share with you many similar feelings, Mr. Chairman. When I was Solicitor of the Department of the Interior, I heard the first vibrations coming from the Law of the Sea negotiations, and very frankly, I was frustrated as much as you and other members of the committee, no doubt have been.

As I have worked into the issue and gained a little more knowledge, and particularly, in just the last few weeks in discussions with Mr. Ratiner, having learned what is going on up in New York City, I am more optimistic presently than I have been at any time in the last several years, to the extent that I am willing to wait until we know the results of these negotiations, to see what fruits may be more in the near term before we make a final assessment on going for ward with some legislation.

I am not willing to wait around forever myself, Mr. Chairman.

Mr. MURPHY. On page 2 you say decisions to make such substantial capital investments by our ocean miners of $300 million to $600 mil lion for each planned minesite will have to be made within the next 18 months.

Yesterday, Mr. Ratiner said perhaps we can expect at best a treaty document, just a document, at summer's end, and that could be 8 months. He does not know how many countries have to sign to ratify that treaty. That could be years based on past experience.

He also said hopes of meeting this schedule are only a "faint glimmer."

Given this long-shot assessment, do you not think the Congress is on safe ground to proceed with unilateral legislation and, in fact, would not the Congress be derelict in its duty if it did not proceed?

Mr. FRIZZELL. I think if it were not for the fact that we had some hopeful signs in the committee I negotiations that the answer to your question might well be yes, in the affirmative. But, I think we are down to the point in those negotiations in which we are going to know in the very near term whether or not they can be successfully pursued or not Mr. Chairman. It is because of that ray of hope that we are willing to take another last look at it in the next few weeks, and in the next month or two, and see where we are at that time, before we make a final judgment on the issue that you raise.

Mr. MURPHY. Have you seen any change in the way the Group of 77 is voting in other areas of the United Nations since the Geneva Conference?

Mr. FRIZZELL. I am informed by Mr. Ratiner that Group 77 is not negotiating any other treaties with us, other than on Committee I on the Law of the Sea.

I do not know how indicative their vote in other forums would be toward these negotiations, Mr. Chairman.

Mr. MURPHY. I would think there would be a relationship between their general attitudes and their cohesiveness in other foreign policy areas, and their opinion and actions in Committee I.

Mr. FRIZZELL. I think that would be a general truism, but I think you have to recognize that they also have something to lose in the Committee I negotiations, as well as something to gain.

Mr. MURPHY. What do they have to lose?

Mr. FRIZZELL. Control.

Mr. MURPHY. Control of what?

Mr. FRIZZELL. Of the resources.

Mr. MURPHY. What control do they have of the resources, or ability to control?

Mr. FRIZZELL. The results of the LOS treaty negotiations would either give them more or less control of those resources.

Mr. MURPHY. With the exception of the question we had to ask three times yesterday, with regard to those underdeveloped countries, and to this type of mineral resource today, whether they want to control land-based resources through the Law of the Sea.

Mr. FRIZZELL. As I say, Mr. Chairman, I think that all of these issues need to be looked at closely in the next 60 to 90 days, but I think judgments at this time would be premature, until we know, in fact, what directions those negotiations are going to take.

It may well be true that in a few months I will be back, or some member of this administration will be back, and we will find no room for disagreement on that premise.

It is premature to make a judgment at this time, Mr. Chairman.

Mr. MURPHY. You say on page 2 that through the Mining and Minerals Policy Act of 1970 the Department of the Interior is mandated to "foster and encourage the development of economically sound and stable domestic mining, minerals and metals industries."

Now, you say in the case of ocean mining you have diligently sought to fulfill this responsibility.

Have these efforts been carried in concert with, or consultation with the ocean mining industry?

Mr. FRIZZELL. At all stages and steps.

Mr. MURPHY. If that is the case, then why is the industry so distraught, and why are they continuously seeking relief from the committee?

Mr. FRIZZELL. For the same reason I think you are distraught, and I am, Mr. Chairman, that heretofore the treaty negotiations have not been going well.

Mr. MURPHY. Well, after what I saw in Caracas and Geneva I can certainly understand what the problems of that industry are, and why the stockholders and the boards are ready right now not to commit any capital to ocean mining, and just scrap the whole program, which would take the U.S. private enterprise completely out of deep ocean mining.

Do you want to respond to that?

Mr. FRIZZELL. I think the more knowledgeable members of that industry recognize the new events and directions of the last few weeks in New York, and understand that it may well be worth waiting another couple of months, after 5 or 6 or 10 years, to see the outcome before they jump. I believe that industry members feel that they have something to gain from those negotiations just as the U.S. Government does for the country as a whole.

Mr. MURPHY. Will you supply for the record the references to DOI's ocean mining activities referred to at the bottom of pages 3 and 4 of your statement?

Mr. FRIZZELL. Yes.

[The document deferred to follows:]

OCEAN MINING ACTIVITIES DEPARTMENT OF THE INTERIOR

Secretarial-level participation in the initial formulation of United States oceans policy and law of the sea positions in conjunction with the Departments of Defense and State, leading to promulgation in 1970 of a Presidential oceans policy.

Ongoing responsibility for policy formulation and advice to the Department of State in respect of the ocean mineral resource aspects of the law of the sea negotiations.

Liaison with industry concerning their technical progress as well as the potential impacts of legal and political developments on their activities includng periodic visits by Interior representatives to monitor technology development.

Preparation of analyses of the regulatory options for deep ocean mining, and the economic impact of those options, to serve as a basis for regulatory schemes proposed in law of the sea negotiations.

Deep ocean resource mapping through the marine geology program of the Geological Survey.

Developing estimates of the economic potential of deep ocean resources.

Establishing an information base on technological progress in the ocean mining industry.

Mining technology research on OCS hardrock mining, environmental studies including gathering baseline data and studying environmental effects of mining technology.

Transferred to NOAA By Reorganization Plan No. 4 of 1970.

Nodule processing research.

Establishment in 1972 of a joint Department of the Interior, Department of Commerce committee, chaired by Interior, to study technical aspects of ocean mining to prepare a base for interim ocean mining legislation and the drafting of an Environmental Impact Statement.

Presentation in 1973 to the Congress of an official assessment of the status of the ocean mining industry, prepared by the Bureau of Mines.

Public appearances before academic groups, Government/industry seminars, etc., for the purpose of promoting interest and knowledge of the importance of ocean mining and the potential obstacles to its development.

Development within Bureau of Mines and the Geological Survey of basic data utilized in intergovernmental review of U.S. economic/mineral resources objectives in the law of the sea.

Drafting proposed interim legislation for ocean mining.

Completion of draft Environmental Impact Statement on ocean mineral resource development submitted through Department of State for public comment.

Economic analyses of potential profitability of various ocean mining industry models by Bureau of Mines.

Initiation of outside contract studies to analyze the state-of-the-art of ocean mining technology, to develop topographic and seismic data charts needed for ocean mineral assessment, and to assess economic and regulatory conditions of ocean mining to define strategic and regulatory alternatives available to the Government.

Establishment of a systematized public information effort involving regular mailings to industry and Government officials as well as private individuals in this and other countries who are involved in ocean mining related activities.

Analyses of the potential impact of ocean mining on availability of minerals supply to the United States.

Mr. MURPHY. What is the Department's legal authority to engage in ocean mining?

Is it not true that this authority was transferred to the Department of Commerce under Reorganization Plan No. 4?

Mr. FRIZZELL. Mr. Chairman, with respect to the first part of your question, the ocean mining activities of the Department of Interior, this is conducted pursuant to the authority of the Department granted from various statutes.

Let me be more specific. The Bureau of Mines, for instance, is authorized by 30 U.S.C. to conduct a broad range of scientifc and technical investigations concerning mining and mineral substances for the use of the United States.

The Geological Survey's authority to examine the geological structure, mineral resources and products of the national domain is expanded to authorize such examination outside of the national domain pursuant to 43 U.S.C. 31 sub (b).

In addition, the Mining and Minerals Policy Act directs the Secretary of Interior in the exercise of his statutory authority to foster and encourage development of economically sound domestic mining industries.

Now, as to the second part of your question, whether or not some or all of Interior's ocean mining-related authorities, were transferred to the Department of Commerce, the Department of Interior recognizes, and has implemented and supported Reorganization Plan No. 4 of 1970, which has been cited in some quarters as the source of authority for the Department of Commerce activities in ocean mining.

However, that reorganization plan transferred only a research facility of the Bureau of Mines, called the Marine Minerals Technology Center. The functions of that facility were technical in nature and, in fact, did not include programs directly related to ocean mining.

Indeed, ocean mining related programs were conducted elsewhere in the Bureau of Mines, and in the Geological Survey.

Mr. MURPHY. What is the level of funding last year and this year for ocean mining?

Mr. FRIZZELL. Specific funding within the Department for ocean mining is identified in the office administered by Mr. Ratiner, known as the Ocean Mining Administration.

This office is under the allocation for the Assistant Secretary for Energy and Minerals. Specifically, approximately $88,000 is provided for the Ocean Mining Administration in the Secretary's budget.

That does not include, however, Mr. Chairman, an additional fund of approximately $85,000 that falls under both Geological Survey and Bureau of Mines, wherein they have contributed personnel and funds to ocean mining activities.

Mr. MURPHY. Was not that $88,000 almost stricken from the appropriations budget?

Mr. FRIZZELL. It certainly was, and thanks to your good auspices it was restored.

Mr. MURPHY. Mr. de la Garza?

Mr. DE LA GARZA. No questions.

Mr. MURPHY. Mr. Mosher?

Mr. MOSHER. Mr. Frizzell, at the bottom of the first page of your testimony you say we will be ready to take any necessary action once we can project the results of the ongoing deep seabead negotiation at the Law of the Sea Conference.

You say, once we can project.

I judge from what you have just said to the Chairman, that this might be as soon as a couple of months from now.

Is that what you are saying?

Mr. FRIZZELL. That is what I hope to infer, and reaffirm at this time, Mr. Mosher.

Mr. MOSHER. You are that optimistic?

Mr. FRIZZELL. I am willing to remain optimistic for that period of time, after which I could not agree more with this committee, that definitive action of some type needs to be taken. You cannot project optimism forever.

Mr. MOSHER. Just before that sentence I read to you, you said "the administration is continuing to explore the question of appropriate ocean mining legislation."

Now, I judge from what you are saying that within 2 or 3 months if there has been no positive, hopeful action in the Law of the Sea Conference the administration is prepared to present or submit appropriate legislation.

Would you anticipate that the administration bill would be distinctively different from the type of legislation we have before us in either of these bills that this committee is now considering?

Mr. FRIZZELL. I think the best I could say would be that the Department of Interior would think it would be appropriate to formulate such an ocean mining policy and legislation.

That does not mean that we would be able to sell that attitude in all quarters within the administration, but hopefully we will be artful advocates towards that end. However, I think it would be presumptuous at this stage, to try to define in any more detail the exact form of such legislation, Mr. Mosher.

Mr. MOSHER. Well, you say that the administration is continuing to explore this.

Now, I guess you are saying that you do not presume to speak for the administration.

Mr. FRIZZELL. Let me say and put it this way.

Through such events as this committee's hearings as well as through our efforts, we have elevated this issue within the administration to the point that it will hopefully be resolved in the very near future, and many in the administration have been receptive to such a resolution.

I cannot tell you what the outcome will be, but at least we are addressing the issue now.

Mr. MOSHER. I will get back to my original question.

Would you anticipate that any administration bill, or any Interior Department bill would contain concepts, or mechanisms quite different from the legislation that is now before this committee?

Mr. FRIZZELL. I do not think you could approach legislation in this area without addressing some of the very same issues that this committee has dealt with. We will have to meet those issues. They will have to be addressed, and I would not anticipate that any administration-recommended legislation would be dramatically different.

Mr. MOSHER. No further questions.

Mr. DE LA GARZA. [presiding]. Mr. Forsythe?

Mr. FORSYTHE. Thank you, Mr. Chairman.

You know, so much of this, Mr. Frizzell, reminds us of going through the Law of the Sea in the past number of years, and it seems almost the same.

I think that I recall about 2 years ago we had substantial testimony at that point in time when industry was at the point of having to make this major commitment of investment, or we were going to lose the whole show.

What has held industry back from that, and still kept them viable in this 2-year period, when you now say that in 18 months we will have a treaty?

Mr. FRIZZELL. I think, and of course, you are going to have representatives of industry later here, but I think they would have to admit 2 years ago, or 18 months ago they were not on the verge of development.

They are closer to it today, Mr. Forsythe, certainly, but not 2 years ago. At that time they were doing the things necessary to gain that capability, and they are there now.

Two years ago things did not look too rosy for any type of a successful negotiation in Committee I. They look better now.

Industry now has the capability, as of 1976. Simultaneously, we hope we are on the verge of some breakthroughs in the negotiations in Committee I. We are going to know very soon. That is why we think it is judicious, to wait for the upcoming negotiations.

We are not asking, as we were 2 years ago: let us wait until New York 2 years hence. We are saying in a couple or three months we ought to know.

Mr. FORSYTHE. I was encouraged yesterday when Mr. Ratiner said that the Group of 77, these nations really do look at this as their last chance if there is going to be a law of the sea, and more particularly, he said seabed mining. He mentioned that it would have to happen at this time.

Do you fully agree with that?

Have you looked and assessed where we are in New York?

Mr. FRIZZELL. I, too, am relying on Mr. Ratiner's assessment, because he is our expert in that area, and he informs me of that as well.

Mr. FORSYTHE. In view of that, you have now just said not months. You have said 60 or 90 days, and maybe it is even a shorter period before you are going to find where there is real movement in the law of the sea, and the time that it takes for legislation to wind its process through this Congress, would you not agree that we had better keep moving rather rapidly here in our hearings, and this whole process, so that we are going to have a chance to be with you when you want it?

Mr. FRIZZELL. I guess the only caveat would be that we would hope the form of that legislation would not tend to injure, or inhibit the forthcoming negotiations.

I think up to the point of final passage of such legislation forward movement does not hurt too much.

Mr. FORSYTHE. Thank you.

Mr. MURPHY. [presiding]. Mr. Oberstar?

Mr. OBERSTAR. Thank you very much, Mr. Chairman.

Mr. Frizzell, what other minerals of interest are there on the ocean bottom besides manganese?

Mr. FRIZZELL. May I merely defer to those more scientifically oriented, and have Dr. Fisher answer your question?

Mr. FISHER. Primarily nickel and cobalt. In addition to the manganese, there are a variety of other minerals, some 20 or 25 that may be associated with the nodules, but the prime commercial concerns are nickel and cobalt in addition to manganese.

Mr. OBERSTAR. Copper as well?

Mr. FISHER. Copper would be, yes.

Mr. OBERSTAR. How much of our manganese do we import now?

Mr. FRIZZELL. I have those figures. Your question was with copper and manganese?

Mr. OBERSTAR. Manganese.

Mr. FRIZZELL. Copper is 98 percent. Excuse me, sir, cobalt is 98 percent, and copper 18 percent, and nickel 73 percent.

Mr. OBERSTAR. We import 73 percent of our nickel requirements?

Mr. FRIZZELL. Yes.

Mr. OBERSTAR. Only 25 pounds of nickel produced in the United States, and we use a lot more than that.

Do you have any concern about, you, speaking for the administration now, about the development of resource cartels, like OPEC?

Mr. FRIZZELL. Certainly, we have concern.

Mr. OBERSTAR. You have information of any others that are being established?

Mr. FRIZZELL. Dr. Fisher will answer.

Mr. FISHER. There have been others established, but not obviously with the effectiveness of OPEC.

This does constitute a potential threat and concern, and I think this is one area where we depend to such large degrees as we do with a couple of minerals just cited here on importation.

This is always a very real threat, and one we should be aware of.

Mr. OBERSTAR. The resource cartel that was established last year, if my memory serves me right, is called CIPEC, I believe, by Zaire and other copper producing countries, and we import a substantial amount of copper.

Nickel is usually associated with the development of copper deposits.

Would you not be concerned about these countries being able to put together an effective cartel, and bringing together some pressure on the United States?

Mr. FRIZZELL. I guess the most optimistic thing that we can reply in that regard is that despite its formation it has not been successful.

That does not mean it might not adopt practices in the future that would be successful, and that is why it concerns us, but to date, they have not been successfully controlling the market, and establishing a cartel.

Mr. OBERSTAR. That is true, and that is something we said about Saudi Arabia and other Middle Eastern countries 10 or 15 or 20 years ago.

For that reason, I think that the administration ought to be more concerned, and more determined to move ahead with an effective program for deep seabed mineral development.

I would like to come back to your statement a moment ago that it would be premature to make a decision on this legislation at this time.

Last year just about this time we heard the same statement made by the State Department and other representatives of the administration about the Law of the Sea Conference, and their high hopes for its favorable outcome on the 200-mile limit legislation we were considering then.

Well, they were wrong, and I kind of suspect you are going to be just as wrong about waiting now.

What makes you more optimistic? That is my question.

Mr. Frizzell. Well, if you do not mind, I would like to defer to the man who has been there over the past years, and has just returned from those negotiations, and he will tell you why he is optimistic.

Mr. Ratiner, will you respond?

Mr. Ratiner. Mr. Oberstar, we did not get into this too much yesterday, but essentially the optimism comes from the fact that the principal developing country negotiators have now brought about a situation in which new treaty articles have emerged on critical issues.

For example, no longer do the treaty articles require direct price and production controls. Since 1968 this has been one of the most significant demands of developing countries in the deep seabed negotiations.

A second example is that proposed new treaty articles now recognizes the importance of increasing the availability of raw materials to meet the world's needs. That is a second major achievement.

In the past, the developing countries have insisted that the Assembly of the international organization which would deal with seabed mining would be a one nation, one vote Assembly. It would have the supreme policymaking powers for the entire international Authority.

That demand by developing countries is now eliminated in the treaty articles to which I referred earlier. Instead, provision is made only for a power in the Assembly to make resolutions and recommendations of a general character.

A new voting system in that Assembly has been incorporated in the new treaty articles, which requires a two-thirds vote of the members of the Authority rather than two-thirds of the members present and voting in order for the Assembly to take a decision on a question of substance.

We have done a little preliminary and tentative research on that, and we find that there is no vote taken at the United Nations since 1945 in which there was an absolute two-thirds majority in favor of a proposition which the United States opposed.

Moreover, the article which deals with the Assembly's powers and functions also says that if within 90 days after the Assembly adjourns, more than one-third of the members of the Authority object to a decision, that decision would be rescinded.

This is a postdecision cooling off period of great significance. These new treaty articles may indicate fundamental changes in the willing ness of developing countries to structure an international organiza tion which might be, in fact, one that the American people could feel comfortable with.

The developing countries are very keenly aware of the dissatisfaction which now exists in the United States with the way in which the United Nations has been functioning. In our recent discussions, developing nations have made genuine attempts to try to structure the international Authority so that countries like the United States can feel adequately protected.

For years, one of the key issues in this negotiation on the part of the developing countries has been to give the international Authority the power to administer the whole of the deep seabed area, including all other uses of the area, scientific research, military activities, and so on.

That demand has now been dropped in these new treaty articles, and the Authority would only deal with the administration of the resources of the area.

There are many other things that came out of the recent New York session, but these are among the most critical results that give us reason to think there may be a genuine turnaround in the developing countries' views.

Mr. OBERSTAR. That is a much more optimistic and informative statement than you gave us yesterday.

Thank you very much.

Mr. MOSHER. Would the gentleman yield?

Mr. OBERSTAR. Certainly.

Mr. MOSHER. This is an impressive list.

What have you given in your preliminary negotiations? What has been required of you in either "expressed" or "implied" terms?

What have you had to give in turn to win these concessions?

Mr. RATINER. Mr. Mosher, you have me in an awkward position.

If I say I did not give up anything, the developing countries might be very hurt. They will read this transcript.

I think it is fair to say the negotiation was approached in New York in a spirit of compromise and accommodation.

Things are not in the new treaty articles exactly as the United States would have wanted them there, but the fact is that the developing countries were aware that the single negotiating text in Committee I that emerged from Geneva, to which Mr. Murphy referred yesterday as an unmatigated disaster, is regarded by the industrialized countries as representing only the views of the developing countries. Therefore, for the moment the onus is very much on the developing countries to come forward and prove to us their willingness to compromise.

We have always taken what we regarded as a middle-of-the-road position in this negotiation.

Now, we are seeing the developing countries come to the middle of the road.

Mr. MOSHER. But you are saying, I judge, that the spokesmen for the developing countries do feel that there is implied, at least, some give on our part?

Mr. RATINER. We have tried to be as flexible as possible in the discussion of issues addressed in these new treaty texts without conceding any of the many major national interests we have in the negotiation.

Mr. MOSHER. Would the gentleman continue to yield?

Mr. OBERSTAR. Yes.

Mr. MOSHER. Who among the other industrial nations are our immediate allies, and in agreement with our position at this point in these negotiations?

Mr. RATINER. We work very closely with, and tend to be in harmony with the Soviet Union, Japan, France, the United Kingdom, the Federal Republic of Germany, and a variety of other countries, most of which come from the European community, but needless to say, there has been a pattern over the years of industrialized countries on the one side and developing countries on the other side.

Mr. Mosher, that pattern is also beginning to break up. The consuming nations among the developing countries, as I mentioned yesterday, are starting to be more keenly aware of their need for resources and raw materials at the lowest possible prices, and therefore, the traditional grouping of developing versus developed countries is starting to break down.

Mr. MOSHER. Thank you.

Mr. DE LA GARZA. Would the gentleman yield to me there?

Mr. OBERSTAR. Yes.

Mr. DE LA GARZA. Mr. Ratiner, that list of so-called concessions, how many were made related to the U.S. initiatives in the beginning?

Mr. RATINER. Mr. de la Garza, I am not sure I understand your question.

Mr. DE LA GARZA. Were all of those concessions made at the request of the United States?

Mr. RATINER. Yes; for all practical purposes.

Mr. DE LA GARZA. And how many of the other countries?

Mr. RATINER. In the Committee I negotiation, Mr. de la Garza, because of the complexity of the issues, and the vast number of issues, there is a tendency for certain countries to emerge more or less as spokesmen for large groups of countries.

The positions which I have outlined today are sponsored and shared by many industrialized countries, but the initiative for putting them forward has generally fallen to the United States.

Mr. DE LA GARZA. We are not spokesmen for positive advancement. We are the scapegoat. Everybody blasts us.

We are not the one that speaks for the other countries at that Conference.

Mr. RATINER. We do not speak for the other countries.

The Conference is composed of all sovereign states, but there is a tendency in Committee I for developing countries to look to the United States, in part, for leadership in presenting the views of the industrialized countries on these issues.

Mr. DE LA GARZA. I would say it was the reverse. We are the ones who are blasted all the time by the Group of 77, trying to embarrass us on the floor and off the floor, and there they pacify us by having private discussions with you off the record.

Mr. RATINER. These new results I am talking about are not simply private discussions.

The Chairman of Committee I has now produced new texts of treaty articles, and they bear his own initials. I submitted them yesterday for the record. In the past we have made the comment that private discussions revealed more optimism than, in fact, was apparent from the single negotiating text.

Now, we are saying that there are new treaty texts which give concrete meaning to what degree of optimism we have.

Mr. DE LA GARZA. I thank the gentleman for yielding.

Mr. OBERSTAR. May I have additional time, Mr. Chairman?

Mr. MURPHY. The gentleman may proceed.

Mr. DE LA GARZA. I did not take any of my own time, Mr. Chairman, and I am happy to yield mine to the gentleman from Minnesota.

Mr. OBERSTAR. Mr. Frizzell, the treaty side, and considerations for the moment aside, how do you view the issue of the right to seabed minerals and mining?

Who holds that right?

Is it the U.S. Government, or do companies have a right?

If not, how do they gain rights to mining, or are they to be considered something other than rights, a permit to be granted by the United States?

I would like to know what view the Department holds of those questions.

Mr. FRIZZELL. I am told by my adviser that both States and private companies now have those types of rights under private law.

Obviously, the precise determination of those rights can either be negotiated through the Committee I in the Law of the Sea Conference, or as this committee well knows, individual governments can establish what those rights are. I do not think any legislation in this area would assert necessarily ownership. It would just offer deep seabed minerals through a licensing of private nationals under the jurisdiction of this Government.

Mr. OBERSTAR. You would view it as a licensing, rather than the establishment of rights under the Mineral Leasing Act, or the Mining Act of 1872?

Mr. FRIZZELL. That has been my uneducated concept; yes.

Mr. OBERSTAR. Now, are you trying to sound like a country lawyer, as the former Solicitor of the Department of Interior?

Now, come on here.

I think this is very important, because considerations obviously are going to be part of the treaty, but if we do not have a treaty and this committee proceeds with legislation, and one of the things we want to know is how are companies going to get access to mining? Is licensing the approach? Is that what you are saying?

Mr. FRIZZELL. Yes, but of course, problems would remain, even with a license. Industry would still be concerned over what happens when they get the license, and they get out there and start mining, as you well know.

I cannot see an assertion through legislation of doing too much more than accomplishing the license objective.

The fisheries bill asserted jurisdiction over territory. This would not.

This, Mr. Oberstar, would be more in the nature of a licensing.

Mr. OBERSTAR. But this is part of the point you make on page 7 in your testimony, and I quote: "Measures to stabilize the investment climate for ocean mining." An establishment of the rights and conditions under which mining would be undertaken would be part of that business of stabilizing the investment climate.

I think it would be very helpful for us to have some clear notion of how the Department would proceed to permit the mining of metals from the ocean floor.

Mr. FRIZZELL. What I had in mind in the specific reference on page 7, very candidly, did not say that. Unfortunately, this time I used words not what they mean for how they can be interpreted.

What I had in mind was some type of insurance scheme, obviously, to give that assurances to the industry, because they cannot risk the large amounts of capital necessary for ocean mining without some type of assurance.

Mr. OBERSTAR. Now, on that same page you talk about the "need for the Government to monitor and investigate the state of art, nodule recovery technologies, to get at the questions of the efficiency, safety and conservation."

What do you mean about "efficiency and safety?" Are you going to require mining companies to file mining plans that detail the efficiency of their operation? Is that a concern of Government?

Safety, yes; conservation, yes, but what do you have in mind by safety, and what do you have in mind by conservation and efficiency?

Mr. FRIZZELL. What I had in mind was efficiency in the conservation sense, not in the economic sense.

I know that there is economic risk in ocean mining ventures, but the Government's concern is that we not waste the resources wherever they are found.

Mr. OBERSTAR. That is true.

Mr. FRIZZELL. And that is what I had in mind when I referred to efficiency.

Yes, we are talking about laying out size of blocks and determining the length of time for leasing rights to be granted rather than allowing leases to go on ad infinitum, for ever and ever, so that a miner could "sit" on the resource, if you will. To do this we need to find out what resources exist and then to learn how to make efficient use of those resources.

Mining plans are to be submitted in all likelihood.

Mr. OBERSTAR. Do you have some guidelines?

Mr. FRIZZELL. Sharing data.

Mr. OBERSTAR. Do you have some guidelines already developed within the Department looking toward that kind of program?

Mr. FRIZZELL. We have them formulated both in case an international regime is agreed upon and in case there is a domestic program.

We have a big headstart already, because we deal with this type of problem on the Outer Continental Shelf, and in other resource recovery programs.

Mr. OBERSTAR. Well, I asked the question because Interior does have a large role in mining on land, on the Outer Continental Shelf, and it puzzled me why the guidelines for this kind of mining should be so much different from other mining.

Mr. FRIZZELL. Well, I do not think the broad, general thrust would be so much different.

The very fact that the nature of this resource is many feet beneath the ocean bed might well dictate that some different rules and regulations would have to apply as opposed to onshore recovery of minerals.

Mr. OBERSTAR. Now, what is so different about metallurgical processing techniques, metals recovered from the ocean bottom, as compared to metals recovered from any other source?

Mr. FRIZZELL. I think the answer to your question is that they are substantially similar.

What I had reference there to, of course, is that in conjunction with the efforts of NOAA we need environmental data in this area. I think we have to ensure the environmental safeguards on this type of mining. Some work has been done on this in Lake Superior. We also need to investigate problems associated with tailings.

Mr. OBERSTAR. For discharge of any wastes, but not for the recovery.

Mr. FRIZZELL. I am referring to disposal of waste from processing of nodules as well as utilization of tailings.

Mr. OBERSTAR. That is a separate issue from recovery.

Mr. FRIZZELL. It is.

Mr. OBERSTAR. Well, I asked the questions because it seems to me that again the administration has come in with a laundry list of the things that ought to be done, reasons, or excuses for abating and delaying action on legislation.

It seems to me that you have raised a number of questions that are really not serious problems, but rather excuses for not acting on legislation.

Mr. FRIZZELL. Well, Mr. Oberstar, as you know, you always put your best foot forward, and we do feel that at this particular time and moment enactment of legislation may preempt or hurt the negotiations.

Mr. OBERSTAR. That is the real problem?

Mr. FRIZZELL. Yes. We could not agree more, once that issue is resolved, these problems need to be addressed and solved and implemented.

Mr. OBERSTAR. And my question is, is the Department addressing itself to a meaningful way?

Mr. FRIZZELL. We are, sir.

Mr. OBERSTAR. What do you mean by the term "near term" on page 6. and the "near term these are things that ought to be done?" Would you put a time frame on "near term?"

Mr. FRIZZELL. I would say, one, no more than 2 years.

Mr. OBERSTAR. And that against the backdrop of Mr. Ratiner's statement yesterday of 1 year to 18 months of getting ahead with an effective and deep seabed mining program.

Mr. FRIZZELL. I am glad we are in agreement. I did not know he said that yesterday.

Mr. OBERSTAR. Thank you, Mr. Chairman.

Mr. MURPHY. Mr. Frizzell, back to the line of questioning I was on before I yielded, we have gone to the level of funding in this year in ocean mining, which was around $88,000, and we have actually gotten to the question of jurisdictional disputes between Interior and Commerce on ocean mining.

Where do you stand on solving that dispute?

Mr. FRIZZELL. My direct testimony indicated that former Secretary Morton, when he was still at the Department of Commerce, met with Secretary Kleppe in December of last year, recognizing that this jurisdictional dispute cannot languish forever.

It just must be solved.

Subsequently, Secretary Kleppe asked if I would take on the issue for him, and I have had several meetings with Dr. White in NOAA and his staff and mine have met.

We have come up with a white paper, if you will, that lays out limited areas where we agree, substantial areas where we disagree, legitimate areas of functioning for both Commerce and the Ocean Mining administration within Interior. Following preparation of that paper, I went back to the Secretary of Interior and said I think we have several options now because we are truly in somewhat of a stalemate; we cannot resolve all these issues between myself and Dr. White, although we made a good effort. It is time either to get with the new Secretary of Commerce and resolve them, give one, take one, or failing that, perhaps we should go to our official arbitrator within the executive branch, the Office of Management and Budget.

I have elevated the issue to that level. The secretaries are taking a look at it right now, and I think that it will be resolved, and must be in the near term.

Mr. MURPHY. If the Congress passes this legislation, do you feel Interior should have jurisdiction over it?

Mr. FRIZZELL. I am not free, Mr. Chairman, to take a partisan position, because the issue has not been resolved by OMB, and I am enough of a team player that however this administration decides this issue I am going to support that decision.

Mr. MURPHY. Do you think your agency is better qualified for this responsibility than the Department of Commerce?

Mr. FRIZZELL. I think our background and our expertise in this field gives us a head start on any other department of the executive branch.

Mr. MURPHY. What do you think Commerce's role should be in ocean mining?

Mr. FRIZZELL. Essentially the environmental assessment that they are doing now presently.

Mr. MURPHY. In your judgment, did the creation of this administration, that is the Ocean Mining Administration, anticipate, or presume a congressional decision to vest ocean mining regulatory authority in the Department of the Interior?

Mr. FRIZZELL. The Ocean Mining Administration was established for two reasons.

First, it upgrades the policy planning functions previously carried on by Interior, and we felt that this was warranted in view of the intensified industry activities, and the anticipated approach of the final stages of the Law of the Sea Conference.

In addition, the Ocean Mining Administration, within the department, provides better coordination for ocean mining activities throughout the department by reviewing budgets, and providing general supervision of relevant programs of the Bureau of Mines and the Geological Survey.

It is important to note the establishment of the Ocean Mining Administration reorganized and updated ongoing activities, but did not assume any new statutory authorities.

To clarify the exact nature of the functions assigned to Mr. Ratiner's office I will, with your permission, submit for the record the official organizational statement published in the Department of Interior manual.

[The information referred to follows:]

[From Department of the Interior departmental manual]

ORGANIZATION, OTHER DEPARTMENTAL OFFICES, OCEAN MINING ADMINISTRATION

This Departmental Manual Release, 111 DM 16, provides an organization description for the Ocean Mining Administration (OMA) which was established by Secretarial Order No. 2971 dated February 24, 1975. OMA, headed by an

Administrator, is under the jurisdiction of the Assistant Secretary-Energy and Minerals.

The provisions of Secretarial Order No. 2971 have been incorporated into 111 DM 16. Therefore, Secretarial Order No. 2971 is hereby superseded by this Manual Release.

RICHARD R. HITE,
Deputy Assistant Secretary of the Interior.

CHAPTER 16. OCEAN MINING ADMINISTRATION

.1 *Creation and Purpose.*—The Ocean Mining Administration (OMA) was established by Secretarial Order No. 2971 dated February 24, 1975. The OMA is the focal point for policy development for the Assistant Secretary-Energy and Minerals on issues requiring the promotion and continuation of a domestic ocean mining capability; reviews budget and program activities of other departmental organizational units conducting technology and resource assessments relating to mineral resources of the seabed beyond the area of national jurisdiction; recommends policy on ocean minerals issues involved in international negotiations, including United States jurisdiction over the mineral resources of the continental shelf; and participates in such negotiations.

.2 *Authority.*—The legislative authority to engage in activities described herein exists in various statutes conferring on the Department of the Interior responsibilities relating to mineral resources including 43 U.S.C. 31(b) and 30 U.S.C. 3. Establishment of the OMA is in accordance with the authority provided by Section 2 of Reorganization Plan No. 3 of 1950 (64 Stat. 1262).

.3 *Functions.*

A. *Policy Planning.*—The OMA is responsible for policy planning for the development of the mineral resources of the deep seabed beyond the continental shelf, as well as the mineral resources of Antarctica, and for jurisdictional issues in international negotiations relating to the resources of the continental shelf. Relevant responsibilities include:

(1) assessing legislative requirements for the promotion and continuation of a domestic ocean mining capability, to include the implementation of the ocean mining provisions of any international treaty, or alternatively, of a domestic ocean mining program, and the protection of ocean mining investments against the unusual risks associated with such activities;

(2) preparing draft legislation, in consultation with other agencies; studying possible content of any domestic ocean mining regulations;

(3) recommending policies to be pursued in international negotiations concerning ocean mineral resources; and assisting the Department of State in the conduct of such negotiations;

(4) conducting liaison with interested public and the industry as appropriate to carry out the responsibilities of the OMA and serving as the coordinator for departmental consultations in this regard;

(5) conducting studies of ocean mineral resource development, the evaluation of ongoing public and private programs relating to such development, domestic and international legal and economic requirements for the operation of an ocean mining industry, and such other studies as may be required for the discharge of the OMA's functions.

B. *Management and Coordination.*—The OMA provides central management focus for Department of the Interior activities relating to seabed mineral resources beyond national jurisdiction by reviewing budget and program activities of other departmental organizational units for consistency with overall ocean mineral resource policy and program objectives. Relevant activities include:

(1) Programs of the Geological Survey relating to the study of (i) the geology, geophysics, geochemistry and origin of marine minerals; (ii) marine mineral resource assessments; and (iii) mineral products retrieved from the world's seabed;

(2) Bureau of Mines activities concerned with economic and statistical analysis of minerals commodities, both foreign and domestic, to ensure that the availability of sea-based minerals is properly taken into account;

(3) Scientific investigations of the Bureau of Mines concerning utilization of mineral substances from the seabed with a view to improving efficiency, economic development and preventing wastes in the metallurgical and other min-

eral industries as well as inquiries into the economic conditions and technological aspects affecting development of ocean mineral resources.

C. *Interdepartmental Coordination.*—The OMA coordinates and acts as principal contact within the Department of the Interior for the Department's participation in Executive Branch consideration of United States policy with respect to development of ocean mineral resources. In this regard the OMA:

(1) conducts liaison and coordinates the implementation of Departmental programs with other concerned government agencies;

(2) participates in and represents the Secretary in advising the Department of State on international negotiations concerning ocean mineral resources, with particular emphasis on negotiations involving seabed minerals beyond national jurisdiction;

(3) represents the Department of the Interior on interdepartmental committees dealing with ocean mineral resources, including those on the law of the sea, Antarctic resources and other appropriate interagency committees;

D. *Environmental Impact Statement.*—The OMA coordinates the carrying out of the Department of the Interior's responsibilities with respect to drafting any required Environmental Impact Statements for deep ocean mining.

E. *Public Information.*—Where deemed necessary by the Administrator, the OMA sponsors studies, workshops, and symposiums to promote knowledge concerning the science and technology of ocean mining. Periodic reports are issued by the Administrator to provide policy guidance, develop background information to support Environmental Impact Statements, and inform the general public of the status of ocean mining and related research.

.4 *Organization.*—The OMA has the following organizational components:

A. *Administrator.*—The Administrator of the OMA formulates and executes the basic policies for carrying out the functions described above and such other tasks as may be assigned by the Secretary of the Interior and the Assistant Secretary-Energy and Minerals. He directs and coordinates the activities of the OMA, supervises the maintenance of public and industrial relations and where appropriate, approves the terms and conditions of any contracts relating to ocean mineral resources.

The Administrator exercises the functions of the Assistant Secretary-Energy and Minerals as directed, with respect to his responsibilities for contracts to non-Governmental institutions for necessary studies.

B. *Office of the Administrator.*—The Administrator is assisted in his responsibilities by a staff composed of international legal, economic and political affairs experts, scientific and environmental specialists, and administrative support staff.

Mr. MURPHY. What you just said may be true, but the fact is there would not be an Ocean Mining Administration if I had not gone to the House Appropriations Committee and kept the money in for one purpose, and that was to have continuity in the conclusion of the Law of the Sea through this fiscal year, and that was to retain Ratiner's office for that purpose.

Mr. FRIZZELL. And we privately applaud those efforts, Mr. Chairman.

Mr. MURPHY. But not for the purposes that you have just mentioned, but merely for that purpose, and that is to conclude this conference.

What ocean mining programs does Interior plan to go forward with in the immediate future?

Mr. FRIZZELL. I would like to rely on Mr. Ratiner who heads that office to give you an answer.

Mr. MURPHY. Outside of New York.

Mr. RATINER. Mr. Chairman, what I would like to do is briefly summarize the work that needs to be done. The first task is the acquisition of a sufficient data base, so that Government has credibility in respect of the public when it recommends detailed rules and regulations for ocean mining.

We need more information about the resources, their distribution, and about the methods of recovering those resources.

In addition, we need to determine for example, would be a fair royalty.

There are a whole host of pieces and bits of information that Government needs before it can endorse a particular systematic approach to resource management.

During the course of the next couple of years these are the kinds of programs that would need to be initiated, and the kind of information we would need to develop so we could be in a credible posture when we come before Congress and the public and recommend certain regulatory approaches to ocean mining.

Mr. MURPHY. Mr. Frizzell, would you give this committee a list of the major studies and analytical pieces done on ocean mining?

Mr. FRIZZELL. I would be pleased to do so.

Mr. MURPHY. That is, by the Department of Interior since 1967.

Mr. FRIZZELL. We will submit that for the record, and I would like to indicate to you now, if I may, some of the major kinds of work that we have undertaken.

This would include geological surveys, technical papers, locating and submitting the magnitude of manganese nodule deposits, and the primary Government studies of regulatory approaches to ocean mining industry.

The Bureau of Mines has provided metallurgical processing studies, and some economic analyses of various problems of the ocean mining industry.

In addition, contracts have been let to further our technology assessment of industry progress, and the Ocean Mining Administration will shortly release a study of ocean mining costs.

[The following was received for the record.]

MAJOR DEPARTMENT OF THE INTERIOR TECHNICAL STUDIES, POLICY ANALYSES AND STATEMENTS RELATING TO OCEAN MINING

I. TECHNICAL STUDIES

A. *Geological Survey*

Publications and Papers Containing Data on Manganese Nodules:

Albers, J.P., Carter, M.D., Clark, A.L., Coury, A.B., and Schweinfurth, S.P., 1973, Summary Petroleum and Selected Mineral Statistics for 120 Countries, Including Offshore Areas: U.S. Geological Survey Professional Paper 817.

Berryhill, H.L., 1974, The Worldwide Search for Petroleum Offshore—A Status Report for the Quarter Century, 1947–1972: U.S. Geological Survey Circular 694.

Bischoff, J.L., 1975, Geological and Geochemical Properties of a NE Pacific Sediment Core: Preliminary Results of a U.S. Geological Survey Study of Site C, Deep Ocean Mining Environmental Study.

Brobst, D.A., and Pratt, W.P., (Editors), 1973, United States Mineral Resources: U.S. Geological Survey Professional Paper 820 (contains 66 papers).

Corwin, Gilbert, and Berryhill, Jr., Henry L., 1973, Interim Revision and Updating of World Subsea Mineral Resources: U.S. Geological Survey Miscellaneous Geologic Investigations, Map I–632.

McKelvey, V.E., and Wang, F.F.H., 1970, Preliminary Maps, World Subsea Mineral Resources, U.S. Geological Survey Miscellaneous Geologic Investigations, Map I–632.

Mineral Resource Perspective 1975: U.S. Geological Survey Professional Paper 940.

Subsea Mineral Resources and Problems Related to Their Development, 1969: U.S. Geological Survey Circular 619.

Woo, C.C., 1975, Surface textures and the Ferromanganesenucleation of Proj. DOMES Mn-Nodules, U.S. Geological Survey memo, December 12, 1975.

Wright, N.A. and Williams, P.L., 1974, Mineral Resources of Antarctica: U.S. Geological Survey Circular 705.

Publications and Papers Relevant to Deep Seabed Geology: [See Attachment A.]

B. Bureau of Mines

Specific Publications and Papers on Ocean Mining:

Heady, H.H. Collection and Analysis of Marine Manganese Nodules, OFR 7-67, 1967.

Rosenbaum, J.B., J.T. May, and J.M. Riley. Gold in Sea Water—Fact or Fancy. Mines Magazine, v. 5, No. 9, September 1969.

Handsman, M. and A. Kaufman. Ocean Mining: Today and Tomorrow, paper presented to Marine Technology Society Conference, 1969.

Brooks, P.T., K.C. Dean, and J.B. Rosenbaum. Experiments in Processing Marine Nodules. Proc. 9th Internat. Mineral Processing Cong., Prague, Czechoslovakia, June 1-6, 1970, v. 1.

Brooks, P.T. and D.A. Martin. Processing Manganiferous Sea Nodules. BuMines RI 7473, January 1971.

Ely, Northcutt. Summary of Mining and Petroleum Laws of the World, IC 8482, 1970.

Conceptual Evaluation of Deep Ocean Nodules Technology and Economics of Mining and Processing, February 1975.

Position Paper on Ocean Mining, Twin Cities Research Center, July 1975.

General Publications on Minerals Supply-Demand Applicable to Ocean Mining Studies:

Mineral Facts and Problems, 1975 Edition, Bulletin 667 (quinquennially)

Minerals Yearbook, Volume I. Metals, Minerals, and Fuels (annually)

Minerals Yearbook, Volume III, Area Reports: International (annually)

Commodity Data Summaries (annually)

Mineral Industry Surveys (weekly, monthly, quarterly, and/or annually)

(See Attachment B containing a list of commodity reports on 100 commodities.)

C. Other

Hypothetical Marketing Situation for Nickel, attachment to statement by Leigh S. Ratiner before Subcommittee on Oceanography of House Merchant Marine and Fisheries Committee, March 1, 1973.

Economic Implications of Deep Sea Mining for World Markets in Nickel, Copper, Manganese and Cobalt, study submitted to Senate Interior and Insular Affairs Committee, March 7, 1973.

Revision of the Secretary-General's Report on the Economic Implications of Deep Sea Mining, submitted to the Senate Interior and Insular Affairs Committee, July 9, 1973.

Draft Environmental Statement proposed for United States Involvement in Law of the Sea Negotiations Governing the Mining of Deep Seabed Hard Mineral Resources Seaward of the Limits of National Jurisdiction, prepared by the U.S. Department of the Interior, Office of the Assistant Secretary-Energy and Minerals, March 1974.

Economic Evaluation of Ocean Mining, draft study soon to be released by Ocean Mining Administration.

D. Studies currently under contract

Bureau of Mines funded research:

"Assessment of Economic and Regulatory Conditions Affecting Ocean Minerals Resource Development," Massachusetts Institute of Technology.

"Study of Sedimentology and Geology of Eastern Pacific Ocean Bottom," Scripps Institution of Oceanography, Modification of Bureau of Mines Grant USDI-60-254024.

"Investigation of the Bathymetry and Seismicity as a Basis of Mineral Assessment of the North Equatorial Pacific," Lamont-Doherty Geological Observatory of Columbia University.

Office of Minerals Policy Development funded research:

"Technological and Economic Assessment of Ocean Mining," Arthur D. Little.

II. POLICY ANALYSES AND POSITION PAPERS

"Alternative Rules and Provisions Governing Exploration and Exploitation of Seabed Mineral Resources beyond the Limits of National Jurisdiction," prepared by Interior for Law of the Sea Task Force, Regime Working Group, June 2, 1970.

"Draft United Nations Convention on the International Sea-bed Area: United States Working Paper," submitted to UN Committee on Peaceful Uses of Seabed and Ocean Floor beyond the Limits of National Jurisdiction (appendices largely prepared by Interior), August 3, 1970.

Internal Working Papers of Interior/Commerce Interim Policy Working Group and ad hoc Environmental Task Force, chaired by Interior, 1972.

Mendelsohn, Allan I., Consultant to Interior. "OPIC—A Potential Insurer of Deep Sea Hard Mineral Mining Projects," March 1973.

Mendelsohn, Allan I., Consultant to Interior. "MARAD and Ship Mortgage Insurance—another USG Insurance Program," a study of the potential application to ocean mining, March 12, 1973.

"Precedents in International Law for Provisional International Organizations," study prepared by staff of the Solicitor, May 1, 1973.

Charney, Jonathan I., Consultant to Interior. "Proposed United States Working Paper on a Provisional Convention on the Law of the Sea for Submission to the Third United Nations Conference on the Law of the Sea" and "Background Memorandum on Proposed Working Paper," June 6, 1974.

"United States Working Paper on Economic Effects of Deep Seabed Exploitation," submitted to Committee I of the Law of the Sea Conference (largely prepared by Interior), August 8, 1974.

"United States Working Paper on Draft Appendix to the Law of the Sea Treaty Concerning Mineral Resource Development in the International Seabed Area," submitted to Committee I of the Law of the Sea Conference (largely prepared by Interior), August 13, 1974.

Internal Departmental Study proposing a "Deep Ocean Minerals Initiative," January 6, 1975.

"Draft Bill to Encourage the Development of Ocean Mineral Resources, to Provide for the Provisional Entry into Force of a Treaty on the Law of the Sea and for Other Purposes," February 7, 1975.

"Draft Bill to Provide for the Provisional Entry into Force of a Treaty on the Law of the Sea, to Encourage the Development of a Domestic Ocean Mining Capability and for Other Purposes," October 31, 1975.

[The following are subjects upon which additional studies have been prepared by the Department of the Interior during 1970–76.]

Comparative analyses of different versions of Single Negotiating Text.

Comparisons of various proposals for deep seabed regime and machinery.

Consultations with foreign delegations on deep seabed negotiations.

Decision-making procedures in the international deep seabed machinery.

Detailed analyses of Committee I Single Negotiating Text, Annex I to the Single Negotiating Text, and regime and machinery texts prepared by Committee I Working Group Chairman.

Detailed comments and policy considerations on law of the sea economic issues.

Economic implications of deep seabed exploitation.

Elements of a deep seabed minerals recovery regime.

Issues concerning revenues from manganese nodules.

Negotiating issues in Committee I, both substantive and tactical.

Ocean mining interim policy.

Proposals on economic implications.

Proposed amendments to Single Negotiating Text.

Regulations for deep seabed exploration and exploitation.

Resource implications of different depth limitations to coastal State seabed jurisdiction.

Resource implications of different limits to coastal State seabed jurisdiction.

Resource implications of different seabed limits for islands.

III. STATEMENTS

A. Before congressional committees

Subcommittee on International Organizations and Movements of the House Committee on Foreign Affairs. Statement on Interim Report on the United Nations and the Issue of Deep Ocean Resources—Pursuant to H. Res. 179 by

Dr. Harold L. James, Chief Geologist, U.S. Geological Survey, accompanied by Thomas Howard, Director, Mining Research, Bureau of Mines, October 19, 1967.

Subcommittee on International Organizations and Movements of the House Committee on Foreign Affairs. Statement on The Oceans: A Challenging New Frontier—Pursuant to H. Res. 179 by Frank Cotter, Division of Public Lands, Solicitor Office, June 12, 1968.

Subcommittee on International Organizations and Movements of the House Committee on Foreign Affairs. Statement on The Oceans: A Challenging New Frontier—Pursuant to H. Res. 179 by Hon. Edward Weinberg, Solicitor, June 12, 1968.

Subcommittee on International Organizations and Movements of the House Committee on Foreign Affairs. Statement on The Oceans: A Challenging New Frontier—Pursuant to H. Res. 179 by Dr. William T. Pecora, Director, U.S. Geological Survey, July 25, 1968.

Subcommittee on Oceans and Atmosphere of the Senate Committee on Commerce. Statement on Hearings on the Law of the Sea by Leigh S. Ratiner, October 3, 1972.

Subcommittee on Oceanography of the House Committee on Merchant Marine and Fisheries. Statement in Hearings on H.R. 9 by Leigh S. Ratiner, March 1, 1973.

House Committee on Merchant Marine and Fisheries. Statement in Maritime Briefings by Leigh S. Ratiner, Director for Ocean Resources, April 9, 1973.

Subcommittee on Minerals, Materials and Fuels of the Senate Committee on Interior and Insular Affairs. Statement on Mineral Resources of the Deep Seabed—Hearings on S. 1134 by Leigh S. Ratiner, June 14, 1973.

Subcommittee on Minerals, Materials and Fuels of the Senate Committee on Interior and Insular Affairs. Statement in Status Report on the Law of the Sea Conference by Leigh S. Ratiner, Special Assistant to the Assistant Secretary for Energy and Minerals, September 17, 1974.

Subcommittee on Minerals, Materials and Fuels of the Senate Committee on Interior and Insular Affairs. Statement on Recent Developments in Deep Seabed Mining by Jack W. Carlson, Assistant Secretary for Energy and Minerals, accompanied by Leigh S. Ratiner, Administrator, Ocean Mining Administration, March 19, 1975.

Subcommittee on Mines and Mining of the House Committee on Interior and Insular Affairs. Statement in Oversight Hearings for the Bureau of Mines, Geological Survey, and Ocean Mining Administration by Thomas Falkie, Director, Bureau of Mines, accompanied by T.A. Henrie, Associate Director, Minerals and Materials, R&D, March 4, 1975.

Subcommittee on Mines and Mining of the House Committee on Interior and Insular Affairs. Briefing on Ocean Mining Administration activities by Leigh S. Ratiner, Administrator, Ocean Mining Administration, March 4, 1975.

Subcommittee on Oceanography of the House Committee on Merchant Marine and Fisheries. Statement in Hearings on the Law of the Sea by Leigh S. Ratiner, Administrator, Ocean Mining Administration, May 16, 1975.

Subcommittee on Oceans and International Environment of the Senate Committee on Foreign Relations. Statement in Hearings on achievements of the Geneva Session of the Law of the Sea Conference by Leigh S. Ratiner, Administrator, Ocean Mining Administration, May 22, 1975.

Subcommittee on Minerals and Fuels of the Senate Committee on Interior and Insular Affairs. Statement in Hearings on the Law of the Sea Conference by Leigh S. Ratiner, Administrator, Ocean Mining Administration, June 4, 1975.

Subcommittee on Minerals, Materials and Fuels of the Senate Committee on Interior and Insular Affairs. Statement in Hearings on S. 713 by Leigh S. Ratiner, Administrator, Ocean Mining Administration, October 29, 1975.

Subcommittee on Oceanography of the House Committee on Merchant Marine and Fisheries. Statement on H.R. 11879 and Law of the Sea by Leigh S. Ratiner, Administrator, Ocean Mining Administration, February 23, 1976.

Subcommittee on Oceanography of the House Committee on Merchant Marine and Fisheries. Statement on Ocean Mining Jurisdiction by Hon. Kent Frizzell, Under Secretary of the Interior, February 24, 1976.

B. *Before United Nations Law of the Sea meetings*

Statement on Progress in the Exploration and Exploitation of Hard Minerals from the Seabed. Presented to the Economic & Technical Subcommittee of the UN Committee on the Peaceful Uses of the Seabed and Ocean Floor beyond the Limits of National Jurisdiction by V.E. McKelvey, Geological Survey, March 13, 1969.

Statement on Potential Ill Effects of Subsea Mineral Exploitation and Measures to Prevent Them. Presented to the Economic & Technical Subcommittee of the UN Committee on the Peaceful Uses of the Seabed and Ocean Floor beyond the Limits of National Jurisdiction by V.E. McKelvey, Geological Survey, March 17, 1969.

Statement on Implications of Geologic and Economic Factors to Seabed Resource Allocation, Development and Management. Presented to the Economic & Technical Subcommittee of the UN Committee on the Peaceful Uses of the Seabed and Ocean Floor beyond the Limits of National Jurisdiction by V.E. McKelvey, Geological Survey, March 24, 1969.

Statement on International Machinery Governing Exploration and Exploitation of Sub-sea Mineral Resources beyond the Limits of National Jurisdiction. Presented to the Economic & Technical Subcommittee of the UN Committee on the Peaceful Uses of the Seabed and Ocean Floor beyond the Limits of National Jurisdiction by V.E. McKelvey, Geological Survey, August 20, 1969.

Statement on the Merits of Alternative Rules and Provisions Governing the Exploration of Seabed Mineral Resources beyond the Limits of National Jurisdiction. Presented to the Economic & Technical Subcommittee of the UN Committee on the Peaceful Uses of the Seabed and Ocean Floor beyond the Limits of National Jurisdiction by V.E. McKelvey, March 11, 1970.

Continuation of March 11, 1970. Statement by V.E. McKelvey, Geological Survey, March 13, 1970.

Statement on International Regime for the Deep Seabed, including Rules and Recommended Practices. Presented to the Economic & Technical Subcommittee of the UN Committee on the Peaceful Uses of the Seabed and Ocean Floor beyond the Limits of National Jurisdiction by V.E. McKelvey, Geological Survey, August 13, 1970.

Statement on Mineral Production beyond the 200-Meter Depth. Presented to the Enlarged UN Committee on the Peaceful Uses of the Seabed beyond the Limits of National Jurisdiction—Subcommittee I by V.E. McKelvey, Geological Survey, March 25, 1971.

Statement on Economic Implications of Sub-sea Mineral Production beyond the Limits of National Jurisdiction. Presented to the Enlarged UN Committee on the Peaceful Uses of the Seabed beyond the Limits of National Jurisdiction—Subcommittee I by V.E. McKelvey, Geological Survey, August 4, 1971.

Statement on U.S. Firms Engaged in Deep Sea Mineral Studies. Presented to the Enlarged UN Committee on the Peaceful Uses of the Seabed beyond the Limits of National Jurisdiction—Subcommittee I by V.E. McKelvey, Geological Survey, March 14, 1972.

Statement on Economic Aspects of Deep Seabed Mineral Exploitation. Presented to the Third UN Conference on the Law of the Sea—Committee I by Leigh S. Ratiner, U.S. Representative in Committee I, August 8, 1974.

Statement on Deep Seabed Rules and Regulations. Presented to the Third United Nations Conference on the Law of the Sea—Committee I by Leigh S. Ratiner, U.S. Representative in Committee I, August 8-9, 1974.

Statement on Conditions of Deep Seabed Exploitation—Committee I. Presented to the Third United Nations Conference on the Law of the Sea—Committee I by Leigh S. Ratiner, U.S. Representative in Committee I, August 19, 1974.

Statement on Machinery Issues. Presented to the Third United Nations Conference on the Law of the Sea—Committee I by Leigh S. Ratiner, U.S. Representative in Committee I, April 28, 1975.

C. General

"The Development of Ocean Minerals and the Law of the Sea." Statement by Charles F. Luce, Under Secretary of the Interior, before the National Institute on Marine Resources, American Bar Association, June 8, 1967.

"Ocean Minerals and the Law." Article by Hollis M. Dole, Assistant Secretary of the Interior, in *Natural Resources Lawyer*, Vol. 2, No. 4, pp. 342–359 (November 1969).

"Rules Governing Seabed Mineral Exploration and Exploitation contained in the U.S. Draft Convention on the International Seabed Area." Statement by V.E. McKelvey before the Asian-African Legal Consultative Committee, Twelfth Session, Colombo, January 20, 1971.

"Recent U.N. Developments concerning the Seabeds." Article by David P. Stang, Office of the Secretary, in *Marine Technology*, Vol. 1, pp. 593–610 (1970).

"Ocean Politics and the United Nations." Article by Hollis M. Dole and David P. Stang in *Oregon Law Review*, Vol. 50 (Spring 1971).

"United States Ocean Mineral Resource Interests and the United States Conference on the Law of the Sea." Article by Leigh S. Ratiner and Rebecca L. Wright, in 6 *Natural Resources Lawyer* 1 (Winter 1973).

"Public Policy and Debate on S. 2801." Speech by Leigh S. Ratiner before the Manganese Nodule Symposium, Honolulu, Hawaii, October 16, 1972.

"Local Impacts of the Law of the Sea Conference." Speech by Leigh S. Ratiner at the University of Washington, Seattle, Washington, October 1972.

"Using the Law of the Sea to Promote International Prosperity." Speech by Leigh S. Ratiner at the Financial Times Conference, London, February 17, 1974.

"Who Owns the Seas: Problems of Mineral Exploitation and National Rights." Speech by Leigh S. Ratiner at the International Studies Council Program, University of New Hampshire, Durham, N.H., April 4, 1974.

"Conflict and Order in Ocean Relations." Participation in panel discussion by Leigh S. Ratiner. Conference sponsored by Ocean Policy Project, SAIS, Johns Hopkins University, Washington, D.C. October 21, 1974.

"A New Law of the Sea." Participation in panel discussion by Leigh S. Ratiner at the Third Annual Wolfgang Friedmann Series in International Law, Columbia University, New York, N.Y., November 14, 1974.

"The Science, Engineering, Economics and Politics of Ocean Hard Mineral Development." Speech by Leigh S. Ratiner, at the 4th Annual Sea Grant Lecture and Symposium, MIT Sea Grant Program, Cambridge, Mass., October 16, 1975.

Speech on Ocean Mining given by Leigh S. Ratiner before the American Mining Congress, San Francisco, Calif., October 1, 1975.

Remarks of Thomas S. Kleppe, Secretary of the Interior, before the American Oceanic Organization, Washington, D.C., February 27, 1976.

Some of the studies listed in this document bear a security classification.

Clifton, H.E., Hubert, A., and Phillips, R.L., 1967, Marine Sediment Sample Preparation for Analysis for Low Concentrations of Fine Detrital Gold: U.S. Geological Survey Circular 545.

Clifton, H.E., and Phillips, R.L., 1972, Physical Setting on the Tektite Experiments: Results of the Tektite Program: Ecology of Coral Reef Fishes, Natural History Museum Los Angeles County Science Bulletin 14, pp. 13–16.

Cook, H.E., 1970 Deep Sea Drilling Project, Leg 9 Scientists, 1970, Preliminary interpretations of the Deep Sea Drilling Project, Leg 9, Equatorial Pacific: Geotimes, v. 15, No. 4, pp. 11–13.

Cook, H.E., 1971, Iron and manganese rich sediments overlying oceanic basaltic basement, equatorial Pacific, Leg 9, DSDP: Geol. Soc. America Abs., v. 3, No. 7, pp. 530–531.

Cook, H.E., Robinson, P.T., 1971, Sea-floor basalts cored from the equatorial Pacific, Leg 9, Deep Sea Drilling Project: Geol. Soc. America Abs., v. 3, No. 7, p. 531.

Cook, H.E., 1974, Deep Sea Drilling Project, Leg 33, Scientists, 1974, Deep Sea Drilling Project, Leg 33, Testing a hot spot theory: Geotimes, v. 19, No. 3, pp. 16–20.

Cook, H.E., Schlanger, S.O., Jackson, E.D., Boyce, R.E., Jenkyns, H. Johnson, D.A., Kaneps, A.G., Kelts, K.R., Martini, E., McNulty, C.L., and Winterer, E.L., 1974, Linear Island Chain Chronologies: Leg 33 Deep Sea Drilling results from the Line and Tuamotu Islands: Geol. Soc. America Abs., v. 6, No. 7, p. 941.

Cooper, A., Scholl, D.W., and Marlow, M.S., 197–, Magnetic lineations in the Bering Sea Marginal Basin: EOS, Trans. Amer. Geophys. Union, v. 55, p. 232.

Grow, J.A., 1973, The Crustal and Upper Mantle Structure of The Central Aleutian Arc, G.S.A. Bull., 84, 2169–2192.

Grow, John A., and Tanya Atwater, 1970, Mid-Tertiary Tectonic Transition in The Aleutian Arc, Geol. Soc. Amer. Bull., v. 81, pp. 3715–3732.

Klitgord, K., Mudie, J.D., Grow, J.A., and Larson, P., 1972, Recent Sea-Floor Spreading on the Chile Ridge, (abstract), Trans. AGU (EOS, 53(11), 973.

Klitgord, K.D., Mudie, J.D., Larson, P.A., and Grow, J.A., 1973, Fast Sea-Floor Spreading on the Chile Ridge, Earth and Planetary Science Letters, v. 20, 93–99.

MacLeod, N.S., and Snavely, P.D., Jr., 1971, Plate tectonics and the Tertiary geology of western Oregon and Washington: in Symposium on Tectonism of the Pacific Northwest, Moen, A.D., (ed.) : EOS Trans. Amer. Geophys. Union, v. 52, No. 9, pp. 1640–1641.

Marlow, M.S., Scholl, D.W., and Buffington, E.C., 1968, Buldir Depression and Extensional Deformation of the Aleutian Ridge, Alaska: Transactions, American Geophysical Union, Vol. 49, No. 4, p. 695.

Marlow, M.S., Scholl, D.W., and others, 1970, Geophysical and geological investigations of Buldir depression, Aleutian Ridge: Marine Geology, v. 8, pp. 85–108.

Marlow, M.S., 1972, Tectonic history of western Aleutian Ridge-Trench System: Ph.D. Thesis, Stanford University, 102p.

Marlow, M.S., Scholl, D.W., and Garrison, L.E., 1972, Evidence (?) of underthrusting from seismic reflection profiles across the Puerto Rico and Aleutian Trenches: Trans. Am. Geophys. Union, v. 53, p. 1114.

Marlow, M.S., Scholl, D.W., and Buffington, E.C., 1973, Tectonic history of the central Aleutian arc: Geol. Soc. America Bull. 84. pp. 1555–1574.

Marlow, M.S., Scholl, D.W., and Buffington, E.C., 1973, Comments on paper by M.L. Holmes, R.E. von Huene, and D.A. McManus, Seismic reflection evidence supporting underthrusting beneath the Aleutian Arc near Amchitka Island: Journ. Geophys. Res., 78, pp. 3517–3522.

Marlow, M.S., Scholl, D.W., and Garrison, L.E., 1973, Comparative geologic histories of the Aleutian and Lesser Island arcs: Geol. Soc. America Abstracts with Programs, v. 5, pp. 77–78.

Marlow, M.S., and Scholl, D.W., 1973, Comparative geologic histories of the Aleutian and Lesser Antilles Island arcs: Geol. Soc. America Abstracts with Programs, v. 5, No. 1, pp. 77–78 (abs).

Marlow, M.S., Scholl, D.W., Buffington, D.C., and Alpha, T.R., 1973a, Tectonic history of the Central Aleutian Arc: Geol. Soc. America, v. 84, pp. 1555–1574.

Moore, G.W., 1970, Sea-floor spreading at the junction between Gorda Rise and Mendocino Ridge: Geo. Soc. America Bull., v. 81, pp. 2817–2824.

Nelson, C.H., Hopkins, D.M., and Scholl, D.W., 197–, Cenozoic sedimentary and tectonic history of the Bering Sea, in Hood, Donald, ed., Proceedings for International Symposium for Bering Sea Study, Published by International Decade of Ocean Exploration, 30p. (in press).

Nelson, C.H., Hopkins, D.M., and Scholl, D.W., 1974, Tectonic setting and Cenozoic sedimentary and tectonic history of the Bering Sea, in Herman, Yvonne, ed., Arctic Oceanography, Springer-Verlag Publishers, New York, 28p., (in press).

Reimnitz, Erk, von Huene, Roland, and Wright, F.F., 1970, Detrital gold and sediments in Nuka Bay, Alaska: U.S. Geol. Survey Prof. Paper 700–C, pp. C35–C42.

Scholl, D.W., von Huene, Roland, and Ridlon, J.B., 1968, Spreading of the ocean floor: Undeformed sediments in Peru-Chile Trench: Science, v. 1959, pp. 869–871.

Scholl, D.W., and von Huene, R., 1969, Geologic implications of Cenozoic subsidence and fragmentation of continental margins: Am. Assoc. Petroleum Geologists Bull., v. 49, pp. 740–741 (abs).

Scholl, D.W., 1969, Geologic significance of continental slope basement rocks, Pacific margin: Geol. Soc. America, Special Paper 121, p. 266 (abs).

Scholl, D.W., Christensen, M.N., von Huene, R., and Marlow, M.S., 1969, Seafloor spreading the volume of sediment in the Peru-Chile Trench: Geol. Soc. America, Abstract with Programs for 1969, pt. 7, p. 199.

Scholl, D.W., Greene, H.G., Addicott, W.O., Evitt, W.R., Pierce, R.L., Mamay, S.H., and Marlow, M.S., 1969 Adak "Paleozoic" site Aleutians—In fact of Eocene age: Am. Assoc. Petroleum Geologists Bull., v. 53, p. 459 (abs).

Scholl, D.W., and von Huene, R. 1970, Comments on paper by R.L. Chase and E.T. Bunce, "Underthrusting of the eastern margin of the Antilles by the floor of the western north Atlantic Ocean, and origin of the Barbados Ridge": Jour. Geophys. Res., v. 75, pp. 488–490.

Scholl, D.W., Christensen, M.N., von Huene, R., and Marlow, M.S., 1970, Peru-Chile Trench sediments and sea-floor spreading: Geol. Soc. America Bull., v. 81, pp. 1339–1360.

Scholl, D.W., and Buffington, E.C., 1970, Structural evolution of Bering continental margin: Cretaceous to Holocene: Am. Assoc. Petroleum Geologists Bull., v. 54, No. 12, p. 2503 (abs).

Scholl, D.W., Creager, J.S., Boyce, R.E., Echols, R.J., Fullam, T.J., Grow, J.A., Koizumi, Itaru, Lee, J.H., Ling, Hsin-Yi, Supko, P.R., Stewart, R.J., Worsley, T.R., Ericson, A., Hess, J., Bryan, G., and Stoll, Robert, 1971, Deep Seat Drilling Project Leg 19: Geotimes, 1971.

Scholl, D.W., and Marlow, M.S., 1972, Ancient trench deposits and global tectonics: A different interpretation: Geol. Soc. America Abstracts with Programs, v. 4, No. 3, p. 232 (abs).

Scholl, D.W., and Marlow, M.S., 1972, The sedimentary sequence in Modern Pacific trenches, and the apparent rarity of similar sequences in deformed circumpacific eugeosynclines: Proceedings Modern and Ancient Geosynclinal Sedimentation, a Conference, Dept. Geol. Univ. Wisconsin, No. 10–11, 1972 (abs).

Scholl, D.W., and Creager, J.S., 1973, Geologic synthesis of Leg 19 (DSDP) results; far north Pacific and Aleutian Ridge and Bering Sea, in Creager, J.S., Scholl, D.W., and others, Initial Reports of the Deep Sea Drilling Project, v. 19, U.S. Government Print. Office, Wash., D.C., pp. 897–913.

Scholl, D.W., Creager, J.S., and others, 1973, Initial Report of the Deep Sea Drilling Project, v. 19, U.S. Government Print. Office, Wash., D.C., 913p.

Scholl, D.W., Marlow, M.S., and Buffington, E.C., 1974, How to form the Aleutian-Bering Sea region in two easy steps: Geol. Soc. America Abstracts with Programs, v. 6, No. 3, p. 250.

Scholl, D.W., and Marlow, M.S., 197–, Ancient and modern trench deposits, some different interpretations: Am. Assoc. Petroleum Geologists, Special Paper, (in press).

Scholl, D.W., Buffington, E.C., and Marlow, M.S., 197–, Plate tectonics and the structural development of Aleutian-Bering Region: Geol. Soc. America Memoir 151, (in press).

Scholl, D.W., and Marlow, M.S., 197–, The sedimentary sequence in modern Pacific trenches, and the deformed circumpacific eugeosynclines, in Dott, R.H., Jr., and Shaver, R.H., eds., Geosynclinal Sedimentation: Soc. Econ. Paleotologists and Mineralogists Spec. Paper 19, (in press).

Scholl, D.W., 197–, The Western Pacific; Island arcs, marginal seas, geochemistry: P.J. Coleman, ed., Crane, Russak & Co.: A review: Science, (in press).

Silver, E.A., 1969, Tectonic implications of the structure of the Gorda Escarpment and of the magnetic anomaly pattern north of the escarpment: Geol. Soc. America, 82nd Ann. Mtg., v. 80, pp. 206–207.

Silver, E.A., 1970, Gorda Basin deformation related to triple junction tectonics: Geol. Soc. America, 83rd Ann. Mtg., v. 2, No. 7, p. 684.

Silver, E.A., and Curray, J.R., 1971, Structure of the continental margin and distribution of basement rock types off central California: Geol. Soc. America, 67th Ann. Mtg., Cordilleran Section.

Silver, E.A., 1971, Transitional tectonics and Late Cenozoic structure of the continental margin off northernmost California: Geol. Soc. America Bull v. 82, No. 1, pp. 1–22.

Silver, E.A., 1971, Tectonics of the Mendocino Triple Junction: Geol. Soc. America Bull., v. 82, pp. 2965–2978.

Silver, E.A., Curray, J.R., and Cooper, A.K., 1971, Tectonic development of the continental margin off central Calif.: Geological Society of Sacramento, Annual Field Trip Guidebook, pp. 1–10.

Silver, E.A., 1971, Small Plate Tectonics of the Northeastern Pacific: Geol. Soc. America Bull., v. 82, pp. 3491–3496.

Silver, E.A., 1972, Pleistocene Tectonic Accretion of the continental slope off Washington: Marine Geology, v. 13, pp. 239–249.

Silver, E.A., Jackson, E.D., and Dalrymple, G.B., 1972, Hawaiian-Emperor chain and its relation to Cenozoic Circumpacific tectonics: Geol. Soc. America Bull., v. 83, pp. 601–618.

Silver, E.A., 1974, Geometrical principles of plate Tectonics: in San Joaquin Geological Soc. Short Course, Geological Interpretations from global Tectonics with applications for Calif. geology and petroleum exploration.

Silver, E.A., 1974, Basin development along translational continental margins: in San Joaquin Geological Soc. Short Course, Geological interpretations from global Tectonics with applications for Calif. geology and petroleum exploration, W.R. Dickinson, Ed., pp. 6–1 to 6–5.

von Huene, Roland, Scholl, D.W., and Shor, George G. Jr., 1968, Hypothesis of thrusting at continental margins in light of recent marine geophysical observations: Transactions of the American Geophysical Union, v. 49, No. 4 (abs).

von Huene, Roland, Scholl, D.W., and Ridlon, J.B., 1968, Submarine trenches and deformation: Science, v. 160, No. 3831, p. 1024.

von Huene, Roland, 1969, Geological structure between the Murray fracture zone and transverse ranges: Marine Geology, v. 7, No. 6.

von Huene, Roland, and Shor, George G. Jr., 1969, The structure and tectonic history of the eastern Aleutian Trench: Geol. Soc. America Bull., v. 80, No. 10, pp. 1889–1902.

von Huene, Roland, and Scholl, David W., 1969, Tectonic implications of structures in stratified sequences at the base of Pacific continental margins: Am. Assoc. Petroleum Geologists Bull., v. 53, pp. 747–748 (abs).

von Huene, Roland, Wright, F.F., and Lathram, Ernest, 1969, Tectonic features of the continental shelf in the northeastern Gulf of Alaska: Transactions, Amer. Geophys. Union, v. 49, p. 207 (abs).

von Huene, Roland, 1971, A possible relationship between the Transverse Ranges of California and the Murray Fracture: Geol. Soc. America Program with Abstracts, v. 3, No. 2, p. 213.

von Huene, Roland, 1971, Initial reports reports of the Deep Sea Drilling Project: Book Review, Marine Geology, v. 10, pp. 145–149.

von Huene, Roland, Kulm, LaVerne D., Duncan, John R., Kling, Stanley A., Musich, Lillian M., Piper, David J.W., Pratt, Richard M., Schrader, Hans-Joachim, Weser, Oscar, and Wise, Sherwood W., 1971, Deep Sea Drilling Project, Leg 18: Geotimes, v. 16, No. 10, pp. 12–15.

von Huene, Roland, 1972, Structure of the continental margin and tectonism at the eastern Aleutian Trench: Geol. Soc. American Bull., v. 83.

FREQUENCY OF REGULARLY ISSUED BUREAU OF MINES COMMODITY REPORTS

[W=weekly, M=monthly, Q=quarterly, A—annually]

MINERAL INDUSTRY SURVEYS

Abrasive Materials (A)
Aluminum (M,A)
Antimony (Q,A)
Asbestos (A)
Barite (A)
Bauxite (Q)
Beryllium (A)
Bismuth (Q,A)
Boron (A)
Bromine (A)
Cadmium (Q,A)
Calcium-magnesium chloride (A)
Carbon black (Q,A)
Cement (M,A)
Cesium and rubidium (A)
Chromium (M,A)
Clays (A)
Coal, bituminous (W,A)
Coal, Bituminous distribution (Q)
Coal, anthracite (W,A)
Coal, anthracite distribution (A)
Cobalt (M,A)
Cobalt refiners (Q)
Coke and coal chemicals (M,A)
Coke distribution (A)
Coke producers (A)
Columbium and tantalum (A)
Copper industry (M,A)
Copper production (M)
Copper sulfate (Q)
Diatomite (A)
Feldspar (A)

Ferroalloys (semiannual)
Ferrosilicon (Q,A)
Fluorspar (Q,A)
Gem stones (Q,A)
Gold and silver (M,A)
Graphite (A)
Gypsum (M,A)
Iodine (A)
Iron and steel (A)
Iron and steel scrap (M,A)
Iron ore (M,A)
Kyanite and related materials (A)
Lead industry (M,A)
Lead, primary production (M)
Lime (M,A)
Liquefied petroleum gasses & ethane sales (A)
Lithium (A)
Magnesium, primary (Q,A)
Magnesium and magnesium compounds (A)
Manganese (M,A)
Mercury (Q,A)
Mica (A)
Mineral production, world (A)
Minor nonmetals (A)
Molybdenum (M,A)
Natural gas (M,A)
Natural gas liquids (M)
Natural gas processing plants (bi-annually)
Natural gas production, world (A)
Nickel (M,A)
Nitrogen (A)
Peat (A)
Peat producers (A)
Perlite (A)
Petroleum and petroleum products:
    Asphalt sales (A)
    Aviation turbine fuels (A)
    Burner fuel oils (A)
    Crude oil production, world (A)
    Crude oil and products pipeline mileage (tri-annually)
    Diesel fuel oils (A)
    District V petroleum statement (M,A)
    Fuel oil and kerosine sales (A)
    Fuel oils by sulfur content (M)
    Motor gasolines (summer) (A)
    Motor gasolines (winter) (A)
    Pertroleum refineries in U.S. (A)
    Petroleum statement, advance release (M)
    Petroleum statement (M,A)
Phosphate rock (M,A)
Platinum group metals (Q,A)
Potash (A)
Pumice and volcanic cinder (A)
Rare earth elements and thorium (A)
Rhenium (A)
Salt (A)
Sand and gravel (A)
Selenium (Q)
Selenium and tellurium (A)
Slag, iron and steel (A)
Sodium compounds (A)
Stone (A)
Sulfur (M,A)
Talc, soapstone, and pyrophyllite (A)
Tin (M,A)

Titanium (Q,A)
Tungsten (M,A)
Uranium (A)
Vanadium (M,A)
Vermiculite (A)
Zinc industry (M,A)
Zinc production (M)
Zinc oxide (M)
Zirconium and hafnium (A)

OTHER REPORTS

Commodity data summaries (covers 95 commodities) (A)
Minerals and materials (covers 15 commodities) (M)
International coal trade (M)
International petroleum annual (A)
Mineral trade notes (M)
Minerals yearbook, vol. I (covers 92 commodities) (A)
Minerals yearbook, vol. II (covers 50 states) (A)
Minerals yearbook, vol. III (covers 157 countries) (A)
Mineral facts & problems (covers 89 commodities) (every 5 years)

Mr. MURPHY. There have been press reports that the Department of the Interior prepared ocean mining legislation last year. Is this true?

Are you pressing for any legislation in this field within the administration now?

Mr. FRIZZELL. It is true that the Department of the Interior has prepared draft legislation designed to encourage continued ocean mining activity by American industry during the period prior to the coming into force of the Law of the Sea Treaty.

We felt that the continuing delays, and until recently an apparent stalemate in that of the Sea Conference on ocean mining issues presented a significant enough risk that U.S.-owned ocean mining companies would either severely cut back or abandon their development plans.

In order to protect our national interest in developmnet of ocean mineral resources we sought to formulate a legislative program that would both encourage ocean miners, and still be consistent with our Law of the Sea negotiations, and we continue to work to refine the technical aspects of that legislation.

Mr. MURPHY. Will you send us a copy of those proposals?

Mr. FRIZZELL. Until we would get the appropriate clearance, we would not be able to, Mr. Chairman.

Mr. MURPHY. What is the appropriate clearance?

Mr. FRIZZELL. The Office of Management and Budget.'

Mr. MURPHY. Would you communicate to OMB that the committee would like to take under advisement proposals in the ocean mining field considered by the Department?

Mr. FRIZZELL. I shall do so.

Mr. MURPHY. I have some other questions which I will submit to you in writing, and if you will respond to those, I would appreciate it.

Time is running out, and we have some other witnesses that we would like to proceed with.

Mr. FRIZZELL. Thank you for the opportunity today.

Mr. MURPHY. As a final note, would you give us a brief assessment of what you feel the value of deep ocean resources is to the United States?

Mr. FRIZZELL. I have some figures here that have been prepared by my staff, to the extent that their estimates of the total value of seabed mineral production by 1985 would exceed $1 billion in 1975 dollars.

That is conceivably a $1 billion decrease in our mineral import costs, and we also project that the total private investment for a capacity in the year 1985 would range from $2 billion to $3 billion.

According to information developed by the Bureau of Mines, Geological Survey, and the Ocean Mining Administration such production would reduce our nickel imports by over 50 percent, eliminate totally our cobalt imports, would reduce our copper imports by 30 percent, and possibly reduce manganese ore imports by more than 50 percent.

Mr. MURPHY. You might mention that to the OMB when you give them my request.

Mr. FRIZZELL. We shall do so, and it should be a strong argument.

Mr. MURPHY. Thank you, I appreciate your testimony this morning. Our next witness is Mr. Northcutt Ely.

STATEMENT OF NORTHCUTT ELY, COUNSEL IN INTERNATIONAL LAW MATTERS TO DEEPSEA VENTURES, INC.

Mr. ELY. Mr. Chairman, I was honored by the committee's invitation to discuss H.R. 11879, a bill to promote the orderly development of hard mineral resources of the deep seabed, pending adoption of an international regime relating thereto.

Mr. Chairman, since time is short, and I have submitted a prepared statement, which I honestly hope you have read, or will read, I shall summarize portions of it.

I should say that the views I am expressing are my own. They were developed in the course of several years in which I have served as a member of professional committees concerned with this subject, in the International Law Association, the American Bar Association, the National Petroleum Council, and more recently as counsel to Deepsea Ventures, Inc., a company which is ready to commence active mining of deep sea nodules.

Mr. John Flipse is president of that company, and will appear before you at a later time to testify on behalf of the company.

I shall restrict my discussion today primarily to the questions of international law, and what I conceive to be national policy involved in this bill.

I strongly favor the enactment of this bill, Mr. Chairman.

Later on, if the committee wishes, I may have some amendments to suggest, but they will be in accord with the bill's objectives, which are excellent.

Before this committee I do not need to dwell upon the importance of the resource, nor of our Nation's dependence on the minerals it contains.

We are, indeed, now dependent upon foreign sources for approximately 100 percent of our manganese—there are 3-year averages of reports by the Bureau of Mines—88 percent of our nickel, 20 percent of our copper, and 100 percent of our cobalt requirements.

Moreover, the sources of these supplies are, in general, insecure cartels.

We are confronted by policies in the United Nations that favor these cartels, which will continue to grow in number and influence.

For example, article 5, and this is at the bottom of page 2 of my statement, of the Charter of Economic Rights and Duties of States adopted by the U.N. General Assembly, at its 29th session, declares that:

All States have the right to associate in organizations of primary commodity producers in order to develop their national economies, to achieve stable financing for their development and, in pursuance of their aims, to assist in the promotion of sustained growth of the world economy, in particular, accelerating the development of developing countries.

Correspondingly, all States have the duty to respect that right be refraining from applying economic and political measures that would limit it.

I may say of the nine countries which presently supply more than 90 percent of U.S. imports of manganese, nickel, cobalt and copper, not one joined with the United States to vote against this resolution.

Arguments have been made that the mineral exporting nations will not be able to operate effectively as cartels.

Six years ago we heard the same statement about the petroleum exporting countries, and now we have OPEC.

Existing metal producing cartels include the Intergovernmental Committee of Copper Exporting Countries, the Iron Ore Exporters Association, the International Bauxite Association, the International Tin Council, the International Cadmium Institute, the International Association of Mercury Producers, the International Phosphate Rock Export Association, and the Primary Tungsten Association.

Other cartels are in the process of being formed. Given time, these cartels can be expected to realize their ambitions of maximizing revenues from their mineral resources at the expense of consumers in industrialized nations, just as OPEC has.

As we all know, there are tremendous deposits of manganese nodules lying on the seabed beyond the limits of national jurisdiction.

I discuss in my prepared statement, at some length, the existing international law which is to the effect that there now exists in nations, and in their nationals, under the existing freedoms of the seas doctrine, the right to discover, mine, take away and use these nodules, so long as the operation does not unreasonably interfere with other freedoms of the seas, such as fishing, navigation, and so on.

This is assumed by the State Department and by the Government witnesses who have appeared before you.

I shall place in the record, if I may, an opinion I prepared, dated November 14, 1974, which was submitted to the State Department in support of Deepsea Ventures' claim to a specific deposit they have discovered.

Mr. MURPHY. Without objection that report will be included in the permanent files of the committee.

Mr. ELY. Thank you, Mr. Chairman.

Nor has this existing freedom of the seas been effectively impaired by any action taken so far by the General Assembly of the United Nations.

I say "so far", Mr. Chairman, because it is quite true that the General Assembly has taken action hostile to deep sea mining: First, by the passage of a moratorium resolution to which the United States objected, and second, by the passage of a declaration of principles for which, unfortunately, the United States voted.

The declaration of principles may be taken as somewhat ambiguous. This is because it says merely that no nation or person shall have the right to appropriate any portion of the area beyond existing national jurisdiction, and that no nation or person may acquire rights to manganese nodules which are incompatible with the regions to be established at some time in the future. The point to be made, however, is that, as a matter of international law, neither the moratorium resolution nor the declaration of principles is binding on the United States or its nationals.

If, under international law, we have the right to take and use these nodules, what is industry waiting for?

Why do we want legislation?

Let me take up first the matter of a treaty before I discuss legislation.

Assurances by the United States negotiators to the Congress are variously worded on several points.

First, that we do indeed have existing rights to mine deep sea nodules; second, that integrity of investments would be protected in the interim before there is a treaty, and, third, that they would be protected in the treaty itself, and that we shall receive diplomatic protection during this interim, as well as diplomatic protection of the guarantees to be given us by the treaty.

These are assurances from the executive department, transient utterances of individuals.

However, it is only Congress that can give these assurances, and only by legislation.

International law on which we may now rely does not prescribe any detailed regulation of any deep seabed mining activities, and, for example, the size of the area, the duration of the rights, the work or diligence requirements to keep a right alive, environmental restrictions, and so on.

These are matters that could be dealt with in a multilateral convention, or in bilateral treaties within the countries capable of carrying out such activities, or the domestic activities controlling the activities of the legislating state.

As to the first of these, over the past 6 years, the efforts of the United States negotiators to achieve a multilateral convention have been repeatedly frustrated by the developing nations.

I shall come, after the discussion of my prepared testimony, to the discussion made here by Mr. Ratiner as to the development for which he feels a glimmer of hope. But the most recent sessions of the Law of the Sea negotiations produced a "Single Negotiating Text," which the Government witnesses here have quite accurately characterized as a disaster.

I may say that this was disaster number two. The senior disaster was the floating promulgation by the United States negotiators in 1970 of a draft treaty.

This draft treaty proposed the creation of the International Seabed Resource Authority, which the developing countries have seized upon and distorted to their own advantage, it, like the present proposal in the document Mr. Ratiner has given you, would consist of a council and an assembly, a secretariat supplemented by three commissions, three councils, and a tribunal.

In other words, the three branches of Government, legislative, executive and judicial, Mr. Chairman.

Once duly created, this sea monster would have a perpetual life. You could not escape from it.

Now the United States has been consistently outvoted in the United Nations General Assembly, but there is one important difference between the General Assembly of the United Nations and the assembly that we propose, and which the current treaty negotiations have eargerly seized upon: namely, that while, as Ambassador Moynihan has said, the Assembly of the United Nations only pretends to be a parliament—it has no legislative powers; all we have agreed to is to listen to its recommendations—the new International Seabed Resource Authority would indeed have legislative powers, and it is a minor matter whether it votes by majority or two-thirds, or whatever.

The resolutions adopted by the Assembly of the United Nations should have taught us a lesson in the last 5 years.

The resolution condemning the United States presence in Guam within the last 3 months was passed by a vote of 108 to 1. Not a single ally voted with us to oppose this resolution.

The notion that we are safe in a new Assembly, because it takes two-thirds of the parties to the authority to vote, is answered by that type of vote.

The vote to establish a charter of economic rights and duties of States passed January 15, 1975, declares, among other things, the right of developing Nations to form producer cartels, and the duty of industrialized nations not to interfere with such cartels.

It also declares the right to nationalize foreign investment, and determine the compensation therefor by domestic law, rather than international law.

This, Mr. Chairman, was adopted by a vote of 120 to 6, the 6 being the United States, Belgium, Denmark, West Germany, Luxembourg, and the United Kingdom.

On the vote of the Assembly to expel Taiwan from the United Nations, of the 20 NATO nations, 1 voted against explusion, and, thanks to the position of the United States, that 1 was the United States itself; not a single ally voted with us.

Now, it is naive to expect the Congress to accept the assurance that, if this new legislature is created, somehow we can control it.

The original proposal in 1970, made by the U.S. delegation, contained a provision that the governing power should be in a Council, not an Assembly.

The Council was to consist of 24 States, of which 6 should be the most advanced industrially, and the other 18, making up the others, to be of another category.

It provided that any substantive matter must have the affirmative, passed affirmatively by the 2 blocs, the 6 and the 18.

I was a member of the National Petroleum Council Committee that considered this. We expressed total shock. But we were reassured by the Government negotiators at that time that we could relax because the United States would never accept a treaty that did not contain this weighted voting provision, and that if the treaty did not contain such a provision, the U.S. negotiators would not sign it.

You do not have that type of assurance before you today from the Government witnesses at all, and it was naive from the beginning for our negotiators to expect that the less developed countries would move to the back of the bus, and that the show would be run from the front of the bus, by the six most industrially developed countries.

This is the type of self-deception that has characterized the negotiation of this treaty on the part of the United States from the beginning.

This new Assembly, with the power to legislate, we may scarcely add, would be dominated by the same unfriendly nations that Ambassador Moynihan has been contending with so gallantly in the United Nations.

The county's supplies would become all the more vulnerable to price fixing, and we would be required, by the Single Negotiating Text, to turn over our technology.

The material given you by Mr. Ratiner itself provides that the Council must approve any work program before a company can undertake it.

While he assures you the technology would not be required to be turned over, can you imagine the hostile Council permitting an American company to operate without divulging and turning over its technology? If it does not meet the conditions set by the council, the work program is not approved.

The problem has come to rest in the U.S. Congress. The Congress has been told repeatedly in the last 6 years, "Wait until manana. We will have a treaty. Please do not rock the boat."

Congress, finally discontented with this continual procrastination, passed a fisheries bill.

We were told by the U.S. negotiators that the passage of such a bill would be catastrophic. It would be the end of the treaty negotiations.

Well, the world has not ended. The sun has been rising on time every day, and the bureaucrats in the United Nations have been going to work every day.

The fisheries bill was a salutary exercise, and instruction by the Congress to United States negotiators of the mining bill will be too.

Mr. Chairman, it is time that our negotiators had clear direction from the Congress as to the type of treaty that the American public will accept; and it certainly will not accept either the U.S. proposal of 1970, nor the Single Negotating Text, these twin disasters. Nor, in my opinion, will it, or should it, accept the "glimmer of hope" now displayed by Mr. Ratiner, as emanating from New York.

Mr. Chairman, it is time for Congress to act, if the decisions must be made in 1976 by the mining companies in order to get production in the early 1980's. Now is the time for decision.

We cannot afford to have this decision put off by a moratorium. And all further treaty negotiations will do is provide a moratorium, because no investor is going to risk a nickel in deep sea mining if a treaty containing the hostile provisions of the 1970 U.S. proposal, the Single Negotiating Text, or the material handed to you yesterday by Mr. Ratiner are floating around awaiting ratification by the U.S. Senate to become the law of the land. Such a treaty would render our investments worthless.

Let me come now to page 17 of my testimony, to the particular provisions of H.R. 11879.

This bill, in my opinion, meets the tests that are required for protection of American interests and the American mining industry.

There is no pretense by Congress here that the United States owns the deep seabed, and is about to grant patents to it. Quite the contrary.

All that you are asked to do is to exercise the constitutional power that Congress has to legislate to control the activities of American nationals anywhere in the world.

The premise of the bill is that there does exist, under international law, the present right of American nationals to mine the deep sea nodules. But, hereafter, by the passage of this bill, this activity will be carried on under reasonable restraints for the protection of the environment and for the limitation of area sizes, so that the United States is not in a position purporting to hog the whole seabed; with reasonable financial provisions; and with the expectations that these minerals will be brought into the United States to be refined, and that the operation shall be carried on without unreasonable interference with other reasonable uses of the ocean.

No one can fairly complain that Congress requires of the American mining industry adherence to a code of behavior we would expect nationals of other States to adhere to. Nor can anyone object to the American Congress saying that, if Americans carry on in the fashion Congress has prescribed, they shall have the diplomatic protection of our country. Nor can anyone fairly object that, if other nations do likewise, as reciprocating States, we will recognize their rights as they recognize ours.

That, Mr. Chairman, is what this bill does. It contains, like most of the world's mining legislation, area 1 limitations, mandatory relinquishments, work requirements, transfer and surrender of the right and application procedures.

The Interior Department does not have to carry on several years of research to establish the need for, or define, these principles. They have to apply to deep sea mining, as they do to mining onshore.

There are two provisions of this bill that deserve particular attention, because they relate to guarantees, and insurance, and at page 18 you will find a reference to them.

Section 13 of the bill is a guarantee provision. It provides that, in the event an international agreement which is inconsistent with the provisions of the act becomes binding on the United States, the United States shall compensate the licensee for losses resulting from "the differing requirements" of the treaty and the act.

Let me pause here a minute to say Mr. Ratiner was asked yesterday whether the U.S. negotiators would accept a treaty less protective of United States interests than your bill, and he gave a candid and honest answer.

The answer was one word: "probably."

If that should happen, and, as a result, hundreds of millions of dollars of American investment should be lost in this high risk enterprise, the American investors are entitled to assurance that, if the United States destroys these rights by a new treaty, compensation shall be made to them.

Otherwise, there is just not going to be any deep sea mining carried on, obviously, with the threat of the probably hostile treaty hanging over us, to borrow Mr. Ratiner's words.

Section 14 is an insurance provision. It provides that, upon payment by the licensee of an annual premium, the United States will insure the "licensee" for any damages suffered through the impairment of the insured investment, or through the removal of hard minerals of the licensed block, by any other person against whom a legal remedy either does not exist, or is unavailable in any legal forum to which the licensee has access.

If insurance is available against such risk in the open market, so be it. If it is not, it is a fair type of insurance for the United States to set up on the payment of reasonable premium.

Mr. MURPHY. Like OPIC?

Mr. ELY. Somewhat similar, but they are not the same.

Mr. MURPHY. The companies would pay a premium for that type of coverage?

Mr. ELY. Yes, sir.

Mr. MURPHY. So the fund, the basic insurance fund, would not be a taxpayers' fund, but it would be an industry fund, payable by premiums from the industry?

Mr. ELY. That is correct.

The initial capital may have to be provided, as in the OPIC case, but the theory is, it would be a self-supporting fund.

There are some points on which in due time I would suggest some amendments to H.R. 11879, but they are totally consistent with your purposes, which are admirable.

I would like to have the bill more clearly state that the issuance of a license to a national of the United States establishes that the United States has determined

One: That the issuance of the license does not conflict with any international obligations of the United States, and that operations carried on in accordance with the license with respect to the area therein described will not unreasonably interfere with other reasonable uses of the high seas.

Two: That the licensee is recognized by the United States as having, as against the United States, reciprocating States, nationals of the United States and nationals of reciprocating States, the exclusive right to explore for, recover, take away, and use, the seabed mineral resources in the area described in the license, in accordance with its terms, for the period of time therein prescribed.

Three: That the licensee is entitled to diplomatic protection of the these three determinations shall have the written concurrence of the United States with respect to operations so conducted, provided that these three determinations shall have the written concurrence of he Secretary of State.

The license is not a patent or grant of anything. It is a certificate by the United States of the entitlement I have spoken of, with a guarantee of diplomatic protection.

I personally favor another addition to the bill, and I am not speaking for Deepsea Ventures, Inc., in this respect.

This would be a provision earmarking a portion of U.S. income taxes, related to operations at the minesite, in an escrow fund, from which Congress can appropriate money, if it so chooses, in fulfillment of provisions of some future treaty which may dedicate revenues from deep sea mining to international purposes.

The point to make clear is that deep sea mining, an extremely high risk, high cost business, cannot, and should not, pay higher taxes than those paid by onshore competitors.

The intent of the proposal is that only U.S. income taxes would be collected from deep sea mining enterprises, and that any contribution to an international fund would be paid out of, not in addition to, U.S. taxes.

The contrary notion, of double taxation, which seems to be buzzing in some foreign heads, would solve all deep sea mining problems very simply, indeed. There would be no mining.

Deep sea miners taking on these added costs and risks cannot bear the additional financial burden, and the Government financial take greater than that borne by their competitors onshore who do not undertake such risks.

The matter of urgency can be best highlighted, I think, by the fact that in the last 5 years, since 1971, when deep sea mining legislation was first introduced in the Congress, the world prices of manganese, nickel, and cobalt increased 130 percent, 65 percent, and 82 percent, respectively.

The costs of equipment have escalated, as have all engineering and industrial construction costs, at a rate of 8 to 10 percent a year.

Mr. Chairman, now is the tme for decision.

Now, let me turn briefly, Mr. Chairman, to the material handed you by Mr. Ratiner.

I must say, first of all, that I have disagreed with Mr. Ratiner on many occasions professionally, but I have high professional respect for him, and personal regard for him.

What I am about to say now is directed not at the gentleman who testified, but at the proposals that he brought before you—and I am grateful to have them disclosed—I presume by direction.

As I have told Mr. Frizzell in my encounters with Mr. Ratiner, the wounds and scars I bear are all in the front, and all above the belt.

If you have this document before you, let me say that my copy is not very legible, which is merciful, because the more clearly you can read it, the more incredible it becomes.

Taking them up in the order in which they are presented, article 9 is headed, "General Provisions Regarding Economic Aspects of Activities in the Area." Paragraph 4 provides instructions to protect against the adverse economic effects of a substantial decline in the mineral export earnings of developing countries for whom export revenues for minerals or raw materials also under exploitation in the area represent a significant share of their domestic product, or foreign exchange earnings, when such decline is caused by activities in the area by three types, and they are:

Number 1: Facilitating through existing forums for such new arrangements as may be appropriate, and in which all affected parties participate, the growth, efficiency and stability of markets for those classes of commodities produced from the Area, at prices remunerative to producers and fair to consumers.

Number 2: During an interim period, total production from the area shall not exceed an amount specified in accordance with article [Blank].

Number 3: A system of compensation in respect of the losses specified above.

Well, now, here are the production controls that I am told were not going to be imposed.

Here is a system of compensation to producing countries if we are permitted to mine.

Here is a promise that whatever we do is not going to significantly reduce income to producing nations.

Where is the American consumer in all of this?

If new supplies are subjected to escalating prices, as in the case of OPEC, that is all right; but if prices come down because new supplies become available from this last great reserve available to the American producer, that is prohibited.

Next is Article XI. Paragraph 1 reads:

The Authority is the organization to which States Parties shall organize and control activities in the area, particularly with a view towards the administration of the resources of the area in accordance with this Convention.

In so doing, the Authority shall promote the objectives set forth in Articles 9, 23 and (Blank).

Paragraph 2:

The Authority is based on the principle of the sovereign equality of all its members.

What has become of the assurance given us that nothing could happen adverse to the interests of the United States, because we would have a blocking vote in the council?

Paragraph 3:

All members, in order to ensure to all of whom the rights and benefits resulting from membership, shall fulfill in good faith the obligations assumed by them in accord with this convention.

In other words, the United States must enforce the treaty against its nationals, the mining companies I have referred to.

Next is article 22, "Functions of the Authority."

Paragraph 7:

Activities in the area shall be conducted directly by the Authority, and on its behalf, by States, parties, or State enterprises, or persons, natural or juridical which possess the nationality of States Parties or are effectively controlled by them.

The key phrase is, "conducted directly by the Authority, and on its behalf." This is a "common heritage of mankind," with the authority as the spokesman of mankind, in other words.

Paragraph 2:

All activities in the area shall be carried out in accordance with a formal written plan of work drawn in accordance with Annex I and approved by the Council after review by the Technical Commission. In the case of activities in the area conducted on behalf of the Authority such plan of work shall be in the form of a contract of exploration and exploitation.

Paragraph 3

The Authority shall exercise effective control of a general and overall nature in respect of the conduct of all activities in the Area in accordance with the provisions of this Convention, Annex I, and the rules, regulations and procedures of the Authority adopted under Article 28 (xi). States Parties who sponsor persons natural or juridical shall assist the Authority by taking all necessary measures to assure compliance by such persons with this Convention, and any contracts they may have with the Authority. Effective control of a general and overall nature.

That is more than just giving little old guidelines and going back home. Effective control of a general and overall nature means the council and the assembly; the perpetual legislative body in which we have one vote is going to exercise the type of control that it thinks corresponds to this mandate. And if somebody does not like it, their Government can go alone to the tribunal for a determination of whether the authority acted ultra vires. You can write that opinion here without leaving the council table.

The next article is 24, "Organs of the Authority."

It says, "There are hereby established as the principal governing, judicial and administrative organs of the authority: an Assembly, a Council, a Tribunal and a Secretariat." These organs represent the three branches of government.

"There is hereby established the Enterprise, the organ through which the Authority will directly carry out activities in the Area."

Article 25 describes the Assembly.

Mr. Ratiner has told you of the great advance made in the last 2 or 3 weeks, namely, that now this Assembly can only act on questions of substance by a two-thirds majority of the members of the Authority.

He has hold you careful research shows that there have been no resolutions opposed by the United States passed by a vote of two-thirds of the members of the General Assembly.

I have cited the votes on two such resolutions: 108 to 1, and 108 to 6.

Mr. Chairman, these were vital resolutions; one would make us get out of Guam, and the other affirms this principle of cartels.

Paragraph 10 of article 25 reads, "upon a request to the President, supported by not less than one-fourth of the members of the Authority, a vote on any matter before the Assembly shall be deferred pending reference to the Tribunal for an advisory opinion on the legality of the proposed action.

Voting on such matters shall be stayed pending delivery of the Tribunal's advisory opinion.

If the advisory opinion is not received during the session in which it is requested, the Assembly will decide when it will meet to vote on the deferred question."

I suppose we could demand that the matter be deferred until the Tribunal approved it. This is not very reassuring.

Now, article 26 does say, "The Assembly shall have the power to lay down general guidelines as to policies to be pursued by the Authority on any question or matter within the competence of the

Authority by adopting resolutions and making recommendations."

This is legislation. And whether a resolution is just a guideline or is a mandate that has to be obeyed will be decided by the Tribunal, naturally.

The Assembly is to set up budgets, make appropriations, and finally, in paragraph 2(x) of article 26, it has the function of "Adoption of criteria, rules, regulations, and procedures for the equitable sharing among States Parties of financial and other economic benefits derived from activities in the area, taking into particular consideration the interest and needs of the developing countries."

In paragriph 2(iv) the Assembly is also given the function of "assessment of the contribution of States Parties to the administrative budget of the Authority."

This new legislation is going to fix the tax, the assessment the U.S. Government must pay. It will fix the budget to make the appropriations.

I greatly prefer that the U.S. Congress carry on these functions with respect to American deep seabed mining, and that these governmental powers not be turned over to a foreign legislature, in which we have one vote, and which is made up of nations who have evidenced their ill will toward our country in repeated actions in the Assembly of the United Nations.

It is a fortuitous coincidence, Mr. Chairman and gentlemen, that this committee is going to mark up this bill on March 15 and 16, on the eve of the resumption by the negotiators of the treaty based on the documents that Mr. Ratiner has given you.

I would hope that in your committee report you would shoot this new "glimmer" down before it gets off the runway, and before this can do the mischief that was done by the floating of the 1970 draft treaty by the same negotiators.

I would ask to place in your record, Mr. Chairman, the 1970 draft treaty.

I do not think it should be forgotten, and, if you want it, I have available here a statement I made before the American Mining Congress on the deep seabed, that traces recent proceedings in the United Nations.

In closing, may I give one statistic? The informal single negotiating text which creates this international regime, and deals with the deep seabed, is itself longer than the U.S. Constitution—some 50 pages of single space.

Proceed with great caution in setting up this irrevocable document.

I am grateful that this committee is taking hold of this problem, and I am hopeful that the Congress will give such clear "guidelines" to the American negotiators, that there is going to be no doubt at all as to what the American public wants.

Thank you, Mr. Chairman and gentlemen.

Mr. Murphy. Thank you, Mr. Ely, for a very fine presentation, and for your obvious expertise in this area.

The documents you referred to will be made a part of the record at this point.

[The documents referred to follow:]

August 3, 1970 *

DRAFT UNITED NATIONS CONVENTION
ON THE INTERNATIONAL SEABED AREA

Working Paper

The attached draft of a United Nations Convention on the International Seabed Area is submitted by the United States Government as a working paper for discussion purposes.

The draft Convention and its Appendices raise a number of questions with respect to which further detailed study is clearly necessary and do not necessarily represent the definitive views of the United States Government. The Appendices in particular are included solely by way of example

CHAPTER I

BASIC PRINCIPLES

ARTICLE 1

1 The International Seabed Area shall be the common heritage of all mankind.

2. The International Seabed Area shall comprise all areas of the seabed and subsoil of the high seas [1] seaward of the 200 meter isobath adjacent to the coast of continents and islands

3. Each Contracting Party shall permanently delineate the precise boundary of the International Seabed Area off its coast by straight lines not exceeding 60 nautical miles in length, following the general direction of the limit specified in paragraph 2. Such lines shall connect fixed points at the limit specified in paragraph 2, defined permanently by coordinates of latitude and longitude. Areas between or landward of such points may be deeper than 200 meters Where a trench or trough deeper than 200 meters transects an area less than 200 meters in depth, a straight boundary line more than 60 nautical miles in length, but not exceeding the lesser of one fourth of the length of that part of the trench or trough transecting the area 200 meters in depth or 120 nautical miles, may be drawn across the trench or trough.

4 Each Contracting Party shall submit the description of the boundary to the International Seabed Boundary Review Commission within five years of the entry into force of this Convention for such Contracting Party Boundaries not accepted by the Commission and not resolved by negotiation between the Commission and the Contracting Party within one year shall be submitted by the Commis-

sion to the Tribunal in accordance with Section E of Chapter IV.

5. Nothing in this Article shall affect any agreement or prejudice the position of any Contracting Party with respect to the delimitation of boundaries between opposite or adjacent States in seabed areas landward of the International Seabed Area, or with respect to any delimitation pursuant to Article 30.

ARTICLE 2 [2]

1. No State may claim or exercise sovereignty or sovereign rights over any part of the International Seabed Area or its resources Each Contracting Party agrees not to recognize any such claim or exercise of sovereignty or sovereign rights.

2. No State has, nor may it acquire, any right, title, or interest in the International Seabed Area or its resources except as provided in this Convention.

ARTICLE 3

The International Seabed Area shall be open to use by all States, without discrimination, except as otherwise provided in this Convention.

ARTICLE 4

The International Seabed Area shall be reserved exclusively for peaceful purposes

ARTICLE 5

1 The International Seabed Resource Authority shall use revenues it derives from the exploration and exploitation of the mineral resources of the International Seabed Area for the benefit of all mankind, particularly to promote the economic advancement of developing States Parties to this Convention, irrespective of their geographic location Payments to the Authority shall be established at levels designed to ensure that they make a continuing and substantial contribution to such economic advancement, bearing in mind the need to encourage investment in exploration and exploitation and to foster efficient development of mineral resources

---

1 NOTE The United States has simultaneously proposed an international Convention which would, inter alia, fix the boundary between the territorial sea and the high seas at a maximum distance of 12 nautical miles from the coast

2 NOTE The preceding Article is not intended to imply that States do not currently have rights under, or consistent with, the 1958 Geneva Convention on the Continental Shelf

2 A portion of these revenues shall be used, through or in cooperation with other international or regional organizations, to promote efficient, safe and economic exploitation of mineral resources of the seabed, to promote research on means to protect the marine environment; to advance other international efforts designed to promote safe and efficient use of the marine environment, to promote development of knowledge of the International Seabed Area, and to provide technical assistance to Contracting Parties or their nationals for these purposes, without discrimination

ARTICLE 6

Neither this Convention nor any rights granted or exercised pursuant thereto shall affect the legal status of the superjacent waters as high seas, or that of the air space above those waters

ARTICLE 7

All activities in the marine environment shall be conducted with reasonable regard for exploration and exploitation of the natural resources of the International Seabed Area

ARTICLE 8

Exploration and exploitation of the natural resources of the International Seabed Area must not result in any unjustifiable interference with other activities in the marine environment.

ARTICLE 9

All activities in the International Seabed Area shall be conducted with strict and adequate safeguards for the protection of human life and safety and of the marine environment.

ARTICLE 10

All exploration and exploitation activities in the International Seabed Area shall be conducted by a Contracting Party or group of Contracting Parties or natural or juridical persons under its or their authority or sponsorship.

ARTICLE 11

1. Each Contracting Party shall take appropriate measures to ensure that those conducting activities under its authority or sponsorship comply with this Convention

2 Each Contracting Party shall make it an offense for those conducting activities under its authority or sponsorship in the International Seabed Area to violate the provisions of this Convention Such offenses shall be punishable in accordance with administrative or judicial procedures established by the Authorizing or Sponsoring Party

3. Each Contracting Party shall be responsible for maintaining public order on manned installations

and equipment operated by those authorized or sponsored by it

4. Each Contracting Party shall be responsible for damages caused by activities which it authorizes or sponsors to any other Contracting Party or its nationals

5. A group of States acting together, pursuant to agreement among them or through an international organization, shall be jointly and severally responsible under this Convention

ARTICLE 12

All disputes arising out of the interpretation or application of this Convention shall be settled in accordance with provi ~ of Section E of Chapter IV.

CHAPTER II
GENERAL RULES

A. Mineral Resources

ARTICLE 13

1. All exploration and exploitation of the mineral deposits of the International Seabed Area shall be licensed by the International Seabed Resource Authority or the appropriate Trustee Party All licenses shall be subject to the provisions of this Convention

2. Detailed rules to implement this Chapter are contained in Appendices A, B and C.

ARTICLE 14

1. There shall be fees for licenses for mineral exploration and exploitation

2. The fees referred to in paragraph 1 shall be reasonable and be designed to defray the administrative expenses of the International Seabed Resource Authority and of the Contracting Parties in discharging their responsibilities in the International Seabed Area

ARTICLE 15

1. An exploitation license shall specify the minerals or categories of minerals and the precise area to which it applies The categories established shall be those which will best promote simultaneous and efficient exploitation of different minerals

2 Two or more licensees to whom licenses have been issued for different materials in the same or overlapping areas shall not unjustifiably interfere with each other's activities

ARTICLE 16

The size of the area to which an exploitation license shall apply and the duration of the license shall not exceed the limits provided for in this Convention

ARTICLE 17

Licensees must meet work requirements specified in this Convention as a condition of retaining an exploitation license prior to and after commercial production is achieved.

ARTICLE 18

Licensees shall submit work plans and production plans, as well as reports and technical data acquired under an exploitation license, to the Trustee Party or the Sponsoring Party, as appropriate, and, to the extent specified by this Convention, to the International Seabed Resource Authority.

ARTICLE 19

1 Each Contracting Party shall be responsible for inspecting, at regular intervals, the activities of licensees authorized or sponsored by it Inspection reports shall be submitted to the International Seabed Resource Authority.

2 The International Seabed Resource Authority, on its own initiative or at the request of any interested Contracting Party, may inspect any licensed activity in cooperation with the Trustee Party or Sponsoring Party, as appropriate, in order to ascertain that the licensed operation is being conducted in accordance with this Convention In the event the International Seabed Resource Authority believes that a violation of this Convention has occurred, it shall inform the Trustee Party or Sponsoring Party, as appropriate, and request that suitable action be taken If, after a reasonable period of time, the alleged violation continues, the International Seabed Resource Authority may bring the matter before the Tribunal in accordance with Section E of Chapter IV

ARTICLE 20

1. Licenses issued pursuant to this Convention may be revoked only for cause in accordance with the provisions of this Convention.

2 Expropriation of investments made, or unjustifiable interference with operations conducted, pursuant to a license is prohibited.

ARTICLE 21

1 Due notice must be given, by Notices to Mariners or other recognized means of notification, of the construction or deployment of any installations or devices for the exploration or exploitation of mineral deposits, and permanent means for giving warning of their presence must be maintained. Any installations or devices extending into the superjacent waters which are abandoned or disused must be entirely removed

2 Such installations and devices shall not possess the status of islands and shall have no territorial sea of their own.

3 Installations or devices may not be established where interference with the use of recognized sea lanes or airways is likely to occur.

B. Living Resources of the Seabed

ARTICLE 22

Subject to the provisions of Chapter III, each Contracting Party may explore and exploit the seabed living resources of the International Seabed Area in accordance with such conservation measures as are necessary to protect the living resources of the International Seabed Area and to maximize their growth and utilization.

C. Protection of the Marine Environment, Life and Property

ARTICLE 23

1. In the International Seabed Area, the International Seabed Resource Authority shall prescribe Rules and Recommended Practices, in accordance with Chapter V of this Convention, to ensure

a The protection of the marine environment against pollution arising from exploration and exploitation activities such as drilling, dredging, excavation, disposal of waste, construction and operation or maintenance of installations and pipelines and other devices;

b. The prevention of injury to persons, property and marine resources arising from the aforementioned activities,

c The prevention of any unjustifiable interference with other activities in the marine environment arising from the aforementioned activities.

2. Deep drilling in the International Seabed Area shall be undertaken only in accordance with the provisions of this Convention

D. Scientific Research

ARTICLE 24

1 Each Contracting Party agrees to encourage, and to obviate interference with, scientific research.

2 The Contracting Parties shall promote international cooperation in scientific research concerning the International Seabed Area

a. By participating in international programs and by encouraging cooperation in scientific research by personnel of different countries;

b Through effective publication of research programs and the results of research through international channels,

c. By cooperation in measures to strengthen the research capabilities of developing countries, including the participation of their nationals in research programs

E. International Marine Parks and Preserves

ARTICLE 25

In consultation with the appropriate international organizations or agencies, the International Seabed Resource Authority may designate as international marine parks and preserves specific portions of the International Seabed Area that have unusual educational, scientific or recreational value The establishment of such a park or preserve in the International Trusteeship Area shall require the approval of the appropriate Trustee Party.

CHAPTER III
THE INTERNATIONAL TRUSTEESHIP

ARTICLE 26

1. The International Trusteeship Area is that part of the International Seabed Area comprising the continental or island margin between the boundary described in Article 1 and a line, beyond the base of the continental slope, or beyond the base of the slope of an island situated beyond the continental slope, where the downward inclination of the surface of the seabed declines to a gradient of 1 _____ .[1]

2. Each Trustee Party shall permanently delincate the precise seaward boundary of the International Trusteeship Area off its coast by straight lines not exceeding 60 nautical miles in length, following the general direction of the limits specified in paragraph 1. Such lines shall connect fixed points at the limit specified in paragraph 1, defined permanently by coordinates of latitude and longitude Areas between or landward of such points may have a surface gradient of less than 1 _____ . Where an elongate basin or plain having a surface gradient of less than 1:_____ transects an area having a gradient of more than 1 _____ , a straight boundary line more than 60 nautical miles in length, but not exceeding the lesser of one-fourth of the length of that part of the basin or plain transecting the area having a gradient of more than 1 _____ or 120 nautical miles, may be drawn across the basin or plain

3 Each Trustee Party shall submit the description of its boundary to the International Seabed Boundary Review Commission within five years of the entry into force of this Convention for that Party Boundaries not accepted by that Commission and not resolved by negotiation between the Commission and the Trustee Party within one year shall be submitted by the Commission to the Tri-

bunal for adjudication in accordance with Section E of Chapter IV.[2]

ARTICLE 27

1 Except as specifically provided for in this Chapter, the coastal State shall have no greater rights in the International Trusteeship Area off its coast than any other Contracting Party.

2. With respect to exploration and exploitation of the natural resources of that part of the international Trusteeship Area in which it acts as trustee for the international community, each coastal State, subject to the provisions of this Convention, shall be responsible for:

a. Issuing, suspending and revoking mineral exploration and exploitation licenses;

b. Establishing work requirements, provided that such requirements shall not be less than those specified in Appendix A;

c Ensuring that its licensees comply with this Convention, and, if it deems it necessary, applying standards to its licensees higher than or in addition to those required under this Convention, provided such standards are promptly communicated to the International Seabed Resource Authority,

d. Supervising its licensees and their activities,

e Exercising civil and criminal jurisdiction over its licensees, and persons acting on their behalf, while engaged in exploration or exploitation,

f Filing reports with the International Seabed Resource Authority,

g. Collecting and transferring to the International Seabed Resource Authority all payments required by this Convention,

h. Determining the allowable catch of the living resources of the seabed and prescribing other conservation measures regarding them,

i. Enacting such laws and regulations as are necessary to perform the above functions

3. Detailed rules to implement this Chapter are contained in Appendix C.

ARTICLE 28

In performing the functions referred to in Article 27, the Trustee Party may, in its discretion·

a Establish the procedures for issuing licenses;

b Decide whether a license shall be issued,

c. Decide to whom a license shall be issued, without regard to the provisions of Article 3,

---

1 The precise gradient should be determined by technical experts taking into account, among other factors, ease of determination, the need to avoid dual administration of single mineral deposits, and the avoidance of including excessively large areas in the International Trusteeship Area

2 NOTE Additional consideration will be given to problems raised by enclosed and semi-enclosed seas

d Retain [a figure between 33⅓% and 50% will be inserted here] of all fees and payments required by this Convention,

e Collect and retain additional license and rental fees to defray its administrative expenses, and collect, and retain [a figure between 33⅓% and 50% will be inserted here] of, other additional fees and payments related to the issuance or retention of a license, with annual notification to the International Seabed Resource Authority of the total amount collected,

f. Decide whether and by whom the living resources of the seabed shall be exploited, without regard to the provisions of Article 3.

ARTICLE 29

The Trustee Party may enter into an agreement with the International Seabed Resource Authority under which the International Seabed Resource Authority will perform some or all of the trusteeship supervisory and administrative functions provided for in this Chapter in return for an appropriate part of the Trustee Party's share of international fees and royalties.

ARTICLE 30

Where a part of the International Trusteeship Area is off the coast of two or more Contracting Parties, such Parties shall, by agreement, precisely delimit the boundary separating the areas in which they shall respectively perform their trusteeship functions and inform the International Seabed Boundary Review Commission of such delimitation If agreement is not reached within three years after negotiations have commenced, the International Seabed Boundary Review Commission shall be requested to make recommendations to the Contracting Parties concerned regarding such delimitation If agreement is not reached within one year after such recommendations are made, the delimitation recommended by the Commission shall take effect unless either Party, within 90 days thereafter, brings the matter before the Tribunal in accordance with Section E of Chapter IV.

CHAPTER IV
THE INTERNATIONAL SEABED RESOURCE AUTHORITY

A. General

ARTICLE 31

1. The International Seabed Resource Authority is hereby established

2. The principal organs of the Authority shall be the Assembly, the Council, and the Tribunal.

ARTICLE 32

The permanent seat of the Authority shall be at

ARTICLE 33

Each Contracting Party shall recognize the juridical personality of the Authority The legal capacity, privileges and immunities of the Authority shall be the same as those defined in the Convention on the Privileges and Immunities of the Specialized Agencies of the United Nations

B. The Assembly

ARTICLE 34

1 The Assembly shall be composed of all Contracting Parties

2 The first session of the Assembly shall be convened _____. The Assembly shall thereafter be convened by the Council at least once every three years at a suitable time and place Extraordinary sessions of the Assembly shall be convened at any time on the call of the Council, or the Secretary-General of the Authority at the request of one-fifth of the Contracting Parties

3. At meetings of the Assembly a majority of the Contracting Parties is required to constitute a quorum

4 In the Assembly each Contracting Party shall exercise one vote.

5 Decisions of the Assembly shall be taken by a majority of the members present and voting, except as otherwise provided in this Convention

ARTICLE 35

The powers and duties of the Assembly shall be to:

a. Elect its President and other officers;

b Elect members of the Council in accordance with Article 36,

c. Determine its rules of procedure and constitute such subsidiary organs as it considers necessary or desirable;

d. Require the submission of reports from the Council,

e Take action on any matter referred to it by the Council,

f. Approve proposed budgets for the Authority, or return them to the Council for reconsideration and resubmission,

g. Approve proposals by the Council for changes in the allocation of the net income of the Authority within the limits prescribed in Appendix D, or return them to the Council for reconsideration and resubmission,

h. Consider any matter within the scope of this Convention and make recommendations to the Council or Contracting Parties as appropriate;

i. Delegate such of its powers as it deems necessary or desirable to the Council and revoke or modify such delegation at any time,

j. Consider proposals for amendments of this Convention in accordance with Article 76.

C. The Council

ARTICLE 36

1. The Council shall be composed of twenty-four Contracting Parties and shall meet as often as necessary

2. Members of the Council shall be designated or elected in the following categories

a The six most industrially advanced Contracting Parties shall be designated in accordance with Appendix E,

b Eighteen additional Contracting Parties, of which at least twelve shall be developing countries, shall be elected by the Assembly, taking into account the need for equitable geographical distribution.

3 At least two of the twenty-four members of the Council shall be landlocked or shelf-locked countries.

4. Elected members of the Council shall hold office for three years following the last day of the Assembly at which they are elected and thereafter until their successors are elected.

Designated members of the Council shall hold office until replaced in accordance with Appendix E.

5 Representatives on the Council shall not be employees of the Authority

ARTICLE 37

1. The Council shall elect its President for a term of three years

2 The President of the Council may be a national of any Contracting Party, but may not serve during his term of office as its representative in the Assembly or on the Council

3. The President shall have no vote

4. The President shall

a. Convene and conduct meetings of the Council,

b Carry out the functions assigned to him by the Council

ARTICLE 38

Decisions by the Council shall require approval by a majority of all its members, including a majority of members in each of the two categories referred to in paragraph 2 of Article 36.

ARTICLE 39

Any Contracting Party not represented on the Council may participate, without a vote, in the consideration by the Council or any of the subsidiary organs, of any question which is of particular interest to it.

ARTICLE 40

The powers and duties of the Council shall be to·

a Submit annual reports to the Contracting Parties;

b Carry out the duties specified in this Convention and any duties delegated to it by the Assembly,

c. Determine its rules of procedure;

d. Appoint and supervise the Commissions provided for in this Chapter, establish procedures for the coordination of their activities, and determine the terms of office of their members;

e. Establish other subsidiary organs, as may be necessary or desirable, and define their duties;

f Appoint the Secretary-General of the Authority and establish general guidelines for the appointment of such other personnel as may be necessary,

g. Submit proposed budgets to the Assembly for its approval, and supervise their execution;

h. Submit proposals to the Assembly for changes in the allocation of the net income of the Authority within the limits prescribed in Appendix D;

i Adopt and amend Rules and Recommended Practices in accordance with Chapter V, upon the recommendation of the Rules and Recommended Practices Commission,

j. Issue emergency orders, at the request of any Contracting Party, to prevent serious harm to the marine environment arising out of any exploration or exploitation activity and communicate them immediately to licensees, and Authorizing or Sponsoring Parties, as appropriate;

k Establish a fund to provide emergency relief and assistance in the event of a disaster to the marine environment resulting from exploration or exploitation activities;

l. Establish procedures for coordination between the International Seabed Resource Authority, and the United Nations, its specialized agencies and other international or regional organizations concerned with the marine environment;

m. Establish or support such international or regional centers, through or in cooperation with other international and regional organizations, as may be appropriate to promote study and research of the natural resources of the seabed and to train nationals of any Contracting Party in related science and the technology of seabed exploration and exploitation, taking into account the special needs of developing States Parties to this Convention,

n Authorize and approve agreements with a Trustee Party, pursuant to Article 29, under which the International Seabed Resource Authority will perform some or all of the Trustee Party's functions

ARTICLE 41

In furtherance of Article 5, paragraph 2, of this Convention, the Council may, at the request of any Contracting Party and taking into account the special needs of developing States Parties to this Convention:

a. Provide technical assistance to any Contracting Party to further the objectives of this Convention;

b Provide technical assistance to any Contracting Party to help it to meet its responsibilities and obligations under this Convention,

c Assist any Contracting Party to augment its capability to derive maximum benefit from the efficient administration of the International Trusteeship Area.

D. The Commissions

ARTICLE 42

1 There shall be a Rules and Recommended Practices Commission, an Operations Commission, and an International Seabed Boundary Review Commission.

2. Each Commission shall be composed of five to nine members appointed by the Council from among persons nominated by Contracting Parties The Council shall invite all Contracting Parties to submit nominations

3. No two members of a Commission may be nationals of the same State.

4. A member of each Commission shall be elected its President by a majority of the members of the Commission.

5 Each Commission shall perform the functions specified in this Convention and such other functions as the Council may specify from time to time

ARTICLE 43

1 Members of the Rules and Recommended Practices Commission shall have suitable qualifications and experience in seabed resources management, ocean sciences, maritime safety, ocean and marine engineering, and mining and mineral technology and practices They shall not be full-time employees of the Authority.

2 The Rules and Recommended Practices Commission shall:

a Consider, and recommend to the Council for adoption, Annexes to this Convention in accordance with Chapter V;

b Collect from and communicate to Contracting Parties information which the Commission considers necessary and useful in carrying out its functions

ARTICLE 44

1 Members of the Operations Commission shall have suitable qualifications and experience in the management of seabed resources, and operation of marine installations, equipment and devices.

2. The Operations Commission shall:

a Issue licenses for seabed mineral exploration and exploitation, except in the International Trusteeship Area;

b Supervise the operations of licensees in cooperation with the Trustee or Sponsoring Party, as appropriate, but shall not itself engage in exploration or exploitation,

c Perform such functions with respect to disputes between Contracting Parties as are specified in Section E of this Chapter;

d Initiate proceedings pursuant to Section E of this Chapter for alleged violations of this Convention, including but not limited to proceedings for revocation or suspension of licenses;

e. Arrange for and review the collection of international fees and other forms of payment;

f Arrange for the collection and dissemination of information relating to licensed operations;

g Supervise the performance of the functions of the Authority pursuant to any agreement between a Trustee Party and the Authority under Article 29;

h. Issue deep drilling permits.

ARTICLE 45

1. Members of the International Seabed Boundary Review Commission shall have suitable qualifications and experience in marine hydrography, bathymetry, geodesy and geology They shall not be full-time employees of the Authority.

2. The International Seabed Boundary Review Commission shall:

a Review the delineation of boundaries submitted by Contracting Parties in accordance with Articles 1 and 26 to see that they conform to the provisions of this Convention, negotiate any differences with Contracting Parties, and if these differences are not resolved initiate proceedings before the Tribunal in accordance with Section E of this Chapter,

b Make recommendations to the Contracting Parties in accordance with Article 30,

c At the request of any Contracting Party, render advice on any boundary question arising under this Convention.

E. The Tribunal

ARTICLE 46

1 The Tribunal shall decide all disputes and advise on all questions relating to the interpretation and application of this Convention which have been submitted to it in accordance with the provisions of this Convention In its decisions and advisory opinions the Tribunal shall also apply relevant principles of international law

2. Subject to an authorization under Article 96 of the Charter of the United Nations, the Tribunal may request the International Court of Justice to give an advisory opinion on any question of international law.

ARTICLE 47

1. The Tribunal shall be composed of five, seven, or nine independent judges, who shall possess the qualifications required in their respective countries for appointment to the highest judicial offices, or shall be lawyers especially competent in matters within the scope of this Convention. In the Tribunal as a whole the representation of the principal legal systems of the world shall be assured

2. No two of the members of the Tribunal may be nationals of the same State

ARTICLE 48

1. Each Contracting Party shall be entitled to nominate candidates for membership on the Tribunal The Council shall elect the Tribunal from a list of these nominations

2. The members of the Tribunal shall be elected for nine years and may be re-elected, provided, however, that the Council may establish procedures for staggered terms Should such procedures be established, the judges whose terms are to expire in less than nine years shall be chosen by lots drawn by the Secretary-General

3. The members of the Tribunal shall continue to discharge their duties until their places have been filled. Though replaced, they shall finish any cases which they may have begun.

4. A member of the Tribunal unable to perform his duties may be dismissed by the Council on the unanimous recommendation of the other members of the Tribunal.

5. In case of a vacancy, the Council shall elect a successor who shall hold office for the remainder of his predecessor's term.

ARTICLE 49

The Tribunal shall establish its rules of procedure; elect its President, appoint its Registrar and determine his duties and terms of service; and adopt regulations for the appointment of the remainder of its staff

ARTICLE 50

1. Any Contracting Party which considers that another Contracting Party has failed to fulfill any of its obligations under this Convention may bring its complaint before the Tribunal

2. Before a Contracting Party institutes such proceedings before the Tribunal it shall bring the matter before the Operations Commission.

3. The Operations Commission shall deliver a reasoned opinion in writing after the Contracting

Parties concerned have been given the opportunity both to submit their own cases and to reply to each other's case

4 If the Contracting Party accused of a violation does not comply with the terms of such opinion within the period laid down by the Commission, the other Party concerned may bring the matter before the Tribunal

5. If the Commission has not given an opinion within a period of three months from the date when the matter was brought before it, either Party concerned may bring the matter before the Tribunal without waiting further for the opinion of the Commission

ARTICLE 51

1 Whenever the Operations Commission, acting on its own initiative or at the request of any licensee, considers that a Contracting Party or a licensee has failed to fulfill any of its obligations under this Convention, it shall issue a reasoned opinion in writing on the matter after giving such party the opportunity to submit its comments

2. If the Party concerned does not comply with the terms of such opinion within the period laid down by the Commission, the latter may bring a complaint before the Tribunal

ARTICLE 52

1 If the Tribunal finds that a Contracting Party or a licensee has failed to fulfill any of its obligations under this Convention, such party shall take the measures required for the implementation of the judgment of the Tribunal

2 When appropriate, the Tribunal may decide that the Contracting Party or the licensee who has failed to fulfill its obligations under this Convention shall pay to the Authority a fine of not more than $1,000 for each day of the offense, or shall pay damages to the other party concerned, or both.

3 In the event the Tribunal determines that a licensee has committed a gross and persistent violation of the provisions of this Convention and has not within a reasonable time brought his operations into compliance with them, the Council may, as appropriate, either revoke his license or request that the Trustee Party revoke it The licensee shall not, however, be deprived of his license if his actions were directed by a Trustee or Sponsoring Party.

ARTICLE 53

If disputes under Articles 1, 26 and 30 have not been resolved by the time and methods specified in those Articles, the International Seabed Boundary Review Commission shall bring the matter before the Tribunal

ARTICLE 54

1. Any Contracting Party, which questions the legality of measures taken by the Council, the Rules

and Recommended Practices Commission, the Operations Commission, or the International Seabed Boundary Review Commission on the grounds of a violation of this Convention, lack of jurisdiction, infringement of important procedural rules, unreasonableness, or misuse of powers, may bring the matter before the Tribunal

2 Any person may, subject to the same conditions, bring a complaint to the Tribunal with regard to a decision directed to that person, or a decision which, although in the form of a rule or a decision directed to another person, is of direct concern to the complainant.

3 The proceedings provided for in this Article shall be instituted within a period of two months, dating. as the case may be, either from the publication of the measure concerned or from its notification to the complainant, or, in default thereof, from the day on which the latter learned of it.

4. If the Tribunal considers the appeal wellfounded, it should declare the measure concerned to be null and void, and shall decide to what extent the annulment shall have retroactive application

ARTICLE 55

1. The organ responsible for a measure declared null and void by the Tribunal shall be required to take the necessary steps to comply with the Tribunal's judgment.

2 When appropriate, the Tribunal may require that the Authority repair or pay for any damage caused by its organs or by its officials in the performance of their duties.

ARTICLE 56

When a case pending before a court or tribunal of one of the Contracting Parties raises a question of the interpretation of this Convention or of the validity or interpretation of measures taken by an organ of the Authority, the court or tribunal concerned may request the Tribunal to give its advice thereon

ARTICLE 57

The Tribunal shall also be competent to decide any dispute connected with the subject matter of this Convention submitted to it pursuant to an agreement, license, or contract

ARTICLE 58

If a Contracting Party fails to perform the obligations incumbent upon it under a judgment rendered by the Tribunal, the other Party to the case may have recourse to the Council, which shall decide upon measures to be taken to give effect to the judgment When appropriate, the Council may decide to suspend temporarily, in whole or in part, the rights under this Convention of the Party failing to perform its obligations, without impairing the rights of licensees who have not contributed to the failure

to perform such obligations. The extent of such a suspension should be related to the extent and seriousness of the violation.

ARTICLE 59

In any case in which the Council issues an order in emergency circumstances to prevent serious harm to the marine environment, any directly affected Contracting Party may request immediate review by the Tribunal. which shall promptly either confirm or suspend the application of the emergency order pending the decision of the case

ARTICLE 60

Any organ of the International Seabed Resource Authority may request the Tribunal to give an advisory opinion on any legal question connected with the subject matter of this Convention.

F. The Secretariat

ARTICLE 61

The Secretariat shall comprise a Secretary-General and such staff as the International Seabed Resource Authority may require. The Secretary-General shall be appointed by the Council from among persons nominated by Contracting Parties He shall serve for a term of six years, and may be reappointed.

ARTICLE 62

The Secretary-General shall

a. Be the chief administrative officer of the International Seabed Resource Authority, and act in that capacity in all meetings of the Assembly and the Council,

b. Report to the Assembly and the Council on the work of the International Seabed Resource Authority,

c Collect, publish and disseminate information which will contribute to mankind's knowledge of the seabed and its resources;

d Perform such other functions as are entrusted to him by the Assembly or the Council

ARTICLE 63

1. In the performance of their duties the Secretary-General and the staff shall not seek or receive instructions from any government or from any other external authority They shall refrain from any action which might reflect on their position as international officials responsible only to the International Seabed Resource Authority

2 Each Contracting Party shall respect the exclusively international character of the responsibilities of the Secretary-General and the staff and shall not seek to influence them in the discharge of their responsibilities

ARTICLE 64

1. The staff of the International Seabed Resource Authority shall be appointed by the Secretary-General under the general guidelines established by the Council.

2 Appropriate staffs shall be assigned to the various organs of the Authority as required

3. The paramount consideration in the employment of the staff and in the determination of the conditions of service shall be the necessity of securing the highest standards of efficiency, competence, and integrity. Due regard shall be paid to the importance of recruiting the staff on as wide a geographical basis as possible

G. Conflicts of Interest

ARTICLE 65

No representative to the Assembly or the Council nor any member of the Tribunal, Commissions, subsidiary organs (other than advisory bodies or consultants), or the Secretariat, shall, while serving as such a representative or member, be actively associated with or financially interested in any of the operations of any enterprise concerned with exploration or exploitation of the natural resources of the International Seabed Area.

CHAPTER V

RULES AND RECOMMENDED PRACTICES

ARTICLE 66

1. Rules and Recommended Practices are contained in Annexes to this Convention

2. Annexes shall be consistent with this Convention, its Appendices, and any amendments thereto Any Contracting Party may challenge an Annex, an amendment to an Annex, or any of their provisions, on the grounds that it is unnecessary, unreasonable or constitutes a misuse of powers, by bringing the matter before the Tribunal in accordance with Article 54.

3. Annexes shall be adopted and amended in accordance with Article 67. Those Annexes adopted along with this Convention, if any, may be amended in accordance with Article 67.

ARTICLE 67

The Annexes to this Convention and amendments to such Annexes shall be adopted in accordance with the following procedure:

a. They shall be prepared by the Rules and Recommended Practices Commission and submitted to the Contracting Parties for comments;

b. After receiving the comments, the Commission shall prepare a revised text of the Annex or amendments thereto;

c. The text shall then be submitted to the Council which shall adopt it or return it to the Commission for further study;

d. If the Council adopts the text, it shall submit it to the Contracting Parties,

e. The Annex or an amendment thereto shall become effective within three months after its submission to the Contracting Parties, or at the end of such longer period of time as the Council may prescribe, unless in the meantime more than one-third of the Contracting Parties register their disapproval with the Authority,

f The Secretary-General shall immediately notify all Contracting States of the coming into force of any Annex or amendment thereto.

ARTICLE 68

1. Annexes shall be limited to the Rules and Recommended Practices necessary to

a. Fix the level, basis, and accounting procedures for determining international fees and other forms of payment, within the ranges specified in Appendix A;

b. Establish work requirements within the ranges specified in Appendices A and B;

c. Establish criteria for defining the technical and financial competence of applicants for licenses;

d Assure that all exploration and exploitation activities, and all deep drilling, are conducted with strict and adequate safeguards for the protection of human life and safety and of the marine environment;

e. Protect living marine organisms from damage arising from exploration and exploitation activities,

f. Prevent or reduce to acceptable limits interference arising from exploration and exploitation activities with other uses and users of the marine environment;

g Assure safe design and construction of fixed exploration and exploitation installations and equipment,

h. Facilitate search and rescue services, including assistance to aquanauts, and the reporting of accidents;

i. Prevent unnecessary waste in the extraction of minerals from the seabed,

j. Standardize the measurement of water depth and the definition of other natural features pertinent to the determination of the precise location of International Seabed Area boundaries,

k Prescribe the form in which Contracting Parties shall describe their boundaries and the kinds of information to be submitted in support of them,

l Encourage uniformity in seabed mapping and charting,

m. Facilitate the management of a part of the International Trusteeship Area pursuant to any agreement between a Trustee Party and the Authority under Article 29,

n Establish and prescribe conditions for the use of international marine parks and preserves

2 Application of any Rule or Recommended Practice may be limited as to duration or geographic area, but without discrimination against any Contracting Party or licensee.

ARTICLE 69

The Contracting Parties agree to collaborate with each other and the appropriate Commission in securing the highest practicable degree of uniformity in regulations, standards, procedures and organizations in relation to the matters covered by Article 68 in order to facilitate and improve seabed resources exploration and exploitation

ARTICLE 70

Annexes and amendments thereto shall take into account existing international agreements and, where appropriate, shall be prepared in collaboration with other competent international organizations. In particular, existing international agreements and regulations relating to safety of life at sea shall be respected

ARTICLE 71

1 Except as otherwise provided in this Convention, the Annexes and amendments thereto adopted by the Council shall be binding on all Contracting Parties.

2 Recommended Practices shall have no binding effect

ARTICLE 72

Any Contracting Party believing that a provision of an Annex or an amendment thereto cannot be reasonably applied because of special circumstances may seek a waiver from the Operations Commission and if such waiver is not granted within three months, it may appeal to the Tribunal within an additional period of two months

CHAPTER VI
TRANSITION

ARTICLE 73

1 There shall be due protection for the integrity of investments made in the International Seabed Area prior to the coming into force of this Convention

2 All authorizations by a Contracting Party to exploit the mineral resources of the International Seabed Area granted prior to July 1, 1970, shall be continued without change after the coming into force of this Convention provided that

a Activities pursuant to such authorizations shall, to the extent possible, be conducted in accordance with the provisions of this Convention,

b New activities under such previous authorizations which are begun after the coming into force of this Convention shall be subject to the regulatory provisions of this Convention regarding the protection of human life and safety and of the marine environment and the avoidance of unjustifiable interference with other uses of the marine environment,

c Upon the expiration or relinquishment of such authorizations, or upon their revocation by the authorizing Party, the provisions of this Convention shall become fully applicable to any exploration or exploitation of resources remaining in the areas included in such authorizations,

d Contracting Parties shall pay to the International Seabed Resource Authority, with respect to such authorizations, the production payments provided for under this Convention.

3 A Contracting Party which has authorized exploitation of the mineral resources of the International Seabed Area on or after July 1, 1970, shall be bound, at the request of the person so authorized, either to issue new licenses under this Convention in its capacity as a Trustee Party, or to sponsor the application of the person so authorized to receive new licenses from the International Seabed Resource Authority Such new license issued by a Trustee Party shall include the same terms and conditions as its previous authorization, provided that such license shall not be inconsistent with this Convention, and provided further that the Trustee Party shall itself be responsible for complying with increased obligations resulting from the application of this Convention, including fees and other payments required by this Convention

4 The provisions of paragraph 3 shall apply within one year after this Convention enters into force for the Contracting Party concerned, and in no event more than five years after the entry into force of this Convention

5 Until converted into new licenses under paragraph 3, all authorizations issued on or after July 1, 1970, to exploit the mineral resources of the International Seabed Area shall have the same status as authorizations issued under paragraph 2 Five years after the entry into force of this Convention all such authorizations not converted into new licenses under paragraph 3 shall be null and void

6 Any Contracting Party that has authorized activities within the International Seabed Area after July 1, 1970, but before this Convention has entered into force for such Party, shall compensate its licensees for any investment losses resulting from the application of this Convention.

ARTICLE 74

1. The membership of the Tribunal, the Commissions, and the Secretariat shall be maintained at

a level commensurate with the tasks being performed

2. In the period before the International Seabed Resource Authority acquires income sufficient for the payment of its administrative expenses, the Authority may borrow funds for the payment of those expenses. The Contracting Parties agree to give sympathetic consideration to requests by the Authority for such loans.

CHAPTER VII
DEFINITIONS

ARTICLE 75

Unless another meaning results from the context of a particular provision, the following definitions shall apply:

1. "Convention" refers to all provisions of and amendments to this Convention, its Appendices, and its Annexes.

2. "Trustee Party" refers to the Contracting Party exercising trusteeship functions in that part of the International Trusteeship Area off its coast in accordance with Chapter III.

3. "Sponsoring Party" refers to a Contracting Party which sponsors an application for a license or permit before the International Seabed Resource Authority. The term "sponsor" is used in this context.

4. "Authorizing Party" refers to a Contracting Party authorizing any activity in the International Seabed Area, including a Trustee Party issuing exploration or exploitation licenses The term "authorize" is used in this context. In the case of a vessel, the term "Authorizing Party" shall be deemed to refer to the State of its nationality.

5. "Operating Party" refers to a Contracting Party which itself explores or exploits the natural resources of the International Seabed Area.

6. "Licensee" refers to a State, group of States, or natural or juridical person holding a license for exploration or exploitation of the natural resources of the International Seabed Area

7. "Exploration" refers to any operation in the International Seabed Area which has as its principal or ultimate purpose the discovery and appraisal, or exploitation, of mineral deposits, and does not refer to scientific research The term does not refer to similar activities when undertaken pursuant to an exploitation license.

8. "Deep drilling" refers to any form of drilling or excavation in the International Seabed Area deeper than 300 meters below the surface of the seabed.

9. "Landlocked or shelf-locked country" refers to a Contracting Party which is not a Trustee Party.

CHAPTER VIII
AMENDMENT AND
WITHDRAWAL

ARTICLE 76

Any proposed amendment to this Convention or the appendices thereto which has been approved by the Council and a two-thirds vote of the Assembly shall be submitted by the Secretary-General to the Contracting Parties for ratification in accordance with their respective constitutional processes It shall come into force when ratified by two-thirds of the Contracting Parties, including each of the six States designated pursuant to subparagraph 2(a) of Article 36 at the time the Council approved the amendments Amendments shall not apply retroactively.

ARTICLE 77

1 Any Contracting Party may withdraw from this Convention by a written notification addressed to the Secretary-General The Secretary-General shall promptly inform the other Contracting Parties of any such withdrawal

2 The withdrawal shall take effect one year from the date of the receipt by the Secretary-General of the notification.

CHAPTER IX
FINAL CLAUSES

ARTICLE 78

APPENDIX A
TERMS AND PROCEDURES
APPLYING TO ALL
LICENSES IN THE INTERNATIONAL SEABED AREA

1. Activities Requiring a License or a Permit

1.1. Pursuant to Article 13 of this Convention, all exploration and exploitation operations in the International Seabed Area which have as their principal or ultimate purpose the discovery or appraisal, and exploitation, of mineral deposits shall be licensed.

1.2. There shall be two categories of licenses:

(a) A non-exclusive license shall authorize geophysical and geochemical measurements, and bottom sampling, for the purposes of exploration. This license shall not be restricted as to area and shall grant no exclusive right to exploration nor any preferential right in applying for an exploitation license. It shall be valid for two years following the date of its issuance and shall be renewable for successive two-year periods.

(b) An exploitation license shall authorize exploration and exploitation of one of the groups of minerals described in Section 5 of this Appendix in a specified area. The exploitation license shall include the exclusive right to undertake deep drilling and other forms of subsurface entry for the purpose of exploration and exploitation of minerals described in paragraphs 5.1(a) and 5.1(c) The license shall be for a limited period and shall expire at the end of fifteen years if no commercial production is achieved

1.3. The right to undertake deep drilling for exploration or exploitation shall be granted only under an exploitation license.

1.4. Deep drilling for purposes other than exploration or exploitation of seabed minerals shall be authorized under a deep-drilling permit issued at no charge by the International Seabed Resource Authority, provided that

(a) The application is accompanied by a statement from the Sponsoring Party certifying as to the applicant's technical competence and accepting liability for any damages that may result from such drilling,

(b) The application for such a permit is accompanied by a description of the location proposed for such holes, by seismograms and other pertinent information on the geology in the vicinity of the proposed drilling sites, and by a description of the equipment and procedures to be utilized,

(c) The proposed drilling, including the methods and equipment to be utilized, complies with the requirements of this Convention and is judged by the Authority not to pose an uncontrollable haz-

ard to human safety, property, and the environment,

(d) The proposed drilling is either not within an area already under an exploitation license or is not objected to by the holder of such a license;

(e) The applicant agrees to make available promptly the geologic information obtained from such drilling to the Authority and the public.

2. General License Procedures

2.1. An Authorizing or Sponsoring Party shall certify the operator's financial and technical competence and shall require the operator to conform to the rules, provisions and procedures specified under the terms of the license

2.2. Each Authorizing or Sponsoring Party shall formulate procedures to ensure that applications for licenses are handled expeditiously and fairly.

2.3. Any Authorizing or Sponsoring Party which considers that it is unable to exercise appropriate supervision over operators authorized or sponsored by it in accordance with this Convention shall be permitted to authorize or sponsor operators only if their operations are supervised by the International Seabed Resource Authority pursuant to an agreement between the Authorizing or Sponsoring Party and the International Seabed Resource Authority. In such event fees and rentals normally payable to the International Seabed Resource Authority will be increased appropriately to offset its supervisory costs.

3. Exploration Licenses—Procedures

3.1. All applications for exploration licenses and for their renewal shall be accompanied by a fee of from $500 to $1,500 as specified in an Annex and a description of the location of the general area to be investigated and the kinds of activities to be undertaken A portion [a figure between 50% and 66⅔% will be inserted here] of the fee shall be forwarded by the Authorizing or Sponsoring Party to the Authority together with a copy of the application.

3.2. The Authorizing or Sponsoring Party shall transmit to the Authority the description referred to in paragraph 3 1 and its assurance that the activities will not be harmful to the marine environment.

3.3. The Authorizing or Sponsoring Party may require the operator to pay, and may retain, an additional license fee not to exceed $3,000, to help cover the administrative expenses of that Party.

3.4. Exploration licenses shall not be renewed

in the event the operator has failed to conform his activities under the prior license to the provisions of this Convention or to the conditions of the license.

4. Exploitation Licenses—Procedures

4.1. All applications for exploitation licenses shall be accompanied by a fee of from $5,000 to $15,000, per block, as specified in an Annex. A portion [a figure between 50% and 66⅔% will be inserted here] of the fee shall be forwarded by the Authorizing or Sponsoring Party to the Authority together with a copy of the application.

4.2. Pursuant to Section 5 of this Appendix, applications shall identify the category of minerals in the specific area for which a license is sought

4.3. When a license is granted to an applicant for more than one block at the same time, only a single certificate need be issued

4.4. The Authorizing or Sponsoring Party may require the operator to pay, and may retain, an additional license fee not to exceed $30,000, to help cover the administrative expenses of that Party.

4.5. The license fee described in paragraph 4.1 shall satisfy the first two years' rental fee.

5. Exploitation Rights—Categories and Size of Blocks

5.1. Licenses to exploit shall be limited to one of the following categories of minerals:

(a) Fluids or minerals extracted in a fluid state, such as oil, gas, helium, nitrogen, carbon dioxide, water, geothermal energy, sulfur and saline minerals

(b) Manganese-oxide nodules and other minerals at the surface of the seabed.

(c) Other minerals, including category (b) minerals that occur beneath the surface of the seabed and metalliferous muds.

5.2. An exploitation license shall be issued for a specific area of the seabed and subsoil vertically below it, hereinafter referred to as a "block". The methods for defining the boundaries of blocks, and of portions thereof, shall be specified in an Annex.

5.3. In the category described in paragraph 5.1(a) the block shall be approximately 500 square kilometers, which shall be reduced to a quarter of a block when production begins. Each exploitation license shall apply to not more than one block, but exploitation licenses to a rectangle containing as many as 16 contiguous blocks may be taken out under a single certificate and reduced by three quarters to a number of blocks, a single block, or a portion of a single block when production begins The relinquishment requirement shall not apply to licenses issued for areas of one quarter of a block or less.

5.4. In the category described in paragraph 5.1(b) the block shall be approximately 40,000 square kilometers, which shall be reduced to a quar-

ter of a block when production begins. Each exploitation license shall apply to not more than one block, but exploitation licenses to a rectangle containing as many as four contiguous blocks may be taken out under a single certificate and reduced to a single block, or to a portion of a single block, comprising one-fourth their total area, when production begins The relinquishment requirement shall not apply to licenses issued for areas of one quarter of a block or less

5.5. In the category described in paragraph 5.1(c) the block shall be approximately 500 square kilometers, which shall be reduced to one eighth of a block when production begins Each license shall apply to not more than one block, but exploitation licenses to as many as 8 contiguous blocks may be taken out under a single certificate and reduced to a single block, or to a portion of a single block, comprising one eighth their total area, when production begins The relinquishment shall not apply to licenses issued for one eighth of a block or less.

5.6. Applications for exploitation licenses may be for areas smaller than the maximum stated above

5.7. Operators may at any time relinquish rights to all or part of the licensed area

5.8. Commercial production shall be deemed to have commenced or to be maintained when the value at the site of minerals exploited is not less than $100,000 per annum The required minimum and the method of ascertaining this value shall be determined by the Authority.

5.9. If the commercial production is not maintained, the exploitation license shall expire within five years of its cessation, but when production is interrupted or suspended for reasons beyond the operator's control, the duration of the license shall be extended by a time equal to the period in which production has been suspended for reasons beyond the operator's control.

6. Rental Fees and Work Requirements

Rental Fees

6.1. Prior to attaining commercial production the following annual rental fees shall be paid beginning in the third year after the license has been issued:

(a) $2-$10 per square kilometer, as specified in an appropriate Annex, for the category of minerals described in paragraph 5 1(a) above;

(b) $2-$10 per 100 square kilometers for the category of minerals described in paragraph 5 1(b) above, and

(c) $2-$10 per square kilometer for the category of minerals described in paragraph 5 1(c) above

6.2. The rates in paragraph 6.1 shall increase at the rate of 10% per annum. calculated on the original base rental fee, for the first ten years after the third year, and shall increase 20% per annum, calculated on the original base rental fee, for the following two years.

6.3. After commercial production begins, the annual rental fee shall be $5,000-$25,000 per block, regardless of block size

6.4. The rental fee shall be payable annually in advance to the Authorizing or Sponsoring Party which shall forward a portion [a figure between 50% and 66⅔% will be inserted here] of the fees to the Authority The Authorizing or Sponsoring Party may require the operator to pay, and may retain, an additional rental fee, not to exceed an amount equal to the amount paid pursuant to paragraph 6 1 through 6 3, to help cover the administration expenses of that Party

Work Requirements

6.5. Prior to attaining commercial production, the operator shall deposit a work requirement fee, or post a sufficient bond for that amount, for each license at the beginning of each year

6.6. The minimum annual work requirement fee for each block shall increase in accordance with the following schedule

Para. 5.1(a) and (c) minerals

Years	Amount per annum
1-5	$ 20,000
6-10	180,000
11-15	200,000
Total	$2,000,000

Para. 5.1(b) minerals

Years	Amount per annum
1-2	$ 20,000
3-10	120,000
11-15	200,000
Total	$2,000,000

The minimum annual work requirement fee for a portion of a block shall be an appropriate fraction of the above, to be specified in an Annex

6.7. The work requirement fee shall be refunded to the operator upon receipt of proof by the Authorising Party or Sponsoring Party that the amount equivalent to the fee has been expended in actual operations Expenditures for on-land design or process research and equipment purchase or off-site construction cost directly related to the licensed block or group of blocks shall be considered to apply toward work requirements up to 75% of the amount required

6.8. Expenditures in excess of the required amount for any given year shall be credited to the requirement for the subsequent year or years

6.9. In the absence of satisfactory proof that the required expenditure has been made in accordance with the foregoing provisions of this section, the deposit will be forfeited

6.10. If cumulative work requirement expenditures are not met at the end of the initial five-year period, the exploitation license shall be forfeited

6.11. After commercial production begins the operator shall make an annual deposit of at least $100,000 at the beginning of each year, or shall post a sufficient bond for that amount, which shall be refunded in an amount equivalent to expenditures on or related to the block and the value of production at the site

6.12. If production is suspended or delayed for reasons beyond the operator's control, the operator shall not be required to make the deposit or post the bond required in paragraph 6.11.

7. Submission of Work Plans and Data Under Exploitation Licenses Prior to Commencement of Commercial Production

7.1. Exploitation license applications shall be accompanied by a general description of the work to be done and the equipment and methods to be used The licensee shall submit subsequent changes in his work plan to the Sponsoring or Authorizing Party for review

7.2. The licensee shall furnish reports at specified intervals to the Authorizing or Sponsoring Party supplying proof that he has fulfilled the specified work requirements Copies of such reports shall be forwarded to the Authority

7.3. The licensee shall maintain records of drill logs, geophysical data and other data acquired in the area to which his license refers, and shall provide access to them to the Authorizing or Sponsoring Party on request.

7.4. At intervals of five years, or when he relinquishes his rights to all or part of the area or when he submits a production plan as described in Section 8 of this Appendix, the operator shall transmit to the Authorizing or Sponsoring Party such maps, seismic sections, logs, assays, or reports, as are specified in an Annex to this Convention. The Authorizing or Sponsoring Party shall hold such data in confidence for ten years after receipt, but shall make the data available on request to the Authority for its confidential use in the inspection of operations.

7.5. The data referred to in paragraph 7 4 shall be transmitted to the Authority ten years after receipt by the Authorizing or Sponsoring Party, and made available by the Authority for public inspection. Such data shall be transmitted to the Authority immediately upon revocation of a license

8. Production Plan and Producing Operations

8.1. Prior to beginning commercial production the licensee shall submit a production plan to the Authorizing or Sponsoring Party and through such Party to the Authority

8.2. The Authorizing or Sponsoring Party and the Authority shall require such modifications in the plan as may be necessary for it to meet the requirements of this Convention

8.3. Any change in the licensee's production plan shall be submitted to the Authorizing or Sponsoring Party and through such Party to the Authority for their review and approval.

8.4. Not later than three months after the end of each year from the issuance of the license the licensee shall transmit to the Authorizing or Sponsoring Party for forwarding to the Authority production reports and such other data as may be specified in an Annex to this Convention

8.5. The operator shall maintain geologic, geophysical and engineering records and shall provide access to them to the Authorizing or Sponsoring Party on its request In addition, the operator shall submit annually such maps, sections, and summary reports, as are specified in Annexes to this Convention

8.6. The Sponsoring or Authorizing Party shall hold such maps and reports in confidence for ten years from the time received but shall make them available on request to the Authority for its confidential use in the inspection of operations

8.7. Such maps and reports shall be transmitted to the Authority and shall be made available by it for public inspection not later than ten years after receipt by the Sponsoring or Authorizing Party.

9. Unit Operations

9.1. Accumulations of fluids and other minerals that can be made to migrate from one block to another and that would be most rationally mined by an operation under the control of a single operator but that lie astride the boundary of adjacent blocks licensed to different operators shall be brought into unit management and production

9.2. With respect to deposits lying astride the seaward boundary of the International Trusteeship Area, the Operations Commission shall assure unit management and production, giving the Trustee and Sponsoring Parties and their licensees a reasonable time to reach agreement on an operation plan

10. Payments on Production

10.1. When commercial production begins under an exploitation license, the operator shall pay a cash production bonus of $500,000 to $2,000,000 per block, as specified in an Annex to this Convention, to the Authorizing or Sponsoring Party.

10.2. Thereafter, the operator shall make payments to the Authorizing or Sponsoring Party which are proportional to production, in the nature of total payments ordinarily made to governments under similar conditions Such payments shall be equivalent to 5 to 40 percent of the gross value at the site of oil and gas, and 2 to 20 percent of the gross value at the site of other minerals, as specified in an Annex to this Convention The total annual payment shall not be less than the annual rental fee under paragraph 6 3

10.3. The Sponsoring Party shall forward all payments under this section to the Authority The Authorizing Party shall forward a portion [a figure between 50% and 66⅔% will be inserted here] of such payments to the Authority

11. Graduation of Payments According to Environment and Other Factors

11.1. The levels of payments and work requirements, as well as the rates at which such payments and work requirements escalate over time, may be graduated to take account of probable risk and cost to the investor, including such factors as water depth, climate, volume of production, proximity to existing production, or other factors affecting the economic rent that can reasonably be anticipated from mineral production in a given area

11.2. Any graduated levels and rates shall be described and categorized in an Annex in such a way as to affect all licensees in each category equally and not to discriminate against or favor individual Parties or groups of Parties, or their nationals

11.3. Any increases in such levels of payments or requirements shall apply only to new licenses or renewals and not to those already in force

12. Liability

12.1. The operator and his Authorizing or Sponsoring Party, as appropriate, shall be liable for damage to other users of the marine environment and for clean-up and restoration costs of damage to the land environment

12.2. The Authorizing or Sponsoring Party, as appropriate, shall require operators to subscribe to an insurance plan or provide other means of guaranteeing responsibility, adequate to cover the liability described in paragraph   .[1]

13. Revocation

13.1. In the event of revocation pursuant to Article 52 of this Convention, there shall be no reimbursement for any expense incurred by the licensee prior to the revocation The licensee shall, however, have the right to recover installations or equipment within six months of the date of the revocation of his license Any installations or devices not removed by that time shall be removed and disposed of by the Authority, or the Authorizing or Sponsoring Party, at the expense of the licensee.

14. International Fees and Payments

14.1. The Authority shall specify the intervals at which fees and other payments collected by an Authorizing or Sponsoring Party shall be transmitted

14.2. No Contracting Party shall impose or collect any tax, direct or indirect, on fees and other payments to the Authority

14.3. All fees and payments required under this Convention shall be those in force at the time a license was issued or renewed

14.4. All fees and payments to the Authority shall be transmitted in convertible currency.

---

1 *NOTE* More detailed provisions on liability should be included

APPENDIX B

TERMS AND PROCEDURES APPLYING TO LICENSES
IN THE INTERNATIONAL SEABED AREA BEYOND
THE INTERNATIONAL TRUSTEESHIP AREA

1. Entities Entitled to Obtain Licenses.

1.1. Contracting Parties or a group of Contracting Parties, one of which shall act as the operating or sponsoring Party for purposes of fixing operational or supervisory responsibility, are authorized to apply for and obtain exploration and exploitation licenses Any Contracting Party or group of Contracting Parties, which applies for a license to engage directly in exploration or exploitation, shall designate a specific agency to act as operator on its behalf for the purposes of this Convention.

1.2. Natural or juridical persons are authorized to apply for and obtain exploration and exploitation licenses from the International Seabed Resource Authority if they are sponsored by a Contracting Party.

2. Exploration Licenses—Procedures

2.1. Licenses shall be issued promptly by the Authority through the Sponsoring Party to applicants meeting the requirements specified in Appendix A.

3. Exploitation Licenses—Procedures

3.1. The Sponsoring Party shall certify as to the technical and financial competence of the operator, and shall transmit the operator's work plan.

3.2. An application for an exploitation license shall be preceded by a notice of intent to apply for a license submitted by the operator to the Authority and the prospective Sponsoring Party. Such a notice of intent, when accompanied by evidence of the deposit of the license fee referred to in paragraph 4.1 of Appendix A, shall reserve the block for one hundred and eighty days Notices of intent may not be renewed

3.3. Notices of intent shall be submitted sealed to the Authority and opened at monthly intervals at previously announced times.

3.4. Subject to compliance with these procedures, if only one notice of intent has been received for a particular block, the applicant shall be granted a license, except as provided in paragraphs 3 6 through 3.8.

3.5. If more than one notice of intent to apply for a license for the same block or portion thereof is received at the same opening, the Authority shall notify the applicants and their Sponsoring Parties that the exploitation license to the block or portion thereof will be sold to the highest bidder at a sale to be held one hundred and eighty days later, under the following terms:

(a) The bidding shall be on a cash bonus basis and the minimum bid shall be twice the license fee,

(b) Bids shall be sealed,

(c) The bidding shall be limited to such of the original applicants whose applications have been received in the interim from their Sponsoring Parties,

(d) Bids shall be announced publicly by the Authority when they are opened In the event of a tie, the tie bidders shall submit a second sealed bid to be opened 28 days later,

(e) The final award shall be announced publicly by the Authority within seven days after the bids have been opened

3.6. In the event of the termination, forfeiture, or revocation of an exploitation license to a block, or relinquishment of a part of a block, the block or portion thereof will be offered for sale by sealed competitive bidding on a cash bonus basis in addition to the current license fee. The following provisions shall apply to such a sale:

(a) The availability of such a block, or portion thereof, for bidding shall be publicly announced by the Authority as soon as possible after it becomes available, and a sale following the above procedures shall be held within one hundred and eighty days after a request for an exploitation license on the block has been received,

(b) The bidding shall be open to all sponsored operators, including, except in the case of revocation, the operator who previously held the exploitation license to the block or to the available portion thereof,

(c) If the winning bid is submitted by an operator who previously held the exploitation right to the same block, or to the same portion thereof, the work requirement will begin at the level that would have applied if the operator had continuously held the block

3.7. Blocks, or portions thereof, contiguous to a block on which production has begun shall also be sold by sealed competitive bidding under the terms specied in paragraph 3 6.

3.8. Blocks, or separate portions thereof, from which hydrocarbons or other fluids are being drained, or are believed to be drained, by production from another block shall be offered for sale by sealed competitive bidding under the terms specified in paragraph 3.6 at the initiative of the Authority.

3.9. Geologic and other data concerning blocks, or portions thereof, open for bidding pursuant to paragraph 3 6 through 3 8, which are no longer confidential, shall be made available to the public prior to the bidding date Data on blocks, or separate portions thereof, for which the license has been revoked for violations shall be made available to the public within 30 days after revocation.

3.10. Exploitation licenses shall only be transferable with the approval of the Sponsoring Party and the Authority, provided that the transferee meets the requirements of this Convention, is sponsored by a Contracting Party, and a transfer fee is paid to the Authority in the amount of $250,000 This fee shall not apply in transfers between parts of the same operating enterprise.

4. Duration of Exploitation Licenses

4.1. If commercial production has been achieved within fifteen years after the license has been issued, the exploitation license shall be extended automatically for twenty additional years from the date commercial production has commenced.

4.2. At the completion of the twenty-year production period referred to in paragraph 4.1, the operator with the approval of the Sponsoring Party shall have the option to renew his license for another twenty years at the rental fees and payment rates in effect at the time of renewal.

4.3. At the end of the forty-year term, or earlier if the license is voluntarily relinquished or expires pursuant to paragraph 5.9 of Appendix A, the block or blocks, or separate portions of blocks, to which the license applied shall be offered for sale by competitive bidding on a cash bonus basis. The previous licensee shall have no preferential right to such block, or separate portion thereof.

5. Work Requirements

5.1. The annual work requirements fee per block shall be specified in an Annex in accordance with the following schedule:

Para. 5.1(a) and (c) minerals

Years		Amount per annum	
1-5	$	20,000 -	60,000
6-10	....	180,000 -	540,000
11-15	....	200,000 -	600,000
Total .	....	$2,000,000 - 6,000,000	

Para. 5.1(b) minerals

Years		Amount per annum	
1-2	$	20,000 -	60,000
3-10		120,000 -	360,000
11-15		200,000 -	600,000
Total	....	$2,000,000 - 6,000,000	

The minimum annual work requirement fee for a portion of a block shall be an appropriate fraction of the above, to be specified in an Annex.

5.2. Work expenditures with respect to one or more blocks may be considered as meeting the aggregate work requirements on a group of blocks originally licensed in the same year, to the same operator, in the same category, provided that the number of such blocks shall not exceed sixteen in the case of the category of minerals described in paragraph 5.1(a) of Appendix A, four in the case of the category of minerals described in paragraph 5 1(b) of Appendix A and eight in the case of the category of minerals described in paragraph 5 1(c) of Appendix A.

5.3. Should the aggregate work requirement fee of $2,000,000 to $6,000,000 be spent prior to the end of the thirteenth year, an additional work requirement fee of $25,000-$50,000, as specified in an Annex, shall be met until commercial production begins or until expiration of the fifteen-year period

5.4. After commercial production begins, the operator shall at the beginning of each year deposit $100,000 to $200,000 as specified in an Annex, or with the Sponsoring Party post a bond for that amount. Such deposit or bond shall be returned in an amount equivalent to expenditures on or related to the block and the value of production at the site A portion [a figure between 50% and 66⅔% will be inserted here] of any funds not returned shall be transmitted to the Authority

6. Unit Management

The Operations Commission shall assure unit management and production pursuant to Section 9 of Appendix A, giving the licensees and their Sponsoring Parties a reasonable time to reach agreement on a plan for unit operation.

APPENDIX C
TERMS AND PROCEDURES FOR LICENSES IN
THE INTERNATIONAL TRUSTEESHIP AREA

1. General

1.1. Unless otherwise specified in this Convention, all provisions of this Convention except those in Appendix B shall apply to the International Trusteeship Area

2. Entities Entitled to Obtain Licenses

2.1. The Trustee Party, pursuant to Chapter III, shall have the exclusive right, in its discretion, to approve or disapprove applications for exploration and exploitation licenses.

3. Exploration and Exploitation Licenses

3.1. The Trustee Party may use any system for issuing and allocating exploration and exploitation licenses

3.2. Copies of licenses shall be forwarded to the Authority.

4. Categories and Size of Blocks

4.1. The Trustee Party may license separately one or more related minerals of the categories listed in paragraph 5 1 of Appendix A

4.2. The Trustee Party may establish the size of the block for which exploitation licenses are issued within the maximum limits specified in Appendix A

5. Duration of Exploitation Licenses

5.1. The Trustee Party may establish the term of the exploitation license and the conditions, if any, under which it may be renewed, provided that its continuance after the first 15 years is contingent upon the achievement of commercial production

6. Work Requirements

6.1. The Trustee Party may set the work requirements at or above those specified in Appendix A and put these in terms of work to be done rather than funds to be expended

7. Unit Management

7.1. When a deposit most rationally extracted under unit management lies wholly within the In-ternational Trusteeship Area, or astride its landward boundary, the Trustee Party concerned shall assure unit management and production pursuant to Section 9 1 of Appendix A, and shall submit the plan for unit operation to the Operations Commission

7.2. With respect to deposits lying astride a boundary between two Trustee Parties in the International Trusteeship Area, such Parties shall agree on a plan to assure unit management and production, and shall submit the operation plan to the Operations Commission

8. Proration

8.1. The Trustee Party may establish proration, to the extent permitted by its domestic law.

9. Payments

9.1. Pursuant to Subparagraph (e) of Article 28, the Trustee Party may collect fees and payments related to the issuance or retention of a license in addition to those specified in this Convention, including but not limited to payments on production higher than those required by this Convention

9.2. The Trustee Party shall transfer to the Authority a portion [a figure between 50% and 66⅔%] will be inserted here] of the fees and payments referred to in paragraph 9 1 except as otherwise provided in paragraphs 3 3, 4 4 and 6 4 of Appendix A.[1]

10. Standards

10.1. The Trustee Party may impose higher operating, conservation, pollution, and safety standards than those established by the Authority, and may impose additional sanctions in case of violations of applicable standards.

11. Revocation

11.1. The Trustee Party may suspend or revoke licenses for violation of this Convention, or of the rules it has established pursuant thereto, or in accordance with the terms of the license.

1 NOTE Further study is required on the means to assure equitable application of the principle contained in paragraph 9 2 to socialist and non-socialist parties, and their operations.

APPENDIX D
DIVISION OF REVENUE

1. Disbursements

1.1. All disbursements shall be made out of the net income of the Authority, except as otherwise provided in paragraph 2 of Article 74.

2. Administrative Expenses of the International Seabed Resource Authority

2.1. The Council, in submitting the proposed budget to the Assembly, shall specify what proportion of the revenues of the Authority shall be used for the payment of the administrative expenses of the Authority.

2.2. Upon approval of the budget by the Assembly, the Secretary-General is authorized to use the sums allotted in the budget for the expenses specified therein.

3. Distribution of the Net Income of the Authority

3.1. The net income, after administrative expenses, of the Authority shall be used to promote the economic advancement of developing States Parties to this Convention and for the purposes specified in paragraph 2 of Article 5 and in other Articles of this Convention.

3.2. The portion to be devoted to economic advancement of developing States Parties to this Convention shall be divided among the following international development organizations as follows: [1]

3.3. The Council shall submit to the Assembly proposals for the allocation of the income of the Authority within the limits prescribed by this Appendix.

3.4. Upon approval of the allocation by the Assembly, the Secretary-General is authorized to distribute the funds.

---

[1] *NOTE* A list of international and regional development organizations should be included here, indicating percentages assigned to each organization

APPENDIX E
DESIGNATED MEMBERS OF THE COUNCIL

1 Those six Contracting Parties which are both developed States and have the highest gross national product shall be considered as the six most industrially advanced Contracting Parties

2. The six most industrially advanced Contracting Parties at the time of the entry into force of this Convention shall be deemed to be

....

They shall hold office until replaced in accordance with this Appendix.

3. The Council, prior to every regular session of the Assembly, shall decide which are the six most industrially advanced Contracting Parties It shall make rules to ensure that all questions relating to the determination of such Contracting Parties are considered by an impartial committee before being decided upon by the Council

4 The Council shall report its decision to the Assembly, together with the recommendations of the impartial committee.

5 Any replacements of the designated members of the Council shall take effect on the day following the last day of the Assembly to which such a report is made

328

MINING RIGHTS IN THE DEEP SEABED

Northcutt Ely*

Presented Before the American Mining Congress
San Francisco, California

OCTOBER 1, 1975

Of the Law Offices of Northcutt Ely, Washington, D. C.

329

MINING RIGHTS IN THE DEEP SEABED

Northcutt Ely*

Presented before the
American Mining Congress
San Francisco, California

October 1, 1975

*Of the Law Offices of Northcutt Ely, Washington, D.C.

MINING RIGHTS IN THE DEEP SEABED

Contents

MINING RIGHTS IN THE DEEP SEABED

Northcutt Ely*

Introduction

The subject of this discussion is the international law applicable to
the acquisition and enjoyment of rights to mine the minerals of the deep
seabed beyond the limits of national jurisdiction. [1] The discussion is keyed
to a claim filed in November 1974 with the State Department by Deepsea
Ventures, Inc., giving notice of discovery of a deposit of manganese nodules

---

*Mr. Ely wishes to acknowledge the valued assistance of his associate,
Robert F. Pietrowski, Jr.

[1] By the expression "limits of national jurisdiction" is meant the geographical
limit of the exclusive sovereign rights of coastal States to govern the exploration and exploitation of the mineral resources of the seabed and subsoil in areas
adjacent to their coasts. This sort of jurisdiction extends beyond the limits of
the territorial sea. Under existing conventional and customary law, these
limits, in the author's opinion, are coextensive with the geomorphic features
of the continental margin abutting the particular State's coast, i.e., the continental shelf, continental slope, and a "grey area" encompassing the portion
of the continental rise landward of the junction between the rocks of the continent and those of the abyssal ocean floor. This corresponds with the concept
of "prolongation of the land territories" of the coastal State articulated by the
International Court of Justice in the North Sea Continental Shelf Cases, /1969/
I.C.J. 3. Under some of the proposals now current in the Law of the Sea negotiations, the corresponding limits of national jurisdiction would be the seaward
limits of the continental margin (not yet specifically defined), or 200 nautical
miles from the baseline from which the breadth of the territorial sea is measured. Some proposals would encompass whichever of these two areas is
greater. For purposes of the present discussion, it makes no difference what
the limits of national seabed jurisdiction are taken to be, because the seabed
resource in question is assumed, by hypothesis, to be seaward of all such limits.

within stated coordinates in the deep seabed of the Pacific beyond the limits
of national jurisdiction of any State, and asking diplomatic protection. 2/ The
issues discussed, however, are of general application.

The presentation will be in the following order:

(i) The nature of the resource;

(ii) The significance of seabed hard minerals to the United States;

(iii) The availability of the resource under present international law, with
particular reference to the procedure followed in the case of Deepsea Ventures'
discovery;

(iv) The current Law of the Sea negotiations, and the potential effect of a
treaty on the availability of minerals from the deep seabed.

(v) Finally, an evaluation of alternatives to a general Law of the Sea treaty.

When we talk about seabed mining, we are dealing with the latest in the
evolution of a very long history of relationships between consumers, governments, landowners and miners. In 1912, Herbert Hoover and his wife, Lou
Henry Hoover, translated Agricola's classic mining law treatise, De Re Metallica, 3/ into English. Mr. Hoover added a footnote of his own, observing:

2/ The writer participated in the preparation and filing of that notice, and
rendered an opinion to Deepsea Ventures November 14, 1974, which accompanied it, and was made public. This paper, in all other respects, states
the author's personal views, and no client is responsible for them.

3/ Agricola, De Re Metallica 82, n. 6 (H. & L. H. Hoover transl. 1912).

"There is no branch of the law of property, of which
the development is more interesting and illuminating from
a social point of view than that relating to minerals. Unlike
the land, the minerals have ever been regarded as a sort of
fortuitous property, for the title of which there have been
four principal claimants--that is, the Overlord, as represented by the King, Prince, Bishop, or what not; the Community
or the State, as distinguished from the Ruler; the Landowner;
and the Mine Operator, to which class belongs the Discoverer.
The one of these that possessed the dominant right reflects vividly
the social state and sentiment of the period. The Divine Right
of Kings; the measure of freedom of their subjects; the tyranny
of the land-owning class; the rights of the Community as opposed
to its individual members; the rise of individualism; and finally,
the modern return to more communal view, have all been reflected
promptly in the mineral title. Of these parties the claims of the
Overlord have been limited only by the resistance of his subjects;
those of the State limited by the landlord; those of the landlord by
the Sovereign or by the State; while the miner, ever in a minority
in influence as well as in numbers, has been buffeted from pillar
to post, his only protection being the fact that all other parties
depended upon his exertion and skill. " (Emphasis added.)

While the miner's position on land, vis-a-vis the overlord, the State, and

the landlord, has changed very little since Mr. Hoover wrote that passage,

when the miner goes beneath the sea and beyond the territorial jurisdiction of

a State, he encounters a new set of forces. One is the amorphous but formid-

able jellyfish consisting of the general body of international law. The other is

a ravenous shark attracted by the miner's first tentative undersea movements.

It might aptly bear the sobriquet of "Jaws," but is known more formally as the

International Seabed Resource Authority, now being structured, not in Holly-

wood, but in another never-never land.

1. The nature of the resource

We are talking here primarily about manganese nodules, and sec-
ondarily about hydrocarbons.

A. Manganese nodules

Manganese nodules, as we all think we know, are strange potato-shaped
concretions of metal oxides, primarily manganese, silica, iron, copper,
cobalt, and nickel. They range in size from marbles up to grapefruit.
When sliced through the center, they resemble gallstones, in that a
large number of thin concentric shells are seen to have been deposited
around a central nucleus of some quite different material, often a grain of
sand or a piece of shell. They lie on the surface of the seabed in populations of varying density, covering as much as 60 percent of the area in
some deposits. These deposits are scattered over literally thousands
of square miles of the seabed in the Pacific, Indian, and some other
oceans, usually in very deep water. Depths of the order of 15,000 feet are
not uncommon. The total quantity of seabed nodules has been estimated, on
a very approximate basis, to be in the trillions of tons. There seems to be
a tendency for these populations to be most dense in the vicinity of sea
mounts, which are like isolated mountain peaks that do not reach the surface.
As to why and how the nodules were formed, I have yet to hear an expert

give an explanation that, as a layman, I could understand and believe, or that his fellow experts would applaud.

Two things do seem to be proved, however. The first is that technology now exists to harvest the nodules and raise them vertically through several miles of water to ships on the surface. The second is that technology now exists to refine the nodules and separate out the metals that they contain, primarily as on-shore operations. In both respects the techniques are proprietary. They have been developed by American companies, several of which now have foreign companies as associates in one relationship or another.

Some nodules contain a score or more metals, but those of primary importance to the American economy are manganese, copper, nickel, and cobalt. I will come to their degree of importance in a moment.

Some features of the production problem need to be identified more specifically before we discuss the legal problems that they generate.

Item: The legal problem is not how to police a gold rush, where competitors can be expected to try to jump each other's claims. Quite the contrary. The topography of the seabed is such that, after discovery of a promising mine site, prolonged, detailed mapping, by very sophisticated methods is necessary before the mining equipment can be designed for that particular area. One must know what the gradients are, where the canyons are located, what obstacles must be avoided, what weight the underlying ooze will support, what distribution of weight is required, what kind of force is to be applied from the surface, how the harvesting mechanism can best be guided, how the surface vessel is to be kept in position, what kinds of accidents to seabed equipment and lifting mechanisms must be provided against, and so on.

Item: The metallurgical problems involved in refining nodules of different deposits located only a few hundred miles apart may differ so completely as to render the refining process that is developed for the one uneconomical for the other. Huge investments are required. The production equipment for a single deposit, at present prices, may cost $200 million to $300 million. The specialized refining for that deposit may cost another $150 million.

The last thing in the world that an investor wants is to discover that he has been spending his money on a deposit that someone else claims, when there are plenty of free areas available. What he does need is public disclosure of the location of all claims, not so that he can go there and poach, but so that he can avoid those areas. Conversely, he needs a system that will give him protection for a discovery, so that others will not inadvertently invade it. I use the word inadvertently deliberately, for the reasons I have stated.

Moreover, the cost of these operations is such that less than a dozen will probably be operational within the next decade and a half. In the nature of things, they will be widely scattered.

There is no urgent international administrative problem

Another comment or two, before we leave the physical problem.

The first is as to size and duration and productivity of the operation. It seems to be generally agreed, by those who are spending their money on research, that the economic size of each operation will be geared to the gathering of up to three million tons of nodules per year, and that the commercial operation should continue for some 40 years. This, related to average population densities, requires a production area of some 30,000 square kilometers, and, in turn, a preliminary exploration area of about 60,000 square kilometers.

The second relates to environmental impact. As the nodules lie on the surface of the seabed, the gathering operation is not at all like an open pit copper mine. When the nodules are all scooped up, the seabed will look much as it did before. From an environmental viewpoint, it would seem a good deal better to mine copper from the deep seabed in this temporary scraping operation, thousands of miles from shore, than from an open pit in Montana or Arizona, which will be a permanent new feature of the landscape.

The third comment relates to timing. We are assured that the technology of nodule recovery and refining has progressed to the point where capital is available in the amounts required to finance the costly mapping, exploration and evaluation of the sites already discovered, and construction of preliminary pilot-plant refinery operation. Most of the

8

first stages can be commenced in a matter of months, to be followed by full-scale operations in a few years. The hurdles are not technological, but legal, as we shall see.

B. Hydrocarbons

Hydrocarbons, we have been taught, occur in sedimentary deposits. The submarine reservoirs, we have also been told, are situated primarily on the margins of the continents and in the beds of the marginal or semi-enclosed seas of the world. These are the areas which are or will become subject to exclusive coastal State authority, and are therefore excluded from our present inquiry.

But the reports of the National Petroleum Council[4/] indicate the probable existence of some important hydrocarbon deposits in the areas seaward of national jurisdiction. It is reported that the technology for finding and producing oil in some parts of the ocean depths up to 3,000 feet is in an advanced state of development, and will probably be ready for use in the mid-80's. The deep sea jurisdictional problem with respect to hydrocarbons is less pressing than it is with respect to hard minerals only because the continental margins, in which the jurisdictional issue is almost completely resolved in favor of the coastal State, are much more attractive from the viewpoint of cost than is the deep seabed. Thus it can be said that the petroleum industry has an interest in resolving the deep

---

4/ E.g., National Petroleum Council, Ocean Petroleum Resources, Fig. 1, Table 4, p. 19 (1975).

seabed jurisdictional problem which is parallel with that of the hard mineral industry, but which is less urgent, for the reasons that I have stated. Accordingly, the present discussion will deal mainly with hard minerals.

2.   The significance of seabed hard minerals to the United States

At the present time, the United States is dependent on foreign sources for 95 percent of its manganese, 74 percent of its nickel, 20 percent of its copper, and 98 percent of its cobalt requirements. In 1974, imports of these four minerals alone contributed 900 million dollars to the U.S. balance of payments deficit.

Domestic demand for manganese, nickel, copper, and cobalt is forecast to increase at annual compound rates of 2 percent, 3 percent, 3.5 percent, and 2.6 percent, respectively, through 1980, indicating a doubling of demand in about one generation. Since domestic reserves of these minerals are already inadequate to meet U.S. demand (indeed, the United States has no manganese reserves), this increased demand will have to be met by supplies originating outside of the United States. But the world demand is also increasing, and is expected to treble by the end of this century.

Notwithstanding this projected increase in demand, the U.S. Department of the Interior has estimated that by a date as early as 1990 the United States can be self-sufficient in nickel, copper, and cobalt, and can reduce imports of manganese to 23 percent of consumption, provided that American companies go forward with their deep sea mining operations now.

On the other hand, if American companies are unable to proceed with their deep sea mining operations, and the United States continues to be dependent on foreign sources for manganese, nickel, copper, and cobalt, the economic welfare and national security of the United States will be in jeopardy. 'As we

11

shall see, the obstacles which stand in the way of substantial American self-sufficiency in these minerals are not found in the existing law of the sea, but in the threat of creation of a new international regime which will throttle this infant industry before it leaves the cradle.

The importance of these minerals to the United States is manifest. Manganese, nickel, and cobalt are important in the manufacture of steel; copper is a basic industrial metal. There are no satisfactory substitutes for manganese or nickel in their primary uses. Nickel is the only satisfactory substitute for cobalt. Substitutes exist for some, but not all, uses of copper.

The dangers inherent in our present supply deficits for these minerals are also obvious. We should have learned from the OPEC experience. But the same arguments that were used in 1970 to support the contention that OPEC would never be an effective cartel [5] are being put forth today to support the proposition that the hard mineral exporting nations will never be able to effectively control prices and production.

Production and reserves of manganese, nickel, copper and cobalt are concentrated in even fewer countries than are production and reserves of petroleum. Five nations control 99 percent of the free world's manganese reserves; two nations control 66 percent of the free world's nickel reserves;

---

[5] See, e.g., The Oil Import Question: A report on the relationship of oil imports to the national security by the Cabinet Task Force on Oil Import Control, para. 204(c), p. 21 (Feb. 1970); Charles River Associates, An Analysis of the United States Oil Import Quota 95 (1970).

12

six nations control 75 percent of the free world's copper reserves; and
five nations control 99 percent of the free world's cobalt reserves. [6/]
And, as in the case of petroleum, increased world demand and competition
among buyers has eroded the bargaining power of the buyers relative to that
of the mineral exporting governments. . oreover, the very nations which
presently supply the U. S. hard minerals deficit have repeatedly expressed
their intentions to maximize revenues from mineral exports.

At its 29th session, the United Nations General Assembly adopted a
resolution entitled, "The Charter of Economic Rights and Duties of States." [7/]
Article 5 of this resolution provides:

> "All States have the right to associate in organizations
> of primary commodity producers in order to develop their nation-
> al economies, to achieve stable financing for their development
> and, in pursuance of their aims, to assist in the promotion of sus-
> tained growth of the world economy, in particular accelerating
> the development of developing countries. Correspondingly all
> States have the duty to respect that right by refraining from apply-
> ing economic and political measures that would limit it."

Thus, the resolution asserts (1) a positive right to form commodity
cartels, and (2) a correlative duty not to resist the objectives of such cartels.
Other of the resolution's provisions make clear that the right asserted in
Article 5 is intended to attach only to the developing countries, while the duty
asserted in that article is meant to bind the developed nations. For example,

---

6/ U. S. Department of the Interior, Commodity Data Summaries 1975 (1975).

7/ A/RES/3281 (XXIX) (January 15, 1975).

13

rticle 14 provides in part:

". . . States shall take measures aimed at securing additional
benefits for the international trade of developing countries so
as to achieve a substantial increase in their foreign exchange
earnings, the diversification of their exports, the acceleration
of the rate of growth of their trade, taking into account their
development needs, an improvement in the possibilities for
these countries to participate in the expansion of world trade
and a balance more favourable to developing countries in the
sharing of the advantages resulting from this expansion, through,
in the largest possible measure, a substantial improvement in
the conditions of access for the products of interest to the developing countries and, wherever appropriate, measures designed to
attain stable, equitable and remunerative prices for primary products."

Article 24 provides:

"All States have the duty to conduct their mutual economic
relations in a manner which takes into account the interests of
other countries. In particular, all States should avoid prejudic-
ing the interests of developing countries."

And Article 28 provides:

"All States have the duty to co-operate in achieving adjust-
ments in the prices of exports of developing countries in relation
to prices of their imports so as to promote just and equitable terms
of trade for them, in a manner which is remunerative for producers
and equitable for producers and consumers."

The Charter of Economic Rights and Duties of States is important here

because it articulates the aspirations of the mineral exporting nations. Of

the nine countries [8/] which presently supply more than 90 percent of U.S. im-

ports of manganese, nickel, copper, and cobalt, not one joined with the United

States to vote against the resolution. In general, these nations, like the OPEC

8/ Brazil, Canada, Chile, Finland, Gabon, Norway, Peru, South Africa, and
Zaire.

14

nations, seek absolute control (i.e., free from any meaningful contract restrictions) over the production and prices of their commodities. This point of view,
while understandable, is nevertheless inimical to United States interests. Its
prevalence among the mineral exporting nations of the world underscores the
need for American companies to begin deep sea mining operations as soon as
possible.

3. The legal and political prerequisites to a successful ocean mining industry

If deepsea mining production and refining technology has reached the point where this industry is ready to proceed, and the Nation's thirst for the four major seabed minerals is as serious as the foregoing figures make it out to be, what additional problems stand in the way of success? What assurances does the industry need?

It needs, in this new environment, what every mining venture has always needed, a combination of the following factors:

First, a right to freely explore areas not owned by others.

Second, if a discovery of a mineral deposit is made, the exclusive right to evaluate and utilize that deposit.

Third, security of tenure, that is, a right to be protected against loss of the discovered deposit, either in consequence of "poaching" by a competitor, or seizure by a sovereign. Historically, the industry has wanted its security of tenure to be evidenced by a piece of paper issued by a sovereign, or by a landowner whose title the sovereign recognizes.

Fourth, freedom to take away and use or sell the recovered minerals.

Fifth, freedom from governmental restrictions on production or prices, which may make the operation uneconomic.

Sixth, knowledge, in advance of investment, of the probable range of burdens of taxation and other elements of "governmental take," so that the miner's investment will not be rendered worthless by an uncompensated change in the rules after the investment is irrevocably committed.

16

Other assurances may be sought, but, given these six in reasonable
degree, the mining industry has historically been willing to venture its capital
in this highly risky business. The problem has always been, as it is here,
how to attract capital, which is required by the mining industry in very large
amounts per unit of production. This requires reasonable assurance that a
profit, large in comparison with risk-free investments, will be realized in
addition to amortizing a very high investment during the limited life of the
mineral deposit. With respect to manganese nodules, the financial risk is
obviously increased enormously by the physical problem of finding and producing minerals under a wet and shifting overburden of some three miles of salt
water, and lifting these minerals to the surface by means of operations conducted in the teeth of all of the perils of the sea.

So much for necessary rights. How about the miner's correlative
obligations? The historical ones have been these, as Mr. Hoover's note to
De Re Metallica pointed out:

First, the miner, as in the case of any industrial operations, must pay
taxes to the government or governments having jurisdiction over the operation.
This jurisdiction may be in personam, as lawyers say, that is, the right of a
government to tax its nationals, whether or not they are operating within the
national territory. Or it may be taxation in rem, that is, taxes of one sort or
another resting on the jurisdictional basis that the operation, regardless of
nationality of its owners, is carried on within the jurisdiction of the taxing State.

17

Second, the miner is subject to an obligation to pay compensation to the owner of the minerals for the right to mine them. This may take the form of royalties on production, or surface rentals, or hybrids of these. Where the owner of the minerals is not the State, this obligation is naturally quite distinct from the obligation to pay taxes. Where the owner of the minerals is the State, the two obligations can become quite blurred. Indeed, the trend in recent petroleum legislation has been to meld together the equity interest of the miner, the proprietary interest of the State, and the State's taxing power as sovereign, and to produce, as a resultant of these forces, arrangements in the nature of joint ventures, or participation agreements, or working contracts in which the company, as the sovereign's agent, is paid in oil. These devices are all premised on the government's ownership of the resource, a premise lacking in the areas of the deep seabed beyond the limits of national jurisdiction.

Third, we can now add an obligation of more recent recognition: to operate with the minimum practicable damage to the environment. But, correlatively, the miner is entitled to know the character and extent of this restriction before he makes his irrevocable financial commitment.

Fourth, the miner is subject to the State's police power, exercised for the protection of its citizens' health and safety (including, of course, the labor force of the mine), and for the protection of the mineral deposit against waste -- a power developed and confirmed in the statutes and cases dealing with petroleum operations. It goes without saying that this industry is also subject to all the laws that apply to other businesses, including the antitrust laws, and those

18

governing production, transportation, refining, and sale of all industrial materials.

I propose now to consider how these essential rights and obligations of the miner can best be balanced and regulated when the mineral deposit is beyond the limits of national jurisdiction.

Three facets of this problem suggest themselves: (1) the situation under existing international law, (2) the current treaty proposals, and (3) possible alternatives to a treaty, if the existing international law is to be changed or supplemented.

As we shall see, under the existing law of the sea, the deep seabed minerals are not subject to the sovereignty or ownership of any State, and so no State can hold the consumers of the world at ransom for the right of access to them. And, as we shall further see, the sharp issue in the pending treaty negotiations is whether this freedom of the seas shall be supplanted by subjecting these minerals to control by a new sort of multi-national sovereignty, with the result that access to these minerals, like petroleum, must be obtained on terms set by a cartel of governments.

- 19

4. The Deepsea Ventures Mining Claim

The problems just stated were put into sharp focus in 1974 when Deepsea Ventures, Inc., one of the principal companies engaged in preparation for mining deep sea manganese nodules, placed the following set of facts[9/] before us, and asked our advice as to how their interests could best be protected.

After describing several years' work in preliminary prospecting, the Company's president, John E. Flipse, stated:

> "As a result of the foregoing activities, attention was concentrated in the California Seamount area of the Clarion Fracture Zone of the Baja California Oceanographic Province, identified during cruises of R/V PROSPECTOR (owned by Deepsea's predecessor in interest) during August 1964 and April/May 1965. Further cruises based thereon resulted, on August 31, 1969, at 1820 local time, in recovery of a particularly significant grab sample of nodules from a station at $15°28'$ N. Latitude $125°00.5'$ W. Longitude. Survey activity on this cruise continued as far south as $15°12.5'$N., $125°02'$W.
>
> "Since August 31, 1969, further surveys during 16 cruises, of three to four weeks duration each, have further defined the extent of the deposit discovered on that date. These activities included the taking of some 294 discrete samples, including the bulk dredging of some 164 tons of manganese nodules from some 263 dredge stations, 28 core stations and three grab sample stations, cutting of some 28 cores, approximately 1,000 lineal miles of survey of sea floor recorded by television and still photography, etc. As a result, the deposit of nodules (hereinafter 'Deposit') identified with the discovery has been proved to extend generally throughout the entire area encompassed by lines drawn as follows:

9/ Affidavit of John E. Flipse, President.

20

From:
(1) Latitude 15°44'N.   Longitude 124°20'W.
A line drawn West to:
(2) Latitude 15°44'N.   Longitude 127°46'W.
And thence South to:
(3) Latitude 14°16'N.   Longitude 127°46'W.
And thence East to:
(4) Latitude 14°16'N.   Longitude 124°20'W.
And thence North to the point of origin;

including approximately 60,000 square kilometers, lying on the
seabed of the abyssal ocean, in water depths between 2300 to 5000
meters. This Deposit is some 1300 kilometers from the nearest
continental margin, and some 1000 kilometers from the nearest
island.

"   dredge heads and mining systems have been designed
by Deepsea Ventures, Inc., for the specific sediments, nodule properties, and water depths at, over and/or under the Deposit, and
process design and pilot plant operations have been tailored to the
nodules of grade and chemical composition of the manganese nodules
in the Deposit. The cost to date of prospecting, exploration, design
and test efforts required to identify and evaluate the potential of the
Deposit has been approximately U.S. $20,000,000. Further explora-
tion, evaluation, and development of the Deposit and associated facilities will consume some three years and cost between U.S. $22,000,000
and U.S. $30,000,000. Such further exploration, evaluation and de-
velopment of the Deposit commenced on 1 November 1974.

"Deepsea intends to commence commercial production of the
Deposit within 15 years at an initial rate of approximately 1.35 million wet metric tons of manganese nodules per year, which rate may
be expanded according to market conditions to as much as 4 million
wet metric tons per year. The company intends to process said
nodules at a land-based processing plant which will yield as the products thereof copper, nickel, cobalt and manganese and other products."

The coordinates of the "deposit" placed it between Hawaii and Baja

California.

The ultimate question was whether the discoverer would be better
protected by making the discovery public, and claiming our government's
diplomatic protection, or keeping it secret. We advised the former course
for reasons which will be discussed later.

Accordingly, Deepsea, on November 14, 1974, filed with the
Secretary of State a "Notice of Discovery and claim of exclusive mining
rights and request for diplomatic protection and protection of investment
by Deepsea Ventures, Inc."

It said:

"Notice of Discovery and Claim of Exclusive Mining Rights

"Deepsea Ventures, Inc., (hereinafter 'Deepsea'), hereby
gives public notice that it has discovered and taken possession of,
and is now engaged in developing and evaluating, as the first stages
of mining, a deposit of seabed manganses nodules (hereinafter 'Deposit'). The Deposit, illustrated by the sketch annexed as Exhibit B,
is encompassed by, and extends to, lines drawn between the coordinates numbered in series below, as follows:"

Here followed the coordinates previously quoted.

The document continued:

"These lines include approximately 60,000 square kilometers
for purposes of development and evaluation of the Deposit encompassed
therein, which area will be reduced by Deepsea to 30,000 square kilometers upon expiration of a term of 15 years (absent force majeure)
from the date of this notice or upon commencement (absent force majeure) of commercial production from the Deposit, whichever event
occurs first. The Deposit lies on the abyssal ocean floor, in water
depths ranging between 2300 to 5000 meters and is more than 1000
kilometers from the nearest island, and more than 1300 kilometers
seaward of the outer edge of the nearest continental margin. It is
beyond the limits of seabed jurisdiction presently claimed by any
State. The overlying waters are, of course, high seas.

"The general area of the Deposit was identified in August of 1964 by the predecessor in interest of Deepsea, and the Deposit was discovered by Deepsea on August 31, 1969."

After describing the work done, and in progress, the claim

continued:

"Deepsea, or its successor in interest, will commence commercial production from the Deposit within 15 years (absent force majeure) from the date of this Claim, and will conclude production therefrom within a period (absent force majeure) of 40 years from the date of commencement of commercial production whereupon the right shall cease.

"Deepsea asserts the exclusive rights to develop, evaluate and mine the Deposit and to take, use, and sell all of the manganese nodules in, and the minerals and metals derived, therefrom. It is proceeding with appropriate diligence to do so, and requests and requires States, persons, and all other commercial or political entities to respect the exclusive rights asserted herein. Deepsea does not assert, or ask the United States of America to assert, a territorial claim to the seabed or subsoil underlying the Deposit Use of the overlying water column, as a freedom of the high seas, will be made to the extent necessary to recover and transport the manganese nodules of the Deposit.

"It is Deepsea's intention, by filing this Claim in your office and in appropriate State recording offices, to publish this Claim and provide notice and proof of the priority of the right of Deepsea to the Deposit, and its title thereto.

"We ask that this Claim, and all of the annexed Exhibits, be made available by your office for public examination.

"Request for Diplomatic Protection and Protection of Integrity of Investment

23

"Deepsea respectfully requests the diplomatic protection of the United States Government with respect to the exclusive mining rights described and asserted in the foregoing Claim, and any other rights which may hereafter accrue to Deepsea as a result of its activities at the site of the Deposit, and similar protection of the integrity of its investments heretofore made and now being undertaken and to be undertaken in the future.

"This request is made prior to any known interference with the rights now being asserted, and prior to any known impairment of Deepsea's investment. It is intended to give the Department immediate notice of Deepsea's Claim for the purpose of facilitating the protection of Deepsea's rights and investments should this be required as a consequence of any future actions of the United States Government or other States, persons, or organizations.

"The protection requested accords with the assurances given on behalf of the Executive Department to the Congress of the United States, including those by Ambassador John R. Stevenson, by Honorable Charles N. Brower, and by Honorable John Norton Moore, as follows:"

(We quote these later on, in the present paper.)

5. <u>Mining rights in the deep seabed under existing international law</u>

Several related problems of international law were involved in the protection of Deepsea's discovery:

First, whether the right to discover, take and use the minerals of the
seabed, in areas beyond national jurisdiction, is one of the freedoms of the
sea, available to all States and their nationals;

Second, whether the first discoverer has a right to the exclusive utilization of the discovered deposit, and, if so, how this priority is to be established;

Third, how this exclusive right, if it exists, may be maintained and
enforced.

Beyond these questions there lurked the further one of the possible impact of a new treaty governing operations in seabed areas beyond national jurisdiction. We will come to that later.

The sources of international law are generally considered to be fairly
identified in Article 38.1 of the Statute of the International Court of Justice,
<u>i.e.</u>, (a) international conventions establishing rules recognized by the con-
testing States, (b) international custom, (c) general principles of law recognized by civilized nations, and (d) as subsidiary sources, judicial decisions
and teachings of the most highly qualified "publicists."

These sources of law enable a quick answer to the first question, whether
under existing law the mining of deep sea minerals may be considered to be one
of the freedoms of the sea. The answer is "yes."

The U. S. State Department has repeatedly advised the Congress that deep sea mining, if presently undertaken, would be a valid exercise of the freedom of the seas doctrine and the rights embodied in the Convention on the High Seas. Some of these assurances deserve quotation.

In 1970, the Legal Adviser of the Department of State, in a letter to the Chairman of the Senate Special Subcommittee on the Outer Continental Shelf, referring specifically to U. S. miners who may wish to mine the manganese nodules of the international seabed area (the "deep seabed"), stated:

> "The Department does not anticipate any efforts to discourage U.S. nationals from continuing with their current exploration plans. In the event that U.S. nationals should desire to engage in commercial exploitation prior to the establishment of an internationally agreed regime, we would seek to assure that their activities are conducted in accordance with relevant principles of international law, including the freedom of the seas and that the integrity of their investment receives due protection in any subsequent international agreement." 10/

In 1973, Charles N. Brower, Acting Legal Adviser, told the Congress:

> "At the present time, under international law and the High Seas Convention, it is open to anyone who has the capacity to en-

10/ Letter of January 16, 1970, from John R. Stevenson, Legal Adviser, Department of State, to Lee Metcalf, Chairman, Special Subcommittee on the Outer Continental Shelf, U.S. Senate, reproduced in Hearings before the Special Senate Subcommittee on the Outer Continental Shelf, 91st Cong., 1st and 2d Sess., 211 (1970).

gage in mining of the deep seabed subject to the proper exercise of high seas rights of other countries involved."[11]

In 1973, John Norton Moore, then State Department Counselor on International Law, testified before the Subcommittee on Minerals, Materials and Fuels of the Senate Committee on Interior and Insular Affairs. When asked, "Is there any legal reason at the present time why a company shouldn't continue to prospect and explore the deep seabed pending this international agreement," Mr. Moore replied:

> "No; I think there is not. It is certainly the position of the United States that the mining of the deep seabed is a high-seas freedom and I think that would be a freedom today under international law. And our position has been that companies are free to engage in this kind of mining beyond the 200-meter mark subject to the international regime to be agreed upon, and of course, assured protection of the integrity of investment in that period."[12]

In 1974, Mr. Moore, who had become Chairman, National Security Council Interagency Task Force on the Law of the Sea, told Congress:

> "The Executive Branch continues to hold the view that deep seabed mineral exploitation constitutes a reasonable use of the high seas and is presently permitted under international law."[13]

The United States Senate Committee on Interior and Insular Affairs, in its 1974 Report to Accompany S. 1134 (Deep Seabed Hard Minerals Act), said:

> "/To/ the extent that /manganese/ nodules are located outside the territorial limits and beyond the Continental Shelf of any nation,

---

11/ Hearings before the House Subcommittee on Oceanography of the Committee on Merchant Marine and Fisheries, 93d Cong., 1st Sess. 50 (1974).

12/ Hearings before the Senate Subcommittee on Minerals, Materials and Fuels, 93d Cong., 1st Sess. 247 (1973).

13/ Hearings before the Senate Subcommittee on Minerals, Materials and Fuels, 93d Cong., 2d Sess. 994 (1974).

the nodules are available for utilization by any nation with the ability to develop them. "14/

There is plenty of support for these conclusions of the State Department and of the Senate Committee to be found in the practice of States, the travaux preparatoires of the 1958 Convention on the High Seas, and the writings of legal scholars. These are cited in our opinion of November 1974. But for present purposes it is enough to say that American companies are entitled to rely upon these assurances from the State Department, and Deepsea Ventures did so in filing with that Department its notice of claim and request for diplomatic protection.

Second, as to whether an exclusive right can be established in a deep sea mineral deposit by discovery and occupancy.

The historical practice of States affords a favorable answer.

A starting point is found in the general rules relating to discovery, possession, and consolidation of title found in cases deciding disputes over land territories, e.g., the Island of Palmas Case, 15/ the Clipperton Island Award, 16/ and the Legal Status of Eastern Greenland Case. 17/

14/ S. Rep. No. 93-1116, 93d Cong., 2d Sess. 1 (1974).

15/ 2 U.N. Rep. Int'l Arb. Awards 829 (1928).

16/ 2 U.N. Rep. Int'l Arb. Awards 1105 (1931); transl. 26 Am. J. Int'l L. 390 (1932).

17/ 3 Hudson World Court Reports 148 (1938).

28

But it is not necessary to apply here the tests which might determine a claim of territorial sovereignty as between contesting nations. We are dealu here with a lesser claim, restricted to the exclusive use of a single natural resource, not claimed by any other State, and to be used for a limited time. The question is the restricted one of whether a State or its nationals may acquire an exclusive right to the use of such a resource, beyond the limits of national jurisdiction of any State, by discovery, occupation to the extent that circumstances permit, and the use of the resource. The answer is quite clearly in the affirmative.

Since time immemorial, international law has recognized in States the competence to establish their exclusive jurisdiction, by discovery and exploita tion, of natural resources belonging to no one, even though lying outside their own national jurisdiction. [18]

There has been general acquiescence by the community of nations in

_____

[18] The States which have exercised powers of control beyond their areas of national jurisdiction include Algeria (coral), Australia (pearl), the Bahamas (sponge), British Honduras (sponge), Ceylon (chank and pearl), Cuba (sponge), England (oyster), Egypt (sponge), France (oyster), Greece (sponge), Ireland (oyster), Italy (coral), Japan (coral), Libya (sponge), Mexico (pearl), Panama (pearl), the Persian Gulf States (pearl), the Philippines (pearl), Sicily (coral), Tunisia (coral and sponge), Turkey (sponge), and Venezuela (pearl). For descriptions and analyses of these various rights, see the testimony of the Honorable Philip C. Jessup in U.S. v. Maine, et al., Sup. Ct. No. 35, Original, October Term 1973, and the sources cited therein.

these exclusive rights, and they have been widely recognized by publicists. [19]

Moreover, private individuals have established similar rights in the same way

by discovery, possession to the extent permitted by circumstances, and utili-

zation. Examples are found in the decisions relating to rights in wrecks dis-

covered by salvagers beyond the then limits of national jurisdiction; [20] cases

deciding controversies between whalers; [21] on land, the celebrated Spitz-

bergen coal controversy, [22] in which the United States successfully asserted

the exclusive right of an American company to a coal deposit that it had dis-

covered in terra nullius, a no man's land; and the Guano Island cases in which

Congress instructed the Secretary of State to defend the rights of American

nationals who had discovered guano deposits on unoccupied and unclaimed

islands. [23]

---

[19] See, for example, E. Vattel, The Law of Nations or the Principles of Natural Law (1758), in Classics of International Law (C. Fenwick transl. 1916); T. Fulton, The Sovereignty of the Sea 696-98 (1911); International Law Association, Report of the Forty-Fourth Conference 90 (1952), Jonkheer P.R. Feith, Rapporteur; L. Oppenheim, International Law 628 (H. Lauterpacht 8th Ed. (1955); P. C. Jessup, prepared testimony in United States v. Maine, et al., 104 (1974); Waldock, The Legal Basis of Claims to the Continental Shelf, 36 Grotius Society 115, 118 (1951), quoted with approval in the Report of the Special Master in United States v. Maine, et al.

[20] The Tubantia, L.R. /1924/ P.78.

[21] Ghen v. Rich, 8 F. 159 (D. Mass. 1881); Swift v. Gifford, 2 Low. 110 (D. Mass. 1872).

[22] Goldie, A General International Law Doctrine for Seabed Regimes, 7 Int'l Lawyer 776, 807-10 (1973).

[23] 1 J. Moore, Int'l Law Digest 556-80 (1906).

The key element of the right in all of these extraterritorial cases was possession. And the possession need not be absolute or literal; what is required is a degree of possession consistent with the physical realities, as the salvage and whaling cases sensibly pointed out. This criterion, and the companion test of the absence of prior claims of the same character, find their logical roots in the controversies between States over uninhabited territories that have attracted contact by representatives or nationals of the competing States--as in the controversies over Greenland, Clipperton Island, and Las Palmas Island. The rationale as to the degree of control which creates an exclusive right is the same whether the claimant is a State or an individual, even though we must be clear that in the case of the private person we are talking only about the degree of control necessary to give an exclusive possessory right rather than sovereignty, as in the case of the cited quarrels between States.

The right, being one to take and use specific resources, is like a profit a prendre or usufruct, and so ceases on completion of extraction of the nodules. It does not constitute the acquisition of permanent title, comparable to fee simple, in the seabed itself. As to the degree of occupation required to consolidate the right after discovery, it deserves repetition to say that the law requires only what is possible and reasonable. Manifestly, it is not possible to physically occupy at one time the whole area encompassing the deposit, which lies more than two miles below the surface of the sea, and which, under

existing technology, will be "swept" in successive parallel or concentric paths
or furrows. The required legal nexus between the owner and the res is correlative with the practicable physical nexus between the owner's vessel and the
submerged deposit--a degree of control which, though remote, is nevertheless sufficiently real and positive to enable the deposit to be gathered, brought
to the surface, and carried away. As to the size of the area, we have accepted
the hypothesis of the States[24] which have active programs of ocean mining
that an area of 60,000 square kilometers during the exploration phase, re-
ducible to 30,000 square kilometers during the production phase, is essential
to economic operation. If so, the recovery of samples which prove the existence of the deposit of nodules over such an area suffices, in our opinion, to
encompass the whole area in the mining right thus initiated.

Accordingly, we gave our opinion that Deepsea had effectively established
its possessory title to the deposit, by discovery and subsequent extensive and
costly activities in exploring and evaluating it, including the recovery of a large
quantity of nodules from points scattered over the whole area, and the perfec-
tion of a processing system keyed to the composition and characteristics of
this particular deposit. The possessory title, initiated by discovery, has
thus been maintained by the exercise of due diligence.

We recommended that, to protect Deepsea's priority, public notice of
the claim should be given, by notice to the State Department and publication,

---

24/ See, e.g., U.N. Doc. A/CONF. 62/C. 1/L. 6 (1974); U.N. Doc. A/CONF.
62/C. 1/L. 8 (1974); U.N. Doc. A/CONF. 62/C. 1/L. 9 (1974).

and by making the same of record in appropriate public agencies. As we have noted, this was done.

The requirements of due diligence in the future maintenance of title would appear to be more than adequately met by the program of work and expenditures now under way.

This brings us to the third question: How can such a possessory right be protected and enforced?

International law being the "law of nations," private persons, including corporations, have traditionally been considered not to have rights under international law, although international tribunals have for many years implicitly recognized such rights (and obligations). Today, the writings of legal scholars suggest that the "traditional" view has become an anachronism, and that international law may be said to recognize the rights of private corporations. However, it is still true that if a corporation's rights are abused by a foreign State or a national thereof, the corporation must rely on its government for vindication of those rights, or seek redress in the courts of the State responsible for the injury. Thus it appears that while an American mining company may acquire rights under international law to mineral resources in seabed areas beyond national jurisdiction independently of any claim by the United States Government to those resources, nevertheless, if these rights are violated by a foreign State, or its nationals, the American company must rely on the U.S. State Department for protection of its rights, through diplomatic channels or before international tribunals.

Under U.S. law, such protection is discretionary with the State Department, but State Department officials, testifying before Congress, have repeatedly given assurances that diplomatic protection, including protection of the integrity of investments, would be afforded by the United States if the rights of U.S. mining companies operating in the deep seabed should be infringed. These assurances have been so emphatic, and repeated so often, that a repudiation of them would inspire more than the usual congressional exasperation associated with a diplomat's forgetfulness.

34

6. <u>How deep sea mining would be affected by pending treaty proposals</u>

We come now to potential changes in the law, international and domestic, that might affect deep sea mining.

The effects of four kinds of action must be considered.

First, what attention must be paid to the resolutions which the Assembly of the United Nations has passed. These include primarily a moratorium resolution in 1969, and a Declaration of Principles in 1970.

The 1969 resolution, which was aimed squarely at deep sea mining said:

> "The General Assembly. . . /d/eclares that, pending the establish-
> ment of the aforementioned international regime:
> (a) States and persons, physical or juridical, are bound to refrain
> from all activities of exploitation of the resources of the area of
> the sea-bed and ocean floor, and the subsoil thereof, beyond the
> limits of national jurisdiction;
> (b) No claim to any part of that area or its resources shall be
> recognized. " 25/

It was passed by a vote of 62 to 28, with 28 abstentions. The United States and other industrialized nations voted against it.

The 1970 Declaration of Principles, a rather prolix document, contains several paragraphs related to deep sea mining, of which the following are examples:

> "The General Assembly. . . /s/olemnly declares that:
> "1. The sea-bed and ocean floor, and the subsoil
> thereof, beyond the limits of national jurisdiction (here-
> inafter referred to as the area), as well as the resources
> of the area, are the common heritage of mankind.

25/ G.A. Res. 2574 D (XXIV), 24 UN GAOR, Supp. 30 at 11, U.N. Doc. A/7630 (1969).

"2. The area shall not be subject to appropriation by any means by States or persons, natural or juridical, and no State shall claim or exercise sovereignty or sovereign rights over any part thereof.

"3. No State or person, natural or juridical, shall claim, exercise or acquire rights with respect to the area or its resources incompatible with the international regime to be established and the principles of this Declaration.

"4. All activities regarding the exploration and exploitation of the resources of the area and other related activities shall be governed by the international regime to be established. . . . "

This Declaration was adopted by a vote of 108 to 0, with 14 absentions. The United States voted for it. While it is possible to parse this language in such a way as to avoid the outright prohibition of interim mining uttered in the 1969 resolution, realism requires it to be put in the same hostile category.

But State Department representatives have consistently told Congress that these particular resolutions do not have the force of law, and are merely advisory. [26]

The International Court of Justice had this to say about the U.N. resolutions generated in preparation for the Third Law of the Sea Conference:

"The Court is also aware of present endeavours, pursued under the auspices of the United Nations, to achieve in a third Conference on the Law of the Sea the further codification and progressive development of this branch of the law, as it is of various proposals and preparatory documents produced in this framework, which must be regarded as manifestations of the views and opinions of individual States

---

26/ Re the 1969 resolution:

"The United States considers the recommendation contained in the Moratorium Resolution an important statement to be given weight in the determination of United States policy. The United States is not, however, obligated to implement the (Footnote continued on following page).

36

and as vehicles of their aspirations, rather than as expressing principles of existing law. "27/

(Footnote continued from preceding page)

26/ the recommendations and has made clear its opposition to
the concept." Letter of January 16, 1970, from John R.
Stevenson, Legal Adviser, Department of State, to Lee
Metcalf, U.S. Senate, reproduced in Hearings before the
Senate Special Subcommittee on the Outer Continental Shelf,
91st Cong., 1st and 2d Sess., 210 (1970).

Re the 1970 resolution:

"Some states have suggested that it is possible to
interpret the 'Declaration of Principles' (General Assembly
Resolution 2749 of December 17, 1970) as legally prohibit
ing the exploitation of the deep seabed until the new international regime and machinery for that exploitation comes
into effect. These states derive this interpretation from
their understanding of the common heritage of mankind concept. The United States, however, has consistently maintained that its interpretation of the 'Declaration of Principles'
does not permit the derivation of a 'moratorium effect' from
this resolution." Hon. John Norton Moore, Hearings before
the Senate Subcommittee on Minerals, Materials and Fuels,
93d Cong., 2d Sess., 994 (1974).

27/ Fisheries Jurisdiction Case (United Kingdom v. Iceland), /1974/ I.C. J.
Rep. 3, 23-24; Fisheries Jurisdiction Case (Federal Republic of Germany
v. Iceland), /1974/ I.C.J. Rep. 175, 192.

Judge Lauterpacht had said much the same thing, in another connection, in 1955:

"Although decisions of the General Assembly are
endowed with full legal effect in some spheres of the activity
of the United Nations and with limited legal effect in other
spheres, it may be said, by way of a broad generalisation,
that they are not legally binding upon the Members of the
United Nations. . . . /I/n general, they are in the nature of
recommendations and it is in the nature of recommendations
that, although on proper occasions they provide a legal
authorization for Members determined to act upon them
individually or collectively, they do not create a legal obligation to comply with them." Advisory Opinion on Voting Procedure /1955/ 1 I.C.J. 67.

37 -

So much for the Assembly resolutions. We should apparently regard
the unfortunate vote of the American representative for the 1970 resolution
as being due to a bad telephone connection with Washington.

Second, what provisions regarding deep sea mining can we expect to
come out of the Law of the Sea Conference when it reconvenes in 1976?

Four groups of signals have appeared.

(1) At the Caracas session of the Conference, in 1974, the Group of
77 (now 105) countries of the Third and Fourth World produced a set of "Basic
Conditions," which, keyed to the creation of an international authority which
would have jurisdiction in the seabed area seaward of the areas of national
jurisdiction, said, among other things:[28]

> "1. The area and its resources being the common
> heritage of mankind, the title to the Area and its resources
> and all other rights in the resources are vested in the Authority
> on behalf of mankind as a whole. These resources are not
> subject to alienation.

> "2. Title to the minerals and all other products derived
> from the resources shall not pass from the Authority except in
> accordance with the rules and regulations laid down by the
> Authority and the terms and conditions of the relevant contracts,
> joint ventures or any other such form of association entered
> into by it.

> * * * * *

> "4. All contracts, joint ventures or any other such form
> of association entered into by the Authority relating to the explora-
> tion of the Area and the exploitation of its resources and other
> related activities shall ensure the direct and effective control of
> the Authority at all times, through appropriate institutional
> arrangements.

---

[28] "First Committee: Text prepared by the Group of 77 and circulated in
accordance with the decision taken by the Committee at its informal meeting
on 16 August 1974": A/CONF.62/C.1/L. (16 August 1974).

368

* * * * *

"9. The Authority may, if it considers it appropriate, enter into a joint venture or any other such form of association with any person, natural or juridical, to undertake one or more stages of operations, provided, however, that the Authority shall have financial control through majority share and administrative control in such joint venture or other form of association.

"10. The Authority shall ensure security of tenure to a contractor within the terms of the contract provided he does not violate the provisions of the Convention and the rules and regulations laid down by the Authority.

"11. In case of a radical change in circumstances or 'force majeure', the Authority may take appropriate measures, including revision, suspension or termination of the contract.

"12. Any person, natural or juridical, entering into a contract, joint venture or any other such form of association with the Authority may be required to provide the funds, materials, equipment, skill and know-how necessary for the conduct of operations at any stage or stages, and to deposit a guarantee.

"13. Any responsibility, liability or risk arising out of the conduct of operations shall lie only with the person, natural or juridical, entering into a contract with the Authority.

* * * * *

"16. The Authority shall have the right to take at any time the necessary measures in order to apply the provisions contained in this Convention, particularly those relating to regulation of production.

"17. The applicable law shall be solely the provisions of this Convention, the rules and regulations laid down by the Authority, and the terms and conditions of the relevant contracts, joint ventures and any other such form of association entered into by the Authority."

The theme of these "Basic Conditions" has been reiterated in numerous forums. For example:

Programme of Action on the Establishment of a New International

Order.[29] This resolution of the Assembly commends the OPEC nations for

their success in controlling oil prices, and calls upon other developing nations

to form producer cartels for other natural resources. The program "invites"

the industrialized nations to make financial contributions to the developing

nations, to cancel or renegotiate existing debts of the developing nations, and

to defer payments by the developing nations for imports of certain commodities

and goods.

Charter of Economic Rights and Duties of States. [30] This charter

promulgated by the Assembly, declares among other things the right of

developing nations to form producer cartels, and the duty of industrialized

nations not to interfere with such cartels. It also declares the right to

nationalize foreign investment and to determine the compensation therefor

by domestic law rather than by international law. It was adopted by a vote

of 120 to 6, the six being the United States, Belgium, Denmark, West Ger-

many, Luxembourg, and the United Kingdom.

The Conference of Developing Countries on Raw Materials.[31] The

documents from this conference expand the theme of producer cartels. For

example, the Action Program declares that:

> "[C]ooperation among developing countries in the field
> of raw materials and other primary commodities should
> aim to achieve the following main objectives:
> (a) to strengthen the negotiating position of the developing
> countries in relation to the developed countries;
> (b) to secure for the developing countries control over their

---

29/ A/RES/3202 (S-VI) (May 1, 1974).
30/ A/RES/3281 (XXIX) (January 15, 1975).
31/ TD/B/C.1/L.45 (February 17, 1975).

natural resources;
(c) to expand the markets for, and increase the returns
from the exports of commodities produced by developing
countries. . . ."

The conference condemned "the elements of economic pressure and

coercion such as those contained in the United States' Trade Bill, aimed at

impeding action by the raw material producing developing countries," and

denounced these elements as "a violation of numerous international regula-

tions and especially of Articles 2 and 5 of the Charter of Economic Rights and

Duties of States. . . ." 32/

The United Nations Industrial Development Organization Lima Declara-

tion 33/ provides more of the same. This document declares, inter alia:

"That every State has the inalienable right to exercise
freely its sovereignty and permanent control over its natural
resources, both terrestrial and marine, and over all economic
activity for the exploitation of these resoures in the manner
appropriate to its circumstances, including nationalization in
accordance with its laws as an expression of this right, and that
no State shall be subjected to any forms of economic, political
or other coercion which impedes the full and free exercise of
that inalienable right;

"That special attention should be given to the least
developed countries, which should enjoy a net transfer of resources from the developed countries in the form of technical
and financial resources as well as capital goods, to enable the
least developed countries in conformity with the policies and
plans for development, to accelerate their industrialization;

"That the unrestricted play of market forces is not the
most suitable means of promoting industrialization on a world
scale nor of achieving effective international co-operation in
the field of industry and that the activities of transnational corporations should be subject to regulation and supervision

---

32/ Resolution 1.
33/ ID/B/155/Add. 1 (April 14, 1975).

ın order to ensure that these activities are compatible with
the development plans and policıes of the host countries,
taking into account relevant international codes of conduct
and other instruments;

"That it is urgently necessary that the developing
countries change theır tradıtıonal method of negotıatıon wıth
the developed countries. To bring this about, they must
undertake joint action in order to strengthen their negotıat
ıng position vıs-a-vıs the developed countries. For thıs purpose, the developıng countries must consider all possible
means of strengthenıng the actıon of producers' assocıations
already established, encourage the creatıon of other assocıatıons for the prıncıpal commodities exported by them, and
establish a mechanism for consultation and co-operatıon
among the various producers' assocıatıons for the purpose
of the co-ordination of theır actıvities and for their mutual
support, ın particular as a precaution against any economic
or other form of aggression;

"That developing countries should use effectıve means
of strengthening their bargaınıng power individually and
collectively to obtain favourable terms for the acquisition of
technology, expertise, licenses and equipment, fair and
remunerative prices for their prımary commodities and
improved and substantially liberalızed access to the developed
countries for theır manufacturers."

So the "Basıc Conditions" are merely the outer layer of the onion.

If these "Basıc Conditions," thus annotated, become the law, there

would be no deep sea mınıng problem because there would be no mining there.

(2) The second signal: At the close of the Geneva sessıon of the

Law of the Sea Conference ın 1975, an "Informal Single Negotiating Test"[34]/

---

[34]/ A/CONF.62/WP.8. The "Single Negotiatıng Text" can be found in Hearings before the Subcommittee on Minerals, Materials and Fuels of the Committee on Interior and Insular Affaırs, United States Senate, Part 3, June 4,
1975, in Appendix III, pp. 1269-1395. The portion reported by the Chairman
of the Fırst Committee commences at p. 1279; the Second Committee at p.
1320; the Third Committee at p. 1371.

- 42

was published. While it purports to commit no one, it is likely to acquire a very significant status when the Conference reconvenes in 1976. It sets the structure of future negotiations. Changes can be made by amendment, but each amendment will require a vote.

On our problem, the Single Negotiating Text proposes:

"Article 4

"1. No State shall claim or exercise sovereignty or sovereign rights over any part of the Area or its resources, nor shall any State or person, natural or juridical, appropriate any part thereof. No such claim or exercise of sovereignty or sovereign rights, nor such appropriation shall be recognized.

"2. States or persons, natural or juridical, shall claim, acquire or exercise rights with respect to the minerals in their raw or processed form derived from the Area only in accordance with the provisions of this Convention. Otherwise, no such claim, acquisition or exercise of rights shall be recognized

* * * * *

"Article 21

"1. The Authority is the organisation through which States Parties shall administer the Area, manage its resources and control the activities of the area in accordance with the provisions of this Convention.

"2. The Authority is based on the principle of the sovereign equality of all of its Members.

"3. All Members, in order to ensure to all of them the rights and benefits resulting from membership, shall fulfil in good faith the obligations assumed by them in accordance with this Convention.

"Article 22

"1. Activities in the Area shall be conducted directly by the Authority.

"2. The Authority may, if it considers it appropriate, and within the limits it may determine, carry out activities in the Area or any stage thereof through States Parties to this Convention, or State enterprises, or persons natural or juridical which possess the nationality of such States or are effectively controlled by them or their nationals, or any group of the foregoing, by entering into service contracts, or joint ventures or any other such form of association which ensures this direct and effective control at all times over such activities.

"3. Notwithstanding the provisions of paragraphs (1) and (2) of this article and in order to promote earliest possible commencement of activities in the area, the Authority, through the Council shall:

(i) identify as early as practicable after coming into force of this convention ten economically viable mining sites in the Area for exploration and exploitation of no more than. . (size, etc.);

(ii) enter into joint ventures in respect of these sites with States Parties to this Convention or State-enterprises or persons natural and juridical which possess the nationality of such States or are effectively controlled by them or their nationals or any group of the foregoing. Such joint ventures shall be subject to the conditions of exploration and exploitation established by and under this Convention and shall always ensure the direct and effective control of the Authority at all times.

"4. In entering into such joint ventures as provided for in para. 3 (ii) of this article, the Authority may decide on the basis of available data to reserve certain portions of the mining sites for its own further exploitation.

"Article 23

"1. In the exercise of its functions the Authority shall take measures pursuant to this Convention to promote and encourage activities in the Area and to secure the maximum financial and other benefit from them.

"2. The Authority shall avoid discrimination in the
granting of opportunities for such activities and shall, in
the implementation of its powers, ensure that all rights
granted pursuant to this Convention are fully safeguarded.
Special consideration by the Authority under this Convention for the interests and needs of the developing countries,
and particularly the land-locked among them, shall not be
deemed to be discrimination.

"3. The Authority shall ensure the equitable sharing
by States in the benefits derived from activities in the Area,
taking into particular consideration the interests and needs
of the developing countries whether coastal or land-locked. "

While this language is not as full of spikes as that of the "Basic Condi-

tions" of the Group of 77, it is quite unacceptable as a basis for government

of the deep seabed. The key is the full control vested in an international

authority, with directions to conduct operations directly (even though it may,

in its discretion, enter into joint venture arrangements which it will control),

and in any event to operate under a mandate to maximize financial benefits

and avoid or minimize the effects of production of deep seabed minerals on

the revenues of mineral-producing developing countries.

(3) The third signal: The Group of 77 rejected this victory for their

etatist views as not good enough.

The American negotiator, in the First Committee, Mr. Leigh Ratiner,

reported to the Senate Committee on Interior and Insular Affairs:[35]

---

[35] Hearings before the Senate Subcommittee on Minerals, Materials and
Fuels, 94th Cong., 1st Sess. 1182 (1975).

"Mr. RATINER. . . But I must tell you what some of the areas
are in which there was no progress and also no sign of progress
in the future.

"First, Mr. Chairman, the developing countries as a group
presently hold intransigent views on the question of whether the
international seabed authority should be empowered to exploit
the whole of the area to the exclusion if the authority are desirous of states and private companies, they have said the authority
must have this power and we have said it may not have this power.

"Second, they hold with almost equal vigor the view that
ultimately, decisions policies on the actions of the authority must
be subordinated to all organs of the authority must be subordinate
to a one-nation one-vote assembly. We do not agree to this
approach. We cannot agree to it in the interest of preserving the
objectives of the United States in the deep seabed.

"Third, Mr. Chairman, they insist, and there is no sign of
flexibility that even if the authority chooses to exploit the area
through a contractual mode, that is, in cooperation with private
companies and sovereign states, it must be almost entirely
free to dictate the terms and conditions of contract particularly
those relating to the transfer of technology and profits. They
feel to insure a strong bargaining position in such contractual
negotiations, the authority must have the right to keep the seabed area closed until the authority decides to open it.

"Mr. Chairman, they believe the foregoing three points and
again, I am starting my opinion of what the developing countries
believe as a group--that is 105 countries. They believe the three
points I just made are the absolute minimum that they must achieve
in committee I in order to insure their control over the raw materials
of the seabed. This is a foreign policy objective of many, if not
all developing countries in the world today. This policy, as
Ambassador Stevenson has pointed out, is pursued actively in every
international form to which they have access. And as you see,
characterized as the creation of a new economic order. " (Trans-
cription errors are as in printed testimony.)

(4) The fourth signal: Secretary Kissinger, in a speech to the Ameri-

can Bar Association August 11, 1975, said this about American objectives in

the treaty negotiations which will resume in 1976:

46

"The United Nations has declared the deep seabeds
to be the 'common heritage of mankind.' But this only
states the problem. How will the world community manage the clash of national and regional interests or the
inequality of technological capability? Will we reconcile
unbridled competition with the imperative of political
order?

"The United States has nothing to fear from competition. Our technology is the most advanced, and our
Navy is adequate to protect our interests. Ultimately,
unless basic rules regulate exploitation, rivalry will
lead to tests of power. A race to carve out exclusive
domains of exploitation on the deep seabeds, even without claims of sovereignty, will menace freedom of navigation and invite a competition like that of the colonial powers
in Africa and Asia in the last century.

"This is not the kind of world we want to see. Law has
an opportunity to civilize us in the early stages of a new
competitive activity.

"We believe that the Law of the Sea Treaty must preserve the right of access presently enjoyed by states and
their citizens under international law. Restrictions on
free access will retard the development of seabed resources. Nor is it feasible, as some developing countries
have proposed, to reserve to a new international seabed
organization the sole right to exploit the seabeds.

* * * * *

"The United States has devoted much thought and consideration to this issue. We offer the following proposals:

"--An international organization should be created to
set rules for deep seabed mining.

"--This international organization must preserve the
rights of all countries, and their citizens, directly to
exploit deep seabed resources.

"--It should also insure fair adjudication of conflicting interests and security of investment.

"--Countries and their enterprises mining deep seabed resources should pay an agreed portion of their
revenues to the international organization, to be used
for the benefit of developing countries.

"--The management of the organization and its
voting procedures must reflect and balance the interests
of the participating states. The organization should
not have the power to control prices or production rates.

" If these essential U.S. interests are guaranteed, we can agree that this organization will also have the right to conduct mining operations on behalf of the international community primarily for the benefit of developing countries.
"--The new organization should serve as a vehicle for cooperation between the technologically advanced and the developing countries. The United States is prepared to explore ways of sharing deep seabed technology with other nations.
"--A balanced commission of consumers, seabed producers and land-based producers could monitor the possible adverse effects of deep seabed mining on the economies of those developing countries which are substantially dependent on the export of minerals also produced from the deep seabeds. "

One can compare this statement of objectives with those uttered by the Group of 77, and make his own book on the outcome. My own view is that if a treaty is signed on the subject of deep sea mining that is acceptable to the less developed countries which muster 105 of 140 votes, it will be a treaty that the United States should not accept. The only hope for an agreement that would deserve American signature and ratification, and it is a slender one, is that this conference, like that in 1958, will separate out the various subjects into separate conventions, probably with different signatory States and different lists of ratifying countries. The result would be what Dean Rusk has called a "family of treaties, " with differing lists of adherents. This technique would enable agreements to be reached on the more sensible provisions of this treaty, dealing with the territorial sea, passage through straits and archipelagos, the 200-mile economic zone, etc. , while sinking without a trace the International Seabed Resource Authority, the "Floating Chinese Pagoda, " manned by a crew hostile to American interests. There are other and better ways of dealing internationally with deep sea mining than by the creation of this sea monster,

endowed with a perpetual life. We will come to these in a moment.

Looking back over this melancholy record, the pointed remarks of

Ambassador Daniel P. Moynihan come to mind. In his article, "The United

States in Opposition, " in 59 Commentary No. 3, p. 31, March 1975, he reviewed

the unhappy experience of the United States in negotiating with the Third World

in the United Nations. Among other things, he said:

Quoting a Chinese statement in 1974 (p. 35):

"These days, the United Nations often takes on the
appearance of an international court with the Third World
pressing the charges and conducting the trial. "

He goes on:

"Clearly at some level--we all but started the United
Nations--there has been a massive failure of American diplomacy "

He speaks (p. 35) of the

" blind acquiescense and even agreement of the
United States which kept endorsing principles for whose
logical outcome it was wholly unprepared and with which it
could never actually go along. "

This is his crusher, which would be a fitting epitaph for the American

Law of the Sea negotiating policy:

"In Washington, three decades of habit and incentive have created patterns of appeasement so profound as
to seem wholly normal. Delegations to international conferences return from devastating defeats proclaiming
victory. In truth, these have never been thought especially
important. Taking seriously a Third World speech about,
say, the right of commodity producers to market their
products in concert and to raise their prices in the process,
would have been the mark of the quixotic or the failed. "

49

Perhaps it is time to take Ambassador Moynihan s advice (p. 41):

"What then does the United States do?

"The United States goes into opposition. " (His emphasis.

50

7. "Interim Arrangements"

In conclusion, I come now to the "interim arrangements" that might permit ocean mining to go ahead pending American ratification of a treaty. It is likely to be a rather long interim, in my opinion, because no treaty is in the offing that American public opinion would accept. But the euphemism of "interim arrangements" is a politer term than calling them alternatives to a treaty. By some name, some means must be found to enable American technology to make seabed minerals available to the world's consumers. What are the possibilities?

Secretary Kissinger, in his August 11, 1975, speech to the American Bar Association, after outlining American objectives in the oncoming resumption of treaty negotiations, had this to say about encouragement of "current investments" in deep seabed mining:

> "The United States will continue to make determined efforts to bring about final progress when the Law of the Sea Conference reconvenes in New York next year. But we must be clear on one point: The United States cannot indefinitely sacrifice its own interest in developing an assured supply of critical resources to an indefinitely prolonged negotiation. We prefer a generally acceptable international agreement that provides a stable legal environment before deep seabed mining actually begins. The responsibility for achieving an agreement before actual exploitation begins is shared by all nations. We cannot defer our own deep seabed mining for too much longer. In this spirit, we and other potential seabed producers can consider appropriate steps to protect current investment and to insure that this investment is also protected in the treaty."

How is this to be done?

One alternative to a treaty is domestic legislation controlling American nationals in their deep seabed mining operations, and offering to other nations reciprocal recognition of mining claims which their nationals may disclose in a uniform system of registration. It is a familiar theme. The Administration's spokesmen have promised the congressional committees that a position would be stated in the near future.

Senator Metcalf has called a meeting of his subcommittee of the Interior and Insular Affairs Committee October 29 to hear the Administration position. It can be assumed to be unchanged: do nothing until after the next session of the Law of the Sea Conference.

To this Administration position, as one concerned citizen, I respectfully but emphatically dissent. It has become clear that the existing regime of freedom of the seas promises more seabed minerals for American defense and for the American consumer than any treaty now on the drawing boards could possibly do. The American people have everything to lose and nothing to gain by the creation of a new supergovernment to have control in any degree whatever of our access to the minerals of the seabed, now freely available to us under existing law. American foreign policy suffered a self-inflicted wound by taking the initiative, in 1970, in launching a proposed treaty which would create the Seabed Resource Authority--a seagoing government comprising a legislature, an executive, a judiciary, a secretariat, and five powerful commissions. The irrevocable creation of such a new force, dominated by nations hostile to

American interests, is a contingency to be avoided at all costs, but the incredible fact is that the State Department itself proposed the launching of this
Seabed Resource Authority, and has been poised impatiently with the champagne
bottle overhead for five years now, eager to christen it. Put that bottle down.
Stop telling Congress to come back manana. Treat Congress as kindly as you
do the Group of 77.

Another alternative is possible action by the Executive. Several constructive courses are open.

One would be a policy statement by the President, to put more iron in
the blood of our negotiators before the 1976 session of the Law of the Sea Conference begins.

Another would be a Presidential Proclamation to regulate activities of
American nationals, in lieu of legislation, until a satisfactory (I emphasize
satisfactory) treaty is ratified by the United States.

The key feature of domestic action, whether in the legislative or executive branch, ought to be the avoidance of creation of a new international government (the precise reverse of present policy), the preservation of the freedom
of the seas, limitations on size and duration of claims, requirements of diligence in production, prohibition of price-fixing and production controls, and
reciprocal undertaking by the maritime powers to respect the operations of
one another's nationals. If Congress should decide to dedicate to some international fund a portion of the federal tax revenues derived from deep seabed

mining, so be it. But these contributions ought not to be added to the tax burden on this high risk business, which must compete with land-based mines paying no such international tax.

The time has come, in my personal opinion, for the President to speak out and for the Congress to act for the protection of American interests in marine minerals. Early passage by Congress of deep sea mineral legislation would be a plain signal to all negotiators--American and foreign--as to the kind of treaty on this subject that the Senate is prepared to ratify. It would be an equally plain signal that negotiation of a treaty which does not protect American resource interests to the extent that Congress would protect them is a waste of everybody's time, because American public opinion would not accept it and the Senate would not give consent to its ratification.

Mr. MURPHY. Mr. Mosher?

Mr. MOSHER. Well, I agree with you, Mr. Chairman. It is a very impressive statement.

Mr. MURPHY. And somewhat provocative.

Mr. MOSHER. As it should be. We need some stimulation.

Mr. Ely, in the statement you have supported very strongly H.R. 11879.

Now, as you probably know, there are other pieces of legislation before us, H.R. 1270, introduced by the gentleman from Virginia.

Are you familiar with that bill?

Mr. ELY. Yes, Mr. Mosher, and I should hasten to say this is an inadvertence on my part.

I would endorse all three bills before you. I was invited to testify on only one.

I do not intend any criticism of the other bills at all.

Mr. MOSHER. Do you want to discuss any personal preferences as to whether the responsibilities for this function, if the Congress passed any of this legislation, whether the administration of it should be in the Commerce Department or the Interior Department?

Mr. ELY. Well, Mr. Mosher, let me evade your question in two steps.

One: The correction of the errors of the Secretary of the Interior has been a small, but steady source of income to me for 40 years. I should be very much distressed if anything happened to him.

I am assured the Secretary of Commerce would be equally prolific, and I should not worry.

Mr. MOSHER. In other words, you do not express any preference? You have no advice for us?

Mr. ELY. My second escape is that in these 40 years, whenever I have been pursued in this Washington jungle, by governmental dinosaurs, I tried to find another dinosaur to sic on him, and I should not like to get squashed between these two by taking sides.

I have no doubt the one that comes out on top is going to eat me.

Mr. MOSHER. Mr. Chairman, did we formally move to put in the record the full statement of Mr. Ely?

If we did not, I would so move.

Mr. MURPHY. Without objection, the complete statement of Mr. Ely will be printed in the record, as well as the enclosures, but not that last document which you waved, which I think was the "Single Negotiating Text," there have been a number of those floating around, official and unofficial, and rather than encumber the record with something that flies on the shuttle in February, we will wait until we have something more substantive to put into the record to represent just what is the "Negotiating Text."

[The statement referred to follows:]

STATEMENT OF NORTHCUTT ELY

1. INTRODUCTION

I was honored by the Committee's invitation to discuss H.R. 11879, "a bill to promote the orderly development of hard mineral resources of the deep seabed, pending adoption of an international regime relating thereto."

The views that I will express are my own, developed in the course of several years in which I have served as a member or chairman of various professional committees which have written reports on the law of the sea, and in the preparation of opinions for clients. I am currently counsel, in international law matters, to Deepsea Ventures, Inc., one of the companies which is actively preparing to mine the minerals of the deep seabed. Mr. John E. Flipse, president and chairman of the executive committee, will appear at a later time, and will present the views of that company.

I strongly favor the enactment of this bill. Later on, if the Committee wishes, I may have some amendments to suggest, but they will be in accord with the bill's objectives, which are excellent.

2. THE RESOURCE AND ITS IMPORTANCE TO THE AMERICAN CONSUMER

Manganese nodules are small, potato-shaped concretions of metal oxides. They occur at water depths of 6,500 feet or more, where they lie on the surface of the seabed in vast deposits. Nodules of commercial interest generally occur at depths of 15,000 to 20,000 feet.

Nodules vary greatly in size and composition. A typical nodule may contain 30 or more minerals. Four of these minerals are presently of major commercial importance: maganese, nickel, cobalt, and copper.

All four of these minerals are of vital importance to the American consumer. Maganese, nickel, and cobalt are used primarily to make steel. Copper is a basic industrial metal. Like petroleum, these four minerals are basic ingredients of the United States economy. And, like petroleum, these minerals are in alarmingly short supply in the United States. At the present time, the United States is dependent on foreign sources for approximately 100 percent of its maganese, 88 percent of nickel, 20 percent of its copper, and 100 percent of its cobalt requirements. Moreover, the sources of these supplies are, in general, insecure. Maganese is imported primarily from Gabon, Brazil, Zaire, France, India and South Africa; cobalt from Zaire and Belgium; nickel from Canada; and copper from Chile, Peru, and Canada. Of these nations, only Canada, Belgium, and France would appear to qualify as "secure" sources; however, Canada has proven an unreliable source of oil and natural gas. And the cobalt which is imported from Belgium is mined in Zaire. Our current supplies of these four vital minerals are thus vulnerable to both price-fixing and curtailment. And recent actions by the mineral-exporting nations—both within and without the United Nations—evidence an ominous determination on the part of these nations to follow the OPEC example. For example, Article 5 of the "Charter of Economic Rights and Duties of States," adopted by the United Nations General Assembly at its 29th session, declares:

"All States have the right to associate in organizations of primary commodity producers in order to develop their national economies, to achieve stable financing for their development and, in pursuance of their aims, to assist in the promotion of sustained growth of the world economy, in particular accelerating the development of developing countries. Correspondingly all States have the duty to respect that right by refraining from applying economic and political measures that would limit it."

The resolution asserts both a positive right to form commodity cartels, and a correlative duty not to resist the objectives of such cartels. Other provisions of the resolution make clear that the right is intended to be available only to developing countries, while the duty is intended to bind the developed nations. Of the nine countries which presently supply more than 90 percent of U.S. imports of manganese, nickel, cobalt, and copper, not one joined with the United States to vote against this resolution.

Arguments have been made to the effect that the mineral-exporting nations will not be able to operate effectively as cartels. It is argued that the mineral-exporting nations are so diverse economically, politically, and culturally that agreement among them is unlikely. It is argued that the mineral-exploring nations do not have the capital surplus required to impose production cutbacks. Also, it is argued that the mineral-importing nations can deter cartels by establishing stockpiles. Six years ago, these same arguments were being made to support the proposition that OPEC would never be an effective petroleum cartel.

Another argument—one that was not made in connection with OPEC—is that the mineral-importing nations may substitute one mineral for another. This is true for some minerals, provided the substitute is not also controlled by a cartel. But the substitution argument is not convincing when applied to maganese, nickel, and cobalt. There are no substitutes for manganese or nickel in their primary uses; nickel and cobalt are the only satisfactory substitutes for each other.

Existing metal producer cartels include the Intergovernmental Committee of Copper Exporting Countries (Cipec), the Iron Ore Exporter's Association, the International Bauxite Association, the International Tin Council, the International Cadmium Institute (Incadin), the International Association of Mercury Producers, the International Phosphate Rock Export Association, and the Primary Tungsten Association. Other cartels are in the process of being formed. Given time, these cartels can be expected to realize their ambitions of maximizing revenues from their mineral resources at the expense of consumers in industrialized nations, just as OPEC has.

3. AN ALTERNATIVE TO DEPENDENCE ON FOREIGN SUPPLIES : DEEP SEA MINING UNDER EXISTING INTERNATIONAL LAW

As already mentioned, manganese nodules of commercial interest generally occur at water depths of 15,000 to 20,000 feet. American companies, operating at their own risk, have developed and proved the techniques to recover and refine them. Such depths are well beyond the limit of national seabed jurisdiction as defined by existing international law. Therefore, the numerous deposits of manganese nodules which occur throughout the world's oceans are not subject to the jurisdiction of any state. They are available to all countries and their nationals, in the exercise of the freedom of the seas. Under existing international law, however, exclusive rights to nodules (not to the seabed on which they lie) may be acquired by discovery of a deposit accompanied by public notice, and followed by reduction to possession with reasonable diligence.

This notion is not new to international law. Indeed, numerous nations have in the past acquired exclusive rights to resources lying on the seabed in areas beyond the limits of national jurisdiction by discovery and occupation, in the sense of continuing exploitation. Prior to 1945, the limits of national seabed jurisdiction coincided with the limits of the territorial sea. The so-called "doctrine of the continental shelf," ascribing to the coastal state exclusive sovereign rights in the seabed resources of the submarine areas adjacent to its coasts. seaward of the territorial sea, was unknown in international law. Since national seabed jurisdiction stopped with the territorial sea prior to emergence of the continental shelf doctrine, the continental shelf and the deep seabed were at that time legally identical; both were seabed areas beyond national jurisdiction. Yet, during the long period of time that this state of affairs existed, a number of nations acquired exclusive rights to exploit, and regulate the exploitation of. seabel resources beyond territorial waters, and, hence, beyond what at the time was the limit of national jurisdiction. These rights received universal acquiescence. The resources concerned included coral, pearl, oyster, chank, and sponge fisheries.

Between 1945 and 1950, the doctrine of the continental shelf developed and extended national jurisdiction to the resources of the continental shelf, without affecting the status of the overlying waters as high seas. This new concept encompassed certain areas in which coastal states had previously exercised control over seabed resources independently of any notion of sovereignty, and solely in the exercise of the right of discovery and use as one of the freedoms of the high seas. The previous state practice thus remains as evidence of the law applicable to what remains of the seabed beyond national jurisdiction, namely, the deep seabed. This practice is part of the freedom of the high seas doctrine under which every state has several (not joint) rights to navigate on and exploit the resources of the high seas and its seabed, subject to the equal rights of all other states.

The continental shelf doctrine expanded the limits of exclusive coastal state seabed resource jurisdiction, but did not alter or diminish in the least the pre-existing rights of all states and their nationals to take and use the seabed minerals beyond the limits of national jurisdiction, whatever those limits might be.

The 1958 Geneva Convention on the High Seas. which condified existing customary law, is consistent with the proposition that exclusive rights may be acquired to resources in the deep seabed. It does not expressly mention deep sea mining, but it did not need to. Article 2 lists as the freedoms of the high seas freedom of navigation, freedom of fishing, freedom to lay submarine cables and pipelines, freedom to fly over high seas, and other freedoms "which are recognized by the general principles of international law." That the freedom to exploit resources in seabed areas beyond national jurisdiction is included in the last category is indicated by the travaux prepartoires of the Convention. The 1955 Report of the International Law Commission, the body which drafted the Convention, states:

"The list of freedoms of the high seas contained in this article [i.e., Article 2] is not restrictive; the Commission has merely specified four of the main freedoms. It is aware that there are other freedoms, such as the freedom to explore or exploit the subsoil of the high seas . . ."

And the Commission's 1956 Report states:

"The Commission has not made specific mention of the freedom to explore or exploit the subsoil of the high seas. It considered that apart from the case of the exploitation or exploration of the soil or subsoil of a continental shelf—a case dealt with separately . . . [in the Convention as the Continental Shelf]— such exploitation has not yet assumed sufficient practical importance to justify special regulation."

The fact that the Convention is a codification of existing customary law, coupled with the fact that customary law for centuries recognized exclusive possessory rights in seabed areas beyond national jurisdiction, indicates that deep sea mining is a freedom protected by the 1958 Convention on the High Seas.

Nor has this freedom been diminished in any way by recent events in the United Nations or the Law of the Sea negotiations. It is true that the General Assembly passed a "Moratorium Resolution" in 1969 which purports to prohibit exploitation of the deep seabed, and a "Declaration of Principles" in 1970 which declares that the resources of the deep seabed are "the common heritage of mankind" and that no nation or person may acquire rights to these resources which are incompatible with "the international regime to be established." However, these resolutions have no binding effect on the United States or any other member of the General Assembly. The powers of the General Assembly are set forth in Articles 10 through 17 of the United Nations Charter. These powers do not include the legislative authority to enact rules of international law. A proposal to give the General Assembly such authority was expressly rejected at the San Francisco Conference of 1945. Hence, resolutions of the General Assembly are recommendatory, not obligatory.

This fact has been recognized in opinions of the International Court of Justice and in the writings of publicists. Indeed, the International Court of Justice, in its recent decision in the Fisheries Jurisdiction Cases, declared that the various proposals and preparatory documents produced in anticipation of the Third United Nations Conference on the Law of the Sea do not constitute expressions of existing international law. The State Department's position is in accord with this view. In his statement at the closing plenary session of the 30th United Nations General Assembly, U.S. Representative Daniel P. Moynihan stated:

"Both Assemblies are now concluded, and the time is at hand to ask whether anything can be learned from them. For we do not want them forgotten. To the contrary, there are events that occurred in the 30th Assembly which the United States will never forget. . . .

"The first lesson is the most important, which is that the General Assembly has been trying to pretend that it is a parliament, which it is not. It is a conference made up of representatives sent by sovereign governments which have agreed to *listen* to its recommendations—recommendations which are, however, in no way binding."

With respect to the 1969 Moratorium Resolution and the 1970 Declaration of Principles specifically, U.S. Representatives to the Law of the Sea negotiations have asserted that neither resolution is binding on the United States.

Unless and until a treaty that alters existing customary law becomes binding on the United States, this Nation and its nationals are free to exploit manganese nodules in the deep seabed.

Thus, under existing international law, the United States has an alternative source of supplies of manganese, nickel, cobalt, and copper. This source is not within the territorial jurisdiction of the United States, but neither is it within the territorial jurisdiction of any other country. All that the United States or its nationals—or any other country or its nationals—need do to acquire rights to this alternative source is to begin diligent efforts to exploit it. The U.S. Department of the Interior has estimated that by 1990 the United States can totally eliminate all imports of nickel, copper, and cobalt, and can reduce imports of manganese to 23 percent of consumption, *provided* that the American mining industry proceeds with its deep sea mining operations now.

But several years of lead time—anywhere from five to fifteen—are required for the successive stages of detailed mapping and testing of a selected site, design and construction of equipment to mine that specific site, and to design and construct the plant on shore which will process the minerals recovered.

Thus, if production is to commence even as early as the mid-1980's, industry's decisions must be made now, in 1976.

This brings us to the need for certain decisions by the Congress.

4. THE NEED FOR UNITED STATES LEGISLATION

It may be asked, if existing international law permits deep sea mining operations, what are U.S. companies waiting for? The requisite technology, in pilot form, existed several years ago. The answer is that U.S. companies are waiting for a more precise definition of their rights and obligations under U.S. law before committing the vast sums of capital required for site-specific, commercial deep sea mining operations, and a guarantee by the United States Government that these investments will be given diplomatic protection from interference by foreign states and international agencies, and, most important, protection from impairment in consequence of an international treaty ratified by the United States. Assurances along these lines, variously worded, have been given to Congressional committees by spokesmen of the Executive department from time to time, but these are subjects on which only Congress can speak authoritatively. This bill would do that.

First, as to the desirability of legislation, quite aside from the danger posed by a potentially hostile treaty:

International law permits the acquisition of exclusive rights to manganese nodules in seabed areas beyond national jurisdiction, as we have said. But international law does not prescribe the detailed regulation of deep sea mining activities. For example, international law does not prescribe the size of the area which may be exploited, the duration of the rights acquired in the deep seabed, the work or diligence obligations that attach as conditions to such rights in order to keep those rights in force, the environmental restrictions applicable to deep sea mining operations, etc.

These matters could be dealt with in a multilateral convention, in bilateral treaties, or in domestic legislation.

Over the past six years, the efforts of U.S. negotiators at the ongoing Law of the Sea conferences to achieve a multilateral convention have been repeatedly frustrated by the developing nations. The objective of the developing nations is to control access to the resources of the deep seabed, and to determine the conditions under which the United States and other industrialized nations may exploit these resources. This objective would be accomplished by the creation of an "International Seabed Authority" to be controlled by the developing nations. There are two principal motives for this objective. First, many of the developing nations are mineral exporters, and these nations do not want competition from the deep seabed. They want to retain their present monopolies with respect to the minerals which they export. Second, those developing nations which are not mineral exporters generally want to share in the "profits" which they imagine will result from deep sea mining; these nations do not wish to (and are generally unable to) risk any capital, however. They view the Law of the Sea negotiations, and the treaty which they hope will result from these negotiations, as a means of achieving a share in the profits without risk.

The most recent session of the Law of the Sea negotiations produced "single negotiating texts" which will serve as the starting point for future negotiations. The single negotiating text for Committee I (the Committee responsible for drafting articles relating to the deep seabed) places absolute control of all deep sea mining in the "International Sea-bed Authority," an agency effectively controlled by developing nations. This agency has the authority to determine which, if any, nations may mine the deep seabed, and the conditions under which these nations must operate. The agency has the power to control production and prices of the minerals produced. The agency also has the responsibility to insure that production from the deep seabed does not adversely affect exports of land-based minerals by developing nations and the price of such exports. Under the provisions of the single negotiating text, the United States would find itself in far worse position than it now is without a treaty. For it not only would continue to be dependent on foreign sources for its strategic hard minerals, but, if it should become a party to such a treaty, it would have irrevocably conceded to a new international legislature the power now lacking in the General Assembly of the United Nations to legislate and to enforce its legislation. This body, we need scarcely add, would be dominated by the same unfriendly nations that Ambassador Moynihan has been contending with so gallantly in the United Nations. Our country's supplies would become all the more vulnerable to curtailment and price fixing. Moreover, the single negotiating text would have the United States turn over its technology to the developing nations.

It is unthinkable that the United States Senate would ratify a treaty bearing any resemblance to the Committee I single negotiating text. And, even if such a treaty were to become binding on the United States, no U.S. company could possibly operate under it. U.S. companies would, of necessity, be forced to seek participation in consortiums of nationals of states that chose not to ratify the treaty.

It is, of course, hoped that the U.S. negotiators will be able to reverse the present trend of the Committee I negotiations and achieve agreement on a treaty which protects the interests of U.S. companies and U.S. consumers. The American negotiators, however, suffer from a self-inflicted wound, which may prove fatal. I refer to the 1970 draft treaty tendered by the United States as a working paper. It proposed creation of the International Seabed Resource Authority to consist of the three branches of government: a legislature consisting of a council of 24 nations and an assembly of all signatory states; an executive Secretariat supplemented by three Commissions; and a tribunal of five to nine judges. The major policy justification for the creation of the International Seabed Resource Authority was that it would entice other coastal states to accept the so-called "narrow shelf" doctrine, under which coastal state seabed jurisdiction stopped at the 200 meter isobath. The United States sought agreement on the narrow shelf principle in 1970 because at that time it was believed that extension of coastal state jurisdiction beyond the 200 meter isobath would ultimately impinge on the freedom of the high seas. However, the narrow shelf doctrine was never accepted by other coastal states and is no longer an objective of the United States. Thus, the U.S. policy justification for the International Seabed Resource Authority has evaporated. But the United States did not withdraw its proposal, and the developing countries have eagerly seized on this American scheme, modifying it to their advantage. The Assembly, which would operate on a "one nation one vote" basis, would of course be dominated by the same states that have dedicated themselves to making life miserable for our country in the General Assembly of the United Nations. There would be one difference between the two Assemblies, a catastrophic one: Whereas, as Ambassador Moynihan has said, the General Assembly of the United Nations has no legislative powers, and only pretends to be a parliament, the seagoing Assembly now proposed would be a real parliament, issuing legislation which would be enforced by its executive and judicial arms. Whatever justification there might have been for this naive American proposal in 1970, the last five years should have taught us better. But I see no prospect that the American negotiators can, or indeed want to, extricate themselves from this trap that they have dug for themselves.

The treaty prospect is thus not encouraging. The danger is not so much that agreement will not be reached. The danger is that agreement will be reached on the terms demanded by the less developed countries, with respect to resources of the deep seabed, dressed in the customary doubletalk that masks diplomatic defeats.

Furthermore, even if a satisfactory treaty is eventually signed, it will probably take years for the treaty to enter into force and be implemented. The 1958 Geneva Convention on the Continental Shelf did not enter into force for the United States until 1964, six years after it was signed. And today, eighteen years after signature, this convention has been ratified by only 54 nations. Hence, a multilateral treaty does not appear to be a realistic, near-term solution to the problem of defining rights and obligations in the deep seabed.

Nor do bilateral treaties dealing with this problem appear to be forthcoming. The policy of the United States Government has been to achieve a multilateral treaty within the framework of the Law of the Sea negotiations. Consequently, there has been no significant effort to negotiate bilateral treaties relating to deep sea mining.

Thus the problem has come to rest in the United States Congress. To date, U.S. companies have invested some 150 million dollars in the preliminary stages of deep sea mining. These companies have mapped and studied large areas of the ocean floor, and have recovered samples from manganese nodule deposits located all over the world. Potential mining sites have been identified, and one company, Deepsea Ventures, Inc., of Gloucester, Virginia, has publicly disclosed its discovery and claimed exclusive rights under international law to a specific deposit of manganese nodules on the abyssal floor of the Pacific Ocean. Deepsea Ventures and other U.S. companies are now ready to begin development of the mine sites they have discovered. But the contemplated operations will require vast sums of capital. Current estimates of the capital cost of a deep sea mining project range from 250 to 400 million dollars. These amounts are far in excess of what U.S. mining companies can generate internally. The capital required for deep sea mining operations must be acquired with the assistance of large lending institutions. And neither the mining companies nor the lending institutions are willing to risk such large sums of capital in deep sea mining operations until three types of political problems are solved:

(1) the rights and obligations of U.S. companies under United States laws should be identified and made clear, including recognition of their exclusive rights as against other U.S. nationals;

(2) as against foreigners, U.S. investments in deep sea mining must be assured diplomatic protection, and access to an insurance fund against foreign interference;

(3) as against the possibility that the United States will ratify a treaty which subjects these investments to the control of a new international body, the deep sea mining investors must be assured, first that the United States will fully protect those investments in any such treaty, and, second, if it does not, that full compensation for the lost values will be paid. No one asks for any guarantees against failure of the technology or against market fluctuations. But protection against the political hazards, particularly those that might be self-imposed by U.S. ratification of a bad treaty, is essential and is fair.

5. H.R. 11879

The proposed bill meets these tests.

The major provisions of H.R. 11879 are these:

H.R. 11879 would license U.S. companies to explore for and exploit manganese nodules in seabed areas beyond national jurisdiction. Exploration and exploitation rights conferred by the U.S. Government under the act would be exclusive as against persons subject to the jurisdiction of the United States or a reciprocating state.

A reciprocating state is defined as one which has enacted similar legislation, and accords the same recognition to rights of U.S. nationals as this act accords to nationals of the reciprocating state. In a sense, what is contemplated is a series of bilateral arrangements with the other nations which are capable of carrying on deep sea mining, effectuated by enactment of reciprocal legislation. Once this is done, the next step will be relatively simple: conversion of these bilateral arrangements into the form of executed agreements, corresponding to this act of Congress. The important thing is that the Congress, by this legislation, stipulates the kind of arrangement that will be acceptable, and provides for unilateral accomplishment of its objectives if necessary. I may add that enactment of this legislation would be a clear signal to the U.S. negotiators in the present Law of the Sea conferences as to what Congress expects of them. In this respect, it would have a significance similar to that offered by the recent enactment of the fisheries bill.

H.R. 11879, like most of the world's mining legislation, provides for areal limitations, mandatory relinquishment, work obligations, duration of the mining right, transfer and surrender of the right, penalties, and application procedures. It also makes provision for environmental regulations and judicial review of administrative action.

Section 13 of the act is a guaranty provision. It provides that, in the event an international agreement which is inconsistent with the provisions of the act becomes binding on the United States, the United States shall compensate the licensee for losses resulting from "the differing requirements" of the treaty and the act.

Section 14 is an insurance provision. It provides that, upon payment by the licensee of an annual premium, the United States will insure the licensee "for any damages suffered through the impairment of the insured investment, or through the removal of hard minerals from the licensed block, by any other person against whom a legal remedy either does not exist or is unavailable in any legal forum to which the licensee has access."

Sections 13 and 14 go a long way toward establishing the stable investment climate required for the commitment of capital by U.S. mining companies and lending institutions. One important contingency which is not covered by these provisions—and the omission appears to be inadvertent—is the possibility that the *administration* of a future treaty may be inconsistent with the act, even though the treaty itself is not. This can be readily amended.

A second problem with H.R. 11879, also readily remedied, is that it does not expressly recognize that property rights may be acquired in manganese nodules. This omission becomes important if a U.S. company's investment is jeopardized as a result of acts by another party, and either (1) the particular injury does not give rise to compensation under the act, or (2) the compensation provided for in the act is inadequate. And recovery against a trespasser subject to judicial process would be greatly facilitated by express recognition in the act that the licensee can acquire property rights in the nodules (not the seabed or subsoil), under international law.

To meet this problem, I suggest that the bill clearly state that the issuance of a license to a national of the United States establishes that the United States has determined (1) that the issuance of the license does not conflict with any international obligations of the United States, and that operations carried on in accordance with the license with respect to the area therein described will not unreasonably interfere with other reasonable uses of the high seas; (2) that the licensee is recognized by the United States as having, as against the United States, reciprocating States, nationals of the United States and nationals of reciprocating States, the exclusive right to explore for, recover, take away, and use, the seabed mineral resources in the area described in the license, in accordance with its terms, for the period of time therein prescribed; and (3) that the licensee is entitled to diplomatic protection of the United States with respect to operations so conducted, provided that these three determinations shall have the written concurrence of the Secretary of State.

I would personally favor another addition to the bill. This would be a provision earmarking a portion of U.S. income taxes, related to operations at the mine site, in an escrow fund from which Congress can appropriate money, if it so chooses, in fulfillment of provisions of some future treaty which may dedicate revenues from deep sea mining to international purposes. The point to make clear is that deep sea mining, an extremely high risk, high cost business, cannot and should not pay higher taxes than those paid by onshore competitors. The intent of my proposal is that only U.S. income taxes would be collected from deep sea mining enterprises, and that any contribution to an international fund would be paid out of, not in addition to, U.S. taxes. The contrary notion, of double taxation, which seems to be buzzing in some foreign heads, would solve all deep sea mining problems very simply indeed. There would be no mining.

6. THE ELEMENT OF URGENCY

At hearings held before the Senate Subcommittee on Minerals, Materials, and Fuels in 1972, the president of Deepsea Ventures was asked how long it would take for commercial operations to become feasible if deep sea mining legislation were enacted. He replied:

"[B]asically it would be 2 years of developmental work followed by 3 years of actual construction. During the developmental work, the design of the mining equipment and the processing plant would go ahead; then the 3 years would be devoted to building the actual mining equipment and processing the plant, debugging it, testing it so it would function smoothly. But we feel 5 years from the go-ahead, we will have metal in the market-place."

Other companies might need longer lead times. Four years later, U.S. industry—and the U.S. consumer—is still waiting for the "go-ahead."

If deep sea mining legislation is enacted in 1976, U.S. companies will be able to make the investments in 1976 required to achieve commercial production, at the earliest, by 1981. If legislation is not enacted, the necessary investments cannot be made, and commercial production must be postponed even further into the future. The effect of this postponement on the United States is illustrated by the fact that between 1971, when deepsea mining legislation was first introduced in the United States Congress, and the present time, world prices of manganese, nickel, and cobalt have increased 130 percent, 65 percent, and 82 percent. respectively. These increases resulted in additional outflows of hundreds of millions of dollars from the United States to the mineral-exporting nations.

Since the introduction of deep sea mining legislation in 1971, the State Department has requested that Congress postpone enactment of the legislation so as not to jeopardize the on-going law of the sea negotiations. Five years later, we appear to be no closer to a satisfactory treaty, and America's hard-minerals posture has deteriorated significantly. On March 5, 1974, Ambassador John Norton Moore testified before the Senate Subcommittee on Minerals, Materials, and Fuels. When asked by the Chairman of the Subcommittee how long Congress should wait to enact deep sea mining legislation, Ambassador Moore answered:

"[W]e share the concern expressed by you, Mr. Chairman, and the other sponsors of this bill, that we not wait forever. We are interested in a good legal regime to make certain that a timely and reasonable investment climate will exist no later than the end of 1975. Our commitment to the international conference is a commitment to make every effort to achieve a timely and successful conclusion of such a regime by an international agreement which we felt would be a preferable way to achieve the objectives of this bill.

"If, however, it is not possible to achieve a timely and successful agreement, an agreement that would provide a legal regime by the date set out in this bill—January 1, 1976—and a legal regime which would encourage investment and provide reasonable conditions under which that investment is to take place, then we would certainly wish very carefully to consider the kinds of alternative legislative approaches that would be necessary to provide that kind of stable investment climate."

I respectfully submit that "the end of 1975" has come and gone, and that the United States still has not achieved an agreement which provides a "reasonable investment climate." I urgently recommend—in the interests of American industry and the American consumer—that H.R. 11879 be reported out of this Committee at the earliest possible date.

Mr. ELY. Thank you very much, Mr. Chairman.

Mr. MURPHY. Mr. Forsythe, any questions?

Mr. FORSYTHE. I have no questions.

I thank the witness for his statement.

Mr. MURPHY. Mr. Ely, if we do not act legislatively in the Congress, and if the Law of the Sea Conference fails to come to any conclusion, what happens to the American ocean mining industry?

Mr. ELY. This is a matter for company decision.

When Mr. Flipse appears, I would hope you would address that question to him.

Speaking as a lawyer, I would expect that development would go ahead if the treaty went away, and that we would hope that legislation would come along.

The danger is not the failure of the treaty, but the probability that a treaty will be brought back that the Senate will not and should not accept, and we will have a period of many years of uncertainty.

Mr. MURPHY. You discussed, and intimated, that there are cartels in the mining industry today.

Do you feel with the proposals of the Law of the Sea that we create another ocean mining cartel, and that we probably can see the price of all those metals rising from, let us say, $5 per barrel, to $15.50 a barrel, just to use some familiar terms here?

Mr. ELY. First, if a treaty sets up a council and an assembly, and so on, with the powers that are explicit in the "Single Negotiating glimmer documents of the last 2 weeks, in my view we would have, in effect, a cartel, but an international government cartel in effect, administered by the new International Seabed Resource Authority, to which we could not object.

If there is no treaty, if mining proceeds under the legislation before you, there will not be any American cartel, I can assure you.

The antitrust laws apply to it, and I would have no objection to having that made explicit.

I would think it is impossible for any foreign combination, governmental or private, absent a treaty, to control enough of the seabed surface to exclude competitive American industry from going out there and bringing home the minerals at the lowest possible cost.

Mr. MURPHY. Do you have any feel, or information as to how the administration would react to a bill that the Congress might pass in this area?

Mr. ELY. No, I have no information at all.

You have the warnings that have been uttered from time to time.

My own expectation is that the administration would be sensible enough to approve your bill.

I think if the administration did not, it would be taking a most un fortunate step from its viewpoint. I say that, speaking as a card carrying Republican.

I would think that rejection by this administration of a measure of the eminent common sense that the three bills before this commit tee would be not only a melancholy event, but a very serious political mistake, melancholy from the viewpoint of the American consumer.

Mr. MURPHY. Do you feel that the State Department would recommend a veto because of their advocacy of this treaty process?

Mr. ELY. I make no predictions.

The danger is that these negotiations have been carried on for 8 years by gentlemen who have dedicated a substantial portion of their career to this single task. They have taken on a life of their own.

I have not the slightest doubt the recommendation from the third and fourth echelon down would be to veto, and I think the common sense of President Ford would reject such advice.

Mr. MURPHY. I have some other questions, particularly those in reaction to some of Mr. Ratiner's questions, and some of his objections to the legislation that I am going to give to you, and I would ask you to respond in writing to the committee, and when I receive them back they will be printed in the record as an extension of this testimony.

We do have the second bells on a rollcall on the floor, but I want to thank you for your appearance here this morning.

The subcommittee will stand adjourned, subject to the call of the Chair.

[The following questions were submitted by Cong. John Murphy and answers supplied by Mr. Ely. Also, Mr. Ely furnished the follow ing letter for inclusion in the printed record:]

ANSWERS OF NORTHCUTT ELY TO WRITTEN QUESTIONS SUBMITTED BY THE HONORABLE JOHN M. MURPHY CONCERNING H.R. 11879

Question 1. Would you care to comment on the proposed amendments to the Single Negotiating Text which Mr. Ratiner submitted yesterday? How do they compare, in your estimation, with the original Engo document?

Answer. First, it should be noted that, while the Committee I Single Negotiating Text contains some 75 articles and a 21 paragraph Annex, the proposed amendments referred to in the question concern only nine articles. Thus, most of the Single Negotiating Text, including the entire Annex, is not directly affected by these proposed amendments.

By way of comparison, it may be noted that, in December of 1975, the U.S. negotiators prepared a set of proposed amendments which in their opinion represented a satisfactory treaty; these amendments deleted or modified 56 of the 75 articles of the Single Negotiating Text, and 19 of the 21 paragraphs of the Annex.

If such extensive amendment was necessary to produce a treaty which the U.S. negotiators themselves considered satisfactory, it is difficult to understand how the minimal changes represented by the nine amendments submitted to this Committee can be considered encouraging.

Nor are the articles which are unaffected by the nine proposed amendments of only minor significance. For example, there is no proposed amendment to Article 1, which gives the Authority a definitional basis for extending its jurisdiction beyond the seabed to include (1) the water column and surface activities and (2) land-based processing and marketing activities. There are no proposed amendments to Article 11, which requires transfer of technology and scientific knowledge (including patented technology presently protected by our laws). There is no proposed amendment to Article 23, which provides that the Authority shall take measures "to secure [presumably to itself] the maximum financial and other benefit[s] from" deep sea mining activities. Article 23 also provides that the Authority, "in the granting of opportunities for such activities" and "in the implementation of its powers," may discriminate in favor of developing countries. There is no proposed amendment to Article 27, which gives the developing countries voting control of the Council. There is no amendment to Article 28, which defines the powers and functions of the Council; Article 28 should vest primary policy making power in the Council. There is no proposed amendment to Article 30, which would have the Economic Planning Commission ensure that world mineral prices do not decline at the expense of the developing countries. There is no amendment to Article 44, which would require members of the Authority, including the United States, to pay unlimited expenses of the Enterprise, to the extent such expenses cannot be met by the Enterprises' revenues. There is no proposed amendment to paragraph 2 of the Annex, which implies that the Authority is the owner of title to all seabed resources. There is no proposed amendment to paragraph 3 of the Annex, which gives the Authority power to determine what parts of the deep seabed shall be open to exploitation. Paragraph 3 also implies that the Authority may close the Area, which may be opened to economic activity only at the discretion of the Authority. There is no proposed amendment to Paragraph 6 of the Annex, which gives the Authority "direct and effective fiscal and administrative control" over all stages of every operation entered into pursuant to the treaty. And there is no proposed amendment to Paragraph 8 of the Annex, which gives the Authority power to control access to the deep seabed, and which implies that the Assembly will establish a basic resource policy, including production controls, that will govern access to the deep seabed. These examples are representative but are not all-inclusive. Many of the other unaffected articles and Annex provisions concern matters of vital importance to the American public.

Nor is it any answer to say that additional proposed amendments are being drafted by the Chairman of Committee I. The nine proposed amendments submitted to this Committee are unacceptable, and there is no reason to expect that additional amendments will be any better. It is true that some of the amendments proposed represent minor improvements over the original version; for example, the proposed amendment to Article 25 that would require a two-thirds majority vote in the Assembly on matters of substance, rather than a two-thirds majority of those present and voting, is, on its surface, more favorable to the United States than the original version. But, as a practical matter, this amendment is of no consequence; even with the two-thirds majority vote provision, the United States would be at the mercy of the developing countries in the Assembly, as evidenced by recent voting patterns in the United Nations General Assembly. This amendment may represent a concession on the part of the developing countries, but it is a concession that does the United States no good. Moreover, it is a concession which costs the developing countries nothing.

Other of the proposed amendments are actually more onerous than the original articles. The proposed amendment to Article 9, for example, expands the power of the Authority to prevent declines in the mineral export earnings of developing countries by adding three new paragraphs; the first authorizes the control of mineral markets by cartels, the second establishes production controls during "an interim period," and the third provides for compensation to countries that have experienced declines in mineral export earnings. Proponents of this amendment would point to the language that limits Article 9's application to cases "when such decline [in mineral export earnings] is caused by activities in the Area." This provision offers little comfort. The reason that deep sea mining is so important to the United States is that it offers an alternative to dependence on insecure foreign sources for certain vital minerals. If the United States achieves self-sufficiency with respect to these minerals, the mineral export earnings of certain developing countries may well decline. So what? Why should the American consumer subsidize these countries? They have never charged us less than the market would bear for the minerals they export to the United States.

The proposed amendment to Article 9 would also require "equitable sharing in and distribution of financial and other economic benefits . . . taking into particular consideration the interests and needs of the developing countries . . . consistent with Articles 11, 18 and 23." (Article 11 requires transfer of technology "so that all States may benefit therefrom"; Article 18 provides that "participation in the activities in the Area" by land-locked countries shall be promoted; and Article 23 provides that the Authority shall secure maximum financial benefits from the deep seabed, and may discriminate in favor of developing countries.) Determination of what constitutes "equitable sharing in and distribution of financial and other benefits" is ultimately left to the developing countries.

The proposed amendment to Article 21 merely paraphrases the original version, except for the addition to the first paragraph of the sentence "in doing so the Authority shall promote the objectives set forth in Articles 9, 23 and . . ." The objectives set forth in Articles 9 and 23 are (1) maintenance of mineral export earnings of developing countries, (2) maximizing the financial benefits that accrue to the Authority, and (3) discrimination in favor of the developing countries.

The proposed amendment to Article 22 provides that mining operations in the deep seabed may be conducted only by the Authority or on its behalf. It provides further that all activities must be conducted pursuant to a work plan approved by the Council (the Council may decide matters of substance by a two-thirds majority vote of those members present and voting). The proposed amendment to Article 22 also provides that, "The Authority shall exercise effective control of a general and overall nature in respect of the conduct of all Activities in the Area . . ." This provision is a carte blanc delegation of foreign authority over United States operations in areas beyond the national jurisdiction of any state.

Article 26 remains substantially unchanged, except for the addition of a provision which in very general terms applies the "separation of powers" principle to the organs of the Authority.

The amendment to Article 25 changes the vote required for decisions on questions of substance from a two-thirds majority of those members present and voting to a two-thirds majority of the membership. As I have already explained, this amendment is of no value to the United States. In recent months, the U.N. General Assembly has passed a number of resolutions that are hostile to U.S. interests by majority votes that exceeded two-thirds of the U.N.'s membership. We can expect similar voting patterns in any assembly created for purposes of governing the deep seabed.

The amended version of Article 26 differs little in substance from the original version. The only concession to the developed nations appears to be the requirement that the Assembly, in establishing subsidary organs, take "due account . . . of . . . the need for members highly qualified and competent in the relevant technical matters dealt with by such organs." This rather nebulous provision in no way enhances the rights of developed countries to *operate* in the deep seabed.

The amendment to Article 26 also adds a provision that gives the Assembly the power to assess contributions to the Authority to be paid by members "in accordance with the general assessment scale used by the United Nations."

Thus, it appears that the United States would be required to subsidize the Authority until such time as income from the deep seabed is sufficient to finance the Authority.

Question 2. On page 5 of your testimony, you refer to accepted exploitation beyond areas of national jurisdiction of "coral, pearl, oyster. chank and sponge fisheries." What countries carried out that exploitation? Were any of those countries the same that now want to keep us from exploiting the mineral resources of the sea?

Answer. Nations which acquired, by exploitation, exclusive rights in seabed areas that were, at the time, beyond the limits of national jurisdiction include Algeria, Australia (Western Australia, Northern Territory, and Queensland), the Bahamas, British Honduras, Ceylon (Gulf of Manaar and Palks Strait). Cuba, England, Egypt. France, Greece (Dodecanese Islands), India (Malabar and Coromandel Coasts), Indonesia (Aru Islands). Ireland. Italy, Japan, Libya (Cyreniaca and Tripolitania), Mexico, Nicaragua (Pearl Keys. Laguna de Perlas, and Punta de Perlas), Panama (Archipelago de las Perlas), the Persian Gulf States (Oman and the Trucial Shaikhdoms), the Philippines (Moro Gulf). Scotland, Sicily, Tunisia, Turkey, the United States (Florida), and Venezeula.

Of these nations only Australia, France, Ireland. Italy, Japan and the United Kingdom voted with the United States against the 1969 Moratorium Resolution; Algeria. Ceylon, India. Mexico, Nicaragua. Panama. Tunisia and Venezeula voted in favor of the resolution, and Cuba, Greece, Indonesia, Libya, the Philippines. Turkey, and the United Arab Republic abstained.

Question 3. You state in your testimony that we have the right under existing international law to exploit the deep seabed minerals. I believe Mr. Ratiner acknowledged that fact yesterday. What difficulties would you foresee for a company which went ahead and mined the seafloor tomorrow (besides the obvious investment risk)? Would you anticipate sabotage or explosive mines? Do you expect operations conducted *subsequent* to a Law of the Sea treaty would be safer?

Answer. I personally have no reason to anticipate sabotage of deep sea mining activities. but actions of terrorists are impossible to predict. Presumably, the U.S. government would protect its nationals against such acts of piracy.

A Law of the Sea treaty would not necessarily make deep sea mining operations any safer. That such a treaty would afford any greater physical protection against acts of piracy. or sabotage. than the protection that the United States itself could provide appears to me to be a very doubtful assumption.

Question 4. How secure do you think deep sea mining operations would be if we enacted the legislation being considered by this Committee? How much of the risk do you think should be borne by the U.S. government and how much by the industry?

Answer. Testimony of mining industry witnesses has indicated that H.R. 11879 and similar bills provide the minimum security that is acceptable to U.S. industry.

In my opinion, the normal commercial. economic, and technological risks should be borne by industry. while political risks sould be borne by the government. H.R. 11879 is consistent with this.

Question 5. You mention on page 9 of your statement that the ocean mining industry's decisions need to be made now, in 1976. Mr. Frizzell said that they would have to be made in the next 18 months. Can you account for this difference in opinion? What specific disadvantages do you see resulting from an 18 month delay?

Answer. I cannot account for this difference of opinion.

Industry representatives have testified that further delay of legislation will cause delays, curtailment. and possible abandonment of deep sea mining operations. (See. *e.g..* Hearings on "Current Developments in Deep Seabed Mining" before the Subcommittee on Minerals. Materials and Fuels of the Senate Committee on Interior and Insular Affairs. 94th Cong., 1st Sess. at 16–17 (November 7, 1975).

I do not know what Mr. Frizzell's source of information is. but I would think that industry is the best judge of its own needs, and of the conditions under which it can operate successfully.

Question 6. Except for some minor details. you stated that you strongly support H.R. 11879. Mr. Ratiner has raised some objections to the bill. Would you care to respond to his objections to: the specification of block size: the time frame of the investment; the duration of the license; the minimum expenditure per block; and the procedure for obtaining rights?

Answer. Mr. Ratiner has objected to these provisions because they are based on industry data, and the federal government does not at present have independently verifiable data which would support them. Mr. Ratiner has emphasized, however, that the Interior Department has no reason to doubt the accuracy of the data provided by industry.

In my opinion, the fact that the federal government has not independently obtained technical data on the deep seabed is not a valid reason for further delaying deep sea mining legislation. A similar scarcity of information on the Outer Continental Shelf ("OCS") did not prevent Congress from enacting the Outer Continental Shelf Lands Act in 1953. At that time, virtually all of the geotechnical data on the OCS was industry data. Nevertheless, Congress saw fit to pass the Outer Continental Shelf Lands Act, which provided for, *inter alia*, block size, duration of the lease, procedures for obtaining rights, diligence requirements, and royalties and other expenditures. In 1954, the Department of the Interior issued detailed regulations for the OCS, and conducted the first sale of OCS leases. But the federal government did not begin to gather its own geotechnical data on the OCS until 1965, and the first pre-lease sale evaluation of the OCS by the Department of the Interior did not occur until 1966, *thirteen years after Congress enacted the Outer Continental Shelf Lands Act!*

The need for enactment of domestic deep sea mining legislation is urgent. This legislation will be delayed for years if Congress waits for the federal government to obtain its own geotechnical data on the deep ocean floor. To be useful, such data must relate to the first dozen or so mining sites that industry selects for its investments, out of hundreds of potential first generation sites. Not much would be gained by "pancaking" long-drawn out government investigations of the same sites. That such data is not a prerequisite to legislation is evidenced by the Congress' action with respect to the outer Continental Shelf Lands Act. If this data, when finally collected by industry and reviewed by government, indicates that either the legislation or the regulations should be amended, such amendment can be accomplished at that time. But we certainly do not have to wait until then to enact legislation.

Question 7. How would you respond to Mr. Ratiner's comment yesterday that Congress should not be passing legislation which would guarantee industry against the efforts of the Executive Branch at the Law of the Sea Conference?

Answer. We have been listening to this same excuse for postponing domestic legislation since 1971. In the meantime, the hard mineral exporting nations have made substantial progress toward the formation of producer cartels, and the world prices of manganese, nickel, and cobalt have increased 130 percent, 65 percent, and 82 percent, respectively.

The Executive Branch has had eight years in which to conclude an acceptable treaty for the deep seabed. Yet there is no evidence that the U.S. negotiators are any closer to achieving agreement on a satisfactory treaty than they were in 1968. To further delay the enactment of domestic legislation would needlessly jeopardize the interests of U.S. industry and the U.S. consumer. Representatives of the Executive Department have repeatedly assured the Congress that the integrity of investments by American industry pending ratification of a treaty would be fully protected. The only way that this can be done is to provide for compensation if the United States hereafter ratifies a treaty which imposes production or price controls or otherwise reduces the value of investments made in the exercise of the freedom of the seas, which the same representatives have assured Congress now entitles American industry to engage in deep sea mining.

Question 8. Could you comment on the proposal which Mr. Ratiner made yesterday to enrich the Federal coffer as a result of industry activities? I assume he was talking about some kind of royalty system such as the Interior Department now conducts with regard to the oil and gas recovered from our Outer Continental Shelf.

Answer. The drafters of H.R. 11879 have been careful to avoid any language in that bill which could be interpreted as extending U.S. jurisdiction to minerals not actually being exploited by entities of the United States, or to any part of the deep seabed.

In virtually all of the world's mining legislation, including that of the United States, the right to a royalty payment implies a right of ownership or control with respect to either the minerals to which the royalty is applied, or the land on which such minerals are found. Consequently, a royalty provision in H.R. 11879 could be construed as evidence that the bill extends U.S. territorial jurisdiction to the deep seabed, notwithstanding disclaimers in the bill to the contrary. A royalty provision would thus play into the hands of the Third World nations, who will miss no opportunity to denounce any deep sea mining legislation that is enacted by the United States.

For this reason, federal revenues from deep sea mining operations should be collected as income taxes on domestic activity and not as royalties.

——————

DEEPSEA VENTURES, INC.,
Gloucester Point, Va., November 14, 1974.

Notice of Discovery and Claim of Exclusive Mining Rights, and Request for Diplomatic Protection and Protection of Investment, by Deepsea Ventures, Inc.

Hon. HENRY A. KISSINGER,
Secretary of State, U. S. Department of State,
Washington, D.C.

MY DEAR MR. SECRETARY: Deepsea Ventures, Inc., a Delaware corporation having its principal place of business in the County of Gloucester, The Commonwealth of Virginia, U.S.A., respectfully makes of record, by filing with your office this *Notice of Discovery and Claim of Exclusive Mining Rights and Request for Diplomatic Protection and Protection of Investment, by Deepsea Ventures, Inc.* (hereinafter "Claim"), as authorized by its Board of Directors by resolution dated 30 October 1974, a certified copy of which is annexed hereto as Exhibit A.

NOTICE OF DISCOVERY AND CLAIM OF EXCLUSIVE MINING RIGHTS

Deepsea Ventures, Inc., (hereinafter "Deepsea"), hereby gives public notice that it has discovered and taken possession of, and is now engaged in developing and evaluating, as the first stages of mining, a deposit of seabed manganese nodules (hereinafter "Deposit"). The Deposit, illustrated by the sketch annexed as Exhibit B, is encompassed by, and extends to, lines drawn between the coordinates numbered in series below, as follows:
From :

(1) Latitude 15°44′ N, Longitude 124°20′ W : a line drawn West to : (2) Latitude 15°44′ N, Longitude 127°46′ W ; and thence South to : (3) Latitude 14°16′ N, Longitude 127°46′ W ; and thence East to : (4) Latitude 14°16′ N, Longitude 124°20′ W ; and thence North to the point of origin.

These lines include approximately 60,000 square kilometers for purposes of development and evaluation of the Deposit encompassed therein, which area will be reduced by Deepsea to 30,000 square kilometers upon expiration of a term of 15 years (absent force majeure) from the date of this notice or upon commencement (absent force majeure) of commercial production from the Deposit, whichever event occurs first. The Deposit lies on the abyssal ocean floor, in water depths ranging between 2300 to 5000 meters and is more than 1000 kilometers from the nearest island, and more than 1300 kilometers seaward of the outer edge of the nearest continental margin. It is beyond the limits of seabed jurisdiction presently claimed by any State. The overlying waters are, of course, high seas.

The general area of the Deposit was identified in August of 1964 by the predecessor in interest of Deepsea, and the Deposit was discovered by Deepsea on August 31, 1969.

Further exploration, evaluation, engineering development and processing research have been carried out to enable the recovery of the specific manganese nodules of the Deposit and the production of products and byproducts therefrom.

The work done, and in progress, is summarized in the annexed affidavits, Exhibits C and D.

Deepsea, or its successor in interest, will commence commercial production from the Deposit within 15 years (absent force majeure) from the date of this Claim, and will conclude production therefrom within a period (absent force majeure) of 40 years from the date of commencement of commercial production whereupon the right shall cease.

Deepsea has been advised by Counsel, whose names appear at the end hereof, that it has validly established the exclusive rights asserted in this Claim under existing international law as evidenced by the practice of States, the 1958 Convention on the High Seas, and general rules of law recognized by civilized nations.

Deepsea asserts the exclusive rights to develop, evaluate and mine the Deposit and to take, use, and sell all of the manganese nodules in, and the minerals and metals derived, therefrom. It is proceeding with appropriate diligence to do so, and requests and requires States, persons, and all other commercial or political entities to respect the exclusive rights asserted herein. Deepsea does not assert, or ask the United States of America to assert, a territorial claim to the seabed or subsoil underlying the Deposit. Use of the overlying water column, as a freedom of the high seas, will be made to the extent necessary to recover and transport the manganese nodules of the Deposit.

Disturbance of the seabed and subsoil underlying the Deposit will be temporary and will be restricted to that unavoidably occasioned by recovery of the manganese nodules of the Deposit. To facilitate the United States of America's domestic policies and programs of environmental protection, Deepsea will provide, at no cost, reasonable space for U.S. Government representatives of the United States of America on vessels utilized by Deepsea in the development and evaluation of the Deposit. Deepsea does not intend to process at sea the manganese nodules from the Deposit.

It is Deepsea's intention, by filing this Claim in your office and in appropriate State recording offices, to publish this Claim and provide notice and proof of the priority of the right of Deepsea to the Deposit, and its title thereto.

A true copy of this Claim is being filed for recordation in the office of the Secretary of State of the State of Delaware, U.S.A., the State wherein Deepsea is incorporated, and on 15 November 1974 in the office of the Clerk of the Circuit Court of Gloucester County, Virginia, U.S.A., the county and Commonwealth of Deepsea's principal place of business. Copies of this Claim are also being provided to others, as specified in the annexed Exhibit E.

We ask that this Claim, and all of the annexed Exhibits, be made available by your office for public examination.

REQUEST FOR DIPLOMATIC PROTECTION AND PROTECTION OF INTEGRITY OF INVESTMENT

Deepsea respectfully requests the diplomatic protection of the United States Government with respect to the exclusive mining rights described and asserted in the foregoing Claim, and any other rights which may hereafter accrue to Deepsea as a result of its activities at the site of the Deposit, and similar protection of the integrity of its investments heretofore made and now being undertaken, and to be undertaken in the future.

This request is made prior to any known interference with the rights now being asserted, and prior to any known impairment of Deepsea's investment. It is intended to give the Department immediate notice of Deepsea's Claim for the purpose of facilitating the protection of Deepsea's rights and investments should this be required as a consequence of any future actions of the United States Government or other States, persons, or organizations.

The protection requested accords with the assurances given on behalf of the Executive Department to the Congress of the United States, including those by Ambassador John R. Stevenson, by Honorable Charles N. Brower, and by Honorable John Norton Moore, as follows:

"The Department does not anticipate any efforts to discourage U.S. nationals from continuing with their current exploration plans. In the event that U.S. nationals should desire to engage in commercial exploitation prior to the establishment of an internationally agreed regime, we would seek to assure that their activities are conducted in accordance with relevant principles of international law, including the freedom of the seas and that the integrity of their investment receives due protection in any subsequent international agreement." Letter of January 16, 1970, from John R. Stevenson, Legal Advisor, Department of State, to Lee Metcalf, Chairman, Special Subcommittee on the Outer Continental Shelf, U.S. Senate, reproduced in Hearings before the Special Senate Subcommittee on the Outer Continental Shelf, 91st Cong., 1st and 2d Sess. at 210 (1970).

"At the present time, under international law and the High Seas Convention, it is open to anyone who has the capacity to engage in mining of the deep seabed subject to the proper exercise of high seas rights of other countries involved." Statement of Charles N. Brower, Hearings before the House Subcommittee on Oceanography of the Committee on Merchant Marine and Fisheries, 93d Cong., 1st Sess., at 50 (1974).

"It is certainly the position of the United States that the mining of the deep seabed i's a high seas freedom and I think that would be a freedom today under international law. And our position has been that companies are free to engage in this kind of mining beyond the 200-meter mark subject to the international regime to be agreed upon, and of course, assured protection of the integrity of investment in that period." Statement of John Norton Moore, Hearings before the Senate Subcommittee on Minerals, Materials and Fuels, 93d Cong., 1st Sess., at 247 (1973).

The language of these extracts, and other statements similar to them made by these and other responsible officers of the Executive Branch is consistent with the Executive's continuing practice as reflected in a paragraph in President Taft's Message to the Congress of December 7, 1909, where he said:

"The Department of State, in view of proofs filed with it in 1906, showing American possession, occupation and working of certain coal-bearing lands in Spitzbergen [Spitzbergen was at that time recognized as being not subject to the territorial sovereignty of any State] accepted the invitation under the reservation above stated [i.e., the questions of altering the status of the islands as countries belonging to no particular State and as equally open to the citizens and subjects of all States, should not be raised] and under the further reservation that all interests in those islands already vested should be protected and that there should be equality of opportunity for the future." *Annual Message of the President to Congress 7 December 1909*, [1901] For. Rels. of the U.S. IX at XIII (1914).

Deepsea has used its best efforts to ascertain that there are no pipelines, cables, military installations, or other activities constituting an exercise of freedom of the high seas in the area encompassing the Deposit or in the superjacent waters, with which Deepsea's operations might conflict. So far as is known, no claim of rights has been made by any State or person with respect to said Deposit or any other mineral resources in the area encompassing the Deposit and no State or person has established effective occupation of said area.

Initially, approximately 1.35 million wet metric tons of nodules will be recovered by Deepsea from the Deposit per year. In accord with market conditions, this may later be expanded to as much as 4 million wet metric tons per year recovered. Deepsea's processing and refining technology, successfully demonstrated in its pilot plant, will recover copper, nickel, cobalt, manganese, and other products, depending on the market situation and competitive conditions. The recovered weight of the major four metals that the initial 1.35 million wet metric tons of nodules will yield per year will be approximately as shown in Column A below. Column B gives some indication of the dependency of the United States of America upon imports for these four metals.

	A	B
	Production, metric tons	Net U.S. imports (1972) as a percentage of U.S. consumption
Nodules	1,350,000	
Copper	9,150	9
Nickel	11,300	71
Cobalt	2,150	92
Manganese	253,000	93

The importance of these minerals to the economy of the United States does not require elaboration. It has been effectively expressed to the Congress by the Executive Branch.

For your information, the capital stock of Deepsea is at present wholly owned by nationals of the United States. Ninety per cent thereof is owned by Tenneco Corporation, a Delaware corporation, and the other ten per cent is owned by individuals, all of whom are United States citizens. At this date stock options are outstanding which, if all are exercised, will result in acquisition of the following percentages of ownership of Deepsea's capital stock by others:

23.75%—Essex Iron Company, a New Jersey corporation, a wholly owned subsidiary of United States Steel Corporation, a Delaware corporation.

23.75%—Union Mines Inc., a Maryland corporation, a wholly owned subsidiary of Union Miniere, S.A., a Belgian corporation.

23.75%—Japan Manganese Nodule Development Co., Ltd., a Japanese corporation.

Respectfully,

By JOHN E. FLIPSE, *President*.

Counsel:
NORTHCUTT ELY.
L. F. E. GOLDIE.
R. J. GREENWALD.

[Whereupon, at 12:12 p.m., the subcommittee adjourned, subject to the call of the Chair.]

DEEP SEABED MINING

MONDAY, MARCH 8, 1976

House of Representatives,
Committee on Merchant Marine and Fisheries,
Subcommittee on Oceanography,
Washington, D.C.

The subcommittee met, pursuant to call, at 10:10 a.m., in room 1334, Longworth House Office Building, Hon. Paul G. Rogers, presiding.

Mr. Rogers. The subcommittee will please come to order.

This morning and tomorrow we will continue hearings on the subject of deep ocean mining. The purpose of these hearings is to consider unilateral domestic legislation which would authorize ocean mining operations to begin under the regulatory authority of the U.S. Government.

The bills under consideration attempt to provide a stable investment climate which would encourage the development of these deep ocean minerals under current maritime law and in the absence of a Law of the Sea Treaty.

We have invited back some Government witnesses who were either unable to attend the hearings last month, or to whom we would like to address further questions.

In addition, we will be hearing from the industry representatives to gather their comments on the bills before us today.

Finally, we have an economist, a former member of the U.S. Committee One Law of the Sea Treaty team from the Treasury Department, who specializes in anti-trust problems and the economies of cartels. He will discuss the ongoing Law of the Sea negotiations.

So far, these hearings have been very helpful in gathering the various viewpoints of Government and industry, coupled with the testimony we will hear today anad tomorrow from various other interest groups and academicians who have specialized in the Law of the Sea, we should be prepared to move on to markup the legislation before us in the immediate future, and report out a bill that will aid our infant ocean mining industry absent a treaty from the next 8-week session of the Law of the Sea Conference due to convene in New York next week.

We are pleased to have back with the committee today Hon. Carlyle Maw, Under Secretary of State for Security Assistance who is accompanied by Mr. Leigh S. Ratiner, Administrator, Ocean Mining Administration, and we welcome you to the committee, and you may take a position at the witness table, if you desire, and bring any colleagues you have with you.

It is my understanding that, of course, you have given your statement, but it may be that you would like to have additional comments at this time, and if so, the committee welcomes that, and then we will proceed with the questions.

STATEMENT OF HON. CARLYLE MAW, UNDER SECURITY OF STATE FOR SECURITY ASSISTANCE; ACCOMPANIED BY LEIGH S. RATINER, ADMINISTRATOR, OCEAN MINING ADMINISTRATION, DEPARTMENT OF THE INTERIOR

Mr. Maw. Thank you, Mr. Chairman.

Mr. Chairman, I am pleased to be here today, and regret I was out of the country last week, and was not able to present my statement which I had prepared.

I understand that most of the questions were addressed to Mr. Ratiner last week, and I have reviewed his responses, and I think he has done very well.

If you have further questions I shall be happy to elaborate.

Mr. Rogers. Thank you, sir.

Did you have any comments you wanted to make?

Mr. Maw. I think I need not add comments at this point, beyond what has already been put into the record.

I think the administration's position has been fairly and clearly stated, and particularly, the position of the State Department.

We have also had a good review of the ongoing negotiations which are in process.

We like to believe progress is being made. I think it is. How much remains to be seen.

The critical period of negotiations is about to commence beginning next Monday in New York, and it will be a very active session, and we sincerely hope that at the end of the session we can report to you substantial and material progress in the deep seabed issue.

Thank you, Mr. Chairman.

Mr. Rogers. Thank you.

Mr. Ratiner?

Mr. Ratiner. Yes, Mr. Chairman, at the February 23 hearing several matters were raised to which I thought it might be useful to refer very briefly again today.

First, in reviewing the transcript of the February 23 hearings, I noted that a very significant question was asked by the chairman regarding my views as the Administrator of the Ocean Mining Administration on the detailed provisions of the legislation pending before this committee.

In reviewing that transcript, I realized that an erroneous impression could have been left by my answer.

Accordingly, I would appreciate the opportunity of amplifying somewhat the remarks I made in response to that question.

Mr. Rogers. Certainly.

Mr. Ratiner. I said that the U.S. Government does not have independently verifiable data necessary to determine whether the detailed provisions of this legislation are, in fact, accurate, which was one reason, among others, why the administration opposes this legislation. I might add that other reasons of great importance concern the legislation's effect on the Law of the Sea negotiations.

I indicated then that we rely very heavily on industry data and would be in a better position if we had more data that we had obtained ourselves.

I think the erroneous impression that may have been left by that transcript was that we have reason to doubt the accuracy of the data provided by industry. That is most emphatically not the case.

If I can recount our efforts very briefly, we solicited over the past four years a very substantial amount of data from the industry, together with data which was obtained by the U.S. Geological Survey, for example, and we subjected that data to, in a sense, expert cross examination.

I personally assembled a team of Interior Department experts—geologists, oceanographers, and environmentalists, and we met with the industry repeatedly to review their data in what can only be described fairly as a cross examining atmosphere. As a result of those series of meetings, an industry paper was prepared.

I believe that paper has, in fact, found its way into the public record—not in the House, but in the Senate. To the best of our knowledge, it does represent an accurate set of facts upon which, for example, one would determine the appropriate size of blocks to be mined.

While opposing domestic legislation as we do, we have nevertheless relied very heavily on our analysis of that data in the international negotiations which are now occurring, and we intend to continue doing so.

I want to be quite clear on the record however, that the Government does need independently verifiable data.

There is, despite our best efforts to analyze and examine the data submitted by industry, a very significant need for Government to be able to go to the public and indicate that its final decisions on matters affecting resource management are based on its own, independently acquired data.

That is a long term problem, Mr. Chairman. It is one we will have to deal with in the future of ocean mining.

Congressman Murphy did put the question at a rather personal level, if I recall correctly, and said that he realized my views had not been cleared by the Office of Management and Budget. That is correct, they have not.

But if legislation is to pass Congress one day on this subject, the approach I would, as a purely personal view, like to see used essentially would be a system of what I would call prototype licenses or contracts. For a fixed period of time, or perhaps a fixed number of licenses, the Government would be entitled to closely monitor all work done under those licenses and to obtain comprehensive data under the circumstances at very little cost to the Government. Then, on the basis of the information acquired by monitoring these prototype operations over a period of time, let us say 5, 6 or 7 years, the secretary of the department who has regulatory jurisdiction over ocean mining would draft the detailed rules and regulations.

Mr. Chairman, I think this would be a particularly useful ap proach, and I represent it only as my own view, not even the Department of Interior's view for the time being.

That, Mr. Chairman, is what I wanted to say to clarify the record.

A second matter came up during the February 23 hearing. Congressman Murphy indicated that the administration had not returned after it promised, following the Geneva session of the Law of the Sea Conference, to review the "Single Negotiating Text."

We had indicated after Geneva that we were not satisfied with the "Single Negotiating Text" that emerged in Committee I and that we were undergoing comprehensive review of that text which, as you know, is quite lengthy. I promised to return today to describe to the committee the results of that review.

However, I note that the list of witnesses is quite long. While I am prepared to go through the "Single Negotiating Text," if necessary article by article, and indicate the results of the administration's review, I wondered if, in fact, that would be useful to the committee at this point in time.

It may be that, in view of the long list of witnesses, you would prefer that I not do that today and come back at another time when it would not be so onerous for the others who are here assembled.

Mr. Rogers. Yes, I think the committee would prefer that at this time. However, you might submit it for the record so that we can have it, and then we will arrange another session with you.

Mr. Ratiner. I will be happy to do that, Mr. Chairman.

Mr. Rogers. Without objection it will be made a part of the record at this point.

[The modifications to the Committee I Single Negotiating Text which the United States has informally submitted are contained in the document, "Proposed Amendments to the Committee I Single Negotiating Text" at page 140 of this record.]

Mr. Rogers. How much deep sea mining are we doing now?

Mr. Ratiner. We are not doing any deep sea mining in the sense of commercial exploitation of the resources, Mr. Chairman.

Mr. Rogers. We do not allow any off of our shores?

Mr. Ratiner. Well, we neither prohibit or regulate deep ocean mining at the present time.

We believe that ocean mining is a freedom of the seas in that American nationals are free to engage in ocean mining if they please.

In one sense, ocean mining is occurring. The early phase of ocean mining, which is prospecting, exploration, and the development and testing of equipment is occurring right now, at what I regard to be a reasonable pace, looking toward full commercial production by at least some ocean mining companies between 1981 and 1984.

Mr. Rogers. As far as you are aware, there really is none going on in a commercial way at all?

Mr. Ratiner. No, sir, there is no commercial extraction of manganese nodule resources from the deep seabed today.

Mr. Rogers. What is projected? You say they expect to get it by 1981.

What is projected?

Mr. Ratiner. Based on the level of investment which is projected by industry, the work they have done to date, and market factors which will be prevailing in 1981 to 1985, we would predict that two or three companies might each be mining at a full commercial level one major mine site which would be roughly three million tons of manganese nodules per year per mine site. You might see by 1985, if efforts continue at their present pace, perhaps nine million tons of production at that time.

Mr. ROGERS. And what would that represent in investment and income?

Mr. RATINER. Well, I cannot tell you what it would represent in income, but I can tell you what it would represent in investment.

Each mining company has a different level of investment planned, but our own estimates are that it will cost some mining companies up to $600 to $700 million for a single mine site, and others, perhaps $500 million. To be on the safe side, I would estimate the range as between $450 million and $700 million per mine site. Assuming three operations by 1984, that would be an investment of $1.35 billion to $2.1 billion.

Mr. ROGERS. Why can you not give us an estimated income?

Can you not project what inflationary factors, and so forth, would be?

Mr. RATINER. I think this is an area where only the companies can give you any accurate information.

Since they are here today I would prefer, with your permission, to defer to them the response to that question.

Mr. ROGERS. Have they not submitted to you information on what they project?

Mr. RATINER. We are trying to put together a study on costs of ocean mining, both investment and operating costs, to make some predictions as to what we think the overall income would be, but we have not completed that study yet.

Mr. ROGERS. When will it be completed?

Mr. RATINER. We expect to have it momentarily. We hope it will be finished within a few weeks, and published.

Mr. ROGERS. Who is doing it?

Mr. RATINER. My office, the Ocean Mining Administration.

Mr. ROGERS. How long has it been in process?

Mr. RATINER. That particular study has been in process for about 2 months.

Mr. ROGERS. And you anticipate completion in 1 month or 2 months?

Mr. RATINER. I would anticipate it probably in a few weeks.

Mr. ROGERS. A few weeks? Is that a month, or over a month?

Mr. RATINER. Do you want me to fix a final date for it?

Mr. ROGERS. I think it might be interesting for the committee to know when we can have some information.

Mr. RATINER. My staff will not be happy with me for doing it.

Mr. ROGERS. Maybe they will do it if you ask it of them.

Mr. RATINER. I will promise it to you 14 days from today.

Mr. ROGERS. That is excellent. It would be helpful to you to have it when we are in negotiations to show what we can do. And I think it might be helpful to let the Congress make an intelligent judgment, based on projected income and then we can be on with it.

Maybe we ought not to be wasting so much time negotiating if we can go ahead and do something ourselves.

In fact, I am disappointed that we have not done more. We have been talking about this for 10 or 15 years now.

Mr. Forsythe, any questions?

Mr. FORSYTHE. A question just on this point of income.

You certainly have an estimate of the U.S. market value on the quantity.

Mr. RATINER. Yes, Mr. Forsythe, we can supply those kinds of figures for the record if you like.

I was, in fact, referring to somewhat more refined estimates.

Mr. FORSYTHE. Net income?

Mr. RATINER. Yes.

Mr. FORSYTHE. And what are those figures?

Mr. RATINER. I will be happy to supply those figures.

(The information follows:)

Nine million tons of annual ocean mining production in 1984 would represent a gross sales value of approximately $632 million for nickel, $179 million for copper and $112 million for cobalt in terms of 1976 dollars, which do not take into account inflationary factors. While the total gross sales value estimate of $923 million would be increased in the event that manganese was recovered from a portion of the nodule production, estimates of the value of this additional product are highly speculative in view of uncertainty about the quality of seabed manganese to be recovered.

Mr. FORSYTHE. The gross value of the product would give us a measure of what we are talking about.

Thank you, Mr. Chairman.

Mr. ROGERS. I think I will ask counsel, just for the record, to ask certain questions that the committee is anxious to have answered on the record.

Mr. PERIAN. Mr. Maw, Mr. Ratiner, the chief U.S. negotiator in Committee I, is quoted in the March 8, 1976 Newsweek as saying that if the Third World nations reject the compromise text he presented to this committee on February 23, "then the chances for a successful Law of the Sea Conference drops to one in a million."

This text was considered totally inappropriate and unacceptable in testimony, and in representations to this committee presented by members of industry.

Did the so-called Third World caucus consider the text since February 23 as reported in Newsweek, and what were the results of their consideration?

Mr. MAW. Were you addressing that question to me?

Mr. PERIAN. Yes, sir.

Mr. MAW. Well, I will not argue with Mr. Ratiner's odds.

There has been progress since the original negotiating text prepared by the chairman of Committee I.

Whether this progress will be reflected in the Group of 77, we do not know. They are now in session, and we hope that they will go along with the progress that has been made by the committee chairman's amended negotiated text.

We cannot answer where they stand. We do not know yet.

Mr. PERIAN. If the ocean miners reject the text as a "give-away" and as a signal for them to pull out of their deep sea mining ventures, what action will you take?

Mr. MAW. Well, we have not arrived at that point, fortunately. The negotiation is still underway.

As far as we know, the negotiation is going on in good faith, and we will be able to tell you better when we see the results of the next session starting next Monday.

We hope, as I say, to make some advance, but we cannot be certain. If we do not, we will have to meet the issue.

Mr. ROGERS. May I ask here, I presume you have these alternatives already outlined. Are you going in without any alternatives, going into the discussion?

Mr. MAW. We do have options. We do have limits which we think we can go in with.

Our position is well known, we have stated them over and over and the Group of 77 know that we mean what we say.

This, of course, is in the context of an overall treaty, Mr. Chairman. The problems of the deep seabed relate to the problems of the economic zone, and vice versa, so that it moves more slowly than perhaps one would expect if we are only talking about one subject.

They are interrelated, Mr. Chairman, and therefore, the whole process more or less has to move together.

Mr. RATINER. Mr. Chairman, might I supplement Secretary Maw's statement?

It is true that last Tuesday, I believe, one spokesman for the mining industry indicated a high degree of unacceptability for the new compromise text produced by the chairman of Committee I.

First, I would like the record to be clear that I think many of the criticisms leveled at those texts were erroneous, and that I would be happy, at some time when it is convenient for the committee, to engage Mr. Ely in a debate before the committee as to the significance of those texts, or their legal meaning.

Be that as it may, Mr. Chairman, those texts have not been accepted by the United States. They do represent substantial movement forward by the developing countries toward our position, and they have to be seen against the background of other articles yet to be negotiated before we can tell you what their true meaning is.

Indeed, those texts themselves will change as further articles are negotiated. So I think it is a little too soon to conclude, as Mr. Perian seems to have concluded by his question, that those texts are so unacceptable that we probably should proceed immediately with legislation.

Thank you, sir.

Mr. PERIAN. I will point out, Mr. Ratiner, that the conclusion is the committee's, not mine.

Mr. Maw, in your prepared statement of the 23rd you said,

The Law of the Sea Conference provides us with an opportunity, possibly our last, to develop a system which would subject deep seabed mining to widely acceptable international rules embodied in a treaty and related regulations.

What did you mean by "possibly our last opportunity"?

Will the State Department finally concede the uselessness of attempting to obtain a Committee I treaty if the talks bog down again as they did in Geneva?

Mr. MAW. We are looking at an overall treaty on the ocean, not just the seabed, and they are interrelated in the minds of many people. The interrelation is essential, and in order to achieve what we want one place we may have to accept something a little less satisfactory than others.

We have definite priorities which are well known and well stated.

We hope that out of it will come a unified treaty.

Now, time is running against us. I think it is true we have already passed, by both Houses of Congress, a 200-mile fishing bill. If that becomes law we are changing the rules at the seventh inning, and it complicates our problem.

There is no doubt that we are up against a really difficult time achieving a generally accepted Law of the Sea Treaty, and if this negotiation breaks down I have great difficulty seeing how we will get it on the track again.

That is what I mean by probably our last chance.

Mr. PERIAN. In other words, if no settlement is reached, yet in the assessment of the State Department progress has been made, as they have said many times, would you recommend to this committee again putting off domestic legislation until the next session of the Congress? Or do you consider this to be the end of the line?

Mr. MAW. Well, I do not necessarily consider that the session, the Conference, will break up and come to an end 8 weeks hence.

I think we have to judge our progress, and see where we stand. I sincerely hope it does not break up.

Mr. PERIAN. In view of all of this pessimism, how do you view this committee's determination to report out legislation that will provide a recourse for the United States to obtain these critical minerals?

Mr. MAW. We do not believe the passage of unilateral mining legislation will, in any way, bring about or accelerate the achievement of an overall Law of the Sea Treaty at this point in time.

Mr. PERIAN. What do you think it will do for the ocean miners?

Mr. MAW. I think they should bear with us for 8 weeks.

Mr. PERIAN. These are Mr. Murphy's questions. He specifically asked this one.

Assuming that this committee, the House and the Senate work out a piece of legislation, what would be your recommendation or the State Department's recommendation on unilateral legislation in terms of a veto or an acceptance?

Mr. MAW. Well, as you know, we have been quite clear at the State Department that we oppose at this time the enactment of deep sea legislation.

What would happen when, as, and if legislation is offered, it would have to be looked at at the time, and decision made under all cir cumstances then prevailing.

I do not think you can forecast what might be the case on that day.

Mr. PERIAN. Thank you.

Mr. ROGERS. Mr. Forsythe?

Mr. FORSYTHE. Thank you, Mr. Chairman.

Mr. Maw, that 8 weeks seems to pop up as the critical area, and I have heard the testimony of Mr. Ratiner last week.

I think it is unrealistic that the legislative process will produce any legislation during that time, you can take some comfort in that. You will probably not be facing an actual bill on the President's desk in 8 weeks.

As some people have stated who have been closely observing the Law of the Sea, and as we move in, particularly into these negotiations—starting next week—that the progress of this legislation through this committee and through the process here in Washington might help signify the urgency of this nation towards this problem and therefore, would be beneficial for us to continue with the movement of the legislation and the issue as to whether it finally reaches the President's desk is some weeks off?

Mr. MAW. Well, it is hard to forecast the reaction of others to unilateral action.

We have our problem, as I mentioned, with the 200-mile legislation, which is really quite different, of course, than the problem with respect to the pending bills on deep sea mining which, in a sense, unilaterally assert a method of going about setting the rules for deep sea mining.

I would think this would not be accepted as a shove or at least the kind of shove by the developing countries.

It would be more likely accepted as a preemption and not conducive to negotiation.

This is a matter of purely personal judgment and it is very hard to know what your results will be.

Mr. FORSYTHE. In the short time I have been here on this committee we just hear that again and again and our patience is rather difficult to contain. I frankly think that our progress on the law of the fishery zones has had a beneficial effect on the conference, that is the Law of the Sea Conference as a whole.

I think the leadership of this country is moving towards obviously finding ways of making it compatible with the world's needs and the policy is perhaps exhibited this way.

This is more of a statement than a question, I realize. We will keep in touch.

Thank you, Mr. Chairman.

Mr. ROGERS. Mr. Oberstar?

Mr. OBERSTAR. Thank you, Mr. Chairman.

Mr. Maw, you said in response to the question about congressional action, "If the Law of the Sea negotiations break down completely."

I have a view that international conferences do not just breakdown. Once started, they have a momentum of their own, you know, and they have a life of their own and they just kind of continue from one time to another.

There is an international bureaucracy just as there is a Federal bureaucracy and it generates its own life.

It would take a clear cataclysmic confrontation to make a complete breakdown.

What we are going to see I think is just a striking out of this Law of the Sea Conference over a period of time and I think your statement is really a kind of a foot-dragging statement cautioning Congress not to act.

Now, I would rather say that if you do not come to an agreement in these 8 weeks, not if the conference completely breaks down, but if you do not come to any agreement in this upcoming negotiation then what is your position on congressional action in the form of legislation presently before this committee?

Mr. MAW. By way of general comment on your comment this is perhaps the most complex negotiation ever undertaken on a multilateral basis.

The issues are manifold, Mr. Oberstar and the differences of positions are practically incomprehensible.

They have not been going on very long and in many areas there is emerging a consensus which I think is remarkable considering the number of nations involved and the complexity of the issues.

Now, as you know, perhaps committee I is not making the progress, at least in our judgment, that other issues are making although there are sticky points elsewhere.

Since the last conference the intersessional work has produced forward movement. I think it is significant and it is not the kind of thing that will drag out indefinitely. We are seeing that around the world today. People are moving unilaterally in different directions and when that movement gets to a certain point you have a new ball game.

You have the cod war going on between England and Iceland.

You have a breach of relations as a result of that.

We have our problems with Ecuador and Peru. Every time you have confrontation you make negotiation more difficult.

It is our hope to not exacerbate the confrontation and to achieve a generally accepted overall Law of the Sea Treaty that we can accept and it will have the general acceptance throughout the world.

Mr. OBERSTAR. That still does not answer my question of in the event that the negotiations continue on a prolonged basis what is your view of congressional action on pending legislation?

Mr. MAW. Well, I think you have to take that when we see what our failures are and not anticipate them.

I think we have a reasonable chance of coming out of the next session with something that is close enough to being acceptable that you might even want to move toward provisional implementation.

Mr. OBERSTAR. Is there a provisional closing date for the upcoming session?

Mr. MAW. There is a closing date for the upcoming session subject to a second session if the upcoming session decides that a second session is necessary and that would occur late in the summer.

Mr. OBERSTAR. How many days will this session continue?

Mr. MAW. The first one is 8 weeks.

Mr. OBERSTAR. So in 8 weeks then you would be prepared to come back to this committee and report on the progress of those negotiations?

Mr. MAW. We certainly will report back to this committee promptly after that.

Mr. OBERSTAR. What do you see?

Mr. MAW. In the meantime we will keep the committee posted as to our progress.

Mr. OBERSTAR. Oh, yes; I would hope so.

Now, what do you see as the key issues in the Law of the Sea Conference international seabed authority apportionment of profit, technology transfer?

What other issues do you see as key issues?

Mr. Maw. Well, the key issues in Committee I are we must have unrestricted access on reasonable terms.

We are perfectly willing to have others have access or even the authority to have access or an enterprise of the authority but from our point of view we must have unrestricted access on terms we can live with.

We cannot buy the authority with the power to tell us what we can do, how we can do it, what prices we can charge, etcetera.

I appreciate others have exactly the opposite view, Mr. Oberstar.

Mr. Oberstar. What about the issue of apportionment of profits that many of the undeveloped nations are seeking?

Mr. Maw. We have not got to the point of really meeting that one head on.

I think when the time comes I am not sure what the profits are going to be, but I think we are fairly well committed to some needs on the developing world in this regard.

We have informally made suggestions along that line but they have not pushed them but they are too far apart to talk about this.

Mr. Oberstar. So there is no consensus yet nor does there appear to be one on the horizon on the question of apportionment of profits.

Mr. Maw. Well, there is some recognition in the modified text of that possibility.

Mr. Oberstar. What about the question of technology transfer? Mr. Ratiner and I exchanged on that during his last appearance before the committee.

What is your view of the responsibilities of the United States, if any, to offer technology or technological assistance to other nations who might wish to develop deepsea bed resources?

Mr. Maw. In a treaty the principal technology involved, of course, is privately owned and the Government has some technology which might be dealt with under technology transfer arrangements but there is no contemplation of handing company access technology over to anybody.

In the normal course they may license. We do not know. We have this problem in the world in all kinds of industries, not just in the sea bed.

We have a good many agreements and technology transfer agreements with different countries in different areas.

Whether we are speaking to the extent the Government can assist usually to create a climate for investment for the transfer of technology, it is our duty to do so but the government-to-government transfer is a very rare thing.

Mr. Oberstar. What role do you see the International Seabed Authority playing in the development of the deepsea bed resources?

Mr. Maw. Well, we have taken a position quite consistently that it should have a supervisory role but not a directory role: that its power should be limited. It should not make the rules, it should help to carry them out.

There, of course, as you appreciate we are 180 degrees at variance with the Group of 77.

They look at the Authority as being the complete authority on the deep seabed. We do not recognize that possibility.

If you would like a little elaboration on that I will ask Mr. Ratiner to give you more of the details because this is an ongoing problem of which there are many variations.

Mr. OBERSTAR. Would this Authority be the one that would determine where mining could take place and set up a process for bidding on certain areas of the ocean floor for mineral development?

Is that one of its responsibilities as you see it or is that envisioned in the conference negotiations?

Mr. MAW. I am going to ask Mr. Ratiner to pick up that question because there is some give at the moment in the apparent position of the developing countries where there may be a mutual compromise where we can have unimpeded access and at the same have the Authority have rights of exploitation.

Mr. RATINER. I think, Mr. Oberstar, based on the way the treaty negotiations are shaping up now, the emphasis would be on the Authority establishing procedures by which these things are done. However, the basic conditions or rules pursuant to which they would be done would be established in the treaty itself.

For example, there is the key question of who elects the area to be mined. Whether it is the miner or the Authority is one of the matters that is under negotiation and will finally appear as a treaty article.

Our position is that the Authority would establish reasonable block sizes, but the miner would make the selection of the block that he wished to mine.

The Authority would not then have the right to refuse or direct the miner to mine some place else.

That Mr. Oberstar, would simply not be one of the Authority's prerogatives.

Mr. OBERSTAR. Would the International Seabed Authority view itself as apportioning out so many square miles of ocean floor to certain countries within certain geographical distance, within the geographical relationship to certain countries?

How is this thing coming out of the conference, is what I am trying to get at.

Mr. RATINER. There is a view held by a small number of countries, primarily industrialized countries, not developing countries, who would like to see the Authority restrict the number of available mine sites available to one country or its nationals.

This is sometimes referred to in the negotiations as a quota system. Developing countries do not hold this view.

The developing countries are of the view that some provision should be made for reserving seabed areas for developing country use in the future, if and when they have the technology to mine. Within the nonreserved areas, they believe there should be essentially free competition among industrialized countries with no particular limit on what any one country could have.

Therefore, there is in the negotiation a difficulty along the lines you just described, but it is a difficulty between us and our industrialized country allies rather than a difficulty between us and the developing countries.

Mr. OBERSTAR. That is very interesting. I believe you have got to have some means of determining who is going to mine where otherwise you have a gold rush kind of atmosphere surrounding the development of the deepsea minerals and the United States has to look out for its own interests.

At the same time we do not want to engage in international war on the high seas. Obviously, if we can work out a satisfactory arrangement in an international authority of this kind where who mines where can be worked out on a peaceful basis, that is to everyone's interest.

Do I have further time, Mr. Chairman?

Mr. ROGERS. Yes.

Mr. OBERSTAR. Mr. Maw, one of the objectives of our negotiating team as outlined by Mr. Ratiner in his previous presentation to this committee was to develop a stable investment climate for deepsea bed mining.

What factors would you list as being essential to establishing that stable investment climate?

Mr. MAW. Well, I think the first factor is to achieve a general recognition of the stability in question by other governments.

In other words, if we are out there and the only one who claims the ocean, others are going to be against that claim so we must have a consensus on other nations' concern that a particular minesite for example is going to be inviolate for the use of the one who is mining and so we will not be worried about claim-jumping or other problems.

That is the kind of stability you need in order to encourage investment.

Mr. OBERSTAR. That is one factor.

What other factors would you list?

Mr. MAW. Well, recognition that your product is going to be admissable in the world market as yours.

Mr. OBERSTAR. Yes, but then you do not write that into a treaty. You are talking about a general philosophy, a general attitude of building a recognition on the part of other governments.

Mr. MAW. That is correct.

Mr. OBERSTAR. But then there are some specifics that you want to be sure that someone is going to invest $200 million to $300 million in a mining venture and we in northern Minnesota assured a stable investment climate for the iron ore mining industry in 1964 when the State enacted an amendment to the constitution setting conditions under which the tax status of that industry would be treated for the future and that made it possible for $2 billion of private venture capital to be invested in northern Minnesota.

We are talking about $1 billion investment in this operation. What other factors are there going to be besides general good will?

Mr. MAW. All countries in the world recognize the right to control the extraction of the ore and ship it all over the world.

They do not recognize the right of any one country to exploit the deepsea bed.

Mr. OBERSTAR. And that creates a very unstable climate for investment.

Mr. MAW. Correct, and that to be remedied requires a treaty.

Mr. OBERSTAR. And you say just the existence of a treaty is sufficient in itself, that that represents the general recognition?

Mr. Maw. Properly drawn it is the kind of treaty which could be ratified and would give that protection under international law.

Mr. Oberstar. The English diplomatic historian Harold Nicholson once wrote that Americans are unsurpassed negotiators in business-affairs but when it comes to diplomatic negotiation they are bested most often by their adversaries.

I hope that Harold Nicholson's dour comment on American diplomacy of the early 1900's will not prove true in the upcoming Law of the Sea Conference.

Mr. Maw. I am a good listener.

Mr. Oberstar. Thank you.

Mr. Rogers. Mr. Secretary, what is our current policy toward a mining company mining in international waters which was threatened? Would we give protection to that company?

Mr. Maw. I am sorry but I did not hear the question.

Mr. Rogers. What is the current policy? Currently, we can mine under the deep sea I presume. Is that not current policy?

Mr. Maw. Yes.

Mr. Rogers. And if a company does that?

Mr. Maw. Our companies are now experimentally mining.

Mr. Rogers. Yes.

Mr. Maw. And exercising the rights which we think any country has to exploit the deep seabed.

In every right, of course, there are responsibilities, Mr. Chairman.

Mr. Rogers. I understand that. What I am saying is if they were threatened by someone and as long as they were mining the deep seabed underneath the international borders, is it our national policy to give protection to our nationals in that situation?

Mr. Maw. We have done so in the past. I am not sure what our policy is going to be.

Mr. Rogers. Is there any question about it?

Mr. Maw. Well, we have a great deal of trouble with what we claimed were international waters off Ecuador that we have endeavored to protect our tuna fishermen when they were arrested and we paid their fines.

Mr. Rogers. We will presume there is no argument say about international waters.

Mr. Maw. Well, it will be an argument. We are creating arguments on the 200-mile zone.

Mr. Rogers. I am referring to territory outside of 200 miles.

Mr. Maw. It is not universally recognized that we may unilaterally go out there and mine the deepsea bed.

There are many countries in the world who think we do not have that right and we get into this argument which is pretty much rhetoric.

Mr. Rogers. When has there been a change by treaty of what we have been able to do in international waters?

Mr. Maw. The United Nations passed a resolution and we voted for it calling the deepsea bed the common heritage of mankind.

There are a lot of people that deny what I have just asserted, that we have a right to mine at our leisure or pleasure.

Mr. Rogers. You are saying our country has already decided we do not have the right to mine in international waters?

Mr. Maw. I say there is an issue that all people do not agree with us.

Mr. Rogers. I am not sure we can get agreement within the Government from what you are telling me.

Mr. Maw. I think we have agreement in Government that as a State or individual they could have the right to go.

You asked me whether the Navy is going out to protect them if somebody challenges that right.

Mr. Rogers. Yes, I did. I do not know.

Mr. Maw. I do not know whether the Navy is going to do that or not.

Mr. Rogers. I do not think there is a determined position by our Government on that.

Mr. Maw. We are going to have that problem very soon in the 200-mile zone if we are going to call the Navy out to run boats out of that zone that do not recognize our 200 miles.

Mr. Rogers. Well, what I am talking about is where we have companies mining where it has always been acceptable, now you tell me our Government is divided and that it is not really right for a company to go in and do it, that it is an internationally owned zone.

Mr. Maw. There is disagreement in international law among nations and scholars.

Mr. Rogers. And we supported the basis of that disagreement I presume.

Mr. Maw. Unfortunately it has not yet been challenged.

Mr. Rogers. Well, I thought you said we had passed the resolution in the U.N. with our vote.

Mr. Maw. Well, that is correct; but that does not necessarily mean we have given up our right to mine.

Mr. Rogers. Well, it is not very encouraging. I would think that the companies who want to go out and mine, would want to have some assurance and we do not even have a policy as to whether we will protect them or not.

Mr. Maw. That underscores the urgency of this treaty.

Mr. Rogers. Or perhaps law that will set forth a national policy for this country.

Have other nations the same capability as we do in this Nation for deepsea mining?

Mr. Maw. Not that we know of.

Mr. Rogers. So I am not sure what encouragement there is for other nations to get into this very heavily unless they do decide to divide up our properties that our companies might go in and mine.

I see no encouragement for them to sign.

Had you thought of proceeding with a treaty just among the developed countries?

Mr. Maw. That has been suggested as one of many alternative ways of proceeding in this but that ignores the rights of the undeveloped countries.

Mr. Rogers. I understand that, but assuming that they are ready to mine they can come in with us.

Mr. MAW. Well, that is part of it. In order to achieve an overall settlement we hope to have a consensus on the many issues which this is only one of and there are people that think we should ignore the law of the sea and go our own way.

There are other nations that feel the Law of the Sea Treaty is not going to do them any good and they would have sooner whatever conflicts come.

This administration and the prior administration thinks we should, if possible, achieve a negotiated settlement of this complex situation.

Mr. ROGERS. Thank you, so much.

The gentleman from California, Mr. McCloskey.

Mr. MCCLOSKEY. I am just sitting here ex officio, Mr. Chairman, but thank you for the privilege.

Mr. ROGERS. Are there any major developed countries that agree with us who are trying to also bring about a similar approach as our Government is presenting?

Mr. MAW. I think it is fair to say that we started alone on our present position.

Mr. ROGERS. Russia has a position?

Mr. MAW. They are very opposed to the position we take.

Mr. ROGERS. England?

Mr. MAW. Opposed.

Mr. ROGERS. What is the main point of contention?

Mr. MAW. Well, at the moment we are the only country that can go and do the mining and if we go and we preempt the market they take the position that is not cricket.

Mr. RATINER. Mr. Chairman, I might add that the industrialized countries on one vital point, as I elaborated in response to a question from Mr. Oberstar, do feel that we should not be given the freest possible opportunity to monopolize deep seabed resources. But with that exception, on 90 percent of the other significant issues in committee I they do generally support the United States position, and we generally support their position.

There are a number of countries, not very many, but nevertheless quite important, who, by and large, hold the same views in Committee I, and with whom we concert our activities on a regular basis, subject to that one very important point, which I hope will get resolved sooner rather than later.

Mr. ROGERS. Mr. Oberstar?

Mr. OBERSTAR. Thank you, Mr. Chairman.

Mr. Maw. does it not concern you at all that resource cartels, apart from OPEC, are being formed to control the development and distribution of minerals that are in short supply?

Mr. MAW. Well, I am not sure they are being formed in that sense. Some efforts have been made between two or three raw material producers to create an OPEC-type cartel.

Mr. OBERSTAR. Well. CPEC has already been formed, although it is not very effective, but it has been formed, and there are others in bauxite, tin, aluminum.

Mr. MAW. We have, on several occasions, stated the administration's position on raw materials agreements, and the recognition of some of the problems.

We will have compensation problems perhaps in the deep seabed, and we have stated that we are prepared to support a compensatory system of economic adjustment assistance.

We have several commodity agreements already negotiated, as you know, where we try to produce orderly markets, but that is different from the cartels where you have the producers alone trying to establish.

That we do not join. That we do not approve, but we are willing to negotiate in appropriate cases, commodity arrangements, between consumers and producers.

Mr. OBERSTAR. So you are aware and concerned then all the more the United States should be firm and forceful and effective in negotiations because we are talking about deep seabed mineral resources that are in short supply, if not virtually nonexistent in the United States; all the more important for us to negotiate a good and favorable treaty that will generate the widest possible development by the United States of these resources.

Mr. MAW. Precisely.

Mr. OBERSTAR. Now, one further question on pollution abatement.

What consideration is being given in the treaty to adequate measures to prevent pollution of the ocean?

Mr. MAW. Will you take that question?

Mr. RATINER. There are several provisions in the "Single Negotiating Text" to which we still have to make some minor amendments.

By and large, those provisions do provide for the Authority, subject to a general standard set forth in the treaty, to be responsible for ensuring that the marine environment is protected.

Now, we can, if it would be helpful, submit for you separately a listing of the various articles of the treaty which, in fact, provide for that protection.

Essentially, it is a rulemaking system in which the International Seabed Resource Authority is charged with the topics general guidance for regulations which it must establish and enforce.

Mr. OBERSTAR. Well, for instance, if there were plans, and I am just speculating now, I hope you will get this information in in further testimony that the committee will receive, but if there were plans for concentration of raw material at sea, and discharge of waste back into the ocean, I would anticipate this would be something the treaty would address itself to.

Has that issue, in fact, been raised?

Is this part of your negotiations?

Mr. RATINER. Yes, it is, Mr. Oberstar. The issue has been raised, and we are in the process at this moment of refining our position somewhat on precisely what would be the Authority's regulatory and enforcement powers with respect to discharges at sea while a mining ship was either mining or processing at a mine site.

We do want to be careful in this treaty not to give the Authority any more jurisdiction over activities that occur in the water column than is absolutely essential to protect against this precise problem which you have raised.

This is a seabed resource authority, and not an oceans authority. We want to be very careful to structure the marine environment protection provisions in such a way that the Authority does not feel that it also has the authority to regulate general activities in the water column.

There are other international organizations which deal with shipping and discharges from ships. We would like, to the maximum extent practicable, to insure that their jurisdiction is maintained and that the Authority is restricted to things having to do with ocean mining very particularly.

Mr. OBERSTAR. Do those authorities address themselves to the issue of discharges of this nature?

Mr. RATINER. Well, it is a fact that both the Ocean Dumping Convention, and indeed, the Convention on Pollution from Ships left a bit of a vacancy in respect of ocean mining.

These negotiations happened to occur while the Law of the Sea negotiations were in progress, and thus an exemption was provided, particularly in the Ocean Dumping Convention.

In the Committee I section of the Law of the Sea Convention, we will try not to create any conflict between IMCO and the International Seabed Resource Authority.

Mr. OBERSTAR. If your seabed treaty were to incorporate the others simply by reference, you would leave a big hole there that would not be covered.

Mr. RATINER. That is correct, and we are acutely aware of that problem.

Mr. OBERSTAR. Thank you, Mr. Chairman.

Mr. JONES [presiding]. Any other members have further questions? If not, the Chair now recognizes counsel.

Mr. PERIAN. Mr. Ratiner, when we talk about U.S. ocean mining companies, how many such enterprises are we talking about?

Mr. RATINER. Well, there are many ways to characterize that. We generally think of four major companies, four leadership companies, which are International Nickle, Kennecott, Deepsea Ventures and Lockheed.

However, at least three, and possibly four of these companies have partners, in some cases domestic partners and in some cases foreign partners. In terms of the leading technology in the world, it is the United States together with its foreign partners, a number perhaps in the vicinity of between 15 and 25 major worldwide companies, which have a very immediate and very significant interest in deep ocean mining.

Then more peripheral investments have been made by another 20 odd companies in certain experimental work, such as the continuous line bucket dredging system, which was a consortium developed exclusively for the purpose of testing a method of recovering nodules.

It is not a consortium for an integrated mining approach and required very small investments from its members.

I think it would be unfair to put those companies on anything like the level of the four major American companies that I referred to initially.

Mr. PERIAN. So there are essentially four major American companies?

Mr. RATINER. With many partners, all important mining houses, or other major investors.

Mr. PERIAN. I refer to Chairman Murphy's opening statement at these hearings, and I am quoting:

In the opinion of experts at the Law of the Sea Conference the value of the minerals contained in manganese nodules on the ocean floor is estimated at $3 trillion.

Experts also estimate that the nodules are so abundant that it would only take 1 percent of the ocean bottom to satisfy the world's needs for about 50 years.

We had testimony last week from a half dozen scientists from the University of Hawaii who claim that these estimates are very low and that in actuality there are substantially more of these nodules.

You and Mr. Maw have said, in effect, that the foreign nations at the Law of the Sea, feel that the United States would be hogging up the minerals because we are the only ones with the technology.

Does that not seem a little absurd in view of the huge quantities of these nodules, the small number of companies, and the fact that those countries will be catching up in a matter of 10 or 15 years?

Mr. RATINER. Mr. Perian, I want to say first that the figures you have used are wildly speculative, and I realize you did not use the figures, that you are quoting from the experts.

Nobody has any idea what the quantity and value of the resources of the seabed are. Very little survey work of a sufficiently detailed character has been done in the world oceans to arrive at anything but wildly speculative figures.

Nevertheless, it is quite clear that the resource is enormous. That is not wildly speculative. That is a fact, and it is true that the United States, if it were capable of producing all of the manganese nodules which the market would bear for the next 50 years, will be producing an insignificant portion of the total available resource.

Mr. PERIAN. Assuming domestic legislation is needed, do you support the inclusion of insurance provisions in the law?

Mr. RATINER. Mr. Perian, the administration has previously testified, in respect to specific insurance provisions which we have been able to read, study, and analyze, that it was not in favor of those provisions.

What you are asking is a very general question of principle. Would insurance, under certain circumstances in a carefully structured program of insurance seem reasonable? My own view is yes.

Insurance provisions of a certain type at a certain time, at the right time, and for very circumscribed risks would be reasonable. However, the answer in the abstract is really of very little value to the committee.

The present question is whether we should have a certain kind of legislation right now with a certain kind of insurance provision in it. To that, the administration is satisfied the answer is no.

Mr. PERIAN. Given your position, that is you agree that we should have insurance provisions in round numbers, what might that cost the Federal Government?

Mr. RATINER. That is a very easy one, Mr. Perian, because the amount of insurance which the Government could make available can be fixed.

One can establish what one thinks is a reasonable contingent liability based on the knowledge of how much investment there is likely to be, how much ocean mining activity there is likely to be, and what the risks are going to be.

If I were trying to fix an overall limit on insurance liability for the next 3, 4 or 5 years based on the political factors which I know, the number of companies who are about to go into ocean mining and the risks they are facing, I would fix that figure at about $500 million.

Now, I consider that figure to be very low, but probably adequate for the moment.

Mr. PERIAN. Under what conditions would the minerals retrieved from the deep seabed be taxable by the Federal Government?

Mr. RATINER. To take this logically, Mr. Perian, legislation would first have to prohibit American nationals from mining the seabed.

That would be the first step in any legislative scheme.

Mr. PERIAN. Would it prohibit them from bringing minerals from another country to be processed?

Mr. RATINER. You could do that also, but the first step in domestic legislation would have to be a prohibition on mining by American nationals, except as provided in this legislation. Otherwise they would be free to do it.

Once you have established the right to prohibit mining, you would attempt to fix a level of income for the United States as the price for obtaining some sort of rights from the United States, assuming we had rights to confer on ocean mining companies in the deep seabed. The amount of the royalty would presumably be fixed in accordance with what the U.S. Government thought was reasonable, and would leave sufficient profit so as to attract the commercial ventures in the deep seabed.

Mr. PERIAN. Just one final question.

When Mr. Frizzell testified last week, he stated in his testimony that the Department of the Interior has "diligently sought to fulfill its responsibility" in fostering and encouraging "the development of economically sound and stable domestic mining, minerals, and metals industry."

You are the Ocean Mining Administrator. What have you done with regard to deep ocean mining, besides your work directed at the Law of the Sea Conference?

Mr. RATINER. First of all, Mr. Perian, the work done in the Law of the Sea Conference is, in fact, the most significant way that one can promote and encourage the development of an ocean mining capability for the United States.

Until one is satisfied that there can be no treaty, then it is clear that the major burden of establishing an attractive and stable investment climate falls on the negotiators at the Law of the Sea Conference, and in a sense, on the role which the U.S. Government will play when it interfaces with a new International Resource Seabed Authority.

I do not think we should minimize the extent to which that is the primary focus of our intention. It should be, and must be the primary focus.

However, another area which is very significant to the future of ocean mining, and which does not involve the treaty negotiations, is the adequacy of our environmental impact statement.

As you know, the U.S. Government will need to have an environmental impact statement whether it presents a treaty to the Senate, or whether it one day should favor legislation, or produce its own legislation.

To that end, the Department of Interior has, for 4 years, been engaged in an attempt to draft what we would consider a satisfactory programmatic environmental impact statement.

We rely in our work very heavily, of course, on the at sea investigations and environmental assessments, which the National Oceanic and Atmospheric Administration is presently engaged in, referred to as DOMES-1.

Nevertheless, we feel that as part of our responsibility for ocean mining and preparation for the future it is extremely important that we continue to draft an environmental impact statement, perfect it, show it to interested members of the public, and approve the information base that goes into the drafting of that statement.

Another area which we feel is very important to promoting and encouraging the development of a domestic ocean mining capability is having the best possible communications between ourselves and industry, understanding their problems, acquiring as much information as we can about their technology and their plans for the future so that Government does not make any mistakes unwittingly.

We have diligently sought to maintain those contacts on a regular, almost daily basis, so as to insure that we have up to date information, and that we do not put any roadblocks in the way of the industry.

Finally, and again of considerable importance, we have spent considerable effort during the last few years analyzing the possibilities for legislation, either the kind that would implement a Law of the Sea Treaty, if one is forthcoming on a reasonable schedule, or the kind as this committee has before it, which would substitute for a Law of the Sea Treaty, if one is not forthcoming.

Mr. Perian, we have done quite a bit of drafting. We have nothing to show for it because the administration has never agreed that it should put forward legislation.

Nevertheless, the work goes on. We have, in fact, told Congress many times that we are diligently working in this area, which is usually referred to euphemistically as interim policy. What that means is studying various legislative alternatives that could be applied to ocean mining under certain contingencies.

I should also add that we have prepared, drafted and consulted with the industry on what rules and regulations for ocean mining should be applied in the context of a Law of the Sea Treaty.

We have also engaged in active negotiations in the Law of the Sea Conference in respect to those regulations.

Needless to say, having worked out the details of those regulations, they are readily available to us, subject to modification and amendment as we learn new information, as a first draft for domestic purposes, should that become necessary.

In short, we have spent a great deal of time and effort with rather limited resources, trying to be in the best possible posture so that when Government had to take the major step forward, it would be ready to do so with all the necessary actions having been done, and the right materials having been drafted.

There is one area to which I have referred before this committee previously, where inadequacies exist. In my own view, the Government needs to develop more programs to acquire a variety of data so as to put itself in the best possible position for making long-term rules and regulations, either in assistance of an International Seabed Resource Authority pursuant to a treaty, or if that does not come to pass. in order to backstop our domestic ocean mining programs.

Mr. PERIAN. Thank you.

Mr. JONES. I thank you two gentlemen for your appearance here this morning. That concludes your testimony?

Mr. RATINER. Yes, it does, Mr. Chairman.

The Chair now recognizes Hon. James A. Baker, III, Under Secretary, U.S. Department of Commerce.

STATEMENT OF HON. JAMES A. BAKER, III, UNDER SECRETARY OF COMMERCE, ACCOMPANIED BY DR. ROBERT WHITE, ADMINIS-TRATOR OF THE NATIONAL OCEANIC AND ATMOSPHERIC AD-MINISTRATION; MR. BRIAN HOYLE, OFFICE OF GENERAL COUNSEL

Mr. BAKER. Mr. Chairman, I am pleased to have the opportunity to testify before you this morning.

On my right is Dr. Robert White, the very able and distinguished Administrator of our National Oceanic and Atmospheric Administration, and on my left Mr. Brian Hoyle from the Office of General Counsel, National Oceanic and Atmospheric Administration.

A primary concern of the administration in approaching the question of seabed mining legislation is that the mineral requirements of the United States be met in sufficient quantities and at fair market prices. To achieve this goal, we believe a vital and effective marine mining industry is needed. This nation must import 100 percent of its requirements of cobalt and manganese and close to 100 percent of its requirements of nickel. These minerals are available in large quantities in the form of manganese nodules lying on thousands of square miles of the sea floor. The estimated recoverable quantities of these minerals from manganeses nodules are very large in relation to known world reserves.

In order to commence commercial production of these manganese nodules, the marine mining industry needs not only the technical capability, which it now appears to have. but must commit large sums of capital on the order to $500 million to build the mining equipment, vessels and refining facilities necessary to produce and market these minerals.

From discussions that I have had with leaders of the ocean mining industry it is evident that in order to commit this financing the industry must have some guarantee that their investment will not be rendered a total loss through certain actions beyond their control. There are differences within industry regarding the nature of this guarantee.

A widely accepted Law of the Sea Treaty to which the United States is a party would provide this Nation access to a stable supply of the minerals found in the seabed, and would enable American ocean miners to operate in a stable investment climate. A timely treaty acceptable to U.S. interests would thus provide the basic protection to the American ocean mining industry that is needed.

Next Monday the third session of the United Nations Law of the Sea Conference will commence. As previous administration witnesses have advised you, the informal intersessional meetings held in New York in November and February have given us reason for cautious optimism that a satisfactory treaty is obtainable this year.

The imminence of the next session and the preliminary indications that a new negotiating climate may emerge in Committee I leads the administration to the conclusion that we should not support any ocean mining legislation at this time.

However, as Under Secretary Maw and Frizzell indicated in their recent testimony, the administration is continuing to explore the question of appropriate ocean mining legislation so that we will be ready to take any necessary action in light of the results of the ongoing deep seabed negotiations in the Law of the Sea Conference.

In inviting me to testify, you requested that I advise you of the progress of the current discussions between the Departments of Commerce and Interior regarding their roles in marine mining.

As Under Secretary of Interior Frizzell described to you, former Secretary Morton and Secretary Kleppe met in late December to discuss the jurisdiction of their respective Departments over ocean mining. Both Secretaries expressed their desire that the matter be settled between the two Departments. Since then Under Secretary Frizzell and Dr. White, administrator of NOAA, have met and have resolved a number of the issues.

Secretary Richardson and Secretary Kleppe are working on this. Each of them want to continue the close working relationship between Commerce and Interior so that the two Departments' programs will be complementary without unnecessary duplication. No matter how the matter is resolved the expertise of both Departments will be required.

I would like to turn now to the role that the Department of Commerce is playing in the development of this Nation's ocean mining industry.

The Department of Commerce views deep seabed mining as requiring a two-pronged approach. This Government must encourage the development of a sound, technically capable ocean mining industry. At the same time, the Government has a responsibility to ensure that these resources are developed according to a sound resource management program, which ensures that seabed mining is carried out wisely. Of course, any regulations should be kept to the minimum necessary so as not to impair the productive potential of this new industry.

In 1974, in response to the need for better lines of communication with industry, marine scientists, environmental groups, and industry, Commerce created the Marine Petroleum and Minerals Advisory Committee. This Advisory Committee has met regularly under the chairmanship of NOAA Deputy Administrator Howard Pollock. Through the committee, environmental groups and marine scientists have indicated to us their concerns regarding wise resource management.

In addition, industry has conveyed its views on both the Law of the Sea and domestic ocean mining legislation. Since representatives of industry are appearing before this committee today, I shall let them advise you first hand of their concerns.

I might note, however, the mining industry has recommended that the Department work with the industry to promote technology transfer. The Maritime Administration has a keen interest in the latest technology development in the field of marine transport associated with mining.

Within NOAA we intend to effect such a Department/industry relationship. Since the creation of NOAA with the Department of Commerce in 1970, the Department has maintained close contacts with industry, beginning with the Mining Panel of the Ocean Science and Technology Advisory Committee which I mentioned earlier.

Department of Commerce programs focus on a broad front of raw material issues. The Domestic and International Business Administration (DIBA) is a major participant in the development of United States commodity policies concerning, domestic and foreign commodities, including minerals, to assure adequate supply at reasonable prices.

DIBA further provides economic expertise on a wide range of related issues which will assist us in the development of a sound national deep seabed mining policy. Commerce with State and Treasury are members with the President's Economic Policy Board/National Security Council Commodities Policy Group.

NOAA possesses extensive scientific, engineering and administrative competence that enables it to carry out its responsibilities for marine resource management. Other departments in the Government, and industry are looking to the Department of Commerce and NOAA to provide them with environmental impact assessments and technical data from NOAA marine research, which are necessary to the development of governmental ocean mining policies. In 1972, industry, through the Ocean Science and Technology Advisory Committee, requested NOAA to expand its activities in the ocean mining field.

The outgrowth of this recommendation was the Deep Ocean Mining Environmental Study (DOMES) which is nearing the end of its first phase. In the next phase, DOMES in conjunction with industry will carry out a pilot ocean mining project for the purpose of assessing the environmental effects of an actual ocean mining operation.

Perhaps the most important point here is that ocean miners are not dealing with the same problems encountered in land based mining operations. Entirely new technologies are required, for deep seabed mining.

The institutional framework in which deep seabed mining will take place should be a part of the new ocean management programs which this Nation is currently attempting to design, both nationally and internationally. These new ocean management programs must of necessity be interrelated.

The Department of Commerce, through NOAA has specialized expertise that can help advance the understanding of the problems of resource recovery from the deep oceans. Through its office of Marine

Minerals, which coordinates and develops NOAA's ocean mining programs, NOAA has established the infrastructure necessary to provide timely information for use in the development of Government ocean mining policies.

The Department of Commerce considers the development of deep ocean mining resources to be of critical importance to this country. We shall use all our capabilities and experience to encourage that development.

Mr. Chairman, this completes my statement. I will be happy to answer such questions as you or members of the committee have.

Mr. JONES. Thank you.

On page two, your last sentence, first paragraph, you say there are differences within industry regarding the nature of this guarantee.

Could you perhaps give us a little more explanation of what those differences are?

Mr. BAKER. Yes, Sir.

Mr. JONES. And also the position of your department as it relates to these differences.

Mr. BAKER. Well, sir, in our discussions with industry, most of the people we have talked with have indicated that some form of insurance or guarantee of investment, pending a resolution of the Law of the Sea Treaty or some form of permanent domestic legislation, would, in effect, provide that they would at least receive a return of their investment.

Other companies, on the other hand, have indicated to us that insurance alone, providing for a return of their investment, would not be sufficient. They say they would have to have, in order to embark upon this and make the financial expenditures that would be required, they would have to have something more by way of some form of site specific tenure, or insurance, which would go further than just repaying their investment, and would also compensate them for the loss of profits if a commercial profitable operation were interrupted.

Mr. JONES. Thank you, sir.

I notice also on page 2 that you have reason for cautious optimism that a satisfactory treaty is obtainable this year.

Do you honestly feel that the Law of the Sea Treaty can be worked out, concluded in a fair and equitable manner for this Nation in protecting our interests?

Mr. BAKER. Mr. Chairman, in the light of the lack of progress in recent years I think we would say that yes, we do honestly believe that there is reason for cautious optimism.

We believe that the indicated change of position which the prior witnesses this morning have mentioned to you gives us reason for cautious optimism.

The position of the lesser developed countries, we believe, is changing substantially, as evidenced by the intersessional meetings in New York.

Mr. JONES. I wish I could share your optimism, and I hope you are right and I am wrong.

Mr. Oberstar?

Mr. OBERSTAR. Thank you, Mr. Chairman.

I, too, share the Chair's concern about the future of this Conference.

Mr. BAKER. I might say, Mr. Chairman, that this is the first move that could be interpreted as being an optimistic move in the right direction, and that is one reason we are optimistic.

Mr. OBERSTAR. Mr. Baker, could you do a little better job than your predecessor, of specifying for me those specific elements you would consider to be vital to establishment of a stable investment climate?

We know a treaty would be one of those factors, but what elements specifically in a treaty, some of those referred to? I would like to have a catalog of one, two, three, four.

Mr. BAKER. Well, I think that one of the prior witnesses indicated that perhaps the most important element would be guaranteed access, or right to access.

I think that as far as industry is concerned, we would have to have a treaty that did not provide for price or production controls, except perhaps as a part of an overall international commodities agreement that related to minerals other than simply minerals obtained from the deep seabed. Another essential element, I think, would be a mechanism in the Seabed Authority which would be fair, which industry in this country would consider fair and equitable as far as their interests were concerned.

By that I mean some form of assembly or council in which we had a say commensurate with our stake.

Mr. OBERSTAR. That is a little more specific than what we had earlier.

What progress do you see being made toward achievement of those objectives in the International Law of the Sea Conference, and how does the presently written craft treaty respond, in your judgment, to those factors that you have listed as important elements in assuring stability?

Mr. BAKER. Mr. Oberstar, my question to Mr. Ratiner was to the extent to which certain information was classified.

I could not recall the extent to which it was, and he indicated to me that he testified last week, in response to a similar question.

I think that all I should say is that the intersessional meetings in New York indicate that we are making progress on all three of the points that I mentioned as being necessary for stable investment climate, and in the opinion of this Department, in any event, required before we would have a treaty which we would consider acceptable as far as industry is concerned.

Mr. OBERSTAR. Does the legislation pending before this committee, that is, Mr. Murphy's bill, accomplish those objectives, in your judgment?

Mr. BAKER. Yes, sir; I think that we have to say that it accomplishes those objectives, but of course, it is without the framework of a treaty, which as Under Secretary Maw indicated, we believe is the most desirable approach.

Mr. OBERSTAR. And speaking for the Department of Commerce, that agency of government most interested in economic development, then I would assume from that statement that if these treaty negotiations do not result in a treaty you would be prepared to support the legislation?

Mr. BAKER. I think there is a point, yes, sir; at which we would definitely be prepared to support the legislation.

I cannot say that that is after this L.O.S. session. I think a lot depends on the extent of the progress during the session.

If real progress has been made, it may be that the summer session would be the key as to when we would look toward, and when we might expect to have a satisfactory treaty.

To answer your question, I think the Department of Commerce would certainly favor legislation of the type that has been introduced by the chairman.

Our primary problem with it is that we do not favor it at this time.

Mr. OBERSTAR. We will be coming back to you, I am sure, when the Law of the Sea Conference has concluded, and when we are prepared to move again.

Thank you very much.

Mr. JONES. Mr. Oberstar, the Chair would suggest, if it is any classified information you cannot get here, that you call Daniel Schorr.

Mr. Forsythe is recognized.

Mr. FORSYTHE. Thank you, Mr. Chairman.

Mr. Baker, do you agree with the statement we heard that perhaps not these 8 weeks, but this year is perhaps the last chance for reaching the Law of the Sea Treaty?

Mr. BAKER. I think so, yes, sir; unless meaningful progress is made. I would agree with the statement.

Mr. FORSYTHE. Well, you suggested perhaps we would be holding these hearings more in the real world if they were being held 8 weeks from now.

Mr. BAKER. As far as the position of the administration is concerned, I would agree with that: yes, sir.

Mr. FORSYTHE. Apparently, if American industry could go wide open and supply the total needs for perhaps 50 years, they would still only touch an insignificant portion of the resources available.

Do you see that it should be the real concern of our world order that we have been hearing so much about, is it not possible that this is going to be beneficial to mankind, even if it is without a treaty?

Mr. BAKER. I think it could be beneficial to mankind, yes, sir, in the absence of a treaty, but I think the concerns of the lesser developed countries, and even the industrialized countries that are not as far advanced as we are technologically, are indeed, germane.

I think, Mr. Forsythe, they would want a piece of the action.

Mr. FORSYTHE. In the meantime we may well suffer some serious shortages of very important minerals that are just waiting for us.

I will concede that you bring up an issue that was brought up earlier about the 200-mile fisheries legislation, the confrontations that are perhaps going to be involved, and these minerals for sure are not going to go away, where the fish, if they are depleted, may have some problem in coming back.

I think that that is a totally different context involved in this kind of a situation. I might have more patience because the minerals will not disappear, but I am concerned that the fish are disappearing, but somehow I agree that I do not think we can go too long down this road.

We appreciate your testimony.

I thank you. Mr. Chairman.

Mr. JONES. Thank you, Mr. Forsythe.

Mr. McCloskey?

Mr. McCLOSKEY. Thank you very much, Mr. Chairman.

Mr. Baker, on page three of your testimony, you mentioned the committee requested you advise them on the progress of the current discussions between the Department of Commerce and Department of Interior regarding the role of marine mining.

Rather than take the time today, could you submit in writing a list of the issues on which Secretary Kleppe and Secretary Morton have agreed, as well as the points that are still to be resolved?

Mr. BAKER. We will be glad to do so, yes, sir.

Mr. McCLOSKEY. In so doing, I wonder if you could footnote the basic laws underlining the jurisdiction claims of Commerce and In terior.

Mr. BAKER. Yes, sir, be glad to supply that.

[The following was received for the record.]

DEPARTMENT OF COMMERCE

MARINE MINERALS ACTIVITIES

OVERVIEW

The Department of Commerce believes that the development of marine minerals will be necessary if the mineral requirements of the United States are to be met in sufficient quantities and at fair market prices. The development of marine minerals, in the Department's view, will require a two-pronged approach. First, we believe a technically capable, viable, and effective marine mining industry is needed. Second, and of equal importance, marine mineral resources should be developed in an orderly manner according to a sound and wise mineral resource management program designed both to satisfy this nation's mineral needs and protect the quality of the marine environment. Of course, any governmental assistance and regulations must be kept to the minimum necessary.

The Department of Commerce has various activities associated with the development of marine minerals. The Department of the Interior also has various activities associated with marine minerals development. The two Departments are working together to make the marine minerals activities of each Department complementary and without unnecessary duplication. In any event, the expertise of both Departments will be required, as will those of other Federal agencies.

DEPARTMENT OF COMMERCE ELEMENTS

The Department of Commerce's marine minerals activities are managed through several Departmental offices and agencies.

National Oceanic and Atmospheric Administration (NOAA).—NOAA responsibilities related to marine minerals development include prediction and forecasting of weather and oceanic conditions, mapping and charting, oceanographic research, marine environmental impact assessment and prediction, mineral resource technology, environmental assessment technology, education related to the development of marine resources (including practices, techniques, and equipment) and imparting knowledge by instruction, practical demonstration, and publication through marine advisory programs to persons interested or employed in marine resource development related fields. An Office of Marine Minerals within NOAA coordinates these activities.

Office of Energy and Strategic Resource Policy (OESRP).—OESRP is responsible for the development and coordination of Departmental energy and resource policies including those related to marine minerals development. Included are responsibilities for the adequacy of supplies to the U.S. consumer at fair and reasonable prices for internationally traded raw materials including energy. International market trends are closely monitored in the formulation of trade policies.

Domestic and International Business Administration (DIBA).—DIBA's programs relevant to marine minerals development include close and continuing contact with the domestic mining industry regarding production, processes, consumption, and the market situation through the conduct of studies and in the conduct of extensive market research and domestic policy analysis.

Economic Development Administration (EDA)—Pursuant to the Public Works and Economic Development Act, EDA provides funds and assistance to State, local and regional groups for planning programs aimed at creating new sources of income and employment. It provides technical assistance in dealing with impediments to economic progress and opportunities, including support for pilot or demonstration projects. EDA also provides funds and assistance for public works and development facilities needed for new industry and to encourage business expansion in areas of high unemployment or low income families. Business development in economically lagging areas is assisted through loans to private industry.

For a designated redevelopment area, EDA funds and assistance would be available, under appropriate circumstances, to aid in the development of seabed minerals including related activities in the coastal zone.

Maritime Administration (MARAD).—MARAD programs relevant to marine minerals development include Federal ship financing guarantees and related shoreside marine facilities or equipment; subsidy programs for ships built in American shipyards; port development; ship pollution control; development of safety standards on design and construction of special purpose vessels, such as deepsea submersibles for hard mineral exploration and production; and research and development of promising concepts which could be applied to transporting minerals from ocean sites.

National Bureau of Standards (NBS).—Major NBS programs related to ocean minerals activities include the development of standard reference materials for calibration and quality control in water pollution measurements, new measurement techniques, chemical and physical properties of water pollutants. The National Bureau of Standards Institute of Materials Research exercises overall management supervision of these programs.

Marine Mineral Activities of Department of Commerce Elements.—The following is a summary of historical and/or ongoing marine minerals development related activities of the Department of Commerce since approximately 1970. The summary is subdivided to indicate the Departmental agency or element which performed or is performing the activity.

1. National Oceanic and Atmospheric Administration

A. Office of the Administrator

The Deputy Administrator of NOAA serves on the Executive Committee of the Interagency Law of the Sea Task Force.

The Deputy Administrator of NOAA heads the Commerce delegation to meetings of the Third UN Conference on Law of the Sea.

NOAA co-sponsored the June 9–12, 1976 "National Planning Conference on the Commercial Development of the Oceans", which included a marine minerals panel.

B. Office of the Associate Administrator for Marine Resources

Provides policy guidance and overview for all of NOAA's marine resources programs including those conducted by its Office of Marine Minerals and its Manned Undersea Science and Technology Office, and the Environmental Research Laboratories, the Office of Sea Grant, and the National Ocean Survey (1970–1966).

Convened an industrial meeting in 1972 at NOAA's Marine Mining Technology Center (MMTC) in order to review MMTC's program and help define MMTC's role and priority research areas and programs to implement this role. One of the major recommendations of this group was that NOAA sponsor a program to determine the environmental impact of deep ocean mining. The subsequent Deep Ocean Mining Environment Study (DOMES) grew out of this recommendation.

Participated in the development of a preliminary draft environmental impact statement (DEIS) for deep ocean mining (1972–1973), information from which was later incorporated into the Department of State's DEIS for the 1974 Caracas Law of the Sea Conference.

Established in 1975 an Office of Marine Minerals to serve as a focal point for NOAA's marine hard minerals activities and to implement new activities required to facilitate the orderly development of marine mineral resources in an environmentally compatible manner.

1. Office of Marine Minerals (1975–1976)

Sponsored a major marine minerals workshop in March 1976 in which about 80 experts from around the country participated. The workshop's objectives were:

To provide an information base of past and present marine mineral-related activities conducted through the National Sea Grant Program and by other elements of NOAA;

To encourage better communications among those directly involved in marine mineral-related activities; and

To develop information regarding the future directions of NOAA's existing programs and activities needed to further development of marine mineral resources in an environmentally safe manner.

Provides representation on the Working Group on Effects on Fisheries of Marine Sand and Gravel Extraction of the International Council for the Exploration of the Sea.

Provide background support for Law of the Sea negotiations with respect to the deep seabed by assisting in the preparation and review of position papers and providing membership on the Department's delegation to UN sponsored conferences.

Consideration any analysis of interim legislation for ocean mining.

Coordinated hard minerals panel at the National Planning Conference on the Commercial Development of the Oceans (June 1976).

Maintains close liaison with industrial firms and academic institutions which are conducting marine mineral activities or which have interests in the field.

Engaged in the conduct of studies to evaluate environmental and socio-economic impacts of onshore processing associated with deep ocean mining.

Engaged in the development of a detailed technical assessment of marine minerals technology (being performed by the National Academy of Sciences—National Research Council).

2. Manual Undersea Science and Technology Office

Assesses Federal agencies' requirements for the use of manned undersea facilities for the Interagency Committee on Marine Science and Engineering (ICMSE) and serves as a coordinator for the use of such facilities (1972–1976).

Co-sponsor of the French-American Mid-Ocean Undersea Study (FAMOUS) which conducted research that provides additional knowledge regarding the origins of deep ocean marine mineral resources (1974–1975).

Sponsored submersible dives on the East Coast, West Coast and in the Straits of Florida which provided information regarding the origins and characteristics of marine mineral resources (1972–1975).

C. Environmental Research Laboratories (ERL)

NOAA's ERL has been responsible for a number of research studies and related projects through the four activities under its jurisdiction. Some of this work has been carried out by ERL staff and other work has been done by contractors.

1. Marine Minerals Technology Center/Pacific Marine Environmental Laboratory [1]

Investigated heavy mineral placer sampling techniques (ERL staff) (1970).

Developed system for real time electronic positioning and navigation at sea (Barnes, Newman—ERL staff) (1970–1971).

Investigated slurry flow in vertical pipes (Wing—ERL staff) (1970–1971).

Conducted literature search on marine mining environmental impact (Battelle Memorial Institute) (1970).

Conducted laboratory studies on effects of suspended sediments on marine organisms (Padan, Davis and Nudi—ERL staff) (1970–1972).

[1] Ceased operation in 1973; functions of the Center were integrated into ERL's Pacific Marine Environmental Laboratory (PMEL).

Developed technique to detect self-potential field of seafloor metallic ore bodies (Corevin—University of California) (1970–1971).

Geophysical identification and classification of sea floor sediments (Barnes—ERL staff) (1970–1971).

Studied United Kingdom offshore sand and gravel mining industry (Hess—ERL staff) (1970–1971).

Conducted literature search on anchor blocks and laterally loaded piles (Keller, Duncan—University of California) (1970–1972).

Developed diver-operated seafloor sampler (Jenkins—ERL staff) (1971–1972).

Investigated effects of suspension sediment on the eastern lobster (Cobb—ERL staff) (1971–1972).

Continuing laboratory studies on effects of suspended sediments on marine estuarine organisms (Peddicor—University of California, Bodega Marine Lab) (1972–1976).

Studied manganese nodules (infrared microanalysis) (Estep—U.S. Bureau of Mines) (1972).

Deep Ocean Mining Environmental Study (DOMES) (Subdivided as follows).

Continuing baseline studies of benthic organisms (Paul—(Lamont-Doherty Geological Observatory)) (1975–1977).

Investigating geological and geochemical properties of seafloor sediments at selected sites (Bishoff—U.S. Geological Survey) (1975–1977).

Conducted study on environmental impact of manganese nodule mining (Roels—(Lamont-Doherty Geological Observatory) and City University of New York) (1972–1975).

Studying phytoplankton and primary productivity at selected sites (El-Sayed—(Texas A&M University)) (1975–1977).

Studying of zooplankton at selected sites (Hirota—University of Hawaii) (1975–1977).

Studying nutrient chemistry at selected sites (Richards, Anderson—University of Washington (1975–1977).

Studying suspended particulate matter at selected sites (Baker, Feely—PMEL) (1975–1977).

Plume modeling (Ichiye—Texas A&M University) (1975–1977).

Literature search involving benthic smothering (Heezen—(Lamont-Doherty Geological Observatory)) (1975).

Reviewing existing information of fishes, including eggs and larvae in and adjacent to the sites being studied in DOMES (Blackburn—Scripps Institute of Oceanography) (1975–1976).

Providing statistically sound procedures for obtaining replicate benthic samples at selected sites (Jumars—University of Washington) (1976).

Describing bottom water physical oceanography (Hayes—PMEL) (1976).

Conducting literature search for all other aspects of DOMES (Documentation Associates, Inc.) (1976).

2. Atlantic Oceanographic and Meteorological Laboratories (AOML)

Research into metallogenesis at dynamic plate boundaries in order to determine origins of marine mineral resources and to develop criteria to predict their occurrences. (Roma—ERL Staff) (1976).

Provides consultation on seabed resources to the Secretariat of the United Nations.

Conducts marine geological and geophysical research between North America and Africa as part of the Trans-Atlantic Geotraverse Program.

Publication of over fifty scientific papers, representative titles include: Exploration Methods of the Continental Shelf: Geology, Geophysics, Geochemistry: Manganese Crusts of the Atlantic Fracture Zone; Plate Tectonics and Mineral Resources: Rapidly Accumulating Manganese Deposits from the Median Valley of the Mid-Atlantic Ridge; and the Trans-Atlantic Geotraverse Hydrothermal Field (1970–1975).

3. New England Offshore Mining Environmental Study (NOMES) (joint ERL activity)

Investigated geology of test site for NOMES (Setlow—Massachusetts Department of Natural Resources) (1972–1973).

Conducted physical and chemical oceanographic investigations in Massachusetts Bay for NOMES (Ippen, Mollo-Christensen—(Massachusetts Institute of Technology)) (1972–1974).

Conducting baseline study of benthic invertebrates at test site for NOMES (Harris—University of New Hampshire) (1972–1976).

Determined spatial and temporal variability of phytoplankton in Massachusetts Bay as part of NOMES (Hess. Nelson-ERL) (1973–1975).

Mineral and chemical analysis of bottom sediments recovered during sampling at and around test site (Grant—University of New Hampshire) (1972–1974).

Determining spatial and temporal variability of phytoplankton in Massachusetts Bay (Mulligan—University of New Hampshire) (1972–1976).

D. National Ocean Survey

Collection and publication of seismic. bathymetric, magnetic, and gravimetric information for the deep ocean and continental shelf as part of the Marine Geophysics Program (1970–1973).

E. Office of Sea Grant

The Office of Sea Grant is responsible for the performance of work in a number of areas. This work is carried out through the various colleges and universities which are part of the Sea Grant Program. The following is a listing of Office of Sea Grant projects.

Studied hydraulic dredge spoil fate (Oregon State University) (1972–1974)

Conducted an economic evaluation of ocean mineral resource development (Mead. Sorensen—University of California) (1969).

Developing a management program for offshore mining of sand and gravel, (SUNY at Stony Brook) (1975-continuing).

Conducting an evaluation of coastal sand and gravel deposits as construction or specialty materials (Bardsdale—University of Georgia) (1975–1977).

Conducting an evaluation and economic analysis of Southern California's phosphorite and sand-gravel deposits (Fisher, Mead—California State University) (1975–1976).

Conducting marine resources legal research (Wurfel—University of North Carolina) (1970–1977).

Continuing research of the legal aspects of ocean resources exploitation (Knight—Louisiana State University) (1971–1976).

Studying Green Bay manganese (Moore—University of Wisconsin) (1968–1972.)

Studying marine mineral placers (Moore—University of Wisconsin) (1969–1976).

Analyzed the geology of Delaware Bay (Kraft—University of Delaware) (1970–1971).

Conducted seismic reflection surveys of sedimentary structures of Delaware Bay (Sheridan—University of Delaware (1970–1973).

Studied recent sediments of northeastern North Carolina estuaries determining their relation to plio-pleistocene mineral deposits and their implication upon coastal zone management (Riggs—East Carolina University) (1970–1974).

Studying manganese resources (Andrews—University of Hawaii) (1970-continuing).

Studied size analysis and heavy mineral distribution in Delaware Bay sediments (Glass—University of Delaware) (1972).

Conducted inventory of mineral resources off Chesapeake Bay (Nicholas-Virginia Institute of Marine Science) (1972–1973).

Conducted assay of the marine resources of Massachusetts Bay (Lassiter-Massachusetts Institute of Technology) (1973–1974).

Studying offshore sand and gravel resources in California (Henyey, Osborne-University of Southern California) (1974–1976).

Conducting an oceanographic inventory of Southern California shelf sand and gravel deposits (Fischer-University of California) (1974-continuing).

Evaluating confirming strata associated with the principle coastal Georgia aquifer (Woolsey-University of Georgia) (1975–continuing).

Assessing Western Lake Michigan sand and gravel (Meyer-University of Wisconsin) (1975–1979).

Conducted an evaluation and recovery of offshore sand resources (Moberly, Casciano and Palmer-University of Hawaii) (1969–1975).

Analyzed the science and technology of utilizing the bottom resources of the Continental Shelf (Corell-University of New Hampshire) (1969–1975).

Conducted an undersea mineral survey of the Georgia Continental Shelf (Noakes-University of Georgia) (1970–1975).

Studied sediment and water characteristics in the Marine District Eastern Long Island (Brennan-State University College, Cortland, New York (1971–1973).

Conducted copper survey of Lake Superior (Meyer-University of Wisconsin) (1971–1975).

Conducted geophysical investigation of potential aggregate resources in the Georgia coastal area (Harding-University of Georgia) (1972–1974).

Conducted pre-mining survey (Moore-University of Wisconsin) (1972–1975).

Studied relationship of nucleus to ore grade of marine manganese nodules (Moore-University of Wisconsin) (1972–1975).

Conducting research on metal extraction from manganese nodules (Moore-University of Wisconsin) (1975–1978).

Conducting marine lode minerals exploration (Moore—University of Wisconsin) (1975—continuing).

Conducting marine noble metal exploration (Moore—University of Wisconsin) (1975—continuing).

Developed Vibratory Marine Sediment Sampler (Harbor-University of Wisconsin) (1969–1972).

Investigated the geotechnical properties in two seafloor development demonstration areas, a fundamental research and development precursor to applied technologies (Richards, Parks-Lehigh University) (1970–1974).

Studied clean undersea mineral processing (Tiemann-University of Wisconsin) (1971–1974).

Conducting high resolution subbottom profiling (Vine-Woods Hole Oceanographic Institute) (1974–1976).

Developed an accoustic probe for ocean bottom and subbottom surveys (Dow-Woods Hole Oceanographic Institttue) (1974–1975).

Studying metal extraction from manganese nodules (Chapman—University of Wisconsin) (1975–continuing).

2. *Domestic and International Business Administration/Office of Energy and Strategic Resource Policy* [1]

Economic Review of Law of the Sea Treaty (1973). Bureau of Resources and Trade Assistance, in collaboration with NOAA, prepared Commerce Department study on economic implication for U.S. and world markets of future production plans of U.S. companies regarding deep seabed metals.

Law of the Sea Negotiating Conferences. Caracas, Geneva, New York (1974–1975–1976). Bureau of Resources and Trade Assistance provides advice to DOC representatives on Interagency Law of the Sea Task Force, both during Washington preparations and as member of Commerce group on U.S. Delegation, on economic implications of treaty articles relating to deep seabed mining, with particular attention to their relationship to and consistency with U.S. international resources and commodity policy.

Deep Ocean Mining Environmental Study (DOMES) (1974). Bureau of Resources and Trade Assistance, in collaboration with NOAA, developed the economic justification, for the Departmental decision making and subsequent presentation to OMB, to proceed with funding of NOAA's DOMES program.

Consideration and analysis of domestic legislation to regulate deep ocean mining by persons subject to U.S. jurisdiction (1976), Office of Energy and Strategic Resource Policy, Bureau of International Economic Policy and Research, and Bureau of Domestic Commerce.

Bureau of Resources and Trade Assistance participates as part of Commerce supporting staff for the Marine Petroleum and Minerals Advisory Committee (1975–1976). Bureau of Resources and Trade Assistance and Bureau of International Economic Policy and Research prepared special study for subcommittee on existing insurance programs available for deep ocean mining ventures.

Law of the Sea Position Papers (1970–1976). Bureau of Resources and Trade Assistance regularly collaborates with NOAA in reviewing position papers prepared by other agencies.

Congressional Testimony (1970–1976). Bureau of Resources and Trade Assistance regularly collaborates with NOAA in reviewing Executive Branch testimony on proposed legislation concerning marine minerals.

---

[1] The functions and projects of the Bureau of Resources and Trade Assistance in the area of marine minerals are now within the Office of Energy and Strategic Resource Policy.

Bureau of Domestic Commerce and Bureau of Resources and Trade Assistance participated in a technical study of manganese with the National Material Advisory Board's Committee on Technical Aspects of Critical and Strategic Materials.

"The Impact of Proposed New Source Performance Standards on the Nonferrous Smelting Industry, An Interagency Assessment" (U.S. Department of the Interior, U.S. Department of Commerce, and Federal Energy Administration) (July 1975).

Project Independence Availabilities, Requirements, and Constraints on Materials, Equipment, and Construction. Task Force Report under Direction of U.S. Department of Commerce (November 1974) (sections on copper and nickel).

An analysis of the Impact of Alternative Approaches to Significant Deterioration in the Nonferrous Metals Industy (Staff Study A–03–76) (Bureau of Domestic Commerce of the U.S. Department of Commerce) (May 1976).

Nonferrous Resources—"A Five-Year View" (Owens, Romagnoli—U.S. Department of Commerce) (presented to Society of Automotive Engineers, Automotive Engineering Congress and Exposition, Detroit, Michigan (February 24–28, 1975)).

An Analysis of Selected Commodities and Identification of Casual Factors Contributing to Supply Shortfalls (Arthur D. Little, Inc.) (Report to Domestic Business Policy Analysis Staff, Department of Commerce (December 20, 1974)).

Study of the Energy and Fuel Use Patterns in the Nonferrous Metals Industries (Battelle Columbus Labortories) (report to Federal Energy Administration and Department of Commerce (December 31, 1974)).

3. Maritime Administration

Technology Assessment of Offshore Industry (including Ocean Mining) (BDM Corporation) (1975–1976).

National Planning Conference on the Commercial Development of the Oceans (BDM Corporation) (1976). Hard Minerals Panel coordinated by the Office of Marine Minerals—NOAA.

4. National Bureau of Standards

Contingency Planning for Anticipated Technological Crises (Charles River Associates) (1975–1976).

Mr. McCLOSKEY. On page 5 of your testimony you indicate that the mining industry has recommended the department work with the industry to promote technology transfer.

To whom?

Mr. BAKER. I will let Dr. White answer that question.

Dr. WHITE. The technology transfer would be from the research undertaken by the Government, or under Government sponsorship to the industry, to enable them to have whatever information is available as a result of Government expenditures.

Mr. McCLOSKEY. The Government, then, would make available to industry what it had ascertained in its oceanographic research.

What about the research that has already been done by the companies?

Will that be tranasferred to our Government?

Dr. WHITE. Much of that is made available to the Government, and as Mr. Ratiner testified this morning, it is available to us for consideration of things we need to do.

Mr. McCLOSKEY. All of it?

Dr. WHITE. I do not know that all of it is, but a large amount is.

Mr. McCLOSKEY. If industry comes to Government and asks Government's protection, would Commerce require, as a condition to that insurance and protection a license for transfer of all technolgy ascertained by industry to date?

Dr. WHITE. I do not know that we would, Mr. McCloskey.

I do not know that we require a complete transfer of technology from industry to the Government in other areas.

In cases where there are governmental licenses, I think the Government has to ensure that it has sufficient knowledge so that the public interest is fully taken into consideration in its management of the resource but insofar as the technology transfer is concerned, I do not think we do that as a practice.

Mr. McCloskey. I perceive in the past a certain reluctance among competing private corporations to share the results of their research with the Government. Promoting the free enterprise system, as Commerce does, you would promote fair competition among the various companies.

Here, where we are acting in the national interest, as I understand is the thrust of the administration's witnesses, there seems to be an evasion of the ordinary concept of free enterprise competition. The Government is getting involved to protect the competitors; to assist them.

I wonder what extent the Government might in this case require full cooperation on the transfer of technology to the Government.

Dr. White. I am not aware of any discussion, sir.

Mr. McCloskey. Pardon me?

Mr. Baker. We are not aware, either, of any discussions within Government to that effect.

Mr. McCloskey. In your testimony, Mr. Baker, you mentioned Commerce has completed the Marine Petroleum Advisory Committee and you referred to the Mining Panel of the Ocean Science and Technology Committee.

Dr. White. Sir, one is formerly a body of the National Security Industry Association, and the other is a part of an advisory committee to the Secretary of Commerce.

Mr. McCloskey. No further questions.

Mr. Jones. Does counsel have questions?

Mr. Perian. Mr. Baker, the Department of the Interior through its Ocean Mining Administration actively participates in the negotiations at the Law of the Sea Conference.

Is the Department of Commerce an active participant and if so, what is its role?

Mr. Baker. We are represented on the delegation to the Law of the Sea Conference by the deputy administrator of the National Oceanic and Atmospheric Association, Mr. Pollock.

Mr. Perian. Do you find that your perception of the American mining industry's interest at the conference is any different than the perception which the Interior Department has?

Mr. Baker. I did not hear the last part.

Mr. Perian. Is your perception of the American mining industry's interest at the conference any different than the perception which the Interior Department has as expressed here this morning by Mr. Ratiner or Mr. Maw on previous occasions?

Mr. Baker. No, sir.

Mr. Perian. On page 6 of your statement you state that NOAA possesses extensive scientific, engineering and administrative competence that enables it to carry out its responsibilities for marine resource management.

What are NOAA's responsibilities for marine resource management?

Mr. BAKER. Well, we have responsibilities through the office of Marine Minerals which we have established and which I alluded to in my statement.

Assuming that the 200-mile bill becomes law, we will have responsibilities with respect to the fishery management provisions of that legislation.

Mr. PERIAN. Which statutes have assigned these responsibilities to NOAA?

Dr. WHITE. Mr. Perian, I would like to elaborate on that just a bit.

We do have a broad range of responsibilities. We have, of course, authorities dealing with fisheries and coastal zone management, which as you know is becoming increasingly important, and those dealing with the protection of marine mammals, and endangered species.

These are management responsibilities all of which involve managing or developing ocean resources.

Mr. PERIAN. I think you know what I am getting at. There now exists a conflict between who is in charge of ocean mining, the operation run by Mr. Ratiner in the Department of Interior or the operation in the Department of Commerce.

I understand there have been negotiations to finally settle or determine who is really in charge of ocean mining. This committee would like to know when a decision will be made on this issue, and who will then be in charge.

Mr. BAKER. We think a decision will be made in the relatively near future.

I would share the Under Secretary's judgment in that regard and we would hope, sir, that this could be worked out between the Secretaries.

If it cannot be worked out between the Secretaries there are two other routes that could be utilized. One would be to refer the matter to the Office of Legal Counsel in the Attorney General's office for an opinion. The other would be through the normal mechanism of resolution through the Office of Management and Budget and a decision by the President.

Mr. PERIAN. And you say that is in the near future?

Mr. BAKER. We would think that this could be worked out in the reasonably near future. I think both Interior and Commerce are anxious to have a resolution of the dispute. We certainly are looking forward to trying to resolve it at the secretarial level.

Mr. JONES. Would the gentleman yield at that point?

Mr. PERIAN. Certainly.

Mr. JONES. Do you not have a third choice in legislation if necessary, if the Congress decides?

Mr. BAKER. That is correct. I was speaking, sir, in the absence of legislation. You are absolutely right.

Mr. PERIAN. You point out in your testimony that the technical problems the ocean mining industry will encounter are not the same as those encountered in land-based mining operations.

Do you think NOAA is the most appropriate agency for helping in that technology.

Mr. Baker. We think that the matter of mining of the deepsea bed is more an ocean matter, sir, than it is a mining matter. That is our position.

Mr. Perian. Do you think perhaps that the Interior Department should manage ther esources during the actual leasing operation, while the Commerce Department provides the technical expertise needed for environmental assessment and technology development?

Mr. Baker. We are unable to concede now that the Department of Interior should have the management function.

That is the basic question that the dispute revolves around, who should have the management function.

Mr. Perian. For the record, could you provide us with the Office of Marine Minerals staffing and funding levels over the past 5 years?

Mr. Baker. Be glad to do that for you, yes, sir.

[The information follows:]

OFFICE OF MARINE MINERALS 5-YEAR STAFFING AND FUNDING LEVELS

	Permanent positions	Positions allocated to hard minerals	Funding (thousands)
Fiscal year:			
1972		$1\frac{1}{2}$	$97
1973	4	$1\frac{1}{2}$	106
1974	4	$1\frac{1}{2}$	118
1975	5	$1\frac{1}{2}$	140
1976 (initial)	5		160

Mr. Perian. On page 5 you say that since representatives of industry are appearing before this committee today you will let them advise us firsthand of their concerns.

I think we know some of these concerns and so do you. The question is what do you think should be done about them?

Mr. Baker. Well, sir, I think I said earlier that we believe that a comprehensive law of the sea treaty which is acceptable to industry is the best approach to that.

I realize that it has been going on for a long time and if substantial progress is not made at the next session or the session following in the summer, then I think perhaps legislation would certainly be one answer, perhaps the answer at the time.

Mr. Perian. Are you willing to agree then that if this next 8-weeks session is nonproductive, as was Geneva, that perhaps we should go through domestic or unilateral legislation?

Mr. Baker. I think I said this earlier. I believe at that time we should take a hard look at the administration's position if indeed no progress is made at the session in New York.

Mr. Perian. I have no further questions.

Mr. Jones. To the Members of the subcommittee, as you know it is now 12:05 and in all probability within the next 10 or 15 minutes we will be summoned to the House floor for a quorum call.

The three gentlemen representing the industry have agreed to appear jointly at one time. I understand they have a very exciting film which runs 10 or 12 minutes.

What are the wishes of the subcommittee, that we recess at this time until 2:00 p.m. or try to fight it out and take our chances over on the House floor on votes?

Mr. FORSYTHE. I would prefer recessing until 2:00 o'clock.

Mr. JONES. Is that agreeable to you, Mr. Oberstar?

Mr. OBERSTAR. I would just as soon go ahead and if you go right ahead we can respond to the quorum call and continue with the hearing.

Mr. JONES. Mr. McCloskey, would you settle this?

Mr. McCLOSKEY. I am privileged to be here. I am not a member of the subcommittee.

I defer to your wishes, Mr. Chairman.

Mr. JONES. I have always taken a position that once a witness gets at the table and he is interrupted you lose the impact of his statement, the continuity.

Could you come back at 1:30?

Mr. OBERSTAR. One o'clock would be fine with me.

Mr. JONES. Does 1:00 o'clock suit you?

Without objection, the Chair recesses this subcommittee until 1:00 p.m.

(Whereupon, at 12:07 p.m., the subcommittee recessed to reconvene at 1:00 p.m., the same day.)

AFTERNOON SESSION

Mr. JONES (presiding). The subcommittee will come to order now, please.

At this time the Chair recognizes Mr. Flipse, President, Deepsea Ventures, Inc.: Mr. Marne A. Dubs, Director, Ocean Resources Department, Kennecott Copper Corporation; and Mr. Conrad G. Welling, Program Manager, Ocean Mining, Lockheed Missiles & Space Company.

Will you three gentlemen come up, please, as a panel.

Whom shall I recognize as the first witness?

STATEMENT OF A PANEL OF INDUSTRY REPRESENTATIVES CONSISTING OF JOHN E. FLIPSE, PRESIDENT, DEEPSEA VENTURES, INC.: MARNE A. DUBS, DIRECTOR, OCEAN RESOURCES DEPARTMENT, KENNECOTT COPPER CORP., AND CONRAD G. WELLING, PROGRAM MANAGER, OCEAN MINING, LOCKHEED MISSILES & SPACE CO.

Mr. DUBS. I would be glad to lead off, Mr. Chairman.

I am Marne A. Dubs and I will testify today on behalf of the American Mining Congress. However, the views presented are fully supported both by Kennecott Copper Corporation and myself.

In addition, where appropriate I will provide other information to the committee as a representative of Kennecott Copper Corporation.

I note that I have a somewhat abbreviated statement and I ask that my written statement appear in full in the record.

Mr. JONES. Without objection, it will appear at this point in the record.

[The full statement follows:]

STATEMENT OF MARNE A. DUBS, DIRECTOR, OCEAN RESOURCES DEPARTMENT, KENNECOTT COPPER CORP. ON BEHALF OF THE AMERICAN MINING CONGRESS

Mr. Chairman: My name is Marne A. Dubs. I am Director of the Ocean Resources Department of the Kennecott Copper Corporation and also am Chairman of the Committee on Undersea Mineral Resources of the American Mining Congress. I will testify today on behalf of the American Mining Congress. However, the views presented are fully supported both by Kennecott Copper Corporation and myself. In addition, where appropriate, I will provide other information to the Committee as a representative of Kennecott Copper.

The American Mining Congress, recognizing the potential importance of minerals from the seabed, has had an active committee on undersea mineral resources for many years now and includes undersea minerals in its yearly major policy statement. As you know, the American Mining Congress is a trade association composed of U.S. companies who produce most of the nation's metals, coal, and industrial and agricultural minerals. It also represents more than 220 companies who manufacture mining, milling, and processing equipment and supplies, and commercial banks and other institutions serving the mining industry and the financial community.

Kennecott Copper Corporation has been actively investigating the recovery of the mineral resources of the deep seabed since 1962. Since January 1974 it has been Operator for and held a 50% equity interest in an international consortium organized for the development of manganese nodule mining. I have been manager of Kennecott's activities in ocean mining since 1969 and chair the consortium's governing committee. I also serve on the State Department's Advisory Committee on the Law of the Sea and as an expert on the U.S. Delegation to the Law of the Sea Conference. In addition. I am a member of a number of advisory bodies, including the National Advisory Committee on Oceans and Atmosphere, concerned with ocean technology and policy.

Mr. Chairman, I very much appreciate this opportunity to testify before your Committee on this important subject of legislation "to promote the conservation and orderly development of hard mineral resources of the deep seabed, pending adoption of an international regime relating thereto"—H.R. 11879. I am well aware of your own intimate and extensive knowledge of the policy issues involved and the efforts of this Committee extending over a number of years and many hearings on the subject. Accordingly, I will try to avoid plowing old well-tilled ground too much and focus my efforts on the present status of industry and its needs and the effectiveness of the legislation being considered by the Committee in promoting the development of the mineral resources of the deep seabed. However, I must perforce also comment briefly on the Law of the Sea Conference and the jurisdictional issues relating to deep sea mining.

The American Mining Congress has considered these fundamental questions carefully and debated them extensively. The conclusions of this analysis are expressed succinctly in the 1976 American Mining Congress Declaration of Policy. Although the policy statement is short, yet covers the ground of interest thoroughly, I will quote it in part to the Committee. I quote:

"UNDERSEA MINERAL RESOURCES

"Seabed minerals are a major potential source of certain metals and minerals of critical importance to the security and economy of the United States and for which we are presently dependent on foreign sources of supply. Nodules from the floor of the deep ocean may well provide additional supplies of nickel, cobalt and manganese to the United States, supplement the production of domestic copper and assist in the reduction of foreign dependency.

"Many Member of Congress and others in government share our concern over potential shortages of vital mineral commodities. They also share our view that seabed minerals may be an effective means of helping to combat a number of such shortages, and therefore their early recovery should be encouraged.

"The technology of recovering minerals from the depths of the sea and processing them into useful raw materials has been under development by private industry for over 10 years at its own cost. However, the future course of action by industry is threatened by uncertain investment conditions resulting from the failure to achieve either a timely and satisfactory international regime on the law of the sea or domestic legislation which moves towards a stable and predictable investment climate.

"Members of Congress have proposed legislative arrangements in identical bills (S. 713 and H.R. 1270) which constitute a first step in providing the basis for a stable and predictable investment climate for ocean mining. This legislation would regulate the activities of U.S. persons and in no way authorizes any unilateral actions by the United States with respect to the nationals of any other country. This legislation is an appropriate response to the problem of encouraging the development of seabed resources, and we urge its early enactment by Congress.

"The Executive Branch has also recognized the potential of seabed resources to the nation and has carried out negotiations at the Law of the Sea Conference on the basis of protecting United States interests. However, this objective was not achieved at the Law of the Sea Conference either in Caracas in 1974 or in Geneva in 1975. We continue to support the long-range search by the United States for an acceptable law of the sea treaty on the deep seabed, and domestic legislation becomes important for the development of seabed resources.

"However, the Executive Branch has failed to act positively on such legislation even though in testimony before Congress, administration witnesses have stated more than once that failure to achieve a timely (usually taken to be 1975) and successful law of the sea treaty would require domestic legislation. Such legislation is needed now, and we urge the Executive Branch to support legislation such as S. 713/H.R. 1270.

"We urge the administration and the Congress to fund and staff adequately the office of the Ocean Mining Administration to permit it to carry out its mission with respect to seabed mineral resource development. The activities of the National Oceanic and Atmospheric Administration with regard to basic environmental studies and data acquisitions should be continued. We urge that any confusion in regard to the agencies' functions be resolved so that each agency may effectively contribute to the solution of problems within the ambit of its expertise: NOAA in the area of environmental base-line studies and data accumulation; OMA in the area of deep ocean mineral resource development.

"In summary, we endorse these words of the Secretary of State, Henry Kissinger, in his August 11, 1975 speech on law of the sea: 'We cannot defer our own deep seabed mining for too much longer. In this spirit, we and other potential seabed producers can consider appropriate steps to protect current investment, and to ensure that this investment is also protected in the treaty.' We urge that these 'appropriate steps' be taken now and that they be taken in the form of domestic legislation which will not 'defer our own deep seabed mining' but which will encourage the commercial development of seabed resources at an accelerated pace."

The terse language of this policy statement obviously needs to be fleshed out to clarify the intended meanings and provide a back-up rationale. This I will strive to do in my statement today.

Mr. Chairman, Mr. Murphy in his opening statement at the hearing held on February 23, 1976, you stated, and I quote, "There is no question that the only thing holding back this next stage of development is the lack of the proper investment climate." Mr. Murphy, you hit the nail on the head. This is *the* problem of industry. We cannot undertake the approaching very large risk capital expenditures required for developing the resources of the deep seabed unless it is assured that these expenditures will not be made in vain because of adverse political actions over which industry has absolutely no control.

The term "investment climate" itself is a euphemism which is subject to misunderstanding and distortions. H.R. 11879 in Sec. 2(a)(6) on page 2 is more precise in its language; namely, "that United States mining companies . . ., given the necessary security of tenure, are prepared to make the necessary capital investment for such development and processing." Security of tenure means to us the exclusive right to mine a specific area of the seabed for a specific length of time and under specific conditions that will not change during the period of tenure. It is this security of tenure that is the basic and only requirement of industry.

The technical and economic reasons for this have been discussed in previous hearings. I would sum them up by saying that a production facility costing one half billion dollars or more is utterly dependent on an uninterrupted known source of ore of known characteristics and cost. Thus, investment in such a facility is not possible without such a secure ore source.

Industry, then, is seeking a system which will provide this security of tenure. At this time, only the United States Government can provide these exclusive rights in the first instance and seeking to maintain them over their stated term. Industry understands that it may not prove to be possible to maintain these rights without diminution because of other important policy objectives and that, therefore, the Government cannot be committed to the absolute protection of such rights, come what may.

Nevertheless, if, in the process of achieving the best overall solution to all of the public policy questions involved in the Law of the Sea, the Government should after most serious deliberation conclude that it must agree to the diminution of the rights of the ocean miner, then, as in other cases where the Government takes or diminishes the value of property for other public purposes, the Government should provide compensation as a basic constitutional right. Therefore, industry believes that in the event it proves not possible to continue these rights under all circumstances, financial protection must be provided which will compensate for such loss of security of tenure or adverse change in the terms, conditions, and financial arrangements attached thereto. This is the very essence of domestic legislation from industry's point of view.

H.R. 11879 accomplishes the above purpose well enough albeit not perfectly. Sec. 5(b)(1) provides exclusive rights with respect to persons subject to the jurisdiction of the United States or of any reciprocating state. Sec. 16(a) treats the matter of reciprocating states. Sec. 12 recognizes that the Government may not be able to protect the rights under the terms of an international regime. Sec. 13 provides for financial compensation for any economic losses resulting from failure to maintain rights under an international agreement. Sec. 14 provides investment insurance against economic losses resulting from interferences with mining activities by those against whom a legal remedy either does not exist or is unavailable in any legal form to which the licensee has access.

Although the above is the most basic need of industry, many detailed provisions are required for the equitable implementation of the basic provisions for establishing the relationship of ocean mining to domestic laws, and for important matters of public interest and policy other than secure mineral supplies, such as the protection of the marine environment. H.R. 11879 has the necessary detailed provisions which in general appear adequate to the task.

I do not intend to go into detail on the legislation at this point but I will have some specific comments later. The point I want to make with absolute clarity is that H.R. 11879 does satisfy the needs of industry. It falls within the policy statement of the American Mining Congress and is acceptable, with only minor changes, as the equivalent to S. 713 and H.R. 1270 alluded to in the statement.

In the Chairman's letter of invitation to testify before this Committee, you requested that industry discuss the status of the ocean mining industry. I will now turn to this subject. H.R. 11879 states in Sec. 2(a)(6) "that United States mining companies have developed the technology necessary for the development and processing of deep seabed nodules and, given the necessary security of tenure, are prepared to make the necessary capital investment for such development and processing;" and the AMC policy statement says:

"The technology of recovering minerals from the depths of the sea and processing them into useful raw materials has been under development by private industry for over ten years at its own cost. However, the future course of action by industry is threatened by uncertain investment conditions resulting from the failure to achieve a timely and satisfactory international regime on the law of the sea or domestic legislation which moves toward a stable and predictable investment climate."

These statements do truly depict the overall status of development.

However, I appreciate the opportunity to brief the Committee on current developments in ocean mining. There indeed has been substantial progress. I last appeared before this Committee in May 1975. At that time I commented very negatively on the progress made and on the future prospects of progress at the Law of the Sea Conference. A third session of the Conference is scheduled for New York beginning next week. In this Committee's hearing two weeks ago, the prospects of the third session were characterized, even with the vaunted intersessional accomplishments—which were in fact noteworthy considering the Geneva intransigence of the developing world—by you, Mr. Murphy, as "in the realm of a faint glimmer of hope, and nothing more" and our chief negotiator, Mr. Ratiner, replied, "I think that is a reasonable characterization." I can do no better than support that analysis.

Now during this same period of Caracas, Geneva, and intersessional meetings, what has happened in the world of industry and technology? Where do things stand today? Today, industry has progressed to the point where the next steps in unlocking the resources of the deep seabed require very large development expenditures and they are deeply concerned about making such expenditures, since their investment may be negotiated away at a Law of the Sea Conference, and there is no assurance that their own government will afford them protection against interference in the interim period before a treaty. As a result, without a solution to this problem, progress toward commerical recovery will be halted or reduced to an insignificant rate.

It is true that industrial activity in ocean mining has continued high in 1974 and 1975 and ambitious plans have been made for 1976 and subsequently. However, this activity and these plans are based on a prediction and a faith that domestic legislation will be enacted into law and will become effective in 1976.

In the case of my own company, if the above does not occur in the next few months, we would review our development plans in detail. I predict as a result of that review that we would at the very minimum greatly curtail our program. It is also not inconceivable that we would abandon the project. We would find it extremely difficult to embark on a program costing of the order of one hundred million dollars to take us through our next stage of work into commercialization in the absence of appropriate legislation.

Now, what has been happening? Perhaps I should start with the Glomar Explorer. In past Committee hearings, I have extolled the probable merits of this ship and the probability that it could be a tool for achieving early success in ocean mining. I have not changed that view and believe that use of this vessel would in fact accelerate the pace of ocean mining. Its accomplishments, as revealed by the press, are indeed impressive and there is little doubt that it is a further confirmation of our contention that the technology of ocean mining is at hand.

Of course, it appears that one potential ocean miner, The Summa Corporation, has disappeared. However, a new one, Lockheed, has appeared and appears to have a substantive program and serious plans. Their representative is before the Committee today.

In early 1974, Kennecott Copper Corporation announced the establishment of a major consortium to work on ocean mining. It consists of Kennecott, Noranda Mines of Canada, Mitsubishi Corporation of Japan, Consolidated Gold Fields of the United Kingdom and Rio Tinto Zinc of the United Kingdom. A major program has been under way and is essentially on the projected schedule.

In this same period, both Deepsea Ventures and The International Nickel Company (INCO) also announced consortia. The Deepsea Ventures group consists of U.S. Steel, Union Miniere of Belgium, and Tenneco. The INCO group consists of INCO, SEDCO (a U.S. oil drilling contractor), a Japanese group led by Sumitomo, and a West German group containing Metallgesellschaft, Preussag, Saltzgitter, and Rheinbraun. These, like the Kennecott effort, are substantial, serious efforts to bring the mineral resources of the seabed into production.

In addition, the CLB group (Japanese Continuous Line Bucket System) remains active and is planning tests in the Pacific this year. The CLB group has a large number of participants including the French organization CNEXO. In Japan, an association called DOMA, Deep Ocean Mining Association, is carrying out work emphasizing exploration in the Pacific Ocean.

It is somewhat difficult to assess the level of accomplishment of these groups because of their need to protect their own proprietary positions. However, representatives of several are here today and can speak for themselves. My own assessment based on informed observation of the scene is that the "collective" position of the seabed developers is about as follows:

1. They have identified nodule deposits which could provide satisfactory mine sites. Mine site definition will require a large amount of work and substantial expenditures. To carry this work out without protection of investment and assurances for the future ability to mine the site is financially very risky.

2. They have largely solved the metallurgical problems of winning metals from nodules. They have either run pilot plants or will do so in the near future. The next steps will require much larger and more costly pilot plant or demonstration plant tests. These tests must be run with nodules obtained from a mine site which would constitute a known supply for the commercial plant whose design would be based on these tests.

3. Development of the mining systems has progressed from the drawing board and computer stage and away from simple laboratory tests to large-scale at-sea experimentation. Present schedules, as indicated during industry discussions of NOAA's environmental research program, call for several major at-sea tests beginning in late 1976 and continuing through 1978. The costs of such work are very high and in fact are unique in industrial technology development.

In conclusion, there is no longer any doubt about the technical and economic feasibility of ocean mining. The technology is ready; the investment climate is not.

At the risk of boring the Committee I will again emphasize the need for an acceptable investment climate. Looking at it operationally, the miner needs security of tenure over a mine site in order to spend the money necessary to explore completely the mine site, devise a mining plan, develop the expensive equipment to mine and process the minerals, and, finally, to invest in the production facilities. This is the usual basis under which a mining project can be financed and undertaken. Since such security of tenure cannot be obtained under present circumstances, a substitute must be found. This substitute is protection from the risk that the industry will no longer be able to mine or will have investments impaired from financial burdens as a result of a LOS Treaty agreed to by the U.S., and insurance against interference by foreign governments or firms against which no legal remedies are available. This, Mr. Chairman, is the essence of the cure for the present unsatisfactory investment climate, and I hope you will bear with the repetitious nature of this theme song.

I would now like to say a few additional words about the state of the art on ocean mining as seen through the eyes of my own company. We believe we understand quite well the location, metallurgical grade, and tonnage of large manganese nodule deposits of potential commercial interest. We have obtained detailed information on specific potential mine sites with respect to these parameters required for design of mining equipment.

We have tested mining equipment at a 15,000-foot depth on the floor of the Pacific Ocean. This equipment demonstrated successfully certain key aspects of nodule recovery and has given us confidence in our engineering designs. I note that we commented on this on page 21 of Kennecott's 1974 annual report. We believe the technical feasibility of ocean mining is clear.

Finally, we have completed our pilot plant work on the development of a hydrometallurgical process to extract metals from nodules. This unique process is low in energy consumption.

So, we have completed Phase I of our program to bring nodules to commercial reality. We must now tackle Phase II which involves the development of prototype equipment. This effort will be very expensive, requiring massive equipment and large ships. Once committed to these expenditures, there is almost no turning back from commercialization. Thus, we hesitate at this time because of the uncertainty of the investment climate resulting from the law of the sea issues. We have carried it this far on faith. We cannot go very much further. As I stated before if legislation to solve the problem is not enacted into law in the next few months, we will be forced to review our plan in view of the large financial risks such inaction would impose.

As I stated earlier, H.R. 11879 does satisfy the needs of industry. However, some minor changes appear desirable to us. As you may recall, I wrote to you on January 26, 1976, giving the views of the American Mining Congress with respect to legislation. Attached to that letter was a draft bill which showed revisions compared to bills pending at that time. Since H.R. 11879 builds on the previous work of the Committee, these detailed comments are applicable to this bill. Accordingly, Mr. Chairman, I request that my letter of January 26, 1976, with its attached bill, be incorporated in the record of this hearing.

Because of their importance, I want to single out several of these comments in this correspondence. The most significant modification is with respect to the size of the licensing block. H.R. 11879 provides for a 40,000-square-kilometer exploration block with a 75% relinquishment (or a reduction down to 10,000 square kilometers) at the time of conversion into a commercial recovery license. Our strong opinion is that the block size should be 60,000 square kilometers for exploration with a 50% relinquishment, or reduction to 30,000 square kilometers, upon conversion to a commercial recovery license.

The reason for this proposed change is that since 1970 when the 40,000/ 10,000 combination appeared in a U.S. draft treaty, it has become increasingly clear, especially as technological data have been accumulated, that the residual 10,000-square-kilometer site is too small to sustain a reasonable mining operation. The 60,000/30,000 combination would be adequate and is in general accord with proposals made at the Law of the Sea Conference by a number of countries.

A second revision of note we would propose is the deletion of the limitation on the aggregate number of licenses issued by the United States to "30 percentum of an area of the deep seabed which is within a circle with a diameter of one thousand two hundred and fifty kilometers." This is in Sec. 10(a)(3) of H.R. 11879. This deletion would be in conformance with the U.S. position relating to nondiscriminatory access and its opposition to any quota system taken at the U.N. Conference on Law of the Sea.

We also are of the view that an increase in the work requirements in Sec. 8(a) of the pending legislation would not be an unreasonable modification; however, we do not make any specific recommendations. In particular, increasing the block size as we have recommended above, plus the effect of inflationary pressures, indicate such an increase should be considered.

In originally selecting such figures, an effort was made to achieve a balance between work requirements of a magnitude which would ensure good faith exploration, thereby avoiding speculation, and yet would not be so high as to freeze out the smaller operator from a legitimate opportunity to participate in ocean mining.

If you feel we were successful in achieving a reasonable balance, then upward adjustment would be fairly simple: (1) multiply each amount by 150 percentum (to account for the increased block size); (2) then multiply each amount by a factor equal to the cost-of-living index increase since January 1972 and add the product to the amount obtained in (1) above. You may also wish to consider a clause to account for further changes in the cost-of-living index in conjunction with the above.

The remaining revisions in my letter and its attached bill, although not trivial, are principally technical and are for the purpose of clarification. I hope that the Committee will take them into account in its deliberations.

I also have a few additional comments though on H.R. 11879. The first is in regard to the effective date of the Act given in Sec. 24 as January 1, 1977. We urge that this be altered so that the Act takes effect on the date of its enactment. The bill already provides a more than adequate window for Law of the Sea negotiations in the January 1, 1977 date for commercialization in Sec. 5(b)(1). There is nothing gained by setting a future effective date and much is lost because of putting off into the future the establishment of the regulatory machinery under the Act and the settling of priorities on mining sites. In addition, this legislation has continually and for some time now been moved toward some future date and the process should be ended now.

H.R. 11879 contains a section on Reciprocating States, Sec. 16, that has not appeared in previous pending legislation. We believe this to be a good addition and adds strength to the bill. I endorse paragraphs (a) and (b). On the other hand, I have strong reservations on paragraph (c) which instructs the Secretary of State to enter into international agreements with all reciprocating states. My own legal talent is non-existent, but I wonder whether this kind of instruction may be a separation of powers problem. On more pragmatic grounds, I am concerned that the purposes of the Act might be confounded if an interpretation should arise that such international agreements referred to in paragraph (c) must be entered into before the domestic features of the Act become fully operative. I applaud the underlying concept of putting the Reciprocating State concept into real effect rapidly. Perhaps the desired effect could be obtained by changing the preemptive language into a precatory

statement which adjures the Secretary of State to pursue international agreements with Reciprocating States.

In Sec. 7(a) the concept of involvement of the National Oceanic and
Atmospheric Administration in environmental matters has been introduced.
This, we believe, is a good idea. We, too, recognize the expertise of NOAA in
the area of base-line studies and data accumulation and the necessity of their
contribution. However, we believe the wording of paragraph (a) should be
revised so that the words, "acting through the Administrator of the National
Oceanic and Atmospheric Administration," in lines 6 through 8 be struck. We
would then propose a new sentence to be inserted after the end of the present
first sentence (line 13), which would require consultation with NOAA and
charge them with environmental research in this area including the execution
of base-line studies and data. The new paragraph (b) would then fit nicely
into the scheme of things.

The final issue I am concerned with in H.R. 11879 is the jurisdictional
question which appears in Sec. 3(1). Sec. 3(1) reads: "The term 'Secretary'
means, except where its usage indicates otherwise, the Secretary of Commerce."
In all other pending bills, "Secretary" is defined as the Secretary of the Interior.
We are not in accord with the designation of the Secretary of Commerce in
H.R. 11879 and continue to believe the proper administrative authority is the
Secretary of the Interior.

The mining industry has traditionally looked to the Department of Interior
for leadership within the Executive Branch of government with respect to
mineral resource development and appropriate government activity in this
regard. We see no difference on the basis of the occurrence of the resource at
the bottom of the sea.

The Mining and Minerals Policy Act of 1970 (30 U.S.C. 21(a)) specifically
places the responsibility of fostering and encouraging private enterprise in
the development of economically sound and stable domestic mining, minerals,
metal, and mineral reclamation industries on the Secretary of the Interior.
Furthermore, the Secretary is required to include in his annual report to the
Congress ". . . a report on the state of the domestic mining, minerals, and
mineral reclamation industries, including a statement of the trend in utilization
and depletion of these resources, together with such recommendations for
legislative programs as may be necessary to implement the policies of this
section." It is difficult to conceive of a clearer expression of Congressional intent
than the declaration of policy and the assignment of responsibility on the
Secretary of Interior to carry out that policy than is contained in this statute
(P.L. 91-631, 84 stat. 1876). The American Mining Congress concurs both in the
declaration of policy and in the assignment of responsibility made by the Mining
and Minerals Policy Act of 1970.

The reasons we have looked to Interior are also based on their indepth
expertise and understanding of mineral resource technology and policy. The
skills of the U.S. Geological Survey are well known. The expertise and background of the Bureau of Mines, particularly their knowledge of mineral
processing and mining technology, are important. The regulatory arms of
Interior have an understanding of the regulation of the mineral industry.
Finally, the background for formulating and managing the implementation of
policy exists in depth in Interior, particularly in the office of the Assistant
Secretary for Energy and Minerals.

I note that some of the basic attitudes of the Department of Interior
regarding ocean mining were summarized in a speech by Secretary Kleppe
before the American Oceanic Organization on February 27, 1976. I have a news
release summary of that speech and would be glad to provide it for the record
if the Chair so wishes.

Of course, we must also make clear that since the development of the resources
of the deep seabed requires ocean environmental technology, oceanographic
knowledge of many kinds, and meteorological information, the National Oceanic
and Atmospheric Administration can and should provide important research,
data and support for deep ocean mining operations.

Our AMC policy statement expresses our views on the relative roles of
Interior and Commerce. Clearly we believe that each agency, within the ambit
of its expertise, has an important contribution to make to ocean mining. In the
final analysis, though, it is the Secretary of Interior who should be charged
with the administration of the Act.

Mr. Chairman, I noted with some interest the comments of Mr. Ratiner in
the February 23 hearing regarding the substantive provisions of the bill.

I understand his concern for having the capability of assembling independently verifiable data. However, I note that there is in fact much data in the public domain even today which could be used to resolve his concerns. There also appears to be some idea of "Prototype Regulations" and it would be interesting to hear specific ideas. However, I believe it is very late to consider such new initiatives when the present bill is adequate to the task. Nevertheless, I recognize that the Ocean Mining Administration has not yet been adequately staffed and funded to carry out all the activities they need to and are capable of. We noted this in our AMC policy statement saying, "We urge the Administration and the Congress to fund and staff adequately the office of the Ocean Mining Administration to permit it to carry out its mission with respect to seabed mineral resource development."

I have already made some brief comment on the Law of the Sea Conference. I remain quite pessimistic about agreement at the March session or at any time in 1976. Nevertheless, I believe our negotiators are trying hard and in fact made some progress, however far from the end goal, in the intersessional meetings. I note that the U.S. "Proposed Amendments to the Committee I Single Negotiating Text," dated December 1975, represent a basically sound policy approach.

I have also examined the products of the intersessional work on the deep seabed issue which were submitted to this Committee for the record. My perspective on this effort is not that we should agree to these new draft articles but that they represent important steps in putting together a single negotiating text that we would have some real possibility of using for negotiation. As I stated in May before this Committee, the present text is an "unmitigated disaster." The intersessional work has in fact provided some mitigation, but much more is required.

Overall, progress has been made, but this progress may in fact have evaporated before April Fool's Day. In my opinion, there is no treaty on the deep seabed in sight in 1976 and very likely not in 1977.

Mr. Chairman, I have continued too long but it seemed necessary to cover at least superficially the areas you had instructed us to discuss in your invitation to testify. It appears likely to me, and I hope that this is a sound prediction, that the Committee will act on this legislation soon. Accordingly, it seemed necessary to communicate our views reasonably fully.

In conclusion, I believe the early enactment of H.R. 11879 into law—taking into account suggestions for amendments at these hearings—is a proper and urgently needed response to the public need to obtain new secure sources of mineral supply.

I urge the enactment of H.R. 11879 into law.

Mr. Dubs. Thank you, Mr. Chairman.

Mr. Chairman, I very much appreciate this opportunity to testify before your committee on this important subject of legislation "to promote the conservation and orderly development of hard mineral resources of the deep seabed, pending adoption of an international regime relating thereto"—H.R. 11879. I am well aware of your own intimate and extensive knowledge of the policy issues involved and the efforts of this committee extending over a number of years and many hearings on the subject.

Accordingly, I will try to avoid plowing old well-tilled ground too much and focus my efforts on the present status of industry and its needs and the effectiveness of the legislation being considered by the committee in promoting the development of the mineral resources of the deep seabed. However, I must perforce also comment briefly on the Law of the Sea Conference and the jurisdictional issues relating to deep sea mining.

The American Mining Congress has considered these fundamental questions carefully and debated them extensively. The conclusions of this analysis are expressed succinctly in the 1976 American Mining Congress Declaration of Policy. Although the policy statement is short, yet covers the ground of interest thoroughly, I will quote it in part to the Committee. I quote:

Undersea Mineral Resources

Seabed minerals are a major potential source of certain metals and minerals of critical importance to the security and economy of the United States and for which we are presently dependent on foreign sources of supply. Nodules from the floor of the deep ocean may well provide additional supplies of nickel, cobalt and manganese to the United States, supplement the production of domestic copper and assist in the reduction of foreign dependency.

Many Members of Congress and others in Government share our concern over potential shortages ov vital mineral commodities. They also share our view that seabed minerals may be an effective means of helping to combat a number of such shortages, and therefore their early recovery should be encouraged.

The technology of recovering minerals from the depths of the sea and processing them into useful raw materials has been under development by private industry for over 10 years at its own cost. However, the future course of action by industry is threatened by uncertain investment conditions resulting from the failure to achieve either a timely and satisfactory international regime on the law of the sea or domestic legislation which moves towards a stable and predictable investment climate.

Members of Congress have proposed legislative arrangements in identical bills (S. 713 and H.R. 1270 and H.R. 12879) which constitute a first step in providing the basis for a stable and predictable investment climate for ocean mining. This legislation would regulate the activities of U.S. persons and in no way authorizes any unilateral actions by the United States with respect to the nationals of any other country. This legislation is an appropriate response to the problem of encouraging the development of seabed resources, and we urge its early enactment by Congress.

The Executive branch has also recognized the potential of seabed resources to the Nation and has carried out negotiations at the Law of the Sea Conference on the basis of protecting United States interests. However, this objective was not achieved at the Law of the Sea Conference either in Caracas in 1974 or in Geneva in 1975. We continue to support the long-range search by the United States for an acceptable law of the sea treaty on the deep seabed, and domestic legislation becomes important for the development of seabed resources.

However, the Executive branch has failed to act positively on such legislation even though in testimony before Congress, administration witnesses have stated more than once that failure to achieve a timely (usually taken to be 1975) and successful law of the sea treaty would require domestic legislation. Such legislation is needed now, and we urge the Executive branch to support legislation such as S. 713/H.R. 1270.

We urge the Administration and the Congress to fund and staff adequately the office of the Ocean Mining Administration to permit it to carry out its mission with respect to seabed mineral resource development. The activities of the National Oceanic and Atmospheric Administration with regard to basic environmental studies and data acquisitions should be continued. We urge that any confusion in regard to the agencies' functions be resolved so that each agency may effectively contribute to the solution of problems within the ambit of its expertise: NOAA in the area of environmental base-line studies and data accumulation; OMA in the area of deep ocean mineral resource development.

In summary, we endorse these words of the Secretary of State, Henry Kissinger, in his August 11, 1975 speech on law of the sea: "We cannot defer our own deep seabed mining for too much longer. In this spirit, we and other potential seabed producers can consider appropriate steps to protect current investment, and to ensure that this investment is also protected in the treaty." We urge that these "appropriate steps" be taken now and that they will be taken in the form of domestic legislation which will not "defer our own deep seabed mining" but which will encourage the commercial development of seabed resources at an accelerated pace.

The terse language of this policy statement obviously needs to be fleshed out to clarify the intended meanings and provide a backup rationale. This I will strive to do in my statement today.

Mr. Chairman, Mr. Murphy in his opening statement at the hearing held on February 23, 1976, you stated, and I quote:

There is no question that the only thing holding back this next stage of development is the lack of the proper investment climate.

Mr. Murphy hit the nail on the head. This is the problem of the industry. We cannot undertake the approaching very large-risk capital expenditures required for developing the resources of the deep seabed unless it is assured that these expenditures will not be made in vain because of adverse political actions over which industry has absolutely no control.

The term "investment climate" itself is a euphemism which is subject to misunderstanding and distortions. H.R. 11879 in section 2(a)(6) on page 2 is more precise in its language; namely, "that United States mining companies . , given the necessary security of tenure, are prepared to make the necessary capital investment for such development and processing."

Security of tenure means to us the exclusive right to mine a specific area of the seabed for a specific length of time and under specific conditions that will not change during the period of tenure. It is this security of tenure that is the basic and only requirement of industry.

The technical and economic reasons for this have been discussed in previous hearings. I would sum them up by saying that a production facility costing $500 million or more is utterly dependent on an uninterrupted known source of ore of known characteristics and cost. Thus, investment in such a facility is not possible without such a secure ore source.

Industry, then, is seeking a system which will provide this security of tenure. At this time, the U.S. Government can provide these exclusive rights in the first instance and seek to maintain them over their stated term. Industry understands that it may not prove to be possible to maintain these rights without diminution because of other important policy objectives and that, therefore, the Government cannot be committed to the absolute protection of such rights, come what may.

Nevertheless, if, in the process of achieving the best overall solution to all of the public policy questions involved in the Law of the Sea, the Government should after most serious deliberation conclude that it must agree to the diminution of the rights of the ocean miner, then, as in other cases where the Government takes or diminishes the value of property for other public purposes, the Government should provide compensation as a basic constitutional right. Therefore, industry believes that in the event it proves not possible to continue these rights under all circumstances. financial protection must be provided which will compensate for such loss of security of tenure or adverse change in the terms, conditions, and financial arrangements attached thereto. This is the very essence of domestic legislation from industry's point of view.

H.R. 11879 accomplishes the above purpose well enough albeit not perfectly. Section 5(b)(1) provides exclusive rights with respect to persons subject to the jurisdiction of the United States or of any reciprocating state. Section 16(a) treats the matter of reciprocating states. Section 12 recognizes that the Government may not be able to protect the rights under the terms of an international regime. Section 13 provides for financial compensation for any economic losses resulting from failure to maintain rights under an international agreement. Section 14 provides investment insurance against economic losses resulting from interference with mining activities by those against whom a legal remedy either does not exist or is unavailable in any legal form to which the licensee has access.

Although the above is the most basic need of industry, many detailed provisions are required for the equitable implementation of the basic provisions for establishing the relationship of ocean mining to domestic laws, and for important matters of public interest and policy other than secure mineral supplies, such as the protection of the marine environment. H.R. 11879 has the necessary detailed provisions which in general appear adequate to the task.

I will have some specific comments on the legislation at a later point.

The point I want to make with absolute clarity is that H.R. 11879 does satisfy the needs of industry. It falls within the policy statement of the American Mining Congress and is acceptable, with only minor changes, as the equivalent to S. 713 and H.R. 1270 alluded to in the statement.

In the Chairman's letter of invitation to testify before this committee, you requested that industry discuss the status of the ocean mining industry. I will now turn to this subject. H.R. 11879 states in section 2(a)(6) "that United States mining companies have developed the technology necessary for the development and processing of deep seabed nodules and, given the necessary security of tenure, are prepared to make the necessary capital investment for such development and processing;" and the AMC policy statement says:

The technology of recovering minerals from the depths of the sea and processing them into useful raw materials has been under development by private industry for over ten years at its own cost. However, the future course of action by industry is threatened by uncertain investment conditions resulting from the failure to achieve a timely and satisfactory international regime on the law of the sea or domestic legislation which moves toward a stable and predictable investment climate.

These statements do not truly depict the overall status of development.

However, I appreciate the opportunity to brief the committee on current developments in ocean mining. There indeed has been substantial progress. I last appeared before this committee in May 1975. At that time I commented very negatively on the progress made and on the future prospects of progress at the Law of the Sea Conference.

A third session of the conference is scheduled for New York beginning next week. In this committee's hearing two weeks ago, the prospects of the third session were characterized, even with the vaunted intersessional accomplishments—we saw that in the testimony this morning—which were in fact noteworthy considering the Geneva intransigence of the developing world—by you, Mr. Murphy, as "in the realm of a faint glimmer of hope, and nothing more" and our chief negotiator, Mr. Ratiner, replied, "I think that is a reasonable characterization." I can do no better than support that analys̄

Now, during this same period of Caracas, Geneva, and intersessional meetings, what has happened in the world of industry and technology? Where do things stand today? Today, industry has progressed to the point where the next steps in unlocking the resources of the deep seabed require very large development expenditures and they are deeply concerned about making such expenditures, since their investment may be negotiated away at a Law of the Sea Conference, and there is no assurance that their own government will afford them protection against interference in the interim period before a treaty to the Chairman of this committee.

As a result, without a solution to this problem, progress toward commercial recovery will be halted or reduced to an insignificant rate.

It is true that industrial activity in ocean mining has continued high in 1974 and 1975 and ambitious plans have been made for 1976 and subsequently. However, this activity and these plans are based on a prediction and a faith that domestic legislation will be enacted into law and will become effective in 1976.

In the case of my own company, if the above does not occur in the next few months, we would review our development plans in detail. I predict as a result of that review that we would at the very minimum greatly curtail our program. It is also not inconceivable that we would abandon the project. We would find it extremely difficult to embark on a program costing of the order of $100 million to take us through our next stage of work into commercialization in the absence of appropriate legislation.

Now, what has been happening? Perhaps I should start with the Glomar Explorer. In past committee hearings, I have extolled the probable merits of this ship and the probability that it could be a tool for achieving early success in ocean mining. I have not changed that view and believe that use of this vessel would in fact accelerate the pace of ocean mining. Its accomplishments, as revealed by the press, are indeed impressive and there is little doubt that it is a further confirmation of our contention that the technology of ocean mining is at hand.

Of course, it appears that one potential ocean miner, The Summa Corporation, has disappeared. However, a new one, Lockheed, has appeared and appears to have a substantive program and serious plans. Their representative is before the committee today.

In early 1974, Kennecott Copper Corporation announced the establishment of a major consortium to work on ocean mining. It consists of Kennecott, Noranda Mines of Canada, Mitsubishi Corporation of Japan, Consolidated Gold Fields of the United Kingdom, and Rio Tinto Zinc of the United Kingdom. A major program has been under way and is essentially on the projected schedule.

In this same period, both Deepsea Ventures and The International Nickel Company (INCO) also announced consortia. The Deepsea Ventures group consists of U.S. Steel, Union Miniere of Belgium, and Tenneco. The INCO group consists of INCO, SEDCO (a U.S. oil drilling contractor), a Japanese group led by Sumitomo, and a West German group containing Metallgesellschaft, Preussag, Saltzgitter, and Rheinbraun. These, like the Kennecott effort, are substantial, serious efforts to bring the mineral resources of the seabed into production.

In addition, the CLB group (Japanese Continuous Line Bucket System) remains active and is planning tests in the Pacific this year. The CLB group has a large number of participants including the French organization CNEXO. In Japan, an association called DOMA, Deep Ocean Mining Association, is carrying out work emphasizing exploration in the Pacific Ocean.

It is somewhat difficult to assess the level of accomplishment of these groups because of their need to protect their own proprietary positions. However, representatives of several are here today and can speak for themselves. My own assessment based on informed observation of the scene is that the "collective" position of the seabed developers is as follows:

One: They have identified nodule deposits which could provide satisfactory mine sites. Mine site definition will require a large amount of work and substantial expenditures. To carry this work out without protection of investment and assurances for the future ability to mine the site is financially very risky.

Two: They have largely solved the metallurgical problems of winning metals from nodules. They have either run pilot plants or will do so in the near future. The next steps will require much larger and more costly pilot plant or demonstration plant tests. These tests must be run with nodules obtained from a mine site which would constitute a known supply for the commercial plant whose design would be based on these tests.

Three: Development of the mining systems has progressed from the drawing board and computer stage and away from simple laboratory tests to large-scale at-sea experimentation. Present schedules, as indicated during industry discussions of NOAA's environmental research program, call for several major at-sea tests beginning in late 1976 and continuing through 1978. The costs of such work are very high and in fact are unique in industrial technology development.

In conclusion, there is no longer any doubt about the technical and economic feasibility of ocean mining. The technology is ready; the investment climate is not.

At the risk of biring the committee, I will again emphasize the need for an acceptable investment climate. Looking at it operationally, the miner needs security of tenure over a mine site in order to spend the money necessary to explore completely the mine site, devise a mining plan, develop the expensive equipment to mine and process the minerals, and, finally, to invest in the production facilities. This is the usual basis under which a mining project can be financed and undertaken.

Since such security of tenure cannot be obtained under present circumstances, a substitute must be found. This substitute is protection from the risk that the industry will no longer be able to mine or will have investments impaired from financial burdens as a result of a LOS Treaty agreed to by the United States, and insurance against interference by foreign governments or firms against which no legal remedies are available. This, Mr. Chairman, is the essence of the cure for the present unsatisfactory investment climate, and I hope you will bear with the repetitious nature of this theme song.

I would now like to say a few additional words about the state of the art on ocean mining as seen through the eyes of my own company.

We believe we understand quite well the location, metallurgical grade, and tonnage of large manganese deposits of potential commercial interest. We have obtained detailed information on specific potential mine sites with respect to these parameters required for design of mining equipment.

We have tested mining equipment at a 15,000-foot depth on the floor of the Pacific Ocean. This equipment demonstrated successfully certain key aspects of nodule recovery and has given us confidence in our engineering designs. I note that we commented on this on page 21 of Kennecott's 1974 annual report. We believe the technical feasibility of ocean mining is clear.

Finally, we have completed our pilot plant work on the development of a hydrometallurgical process to extract metals from nodules. This unique process is low in energy consumption.

So, we have completed phase I of our program to bring nodules to commercial reality. We must now tackle phase II which involves the development of prototype equipment. This effort will be very expensive, requiring massive equipment and large ships. Once committed to these expenditures, there is almost no turning back from commercialization. Thus, we hesitate at this time because of the uncertainty of the investment climate resulting from the law of the sea issues. We have carried it this far on faith. We cannot go very much further.

As I stated before, if legislation to solve the problem is not enacted into law in the next few months, we will be forced to review our plan in view of the large financial risks such inaction would impose.

As I stated earlier, H.R. 11879 does satisfy the needs of industry. However, some minor changes appear desirable to us.

As you may recall, I wrote to vou on January 26, 1976, giving the views of the American Mining Congress with respect to legislation. Attached to that letter was a draft bill which showed revisions compared to bills pending at that time. Since H.R. 11879 builds on the previous work of the committee, these detailed comments are applicable to this bill.

Accordingly, Mr. Chairman, I request that my letter of January -26- 1976, with its attached bill, be incorporated in the record of this hearing.

Mr. Jones. Without objection, it so ordered.

[The document was not received by the time this hearing went to press.]

Mr. Dubs. Because of their importance, I want to single out several of these comments in this correspondence. The most significant modification is with respect to the size of the licensing block. H.R. 11879 provides for a 40,000-square-kilometer exploration block with a 75-percent relinquishment—or a reduction down to 10,000 square kilometers—at the time of conversion to a commercial recovery license.

The reason for this proposed change is that since 1970 when the 40,000/10,000 combination appeared in a U.S. draft treaty, it has become increasingly clear, especially as technological data have been accumulated, that the residual 10,000-square-kilometer site is too small to sustain a reasonable mining operation. The 60,000/30,000 combination would be adequate and is in general accord with pro posals made at the Law of the Sea Conference by a number of countries.

A second revision of note we would propose is the deletion of the limitation on the aggregate number of licenses issued by the United States to 30 percentum of an area of the deep seabed which is within a circle with a diameter of 1,250 kilometers. This is in section 10(a)(3) of H.R. 11879. This deletion would be in conformance with the United States position relating to nondiscriminatory access and its opposition to any quota system taken at the U.N. Conference on Law of the Sea.

We also are of the view that an increase in the work requirements in section 8(a) of the pending legislation would not be an unreasonable modification; however, we do not make any specific recommendations. In particular, increasing the block size as we have recommended above, plus the effect of inflationary pressures, indicate such an increase should be considered.

In originally selecting such figures, an effort was made to achieve a balance between work requirements of a magnitude which would insure good faith exploration, thereby avoiding speculation, and yet would not be so high as to freeze out the smaller operator from a legitimate opportunity to participate in ocean mining. This kind of balance must be maintained.

If you feel we were successful in achieving a reasonable balance, then upward adjustment would be fairly simple: (1) multiply each amount by 150 percentum—to account for the increased block size; (2) then multiply each amount by a factor equal to the cost-of-living index increase since January 1972 and add the product to the amount obtained in (1) above. You may also wish to consider a clause to account for further changes in the cost-of-living index in conjunction with the above.

The remaining revisions in my letter and its attached bill, although not trivial, are principally technical and are for the purpose of clarification. I hope that the committee will take them into account in its deliberations.

I also have a few additional comments though on H.R. 11879. The first is in regard to the effective date of the act given in section 24 as January 1, 1977. We urge that this be altered so that the act takes effect on the date of its enactment.

The bill already provides a more than adequate window for Law of the Sea negotiations in the January 1, 1977, date for commercialization in section 5(b)(1). There is nothing gained by setting a future effective date and much is lost because of putting off into the future the establishment of the regulatory machinery under the act and the settling of priorities on mining sites.

In addition, this legislation has continually and for some time now been moved toward some future date and the process should be ended now.

H.R. 11879 contains a section on reciprocating states, section 16, that has not appeared in previous pending legislation. We believe this to be a good addition and adds strength to the bill.

I endorse paragraphs (a) and (b). On the other hand, I have strong reservations on paragraph (c) which instructs the Secretary of State to enter into international agreements with whether this kind of instruction may be a separation-of-powers problem. On more pragmatic grounds, I am concerned that the purposes of the act might be confounded if an interpretation should arise that such international agreements referred to in paragraph (c) must be entered into before the domestic features of the act become fully operative. I applaud the underlying concept of putting the reciprocating state concept into real effect rapidly. Perhaps the desired effect could be obtained by changing the preemptive language into a precatory statement which adjures the Secretary of State to pursue international agreements with reciprocating states.

In section 7(a) of the concept of involvement of the National Oceanic and Atmospheric Administration in environmental matters has been introduced. This, we believe, is a good idea. We, too, recognize the expertise of NOAA in the area of baseline studies and data accumulation and the necessity of their contribution.

However, we believe the wording of paragraph (a) should be revised so that the words, "acting through the Administrator of the National Oceanic and Atmospheric Administration," in lines 6 through 8 be struck. We would then propose a new sentence to be inserted after the end of the present first sentence—line 13— which would require consultation with NOAA and charge them with environmental research in this area including the execution of baseline studies, acquisition and baseline data. The new paragraph (b) would then fit nicely into the scheme of things.

The final issue I am concerned with in H.R. 11879 is the jurisdictional question which appears in section 3(1). Section 3(1) reads: "The term 'Secretary' means, except where its usage indicates otherwise, the Secretary of Commerce." In all other pending bills, "Secretary" is defined as the Secretary of the Interior. We are not in accord with the designation of the Secretary of Commerce in H.R. 11879 and continue to believe the proper administrative authority is the Secretary of the Interior.

The mining industry has tradititonally looked to the Department of the Interior for leadership within the executive branch of Government with respect to mineral resource development and appropriate Government activity in this regard. We see no difference on the bases of the occurrence of the resource at the bottom of the sea, in fact we see ocean mining as being more of a matter of mining than oceans.

The Mining and Minerals Policy Act of 1970, 30 U.S.C. 21(a), specifically places the responsibility of fostering and encouraging private enterprise in the development of economically sound and stable domestic mining, minerals, metal, and mineral reclamation industries on the Secretary of the Interior.

Furthermore, the Secretary is required to include in his annual report to the Congress

... a report on the state of the domestic mining, minerals, and mineral reclamation industries, including a statement of the trend in utilization and depletion of these resources, together with such recommendations for legislative programs as may be necessary to implement the policies of this section.

It is difficult to conceive of a clearer expression of congressional intent than the declaration of policy and the assignment of responsibility on the Secretary of the Interior to carry out that policy than is contained in this statute, Public Law 91–631, 84 stat. 1876.

The American Mining Congress concurs both in the declaration of policy and in the assignment of responsibility made by the Mining and Minerals Policy Act of 1970.

The reasons we have looked to Interior are also based on their in-depth expertise and understanding of mineral resource technology and policy. The skills of the U.S. Geological Survey are well known. The expertise and background of the Bureau of Mines, particularly their knowledge of mineral processing and mining technology, are important. More than half the coastline within the mineral processing part of the operation.

The regulatory arms of Interior have an understanding of the regulation of the mineral industry.

Finally, the background for formulating and managing the implementation of policy exists in depth in Interior, particularly in the office of the Assistant Secretary for Energy and Minerals.

I note that some of the basic attitudes of the Department of the Interior regarding ocean mining were summarized in a speech by Secretary Kleppe before the American Oceanic Organization on February 27, 1976. I have a news release summary of that speech and would be glad to provide it for the record if the Chair so wishes.

Of course, we must also make clear that since the development of the resources of the deep seabed requires ocean environmental technology, oceanographic knowledge of many kinds, and meteorological information, the National Oceanic and Atmospheric Administration can and should provide important research, data and support for deep ocean mining operations.

Our AMC policy statement expresses our views on the relative roles of Interior and Commerce. Clearly we believe that each agency, within the ambit of its expertise, has an important contribution to make to ocean mining. In the final analysis, though, it is the Secretary of Interior who should be charged with the administration of the act.

Mr. Chairman, I noted with some interest the comments of Mr. Ratiner in the February 23 hearing regarding the substantive provisions of the bill. He commented on them again this morning. I understand his concern for having the capability of assembling independently verifiable data. However, I note that there is in fact much data in the public domain even today which could be used to resolve his concers. There also appears to be some idea of Prototype Regulations it would be interesting to hear specific ideas.

However, I believe it is very late tot consider such new initiatives when the present bill is adequate to the task.

Nevertheless, I recognize that the Ocean Mining Administration has not yet been adequately staffed and funded to carry out all the activities they need to and are capable of. We noted this in our AMC policy statement saying:

We urge the Administration and the Congress to fund and staff adequately the office of the Ocean Mining Administration to permit it to carry out its mission with respect to seabed mineral resource development.

I have already made some brief comment on the Law of the Sea Conference. I remain quite pessimistic about agreement at the March session or at any time in 1976. Nevertheless, I believe our negotiators are trying hard and in fact made some progress, however far from the end goal, in the intersessional meetings. I note that the U.S. Proposed Amendments to the Committee I Single Negotiating Text, dated December 1975, represent a basically sound policy approach.

I have also examined the products of the intersessional work on the deep seabed issue which were submitted to his committee for the record. My perspective on this effort is not that we should agree to these new draft articles but that they represent important steps in putting together a single negotiating text that we would have some real possibility of using for negotiation.

As I stated in May before this committee, the present text is an unmitigated disaster. The intersessional work has in fact provided some mitigation but much more is required.

Overall, progress has been made, but this progress may in fact have evaporated before April Fool's Day. In my opinion, there is no treaty on the deep seabed in sight in 1976 and very likely not in 1977.

Mr. Chairman, I have continued too long but it seemed necessary to cover at least superficially the areas you had instructed us to discuss in your invitation to testify. It appears likely to me, and I hope that this is a sound prediction, that the committee will act on this legislation soon.

Accordingly, it seemed necessary to communicate our views reasonably fully.

In conclusion, I believe the early enactment of H.R. 11879 into law—taking into account suggestions for amendments at these hearings—is a proper and urgently needed response to the public need to obtain new secure sources of mineral supply.

I urge the enactment of H.R. 11879 into law.

Thank you, Mr. Chairman.

Mr. JONES. Thank you, Mr. Dubs.

The Chair would like to commend you on a very definitive statement, and your specifics, and if I followed you, you have translated it into layman's terms, a private sector in an operation that has gone as far as it can go, until such time it has some assurance from this Government for assistance and protection, is that correct?

Mr. DUBS. That is correct, Mr. Chairman.

Mr. JONES. In your testimony you noted that other foreign nations and companies in other foreign nations had entered into arrangements with your company.

Do you know, as a matter of fact, that is, yourself, what protection or assistance the foreign governments are giving your counterparts with whom you are doing business?

Mr. DUBS. They have not given protection in the guise of say domestic legislation, the kind we are talking about.

However, for example, we have two British participants. The British Government has provided, during the phase I of our program, direct and large financial assistance to the British companies, and it is expected that they will continue to do so.

In the case of the Japanese partner, the Japanese Government has most recently established a policy whereby they will provide substantial assistance to the Japanese companies involved in such consortia.

This, Mr. Chairman, is direct financial assistance.

In the case of Canada, there has been no such direct assistance.

Mr. JONES. Thank you, sir.

I note in your concluding paragraph here you make some reference to April Fool's Day. Are you trying to tell us that we are deluding ourselves if we expect any action on the deep seabed question?

Mr. DUBS. Well, I perhaps meant it to be provocative, but on the other hand, it will represent the end of 2 weeks of the Conference, and as I see the situation, whatever progress has been made from the intersessional meetings will have been brought before a more full body of the Conference, and I think we will be able to judge whether the reception is good or poor.

Mr. JONES. Productive?

Mr. DUBS. Yes.

Mr. JONES. I think this particular question has been before the Conference for what. about 10 years?

Mr. DUBS. Oh, yes; very nearly 10 years. As I recall, it started about 1969.

Mr. JONES. Well, thank you, sir.

Mr. Oberstar, do you have questions?

Mr. OBERSTAR. Thank you. Mr. Chairman.

Mr. Dubs, you have responded to questions that I have asked of other witnesses, the State Department and Interior and others, that never seem to get any answers, and that is what in their judgment constitutes a stable investment climate needed to bring forth the investments from industry to develop seabed resources, and you have made a step in that direction, outlining certain of thoes elements, namely when you referred to security of tenure, including the right to mine, a specific length of time for that mining. and specific conditions without changing during that tenure, and you called for compensation.

Are there other elements that you would consider essential to stable investment climate?

Mr. DUBS. Well, these are the very basic elements. There is not much more really required. and some of the other elements, for example, the, or to take the case in point, the whole reciprocating State concept, is really a means of bringing those States which have the capability to carry out ocean mining, and we know those to be the major developed nations of the world, to bring them into this fold, and this, in turn, reduces, I think, the possibility of any conflict at sea.

Mr. OBERSTAR. If there were no treaty, would you consider that to be an unstable climate for investment?

Mr. DUBS. Well, if there was no treaty and no possibility of a treaty, maybe we better put it back to time zero, and if the issue of a treaty were not now before us at all. I think it is very likely, a very personal opinion of mine. that the natural course of events would see the U.S. Government taking the initiative to establish arrangements with other countries, with an interest in, and a capability for deep ocean exploitation.

Mr. OBERSTAR. It is hard to word the question, since we are dealing with speculative matters, but let us assume the realistic possibility that the treaty negotiations come to a conclusion without any resolution, without specifically resulting in a treaty.

As I suggested to a witness earlier today, the negotiations generate a momentum of their own. They just continue on, which is likely to happen.

Then you obviously, by your definition, have a questionable investment climate.

Then, is it essential for Federal legislation to be enacted in the United States in order to give industry the incentive it needs, and the security to proceed with development?

Mr. DUBS. Yes, I think so, for two or three reasons, Mr. Oberstar.

First, on the high seas we are subject to potential political harassment of all kinds. We do not know what that would be.

If we consider that a freedom of the high seas doctrine, to hold, for example, it is possible that without any protection from our Government, at least I thought I detected some hesitancy in Secretary Maw this morning as far as defining what kind of protection might be forthcoming, and we would feel in that case that we would need some kind of insurance program.

In some ways this is similar to the kind of insurance that has been provided for out of the Overseas Private Investment Corporation.

With respect to the Law of the Sea, I must say that I would still be concerned that even if, you know, it looks as if we are going to drag on forever, even if it were stopped I would be concerned about getting some fundamental protection.

There is somewhat, I would consider to be ideas floating around that might have a potential for entering international law if there is not a firm position taken.

Mr. Oberstar, for example, this whole concept of the common heritage of mankind, which for the United States means that the common heritage of mankind will be defined by the content of a treaty that is eventually negotiated, but for the developing world, the concept of the common heritage of mankind means something quite different.

It means that they own the resources of the seabed. I would consider that, even with the treaty broken off, that we would have to deal with this concept, that is a product, a child of the negotiations over many, many years, as an example.

Mr. OBERSTAR. Yes.

Now, when you talked about one of the conditions for a stable investment climate, and security of tenure, you suggested a specific length of time for developing an ore body, producing from an ore body, if we can refer to the ocean bottom in the most traditional terms.

Mr. DUBS. We can, sir.

Mr. OBERSTAR. You have to have exploration. You have to be able to prove out the ore body by core drilling, or some other measurement means, and then industry has to make a commitment to develop that ore body, and to bring it into production.

Now, how long does it take to do that?

How much of that kind of wrok has to be done?

I realize that you can speak only for your company.

Mr. Dubs. It depends on where you start from. Our particular company started in 1962, so we are 14 years down the stream, and we can see that starting from scratch now and going that far, it does take a long time, because ocean exploration is difficult, it is expensive.

Now, starting where we are today, of course, we do not have to look at quite so much time.

We debated this issue within the Mining Congress Committee on Undersea Mineral Resources. We felt that the 15-year period was very desirable, because it would not penalize those industrial organizations that have not yet entered this field, and we would expect that others would enter the field.

I think the 15-year time period mentioned in the bill makes technical sense, particularly for a company starting from scratch.

For a company that has been in it as long as we have, the time would not have had to be so long.

Mr. Oberstar. How large an area would you consider to be necessary for an economical deposit?

Mr. Dues. We consider that the final mine size of 30,000 square kilometers to be the desirable correct size, and this would provide, depending on how technology develops, this would provide roughly a 20-year mine life for a three-million-ton per year operation.

Mr. Oberstar. Twenty-year mine life and three million tons a year?

Mr. Dues. Yes. Now, this is under the conditions of how we understand the technology today.

As in the case of land mines. I am sure you know, coming from a mining state, as technology changes. it is possible to mine material that a few years ago you were not economically able to, and I do not see any reason why this pattern might not be repeated on the ocean bottom.

Mr. Oberstar. For a 20-year mine life what is the size of investment contemplated?

Mr. Dubs. Well, the size of investment, and since the dollar is somewhat of an illusive target, I would like to talk in terms of maybe mid-1975 dollars.

For an operation that would maybe process three million dry tons per year we would be talking about investments in the range of $500 million to $600 million in 1975 dollars.

Mr. Oberstar. From my own perspective, coming from northern Minnesota, with the taconite industry, that is a very sizable invest ment.

Mr. Dues. It is very sizable. One of the features of deep sea minnig is that it is expensive, and it has to be done at large scale.

Of course, we are dealing with what I would term, loosely speaking, a rich ore, in that there is a high metallic content.

If we considered, for example, recovering the copper, nickel, cobalt, and some of the trace metals, and perhaps a little manganese, we might be talking about a potential sales value of $100 to $130 per ton.

The potential sales then would go along with that scale of opera tions. Again, in 1975 prices it would be in the order of $300 plus million per year.

We are talking then about a very high risk. I think one of the points which also relates to this is that in this next stage of development we are looking at unusually uniquely high development expenditures in that, for example, I will speak only for my own company, we see the next stage as being the construction and test of a very large scale prototype.

Now, we are not talking in tens of millions, but we are talking in excess of $100 million.

That alone, as a developmental expenditure, is very unique, Mr. Oberstar.

Mr. OBERSTAR. What amount of the processing would be done at sea?

Would you have some concentration, and then move the ore concentrate from high seas onto land operation, or would you take the crude from the sea to land processing facilities?

Mr. DUBS. Our own basic approach is a hydraulic approach, whereby we lift the material from the sea bottom by a slurry method suspended in water.

When that material arrives at the surface on the ship there will be fines in the material. There will be some deep sea sediments. These will have to be rejected at sea.

Mr. Oberstar, it would be very difficult not to reject them, but the remainder of the material then, the bulk of the material, would be shipped ashore for processing on shore.

In other words, there would be no at-sea chemical or physical processing, other than this escape of the fines, so the substances would be what I would term natural substances.

Mr. OBERSTAR. You would be returning to the ocean material taken from it without altering it?

Mr. DUES. That is correct, although I think, as you understand, part of the environmental study that is being carried out to get data in the National Oceanic and Atmospheric Administration is to try to obtain specific baseline data on the effect of even this material.

Mr. OBERSTAR. Yes. Well, I realize that.

Is the metallurgy for seabed minerals different from metallurgy required for landbased minerals?

Mr. DUBS. Yes, it is. We cannot process seabed minerals on any existing, and let me be specific, we cannot process manganese nodules on any present landbased plant, and the plant that would be built to handle the manganese nodules could not be expected to process any other ore, and in fact, the process may be more or less depending on where you got your ore, in other words, different nodules will have different trace metals in it.

They will have different concentrations of the primary metals, Mr. Oberstar, and this requires a certain tailoring of the processing plant.

Mr. OBERSTAR. Where is the largest part of your investment required, for onland processing, or sea recovery?

Mr. DUES. More than half of it is on land, and if you look at the at sea part of it, and I am speaking very round about, in very round numbers, perhaps 25 percent of it would be involved in the transport, on the order of 25 percent involved in the transport of stuff from the mining location to shore.

Of course, this transport is using techniques that have been used to transport other ores, so the at-sea mining vessel is perhaps on the order of 25 percent of the whole.

Mr. OBERSTAR. Thank you, Mr. Chairman. I have no other questions. I defer to others, and then if there is time, I would like to come back.

Mr. JONES. Mr. Forsythe?

Mr. FORSYTHE. Thank you, Mr. Chairman.

Mr. Dubs, you may have covered this with Mr. Oberstar, but we have been talking about this $500 million of investment required.

Does that cover both the at-sea and production facilities?

Mr. DUBS. Yes, sir.

Mr. FORSYTHE. Well, one production facility?

Mr. DUES. This would be a single project, one mine, one facility.

Mr. FORSYTHE. And the range, I understand, is somewhat maybe less, maybe 50 percent for a half dozen mines.

Mr. DUBS. Yes.

Mr. FORSYTHE. In this whole question of insurance and protection, after we look at numbers, such as if we did the sole mining for the world supply in the next 50 years, we would hardly touch it.

Just what are we concerned about? You mentioned political harassment.

Are we concerned that someone is going to bring their navy out there?

Just what are we talking about?

Mr. DUBS. Dividing it into the two portions now, one insurance against interference at sea, and No. 2, the Law of the Sea Treaty itself, if we consider now insurance against harassment of various kinds at sea, I could foresee a species of claim jumping, for example.

Let us say we will take a look at a few scenarios. Let us say I have done the exploration work, and the mine development work for a particular area, with the particular unique characteristics, and I now set about to build the production equipment that would mine that ore. It may take me 3 years from that time to get the equipment built.

During that time several kinds of things can happen. It is possible that an organization from another company could attempt in the meantime to mine in the same area, and this would represent an interference which we would not be able to do anything about.

We would have to look to Government to do something about it.

Mr. FORSYTHE. Mining from another company, or a country?

Mr. DUBS. From another country, another company. That possibility clearly exists.

Now, would there be some other kind of interference?

Suppose in the course of detente that it reaches a low moment, and we are out trying to mine, and ships are still within the realm of international law, steaming around, but still interference with the mining operation. That could be another kind of thing.

Mr. Forsythe, we could imagine several of those things. With respect to the Law of the Sea Treaty itself, as we read the various texts that we have before us so far, and notwithstanding the testimony from the State Department people, it is easy to imagine, for example, financial provisions which they have not arrived at all yet that would be very adverse, and we would, in effect, find the miner with a $500 million investment and no opportunity of earning a return on it, much less of getting his investment back, much less earning a return on it.

These all seem to be very real possibilities to us, sir.

Mr. FORSYTHE. The consortium of which Kennecott is the leader, or a part of, includes several of the industrialized nations of the world today, and I believe that there is another that perhaps covers the waterfront so far as those nations with any signs of technical competence and ability to exploit the deep sea are concerned.

If we move away from all these nations at this point in time who are essentially partners in our industry, does that not minimize some of these concerns that industry should have?

Mr. DUBS. It was intended, from the very beginning, to minimize the risks to the extent possible, and it is for that reason, that at least in the case of our own company, that an international consortium arose.

I would say that if legislation such as this had existed on the bill 4 years ago that it would be highly doubtful whether such a consortium would have arisen.

It is a response, and the question is, "Is it enough of a response to satisfy the problem?"

I do not think so, Mr. Forsythe.

Mr. FORSYTHE. I am searching here. If we were to assume the total risk as a nation, and not have this cooperative prospect with other nations in the consortium, I could see more of a problem.

Has the industry attempted to find any other way of insuring these risks, either by domestic or international insurance arrangements, or whatever?

Mr. DUBS. We have not found any hope that such could be accomplished.

In addition to the work that we have done ourselves, we have stimulated the Department of the Interior to take a look at that with their strong interest in marine resource development, and they did not come up with any programs that exist either.

We also, and I think Secretary Baker here this morning mentioned the Marine Petroleum and Minerals Advisory Committee in the Department of Commerce, and that committee stimulated the Department of International and Domestic Business to examine approaches, and they did an in-house study of that also, and did not come up with a system that would satisfy it.

Mr. FORSYTHE. There is no suggestion that there is any seeking of insurance against commercial risk as opposed to outside or international, or whatever?

Mr. DUBS. There is not only no suggestion, there is no interest in that.

We believe that if we can get the political problem solved, and if we are taxed fairly, we can make a go of this new business.

Mr. FORSYTHE. I think that is good to be on the record.

So far as this transfer of technology has been discussed earlier, what is the industry's attitude?

It was mainly pointed out that transfer of technology Government may be able to provide, but when it came to the question of transfer of commercial technology back to the Government, and therefore maybe putting it in the public domain, what is the industry's position here?

Mr. Dues. I have a very negative view of it, sir.

I think the providing of technological data that is necessary to carry out the purposes of Government, let us say, to satisfy conformance with environmental rules and regulations, clearly has to be done, but say the transfer of detailed technology on mineral processing, or the particular design of a pumping system for the Government, that would be very bad.

I even feel nervous sitting alongside these fellows over here now, so that is the way I feel about it.

Mr. Forsythe. Do you believe the Government should be spending taxpayers' dollars to develop technology that should be transferred to you?

Mr. Dues. I would like to see this kind of a role of Government.

I think there are certain larger general questions involved here that require the Government to obtain information itself for public policy and public interest.

They will not help us mine the ocean, except insofar as they might help the Government arrive at regulations and rules that are sensible with respect to mining the ocean.

An example of this, of course, is the question of environmental effect.

It is quite clear that a program carried out on possible environmental effects of ocean mining will be a stimulant to the business as a whole.

Furthermore, such a program carried out by the Government will have a credibility which no amount of work done by industry alone would have.

I think Mr. Ratiner talked about his nervousness with regard to having independent verifiable data with respect to how ocean mining performs.

I think that those are clearly areas where the Government needs to have some investment in technology.

For example, with respect to the assessment of the resource, this is a very sensitive thing with us, incidentally. We have much more data than appears in the public domain, and the total assessment of this resource is particularly sensitive to us at this point, because we have no protection over it.

It seems to me that this resource is so important that it makes sense for the Government to have an independent idea of this resource.

Mr. Forsythe. I see some lines that get a little bit cloudy, and it worries me as to how far the Government goes to spend the taxpayers' money in finding out how much oil we are going to be able to develop in a particular field, and getting quite so deep into this kind of an area.

The Ford Motor Co. did not have much help when they designed the Edsel.

Mr. Dues. I would share that nervousness.

Mr. Forsythe. Thank you very much.

Thank you, Mr. Chairman.

Mr. Jones. Mr. Downing, any questions?

Mr. Downing. Thank you, Mr. Chairman.

It is good to see you gentlemen again. It is good to see my old friend, Mr. Flipse again. The company was an early pioneer in deep sea mining efforts and has been doing remarkable work in this field.

I am sorry I missed hearing your testimony, but I assure you I shall read it.

Mr. JONES. Mr. Flipse has not testified yet, Mr. Downing.

Mr. DOWNING. Oh, he has not?

Mr JONES. No.

Mr. DOWNING. I will hold my questions until after he testifies.

Thank you, Mr. Chairman.

Mr. JONES. Counsel, do you have a question or two.

Mr. PERIAN. Mr. Dubs, the less developed countries have made proposals at the Law of the Sea contracts which, as of now, appear unacceptable to United States Mining interests.

Has the United States ever made a counterproposal which you would support?

Mr. DUBS. I think the document that was referred to this morning, the United States amendments to the single negotiating text; that is for every one of the single negotiating text articles, there is a counter-article by the United States. I think that position is a sounder position, and I personally would support it generally.

I might have the view that it is too big a bundle for the job at hand. Still, from the policy standpoint, it provides the fundamentals.

Mr. PERIAN. That is the text of Mr. Ratiner?

Mr. DUBS. Specifically, this was a text that was printed in 1975. It shows three columns in the book. The first column is the chairman of committee I proposed single negotiating text.

The second column consists of the amendments.

The third column is the complete United States position. This is a good approach for the problem.

Mr. PERIAN. What do you think the chances are for that document surviving?

Mr. DUES. Infinitesimal.

Mr. PERIAN. You mentioned at the beginning of your testimony that you serve on the State Department's Advisory Committee on the Law of the Sea. and as an expert on the United States delegation to the Law of the Sea Conference.

Could you explain what role vou play in both these capacities? Are you frequently consulted? If you are frequently consulted, do they pay any attention to you?

Mr. DUES. Well, first, with respect to the Advisory Committee, I think the Advisory Committee provides an opportunity to have inputs during a policymaking stage. I would say that I probably don't have as warm a feeling toward that as I might simply because it meets infrequently, and oftentimes there is not sufficient time ahead of time to digest material and to be able to comment on it.

With respect to serving as an expert on the United States delegation to the Law of the Sea Conference, I feel that personally I was very fully consulted and had ample opportunity for input. Not all of my inputs were ignored; and I do feel that I had some impact on it. In fact, I would say that I feel very pleased that they have gone in that direction and have utilized whatever talents and information we have.

Mr. Perian. You are generally satisfied that industry has some input into it?

Mr. Dues. Yes.

Mr. Oberstar. Will counsel yield?

Mr. Perian. Yes.

Mr. Oberstar. When negotiations get to the point where somebody on the part of the United States is going to give away something essential to United States industrial development and you point this out, do they act on your concerns?

Mr. Dubs. Well, one can't always—sometimes this kind of thing comes up in circumstances where you are not there. As an expert attached to the delegation, we are hardly privy in the corridor and secret negotiating sessions; so our input cannot be at that point. It has to be before such a kind of negotiation occurs; and we have seen instances where we have been less than happy at what we thought happened. We have expressed that unhappiness, and I think it has had an effect.

Mr. Oberstar. I am sure that there is a great deal of negotiation, probably more negotiation than is carried on in the way you have just described than in the open sessions. Are you privy to that, or are you just considered to be another pesky advisory group?

Mr. Dubs. Well, of course, there is always a problem of classification and sometimes things get classified beyond one's classification level on the committee; and this, then, can be a problem. Things can happen that you do not know about. It would be improper to say everything that goes on we know about. We do not. It is proper to say we have been widely consulted and we have made inputs.

If you said: Is the relationship such that if some very bad thing would happen, you would be sure of having the input to stop it, I would have to answer that I have no way of knowing.

Mr. Oberstar. Thank you very much.

Mr. Perian. How much input did you have into the Pinto document and into the Engo document?

Mr. Dues. No one had any input into the Engo document, but with respect to critiquing and criticizing the various versions of the Pinto document that came into the U.S. delegation, I would say that I had a very full opportunity to input that

Mr. Perian. You state on page 5 that "Security of tenure" is the basic and only requirement of industry.

Do you think a Law of the Sea Treaty could provide this security of tenure?

Mr. Dues. A proper one could.

Mr. Perian. Do you think the proposed structure, i.e., a legislative body which could promulgate laws binding on the United States, would be stable enough to provide security of tenure to the mining industry?

Mr. Dubs. I feel very nervous about that legislative body.

As a matter of fact, if you are referring specifically to the assembly, the assembly as it is constituted in the Anglo-Sino negotiating text, I think that is an entirely unsatisfactory body. We could not live with it and could not depend upon a stable condition to last over a very long time. I think the power of the assembly has to be great circumscribed if a Law-of-the-Sea Treaty is going to result that we can live with.

The assembly is a one-nation-one-vote body; and we know how those votes go.

Mr. PERIAN. What would you say to the charge by Mr. Ratiner at the earlier hearing that by enacting this legislation, Congress would be guaranteeing industry against the efforts and actions of the executive branch?

Mr. DUBS. I read that statement with great interest. There are two ways of looking at that. One way is that that is exactly correct; and it perhaps is one mechanism to prevent negotiating of deals which are maybe against the U.S. interests; so that is one way of looking at it.

Another way of looking at it is that if the negotiator is backed up finally with a firm U.S. position that has been expounded and enacted into law in the Congress, they may find that they can negotiate much more effectively than they now can.

The third way of looking at it is that in one sense it is a bit of sophistry to say that this legislation would prevent achieving a treaty that would be satisfactory to the United States; because if this treaty is to be attained in as brief a time as some of our friends in the State Department would indicate, then how many operations can be licensed before such a treaty came into effect?

In other words, if the treaty is obtained quickly, the exposure of the whole international community to, let us say, this particular legislation is pretty small; so in that sense, it seems to me to be somewhat of a tempest in a teapot.

Mr. PERIAN. You say on page 11 of your statement that "The technology is ready; the investment climate is not."

If legislation is passed this year, how soon could you have the minerals from those nodules in the marketplace?

Mr. DUBS. That date would be in the early part of the eighties, in the period between 1981 and 1982—1983 at the latest.

Mr. PERIAN. What kind of annual production levels do you foresee in the first 5 years of production?

Mr. DUES. Between 10- and 20-million tons per year of nodules. To express that a different way, we have talked about the need of these minerals for the U.S. supply of critical materials. The production of that many modules could supply all the U.S. manganese needed. It could just about supply all the U.S. nickel needs and certainly all the cobalt needs; so it would have a very substantial and marked effect on U.S. mineral economy; and it would supplement copper supplies.

Mr. PERIAN. This comes out to about $125 a ton?

Mr. DUES. As sort of an order of magnitude of sort of a potential sales volume, depending upon how little manganese is presently produced. That is at present prices.

Mr. PERIAN. Is the limitation you refer to on page 13 a limitation to the aggregate number of licenses that the United States can issue or the number that any one licensee can hold?

Mr. DUBS. It really applies to both, but it definitely limits the individual licensee and definitely the United States as a country is written there.

Mr. PERIAN. Thank you.

Mr. Jones. The Chair recognizes Mr. Downing for the purpose of introducing our next witness.

Mr. Oberstar. If I may, I have one further question.

Mr. Jones. The Chair recognizes the gentleman for one question.

Mr. Oberstar. How many jobs would be created by the investment of $500 million or $600 million?

Mr. Dues. I would like to corroborate this in a letter to the Chairman; but it would be in the order of 1,000 or 2,000 jobs.

Mr. Jones. Mr. Downing?

Mr. Downing. Mr. Flipse is no stranger to this committee, as the committee well knows; and it is always a pleasure to have him appear before us.

Mr. Flipse is the president of Deepsea Ventures, which is located on Gloucester, Va. Its headquarters are located there.

He is chairman of the executive committee of Deepsea Ventures, Inc., and also a spokesman for the National Ocean Industry Association.

Mr. Flipse first got me interested in the subject of deep sea mining and that interest has persisted and will persist until we can get something passed which will enable us to mine for deep seabed minerals.

So, Mr. Flipse, it is a pleasure to have you with us, and you may proceed.

STATEMENT OF J. E. FLIPSE, PRESIDENT, DEEPSEA VENTURES, INC AND SPOKESMAN FOR THE NATIONAL OCEAN INDUSTRIES ASSOCIATION

Mr. Flipse. Thank you, Mr. Downing.

After that introduction, perhaps my opening statement is redundant, so I will omit it.

May I request that my complete statement be made a part of the record and I will summarize it and show the subcommittee a movie?

Mr. Jones. Without objection, it is so ordered.

Mr. Flipse. It is a pleasure to appear again before this committee in our continuing effort to develop a constructive working relationship with the Government of the United States during these crucial early years of ocean-mining development.

As requested by the chairman, I shall direct my remarks to the status of the deep sea program and identify those special needs which can be met through actions of the Congress.

Stated simply, our Nation's primary need with regard to the deep seabed is the perpetual and free access of the Nation to deep ocean hard minerals.

Our company's primary need, similarly, is assured access to a chosen ore body whose availability is guaranteed for a reasonable span of time on economic terms which permit its development.

Meeting these mutual needs will assist the United States in developing alternate sources of critical metals while providing the opportunity for our industry to contribute to to maintenance and strengthening of the national economy and to compete in world trade.

Mr. Chairman, at this time, I would like to show a short film which supplements and replaces the written testimony for several pages. I would then like to present the status of our program to the committee.

Mr. JONES. Proceed.

[Mr. Flipse presented a film.]

Mr. FLIPSE. Mr. Chairman, as an update of the film, I would like to report that we have contracted to buy a 20,000-ton modern ore transport vessel to convert to a test ship, and conversion and outfitting plans are well along.

This phase of the program is now fully funded in excess of $15 million.

Off the record.

[Discussion off the record.]

Mr. FLIPSE. If we address as our principal legal and economic problem, the need for an assured ore body for a reasonable length of time and at a reasonable cost, we can identify immediately several corrollaries.

Current international law of the sea, under its freedom of the seas doctrine, gives us the right to mine. It does not, however, provide us with sufficient assurance of continuity of the availability of the ore body.

Our notice to Secretary Kissinger, I believe, makes a clear-cut case for our continuing rights under existing international law, but the uncertainties raised by the uniqueness of this operation, and the "thinness" of the law on the subject, make it inadequate to insure bank support.

Continuing U.N. discussion of the law of the sea and the benign neglect by the U.S. Government, for political reasons, further weakens our position under the freedom of the seas doctrine.

The threat of expropriation of our deposit through international treaty, or irresponsible acts of others which fail to capture the attention of our Department of State, is extremely harmful to the solicitation of economic support.

The inflexible attitude of the developing countries as demonstrated by the Engo text—the Committee I single negotiating text resulting from the 1975 U.S. Conference meeting in Geneva—states conditions which would make private investment in deep seabed mining extremely unattractive.

Indeed, this text would effectively bar exploitation by any agency, international, State, or private, due to its total bias toward control rather than promotion of activity.

Unfortunately, this situation is being fully exploited by the developing countries who recognize the deleterious impact on U.S. industry of a semipermanent state of uncertainty.

The major threat of the Engo text is that price and production controls may be applied by an international body dominated by Third World land-based mineral suppliers.

Further, the text provides that private enterprise may gradually be totally eliminated from deep seabed mining in favor of an international mining monopoly.

The text holds no hope for a binding contract as a basis for continued ocean mining practice but rather assures discriminatory treatment against the developed countries, including our United States.

Deepsea's specific problems are identical with those of the industry in general but are giving us more concern due to our lead in this developing industry.

We recognize fully, as our competition is certain to, that we must design our entire mining, production, and marketing system to a specific, limited deposit of nodules. We realize that even this development work involves many tens of millions of dollars.

To date we have received no specific encouragement by the U.S. Government and therefore are looking to you, the Congress, for the timely definition necessary to permit sound economic planning.

Deepsea is at a critical decision point. We must now plan our mining transportation system based on the location of the processing plant and mine site. An international joint venture has little incentive to accept the tax and environmental costs, incident to American operation, without the type of protection found in the bill now being considered by your committee.

Our economic analyses have indicated clearly that the very large capital investment must be leveraged by debt funds provided at reasonable interest rates. Such funds are available only if the long-term availability of the ore body is assured.

Deepsea also suffers the risk of having our technological lead in the industry eroded. Our policy of protection of the technology through patents, our support of the Department of the Interior and Commerce in explaining to them the real needs of this emerging industry, and our support of this legislative effort lead to disclosures that must be useful to our competition. The passage of suitable legislation will be adequate reward for these disclosures.

The foregoing remarks describe the status of our program and refer, in a general way, to several of our major problems. I would now like to address the specific needs of the American ocean mining industry and Deepsea Ventures, Inc.

Over the past 9 years, we have been faced with an increasingly acrimonious debate on the law of the sea and the status of deep seabed minerals. The record is replete with broken administration promises. President Nixon promised in his declaration of May 1970, that interim arrangements would be made providing security of investment. The 1973 U.N. Law of the Sea Conference was offered, during 1971 and 1972, as the long-range solution to our critical problems.

In 1974, State and Interior Department witnesses repeatedly promised a resolution by 1975 or else they would initiate interim arrangements.

The last carelessly discarded promise was the 1975 State Department assurance that a thorough "study of interim arrangements" would be done and Congress briefed thereon in an effort to offset the disasters of Caracas and Geneva.

These delays and broken promises have manifested themselves in corresponding delays in funding of the ocean mining program of Deepsea Ventures.

Our budget requirements were fully met by Tenneco from 1969 to 1971. However, the then chairman of Tenneco testified before this Committee that further investment in ocean mining would be limited until there was either an international treaty or domestic legislation.

This was indeed the case and our program did not move into its next phase but was continued on a sustaining basis at a low level of funding.

In 1974, Deepsea was able to interest a group of Japanese trading companies, Union Minere of Belgium, and United States Steel Corp. in joining Tenneco in a joint venture, Ocean Mining Associates.

The ocean mining program of Deepsea was restructured as a cautious series of events rather than an aggressive parallel effort as previously envisioned.

Exploration and survey of the mine site was conducted in 1975 and is continuing.

Nineteen seventy-six and early 1977 will be devoted to the at-sea test of the mining system on the claimed mine site. If this work is technically successful, as we expect it to be, the demonstration plant work will be undertaken providing the investment climate justifies this next major investment.

In 1975, both Tenneco and the Japanese group withdrew from Ocean Mining Associates. They are no longer contributing to the financing of the venture and they have no future interest in the venture or in ocean mining.

United States Concessions in Committee I at Geneva in 1975, amplified by Mr. Kissinger's Montreal speech to the American Bar Association, which also contained unilateral concessions, climaxed by Mr. Moynihan's statement of dissapointment concerning the 30th U.N. General Assembly meeting, have presented very little evidence to encourage our directors to make major long-term investments in the ocean.

Mr. Ratiner's new articles modifying the Engo text, as prepared in the intersessional meetings, were presented to this committee last month as the basis for a glimmer of hope.

They are, in fact, the basis for new concern, particularly the acceptance of interim production control as in article 9(a)(ii).

The effect on the board of directors of such inflexibility on the part of the Group of 77, who control the U.N., is markedly negative.

The best offset would be passage of the legislation under consideration today. This action is needed now as industry moves from gate to gate in the several ocean mining programs.

The following comments are submitted on the specific provisions of the legislation before this committee and which are the subject of this hearing. The comments cover the following subjects.

(1) Bureaucratic Jurisdiction; (2) Function and Effect of Licenses; (3) Public Access to Information; (4) Investment Guaranty; (5) Escrow Fund; (6) Eligibility of Consortia Participants; and (7) Block Size, Relinquishment Percent, Work Requirements.

These I will abbreviate:

(1) BUREAUCRATIC JURISDICTION

We have noted that the bills before the committee allocate the various governmental responsibilities and authorities differently. Basically, H.R. 1270 and H.R. 6017 split such responsibilities and authorities in accordance with the historic roles and competences of the Departments of Interior and Commerce.

On the other hand, H.R. 11879 grants all roles—regulatory, scientific, insurance, data management, and environmental—to the Secretary of Commerce.

The Department of Commerce possesses much competence in ocean affairs and has a role to play in connection with ocean mining legislation.

It does not, however, have the competence or the authority to properly discharge responsibilities associated with domestic mineral resource promotion and management.

This is the delegated authority and responsibility of the Department of the Interior, historically and under the Mining and Minerals Policy Act of 1970.

The ocean element in ocean mining is vital, new and exciting but represents less than half of the investment and a small but significant part of the activity.

It refers to a unique overburden covering the particular resource which imposes on the miner the need for unique mining techniques. Once the material is lifted from the seabed and placed aboard a transport vessel, the mining operation—as it proceeds through transfer, beneficiation, processing and marketing—can be reviewed as a normal component of the domestic mining industry and an integral part of the domestic materials base.

The Department of the Interior's accumulated experience in managing and encouraging domestic mining, materials and metals industries should not be ignored in the legislation before this committee just because these resources are found in a unique location, the seabed.

This fact, we feel, would be insufficient reason for Congress to create and fund redundant capacities in the Department of Commerce —where such competence does not now exist—when the broad range of capability and authority already exists in the Department of the Interior.

Having made this plea, it behooves me to note that Government competence in ocean affairs is extremely important in the initial phases of the life of the ocean mining industry. Many functions and facilities of the Department of Commerce are critical to proper and efficient development of the industry.

I have enumerated these capabilities in the written testimony. We urge therefore that this committee look favorably upon the allocation of authorities contained in H.R. 1270 as being the wisest and most efficient uses of existing Government resources.

(2) FUNCTION AND EFFECT OF LICENSES

One of the fundamental objectives of the United States in the Law of the Sea negotiations is to provide the nation with assured access to seabed resources on economic terms.

Such assured access, Mr. Chairman, will be valueless to the miner— or to his nation—unless the products of that access are accorded protection under domestic and transnational law.

The basic protection provided the miner in such law, with regard to minerals produced on land, is the property right in the product which accrues to the miner, and subsequent owners of the product, as a result of his lawful efforts.

With this in mind, there would seem to be a need to provide language in the bills before this committee which expressly provides that exclusive property rights to manganese nodules and the products derived therefrom may be acquired by the miner as a consequence of his lawful activities conducted in conformity with the terms and conditions of the bills as enacted by Congress.

The source of such property rights would be the freedom of the seas doctrine of international law, much the same as present international law provides the basis of such rights to the fisherman.

For this purpose, we suggest language:

(3) PUBLIC ACCESS TO INFORMATION

We endorse the sense of subsection 6(c), which provides for public access to information. This subsection as drafted strikes a reasonable balance between the public's "right to know" and the private company's right to have confidential information it has paid for protected from disclosure to its competitors, both domestic and foreign.

Although we endorse subsection 6(c), we do offer two alternative amendments for our consideration.

First, it would appear desirable that companies submitting information under the legislation under consideration here today be afforded notice and opportunity for hearing before information is made available to the public.

This would, of course, require an exception to Section 522(a) (6) (A) of the Freedom of Information Act, which requires that decisions to grant or deny requests for information be made within 10 working days of the request for disclosure.

But considering the present international politics of deep sea mining, such an exception would appear to be in the interest of the American public. Many of the parties seeking disclosures of information submitted by American mining companies will presumably be foreign—and often hostile—competitors of these companies.

It is imperative that confidential information obtained at the risk and expense of American companies be adequately protected from disclosure to these competitors. But the 10-day limitation provided for the Freedom of Information Act puts considerable pressure on Government agencies to disclose any information requested, regardless of its confidentiality. This is because a decision not to disclose must be supported by a showing that the information requested falls within one of the nine exceptions set forth in the Freedom of Information Act, and it is often difficult for Government officials to make such a showing within 10 days, particularly if the company that submitted the information is not consulted.

This problem could be remedied by requiring that, prior to disclosure, the company that submitted the information be given notice and opportunity for a hearing to show why the information requested should not be disclosed.

As an alternative to this proposal, we would suggest that subsection 6(c) be amended to provide for notice—but not hearing—prior to disclosure.

This is a less desirable alternative, but it would not require an exception to the Freedom of Information Act. Ten days may not be enough time in which to convene hearings, but it is certainly sufficient time in which to notify a company that has submitted information of any request that such information be disclosed.

And if good reason exists to withhold the information, the company should be able to demonstrate such reason to the Government within the time contraints of the Freedom of Information Act.

Alternatively, the company could seek injunctive relief in the courts. This procedure, i.e., notice prior to disclosure, would appear to be the minimum necessary to protect American companies, the American Government, and the ultimate beneficiary of deep-sea mining—the American consumer.

(4) THE INVESTMENT GUARANTEE

It is important to remember that the ratification of a Law of the Sea Agreement is just a beginning step in the process of working out codes of conduct regarding exploitation of deep seabed nodules and the clarification of related rights and obligations of international bodies, nations and persons.

In this regard, the provisions of section 13 of the three bills before this committee should, but do not, expressly provide protection of investment if the administration of the international agreement differs from the terms of that agreement.

This problem can be remedied by inserting into the bill the language and testimony submitted in my formal testimony.

(5) ESCROW FUND

Mr. Chairman, one feels that the timing is right for domestic ocean mining legislation. We can, in spite of Administration assurances of a "glimmer" of hope for the New York City U.N. session, predict that no progress will take place in that forum on deep seabed issues.

However, we should look at the 9-year record of the U.N. debates for positive inputs, particularly those areas of consensus involving principles which do not seek to suppress ocean development, but which reveal generally accepted objectives related to international equity.

One of these principles recognizes the role of manganese nodules in furthering the development of needs of underdeveloped countries.

For this purpose, your committee may wish to reincorporate in your legislation an escrow fund. By this I mean a portion of the tax revenues to be derived by the United States from licensed operations, to be put in escrow for dedication to international marine educational and developmental purposes at such time as a treaty on the subject matter becomes binding on the United States.

The formal testimony suggeests certain sources for such an addition to the bill.

(6) ELIGIBILITY OF CONSORTIA PARTICIPANTS

We note that United States entities, as used in the consortia section of the bills under consideration, is not a defined term.

This creates an uncertainty that domestic corporations, owned in part or whole by foreign capital and subject to the fiscal and admin-

476

istrative authority of the United States, will enjoy equal status with their American-owned consortia partners.

We believe that it is in the national interest that cooperative joint programs of the multinational nature be encouraged by the legislation before the committee.

We urge therefore that the bill contain a definition of United States entities which would encompass all U.S. nationals or corporations or other juridical entitties organized and existing under the laws of the United States or its States, territories or possessions.

(7) BLOCK SIZE, RELINQUISHMENT PERCENT, WORK REQUIREMENTS

Our comments on this subject matter are reflected in a letter to you, dated 26 January, 1976, from the American Mining Congress, which Mr. Dubs has suggested be included in the record.

In that letter, revisions were outlined which would increase the license block size to 60,000 square kilometers with a 50 percent relinquishment upon entering exploitation.

We support Mr. Dubs' contention and the contention of the letter.

Mr. Chairman, this concludes my specific comments on the legislation under consideration.

Let me thank you again, in behalf of the National Ocean Industries Association and the Deepsea Ventures for this opportunity to appear before this committee on this vital matter.

Thank you, sir.

Mr. JONES. Mr. Downing, do you have any questions?

Mr. DOWNING. Just a few, Mr. Chairman.

Mr. Flipse, the recommendations which you made in this presentation, are they made on behalf of the National Ocean Industry Association or on behalf of Deepsea?

Mr. FLIPSE. They were drafted by us and endorsed by the National Ocean Industry Association, and so they are made on behalf of both parties.

Mr. DOWNING. Mr. Flipse, perhaps there is a different governmental climate now than there was when we first started out on this.

We have reason to believe that the President will sign the 200-mile limit. Hopefully, we will see some action on this bill.

Mr. FLIPSE. We are encouraged, Mr. Downing, by the same signs and we hope they will be manifested in action on the bill under consideration.

Mr. DOWNING. Thank you very much.

Mr. JONES. Mr. Forsythe?

Mr. FORSYTHE. Thank you very much.

Your testimony was very, very helpful, but I have no questions.

Mr. DOWNING. Mr. Oberstar?

Mr. OBERSTAR. I found your statement very well done and informative and enlightening. I think the film answered many questions I had on the technology involved.

As one coming from a mining State and mining area, I find this suggestion intriguing, to say the least.

Do you have any substantial disagreement with the answers that Mr. Dubs gave me?

Mr. FLIPSE. I could normally disagree with Mr. Dubs at length on any subject; however, we participated in the preparation of his statement during deliberations of the American Mining Congress; so we fully support his statement.

In response to some of the questions we probably have somewhat a different philosophy. We are not concerned with claim jumping. We sincerely believe anyone who gets into ocean mining will have the identical need that we do, to have a continuously available deposit.

The worst way to get that would be to start work on someone else's claimed deposit. The investment requirements will eliminate the hoopla which went on with the exploration of the West. The extent of these bodies is tremendous, so why argue with me when you can go next door and have your own claim and develop that?

We share his concern that if we lost the right to the body of ore, the investment which becomes considerable, if you are prepared to actually mine the body, would be lost, and so I am sympathetic to that point of view, but less concerned on the claim question.

The other point I think that I would like to amplify in Mr. Dubs' remarks was on the question of the technology transfer.

We believe that the Commerce Department and NOAA are undertaking investigations of the atmosphere and the oceans from a scientific point of view, for other purposes. That technology is highly desirable as background information on which we make predictions and on which we develop our technical systems. The U.S. Navy has developed much data of an unclassified nature which could be useful. The transfer of this technology to the ocean miners will prevent duplication of effort.

We believe that the transfer of technology from industry to the world is provided for in the patent law of the United States and most commercial and developed countries and is probably more than adequate to meet the needs of any lesser developed country.

In fact, at the rate we are progressing, we will probably have our patents expire about the date they become workable. Our exclusive rights to use are rapidly diminishing, as our patents expire. We feel the handling of data is a crutial matter. I made the point in the testimony that we should have the data protected from the Freedom of Information Act and from foreign interests. We are very sensitive about this.

We hope to achieve a technological lead, not a lifetime or perpetual monopoly. Unfair transfer of our technology through the Government requiring it, under some pretext, and then dispensing it to the foreign governments would not right!

Our data rights should be protected and, hence, the specific suggestions as to language.

Except for those two points, I feel very comfortable with Mr. Dubs' statement as well as his answers.

Mr. OBERSTAR. I would agree with your concern about America's acting for other interests and not providing adequate safeguards.

One of the points raised by Mr. Dubs was that a formula be drawn up, if you will, for considering what is a stable investment climate, security of tenure, right to mine, specific length of time for mining, and specific conditions that would not be subject to change during that period of mining time.

Do you agree with that?

Mr. FLIPSE. Most emphatically; yes.

Mr. OBERSTAR. Would you have concern that the negotiating text in the negotiations in the Law of the Sea Conference would lead to the establishment of an International Seabed Authority that would have the right to price controls and production controls?

Mr. FLIPSE. I am very concerned on this point. I would like to state it more emphatically than my diplomatic associate from Kennecott Copper would.

I served as a member of the U.S. delegation to the U.N. Law of the Sea Conference and as an expert adviser on the Interagency Task Force on the Law of the Sea. It has gotten to the point in this U.N. negotiation where positive support of a requirement that we feel is a requirement makes the point nonnegotiable with the lesser developed countries.

In other words, if the treaty does not say we cannot do it, that is the best they can do, because if the U.S. negotiators were to ask for a specific provision that we could do it then, by definition the Group of 77—or 100 plus—say no. Hence, when we give good advice, and Mr. Dubs feels his advice is used much more than mine, which is indubitably so, they say, "Ah, but the article does not say you cannot do it."

I say the treaty must contain positive rights, especially since the proposed rulemakers are fundamentally hostile. I have a very deep concern in this matter. I feel the Committee I single informal negotiating text is not a negotiable document. It can only lead to further haggling and loss of U.S. rights.

I suggest that we go on with something real which is U.S. legislation and let the others get with it so they can move ahead instead of their continuing to block ocean mining. They are winning this argument in the U.N. debate by preventing agreement and the exercise by the U.S. of its existing rights and capabilities.

Mr. OBERSTAR. How would you envision the exploration for ocean minerals to be established under legislation that we are considering?

This is partly a technological question and partly a bureaucratic question.

Is this a function of Commerce or of Treasury?

And, then, how do you go about certifying the agency area that you would like to explore?

Mr. FLIPSE. We were forced, for very practicad reasons to make a claim. We were undertaking highly visible activities in our area of interest, so we filed a claim. We believe that the administration of that claim by the Bureau of Land Management and the Geological Survey of the Department of the Interior, and the submittal to them of geologic and resource data so that they can effectively make decisions regarding the ongoing program, is entirely practical.

We are halfway there in our claim and disclosures relative to it.

The data we have gathered has been shared with Interior and with Commerce, due to their understandable interest in environmental affairs.

I see administration of the Continental Shelf and deep seabed under these two bodies of Interior with the overview for environmental purposes from Commerce as an entirely reasonable way of going ahead.

On Mr. Dubs' numbers, we would make a slight variation. We are projecting a $350 million investment, but we are looking for only 1 million tons of dry material a year, a slightly smaller operation, and we are looking for manganese as an important contributor for the earnings. This will make it competitive within the next 5 to 6 years.

Mr. OBERSTAR. No further questions.

Mr. JONES. Thank you, Mr. Oberstar.

Mr. Flipse, I did not ask you any questions. I thought you did an excellent job on the testimony and with the film, but I think that you and I share the same fear in your belief that if the industry is going to get the green light to go ahead, it must come through the legislative process as the treaty seems to be extremely remote, based upon past experience and circumstances.

Mr. FLIPSE. Very well put. I agree with you completely.

Mr. JONES. Counsel?

Mr. Forsythe?

Mr. FORSYTHE. No questions.

Mr. PERIAN. You talk about Interior managing this as opposed to Commerce.

Is that based on past experience with these two agencies?

Briefly discuss with us the relationships you have had with both of the agencies.

Mr. FLIPSE. We have enjoyed working with both agencies in an educational role. Ours is the newest company with no sales of metals to date, so we have not been managed by Interior or Commerce in the past.

However, Interior is well equipped, and I have worked with some of their program managers and some of their experts—for example, with Dr. McKelvey—and they are well prepared to do the resource management.

The insurance programs and environmental administration can best be done by the Commerce Department.

As H.R. 1270 suggests, these duties would be shared, and I think for the best advantage of the country.

The regretful indecision regarding the jurisdictional matter has prevented the Interior or the Commerce Department from adequately staffing the Ocean Mining Administration or the Office of Marine Mining. Certainly, the Ocean Mining Administration in Interior is not staffed at all except for its very vocal Administrator, but it should be funded.

There are missions that it can achieve with the support of the Bureau of Land Management and the Geologic Survey, so we are saying that the principal responsibilities for resource management would be in Interior, while Commerce would have both the insurance and the environmental responsibilities.

Mr. PERIAN. You mentioned you planned to build a demonstration plant in Belgium. You then said that you will refine the nodules in a plant located in the United States.

What is the purpose of building the plant in Europe?

Mr. FLIPSE. When the parties who were primarily interested in ocean mining from an investment point of view, which included the Japanese trading companies and Tenneco, withdrew from the activity, we were left with the U.S. Steel Co. and the Union Miniere as our financial supporters. Union Miniere in Hoboken, Belgium, has a sister company of considerable technical skills where they have in being a great deal of the equipment that we would otherwise have to buy and use in Gloucester, Va., to run a processing demonstration plant.

So I am sure that you can understand it was a simple economic decision that the demonstration plant, handling 10 to 20 tons of nodules per day in throughput, would utilize those available facilities.

In Coleraine Minn. at the U.S. Steel laboratories, there is also processing work going on.

Again, if you utilize existing facilities, you minimize the costs. It is our Joint Venture's intention, if the law of this land provides protection to both parties in the venture, to domesticate the commercial processing plant in the United States and to run it as an American company in exchange for the protections that would accrue under this legislation.

Union Seas, Inc., Union Miniere's American subsidiary, is an American company wholly owned by Belgian interests. If Union Seas, Inc. is denied the benefits of the legislation, there would be a reconsideration of commercial processing plant location.

As explained in a supplement to our claim filed with Mr. Kissinger, the partners of Ocean Mining Associates are these two companies, and no one else. The ownership of Deepsea Ventures still resides in small part in Tenneco, in smaller part by minority shareholders, and to a major extent—about 68 percent—in U.S. Steel and Union Miniere, through their U.S. subsidiaries.

If the decision is to go ahead in the United States, Deepsea Ventures would be the ongoing company. We are now a service contractor to Ocean Mining Associates who are supplying the funds. This is normal development in this kind of a venture.

There may be additional parties overseas or domestic, depending upon the investment climate.

Mr. OBERSTAR. If counsel will yield.

What work did you mention was going on in Coleraine, Minn.?

That is 20 miles from my home.

Mr. FLIPSE. U.S. Steel has an excellent laboratory there

Mr. OBERSTAR. Yes, they have.

Mr. FLIPSE. They are experimenting with some of the side streams, some of the details of the hydrometallurgy.

Mr. OBERSTAR. Is this heavy media flotation process?

Mr. FLIPSE. No.

It is—analytical—hydrometallurgical work, and some test work. We are doing some and, of course, the Belgian participants are also doing some.

Mr. PERIAN. The administration said you could wait another 18 months or so, is that reasonable?

Mr. FLIPSE. We have just received the funding to convert the test vessel and to go ahead with the mining system test. There will be a decision made no later than the November meeting of our associates on whether to proceed with the investment in the processing work, which is more than the amount being devoted now to the marine work. That is coming very rapidly.

These people are faced with annual reports, meetings with their directors, and it is a very current problem to prepare for this major decision.

We really need the legislation as the sign and seal that the program can go ahead on a prudent basis in the United States.

The sooner we have this, the more likely we are to have a continuing program. These dates are occurring for Mr. Dubs and especially Mr. Welling with horrible regularity when decisions must be made to spend another $10 million or $50 million.

The fact that limited funding has been provided does not mean that the partners will continue if it becomes uneconomic as we move through the various gates. So, we need the legislation as soon as possible.

Mr. JONES. The Chair now recognizes Conrad G. Welling, program manager, ocean mining, Lockheed Missiles & Space Co.

STATEMENT OF CONRAD G. WELLING, PROGRAM MANAGER, OCEAN MINING, LOCKHEED MISSILES & SPACE CO.

Mr. WELLING. Mr. Chairman and members of the committee, my name is Conrad G. Welling. I am program manager, ocean mining, within the Lockheed Missile & Space Co., Inc., in Sunnyvale, Calif.

In this position, I am responsible for planning and direction of Lockheed's ocean mining programs, which include such activities as hardware development, financial and market analysis and planning, testing, and operations.

Ocean mining is located within the ocean systems division, a group responsible for deep ocean technology development, engineering and oceanography. Other projects include the U.S. Navy deep submergence projects, oil recovery systems, and ocean thermal energy conversion.

I am honored to have the opportunity to appear before this committee to present a brief summary of Lockheed's progress in the development of an ocean mining system, and the problems we see in moving ahead in this important area.

I hope that my statements, provided from the perspective of an industrial firm with a long-standing interest in this field, will assist the committee in developing national ocean policy and a posture on this subject.

Lockheed activities in ocean mining extend over a period of more than 12 years, and include the development of mining and processing technology, and related environmental and economic studies.

Through active participation on the American Mining Congress and the National Petroleum Council Committees relating to undersea mineral policy, and through our current support of the National Security Council's Inter-Agency Task Force Advisory Board on Law of the Sea, we have kept well aware of international and domestic activities affecting deep-ocean mining.

Our studies and work over this period have strengthened our opinion that a strong ocean mining industry is a national need, if we are to assure United States self-sufficiency in supply of the critical metals of nickel, copper and cobalt in the years ahead.

Ocean mining activities of Lockheed have been structured to approach the development of an ocean mining system from a total systems viewpoint.

That is, our research and technology developments have been focused on critical limiting technology and the engineering and economic impact, and interaction of major system elements such as the sea floor miner, the lift and surface systems, transportation and processing.

Our studies and research to date have convinced us that the development of an efficient ocean mining system is feasible from the view points of engineering technology and mineral economics.

The fact that an extensive and unique ore body exists on the ocean floor and contains valuable deposits of the minerals I have mentioned, as well as manganese, have been proven beyond question. What is unique about the ore body is that it is a very thin horizontal deposit of nodules on soft soil in very deep water.

The development of a reliable and efficient mining system to recover the ore under these conditions represents a significant technical challenge—feasible but costly.

Our program has been progressing through a series of planned and phased risk management milestones. We have developed a test miner, and have essentially completed on-land system tests of the miner submerged in a test tank and in a large sea floor simulator or mud pit.

In our processing work, we have verified laboratory results of key product element recovery from the feed stock ore in a minipilot plant.

We have now reached a critical milestone in our system development activities. Our technology program to date has been carried out en tirely at Lockheed expense.

These expenditures have been moderate; and, although a great deal has been accomplished over the years, the major system development activity and full-scale onsite system tests still lie ahead.

Our immediate next phase calls for proof testing at sea of the test miner, and initiation of process scale-up, the funding requirements of which exceed our ability to carry out the work alone.

It is commonly known and understood that the total development and capital funding requirements for placing a complete ocean min ing system in production operation, including both mining and the land processing plant, have been estimated at $300 to $500 million.

When these costs are compared with similar data for land mining, i.e., investment capital per annual pound of capacity, the ocean mining venture appears very attractive. Furthermore, the energy requirements are lower.

This is important because the primary metals industry is a large user of energy. But the magnitude of the investment requirement and the length of the payback period makes a stable business climate a vital consideration.

As with any major systems development effort, hardware procurement commitment funding for mining systems, platforms, processing equipment and transport components must be placed several years in advance of delivery date requirements. For example, the funding plan in the case of an operating mining system must allow for 3 to 4 years leadtime for the major capital investments.

In recent months, we have been very actively exploring ways and means and problems associated with moving into the next phase of our program. It is clear from our discussions within industry that major concerns exist within the investment community regarding the lack of a firm U.S. Ocean Policy as to the nature of the legal regime under which the proposed mining industry would operate.

The next step in system development, as I stated earlier, requires a major investment. The high probability of the future establishment of a new international authority which would take control of the seabed resource, imposing currently undefined rules concerning production, price and royalties which have the potential effect of destroying the economic viability of the venture, is an obvious concern to potential investors.

The domestic legislation which has been proposed and has been reviewed and commented upon by the several industrial and commercial organizations is urgently needed. It is needed now. It must provide the U.S. Government's acknowledgement of the need to foster and encourage the fledgling hard minerals deep seabed industry, and provide assurance for security of tenure and freedom of operation.

With regard to the legislation proposed, I would, however, like to direct a few comments to the investment guarantee and insurance provisions.

The investment guarantee, as I read it, will provide the license with compensation in the event an international agreement differs in material respects from the requirements of the act and causes a reduction in value of the licensee's investment resulting from such differing requirements. I believe that such provision is absolutely necessary if the United States is to encourage effective development of existing domestic technologies and capabilities.

For much the same reason the investment insurance, provided in sectiton 14 of the proposed legislation, is urgently needed. However, the purpose of such insurance being the protection of a licensee from otherwise uninsurable risks, I fear it may fail in at least two aspects.

The legislation as currently drafted exempts from payments damages caused by persons against whom a legal remedy exists in any legal forum.

Therefore, damages caused by an insolvent or judgment proof person or group—such as a domestic terrorist group—would not be compensated because a legal remedy might be found to exist, although the remedy itself is worthless.

Second, in the case of damages caused by a foreign national a remedy might theoretically be available in that country, but for all practical purposes not be at all helpful.

For example, as a result of damages caused by a national of a foreign country, the form in a foreign jurisdiction damages caused by a national of a foreign country, the forum in a foreign jurisdiction might decline to make an effective remedy available for political reasons, or refuse to enforce a judgment even if granted, or the country itself might refuse to allow the removal of any funds for its jurisdiction because of currency restrictions.

In order to protect the license and yet insure unnecessary drain is not made on the Government's insurance funds I would suggest that the provisions allowing payments only in situations where remedies are said not to exist be removed and, instead, that the Government be specifically granted subrogation rights based upon any such payments.

This approach would be in accordance with usual insurance practice and would allow the United States to protect the fund while providing essential protection to the licensee.

In summary, we strongly believe that the proposed legislation can create a favorable climate wherein the progress in existing ocean mining development activities can continue on an orderly productive course within normal business venture constraints. We highly recommend enactment of this essential legislation.

I would be most happy to attempt to answer any questions your committee and staff might have.

Again, Mr. Chairman, I would like to express my thanks for this opportunity to present to you Lockheed's view on this most important legislation.

Mr. JONES. Thank you, Mr. Welling, very much, for your testimony.

I didn't find in your testimony that you touched on the controversial question that has been kicked out, the jurisdictional question of regulatory authority as it relates to the Department of Commerce or Department of the Interior.

Do you have any statement on that?

Mr. WELLING. Yes; I do.

I would follow the statements made by my colleagues. We feel that both the Department of the Interior and the Department of Commerce have capabilities in various fields that should be brought to bear upon the problem.

In the case of minerals, the Department of the Interior has extensive experience in the regulation of the materials industry.

In the case of the oceans—and I am separating this—NOAA has extensive expertise.

In the case of the regulation of the environmental effects and in the other areas in which NOAA has developed capabilities. they should be brought to bear. So again I imagine it is one of distinct capabilities in both fields.

Mr. JONES. As this legislation is marked up and finally presented, you would prefer a clear-cut definition of the authority between the two agencies, would you not?

Mr. WELLING. Absolutely.

Mr. JONES. Mr. Oberstar?

Mr. OBERSTAR. Thank you, Mr. Chairman.

You asked one of the questions that I was concerned with. I appreciate your answer.

I am not quite sure how you envision this investment guarantee and this investment insurance. I read your statement ahead of time. I am not quite sure what is to be insured and to what extent, and how you envision damages occurring to an open sea operation.

Mr. WELLING. Well. in my statement here, the part I wanted to stress is, of being able to collect in the event of damages caused by parties, even international or other countries. We believe that adequate protection can be obtained allowing payments by provisions where the Government is granted subrogation rights.

In other words the United States Government provided insurance by the guarantee of payment of damages.

Mr. OBERSTAR. I recognize that there are situations where something serious could happen to an operation. You could bring suit in whatever form, the world court, or the court of the country that caused the damage or the country whose vessel may have caused the damage and find that either their courts won't take jurisdiction or if they do, you can't satisfy a judgment.

I recognize that, but I don't understand what damages you are concerned about, and I don't quite understand how, Mr. Welling, this guarantees reserve, which is explained in section 15 of the bill works out. It says that a guarantee reserve shall be funded by such sums as shall be appropriated.

Are you looking to the Federal Government to totally underwrite these operations?

Mr. WELLING. No; I don't believe so. The problem really stems from the fact that while we could take legal action that resulted in a judgment in our favor, we may be unable to collect the award. This should be taken into consideration in the wording of the bill.

Mr. PERIAN. An analogy can be drawn with the British drilling in the North Sea. They drill in the North Sea, yet they don't own it. They have taken over the jurisdiction. When I asked the members of Parliament how they handled harassment by the Russians' men of war and threats by terrorists, they said, "We protect them with the Royal Air Force and the Royal Navy." This is known by the Russians and the terrorists.

We saw Royal Marines on the rigs with bazookas and heavy weapons and machine guns. They actually go out and protect the equipment of the mining companies and the open waters. Concerning the other issue, one of the plans of the regime in the Law of the Sea Conference was to offer two tracks to the regimes of any area taken over by, say, an American company. One of the tracks would be selected by the regime to go into their bank and the United States company would then have one-half of the other track. So in effect the regime would take over 75 percent of the area designated by the American company.

If that were to happen, what these gentlemen are saying is that they would like the Federal Government which signed this treaty to reimburse them for whatever they may have lost.

I think that is a point that must be explored in much greater length.

I have no further questions.

Mr. JONES. Mr. Forsythe?

Mr. FORSYTHE. No questions.

Mr. JONES. Mr. McCloskey?

Mr. McCLOSKEY. Mr. Welling, if we were to guarantee investments, your judgment is that it is in the Nation's best interest to insure up to $5 million. Would all four of the companies seek such insurance?

Mr. WELLING. I don't think—in the first place, that is a very difficult question to answer. All our efforts have been devoted towards the same effect, that is, two types of insurance.

One, you have the insurance against having to operate under a different set of rules and regulations. That is one insurance. That would be one of degree. In other words, either too heavy taxation or restriction on production or price controls, so that your plant financial feature was seriously derated. That is one type of guarantee.

The other type of guarantee is the one against action on the part of either an individual or nation or some group that physically interfered with your activity, whether it was by actual bombing or some harassment of some kind, sailing a ship around in your area to prevent you from some course of action. Either one of these would present losses to a degree; and my interpretation is not a complete loss of the whole program simply because of the fact that you had at least half of the investment ashore. And assuming that the shore installation was not subject to that kind of harassment.

Mr. McCLOSKEY. We are talking about very serious legislation here. We have four major companies that indicate there must be a stable investment climate. I believe you are willing to invest up to $5 million each, and presumably, you have already invested a substantial part of that. You are asking in section 14 of the act, page 21, that investment insurance be given for any amount invested that might be lost as a result of a Law of the Sea treaty.

The problem I have is that I don't have any relative dollar figures as to what the United States may get out of all of this.

Mr. WELLING. I would like to answer your question in two parts.

One is from the point of view of an insurance company. The insurance company would not have to have assets to cover all the insurance policies because of the distribution of the risks.

Mr. McCLOSKEY. We are talking about $2 billion plus for the risk of the initial investment.

Mr. WELLING. Based on the probability, there is not a $2 billion risk. There may be a portion. That is difficult to answer. Half of the risk is ashore. Half of the investment is ashore. The other half is at sea.

Mr. McCLOSKEY. But if the source is denied, the onshore investment is worthless, isn't it?

Mr. WELLING. I guess one would have to consider that as a possibility, even though a low probability that all four sources were denied operating completely. I assume from many of these scenarios we talked about, it was one of degree where you were limiting the amount, not completely stopping.

Mr. McCLOSKEY. Would you anticipate that if this legislation were enacted all four of the major companies would invest $500 million and proceed to compete with one another?

Mr. WELLING. I think they would. That is the beginning, I think. Absolutely. The market is there. If we have the legislation, and from what the stated plans are of the other companies, the money would be invested. It would be invested for a period of years so that the operations would start in the early 1980's. If this operation were successful, then there is no question about expansion on those operations because the market is there.

Mr. McCloskey. How many years are you away from production, assuming that this legislation is passed tomorrow?

Mr. Welling. Early 1980's—1981 to 1984 is the time frame for achieving full production in the stated capacity.

Mr. McCloskey. Once you achieve full capacity production, how many years will you have to operate to get a return on the investment?

Mr. Welling. This is a kind of difficult question to answer.

Certainly, if the venture is an economic venture, then the return on investment should be achieved within 5 or 10 years.

Mr. McCloskey. Do you think since the Government is sharing the risk, we ought to share the profits?

Mr. Welling. I would say that the money is being invested or committed by the private sector, not by the Government.

Mr. McCloskey. But the money won't be invested unless the Government takes the risk.

Mr. Welling. There are two viewpoints.

One is the normal taxation rate. The Government shares almost 50 percent in the profits with little risks. Second is that we estimate that an expansion of the ocean mining industry by the year 2000 will save $20 million to $30 million in balance of payments if it can take its normal course of expansion based upon a favorable legal climate. These two factors alone are a powerful payback from the point of view of the national interest.

Mr. McCloskey. Does that presuppose an equal share of the market to the companies involved?

Mr. Welling. It is the total amount. The companies may not share an equal amount, but it is a total amount.

Mr. McCloskey. I have no further questions.

Mr. Jones. The Chair recognizes the committee counsel.

Mr. Perian. I would like to point out to Mr. McCloskey that there is one other aspect that the Federal Government has an interest in. What I am concerned with in the Law of the Sea is the sudden development of a cartel or an OPEC in relation to nickel, copper, cobalt and manganese. In 1973 we imported 82 percent of our nickel, 24.6 percent of our copper, but 77 percent of our cobalt and 82 percent of our manganese.

The Ocean Mining Administration said by 1980 we would be self-sufficient in all minerals except manganese, which would be reduced; so the benefit would be that we would become independent in the production of these minerals.

Mr. Jones. Any other questions?

[Mr. Welling's biography follows:]

Biography

Conrad G. Welling is Program Manager of Ocean Mining at the Lockheed Missiles & Space Company, Inc., Sunnyvale, California. He has spent the last twelve years studying and researching in this new field. He is responsible for the new business development, as well as long range planning and direction of engineering production and testing of deep ocean mining systems.

Prior to this, he was Manager of Systems Evaluation and Operations Research at Lockheed. Prior to joining Lockheed he spent twenty years in the Navy as an aviator, a great portion of which was devoted to ocean research and development in the fields of antisubmarine warfare and missiles. Prior to leaving the Navy he directed operations research study of the Polaris Fleet Ballistic Missile System. He received a Masters Degree in electronics from the U.S. Navy Postgraduate School in 1948.

Mr. JONES. The Chair would like to call Mr. James Johnston, representing the Standard Oil Co. of Indiana.

STATEMENT OF JAMES L. JOHNSTON, REPRESENTING THE STANDARD OIL CO. OF INDIANA

Mr. JOHNSTON. This is a first appearance for me testifying before any congressional committee. I have prepared my testimony to make it as brief as possible. In the interest of saving time, I would like to read it.

Mr. JONES. Without objection.

Mr. JOHNSTON. My name is James L. Johnston and I am a senior economist with Standard Oil Co. of Indiana specializing in antitrust economics. Until last August, I was the Treasury representative on the U.S. Delegation to the U.N. Conference on the Law of the Sea—UNCLOS.

My testimony today is a personal statement of my own thoughts as an economist and does not necessarily represent the official views of either organization.

Mr. Chairman, this subcommittee has heard from administration witnesses that they do not support domestic legislation at this time because a glimmer of hope has been detected in the recent unofficial intercessional meetings held in New York.

I am here today to present an economic evaluation of this most recent glimmer of hope in the deep-seated negotiations and to show that U.S. consumers are still seriously threatened with establishment of a worldwide cartel in nickel, copper, cobalt, manganese, and possibly other minerals as well.

Before commenting on the negotiations and the need for domestic legislation it will be useful, I believe, to present a little background on the economics of Government regulation, its relationship to cartels and how cartels exist internationally.

At the outset, it should be observed that organizing a group of producers to act as a monopolist over a long period of time is seldom if ever successful.

The basic problem has to do with gaining continuing compliance among all cartel members to restrict their output according to some formula that maximizes the monopoly rent for the cartel as a whole.

In such an arrangement any member of the cartel has the potential for drawing off more than his share of the monopoly rents by surreptitiously lowering his price and gaining the additional sales.

In the limit such cheating by cartel members drives the price to the competitive level. Any cartel, then, that hopes to maintain its monopoly has to find a mechanism to keep its members from lowering their prices.

Domestically, the enforcement role has most often been played by government regulators, who levy heavy fines and jail sentences on cartel members who charge too low a price.

Internationally, the enforcement problem is more complex. To say the least, it is unseemly for one producer country to send its troops into another country in order to punish the the cartel member who is charging the low price.

Another mechanism must be used, internationally, and most often the necessary element is the active cooperation of the governments of countries which are important consumers of the product supplied by the cartel.

In practice, there are usually three kinds of roles played by the consumer country government.

One is where shipments from a producer country exceed their production quota are barred entry through customs.

This is the system employed under the coffee agreement in the sixties. The second technique is for the governments of major consumer countries to prohibit their nationals from paying a lower than floor price for the commodity or service. This technique is employed for international air travel, and proposed for the new international energy agency and the new coffee agreement.

The third technique is for any government to maintain a large stockpile of the product, although it is an unambiguous gain for producers if the government of a consumer country can be persuaded to perform that function.

The cartel would be even stronger with an international treaty where the consumer country government would finance the stockpile, but empower the producer group to control the purchases from the cartel members. The stockpiling role has been played by the U.S. Government with respect to tin, among other metals.

It is appropriate to note that the State Department has announced its intention to commit the United States to membership in both the new coffee agreement and the tin agreement.

Secretary Kissinger has also announced that the question of joining the copper agreement has the highest priority. Thus, there is ample precedent to justify concern about an international cartel to govern manganese module recovery from the deep seabed. To show the development of these connections, I will turn now to a brief discussion of the deep seabed negotiations.

Perhaps, the event to begin with is the 1970 draft treaty proposed by the United States. This document outlined an elaborate international regulatory body which would be financed from revenues produced from minerals recovered from ocean areas.

The 1970 draft treaty went much further than the simple definition of property rights. Its elaborate structure, which one keen observer dubbed. "the floating Chinese pagoda" provided for virtually unlimited discretion on the part of the international authority to take whatever measures, in its judgment, would protect the environment and conserve the resources from the mythical problem of high grading.

The U.S. Department of the Interior was particularly concerned that nodule miners left to their own devices somehow would violate the rights of the low-grade manganese nodule deposits by not spending the extra sums to recover them. In fact, high grading is efficient because to do otherwise increases the cost of production and forces higher market prices.

About this time, the U.N. General Assembly adopted a resolution supported by the U.S. delegation, designating the resources beyond the limits of national jurisdiction to be the common heritage of mankind. The U.N. General Assembly also adopted a moratorium resolution asking all countries to restrain their nationals from engaging in nodule recovery until UNCLOS produced a treaty. The U.S. delegation voted against the moratorium resolution. However, the course of the negotiations was established. The Group of 77, led by the land-based producers of minerals, set out to stifle the development of this competing source of minerals.

Missing from the 1970 draft treaty were the final detailed rules and regulations which ostensibly would be negotiated at the first substantive session of the UNCLOS in Caracas.

Supposedly these yet unnegotiated rules and regulations would guarantee nondiscriminatory access to all countries including the United States and its nationals to the mineral deposits of the deep seabed.

Treasury Secretary George Schultz, who is an economist of considerable note, remarked about this negotiating strategy that regulation of economic activity is seldom a good idea and regulation by an international organization is never a good idea. Clearly reflected was his abundant experience in international labor and monetary negotiations.

The 10 weeks of negotiation at the Caracas sessions almost ended before the Group of 77, led and supported by the land-based mineral producers, would even permit discussion of rules and regulations. Even then, they concentrated their attention on a set they drafted. The Group of 77 drafted tentatively—I repeat, tentatively —offered to respect the security of contracts but then immediately snatched back the offer with insistence upon complete and effective control of recovery operations by the international authority, overt protection of land-based producers, ownership of the deep seabed and its mineral resources, the transfer of technology and the right to discriminate against our ocean miners.

There was a worldwide cartel in the making, designed with the help of international bureaucrats from the U.N. Secretariat and the U.N. Conference on Trade and Development—UNCTAD.

The cartel even had a proposed headquarters—Jamaica—the location of the international bauxite producers organization, not an isolated coincidence.

In the period between the Caracas and Geneva sessions the U.S. delegation reevaluated its position. Ignoring the emerging cartel, the U.S. negotiators pressed for permission from the President to establish an operating enterprise within the International Authority, financed through overly generous revenue sharing from not only nodule mining but also hydrocarbon recovery from our continental margin.

The International Authority was also to be given half of the nodule deposits prospected by our ocean miners. For protection, U.S. dependence was to rest entirely on voting control in the International Authority's Council which was to be the group directly in charge of ocean mining activity.

The main product of the Geneva session in 1976—the single informal negotiating text—demonstrated that our negotiators had again tragically miscalculated the intentions of the land-based producers and their followers in the Group 77.

Any pretense of voting protection was swept away and the cartel plan emerged full blown.

The only basis on which our ocean miners could operate would be under a contract from the International Authority, where the initial terms and subsequent conditions would be specified by the Authority in its own discretion.

This includes specific control of production. The Authority would even have a permanent organization to monitor world mineral prices and recommend actions which would protect the earnings of land-based mineral exporters.

As for the voting protection, it would be nonexistent. The United States would be hopelessly outnumbered in both the Council and the Assembly; and as if that were not enough, most of the important functions and responsibilities were transferred to the Assembly where the United States would have just one vote out of perhaps 150.

We are now in the last stage of madness. Having finally grasped what the other side is after, our negotiators are now preparing to give it to them under the rubric of "commodity arrangements." As has been discussed, the commodity agreements which we are already involved in, and the ones that we are investigating for membership have in them both the necessary and sufficient conditions for a viable cartel.

The most important feature of the proposed "commodity arrangements" is the U.S. Government's commitment by treaty to accommodate the worldwide cartel.

If these other commodity agreements are any guide, then we may find our Government forcing U.S. consumers to pay floor prices that are above the competitive level, spending tax dollars to finance the purchase of large mineral stockpiles and subjecting our ocean miners to a system of production controls and additional investment uncertainty.

Besides being harmful to U.S. consumers and taxpayers, it is positively disastrous for our ocean miners.

In addition, there is every reason to believe that the emerging metal cartel will devastate the economies of the poorest countries which are just now recovering from the worldwide depression aggravated by the OPEC actions.

Your staff has kindly made available to me the amendments to the single negotiating text that supposedly contain the "glimmer of hope" detected by our negotiators.

As an economist, I still see all the preconditions for a viable cartel in these amendments, and no "glimmer of hope" whatsoever.

Perhaps to the politically naive, it may seem to be a conciliatory move. However, anyone who reads the new text will see that it is still a transparent attempt to keep the U.S. Government in the negotiations, thereby raising the cost of nodule recovery and facilitating the formulation of the cartel.

Mr. Chairman, there is but one way in which the benefits of ocean mineral resources can be fully realized as the common heritage of mankind. That is to have a stable investment climate where a healthy and competitive ocean mining industry can supplement the world's supply of minerals at lower prices.

This will spur the economic growth of all economies, especially those which depend heavily on the capital equipment produced from these minerals, and I say these are the developing countries, particularly.

Regretfully, Mr. Chairman, I must tell you that the U.N. Conference on the Law of the Sea is not going to produce such a solution. If there still remains a way to keep the heritage of mankind from being stolen by the international politicians, then it is through the adoption of domestic legislation such as H.R. 11879 and S. 713. I only hope that enough of your colleagues join you in your efforts before it is too late to achieve this outcome.

Before I conclude my testimony, I would like to comment on the Interior Department's assertion that the ocean mining legislation omits lease payments and some detailed regulatory provisions. It is my view that the present legislation is adequate, and if it has any faults, they arise out of too much discretion and regulatory authority.

One must keep in mind that the cost of political uncertainty also includes concern with what our own Government might do to hinder the development of this infant industry.

More serious, however, are the suggestions for additional charges to be levied on the industry, when a mine site is registered.

In a study prepared by the Treasury during the 1973 economic review of the Law of the Sea, it was observed that the value of a nodule deposit determined, say by an auction, would during the first generation, probably be zero.

The reason primarily is that there are from 100 to 300 prime sites and fewer than that number of likely mining operations.

This implies that until mine sites become scarce, they have no positive market values.

Ignoring this condition by insisting on charging a fee or royalty would not only set a dangerous precedent with regard to ownership of the seabed under international waters, but would also finance elaborate Government involvement in recovery operations—for example, to accommodate the mythical problem of high grading—and consequently stifle the very development we wish to encourage.

Mr. Chairman, I urge the rapid adoption of the ocean mining legislation in essentially its present form, before the U.S. interests in ocean mining are sacrificed to the cartel being fashioned by the U.N. Conference on the Law of the Sea.

Mr. JONES. Mr. Johnston, I want to commend you sincerely for stating, in excellent language, certain fears that I have harbored and entertained for several months, and for several years for that matter; and I think you brought into this hearing an area of concern and one which should be of deep concern to this committee.

I only regret that more are not here to hear you. I commend you for your honesty and your factual report of what is happening to this Nation as our cards are dealt from a stacked deck.

Mr. JOHNSTON. I personally appreciate your kindness.

Mr. JONES. Mr. Oberstar?

Mr. OBERSTAR. I completely agree with that assessment. Your testimony brings a dramatic new element to these hearings.

Repeatedly in previous sessions of this committee, I raised the issue of cartel development. I had the feeling that our United States negotiators pooh-poohed the notion that other countries could form cartels and could bring economic pressure to bear in the way that you have outlined in your statement.

How soon do you feel that it would be before CPEC and other such cartels are brought together in a very effective manner, recognizing that they have made one effort and have not succeeded in bringing pressure to bear, but how long do you think it will be before they can do so, and what are the conditions that would make that possible?

Mr. JOHNSTON. Let me answer the conditions that you should watch for and you can be as good in estimating the date that it will be effective as I.

When the United States commits itself to membership, when that happens, since the United States is the primary consumer of copper in the world, and if the United States can get the other primary consumers of copper to join in that cartel arrangement and help police the restricted output and higher prices among the other producing countries, that is when the cartel will be viable.

Mr. Kissinger, the Secretary of State, has indicated that membership in a copper organization has the highest priority in terms of being investigated by our Government; so I think that probably is the first group that would probably demonstrate viability as a cartel.

Mr. OBERSTAR. You mean Kissinger is calling for U.S. participation in an international cartel?

Mr. JOHNSTON. He doesn't say that. He likes to think, it seems to me, from his statements, that the effective way of coping with problems of raw materials producers is to get the active cooperation of consumer-country governments. I like to think the man has not been getting good economic advice.

Mr. OBERSTAR. I can say that on a wide range of issues that Mr. Kissinger has handled, that we are not the Foreign Relations Committee.

As you have outlined it, the Law of the Sea Conference is really a battleground between the land-based mineral producers and the United States and others who are or may be capable of deep-sea mining?

Mr. JOHNSTON. Yes; I agree.

And at once, that is a problem. If you are trying to get a widely acceptable treaty it may seem to be a weak position. But from another point of view it is a great strength because there can be no treaty except with the United States as an active participant since the United States by and large has the recovery technology, before it loses it, and only it is able to engage in recovery in the foreseeable future.

I think what we have often missed in the negotiations is that we have a position of strength in these negotiations and, instead concentrated on counting the number of delegations that are on one side of the issue versus the number of delegations that are on the other side of the issue.

To some extent that has been exacerbated because of the voting rules that we agreed to during the administrative session of the conference, which allows two-thirds of the conference to essentially formulate the package deal on the whole collection of issues on the Law of the Sea that we will have to face on the vote. We can go into that, but that is a complicated issue.

The United States delegation has talked a lot about the importance of the packaged deal. Now, a packaged deal is good if you can formulate the package, but it is damned bad if you are faced with a package on a take-it-or-leave-it basis. The voting rules in the conference allow two-thirds of the membership—and I needn't tell you that that pretty much means the Group of 77 and no one else—to be able to formulate that package; so the package deal effectively that we are going to be facing is not going to be structured by us; and it is not going to have all the features that we like.

In fact, it will be structured to such a way that will bring us just to the limit of acceptability by United States negotiators.

They will, in turn, come around if, indeed, they choose to accept this all-or-nothing package and present it to the Senate of the United States, who also will have an all-or-nothing decision to make; and all of the other beneficial aspects of the package will be hard for them to vote it down.

Mr. OBERSTAR. So in effect, what we are seeing from the perspective that you gave us is not the view as Government witnesses have laid it out—a concern that the developing nations who do not now have mining technology want to preserve their options for the future—as much as it is the concerns of land-based mineral-producing countries who want to protect their competitive position in the market, and who are going to do everything they can to sabotage this Law of the Sea Conference, either by stringing it out endlessly or by so hamstringing the treaty that it provides no meaningful protection for the United States industry?

Mr. JOHNSTON. I couldn't have said that better.

Mr. JONES. Mr. McCloskey?

Mr. McCLOSKEY. Mr. Johnston. I thank you for the candor of your comments. When I was in Geneva last spring, you were the Treasury representative.

Can you tell me why you were unable to tell me those facts last spring?

Mr. JOHNSTON. Well, part of the story——

Mr. McCLOSKEY. I asked you these questions or at least, related questions.

Mr. JONES. I believe the gentleman answered his own question. He was the Treasury representative.

Mr. JOHNSTON. Mr. McCloskey, part of the testimony today covers new events which have taken place since then.

Mr. McCLOSKEY. But the basic testimony runs counter to the mission as conceived by the delegation in Geneva?

Mr. JOHNSTON. That is right. We saw the problems. We explained the problems at greater length than I really care to remember and I have the scar tissues to prove it, notwithstanding that decisions were made otherwise to proceed, I think not appreciating the serious cartel threat that was emerging.

There is a great deal in getting wrapped up in negotiations and getting involved into mistaking poor people with leaders in developing countries; and those are not always the same sets, nor do they always have the same objectives.

The other problem has to do with this: nobody ever gets successful in the State Department for successfully opposing a bad treaty. The same thing is true in the Defense Department. Nobody gets successful for opposing a bad weapons system.

Mr. McCLOSKEY. Let me just try to get you to expand on that answer.

So far as I know, Secretary Kissinger is the top adviser to the President on the Law of the Sea negotiations. Should I take his Montreal speech as an appropriate and accurate reflection of the United States policy?

Mr. JOHNSTON. Well, as I remember it, he did not read to the people there our instructions. As I review the instructions—it has been some time since I have looked at them, you understand—I didn't see some of the important things stressed in Mr. Kissinger's address that I would hope would have been stressed, and I think particularly in this record, it was how the common heritage could be realized in terms of increasing the world mineral supply at lower prices, and how overly restrictive regulations have a potential for stifling development.

I think I would have great difficulty going down item-by-item in Mr. Kissinger's speech and comparing those items with what I remember to be our instructions.

I don't think it would serve a useful purpose in this public forum to go into that detailed examination.

Mr. McCLOSKEY. No, I am not going to ask you to do that. But I am intrigued by this problem that we face in Congress when we are considering legislation. To try and get an accurate and candid discussion of the problems that face the executive branch is difficult because we don't get an accurate and candid appraisal of the problem. No one dares to contest the policy judgment as seen by the top of the delegation or the top of the Administration.

From your statement, I can only assume that Treasury doesn't find the Law of the Sea Treaty very important to the future of this country.

Is that a fair statement?

Mr. JOHNSTON. I think the Treasury was very concerned, at least they were when I was there, that this emerging treaty might not be in the interest of the United States.

Mr. McCLOSKEY. I recall in 1970, the proposal you mentioned here was drafted by a team which included the present Secretary of Commerce, Elliot Richardson; is that correct?

Mr. JOHNSTON. Mr. Richardson's participation predated mine.

Mr. McCLOSKEY. The 1970 proposal to which you referred is on page 2 of your testimony. Let me go back and read it.

"Perhaps the event to begin with was the 1970 draft treaty proposed by the United States."

That was drawn up by our State Department when Elliot Richardson was Under Secretary?

Mr. JOHNSTON. With considerable input from the Interior Department, especially, and the United States Geological Survey.

Mr. McCLOSKEY. The Secretary Shultz that you referred to was then the Secretary of the Treasury?

Mr. JOHNSTON. Certainly.

Mr. McCLOSKEY. He had input at the time that the 1970 proposal was made?

Mr. JOHNSTON. That is right.

Mr. McCLOSKEY. In 1970, if that is the case, the doubts that the Treasury had gave way to the proposal of the State Department? Is that a fair conclusion?

Mr. JOHNSTON. I think it is also fair to say that in 1970, we were beginning to observe the emergence of the land-based producers as the leaders in the negotiations. I think in 1970 what we ascribed as a potential on the part of the other side was the fact that there were land-based producers in this negotiation and they had in their interest, No. 1, to retard the development of seabed mining or aise the cost of seabed mining.

I think later on they saw that, especially with the detailed regulatory provisions that the United States proposed, not only the potential for being able to retard the development of seabed mining by abberant use of these regulatory provisions, but they began to see the possibility of the worldwide cartel formulation.

It wasn't until later that the new international economic order arose as a rallying cry.

Mr. McCLOSKEY. If I recollect correctly, Secretary Shultz drafted the report which indicated he could see no reason to—how did he put it—"there is nothing to indicate we can't expect an uninterrupted flow of oil from the Mideast until 1985." Isn't that the report?

Mr. JOHNSTON. I can't answer.

Mr. McCLOSKEY. Were you with Treasury then?

Mr. JOHNSTON. No.

Mr. McCLOSKEY. What you are saying is that the perception of the cartel threat in the metal industry has changed since 1970?

Mr. JOHNSTON. I think so. I think in 1970 it is fair to say that the land-based producers were probably only out to restrain a restriction of mining development and perhaps raising the cost of mining development.

Mr. McCLOSKEY. I have the privilege of going up to New York next week to try to understand what our delegation is doing and what the prospects of success may be at the conclusion of that 8 weeks.

Do you see any difference in the attitude of the Treasury Department today than the one you stated last spring as the representative of the Treasury?

Mr. JOHNSTON. Clearly, I have other responsibilities now. I can't follow the day-to-day developments on the part of the Treasury Department policy stands. Information on the extent that they have responded to recent exercises where classified instructions are reviewed is no longer available to me. However, I do think they are still keeping the faith.

Mr. McCLOSKEY. By "keeping the faith," you mean being loyal to whoever heads the delegation?

Mr. JOHNSTON. Trying to secure the U.S. interests.

Mr. McCLOSKEY. The problem that I have is defining the U.S. interests. You have defined a very appropriate and important set of interests including the concerns of ocean miners, the American taxpayer and the American consumer.

What about the national security? How would you compare the issue of passage of straits with the concern of excessive prices or being faced with a cartel in cobalt or copper?

Mr. JOHNSTON. I am glad you asked that. Part of my past includes 3 years with the Rand Corp. studying defense problems; not that I ever looked at the Straits question at that time. But I think there are several things that can be said on the Straits question; in fact, quite a lot of things can be said about the tradeoffs.

To save time here, I can cite a forthcoming chapter and book that will be published by the American Enterprise Institute which addresses an evaluation of the Straits on its own terms.

Mr. McCLOSKEY. I would like to get a copy of that by this Monday.

Mr. JOHNSTON. Yes; I understand its publication is imminent. Mine were the last galleys, and I sent them in a few weeks ago with the corrections. I could send you a copy of my commercial galleys, if you don't mind reading galleys.

Mr. McCLOSKEY. I would appreciate that.

Mr. JOHNSTON. The other thing I have done recently, which compares our security interests, indeed, all the interests, using economic rent as a measure which I submit is more reasonable than one that has been used by the Interior Department.

The Interior Department uses total revenue as a measure of economic importance. That same kind of number has been used to quote the essence of the value of unrestricted navigation.

But looking at the total value of shipping say in the United States, is a flawed measure because it doesn't consider the cost necessary to produce those goods and services. A better measure is economic rent; and for a detailed comparison of that, I would refer you to the National Ocean Policy Study, produced in December 1974, a year ago.

Mr. McCLOSKEY. By whom?

Mr. JOHNSTON. And my paper that I presented before the Syracuse Law School, which uses that context to evaluate the tradeoffs; and if you would like, I have a copy of this, and it could be entered into the record.

[The material referred to follows:]

"Whom the gods would destroy, they first endow with a foreign ministry. Then cultivate the belief that citizens elevated to the ranks of ambassadors and diplomats thereby achieve superhuman sagacity. The final stage of madness comes when—the diplomats having bombed out and chaos been averted only by scrapping the draft treaty that the diplomats believe the gods gave humanity out of godly beneficence—governments and their publics heed the diplomats' pleadings for an early restoration of treaty negotiations and more authority offer concessions."

—Paraphrased from Harry G. Johnson

The Likelihood of a Treaty Emerging From the Third United Nations Conference on the Law of the Sea

(By James L. Johnston*)

On April Fool's Day 1976, the diplomatic elite of more than 140 countries will be starting the fourth session of the Third United Nations Conference on the Law of the Sea (UNCLOS). The latest chapter in this multigenerational epic follows a long series which began before 1958, when the first UNCLOS was held. Four Conventions emerged from the 1958 UNCLOS. Notwithstanding the number of agreements, the significance of the agreements was modest. Essentially the four conventions were a codification of customary international law on ocean usage which evolved over centuries of unilateral actions and domestic legislation.

After this modest success, the delegates met again in 1960 for the second UNCLOS. This time the aim was more ambitious. The goal was to develop a new law of the sea, which would facilitate the recovery of resources and reduce the potential for conflict. The second UNCLOS ended in failure.

In 1967, an obscure U.N. diplomat, Ambassador Arvid Pardo of Malta, became impressed with the value of ocean resources and urged the diplomatic community in a speech before the General Assembly, to declare the ocean resources beyond the limits of national jurisdiction, "the common heritage of mankind." [1] His idea was to finance the economic development of the world's impoverished by giving them the proceeds of the oceans' resources.

The proposal had immediate appeal with adherents to a world order largely because now their schemes could be financed from what were believed to be the limitless resources of the sea. Of course, the view that diplomatic cooperation can somehow overcome economic scarcity is obviously naive. Less obvious is that a diplomatic conference has little chance to define a legal regime to facilitate the recovery of economic resources in the future. In isolation, about the most that can be expected of an international legal conference is to formalize existing relationships. As has already been indicated this was accomplished in 1958 at the first UNCLOS.

But the UNCLOS continues as does the participation by the United States Government. While the chances are slim for a timely and acceptable overall treaty, there is the very real possibility that the continuing negotiations at the UNCLOS will present serious problems for both the United States and the other participating states as well. It will be helpful, I believe, to reduce the complexity of the negotiations into a few diagrams. On that basis it will be easier to see the underlying factors, while avoiding the mass of details associated with this multi-issue conference.

The UNCLOS like its parent, the United Nations, is a parliamentary body in the sense that positions are adopted by negotiation and vote. A useful insight into voting relationships has been provided by Buchanan,[2] who uses the familiar indifference curve diagram of economics. The diagrammatic model in Figure 1 has two issues, x and y. Any point in the space represents a specific mix of x and y. In this model there are three groups of voters. For each group of voters there is a most preferred point and this point is surrounded by a series of convex loci, each one of which traces out a set of x and y packages which are of equal value to the group. Clearly, a locus close to the most preferred point is superior to one which is far away. Another way of thinking of these equal-valued loci is in terms of the likelihood that the voting group will accept the packages of x and y. The probability of accepting the most preferred point would be, of course, 1.0. A particularly relevant loci is the one that encloses all the packages where the probability is at least .5 that the voting group will accept the result.

---

* Presently, senior economic consultant to Standard Oil Company (Indiana) and until August the Treasury representative on the U S delegation to the UNCLOS. The views expressed herein are not necessarily those of either organization.
[1] Arvid Pardo cited in *Hearings Before The Subcommittee On Minerals, Materials and Fuels*, Part 2. Washington : USGPO for the U.S. Senate. 1974. P. 1345
[2] James Buchanan. *The Public Finances*. Homewood, Illinois : Irwin, 1970. Pp. 126–136.

In the next diagram, Figure 2, Arrow's voting paradox[*] is illustrated. For each pair of voting groups there is a set of mutually acceptable packages. If each combination of two voting groups constitutes a majority, then there is no stable solution. Shifting coalitions change from one set of majority packages to another, and that is the paradox. Despite there being a host of acceptable packages, none is a stable equilibrium.

Nor is a stable equilibrium present if there is a package which is unanimously acceptable. Consider the revised diagram in Figure 3 where there is one package that is acceptable to all three groups. In this case, for any pair of voting groups there are many packages which each pair would prefer over the unanimous package. Since the unanimous package is at the corner of three convex sets, any package within a convex (football-shaped) set is preferred by two of the three voting groups. Thus this is the same in essential respects as the previous case, where there is no stable equilibrium. To the extent that the UNCLOS is part of a general class of such negotiations, there may be no equilibrium solution which can be reached.

The basis is now present to view the UNCLOS in the context of the Buchanan paradigm. Consider issue x, the definition of property rights that facilitates the recovery of marine resources such as petroleum, manganese nodules fish, and the abatement of marine pollution. Similarly, one can view issue y to be the degree of navigational freedoms and unrestricted scientific research. The diagram in Figure 4 contains three voting blocs. The point E is preferred by maritime countries and might represent the present state of customary international law with respect to the oceans. In a sense it is the endowment point at which the negotiations began.

The lower point, near the x axis has been labeled "coastal" to indicate that countries boardering on the oceans have a greater relative interest in securing jurisdiction over the ocean resources off their shores. The realm of packages acceptable to coastal countries has been drawn to indicate a concern with avoiding needless disruption of navigational freedoms. Similarly, the frontier of packages acceptable to maritime countries shows a willingness to improve the definition of property rights, if navigational freedoms are not seriously impaired.

A word about an implied assumption is appropriate at this point. The model presumes that improved property rights and navigational freedoms can be maintained simultaneously. Putting it another way, the trade-off is not a zero-sum game where gains on one issue come only at the expense of the other. It should be added that this underlying assumption is not accepted by many of the negotiators on the U.S. delegation. It is their view that any increased resource jurisdiction, necessarily reduces navigational freedoms. They also believe as a corollary, that making economic concessions on resource jurisdictions will buy a larger set of navigational freedoms. The implied assumption of some independence between the two issues is clearly at odds with the alternative view that the negotiations are a zero-sum game. It is left to the reader to evaluate which model is a more accurate and useful reflection of the negotiations.

The position of the United States has been drawn to reflect the fact that it has an important interest in both aspects of the negotiations. Since it has the largest national income, it is understandable that it would have an important national defense interest in maintaining high seas freedoms and a vital stake in all of the economic issues as well. The latter term is used broadly so as to include protecting the environment as an economic interest.

The position of the United States with respect to the other blocs shows the key package-making role which the United States might potentially play. This is not to say that there is a deal which will command unanimous support. Beside the Arrow paradox problem already discussed, there is little, or no common ground, in this observer's opinion, between the maritime and coastal bloc. However, the United States is in the position of choosing which group to negotiate in order to reach an agreement. Perhaps, it would be more correct to say that it *had* the choice, because the U.S. negotiators effectively made the choice before the start of the third UNCLOS. The decision was to strike a bargain with the maritime countries and try to appease coastal states with concessions.

It should be repeated that the diagram in Figure 4 depicts the state of negotiations at the beginning of the third UNCLOS. Since then, the interests

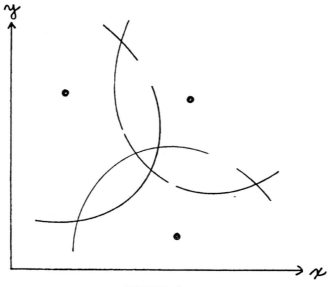

FIGURE 1

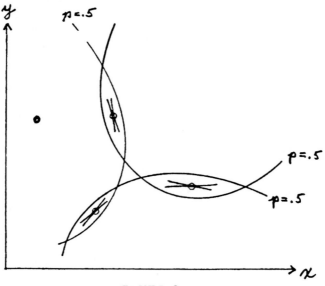

FIGURE 2

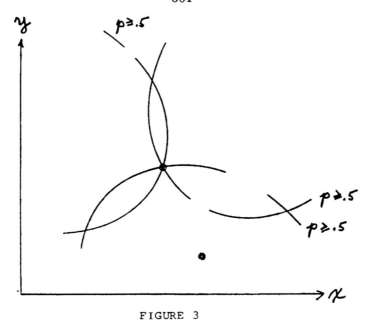

FIGURE 3

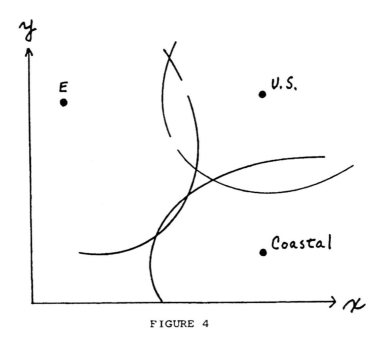

FIGURE 4

seem to have altered in significant ways for both the United States and the other blocs. The new arrangement, as perceived by this observer, is shown in Figure 5.

The most striking change, it is submitted, is the increased willingness of the United States to make concessions on economic issues. What this reflects is the simple fact that one interest is better represented in the delegation and has been successful in shifting the most preferred position (of the U.S. negotiators) away from economic interests, and into a stance where there is less willingness to comprise on navigational and other high seas freedoms. In other words, the U.S. delegation has moved closer to the most preferred position of maritime interests.

Simultaneously, the coastal bloc has shifted toward permitting a greater degree of navigational freedom. Indications, for example from several Latin American countries is that a 200-mile economic zone is becoming an acceptable substitute for a 200-mile territorial sea. This is an important shift for a group that has been the most eloquent proponents of national sovereignty over coastal resources.

There have also been changes to the bloc of maritime countries, but these changes are less easy to perceive in the diagram. Several maritime countries have discovered that there are or may be important petroluem resources in their continental margins. The United Kingdom, Norway and Greece, for example have become increasingly more interested in jurisdiction over their coastal resources. Thus, the number of states in the maritime block have decreased while coastal bloc has increased its numbers.

The landlocked and so-called "geographically disadvantaged states" are also moving toward membership in the coastal bloc. While one might have expected their interests to coincide more closely with maritime countries because of potentially higher transportation costs, however slight, that might come from regulating navigation, in fact they have discovered a potential accommodation with the growing coastal bloc. The landlocked and GDS are now willing to support full resource jurisdiction by coastal states over their adjacent marine resources in exchange for priority access to neighboring fisheries and unrestricted overland access to the sea. Indeed the 45 or so landlocked and GDS are holding the treaty hostage until their demands are met.

Ironically, the United States has nothing to trade in order to resolve this impasse, since it blocks no ocean access and there are no "geographically disadvantaged" countries which wish to participate in its fisheries—except, interestingly, for Cuba. The United States initially tried to appeal to the landlocked and GDS bloc with offers to share petroleum revenues from its continental margin in order to gain their support for continuing the regime of unrestricted navigation. The block apparently perceived that a greater gain was to be obtained by striking a deal with their neigbhoring coastal states. Notwithstanding this negotiating failure, the United States delegation continnes to promote a limited form of revenue sharing, to the chagrin of many of the broad margin states.

Thus, the UNCLOS faces a continuing deadlock and additional economic concessions by the United States cannot help. If there is a potential solution. and that is not certain at least in the near term, then there is only one avenue open to the United States. It must join the coastal bloc by conceding some navigational freedoms. But before this step can be entertained seriously, it is necessary to evaluate the relative worth of each issue. What follows is a first cut attempt at presenting a comparative evaluation of the issues and draws heavily from a report for the National Ocean Policy Study by Robert R. Nathan Associates.[4]

This study is selected because it is virtually unique in correctly going about measuring the relative values of the issues. The Nathan study avoids the error of equating the value of a resource with the total revenue derived from the economic activity. This erroneous approach ignores the costs associated with providing the resource. Gold suspended in ocean water, for example, is presently worthless because the total cost of extraction exceeds the expected total revenue.

---

[4] Robert R Nathan Associates. *The Economic Value of Ocean Resources To The United States.* Washington: National Ocean Policy Study, Senate Committee on Commerce, 1974.

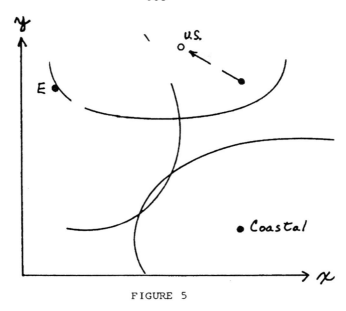

FIGURE 5

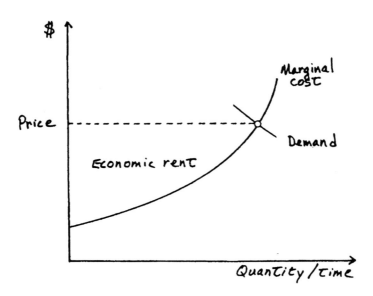

FIGURE 6

Figure 6 illustrates the basic measure, economic rent, used in the evaluation of the issues in the Nathan study. Now, those with training in economics will recognize that the concept is somewhat more complicated than presented here. However, the basic distinction being made in the Nathan study is correct. Economic rent is that part of the price paid for a good that does not affect the quantity supplied.[5] Saying it another way, it is the revenue residual after all of the costs have been accommodated. This will sound to many of you like the definition of profit, net revenue or earnings. Absent government subsidies and other distortions in accounting measures, the two notions are identical. However, in several of these respects there are variations across the UNCLOS issues and it is appropriate to take them into account using economic rent as the measure of worth.

The issue most affected as a result of ranking by economic rent is ocean transportation. First, shipping is only marginally economic as evidenced by the fact that it is primarily an activity of low-income countries which can use low-cost labor to operate the vessels. Few industrially developed countries operate vessels without a subsidy. While the total revenue devoted to ocean transportation is large compared with other national income accounts, the earnings are small. The second reason for small economic rent in ocean transportation is the subsidy program. The Nathan study appropriately subcontracts the subsidy from the earnings of shipping companies to derive its estimate of economic rent. Finally, the issue at stake in the UNCLOS negotiations is not the elimination of all ocean transportation. In the most extreme case, there is some probability ostensibly greater than zero, of having to circumvent or to pay a toll for passage through a few of the international straits. For the United States there are just three that are probably important: Dover, Gibraltar, and Malacca.[6] Notably only one, Malacca, is part of a petroleum transportation route to the United States, and this route will decrease in importance as oil from the Alaskan north slope begins to supply the west coast.

Turning to Figure 7, it is now possible to compare the value of major issues to the United States, using the Nathan estimates. The most striking result is that petroleum is the most important interest for the United States, exceeding the value of all the other U.S. interests combined. Note also that manganese nodules and fisheries are of the same relative value as ocean transportation. Further, the value of fisheries and nodules to the United States is growing and there is reason to believe that the value of ocean transportation is not growing as fast, if at all.

With the Arab oil boycott, the amount of shipborne petroleum has decreased sharply. Idle tankers abound in the world and purchasers of tankers are having considerable difficulty in making payments to the banks which have financed the vessel construction. There is even talk of ship operators forming a cartel in order to recoup part of their losses.

FIGURE 7.—CRUDELY ESTIMATED AND PROJECTED ANNUAL ECONOMIC RENTS ATTRIBUTABLE TO SELECTED OCEAN RESOURCES CONTROLLED BY THE UNITED STATES, 1972-73 TO 2000

[In billions of 1973 dollars]

	1972-73	1985	2000
Oil and gas	3. 90+	7. 70+	9. 40+
Manganese nodules		. 33-. 51	. 65-. 95
Food fish	. 15-. 22	. 19-. 48	. 27-1. 20
Industrial fish	. 01-. 02	. 01-. 02	. 01-. 04
Offshore power		. 04-. 07	. 32-. 54
Transportation		. 14-. 64	?
Recreation	U	U	U
Receptacle for waste	U	U	U

Source: Nathan, "The Economic Value of Ocean Resources to the U.S.," 1974.

Since the Nathan estimates of the value of transportation predated the oil boycott, the projected value in 1985 and the rate of growth would certainly be candidates for a downward reevaluation. This in turn implies that if

---

[5] Armen A. Alchian and William R. Allen. *University Economics.* Belmont, California: Wadsworth Publishing Company, 1972. P. 105.

[6] Nathan. *op. cit.* P. 96.

present value estimates of the stream of rents were used as a measure of relative worth, the value of ocean transportation for the United States would be even further reduced compared with other ocean uses.

Nathan offers no estimates for either the value of recreation or the use of the oceans as a dump for waste. Clearly these values are among the most difficult to estimate. The allocation of resources to both of the activities is complicated since there are externalities present. For example, the oceans are probably being over polluted because no one has the right to charge the correct price for use of the oceans as a dump. But this, in turn, implies that resolution of the problem comes, if at all, with an improved definition of property rights and *not* with steadfastly defending high seas and navigational freedoms. Thus, recreation and pollution are part of the set of economic issues whose importance is enhanced with an improved definition of property rights.

It would appear from what has been said thus far, that the altered position of U.S. delegation viewed from the economic perspective is counterproductive with respect to the U.S. interests, *and* ironically, with respect to reaching agreement with the growing bloc of states striving to extend jurisdiction over their offshore resources.

But the story is incomplete without detailing recent developments at the UNCLOS. As has already been indicated, there now exists an impasse at the UNCLOS because the 45 or so landlocked and geographically disadvantaged states are holding the treaty hostage until they receive priority access to neighboring fisheries and rights to overland passage to the sea. Evidently they perceive a greater gain from being recipients of these concessions than from sharing in oil and nodule revenues. Part of the reason is that the bloc of landlocked and GDS contain some of the most industrially advanced and some of the most important mineral deposits in the world—Switzerland, Austria, Hungary, Czechoslovakia, Zambia and Zaire. Consequently the chances are slim that these countries would receive an important share of revenues from ocean minerals if the basis was some measure of need. The other part of the reason for opting away from revenue sharing is the realization that little revenue would be left for distribution after subtracting (1) the administrative costs of the International Authority, (2) the proposed financing of mineral stockpiles, and (3) compensation to landbased mineral producers for notional losses in their export earnings. In sum, revenue sharing is not very attractive to the only large group for which the concession could have any appeal.

The situation in deep seabed negotiations is quite different. Rather than being at an impasse, there is rather complete concensus among coastal and landlocked alike that a new International Authority should be formed to inhibit nodule production, except as a part of a worldwide mineral cartel. The "new international economic order" has infected the deep seabed negotiations in epidemic proportions. The landbased mineral producers—many of whom are already industrially developed and some of whom are landlocked or GDS— have captured the leadership in these negotiations and are being supported by those idealogically committed to the rhetoric of the "new international economic order" and the redistribution of wealth from industrially developed to the poor of the world which it seems to imply.

Of course, the economic realities are quite at odds with the rhetoric. Forming cartels will largely help the already industrially advanced since they are the major producers of all the higher valued raw materials.

Further, the largest burden will fall on developing countries who will have to pay higher prices for the raw materials, and the capital goods and final products made from them. That the poor of the world have already had their miserable circumstances worsened by the OPEC actions, is mute testimony to the economic realities. That the leaders of these poor countries continue to support the raw materials producers, suggests that personal goals of the leaders sometime diverge from the social goals of the public they represent.

If there has been any dramatic move in the negotiations, it has been away from the sharing of petroleum revenues. African countries who were early supporters, have reversed their position on sharing revenues within 200 miles of the shoreline. States who have the most at stake in avoiding the sharing of revenues beyond 200 miles have been working diligently to head off this provision. Paradoxically, they have had to contend with the U.S. delegation who are actively promoting revenue sharing in the area beyond 200 miles, despite the fact that the United States is a broad margin state having a nonnegligible potential in this area.

Recent nationalizations overseas and the number of dry holes encountered by U.S. oil firms in the Gulf of Mexico, have increased the value of this area. Of course, the portion of the continental margin under the deepest water is the most costly to explore and produce. The fact that the largest portion of the U.S. continental margin is in the harsh arctic climate, also contributes to the costs of recovering this potential. Consequently, at the very time that new discoveries are most important to the United States, our negotiators are apparently willing to add to the cost of recovery in this economically marginal area by promoting an international revenue sharing burden.

Other countries who have broad margins and an even greater stake in their oil potential have cleverly developed revenue sharing formulas where only the United States would have an effective obligation. Thus, the present UNCLOS is dangerously close to overturning the provisions of the Continental Shelf Convention that gives coastal states jurisdiction over their continental margins to the limit of exploitability. Such a condition helps no one except OPEC countries. Ironically, the U.S. attempt to strike a bargain, where clear jurisdiction over the outer continental margin is exchanged for a revenue sharing obligation, ostensibly to enhance agreement, has exactly the opposite effects. Revenue sharing erodes the present definition of property rights and the other broad-margin states are forced to delay if not oppose agreement until the misguided actions by the U.S. delegation can be neutralized.

The developments with respect to the navigation issue have been subtle and not just restricted to the UNCLOS negotiations. First, the military worth of unrestricted passage through straits has been reevaluated and downgraded significantly by Dean Robert Osgood of the School for Advanced International Studies, and ex-National Security Council staffer, in a forthcoming volume to be published by the American Enterprise Institute. Second, the Senate Armed Services Committee was so unimpressed with the national security arguments of the representatives of the Joint Chief of Staff, that they ignored their advice and voted the 200-mile fisheries legislation favorably out of the Committee.

At the UNCLOS the Archepelago states appear to be gaining ground in obtaining acceptance of the idea that they should have jurisdiction in the waters bounded by their islands.[7] Such a regime is reflected in the single informal negotiating texts which were prepared by UNCLOS committee chairman last year in Geneva. Significantly, this was achieved without an elaborate commitment on the part of Archepelago states to avoid restricting navigational freedoms.

The UNCLOS also saw a commitment on the part of the landlocked and GDS to support a coastal state accommodation on residual rights in the 200-mile economic zone.[8] These are the traditional high seas freedoms that are not specifically identified in the regime of the economic zone as coming under coastal state jurisdiction.

Dispute settlement, is probably considered by observers unfamiliar with the negotiations, to be the *sine qua non* of any new law of the sea. The economic logic supports this view, because the value of marine resources depends upon not only upon advancing recovery technology but also upon a stable investment climate. This in turn implies that disputes between firms engaging in resource recovery and coastal states must be subject to a stable, predictable settlement procedure. If it is not, the investment funds and technology will not be forthcoming from outside the coastal state and, most importantly, the value of the marine resources will be virtually zero.

In the face of this, the UNCLOS is showing no inclination for making accommodations along these lines in defining anything but complete discretion for coastal states. The effect, inescapably, is to reduce the derived demand for a timely and satisfactory treaty.

With the foregoing as background, an attempt will be made to predict what to expect at the next sessions of the UNCLOS. The short answer is that nothing will happen in the near term. First an accommodation has to be reached between the bloc of landlocked and GDS and the bloc of coastal states. This accommodation will probably have to be reached within the Group

---

[7] U.N. Third Conference on the Law of the Sea. *Informal Single Negotiating Text*, A–CONF .62–WP.8—Part I, Part II and Part III. 7 May 1975.

[8] The representative of Singapore speaking on behalf of the landlocked and geographically disadvantaged states to the formal session of the Second Committee on April 23, 1975.

of 77. If the U.S. delegation continues to insist on playing a role by offering more concessions in the deep seabed, fisheries and the continental margin, the day when the accommodation will be reached will be delayed.

Time will also be required to essentially return to the starting place in the continental shelf negotiations. That is, where the coastal state has jurisdiction over the full continental margin, unemcumbered by a revenue sharing obligation.

Similarly, dispute settlement negotiations on provisions to facilitate resource recovery especially off the coasts of developing countries, has really not yet begun. Until that happens, with more than the mere 40 or so countries which are now participating, there will be one less incentive to reach agreement.

There are three pieces of domestic legislation currently pending in the U.S. Congress. Each is designed by its sponsors to protect their interests. Of the three—ocean mining, pollution and fisheries—the latter is the closest to adoption. Indeed, the 200-mile fisheries bill is slated for floor debate and vote in the Senate during the current session. The results will be known, in all likelihood, by the time that next session of the UNCLOS begins in New York.

The most important difference between the present Senate bill and the already adopted House bill is the effective date. President Ford has indicated that he would like to give the delegation one more year to negotiate a treaty and then join in supporting domestic legislation if results are not successful.[9] Apparently, the Senate sponsors are taking the President at his word, because they have amended the bill so that it will not begin to take effect until 1977.

With passage of the Senate bill and presuming a successful conference between the House and Senate, the U.S. delegation will be pressured into a desperate attempt to reach agreement by the end of the year. As has already been indicated, moves by the U.S. delegation to offer additional concessions on most economic issues will be counterproductive. There is, however, one disturbing possibility.

Remembering that there is near concensus in the deep seabed negotiations on the part of the other delegations to stop U.S. firms from recovering manganese nodules, the U.S. delegation might be tempted to make the ultimate price-and-production-control concessions, and reach agreement on the structure and powers of the International Authority. Precedent already exists for separate treaties since the first UNCLOS produced four Conventions in 1958.

The next year, indeed the next few months, will bring developments that should determine the outcome of the third UNCLOS. With a little luck UNCLOS will collapse in failure and bring to an end this 17-year diplomatic road show. When this happens all the economic interests of the United States will breathe a sigh of relief.

Mr. McCLOSKEY. When you talk about tradeoffs, what is the value to the United States, dollarwise, of an agreement which fixes a 12-mile territorial sea limitation and a 200-mile economic zone on all of the countries of the world?

Mr. JOHNSTON. In fact, there are several ways of defining property rights in offshore resources if that is the background of the question.

Mr. McCLOSKEY. I am trying to balance the conflicting interests of State, Defense, Commerce, Interior, and Treasury that you have laid out. If you use a value system that is related to dollars and economic benefits, don't you omit this question of an international law which might tell us whether we can send a ship 4½ or 15 miles off someone else's coast?

The international law is to tell us which rights are correct. The Koreans claimed a 12-mile territorial limit following our President's declaration of a 12-mile fishing limit. We contended we had a right to go in within 3 miles of the coast.

Wasn't that the background?

[9] *Ocean Science News.* December 19, 1975. P. 3.

Mr. JOHNSTON. From my experiences at the Rand Corp., defense questions benefit greatly from being analyzed from the economic perspective. I think if you look at the history of defining "rights," they are seldom if ever defined by a treaty except where that treaty essentially codifies the existing practices. To hold out a great hope that this treaty is the superior method for protecting existing rights and codifying new regimes which will enhance the recovery and the development of goods and services, it seems to me, is to ignore the way in which this has taken place in the past.

Generally, this is accomplished by domestic legislation. For example, the Senate on February 19 passed S. 22, which is the new copyright law, and it has in it a provision for reciprocal recognition of patent registrants that register patents in other countries if their legislation is similar to ours.

That came about through domestic legislation, and no one in the State Department contended that that was a unilateral extension of jurisdiction.

With respect to the specific military advantages and the worth of unrestricted passage, I would refer you to Dean Osgood's paper.

He also has a contribution in the forthcoming AEI volume. He goes through and examines all the Straits, from the military perspective, and concludes first of all, there are very few Straits that are of serious importance from a military perspective and of those Straits that are, they are becoming less important because of the improved technology. I think you are better off having firsthand all the details from his report.

However. I would like to make one additional point.

The Conference itself contributes to some extent to customary international law, and we face a real threat that some aspects of the Conference, even if it fails, might be used against U.S. interests, indeed, against our U.S. navigational interests.

It is the Conference itself that is talking about wider bans of jurisdiction, and it is talking about a 200-mile economic zone with many dimensions of resource jurisdiction, whereas the 200-mile fish bill addresses only one specific resource within that same zone.

Mr. McCLOSKEY. Thank you.

Mr. JONES. The Chair recognizes counsel.

Mr. PERIAN. I also was in Geneva for 2 weeks and watched you suffer some of the wounds. You did voice your concerns in some of the meetings that I attended.

Did you ever assess what effect they had on the attainment of the negotiations?

Who really had the final say-so?

Mr. JOHNSTON. Part of the problem in answering that question is that——

Mr. PERIAN. Maybe I can help you.

I have a document here that lists 12 major items concerned with the International Seabed Resource; and the position on these 12 items of the State Department, Treasury Department, Defense Department, Interior, Commerce, OMB and the Council on International Economic Policy.

In all of the positions of the State Department appears the word "Yes."

Treasury is practically diametrically opposed on all issues as is true for every other agency.

The position of the United States at the treaty conference was basically that of the Department of State?

Mr. JOHNSTON. I guess that would be a fair assessment.

Mr. PERIAN. Thank you.

The U.S. position at the deep seabed negotiations has been subject to a great deal of abuse, so much in fact that I understand, and Mr. Murphy understands, that our delegation was advised by some foreign delegates to adopt domestic legislation and withdraw from the deep sea conference.

Do you think that is a viable course for the United States to adopt?

Mr. JOHNSTON. I think that is good advice. I not only think it is good advice, but we have serious problems if we don't accommodate the fact that was given to us.

Ambassador Moynihan has been very helpful describing his situation in the United Nations in New York and thereby giving us some insights into the law of the sea.

He observed that the State Department does not understand conference diplomacy. I am quoting him. He says it is counterproductive to placidly accept the outrageous demands of others. The reason for that is that it sends the wrong signals to the other side about our intentions and what we are willing to accept.

Now, if we don't take the advice of this foreign delegate, it seems to me what we are going to be signaling to him—and surely he will pass it on—is that we are apparently so desperate to reach treaty and we will agree on anything in order to get agreement.

Mr. PERIAN. Your testimony indicates that you are quite concerned about the latest initiatives on commodity arrangements. Should not our negotiators try to reach an agreement?

Mr. JOHNSTON. I know the Administration has testified that in their opinion the UNCLOS negotiations are generally going well, and only the deep seabeds supposedly are holding up the agreement.

Thus, it would seem that just making a few concessions here to get the rest of the package would be worth it, but there are other problems in negotiations.

In the paper that I presented in Syracuse, if you would like to have it for the record, I think you will find that it points out some of these other problems.

Essentially, it points out that not only are some of our initiatives risking U.S. interests but, in fact, they are positively counterproductive toward reaching an early agreement in the treaty. They actually get in the way.

Now, about this package deal; you know we have talked about this before. Let me say again, it is fine if we are constructing the package, but that is not in the cards.

The deal is going to be constructed by the Group of 77, and we are going to be faced with a take-it-or-leave-it decision, as will the Senate.

Mr. PERIAN. Your testimony causes one to wonder who benefits from the kind of arrangements that are under consideration at the Laws of the Sea Conference.

The American ocean and mining industries do not benefit.

Is it just the land-based producers of these minerals that will benefit?

Who are they?

What countries are we talking about?

Mr. JOHNSTON. Well, primarily, you see, taking the lead in negotiators are the primary metals producers, producers of the metals found in the nodules: Chile, Peru, and Brazil, including some other countries that also are mineral producers that in some uses are substitutes for these primary metals, plus there are mineral producers that have an interest in and a stake in justifying some of their past actions and in that group are the OPEC countries.

There are countries also that would aspire to formulate nonmineral cartels and so would like to see approbation of commodity agreements so they could be extended to other commodities.

To answer your question as far as the deep seabed negotiations are concerned, there are two groups that are diametrically opposed. One is mainly the land-based producers of minerals and their supporters, and the other group would be the potential seabed producers of minerals.

I don't know how you bridge that gap. One group wants to halt development of seabed minerals and the other group wants to bring it about.

I am reminded that Evil Knievel tried to bridge a gap recently, and while he wasn't successful in bridging the gap, he was certainly successful in promoting the bridging of the gap.

Mr. PERIAN. One final question.

The legislation under consideration by this subcommittee identifies the Secretary of Commerce as being the one who is primarily responsible for administering the ocean mining program.

Do you agree with that, or do you think it would be more effective if the program were placed under the Secretary of the Interior?

Mr. JOHNSTON. Well, my role as an economist is going to show through, I think.

I can say when I was at Treasury, the Treasury had absolutely no interest in ocean mining.

Mr. JONES. The gentleman doesn't have to qualify his answer. Go ahead.

Mr. JOHNSTON. Competition tends to bring out the best in people. I think that is true for business; and I think it is also true for government.

I know you are going to have to somewhere along the line make some decisions about divvying up some responsibilities in these areas. The final solution will probably be some split in responsibility.

Something you might take into account as you proceed to this decision is not who supposedly knows most about ocean mining, which no one knows very much at all about. Instead, the thing you might keep in mind is what appears to be a dog-in-the-manger attitude on the part of both Interior and Commerce. While they want the responsibility to promote the development, both of them are opposing domestic legislation.

You ought to ask Interior and Commerce to sketch out viable domestic legislation that will promote this industry and perhaps make part of the decision on that basis.

Mr. PERIAN. We have asked them. They have their options, but they are keeping them under wraps until after the next meeting of the LOS.

Mr. JONES. If there are no further questions, and no further business, I want to thank all the witnesses.

I declare this subcommittee adjourned until tomorrow morning at 10:00 o'clock a.m.

[Whereupon, at 4:20 p.m., the subcommittee was adjourned to reconvene tomorrow, Tuesday, March 9, 1976, at 10:00 a.m.]

DEEP SEABED MINING

House of Representatives,
Committee on Merchant Marine and Fisheries,
Subcommittee on Oceanography,
Washington, D.C.

The subcommittee met, pursuant to recess, at 10:40 a.m., in room 1334, Longworth House Office Building, Hon. (Kika) de la Garza, presiding.

Mr. DE LA GARZA. The subcommittee will be in order.

We continue the hearings on H.R. 1270 and other related bills on the deep seabed mining.

Our first witness today will be Mr. Samuel R. Levering, Secretary, United States Committee for the Oceans.

STATEMENT OF SAMUEL R. LEVERING, SECRETARY, UNITED STATES COMMITTEE FOR THE OCEANS

Mr. LEVERING. Right here, sir.

Mr. DE LA GARZA. I will be happy to hear from you at this time, sir.

Mr. LEVERING. Thank you.

Mr. Chairman, I appreciate the opportunity to bring testimony to this committee on these hard mineral bills.

As you know, sir, I had been a witness on other bills before your committee from time to time, and have many good friends among members of your committee.

For those who perhaps do not know, I am an entrepreneur. I have an orchard, and employ about 65 people at peak periods. I know the problems of getting a job done and producing the essential things for people to use.

I am also a member of the Advisory Committee, U.S. delegation to the Law of the Seas, have been on the working groups that have developed United States policy for Committee I, the area of deep seabed mining to which these bills are addressed.

I have been intimately connected with the whole field of deep seabed mining for the last 4½ years, so that it is no new field at all.

This morning I am speaking for myself, and as Secretary of the United States Committee for the Oceans, a private public interest group with former Justice Goldberg and former Governor Sargent of Massachusetts as chairman.

(513)

I am also speaking for a number of other organizations that asked to join in my testimony, the Friends Committee on National Legislation, a Quaker group here in Washington, which I was chairman for 16 years, the Board of Church and Society of the United Methodist Church, the United Methodist Womens Division of the Board of Global Ministries, and the Network, which is a group of Catholic nuns.

After the front page was printed, sir, the Jesuit Association called up and said they wished to join in this testimony, so I am speaking for a very broad group of church organizations Protestant and Catholic. That is the basis of the testimony.

If you do not mind, sir, I would like to file my testimony, and then I would like to speak to the critical issues I think before the committee.

I would simply like this included in the record, and I would like to speak to the issues that seem to me particularly pertinent to this legislation.

Mr. DE LA GARZA. That is perfectly agreeable, sir, and without objection the text of your statement will appear in the record, and you may proceed as you desire.

[The statement referred to follows:]

STATEMENT OF SAMUEL R. LEVERING, SECRETARY, UNITED STATES COMMITTEE FOR THE OCEANS IN BEHALF OF THE UNITED STATES COMMITTEE FOR THE OCEANS, FRIENDS COMMITTEE ON NATIONAL LEGISLATION, BOARD OF CHURCH AND SOCIETY UNITED METHODIST CHURCH, UNITED METHODIST WOMEN'S DIVISION OF THE BOARD OF GLOBAL MINISTRIES AND THE NETWORK—RELIGIOUS LOBBY

Mr. Chairman, I appreciate the opportunity to bring our views on HR 11879 to this committee and its distinguished chairman, Congressman Murphy.

The U.S. Committee for the Oceans, of which I am Secretary, is headed by the Honorary Chairmen, Justice Arthur J. Goldberg and Governor Francis W. Sargent. Louis Henkin, Professor of International Law at Columbia, is Legal Advisor, and the Committee has a distinguished Advisory Board. This is a private public interest group, dedicated to achieving just and effective ocean treaties. We support basic principles of U.S. proposals for the forthcoming Law of the Sea (LOS) Conference.

We know that no generally recognized international law now covers deep seabed hard mineral mining, and that therefore proponents of HR 11879 urge the U.S. to take such actions, even though many legal authorities, both here and abroad, question the legality of such actions.

It can be argued that the *presence* of this bill, and perhaps even more, the state of technological readiness to mine the deep seabed, may spur some delegations to the LOS Conference to reach earlier and better agreement on ocean treaties and institutions. We believe, however, that *passage* of HR 11879 at this time would be a serious mistake and we strongly oppose its passage.

WHY WE OPPOSE PASSAGE OF H.R. 11879

Passage of this bill would direct the Secretary of Commerce to issue licenses to blocks up to 40,000 square kilometers of the deep seabed for ocean mining, *before there is any international agreement*. This unilateral action would still effectively preempt the LOS on possession of the most desirable mining sites. Such unilateral action would be deeply resented by most of the nations of the world, who do not consider that the U.S. has any right to take possession of the sites prior to general agreement at the LOS Conference. The fact that the Bill would not take effect until January 1, 1977, is to real remedy, since the legal provision to take possession of these sites would have been enacted. The result of such unilateral action is not fully predictable, but certainly would make attainment of vital objectives of the U.S. at the LOS Conference much more difficult, if not impossible. It might even result in the break-up of the LOS Conference.

A fuller explanation of the probable damaging effects of passage

Space permits only a brief explanation of the adverse effects which we foresee. One: *Passage of H.R. 11879 Now Would Damage the Interests of the United States.*

We believe that the primary ocean interests of the United States are: Peace and security, stability and orderly development, strengthened by just international law and institutions; development of energy, food and hard mineral resources for our needs, and equitable distribution of royalty revenue from the deep seabed, especially to developing nations; the protection of the marine environment; conservation of living resources; protection of United States rights for navigation, commerce, communication, and scientific research; opportunity and security for American investments and enterprise. We believe that its passage would injure all these interests.

We believe its passage would hinder agreement on just international law and international institutions so badly needed to prevent conflict, settle disputes peacefully, prevent pollution, and supervise orderly development of ocean resources and equitable distribution of net revenues.

We believe that American deep seabed investments and enterprise will have greater opportunity and security under an international authority, operating for the common benefit of mankind, than under the "flag nation" approach promoted by this bill. Certainly security would be questionable for companies attempting to defend expensive deepsea operations against developers, with equal claims, from other nations. Other nations are likely to resist claims unilaterally asserted.

We believe that this bill would injure more United States economic interests than it would help. The chief gainers would be industries which use these metals and who would get them cheaper. Only a part of this would be passed on to the ultimate consumers. The chief United States losers would be investors in land-based mineral production at home and abroad; investors in and exporters (and their workers) to nations whose export income was reduced by seabed production; and U.S. taxpayers, if called upon to reimburse U.S. companies for higher costs if an international regime was established, and in higher military spending in a less friendly world, or in actual conflicts resulting. All U.S. citizens might be losers in a world where we will be increasingly dependent on raw materials from abroad. These metals could be less available or available on less advantageous terms from countries which felt that we had robbed them of their rights to deep seabed resources.

The "reciprocating state" provisions of this bill would amount to the United States signing "blank checks" to honor the claims of those acting through "flag of convenience" nations such as Panama and Liberia, or claims of the Soviet Union, Japan, or others to vast areas of the best seabed mining sites. These claims would be, to all intents and purposes, permanent, with no prostate" "blank checks" were eliminated, unilateral U.S. action would open the vision for adequate ocean environmental protection. Such "blank checks" would seriously damage the interests of the U.S. Even if the "reciprocating door to similar action by other nations, with the U.S. in no position to protest.

Two: *Passage Now Could Prevent Achievement of Important U.S. Objectives at the LOS Conference.*

Here are our judgments on how important U.S. objectives would fare under a widely accepted Law of the Sea treaty (possible even in 1976) and if there is no treaty.

. With a treaty: Agreement on a *12 mile territorial sea* and passage through straits. Shipments of oil and food could be safeguarded from the harassment of ninety-odd coastal nations. Dare anyone risk the possible blockage of over 100 straits, and the denial of access to the open sea?

Without a treaty: Chaos and tragedies such as the Mayaguez may multiply.

With a treaty: Agreement on a *200 mile economic zone.* Most fish could have a chance to survive to feed the hungry. Coastal nations assume the obligation to conserve fish and to allow other nations to catch what they cannot use.

Without a treaty: Coastal states can be expected to claim arbitrary rights for fish and oil that would also restrict the international freedoms of navigation, fishing, and research within 200 miles of shore.

With a treaty: Agreement on *national seabed boundaries*. Disputes over who owns offshore oil are minimized. Legal rights are established.

Without a treaty: Coastal nations can be expected to claim rights not only to 200 miles, but to the entire continental margin, with resulting conflict and confusion. Environmental regulations could be haphazard and revenue sharing nonexistent.

With a treaty: The technologically advanced nations would be prevented from devouring the mineral estate of the deep seabed—declared by the U.N. to be the "common heritage of mankind". The *proposed International Seabed Authority* would embody shared participation by developed and developing states, giving a greater voice to nations who feel excluded from global decision-making. With its own money from nickel, copper and cobalt, its own Tribunal with peaceful enforcement and balanced structure, it could become a model for other global imperatives, such as weapons control.

Without a treaty: The rich get richer as technologically advanced nations mine the manganese nodules at the risk of harassment from embittered losers of the "common heritage." An unprecedented opportunity to move toward a new political and economic order is lost.

With a treaty: *Tribunals and courts of arbitration* rather than gunboats and missiles can settle disputes between all parties, private or public, weak or powerful. The USSR for example, has accepted the principle of binding decisions for fishing disputes—a real breakthrough. Most states make exceptions of boundary disputes.

Without a treaty: More conflict is inevitable. The International Court of Justice has small acceptance. Present machinery for dispute settlement is meager.

With a treaty: *On environmental issues*, allnations assume an obligation to protect the marine environment. The proposed treaty sets up an Authority with environmental control over the international deep seabed.

Without a treaty: Even these small measures could be lost. No treaty means no likely environmental control over deep seabed mining.

With a treaty: On the hotly contested issue as to whether *marine research* is "pure" science or resource and military spying, at least scientists may be assured that basic science could be conducted with less impediment.

Without a treaty: The trend grows toward arbitrary restriction of scientific research without which we are all impoverished and the ocean possibly doomed.

Three: *Proponents' Arguments For Passage Now are Not Fully Persuasive.*

Some proponents say that the United States needs seabed minerals quickly. But presently-known land-based reserves of these metals should last from thirty to more than one hundred years.

Some proponents emphasize the supposed dangers of OPEC-type cartels for these metals. But there are many copper producers with widely different interests. The present association of copper-exporting countries has been unable to prevent a glutted buyers' market. Nickle comes largely from Canada and New Caledonia. Producer cartels for these metals seem highly unlikely. Cobalt comes largely from Zaire, but production could be increased elsewhere. A manganese producers cartel including Brazil, South Africa and Gabon seems quite improbable.

Some proponents stress U.S. balance of payments. Yet balance of payments surpluses are usual with the countries from which the United States imports seabed minerals. Reducing these U.S. imports might force some of these countries to reduce imports from the United States.

Some proponents rightly stress the protection of the U.S. technological lead in deep seabed mining technology. But they have already established international consortia with nationals of the chief developed nations which involve sharing technology. And one U.S. company spokesman spoke of the option of "folding up the tent or moving it", (presumably to a rival country) under certain conditions.

Some proponents say that they must make major investments within 18 months. Postponement for an extra year would subject three or four companies (Deepsea Ventures/Tenneco, Kennecott, International Nickel and possibly Lockheed) to less active investments with interest and other costs probably not over $20 million. This should be compared with the much larger losses to wide U.S. interests (including these companies) if passage now of H.R. 11879 prevented agreement on an acceptable Law of the Sea Treaty.

A larger problem is what kind of world we live in, and what kind of world will best serve the interests of the United States and the people of the world generally. H.R. 11879 assumes that the U.S. and other developed countries, because they have advanced technology, and military power to back it up, should proceed to develop the resources of the deep oceans without regard for the strongly held belief of most developing countries that these resources are equally theirs. This is a throwback to the predatory policies of a century and a half ago, which divided Africa and caused most conflict and injustice.

In our judgment, this is not the kind of world we live in now, and it is not in the interests of the United States to try to recreate this kind of world. The U.S. is living in a world where much of the world's raw material resources are in the hands of developing countries. It is likely that these resources will be available to the U.S. on more favorable terms if development of deep ocean minerals is carried on in an orderly fashion, and in a fashion which is considered equitable and just by developing countries. Cooperative arrangements will do a lot more for long-term stable resource development and utilization. We believe that the interests of the U.S. will be best served by a treaty which not only provides minerals for the U.S., but also is considered just by developing countries.

PASSAGE NOW OF THIS BILL WOULD BE EXTREMELY DANGEROUS

In our judgment, the U.S. has nothing to gain from the passage of this bill now. It has much to lose, damaging the chances to protect other vital interests of the United States: freedom of navigation, commerce, and scientific research; opportunity and security for United States industry to operate off the U.S. ocean environmental protection; conservation of the oceans' living resources; and other coasts; and a peaceful and just international order. We urge you to do as you did to the predecessor bills—make no present effort for passage.

Mr. LEVERING. Good morning, sir.

Mr. OBERSTAR. Good morning.

Mr. LEVERING. The first point I would like to make is something about the proponents of this measure, and the areas in which I agree with them.

I work with Marne Dubs and John Shaw of International Nickel, Jack Flipse of Deepsea Ventures-Tenneco and Lionel Welling of Lockheed. They are fellow members of the LOS Advisory Committee, and have been very close to the negotiations.

Marne Dubs worked with Leigh Ratiner most of the time at the session in Geneva, for instance.

The American policy has been developed and carried out in close cooperation with the mining industry. It is not any question of U.S. policy being on one side and that of industry on the other.

Now, I certainly agree on the advantage of the U.S. industry getting an early start in deep seabed mining, which I assume is one of the main purposes of this legislation.

The resources is major. It will be profitable, in my judgment, and certainly if the U.S. has the capability it should get out there as soon as possible, everything else considered.

I agree with the desirability of major U.S. development of seabed mining. It appears to be a good source of these minerals.

Marne Dubs says that probably there is about as much good ore in the ocean (copper, nickel and cobalt) as there is remaining good reserves on land.

In other words, this is a very major resource. The value of the nodules in the rich area between latitudes 6° and 20° north and longitude 110° and 180° west is estimated at around $3 trillion. That is important money.

It is certainly desirable for the United States to have a large part in the development of these resources. It would be developed within the U.S. balance of payments. Sometimes production outside is a problem.

It would, I agree, be desirable to protect our technological lead to the extent that we can, and it is important to have a resource which is not subject to interruption by action of other producers abroad.

I agree that the first emphasis in any consideration of these bills should be the interest of the United States.

I believe that even Jesus in his Second Commandment said you should love your neighbor as yourself, and that certainly means you want to look out for legitimate interests of your own.

But it is also true that 75 years down the road the interests of the United States are not much different from the interests of the world as a whole.

Temporary advantage may be taken, but in the long run, I do not think very much.

Now, after stating much agreement with the proponents of this bill, and I am a warm friend of many of them, I would now indicate why we oppose passage of this legislation now, and I might add, why we would oppose passage of this type of legislation in the foreseeable future. Legislation of some type might be desirable, even within the next year, but not this bill, in my judgment.

The first reason that we oppose passage of this bill at this time is that the arguments of the proponents are not fully persuasive. Let me indicate why.

NO ASSURED ACCESS

This bill is supposed to give assured access to these minerals, but I do not think it would provide assured access at all.

It is a wide ocean.

The right to mine there is very much in doubt. You have heard that discussed yesterday. Most of the world feels we do not have the right to go out and get them prior to agreement.

On the question of what the common heritage means, the developing countries think it means ownership by the world community, subject to use only after joint decision by the world.

The United States says that the common heritage means whatever the treaty says.

We have not gotten a treaty yet, so in either case our right out there would be strongly disputed by others. Then I think that we would be subject to considerable harassment potentially, and I do not think we, by this bill, would assure access. All we would be doing would be to insure investors, so that some mining could go on until it was interrupted or destroyed by someone calling us on our right to be there.

It would be, really, a sort of a guaranteed testing of the law at the probable expense of the United States taxpayers. I wonder if that is exactly what is wise under these conditions.

FREEDOM OF THE SEAS?

Second, one argument used for this bill is that this is simply a preservation of the freedom of the seas to mine. Of course, the generally accepted international law is that anyone can go out and fish in the high seas, and carry on other activities which do not interfere with the rights of others. But there is a very real difference between fishing and asserting the right to grant exclusive rights for a specific site against American citizens, and by means of reciprocating States, against others.

That in view of many would be a breach of the doctrine of freedom of the seas, and certainly would be strongly contested. Really the old freedom of the seas is no longer applicable, even for fishing. You gentlemen have passed the 200-mile bill, because it does not work there.

I think freedom for the seas for mining is not going to be operable, but I think that if a change is going to be effective, it would have to be by international agreement, rather than by unilateral assertion.

Mr. DE LA GARZA. May I interrupt you there for a moment, sir?

Mr. LEVERING. Please do.

Mr. DE LA GARZA. You used the words, by international agreement, yet, you have been to the Law of the Sea Conference, and have been in Geneva, and by and large, would you say what would you define international agreement as, if you put it side by side with the participating nations, and which nations band together in groups, and where the majority of voting power lies?

Mr. LEVERING. Well, of course, the reciprocating states, it would be an assumption of the right by nations that have the technology and the capital to go out and get these minerals, and to be defended by the navy, if they required it.

Mr. DE LA GARZA. But what I mean, where are the votes at the Law of the Sea Conference, with what nations?

Mr. LEVERING. Now, agreement I think is very possible, even with a 50-50 chance likely this year, that an international seabed authority should be set up with the general guidance over the development, but with the freedom of companies to receive a reasonable number of contracts and carry on their business without interference with some sharing of the revenue with the fund for the developing nations.

This would be with the consent of virtually all nations, and with some benefit to practically all, rather than with the consent of a few, and benefit of only a few at the expense, in their judgment, of the others.

It is a very different kind of set up, sir.

Mr. DE LA GARZA. I do not think you understood my question.

What group of nations does the power lie at the Law of the Sea Conference?

Mr. LEVERING. The vote is with the developing countries, of course. They have well over 100 of the 144 there.

That is not synonymous with power.

Mr. DE LA GARZA. How many of those are coastal states?

Mr. LEVERING. There are well over 100 coastal states, of which over two-thirds are developing.

Mr. DE LA GARZA. What do they call themselves, a group of what?

Mr. LEVERING. Well, it is the Group of 77, but it is actually well over 100 nations that call themselves developing countries.

Of course, that is absurd. Saudi Arabia is in that group, and if it is not developed, it could be.

Of that group, from personal knowledge of very many of them, I think a large majority would agree to a reasonable solution that does provide us with satisfactory access and reasonable terms.

Mr. DE LA GARZA. Well, the leadership in that group of the so-called 77, as you see them operate in Committee I that you have great experience with, is not quite friendly to the United States or the interests of the United States, is it?

Mr. LEVERING. Well, some are, and some are not.

For instance, one of the leaders there is Mr. Thompson Flores of Brazil. The last I heard the United States and Brazil are getting along fine, and Brazil sees a close working association with the United States as a very important part of its future.

That is true of very many other leaders of the Group of 77. For instance, one of the very active ones now is the representative of Chile. I would rather think the present Government of Chile would wish to further the interests of the United States. I am not discounting the fact that the Algerians and some others usually oppose the United States but the United States has many friends in the Group of 77.

Mr. DE LA GARZA. Well, excuse me for interrupting again, but I just wanted to clarify that because international agreement does not necessarily mean the consensus of the membership, but rather you go into voting blocks, and it is not necessarily the best interest of the community of nations, but rather it breaks off into regional or developing nations, or whatever you want to call it.

I want to leave that premise so we do not go under the assumption when we say an international community we mean that every community would have had fair and equal and just treatment.

Mr. LEVERING. I can assure you, sir, that there will be no treaty signed by the United States that does not adequately protect the interests of the United States.

Mr. DE LA GARZA. That you can rest assured.

Mr. LEVERING. That is right, and any agreement which will be reached, and I think can be reached, will be on that premise. The numerous developing countries at this Conference know that anything which they might force through by voting, and did not include the United States and Soviet Union—in general, as you were told yesterday, the United States and the Soviets agree on 90 percent of the issues in the law of the sea—any agreement which did not include these and other large powers would be useless, even if reached. The developing countries know that, and they are not likely to use their voting majority to try to force on us something we cannot accept.

Mr. DE LA GARZA. Please forgive me for interrupting you. You may continue now.

I hope I did not disturb your train of thought.

Mr. LEVERING. Not in the least, and I appreciate the interruption.

Mr. DE LA GARZA. You may continue.

Mr. LEVERING. You did not interrupt me at all, and I intend to go on and discuss the situation in the law of the sea as I see it at the present time.

Mr. DE LA GARZA. You may proceed, sir.

THE TECHNOLOGICAL LEAD

Mr. LEVERING. The third of the arguments which I think does not carry full persuasiveness is the loss of technological lead by the United States. We certainly do not wish to do. But in face of that, the U.S. companies, which are interested in seabed mining, already have formed international consortia with all the major developed countries that might be our competitors, except France.

International Nickel has a consortia that includes the great German group that will be interested, and also a great Japanese group that is a center of economic power, as well as others.

Deepsea Ventures has, of course, a very powerful Belgiam company, one of the largest in the world.

Kennecott has companies in England and Canada and Japan. My guess is that the technology is already in the process of being shared, and I think this is the way things happen in the world now.

The risk is so great politically, as well as economically, that you work together with the companies in the countries that work together with you.

URGENT NEED FOR THE METALS

Now, the statement is made that we need the seabed minerals quickly. But there is at least a 30-year supply of the least plentiful on land, and 100 years supply of others.

Speed in getting these metals for the United States is not important, actually. They say that these would not require us to use foreign exchange, and therefore, would benefit our balance of payments.

It is also true, that with almost no exceptions, we have favorable balances of trade with the countries from which we import these metals. If we cut down imports, they will doubtless find ways to cut down imports from us. On balance, we might be, in the long run, no better off, or even worse.

CARTELS?

Yesterday we had a terrible dragon dragged out before us, a cartel, which was going to surround and eat up the supply and raise the price of these metals for us.

There was at least an indication that Secretary Kissinger was involved in setting up the cartel; that this would be a terrible thing, and so on, and so forth.

Of course, I think first you would want to define a cartel.

A cartel, I believe, is, according to Webster, a combination of producers to limit production and raise prices.

Yesterday, by some strange magic, this was expanded to include commodity agreements between producing and consuming nations which might have no other purpose than to stabilize the price of the commodity with mutual benefits to both the consumer and producers.

For instance, copper in the last few years has varied between 58 cents and $1.10. Such fluctuations at the high level damage us, and at the low level damage somebody else.

Some stabilization might be to our advantage, and to insinuate that our Government, because it is willing to discuss, at least in general terms, a commodity agreement for copper for stabilization of price, and to call that an international cartel, that is about to crawl over and eat us up, is just a stretch of the imagination, in my judgment.

LOSSES TO MINING COMPANIES

Now, there is a very real problem that is raised by proponents, and I certainly have every sympathy with them, and that is that they need money to invest, and they would also not like to see their present investments lying idle.

I certainly would like to see a situation in which they could get money.

I would also like to see their present investment profitably used. I think that is the most valid of the proponents' arguments.

However, I think it might be well to note the size of the investment, and the loss, by letting it lie idle.

The loss in idle investment for all the companies involved, might not be more than $20 million if it was postponed for an extra year, and very much less than that if a decision as to future investment was delayed, say until August, until after the Law of the Sea sessions are through this year.

The statement has been made that decisions have to be made in the next 18 months. That may very well be true, but they do not need to be made, necessarily, in the next 6 months.

While I think there is validity in the argument, I do not think it means, necessarily, passage at this time of this bill.

PROSPECTS FOR A TREATY

Now, let me turn to the argument that there is only a glimmer of hope at the Law of the Sea Conference and that actually there may be not even that. This is a mixed metaphor. Glimmer ought to be a glimmer of light, and I suppose if you carry the metaphor properly, you might say that there is a nonglimmer of darkness, according to some of our witnesses.

From intimate knowledge I think that is simply not true, Mr. Chairman. The intersessional meetings at New York this last February, just a month ago, chaired by Mr. Engo from Cameroon, chairman of Committee I that deals with these matters and participated in by Mr. Thompson Flores of Brazil, representatives from Chile, the Ivory Coast, Singapore and many other from the Group of 77, as well as developed nations, developed a new Engo text to replace part of the single negotiating text which came out in Geneva. The new text makes very marked concessions to the point of view of the United States.

One is the provision that there shall be contracts with companies and other representatives of developed nations. There is no longer any idea that this should be done exclusively by an enterprise under the authority.

There is no provision for production and price control affecting those mining in the ocean. In the past that was one of the old, very strong demands of the producing nations. What has been suggested is that total production from the ocean during an interim period should not be greater than a certain amount. It would not be anyway, because that is all that anybody would want to mine, but this wording would give a sense of security to land-based producers.

The powers of the authority that have been limited to general overall supervision, not arbitrary actions, and subject to review by the Tribunal.

Instead of having an all powerful Assembly, which would be one-nation-one-vote, and would certainly be very dangerous to the United States what the new text proposes is three parallel organs of the Authority.

This would mean that the Council, on which negotiations are not completed, but which would give us good protection, would have the right to carry on the normal operations, and could not be overridden by the Assembly.

There has been very marked improvement in willingness on the part of developing countries to negotiate seriously, and even put on paper things that are acceptable and do protect the interests of the United States.

What will follow, of course, we do not know. The representatives of some developing countries were not present at these meetings. If they are able to convince the Group of 77 that they should turn down the new Engo text, then we are back to square one, and the chances, as Leigh Ratiner told you, of getting agreement this year are very slim.

If, on the other hand, they go along with these, the chances of getting agreement on the general powers and features of a treaty in Committee I are quite good, even this year.

How it turns out we can tell certainly in the next couple of months.

In other words, there has been very real movement, in my judgment, toward a treaty. I agree with many of you that the presence of this legislation in this committee, the fact that it is here, and the technical ability to mine has been a factor in getting more reasonable response.

In other words, if we have the ability to mine, then the fact that sooner or later we will certainly mine, is likely to speed up the negotiating process.

I applaud you in having the hearings here, and I think that serious consideration of what you should do is very much in order. I think that you should be very seriously considering what bill you would actually pass some time next summer or fall, if there is no progress.

WHAT IS BEST FOR THE MINING INDUSTRY

But I think there is a real chance to get something in a treaty which is much more desirable for the American mining industry.

I talked to an official of Tenneco. They have, as you know, withdrawn additional financial support from the consortium that Mr. Fl se of Dee sea Ventures re resents.

This gentleman said he did not want to go out into the ocean unilaterally with a $75 million ship which might be sent to Davey Jones' Locker by a PT boat armed with a Stix missile. He did not want to invest money now in that sort of thing.

He much preferred to go out there under a situation that is generally acceptable, where the danger of harassment would be much less.

I do not know whether his opinion had anything to do with their withdrawing from the consortium, but I do know there are very many members of the hard minerals industry who much prefer a treaty where they will be generally accepted in the oceans than one where they will be, in the eyes of many people, simply taking what does not belong to them.

I know that most responsible members of the mining industry agree that that is the best way to go, through a treaty, and would prefer to do it that way.

DAMAGE TO U.S. INTERESTS

Another reason that I oppose passage at this time is that I think that to pass it now would damage very vital U.S. interests.

As you know, our largest interest is in navigation. We are, by far, the world's maritime Nation. Our world commerce is the greatest.

If we can get a treaty in which these interests are recognized, where we do not need to go through 61 nations' territorial seas or 200-mile economic zones, at their sufferance, to deliver or receive goods from other countries, where oil tankers can go through other countries' waters without harassment, without interdiction as was done at the Suez Canal, this is very important.

The closing of a few straits would be a drastic military problem. Gibralter is one example. Malacca is another. It is much better to have the right to go through, than have the necessity to shoot your way through in an emergency. That is not the best way to operate, if you can avoid it.

The developing world has a large share of the raw material resources. The United States will need to use some of these over a period of years. I think that the terms on which these can be gotten are likely to be much better if these countries feel that they have been fairly treated in the deep seabed, rather than to consider us as taking what they consider is their property equally, without their consent.

I believe you do better in a world where you are considered good neighbors, than if you use your power to take what you want.

REDUCING CONFLICT

The United States has very important interests in stability and orderly development of all the ocean's resources.

It will be of great advantage to the United States if, through a treaty, we know where the outer limit of our economic zone is, rather than have somebody say it is theirs, and we say it is ours. Unilateral carving up of the oceans would be like the dividing up of Africa

160 years ago, which benefitted no one, and brought all kinds of conflict.

The difference now is it might escalate into use of weapons that can destroy all of us. If we can settle the issues in the ocean, such as oil and fisheries, peacefully, it is immensely better.

The United States has more interest in stability and peace in the world than any other country. because we have more to lose. So if we can achieve this, that is all to the good.

The next witness, Dick Frank, will tell you more about the environmental problems, but I think we may make some minor steps for protection of the ocean environment, particularly of the deep ocean, if we can get a treaty. At least, an international body would have the right to set environmental standards there.

If ocean mining is done catch as catch can, some development of the deep ocean probably will be the cheapest and the dirtiest.

FISHING AND WORLD HUNGER

I think that the problem of conservation of the oceans' living resources, and their relation to world hunger can best be dealt with through a treaty.

I hope that the countries, in assuming a 200-mile fishing jurisdiction, will also assume the responsibility to conserve the stock,s which they do not necessarily do, and I would hope even to have some monitoring of their conservation practices.

I would hope that there would be an agreement that if they are not harvesting the proper amount of catch, they would allow other countries to catch the difference, and provide protein for hungry people.

At present, there are 5 million metric tons of fish going to waste off of southern Argentina each year. They claim a 200-mile territorial sea, and they are not catching these fish the last I heard, they do not want others to catch them.

I would like to see an obligation and responsibility for conservation and full utilization fixed in the treaty, as well as the authority to conserve fish in the 200-mile zone.

A treaty is likely to provide ocean scientists with some protection for basic scientific research, not enough, but considerable in the economic zone, more than they would have without a treaty.

SURVIVAL

A very large interest of the United States and the world is in survival.

We, in the religious groups for whom I speak, are simply terrified at the direction in which the nuclear arms race is going.

Two nation nuclear deterrence may work because if one nation hits you, you know where the attack came from, and it will be wiped out also. But with 22, how can you tell? One hundred and twenty two is completely unmanageable, and that is the direction it is going. Unless such weapons as these can be brought under control, and not too long down the road, the future for mankind is very dim, indeed.

Now, armaments are sort of the citadel of national arrogance, and you do not take the citadel first. You have to first get an agreement on the kind of controls which are workable, and an organization that is workable somewhere elsewhere.

We have at least some chance, I think perhaps a 50–50 chance, of getting that kind of control for the deep seabed with an organization with its own money, peaceful enforcement, voting which is neither veto or one nation—one vote, a tribunal with compulsory jurisdiction—a model that can be adapted and applied to armament control and disarmament.

This may be a vain hope, but if so, the hope for mankind is also a vain hope. You have to make progress where you can toward a world in which danger is very much less. In our judgment, the deep seabed is the one place now, and in the next 10 years where you have a chance to start over again if you wish to build an international organization that is really workable for arms control.

The United Nations, as it is now, is not a workable model for arms control.

You will have to start over again, and you can do that in the deep seabed.

IN SUMMARY

This bill assumes, that the interest of the United States are best protected, since we have the technology and the gunboats, by uni lateral action. I do not think so.

I think the interests of the United States are best protected by making every effort to get a treaty which (1) protects the interests of the United States, (2) is considered fair and just by the world generally, and (3) makes real progress toward the kind of organization and peaceful enforcement which could be applied, at least to nuclear weapons.

Therefore every effort should be made to get that sort of a treaty, and this bill should be held in abeyance

I would be sorry if it came to the floor, and was defeated, because I think that would remove pressure toward a treaty I do not think it should be taken to the floor.

If it is taken to the floor, it should be defeated, but I think that would send a mixed message. The best message is that it is here, and you will act if that is what has to be done.

If you do wish to pass unilateral legislation later, much less damage would be done to have legislation providing insurance, but not for a specific site, simply under the doctrine of freedom of the high seas that our mineral people have a right to go and get nodules, which we assert. Since no specific area is named, this is at least plausible.

This would, I think, provide a tideover until something better can be reached. That will take an entire rewriting of the bill.

I was asked by one of the officials of one of the departments who testified before you to help write such a bill, because they thought I was an expert, and I suppose that I am.

It may be that I will help write such a bill in the future. At the present time I think what you should do is hold the bill in the committee, and consider each new development in light of what happens.

Thank you, sir.

Mr. DE LA GARZA. Thank you very much, Mr. Levering.

Mr. Forsythe?

Mr. FORSYTHE. Thank you very much, Mr. Chairman.

I have just a few brief questions.

Mr. Levering, do you agree with several witnesses that pretty much indicated that these present two sessions perhaps of the law of the sea, the ones starting next week, and the one later in the summer, may well be the last chance to pull this together, that unless this movement is sufficient it will be a long time down the road?

Mr. LEVERING. I notice, in talking to delegates from the Group of 77, that a good many of them feel yes, that if there is not real progress this year, that that is it, and it will be catch as catch can, and many of them know that they will suffer too, and perhaps particularly so under those conditions.

When you get successful negotiations, sir, I think it is when people see that their interests are served thereby, and I think the reason that you are getting concessions from the Group of 77 is that they see that their interests would be served in reaching a treaty.

I think our interests would be served also, and I think this is the reason there is a chance of movement, but if nothing happens this year the chance of getting an agreement later is very much less.

I do not say it is the last chance, but at least it will be a largely decreased chance.

Mr. FORSYTHE. Do you believe the signals of this first session in the next 8 weeks are going to be sufficient to indicate progress, perhaps another session this year?

Mr. LEVERING. I think they will be very indicative.

Actually, after the signals of this week and next week from the Group of 77, after that adjourns, and I have talked to some of my friends in that group, I could give you a very good assessment of how much chance there was of reaching agreement this year, unless they reverse themselves, but I think certainly by the end of August we will pretty well know what the situation is.

Mr. FORSYTHE. You are telling me that they probably will know by the middle of May, even earlier than that, the end of the first 8 weeks, but now you have slipped to August already.

Mr. LEVERING. I say that supposing the signs at the end of these 2 weeks is not clear, then you can get some considerable clarification at the end of the 8 week session.

If it is still not clear, then a summer session will tell the tale, in my opinion.

Mr. FORSYTHE. Is it not going to be more difficult if those signals do not come on fairly strong, really in this first session this year?

Mr. LEVERING. Yes, if they are not strong, that makes it more difficult, and the chances are less.

Mr. FORSYTHE. Very much less?

Mr. LEVERING. Yes, I would say very much less.

Mr. FORSYTHE. Really, I am leading to the point that just normal process of this great institution toward early enactment of legisla tion it would seem automatically to provide the time frame within which these signals are going to be very, very clear.

It does seem to me that we should not just sit back and let things drift here, because if, in fact, there is not an ability to come up with a satisfactory resolution, then we are losing a lot of time that may well be important, because I would like to move to the question even if there is success, and acceptable success, so far as our positions are concerned in either the first session or the second section, ratification is going to be a long and tedious process.

Now, I know there is talk of an interim measure.

What do you anticipate, taking the best of all roads that we are going to get agreement?

How soon?

Could an interim measure have sufficient support to be valid?

Mr. LEVERING. Well, there is wide acceptance at the Law of the Sea Conference for including a provision for provisional application of the treaty in this area, which would mean that mining could get underway very quickly prior to ratification.

Ratification by enough nations may be 6 or 8 years away, but I am certain that the United States would insist that it would be accepted, that provisional application of the treaty should get under way upon signature of the treaty, which would mean we could get mining under way very quickly.

Mr. FORSYTHE. That presumes that ultimately, at least for the United States, that it would be a treaty that would be ratifiable.

Mr. LEVERING. That is right. In my judgment, the United States will not sign a treaty that is not ratifiable. I think negotiators at least realize that.

You may differ with them on some things, but I think they know what they face on the Hill.

Mr. FORSYTHE. I am not sure we feel quite that way in some of the negotiations that we have been laboring with here for many, many years.

Mr. LEVERING. I agree with you in other areas.

Mr. Forsythe, we have an ideal setup in the Law of the Sea from one standpoint. The oil industry, Exxon, Gulf and others sit at the side of the one who negotiates when oil interests are involved.

The hard minerals people sit beside the one who is negotiating here, and so on and so on; and I think that realism is forced by those people who will be greatly affected. Maybe that is good.

Mr. FORSYTHE. Well, I hope so.

Thank you, Mr. Chairman.

Mr. LEVERING. Maybe I sit by the side of the oil interests and you would be surprised that we agree on most things.

When the Quakers and Gulf Oil agree, then maybe that is some indication of their looking for common ground.

Mr. FORSYTHE. It gets down to that sticky, 10, 15 or 20 percent, really.

Thank you again, Mr. Chairman.

Mr. LEVERING. I would differ with Gulf on bribery, for instance.

Mr. DE LA GARZA. Mr. Oberstar?

Mr. OBERSTAR. Thank you, Mr. Chairman.

Mr. Levering, what is your position on the 200-mile limit bill that passed the House and the Senate?

Mr. LEVERING. You know, sir, that I testified here, and probably you were here, very strongly in favor of using the Geneva Convention of 1958 for immediate unilateral conservation of fish off our shores.

I knew that conservation was essential and I dug this method up and, as you know, it got rather substantial support in the Senate with the Cranston-Griffin Amendment.

I say now that the way it passed the Senate I certainly am not one who worries too much about it. Conservation is needed. Conservation is provided for, and the date is set late enough so it gives the Law of the Sea a reasonable chance to reach agreement.

Mr. OBERSTAR. Do you see a substantial difference between the 200-mile limit bill as passed, House or Senate, either one, and the Deep Sea Minerals bill?

Mr. LEVERING. Yes, I do; a very sharp difference.

The 200-mile fishery limit bill is, in my opinion, going to do very little damage to our chances of getting a treaty, because it is in line with the consensus already achieved that the coastal States should have fishery management and preference out to 200 miles.

Mr. OBERSTAR. What do you think?

Mr. LEVERING. But the hard mineral bill is quite the opposite.

This would set the precedent for any nation to go out and start mining at this time, which would be against the consensus that has been reached, which is that it should be under international supervision, and would be deeply resented.

I think passing this at this time would have a destructive effect on the Law of the Sea Conference.

I do not think the 200-mile fishery bill will make a major difference.

Mr. OBERSTAR. What do you think about action on this legislation, the Deep Sea Minerals legislation in the event an agreement is not reached in the Law of the Sea on seabed mining?

Mr. LEVERING. If, at the end of August, there has been no agreement, an agreement is not in sight, then I think very probably unilateral legislation should be passed of the insurance type that I suggested. This would not assert any really special right to any specific area.

What is necessary to facilitate mining probably should be done at that time.

That, sir, is my present opinion.

Mr. OBERSTAR. If I understand the rest of your testimony properly, you do not see resource cartels as a threat to the United States.

Mr. LEVERING. In these minerals.

Mr. OBERSTAR. You do not see a pressing U.S. need for the minerals on the sea bottom. You do see the developing nations giving the United States favorable treatment if we keep our hands off the minerals on a unilateral basis.

Mr. LEVERING. Yes, such a treaty is possible.

Mr. OBERSTAR. That is a rosy view of the international scene that I hope our negotiators in New York will not share.

Thank you, Mr. Chairman.

Mr. DE LA GARZA. Mr. Levering, the chairman left a list of questions that he was going to ask you had he been here, and I must apologize for the chairman not being here. He is detained in the Rules Committee trying to secure a rule for other legislation passed by this subcommittee.

Would it be possible to submit these questions to you now, sir, and you return them with your answers for the record at a later time?

Mr. LEVERING. I will be very glad to do so, Mr. Chairman.

Mr. DE LA GARZA. We will do that, and see that the staff gets the questions to you that have been left with me by the chairman.

I just have a couple of further questions.

You mentioned briefly that we, or the United States, was attempt to act unilaterally because we have the gunboats or some statement to that effect.

What I want to ask you is this: other states have acted unilaterally in the fisheries, for example, and have no gunboats at all.

How would you relate that with your statement that we act because we have the gunboats?

Mr. LEVERING. Well, there was at least a debate as to the control of fish offshore and as to action by Ecuador. By the way, their gunboats have gone out and arrested our ships.

Iceland has made such assertions and such gunboats as they have have been harassing the British trawlers.

I would say that nations that have made such assertions, if they have been contested, have used whatever military power they have.

Mr. DE LA GARZA. But their power is minimal.

Chile went out 2,000 miles and I doubt that they have a gunboat.

Mr. LEVERING. But they may think that it is nice to claim, even if you cannot defend it right now. You might defend it later on, sir.

Mr. DE LA GARZA. Well, I just did not feel right to leave the statement unchallenged, that we are going out because we have the gunboats. That is what the Committee of 77 is always accusing us of, and the rest of the world is accusing us of that, and I sort of do not feel right that one of our own here should be saying the same thing, probably not thinking about it in that respect.

Mr. LEVERING. It is simply that power is a factor, sir, in the world today.

Mr. DE LA GARZA. It sure has not been at the United Nations lately.

Mr. LEVERING. Not in votes, but a lot of those resolutions have not amounted to anything anyway, and they should not.

Mr. DE LA GARZA. The only power we have there is sending an Irishman that spoke his mind as our Ambassador.

Mr. LEVERING. Sometimes that is pretty effective. Sometimes it causes more trouble by insulting other people.

Mr. DE LA GARZA. I do not think he insulted anyone. I think he spoke the truth, but that is a matter of personal opinion.

We thank you very much for your contribution today.

Does counsel have any further questions?

Mr. PERIAN. Chairman Murphy has some questions he would like presented to the witness for response.

Mr. DE LA GARZA. We will submit the questions by Chairman Murphy, and if counsel has anything further in the way of clarify ing questions, he will submit them to you.

We appreciate very much your contribution and your appearance here this morning.

Mr. LEVERING. Thank you, sir.

[The questions and responses by Mr. Levering follow:]

QUESTIONS FOR SAMUEL LEVERING FROM CHAIRMAN JOHN M. MURPHY

1. What do you mean when you say the Commission is a "private public interest group"?

Where does your funding come from?

2. What are the Committee's activities?

What do your Honorary Chairmen, Justice Arthur Goldberg and Governor Francis Sargent, do for the Committee?

3. You say at the outset of your statement that your Committee is "dedicated to achieving just and effective ocean treaties." What treaties, to date, has the Committee dedicated itself to?

What role did it play in achieving those "just and effective" treaties?

4. You say that you support the basic principles of U.S. proposals for the forthcoming Law of the Sea Conference." Could you enumerate these "basic principles" which you support?

Do you support even those principles which seem to run directly contrary to basic U.S. interests?

5. You say at the beginning of your statement that "we know that no generally recognized international law now covers deep seabed hard mineral mining."

Are you familiar with the concept of freedom of the high seas? Wouldn't that apply to the exercise of the right to exploit the minerals lying beyond national jurisdiction?

What about the 1958 Geneva Convention on the High Seas? Although deep sea mining is not expressly mentioned, it has been explained to this Committee that mining is clearly one of the freedoms covered in the Convention.

6. I think you have misunderstood the purposes of this bill. You assert that because no generally recognized international law covers deep sea mining, proponents of this legislation have urged Congress to take unilateral action. In fact, however, the purpose of this legislation is to provide the "security of tenure" which industry needs in order to proceed with the costly development of technology *under existing law.* We are making *no new* and *illegal* claims with respect to the deep seabed. We are only making certain guarantees to the American mining industry.

7. You emphasize on p. 1 of your statement that this legislation would authorize the Secretary of Commerce to issue licenses *"before* there is *any international agreement."*

I would like to make two points: First, what would be the point of enacting such legislation *after* an international agreement had been reached? Supposedly if an agreement were reached, that treaty would spell out the procedures for mining the seabed, and make domestic legislation necessary. What you must understand is that we are considering this legislation precisely because *we do not see an agreement forthcoming.*

My second point is that if a treaty *were* to be agreed upon, then American ocean mining companies would be forced to accept the conditions of that agreement. This legislation in no way, as you put it, "preempts the Law of the Sea," but rather provides certain protections in the absence of a treaty and certain insurance in the event a treaty harmful to U.S. mining interests is signed.

8. I do not like the way you refer to the United States "taking possession of the sites prior to general agreement at the Law of the Sea Conference."

The U.S. would not be "taking possession of the sites" in the sense that we might be annexing territory, but rather would only be granting licenses to mine, the nodules located at the site under *specific conditions* for a *specified* amount of time.

9. Could you explain how you feel enactment of the legislation would make "attainment of vital objectives of the U.S. at the Law of the Sea Conference much more difficult, if not impossible?" (p. 1)

10. Could you also explain how enactment of this legislation might "result in the break-up of the Law of the Sea Conference?" (p. 1) On what do you base that opinion?

11. You state repeatedly that you believe passage of this bill would damage the chances for reaching a settlement, would cause the Conference to break up, and then on p. 2 you say that it would actually "injure all these (U.S.) interests." Why do you think passage would actually hurt U.S. interests?

12. Do you think the United States should do everything in its power to reach a settlement at the Law of the Sea, even if it means conceding on certain points which might run counter to U.S. interests?

13. Are you aware that even the negotiators at the Law of the Sea Conference have testified before this Committee that the Engo and Pinto documents which emerged from the Geneva session last year were "unmitigated disasters?"

Would you recommend that the U.S. sign a treaty along the lines of those documents?

14. Mr. Ratiner, chief U.S. negotiator at the Law of the Sea Conference on deep sea mining issues, has characterized the current status of the negotiations as providing only a "glimmer of hope."

Do you still think the U.S. should pursue that elusive treaty?

15. What would you say to the American mining industry spokesmen who claim that further delay severely harms their interests?

16. You say we should wait for a treaty. Certain experts say that we will never obtain an acceptable treaty.

My question is, what benefit is gained by waiting for something that will never arrive? Aren't we in effect "waiting for Godot?"

17. Do you favor the establishment of an international regime which would place a great deal of power in an Assembly?

Aren't you afraid that in such an Assembly where each country has only one vote, policies might be pursued which are directly contrary to U.S. interests?

If yes, then what would the U.S. do: follow the will of the majority or violate international law?

18. I don't understand how on page 2 of your statement you logically arrive at the point where passage of the bill would cause higher taxes to the American taxpayers and would cause us to become increasingly dependent on raw materials from abroad.

It would seem to me that costs would be lower and we would have a more secure domestic supply of minerals if this legislation were enacted.

Would you care to comment?

19. Couldn't we achieve some of the same objectives in bilateral and multilateral agreements if we could not achieve a satisfactory treaty at the Law of the Sea Conference?

20. On page 3 of your statement you predict that if a treaty were not signed, "an unprecedented opportunity to move toward a new political and economic order is lost."

Aren't you concerned that we may just be participating in the establishment of commodity cartels which, if used politically as the oil cartel has been, could cause our economic strangulation?

21. On the last page of your statement you make two points which should be studied together.

First, you state that "much of the world's raw material resources are in the hands of developing countries."

You then recommend pursuing the orderly development of ocean resources "in a fashion which is considered equitable and just by developing countries."

I am concerned that the less developed countries which are land-based producers of minerals will pursue their own self-interest and prohibit through international institutions, such as the Assembly, the development of seabed minerals in order to protect their exports of minerals. Would you care to comment on this?

ANSWERS TO CHAIRMAN MURPHY'S QUESTIONS TO SAMUEL LEVERING

1. A privately funded group, working for the public interest. No member will gain financially from the success of the Committee's work.

All funds come from individuals, chiefly Quakers. The total income, and expenditures of the Committee, including office, salaries, travel, expenses for volunteers, supplies, telephone, etc., are less than $9,000 a year.

2. The Committee works exclusively on matters related to the law of Sea Conference, prospective treaties, related legislation, etc.

Honorary Chairmen, Justice Goldberg and Governor Sargent, provide advice and support.

3. We are working to achieve just and effective ocean treaties at the Law of the Sea Conference.

I am a member of the Advisory Committee to the United States Delegation to the Law of the Sea Conference. I have also attended the Conference sessions at Caracas (10 weeks in the summer of 1974) and Geneva (8 weeks in the spring of 1975). We have had input at both levels.

4. Some basic U.S. principles which we support are:

(a) To clearly define coastal state and international community rights in narrow territorial seas, an economic zone, and the sea beyond.

(b) To ensure freedom of the seas and the air space above for navigation, transportation, communications, and scientific research.

(c) To prevent ocean pollution, to conserve marine life, and to regulate fisheries for optimal sustainable yield.

(d) To establish an effective international authority to supervise the development and use of the resources of the deep seabed for the benefit of all mankind.

(e) To reduce conflict and create stability and security of investments, both oil and mineral, by a clear, equitable and effective treaty for the seabed.

We believe that all these principles are in the U.S. interest, and that none are contrary to it.

5. We are very familiar with the concept of Freedom of the High Seas and with the 1958 Geneva Convention on the High Seas.

But freedom to fish is very different from "freedom" to license a specific area of the international seabed for mining, exclusive relative to other U.S. nationals or those of "reciprocating states".

Whether the United States has such a "right" is very much at issue, with most nations now holding that it has no such right.

6. This is a matter of judgment. To license specific sites, in our view, is to assert a new claim, which many nations would consider illegal.

For U.S. companies to recover nodules, and for the U.S. Government to enact legislation insuring against certain types of risks under certain conditions, without specifying sites, would be less questionable.

7. In our judgment, domestic legislation would be necessary after a treaty is signed, to implement the treaty for U.S. companies. Legislation also would be desirable, as the treaty is being signed, to cover provisional application of this part of the treaty immediately after signature, without waiting for the ratification process.

Passing the present bill would set up a temporary ocean mining system, giving companies rights to up to an estimated 400 million pounds of nickel, copper, and cobalt for $50,000. No widely acceptable treaty is likely to be such a give-away. Passage of this bill would be a constraint against treaty agreement and ratification and a built in loss to U.S. taxpayers if a treaty was ratified.

8. This again is a matter of judgment.

Granting long term license to mine is taking possession of those sites, even though they would be relinquished, after many years, minus their wealth. Agreed, this is not annexing territory, but it is taking the chief value of that territory, without compensation to those who believe that it is as much theirs as ours.

9 For example, vital objectives of the United States include general recognition, through a widely accepted treaty, of freedom of navigation, including unimpeded transit through straits. If this bill should prevent a treaty, this vital U S. interest would be less well protected, and the objective would not be attained.

10. There would be severe reaction by many delegations if this bill was enacted. I know many of these delegates personally.

11. U.S. interests, in our judgment, would be best served by a widely acceptable treaty. Passage of this legislation, would decrease the chances to get such a treaty.

12. The United States should do all that it can to get a widely acceptable treaty that furthers U.S. interests. No concession should be made which seriously damages any important long term interest of the United States.

13. The single negotiating text proposed by Chairman Engo was unsatisfactory to the United States. We, and everyone else, would oppose the U.S. signing a treaty with those provisions.

The proposed Pinto single negotiating test has not been called an "unmitigated disaster" by any U.S. negotiator to our knowledge. With modifications it could be made acceptable to the United States.

14. In our judgment there is much more than "a glimmer of hope" of reaching an acceptable treaty. We believe that the United States should continue to pursue that objective.

15. We would say that six months delay, in our judgment, will not seriously harm their interests. We would also say that the broader interests of the United States should take precedence over the minor loss which might result from that delay.

16. Again this is a matter of judgment. We believe that the gain if a treaty is reached far outweighs the minor loss from a shortterm delay.

17. No, we do not favor the establishment of an International Seabed Authority with an all powerful Assembly based on one nation-one vote.

There is no possibility that the United States would sign such a treaty.

18. Taxpayers would pay if losses occurred, which is very possible if the U.S. licensed sites before making a full effort to achieve a treaty.

Consumers would suffer if raw materials of all types from developing countries were less available.

If seabed minerals were produced by U.S. companies under a widely acceptable treaty, all U.S. interests would benefit.

19. Yes, but in most cases, only partially. If no generally acceptable treaty can be obtained, this should be the next U.S. effort; rather than unilateral action. It is better to get agreement first, rather than say "we are doing it this way—won't you do it our way?"

20. The great opportunity is to establish a workable organization for the deep seabed, without the defests of the U.N., which can be a model for arms control and disarmament. It could also be a successful example of all nations working together to develop an important economic resource for their common benefit.

In our judgment, there is little danger of producer cartels for these metals. There could be a commodity agreement to stabilize the price of copper, which might benefit both consumers and producers.

21. I share your concern. The provisions of the treaty and the structure and voting, the tribunal, and other safeguards in the International Seabed Resources Authority must make certain that this does not happen.

Mr. DE LA GARZA. Our next witness will be Mr. Richard A. Frank, representing the Environmental Defense Fund, and the Center for Law and Social Policy.

STATEMENT OF RICHARD FRANK, REPRESENTING THE ENVIRONMENTAL DEFENSE FUND AND THE CENTER FOR LAW AND SOCIAL POLICY

Mr. FRANK. Mr. Congressman, members of the committee:

I am Richard Frank of the Center for Law and Social Policy in Washington.

Mr. DE LA GARZA. May I interrupt, please, sir?

Would you like to submit your full statement for the record and then paraphrase it if you like?

At this hour, we may be running short of time, just before the noon recess, or you may proceed in whichever way you would prefer to do it.

Mr. FRANK. I would like to summarize my comments, Mr. Congressman, and then have the written statement submitted for the record. I can summarize in about 10 minutes.

Mr. DE LA GARZA. Very well.

Your full statement will appear in the record at this point as though given, and you may continue.

[The prepared statement of Mr. Frank follows:]

STATEMENT OF RICHARD A. FRANK. REPRESENTING THE ENVIRONMENTAL DEFENSE FUND. THE ENVIRONMENTAL POLICY CENTER. THE FRIENDS OF THE EARTH. THE NATIONAL AUDUBON SOCIETY, THE NATURAL RESOURCES DEFENSE COUNCIL, AND THE SIERRA CLUB

Mr. Chairman, Members of the Committee, I am Richard Frank, of the Center for Law and Social Policy in Washington. I appreciate the opportunity to appear today on behalf of six environmental groups—the Environmental Defense Fund, the Environmental Policy Center, the Friends of the Earth, the National Audubon Society, the Natural Resources Defense Council, and the Sierra Club.[1] These national, non-profit organizations, with a combined membership of more than 590,000, have long taken an active interest in protecting the marine environment. They have had a particular interest in the environmental implications of deepsea mining, and have presented their views to the government on this subject in connection with their participation on the Secretary of State's Advisory Committee on the Law of the Sea and through testimony to Congressional committees relating to deep seabed hard minerals legislation similar to H.R. 6017 and H.R. 11879.

In past testimony before Congress, the environmental organizations advocated that it would be unwise at that time to enact legislation which would authorize deepsea mining licensing, exploration, and commercial development. The two basic reasons for that view were (1) that international agreement was an indispensable means to effective environmental regulation of the development of deep ocean resources and that the passage of domestic legislation could adversely affect the possibility of reaching such agreement through the Law of the Sea negotiations, and (2) that adequate environmental analysis had not been undertaken to provide Congress with even a primary understanding of the environmental implications of any legislation sanctioning or promoting deepsea mining.

The situation has somewhat changed, and therefore the nature and focus of this testimony is different.

First, it now seems clear that the international community either will or will not have a Law of the Sea treaty as a result of a conference scheduled to begin next week in New York and a second conference predicted for the summer. Under such circumstances, it does not appear illogical for Congress now to fashion domestic legislation which, in the normal course of events, could be passed at the end of these Conferences and which can easily mesh with the international system developed at the Conference, if the negotiations are successful.

[1] EDF, whose principal place of business is 162 Old Town Road. East Sautauket, NY 11733. has a membership of approximately 57,000 persons and a 700-member Scientists' Advisory Committee. including members residing in 18 foreign countries. EPC, whose principal place of business is 324 C Street, SE. Washington, DC 20003, is a privately funded organization engaging in research, analysis, and representation on energy-connected environmental issues. FOE, whose principal place of business is 529 Commercial Street, San Francisco. CA 94111, has a membership of 20,000 persons and is affiliated with "sister organizations" in 12 foreign countries. The National Audubon Society, whose principal place of business is 950 Third Avenue, New York, NY 10022, has a membership of approximately 340,000 persons. including members in more than 100 foreign countries. NRDC, whose principal office is 15 West 44th Street, New York, NY 10035, and which has additional offices in Washington. DC and Palo Alto. CA, has a membership of approximately 20,000 persons, including members residing in 8 foreign countries. The Sierra Club, whose principal place of business is at 530 Bush Street. San Francisco. CA 94108, has a membership of approximately 150,000 persons, including persons residing in 67 foreign countries.

Second, during prior testimony we expressed a concern in promoting or sanctioning deep sea mining without adequate environmental research and analysis to provide Congress and the American public with a reasonable prediction of what the environmental impacts would be. We remain concerned over the absence of environmental background, but no longer believe that it should be a basis for not proceeding. Indeed, sound legislation would require that environmental studies be undertaken and environmental regulations be imposed and therefore would be an inducement to proceed in an environmentally prudent manner.

Nonetheless, I would like to reiterate the problems being caused by the failure of the Department of the Interior and the Department of Commerce to undertake timely and comprehensive environmental analyses. The reform and extent of the environmental impact from deep seabed mining is, at present, impossible to predict with any degree of accuracy because of the lack of detailed measures relating to, and limited knowledge about, the environments being considered and insufficient data and analysis to forecast the impacts that would be created by large-scale mining operations. Part of the problem is the inherent difficulty of forecasting the effects of a new and developing technology. But the key constraint has been the inadequacy of the government's environmental research and analysis. The government, with an uncoordinated program, has been slow in moving forward with research, e.g., the collection of baseline data. It has thus far failed to establish an adequate work plan to interpret such data and to predict environmental effects on the basis of that data and possible disturbances caused by mining. And, perhaps far more disturbing, the government has not yet committed itself to assessing, nor has developed work plans to assess, such basic and fundamental issues as (a) the impacts at sea and onshore of processing, and (b) the comparative impacts of land and ocean mining. We believe an analysis of comparative impacts is critical; for if deepsea mining is environmentally preferable to onland mining, those concerned with the environment may wish strongly to support the development of deepsea mining. Finally, even in those areas where the government is undertaking analysis, it is proceeding in a rather informal fashion. For example, although industry has indicated a willingness to provide a substantial amount of environmental information, the government has not, in writing, requested that essential information. I mention the above failures of the government to fulfill responsibly its environmental responsibilities because I hope this subcommittee, in its efforts to see that a sensible domestic system is formulated, will assert what influence and pressure it can on the Executive branch in the hope that the Executive branch would do what it should in the environmental area.

In prior testimony, because we believed the passage of domestic legislation should not occur, we did not focus on specific provisions of the bills before Congress. In light of the above comments on timing and environmental analysis, we believe the time is ripe to focus on the specific provisions of the legislation.

The bills. as drafted, should not be passed, and we could not support them. These bills, after all, are essentially the drafts submitted by the mining industry: while they may satisfy the needs of the industry, they should be modified to take into account other parts of the national interest, including environmental protection. Subject to the above comments on timing and environmental analysis, we believe the bills, properly modified, should be passed. The following comments point to specific provisions which are unsatisfactory as drafted and which should be changed and the comments recommend changes. They also point out issues which are not addressed in these bills but which should be addressed in order to make the legislation environmentally acceptable. Most of the comments below do not include recommended language changes. but we would be happy to provide those if the Chairman believes they would be useful. (Our references, unless otherwise stated, are to H.R. 11879.)

1. *The assumption that deepsea mining should be promoted.*—One of the underlying assumptions of the bills is that deepsea mining should be promoted by the U.S. because of possible future supply needs and in light of other factors relating to the national interest. We do not believe that such a conclusion, at present, could be a reasoned judgment because of the incomplete

information on resource need and on environmental impact. The bills should be changed to reflect that many unknowns still exist about resource need, environmental impact, etc., and that these must be resolved by the Executive branch before taking specific steps outlined in the bills.

Section 2(b)(1) of H.R. 11879 states that the purpose of the Act is "to establish a national program to promote the orderly development of certain hard mineral resources of the deep seabed". We do not believe that Congress, on the basis of information before it, can state so categorically that development of deepsea mining should be promoted. In Section 2(a)(7), it is said that it is in the "national interest of the United States to utilize existing technology and capabilities of United States mining companies". No one, including Congress, knows whether existing technology and capabilities are, from an environmental point of view, acceptable; in light of that, Congress should not make a judgment that existing technology should be utilized.

2. *Relationship to envirInmental impact statement and NEPA.*—The bills do not adequately express what we believe to be the intent of Congress with respect to the preparation of environmental impact statements and the opportunity for public input. Under Section 7, "objective environmental standards" are to be established; under Section 19, the responsible government agency is to issue rules and regulations including, *inter alia*, those related to "environmental standards and compliance"; and under Section 5, a decision must be made by the responsible government agency that a prospective licensee will operate in accordance with "guidelines and standards" and that operations under the license will not pose a threat to the marine environment.

In our discussions with members of the Committee staff, we have been led to believe that it is the intent of Congress that the National Environmenal Policy Act should be fully followed, but that it was not necessary to so indicate explicitly in the legislation or to indicate when environmental impact statements would be needed. A programatic environmental impact statement should be prepared before licensing is permitted; regulations should be accompanied by an environmental impact statement; and a project environmental impact statement will be needed before each license can be issued. It would be highly preferable if the legislation spelled this out. Some commentators (the Marine Boatrd Panel of the National Academy of Sciences) have gone further and suggested that regional environmental impact statements should be prepared; we are inclined to believe that regional impact statement may be unnecessary if the programatic statements and individual project statements are adequate, but that is the type of issue that should be considered by this committee.

3. *Timing and standards for environmental guidelines.*—The bills state that licenses may only be issued after the responsible government official determines "that operations under the license will not pose an unreasonable threat to the integrity of the marine environment and that all reasonable precautions will be taken to minimize any adverse effects in that environment." First, as noted earlier, environmental guidelines and standards are to be promulgated. It should be explicitly stated that no license will be issued until the environmental guidelines and standards are prepared. Such an inhibition appears in some bills before Congress, but is not stated in H.R. 6017 or H.R. 11879. Second, the bills set forth, as the underlying standard for environmental guidelines, a best-available-technology requirement.

4. *Prototype or pilot project testing.*—It has been generally agreed by industry, the scientific community, the Executive branch, and the environmental community, that the full implications of a major deepsea mining program will not be understood until we have been able to monitor and analyze the impacts of a few mining operations. We believe, therefore, it is essential that licensing should proceed cautiously and be limited to prototype and pilot projects in the first instance. It would be understood that earlier determinations regarding environmental standards can and will be modified as more information becomes available as a result of the projects and that continued monitoring will occur. These bills do not suggest proceeding with prototype or pilot projects, in their first instance, and they should be changed to state such a policy.

5. *EPA responsibility for environmental standards and enforcement.*—H.R. 6017 places most of the Executive branch authority in the Department of

the Interior. H.R. 11879 places that responsibility in the Department of Commerce. Two types of responsibilities are included, one oriented toward promotion of deep seabed mining and economic regulation, and the other toward environmental standard-setting and enforcement. Environmental protection can be assured only if the same agency is not assigned the responsibility both of promotion and also of environmental regulation. Such dual and some cross-purpose jurisdiction represents an inevitable, potential conflict of interest and results in non-objective decision-making, benefiting those who favor development and harming the national interest. The agency best suited for environmental standard-setting and enforcement duties of the type in question is the Environmental Protection Agency which has responsibilities of this nature in various other areas. Without answering whether the Department of the Interior or the Department of Commerce should be seized with any regulatory or promotional functions, the Environmental Protection Agency should have jurisdiction for environmental regulation. The approval of two agencies would determine the applicant complies with environmental standards, and the other agency would determine perhaps the economic or royalty considerations.

6. *Scope of regulation.*—It is our understanding that the intent of Congress in these bills is that all aspects of deepsea mining would be regulated. However, the bills speak about authorizing "development" of hard mineral resources. "Development" is defined in Section 3(f) as "any operation of exploration and commercial recovery, other than prospecting for the purpose of discovery, recovery, or delivery of hard minerals from the deep seabed." One could misinterpret the bills by concluding that authorization is required for, and regulations and standards apply to, only retrieval and not, for example, processing at sea or other such activities. The bill should be amended explicitly to point out that it covers all activities at sea including retrieval and processing. Furthermore, Congress should consider whether some generic, but perhaps not site-specific, decisions relating to activities on land, such as onland processing, should also be covered.

7. *Jurisdiction.*—The jurisdictional provisions of the bills are quite broad but somewhat vague. U.S. companies have already forewarned the government that if standards by the government are, in the view of the companies, too high or if other countries have significantly lower standards giving competitive advantages to entities operating under their jurisdiction, U.S. companies would attempt to avoid U.S. controls, and mining vessels might fly foreign flags and/or they might incorporate abroad subsidiaries or consortia with which they are associated. But, the U.S. has the responsibility to control those companies in such circumstances when the result may be significant adverse environmental impacts in the ocean. And, of course, if development of U.S. mining industry is in the national .interest, control over that industry is in the national interest. As a consequence, the bills should make clear that they cover U.S. nationals under all circumstances. Jurisdiction should extend to U.S. nationals or subsidiaries of U.S. nationals, even when they are operating a vessel flying a foreign flag, and should extend to activities of consortia which can be said to be controlled by US. nationals.

8. *Preservation of certain areas.*—Until recent years, the earth's resources have most often been exploited without regard to the need to preserve at last some wilderness areas in their natural state for observation, study, enjoyment and use by future generations. It is important that the deep oceans and seabed not suffer for the lack of foresight in this regard. These bills should contain a mandate for the responsible government agency to identify adequate numbers of ocean blocks to be set aside and made not subject to licensing for exploration or commercial development.

9. *Relationships with foreign countries and reciprocity.*—The U.S. has an interest in assuring that other countries adopt adequate environmental regulatory systems, both because the adverse environmental impact of foreign mining vessels effect the oceans and the U.S. uses thereof, and also because failure by other countries to adopt such regulations could put entities subject to U.S. regulation at a competitive disadvantage and would encourage attempts to avoid U.S. regulations. In order to achieve this objective the bills should be changed in two ways. First, some bills contain reciprocity provisions which provide that licenses issued by states which recognize U.S. claims will be recognized by the U.S. (see Section 16 of H.R. 11879). Those provisions should

be changed so that reciprocity would apply only if the reciprocating state also has adequate environmental controls. Second, the legislation should encourage the U.S. Executive branch to make a special effort to assist other governments in their environmental activities; there are a variety of ways in which that could be done, e.g., by including those governments in our environmental impact statement process, by including them in our environmental research, etc.

10. *Liability.*—The bills do not set forth whether and to what extent deepsea mining operators would be liable for pollution damage, nor the means of recovery. The bills should provide that the license should be subject to absolute liability for pollution damage and the Executive branch should be authorized to establish a liability scheme ensuring that claims for all damage will be paid.

11. *Emergency authority.*—Licenses can be revoked, under Section 5(c), for willful, substantial failure to comply with the provisions of the Act or with any regulation promulgated thereunder; however, the revoking authority must provide written notice and the actual revocation may take some time. While it is certainly generally desirable to give the licensee an opportunity to have his case heard, the responsible government agency should have emergency authority either to revoke or suspend a license if the operation is posing an unreasonable threat to the integrity of the marine environment and if the danger is sufficiently imminent and large-scale so that immediate action is necessary.

12. *Review of government inaction.*—Federal courts should have jurisdiction to review any violation of the legislation, including illegal inaction or arbitrary action by government agencies, and a citizen civil action provision should entitle any person to institute such a suit, with attorneys' fees awarded to a prevailing plaintiff.

Thank you, Mr. Chairman.

Mr. FRANK. I appear today on behalf of six environmental groups, the Environmental Defense Fund, the Environmental Policy Center, the Friends of the Earth, the National Audubon Society, the National Resource Defense Council, and the Sierra Club.

These national, nonprofit organizations, with a combined membership of more than 590,000, have long taken an active interest in protecting the marine environment.

When we presented our views to the Congress in the past in connection with deepsea mining legislation, we opposed the passage of legislation for two reasons. We now believe circumstances have changed and therefore, our views have been modified.

We have opposed the passage of legislation first because we believe that international agreement was necessary for international controls on a worldwide basis. It now seems, however, that either through the conference, which will begin next week in New York, or a subsequent conference predicted for the summer, the international community either will or will not have a Law of the Sea treaty and an international regime for deep sea mining.

Under such circumstances it does not appear to us illogical for Congress now to fashion domestic legislation which, in the normal course of events, could be passed at the end of these conferences and which could easily mesh with the international system developed at the conference is the negotiations are successful.

Secondly, during prior testimony, we expressed concern about the absence of environmental impact on deep ocean mining. The situation has not improved substantially. The Department of the Interior and the Department of Commerce have still not undertaken adequate analysis and research.

Nonetheless, we believe that such research and analysis is likely to be spurred by legislation, and the Congress should proceed in spite of the absence of information.

I would like to reiterate this problem at the present time. If this committee is going to consider deep-sea mining legislation, I would hope the committee also would use its influence and pressure to see that the Government undertakes adequate environmental safeguards and adequate analysis.

The Government thus far has proceeded with an uncoordinated program. The Government has been slow in moving forward with research; for instance, the collection of baseline data. Perhaps more disturbing, it has not committed itself to assessing or developing work plans to assess very basic and fundamental issues such as the impact of sea and onshore processing and the comparative impacts of land and ocean mining.

I believe the comparative impacts of land and ocean mining are extremely critical, for if it is shown that ocean mining is environmentally preferable to onland mining, those of us concerned about the marine environment might well want to support ocean mining.

Finally, even in those areas where the Government is undertaking analysis, it is doing so in an informal and haphazard fashion. The industry has indicated, for example, that it is fully prepared in writing to supply the Government with a good deal of information concerning the environmental impact of its activities and its technology; yet the Government has never asked for the information.

Let me now proceed to the bills that are the subject of this hearing and this testimony.

It is our general view that the bills, as drafted, should not be passed. They do not adequately protect the environment. However, subject to the time frame mentioned earlier, we would support passage of the bills, properly modified.

Let me go on to specific comments about provisions in the bills which are now inadequate and should be modified, or to omissions in the bills; and I will suggest some additions in those cases.

Unless I note otherwise, I will be referring to H.R. 11879

First: The assumption that deepsea mining should be promoted—one of the underlying assumptions of the bills is that deepsea mining should be promoted by the United States because of possible future supply needs and in light of other factors relating to the national interest. We do not believe that such a conclusion, at present, could be a reasoned judgment because of the incomplete information on resources need and on environmental impact. The bills should be changed to reflect that many unknowns still exist about resource need, environmental impact, et cetera, and that these must be resolved by the executive branch before taking specific steps outlined in the bills. Section 2(b)(1) of H.R. 11879 states that the purpose of the act is "to establish a national program to promote the orderly development of certain hard mineral resources of the deep seabed." We do not believe that Congress, on the basis of information before it, can state so categorically that development of deep sea mining should be promoted. In section 2(a)(7), it is said that it is in the "national interest of the United States to utilize existing technology and capabilities of U.S. mining companies." No one, including Congress, knows whether existing technology and capabilities are, from an environmental point of view, acceptable; in light of that, Congress should not make a judgment that existing technology should be utilized.

Second: Relationship to environmental impact statement and NEPA—the bills do not adequately express what we believe to be the intent of Congress with respect to the preparation of environmental impact statements and the opportunity for public input. Under section 7, "objective environmental standards" are to be established; under section 19, the responsible government agency is to issue rules and regulations including, inter alia, those related to "environmental standards and compliance"; and under section 5, a decision must be made by the responsible government agency that a prospective licensee will operate in accordance with "guidelines and standards" and that operations under the license will not pose a threat to the marine environment. In our discussions with members of the committee staff, we have been led to believe that it is the intent of Congress that the National Environmental Policy Act should be fully followed but that it was not necessary to so indicate explicitly in the legislation or to indicate when environmental impact statements would be needed. A programmatic environmental impact statement should be prepared before licensing is permitted; regulations should be accompanied by an environmental impact statement; and a project environmental impact statement will be needed before each license can be issued. It would be highly preferable if the legislation spelled this out. Some commentators—the Marine Board Panel of the National Academy of Sciences—have gone further and suggested that regional environmental impact statements should be prepared; we are inclined to believe that regional impact statement may be unnecessary if the programmatic statements and individual project statements are adequate, but that is the type of issue that should be considered by this committee.

Third: Timing and standards for environmental guidelines—the bills state that licenses may only be issued after the responsible government official determines "that operations under the license will not pose an unreasonable threat to the integrity of the marine environment and that all reasonable precautions will be taken to minimize any adverse effects in that environment." First, as noted earlier, environmental guidelines and standards are to be promulgated. It should be explicitly stated that no license will be issued until the environmental guidelines and standards are prepared. Such an inhibition appears in some bills before Congress, but is not stated in H.R. 6017 or H.R. 11879. Second, the bills should set forth, as the underlying standard for environmental guidelines, a best-available-technology requirement.

Fourth: Prototype or pilot project testing—It has been generally agreed by industry, the scientific community, the executive branch, and the environmental community, that the full implications of a major deep sea mining program will not be understood until we have been able to monitor and analyze the impacts of a few mining operations. We believe, therefore, it is essential that licensing should proceed cautiously and be limited to prototype and pilot projects in the first instance. It would be understood that earlier determinations regarding environmental standards can and will be modified as more information becomes available as a result of the projects and that continued monitoring will occur. These bills do not suggest proceeding with prototype or pilot projects, in the first instance, and they should be changed to state such policy.

Fifth: EPA responsible for environmental standards and enforcement—H.R. 6017 places most of the executive branch authority in the Department of the Interior. H.R. 11879 places that responsibility in the Department of Commerce. Two types of responsibility are included, one oriented toward promotion of deep seabed mining and economic regulation, and the other toward environmental standard setting and enforcement.

Environmental protection can be assured only if the same agency is not assigned the responsibility both of promotion and also of environmental regulation. Such dual and some cross-purpose jurisdiction represents an inevitable, potential conflict of interest and results in nonobjective decisionmaking, benefiting those who favor development and harming the national interest.

The agency best suited for environmental standard-setting and enforcement duties of the type in question is the Environmental Protection Agency, which has responsibilities of this nature in various other areas. Without answering whether the Department of the Interior or the Department of Commerce should be seized with any regulatory or promotional functions, the Environmental Protection Agency should have jurisdiction for environmental regulations. The approval of two agencies would thus be required before issuance of a license. The EPA would determine whether the applicant complies with environmental standards, and the other agency would determine perhaps the economic or royalty considerations.

Sixth: Scope of regulation—It is our understanding that the intent of Congress in these bills is that all aspects of deep sea mining would be regulated. However, the bills speak about authorizing development of hard mineral resources. "Development" is defined in section 3(f) as "any operation of exploration and commercial recovery, other than prospecting for the purpose of discovery, recovery, or delivery of hard minerals from the deep seabed." One could misinterpret the bills by concluding that authorization is required for, and regulations and standards apply to, only retrieval and not, for example, processing at sea or other such activities.

The bill should be amended explicitly to point out that it covers all activities at sea including retrieval and processing. Furthermore, Congress should consider whether some generic, but perhaps not site-specific, decisions relating to the activities on land, such as onland processing, should also be covered.

Seventh jurisdiction—The jurisdictional provisions of the bills are quite broad but somewhat vague. U.S. companies have already forewarned the Government that if standards by the Government are, in the view of the companies, too high or if other countries have significantly lower standards giving competitive advantages to entities operating under their jurisdiction, U.S. companies would attempt to avoid U.S. controls, and mining vessels might fly foreign-flag and/or they might incorporate abroad subsidiaries or consortia with which they are associated.

But the U.S. has the responsibility to control those companies in such circumstances when the result may be significant adverse environmental impacts in the ocean. And of course if development of U.S. mining industry is in the national interest, control over that industry is in the national interest.

As a consequence, the bills should make clear that they cover U.S. nationals under all circumstances. Jurisdiction should extend to U.S. nationals or subsidiaries of U.S. nations, even when they are operating a vessel flying a foreign flag, and should extend to activities of consortia which can be said to be controlled by U.S. nationals.

Eight, preservation of certain areas—Until recent years, the earth's resources have most often been exploited without regard to the need to preserve at least some wilderness areas in their natural state for observation, study, enjoyment and use by future generations.

It is important that the deep oceans and seabed not suffer for the lack of foresight in this regard. These bills should contain a mandate for the responsible Government agency to identify adequate numbers of ocean blocks to be set aside and made not subject to licensing for exploration or commercial development.

Nine: Relationships with foreign countries and reciprocity—The U.S. has an interest in assuring that other countries adopt adequate environmental regulatory systems, both because the adverse environmental impact of foreign mining vessels will affect the oceans and the U.S. uses thereof, and also because failure by other countries to adopt such regulations could put entities subject to U.S. regulation at a comparative disadvantage and would encourage attempts to avoid U.S. regulations.

In order to achieve this objective the bills should be changed in two ways. First, some bills contain reciprocity provisions which provide that licenses issued by States which recognize U.S. claims will be recognized by the U.S., as in section 16 of H.R. 11879. Those provisions should be changed so that reciprocity would apply only if the reciprocating State also has adequate environmental controls. Second, the legislation should encourage the U.S. executive branch to make a special effort to assist other governments in their environmental activities; there are a variety of ways in which that could be done, e.g., by including those governments in our environmental impact statement process, by including them in our environmental research, et cetera.

Tenth, liability—The bills do not set forth whether and to what extent deepsea mining operators would be liable for pollution damage, nor the means of recovery. The bills should provide that the licensee should be subject to absolute liability for pollution damage and the executive branch should be authorized to establish a liability scheme ensuring that claims for all damage will be paid.

Eleventh, emergency authority—Licenses can be revoked, under section 5(c), for willful, substantial failure to comply with the provisions of the act or with any regulation promulgated thereunder; however, the revoking authority must provide written notice and the actual revocation may take some time. While it is certainly generally desirable to give the licensee an opportunity to have his case heard, the responsible Government agency should have emergency authority either to revoke or suspend a license if the operation is posing on unreasonable threat to the integrity of the marine environment and if the danger is sufficiently imminent and large-scale so that immediate action is necessary.

Twelfth, review of Government inaction—Federal courts should have jurisdiction to review any violation of the legislation, including illegal inaction or arbitrary action by Government agencies, and a citizen civil action provision should entitle any person to institute such a suit, with attorney's fees awarded to a prevailing plaintiff.

Finally, secrecy—We are concerned about the secrecy provisions of the bill. For example, section 6(a) provides that a variety of information provided by the mining companies to the Government will not be made available to the public. For example, under section 6(a), the Government will hold as secret information the location of the site which is the subject of a license application. That means that if the public wants to comment to the Government about the potential environmental impact, it will be operating in the dark. We do not believe that mining companies need to have this element of secrecy. When a mining company applies for a license it has a priority right to the block in question. One mining company has already disclosed information concerning the coordinates of the area where it proposed to mine.

In light of these circumstances, we believe it should be made clear in the bill that all information, including information concerning the location of the mining site, which is necessary to an analysis of the environment will be made available to the Government and also made available to the public.

In this testimony and in our written statement we have expressed our general views on these provisions. We have not provided specific language changes to effect the changes or the additions we believe should be made. We would be happy to do so if you believe, Mr. Congressman, that would be useful.

Thank you, sir.

Mr. OBERSTAR. (presiding). Mr. Forsythe, any more questions or comments?

Mr. FORSYTHE. Thank you, Mr. Chairman.

Mr. Chairman, I do not have any questions, except to compliment the witness on a very broad and really a good statement.

Mr. FRANK. Thank you, sir.

Mr. OBERSTAR. You have covered many of the concerns that were mine at the outset of these hearings, and some of which I expressed in previous questions to the other witnesses.

Do you have confidence in the various international conventions on marine pollution?

Mr. FRANK. I have no confidence in them, sir, and I think a substantial argument can be made that the international regime for deep sea mining, if there is one, will not adequately protect the marine environment.

The 1973 IMCO Convention, which attempted to provide international environmental protection for vessels has not succeeded, and it is possible that adequate protection will not be achieved for deep sea mining in the Law of the Sea Convention. I think domestic legislation will be necessary, whether we have or do not have an international regime, because domestic legislation may be, in fact, the best means to protect the environment.

Mr. OBERSTAR. You have no confidence in the statement if you were here and heard them yesterday from Mr. Maw of the State Department that they would close loopholes that I pointed out in the Single Negotiating Text.

He would close those loopholes by incorporating the various international conventions on pollution of the marine environment.

You would have no confidence in the ability of that action to provide protection.

Mr. FRANK. I do not have confidence that that action will occur, and I do not have confidence if it would occur, it would provide environmental protection. On the contrary, I think it will not.

Mr. OBERSTAR. The best way to provide protection then, in your analysis, is if there is going to be mining of the sea bottom for the United States to write into legislation, that is, the Congress to write into the legislation the adequate environmental safeguards you have enumerated in your testimony.

Mr. FRANK. Yes. I do not think the Congress can focus on specific safeguards, for example, whether a mining operator would use a self-propelled device or not, what degree of scraping of the ocean bottom would be permitted, or what effluent level will be allowed. I do not think it can go into that detail at the present time. I do believe the legislation should provide a norm—the best technology available—and I believe it has to provide other criteria and requirements so the executive branch will have a clear mandate to act and to act in an environmentally sound fashion.

Mr. OBERSTAR. You do not think we have to incorporate by reference NEPA, as you seem to suggest in your testimony?

Mr. FRANK. Some place in the bill or the legislative history it ought to be clear what the intent is, and that is NEPA has to be followed.

Mr. OBERSTAR. Does not NEPA apply whether or not we pass legislation that incorporates it?

Mr. FRANK. Yes, sir, that is right.

However, Mr. Oberstar, the Government has thus far simply failed to follow NEPA in this area. It has prepared one environmental impact on deep seabed mining. That statement has been inadequate. It is not proceeding to prepare another one, although it talks about it. It has not taken the time to analyze what would be required under NEPA, for example, the comparative impact on land mining and ocean mining.

Mr. OBERSTAR. You would be satisfied, if in the committee report on the bill, should there be one, made reference to the committee's concern that all the provisions of NEPA apply to deep seabed mining?

Mr. FRANK. Yes, sir, would you want me to amplify that?

a programmatic impact statement is required as well as project statements for each license application.

Mr. OBERSTAR. Counsel have questions?

Mr. PERIAN. I was interested in your reference to the 1973 IMCO Conference, and the fact that you did characterize it as unsuccessful in terms of tanker construction.

Mr. FRANK. Yes, sir, would want me to amplify that?

Mr. PERIAN. I think you should, because the conference came out precisely with what the United States delegation wanted, a requirement to use segregated ballast tanks.

Mr. FRANK. The United States delegation proposed segregated ballast, and also double bottoms.

Double bottoms were not accepted.

Mr. PERIAN. Double bottoms were not accepted, because they were, by experience and practice, proven to be unsuccessful.

As a matter of fact, it was shown that they were a threat to the environment.

Mr. FRANK. That is a position of the oil and tanker industry.

Mr. PERIAN. That is the position of the countries of Norway, which has used double bottoms, Great Britain, France.

France wanted to have double bottoms excluded because of the fact that they are dangerous, that a double bottom rupture would probably cause a greater spillage of oil into the sea than any other kind of ship construction.

The ship is also unstable.

Mr. FRANK. That is a position which the oil and tanker industry have espoused. They have never been able to demonstrate that is so.

Mr. PERIAN. The Norwegians did. That is why the vote was 23 to 9. I sat there for 6 months.

Mr. FRANK. I do not accept that view.

Mr. PERIAN. The point is, the ship engineers accepted it.

The conference was made up of ship engineers, not people from the oil industry.

Mr. FRANK. Well, it is unclear whether those delegations were representing an oil industry viewpoint.

Mr. PERIAN. I certainly know what the American viewpoint was.

Mr. FRANK. If I can express my view on the subject, it seems to me IMCO has been notorious for accepting what the industry has wanted to accept, and it did so in this instance. There was no evidence whatsoever that the double bottoms, as you say, are unstable. Chemical tankers use double bottoms, and they are not unstable. All chemical tankers do so.

Let us focus for a minute on segregated ballast. I take it there is a general consensus that segregated ballast should be required because of their substantial environmental benefits. However, segregated ballast has not really been accepted by the convention; it is applicable to vessels ordered only after January 1, 1976, and that means perhaps 98 percent of the vessels which will be plying the oceans for the next 30 years will not have segregated ballast, because all those vessels have been ordered.

There are a variety of other things the Conference did not do. It did nothing with respect to maneuverability—lateral thrust, twin screws, or twin propellers were not considered.

In fact, what the 1973 Convention did was accept what the industry had already adopted, and that is load on top, and load on top really had been mandated by an earlier Convention, and was being put into effect by the industry anyway.

I simply think we disagree on the issue, Mr. Perian.

Mr. PERIAN. No; I respectfully disagree with the witness, because I happened to be a member of the delegation, and I was familiar with the plans of the U.S. delegation.

The double bottom issue was raised simply to scare off the oil tanker shipping nations. The Coast Guard had no desire at all to implement the double bottom concept.

The Coast Guard went there hoping to obtain a segregated ballast treaty, and by the use of the bottom double figures, which had been developed by the oil companies, which originally showed that double bottoms could cause, or could prevent leakage in very minor groundings, this information was developed by Exxon, by Mr. Gray of Exxon, and that information was used, in effect, as a ploy against those countries that did now want double bottoms or segregated ballast.

They settled on segregated ballast as a compromise, which is precisely what the American delegation wanted in the first place.

That is precisely what happened at IMCO.

Mr. FRANK. The Coast Guard, before proceeding over to that Conference had issued an advance notice of the proposed rulemaking which would have required double bottoms. The Coast Guard was depending on one report which recommended double bottoms, and the U.S. position at the Conference was that we should advocate double bottoms. I do not know whether that was all fraudulent, whether the Coast Guard did not intend to have double bottoms, but I base all my testimony on that.

I think we will get no place if we argue on the subject.

Mr. OBERSTAR. The subject of the discussion before us today is not double bottoms, or IMCO, or any other such issue, but the deep seabed mining, and the environmental impact.

We will have to stay on that subject, I am afraid.

Mr. PERIAN. There were many comments made in his prepared statement that reflect the attitude that he just conveyed concerning IMCO.

I was trying to indicate that there were other factors that went into the argument the witness made relative to IMCO, and perhaps this same kind of bias was reached on some of the conclusions made in this statement.

For example, on page 11 you say these bills should contain a mandate for the responsible Government agency to identify adequate numbers of ocean blocks to be set aside and made not subject to license and exploration for commercial development.

Could you amplify on that? We have only four companies in the United States who can mine the approximately 4 million square miles of ocean floor between Hawaii and California.

Mr. FRANK. It seems to me one of the purposes of the bill is to identify areas which should be made available for mining. I think one of the objectives of the bill ought to identify areas, which for one reason or another, should not be available to mining. There is so much ocean, I do not think this will create a problem. I do not think it will create a burden on U.S. mining companies, or the mining companies of the other countries.

There are seabed areas where we should not mine, and it may be later found that intensive mining in one area will be adverse to the environmental impact, because it will retard population of the flora and fauna destroyed in that area. Or it may be that we will find that marine mining is not a compatible use with fishing, and therefore, there may be areas of the ocean which should not be mined because of that.

I am just suggesting here that there ought to be those kinds of limitations—limitations which allow the governmental authority to set aside areas of the ocean floor.

I am not sure this position is inconsistent with the industry position. I have discussed this with industry, and they have not objected.

Mr. PERIAN. Well, your statement would indicate that not too much has been done in the way of environmental impact studies.

Are you aware of the fact that NOAA has spent $3 million thus far on environmental impact studies?

Mr. FRANK. I am fully aware of the DOMES I project. I commented on it about three or four times. I have appeared before NOAA informally, and also at its Advisory Committee.

If you wanted me to tell you all the things that are wrong with DOMES I, and the way NOAA is proceeding, I will be happy to do so.

I think you will also find industry telling you what is wrong with DOMES I. Industry has been more critical of what is going on than I am. But I simplified my thoughts in the statement by simply pointing out that there were gross omissions from the plans of the Federal Government to analyze the environmental impact. These include processing. Processing is not being analyzed. The comparative effect of onland and ocean mining is not being considered. I would think it would be to the benefit of the mining industry, at least the ocean mining industry, if that comparative impact were undertaken.

It may well be, for a variety of means, that ocean mining is environmentally preferable. If so, I think we should know that. Congress should know it. Being one concerned with the ecology, I would like to know it, so I could support deep sea mining fully.

Mr. PERIAN. Is it incomplete? How would you characterize it?

Mr. FRANK. I would characterize it as incomplete.

Mr. PERIAN. Would you prefer that another agency perform that function?

Mr. FRANK. I believe the EPA would perform these functions better.

Mr. PERIAN. What about the Department of Interior?

Mr. FRANK. One problem with both the Department of Commerce and the Department of Interior, I think especially the Department of Interior though, is they promote the development of deep sea mining. I am not against that, but I have suggested in the testimony that to allow the same agency to be responsible for promotion and development, and also for environmental standard setting and enforcement represents an inevitable conflict of interest.

If Interior is going to be given promotional functions, and that might be very sensible, I do not think Interior ought also to do environmental standard setting and regulation.

Interior has prepared one environmental impact statement that was inadequate. It has not moved forward with the other environmental analyses required.

An environmental coordinator has been put in the Ocean Mining Administration, and I commend them for that. However, Mr. Perian, in the Department of Interior, OMA has been unsuccessful in moving forward, in obtaining funds for environmental purposes.

Mr. PERIAN. You would prefer that it be conducted by EPA?

Mr. FRANK. Yes, sir.

Mr. PERIAN. Are you satisfied with the way EPA has handled the ocean dumping legislation this committee passed?

Mr. FRANK. Not entirely.

Mr. PERIAN. Are you happy with any Federal agency in terms of the protection of the environment?

Mr. FRANK. Well, I think EPA has done a fine job in many areas. In ocean dumping, they have made some mistakes in their regulations.

My views about agencies are not black and white. Some agencies have expertise in various areas, and my comment about Interior and Commerce can be explained solely on the fact that there is a conflict of interest, and that would pertain to any agency, not just Interior or Commerce.

Mr. OBERSTAR. We have a quorum call on the House floor in process right now, that is, the call of the House.

If counsel has any further questions, I would request he have those submitted to the witness for response in writing, and any questions that Chairman Murphy has, be submitted in writing for the witness to respond to.

The subcommittee will stand adjourned until 2 p.m., this afternoon.

[The following letter was received in response to the above:]

CENTER FOR LAW AND SOCIAL POLICY,
Washington, D.C., March 15, 1976.

Congressman JOHN M. MURPHY,
Chairman, Subcommittee on Oceanography, Committee on Merchant Marine and Fisheries, U.S. House of Representatives, Washington, D.C.

DEAR MR. CHAIRMAN: Following my testimony before your Subcommittee on March 9, 1976, Mr. Ross of your staff presented me with five written questions and indicated that you would appreciate it if I responded to those questions in writing. The questions and answers are listed below. If you have any additional questions or would like further amplification, please let me know.

1. *Question.*—On page 4 of your statement, you suggest a comparative assessment of the environmental impacts of land and ocean based mining operations. How can you carry out a comparative assessment when in many cases the minerals are not available on land in this country?

Answer.—In situations where the minerals are available on land in this country, that is with respect to nickel and copper, a comparative assessment could easily be prepared. As I mentioned earlier, the comparative assessment is important because it would tell the government whether land mining or ocean based mining is environmentally preferable, and therefore the government could make a judgment about which one should be promoted. It is true that the U.S. imports almost all of its manganese. all of its cobalt, a substantial amount of its nickel, and some of its copper. While we would not have all of the factors or all of the information available to make as comprehensive a comparative assessment as would otherwise be the case, a good deal of environmental information concerning mining abroad is available and the government would simply have to do the best it can.

2. *Question.*—If you were to proceed first with prototype or pilot projects as you suggest on page 8 of your statement, how would you determine who should carry out these pilot programs, especially if competition is strong among the various U.S. firms?

Answer.—It now appears that only four U.S. firms are deeply involved with deepsea mining programs, and of these, two are likely to be ready to proceed with pilot projects earlier than the other two. One possibility of making selections for prototype or pilot projects would be to allow each firm to have one such project; that would avoid choosing among firms. In any event, it is essential that the mining companies understand that the environmental standards will be re-analyzed after the results of the prototype or pilot project are known and that environmental standards may be changed as a result.

3. *Question.*—You recommend on page 9 that the Environmental Protection Agency should have jurisdiction for environmental regulation. To your knowledge does EPA have the necessary expertise to carry out this function with respect to deep ocean mining? Or is this function more properly carried out by NOAA?

Answer.—The Environmental Protection Agency is the agency best suited for jurisdiction for environmental regulation. It presently has responsibility for establishing and enforcing standards in connection with a number of similar activities on deepsea mining. For example, the EPA has responsibility for establishing regulations regarding ocean dumping under the Marine Protection, Research, and Sanctuarties Act, 33 U.S.C. §1401 (Supp. 1976) : water effluent standards under the Federal Water Pollution Control Act, 33 U.S.C. §1251 (Supp. 1976) ; and air quality standards under the Clean Air Act, 42 U.S.C. §1857 (1970). In light of this, I believe the EPA will have more expertise at standard-setting and regulation than NOAA. To the extent that the EPA needs personnel who have familiarity with deepsea mining, such personnel could be easily hired just as NOAA hired personnel recently when NOAA was formed. As to whether the function is clearly "no". NOAA is part of the Department of Commerce and the Department of Commerce has a clear industry orientation and bias. The Department of Commerce is interested in promoting deepsea mining and the prosperity of U.S. companies. I have no quarrel with those functions being carried out by a U.S. agency, but I do not believe that an agency with those functions and biases can or should have an environmental regulatory function also.

4. *Question.*—As a lawyer, do you see any international legal problems arising out of your recommendation No. 7 on page 10? Could the U.S. claim jurisdiction over consortia and subsidiaries in foreign countries?

Answer.—The United States can exercise jurisdiction over its nationals, for example, by stating that its nationals, wherever such consortia or subsidiaries may be, must operate in accordance with U.S. law.

Under both U.S. and international law, the United States could control or forbid participation by U.S. nationals in foreign mining operations. Further, if the United States has jurisdiction over a company (either because it is incorporated in, or does business in, the United States), the United States may indirectly control the company's controlled, foreign affiliates, which otherwise have no relationship to the United States, through the jurisdiction over the parent company (restatement (second) of the foreign relations law of the United States, Reporters Note §27, at 78(1965)). In other words, there is no legal inhibition to the United States' legislating at least certain types of control over a foreign deepsea mining subsidiary of a U.S. corporation. Basically, international law and the courts who have applied it, simply pierce the corporate veil. The United States has exercised this power, for example, in regulations promulgated by the Treasury's Office of Foreign Assets Control (31 C.F.R. §500.329 (1955)). The situation with respect to control over consortia is more difficult. No similar international law doctrine allows the United States to control indirectly a foreign parent through the exercise of jurisdiction over a controlled affiliate in the United States. Consortia agreements may simply be arrangements under which U.S. companies, having developed the technology, would mine and foreign partners would be entitled and obligated to take a percentage of the nodules or processed metals. Under such circumstances, the U.S. partner can be said to have control over equipment and retrieval, and the U.S. may regulate at least these activities.

The United States could exercise jurisdiction over its nationals, or subsidiaries of its nationals, who are operating a vessel flying a foreign flag. The country of registration is also entitled to exercise jurisdiction, but often that country is chosen precisely because its standards are lenient and enforcement infrequent. U.S. entities operating vessels flying foreign flags contend that dual jurisdiction could result in conflicting standards and could not be complied with. The U.S. now has arrangements to take control of vessels owned by U.S. nationals, but flying a foreign flag, in periods of national emergency (46 U.S.C. §5252 (1975). Dual jurisdiction which permits higher standards by one country but takes care to avoid conflicting standards is not illogical, and many situations exist where more than one country has enforcement jurisdiction.

5. *Question.*—With respect to your recommendation No. 10 on page 12 regarding liability for pollution damage, who would be able to claim for pollution damage since the mining activities will almost all occur in water depths of 15,000 feet beyond all areas of national jurisdiction?

Answer.—I should think that the normal tort rules with respect to liability should be followed in terms of who can claim damages for injury. While most nodules are found beyond areas of national jurisdiction, damage from deepsea mining, e.g., damage from the plume, will spread and travel far from the area of actual mining. As a consequence, assets, such as fish stocks, within areas of national jurisdiction may be adversely affected. It may be that even in areas outside national jurisdiction, under normal rules of tort law, some parties may have an adequate interest in a resource to obtain recovery, for example, a coastal state in whose territory an androgenous species, e.g., salmon spawns, may have an adequate property interest in the salmon when they migrate to sea, so that if those salmon are damaged the country would have a claim. I do not believe, however, that we need now decide who should be able to claim for pollution damage. I am merely suggesting that we establish some basic rules so that if pollution damage occurs and if a party is entitled to compensation, it is clear that such compensation will be paid and that adequate funds will be available for the payment of compensation. If a mining company does cause pollution damage to the property interest of another party, I believe that the mining company should have absolute liability for all damage, and I believe the law should so indicate. Furthermore, the law should make some arrangement so that injured parties will be assured compensation, e.g., by requiring bonding or insurance or a compensation fund.

Sincerely yours,

RICHARD A. FRANK.

[Whereupon, at 12:07 p.m., the subcommittee recessed, to reconvene at 2 p.m., the same day.]

AFTERNOON SESSION

Mr. MURPHY [presiding]. The subcommittee will please come to order.

We are pleased to have Jonathan I. Charney, associate professor of law, School of Law, Vanderbilt University, as our next witness.

STATEMENT OF JONATHAN I. CHARNEY, ASSOCIATE PROFESSOR OF LAW, SCHOOL OF LAW, VANDERBILT UNIVERSITY

Mr. CHARNEY. Thank you, Mr. Chairman.

I appreciate the opportunity to come before you to present my views on the pending deep sea mining legislation.

I have already submitted to you copies of my written statement.

Mr. MURPHY. Without objection, the entire statement will be printed in the record at this point as though given and you may proceed to summarize.

[The full prepared statement of Mr. Charney follows:]

STATEMENT OF JONATHAN I. CHARNEY

Mr. Chairman and Members of the Committee: I am Jonathan I. Charney, Associate Professor of Law, Vanderbilt University School of Law. I am here to speak in opposition to passage of any deep sea hard mineral mining bill at this time. My opinion is based on nine years of work in the field of the law of the sea within and without the government, my membership on the United States Public Advisory Committee on the Law of the Sea and my attendance at the Caracas and Geneva Sessions of the Law of the Sea Conference. I believe that enactment of this legislation at this time will have serious adverse consequences to the United States' foreign and domestic interests. More particularly, I oppose this legislation for four reasons. First, it will have a detrimental effect on the law of the sea negotiations. Second, it will violate international law. Third, it will encourage activities harmful to the marine environment without requiring offsetting protections. Fourth, its potential cost to the American taxpayer is enormous.

The United States is currently engaged in serious and extensive negotiations with nearly 150 other nations to achieve a multilateral convention on the law of the sea. Our commitment to achieving this objective stems from a recognition of the many benefits that will flow from international cooperative management of the ocean and its resources. In the area of deep seabed mining, it is hoped that the convention will provide a secure political and legal framework for United States investors, while reducing the possibility of military and other confrontations between competing exploiting nations. The net effect will be to guarantee a stable investment climate, which no domestic legislation can achieve.

The last session of the negotiations in Geneva made substantial progress towards a law of the sea convention. The Committee I single negotiating text that was produced has been the focal point of intense negotiations that have taken place over the last few months. The production of that text represented a large step toward conclusion of a satisfactory treaty on the deep seabed. Even that text which has been highly criticized includes a number of provisions which the United States sought. It provides for the entry into force of the deep seabed portion of the treaty at the earliest opportunity, in order to permit the commencement of ocean mining without further delay. Another important provision creates a tribunal to settle disputes arising from seabed mining activities. And, most significantly, the text shows that Committee I does have agreement on the general structure of a regime for the deep seabed and many details. It is no surprise that a number of economic issues are not yet resolved. Since they are central to the negotiations, they must be last to fall into place. Further elaboration of my views on the status of the negotiations are contained in my article "The International Regime for the Deep Seabed: Past Conflicts and Proposals for Progress," published at page one of volume 17 of the *Harvard International Law Journal.* I am submitting a reprint of that article at this time. Only last week this committee heard testimony that significant progress has been made towards agreement on a Committee I text that is is more in line with United States goals. Mr. Leigh Ratiner of the Department of the Interior even submitted the text of a working text on the matter.

In light of this situation, it is clear that the passage of any deep sea mining act now is likely to upset and significantly set back these negotiations. To enact domestic legislation at this point would fly in the face of our commitment to establish an international system for orderly seabed production. Unilateral action could so alienate the bloc of developing nations with which we are negotiating as to cause the United States to become isolated and prevent it from having any significant impact on the treaty produced by the conference.

A serious disruption in one area of the negotiations will upset negotiating alignments throughout the conference. At the very worst, unilateral action could disrupt the Law of the Sea negotiations entirely.

In my view there is little cost in waiting until the conclusion of these negotiations. First, there is much to gain from a successful Law of the Sea Convention. The stabilizing effect of such a convention would produce very valuable political and economic benefits to the United States. Second, the contents of the negotiating texts indicate that the United States will achieve many results that it wants which it cannot get without a convention. One such result is the establishment of the right of transit passage and overflight through more vital international straits than our navy could keep open by force. The third reason why we should not take unilateral action now is based on my opinion that the negotiations will produce a convention that will include a deep sea regime which would provide a secure economic environment the industry seeks. I believe that unilateral action and the consequent reactions by the international community, on the other hand, are likely to produce only instability, which will prevent seabed mining for a long time.

The cost that the mining industry argues makes waiting unsatisfactory is that of delaying development until the negotiations are concluded. My response to this has two parts. First, as I have already noted, unilateral action is likely to produce an equally unstable investment climate that would continue to inhibit development. Second, from a wider perspective, it is clear that the need for these resources is not yet great enough to justify risking the successful outcome of the negotiations and other worldwide interests. Not only is there no present shortage of the metals likely to be produced from seabed mining but effective international cartelization of these metals by developing countries acting alone is highly improbable.

Let me distinguish the two hundred mile fisheries bill from this situation. I opposed passage of the fisheries bill because I believed that it would have a detrimental effect on the law of the sea negotiations. I believe that unilateral enactment of deep sea mining legislation would present even grater risks to the Conference. Unlike the fisheries zone situation, there is as yet no concensus on many of the specifics of a mining regime. Furthermore, the legislation you are considering is not compatible with the present negotiating texts. Although at some point the legislation may become compatible, its injection into the negotiating picture at this time would be viewed as an extreme act. It would necessarily result in a harder and more extreme posture by the Group of 77. Such a scenario would set the negotiations back by years.

In this age of increasing interdependence, it is important for each country to seek to minimize conflict with other nations. This is the purpose of multilateral negotiations, and to further that purpose it becomes crucial for each country to maintain a good faith negotiating stance during the time that negotiations are in progress. At this stage, while deep sea mining is under negotiation, it is inconsistent with our goal of minimizing world conflict to take unilateral action by passage of this bill. In my opinion, it is simply not worth the cost.

I also believe that current international law ought to deter action on this legislation. It is now a universally recognized principle of international law that the deep seabed and its resources are the common heritage of mankind. Some have argued that this situation permits each country to exploit an area of the deep seabed without the explicit consent of the international community. This view assumes that each nation has a possessory interest in a fraction of the whole.

Although arguments exist to support that view I believe that the reverse is true: each nation has a fractional interest in possession of the whole. This distinction is a familiar one on property law; the interest is joint rather than several. Thus, a nation has no right to exploit the deep seabed absent the consent of the community of nations. Division of the deep seabed into mining blocks described by latitude and longitude as proposed in the bills under consideration would be particularly inconsistent with the state of international law. In fact, such a division would be unprecedented in the law of the sea.

If one takes the view, as I do, that international law is judged not so much by a technical legal analysis but rather in a practical examination of what the community of nations understands nations ought to do, then it is clear that there is a tacit understanding of the community of nations that no nation should unilaterally exploit and deplete the nonrenewable resources of the deep seabed without the consent of the other nations. In language that left no room for doubt, the U.N. General Assembly passed a Moratorium Resolution in 1969 declaring that, pending the establishment of an international seabed regime, no state or person should claim or exercise any rights over the resources of the seabed beyond national jurisdiction. Subsequently, all nations of the world, including the United States acted upon that assumption by engaging in negotiations to develop a regime that would provide the consent of nations to resource exploitation of the deep seabed. Furthermore, no nation has engaged in commercial exploitation during this period.

At the close of the Geneva session of the Law of the Sea Conference last May, the President of the Conference issued a warning against any interim unilateral action to commence exploration and exploitation. This warning was in response to the concern expressed by many nations that some states would violate their commitment to negotiate a multilateral seabed treaty. This concern was particularly acute among the developing countries, who fear that the technological lead held by a few developed countries will prevent the developing countries from realizing any significant share of the profits from seabed mining. However, the same fear is shared by virtually all other developed countries, who do not want to see the United States take the lead in seabed mining.

Although none of the facts that I have just referred to individually creates international law, in my view the net result of this history indicates that the community of nations believes that the United States ought not authorize deep seabed mining, particularly during the pendancy of negotiations. Whether the applicable international law on the subject is a prohibition on deep seabed mining per se or a prohibition from frustrating the conduct of active international negotiations aimed at resolving an international dispute is academic. The important fact to consider is that failure to abide by the obligation is likely to meet with the same community reaction as would follow any other violation of customary international law. It is incumbent on this Committee to take this aspect of international relations into account when considering this legislation.

In addition to creating a risk to the success of the Law of the Sea Conference and a risk of violating international law, the current deep sea mining bills fail to provide adequate protections for preservation of the marine environment. The technology of deep seabed mining is of very recent origin. Neither the mining industry, the scientific community nor the federal government has yet produced satisfactory environmental impact studies which would enable Congress to make a responsible decision as to the permissible scope of mining activity.

From the limited research which has been conducted, it appears that seabed mining will produce a broad spectrum of significant environmental disturbances. These will occur in both phases of the mining cycle: retrieval and processing. A properly detailed analysis of the impact of retrieval operations must address three questions: what is the effect on the ocean floor, the middle layer and the surface?

The ocean floor shelters highly-diversified deep sea fauna, which will inevitably be disturbed as nodules are scraped from the floor and lifted to the surface. The ecological value of these fauna has not yet been established. Some of them, however, have reproductive cycles of two hundred years and, without planned preservation, would rapidly become extinct.[1] Another area for independent study is which mining technique will produce the least overall disruption on the ocean floor.

---

[1] U.S. Dept. of Interior, Draft Environmental Impact Statement Proposed for U.S. Involvement in Law of the Sea Negotiations Governing the Mining of Deep Seabed Hard

The middle layer of the ocean will receive discharges of sediment as the nodules are separated out. A report by the National Academy of Sciences has estimated that a very small scale mining operation of about 5000 tons would produce a daily sedimentary discharge comparable to that of a major river at flood.[2] It will take decades for the sediment to settle down to the ocean bottom.

The major impact of retrieval operations will be felt at the ocean surface. It is possible that discharges of sediment at the surface will disturb the photosynthesis process, impairing the food chain.[3] A similar disruption to the food chain may occur if the discharges discourage the surface feeding of deepsea animals.[4] In addition to these results, scientists have speculated that the relocation of deepsea bacteria and other micro-organisms to the ocean surface may bring them into contact with incompatible surface fauna or even trigger mutant strains harmful to humans working on the surface.[5] Finally, mining operations may cause commercial fishing stocks to migrate or become extinct, which would have severe and worldwide economic consequences.

Most United States deepsea mining companies have expressed a preference for land-based processing, because of the probable financial savings. Whether processing occurs at sea or on land however, similar environmental problems are foreseeable and require study. Approximately 96% of the nodules is waste and will be dumped.[6] Since industry is, for the most part, not interested in the manganese content of the nodules, this mineral will reenter the ocean in huge quantities or produce large land based stockpiles. Toxic reagents used in processing, such as acids and caustics, will also require disposal.

From an environmental standpoint, given the lack of collected data, it is premature for Congress to consider any authorization of deep seabed mining. It is already clear that more stringent controls will be needed than the vague guidelines contained in these bills.

Thus far, the interested mining companies themselves have made the greatest effort to measure the environmental impact of seabed mining. The scientific community has also given the area some attention. Neither group, however, has proceeded beyond an initial analysis of the impact of retrieval operations: the processing phase has been completely overlooked. The most glaring omission in this area is the failure to even identify the problem of waste disposal.

The role of the federal government has been very limited. The State Department, the Commerce Department and the Department of the Interior have conducted preliminary investigations, but have not yet produced the detailed environmental impact statements required by the National Environmental Policy Act of 1969. Although the bills you are considering attempt to provide basic environmental protections, they lack, in addition to evidence of previous environmental assessment, a set of standards and an enforcement mechanism. In particular, no provision for on sight inspection by qualified government agents is included in the bills. Similarly, the bills under discussion, H.R. 6017 and H.R. 11879, make it impossible for private groups interested in protecting the marine environment to comment on whether a license ought to be issued. This situation is due to the fact that section 6(c) of these bills forbid the disclosure of the location of the block to be mined until the license is issued. Obviously, the environmental issues raised by the legislation have not been fully considered.

The fourth reason for my objection to passage of this bill relates to its potential cost to the American taxpayer. The deep sea mining bills under consideration all have a common element: they insure private industry from risks inherent in a commercial enterprise.

. There are two categories of risks that are insured against: loss of investment due to intentional interference with mining operations and loss of investment due to the incompatibility of the regime established by the instant legislation and the international regime. Both protections expose the United States Treasury to large liabilities.

[2] Marine Board Panel on Operational Safety and Marine Mining of the National Academy of Sciences, Mining in the Outer Continental Shelf and in the Deep Ocean (1973) at 100.
[3] Amos, et al, Deep-Ocean Mining: Some Effects of Surface Discharged Deep Water, in Papers from a Conference on Ferromanganese Deposits on the Ocean Floor, O.R. Horn (ed.) 1972).
[4] Dietz, The Sea's Deep Scattering Layers, 207 Scientific American 44 (1962).
[5] Malone, The Possible Occurance of Photosynthetic Microorganisms in Deep Sea Sediments of the North Atlantic, 9 Journal of Phycology 482-88 (1973).
[6] Land-Base Requirements for Deep-Ocean Manganese Nodule Mining by Raymond Kaufman Dee sea Ventures Inc Gloucester Point Vir t ` t n 191

There is no doubt that the international regime will be incompatible with the instant legislation, at least with respect to the fact that the legislation requires no payment of royalties on the minerals produced. It is certain such a payment will be required under the international regime. Thus, it is certain that the international royalties would have to be borne by the United States Treasury. This liability could be enormous particularly due to the fact that every deep sea mining operation licensed by the United States would have a right to make the same claim for compensation. Such a situation would basically entail a direct United States subsidy of deep sea mining.

Direct interference with a mining operation could also require the United States Treasury to pay large amounts of money to the mining companies.

Since the amount of investment is high the potential exposure to the United States Treasury, should an insured event occur, would be in the hundreds of millions or even billions of dollars. In my view, the United States Government ought not assume the risks of private enterprise. Our economic system is based on individual risk taking and no exception should be made here. This is particularly true in light of the amount risked, the significance of the risk involved and the present absence of governmental control of the industry.

Let me make clear that the true nature of the "insurance" or "investment guarantee" provision—the key element in this legislation—is actually a government subsidy. As you know, commercial risks can be insured against by the purchase of insurance. The only value of this legislation to the industry is that the government insurance rates would be lower than private insurance. The difference between the two rates is the amount of subsidy that is being undertaken, not to speak of the virtually limitless fund available in case the insured event occurs. It is sound economic policy that each enterprise should bear the full burden of its costs so that the market can determine which enterprise is most efficient. By subsidizing deep sea mining in this way, the United States will be favoring one method of mineral recovery over others. Before such a step is taken, this fact must be fully realized by the Congress and the public. In my view, the public is not about to subsidize these giant corporations in this new and risky enterprise.

I see no reason why the mistakes made for Lockheed ought to be made for Kennecott Copper, International Nickel and United States Steel and repeated for Lockheed. Furthermore, due to the consortium arrangements, the insurance offered by the United States would also protect against risks assumed by such foreign companies as Union Minière.[7]

In conclusion, as a taxpayer and a citizen, I object to the passage of such an insurance-subsidy provision and believe that on that ground alone the legislation should not be enacted. If one considers the other objections that I have relating to its effect on the negotiations, its likely illegality and the environmental risks, it should be clear beyond doubt that the legislation ought not be enacted.

Mr. Chairman, thank you for this opportunity to speak to the Committee. I hope that my comments have been helpful to you.

Mr. CHARNEY. I should like to summarize and elaborate on aspects of that written statement.

I am associate professor of law at Vanderbilt University School of Law, and I have worked on law of the sea matters for 9 years within and without the Government.

At this time I am a law professor and a member of the U.S. Advisory Committee on the Law of the Sea. I have attended both substantive sessions of the Law of the Sea Conference.

---

[7] Neither Sections 10(b) nor 17 of the two bills under discussion, H.R. 6017 and H.R. 11879, prevent insurance coverage of foreign corporations. Section 10(b) is limited to the prohibitions of Sections 10. Section 17 does not prevent foreign corporations from establishing United States corporations to engage in deep sea mining. In fact, an attempt to forbid foreign corporations from applying for licenses and insurance might violate bilateral treaties that provide for national or most favored nation treatment.

As a result of this work I have come to the conclusion that I have never known a more inopportune time for passage of deep sea mining legislation.

In my view, the law of the sea negotiations are at a pivotal stage.

Last spring's negotiations produced a series of single negotiating texts that moved the negotiations to a stage where mutual accommodations by all participants could result in an acceptable, comprehensive treaty within a very short period of time.

I have written an article on the single text that is found in volume 17 of the "Harvard International Law Journal" which I have submitted along with my statement. It elaborates my views on this single text.

[The document referred to may be found in the files of the subcommittee.]

Mr. CHARNEY. The existence of the single text has caused the pace of the negotiations to increase dramatically.

Last week, Mr. Leigh Ratiner of the Department of the Interior disclosed for the first time that intercessional work had produced new treaty articles. In his testimony to you he indicated the pace of the negotiations had changed significantly and that he had come to believe that a successful conclusion of the negotiations could occur this year.

Mr. Chairman, there is no doubt that these negotiations have entered a very crucial stage. In such a situation, unilateral action by the United States Government to authorize and underwrite deep sea mining, stands a good chance of causing the negotiations to break down.

A collapse or even a significant setback in the Committee I negotiations would send shock waves through the entire Law of the Sea negotiations at a cost to deep sea mining and other Law of the Sea interests.

As I have indicated in my prepared remarks, such unilateral action would be inconsistent with the obligations of the United States. In my view, unilateral action of the kind considered in the bills under discussion would directly injure the very interests of the mining industry that the bills purport to protect.

If one were to analyze the interests of the industry, one would find that the primary interest it has in the creation of a stable, economic climate. Only in that situation can intelligent business decisions be made. The bills under discussion do not assure such a climate,

Mr. Chairman, even the insurance provisions do not fully protect against the risks inherent in the current regime of the deep seabed. In fact, adoption of any of these bills is likely to produce a regime that will be worse and more unstable than that which now exists or is likely to be produced at the Law of the Sea conference. I believe that the reaction of many nations to United States adoption of the Deep Sea Mining bill is likely to be severe and disruptive. More radical nations will be likely to assume control of the group of 77 in Committee I. A deep seabed regime that might be produced in that situation could contain provisions that would be unacceptable to the United States. Although the United States might not become a party to such a treaty, a sufficient number of nations might join it to place the United States in a position that would be in conflict with the vast majority of nations.

In such a situation, I would expect that the risks to industry would be so great that it would either not exploit the deep seabed or do so under the flag of another nation.

The fact that such unpleasant scenarios are possible should sober those that believe the United States unilateral action would produce the necessary stability to assure early deep seabed mining by the United States companies.

In order to hedge against some of the risks of deep seabed mining, the bills would have the United States insure the industry against losses due to interference by other nations or individuals and to guarantee no loss of investment if the legislation is incompatible with the international regime to which the industry must conform.

To put it simply, the bill proposes that the United States taxpayers subsidize Kennecott Copper, International Nickel, United States Steel and Lockheed by guaranteeing that certain risks inherent in private enterprise will not cause a loss of their investment.

The exposure of the American taxpayer under this proposal would be in the hundreds of millions or even billions of dollars. In fact, Mr. Marne Dubs of Kennecott Copper Corp. in a letter to me indicated that in the period of 1975 to 1980 a single company investing in one mine site might spend up to $500 million. Four U.S. corporations might be conducting operations out in the deep seabed during this period. Thus, you are talking about a $2 billion investment which the United States would guarantee under these bills.

In my view, the arguments that the industry has made for such a subsidy—that further delay in development will cause qualified technical teams to be dispersed and that delay will be at the expense of the United States' need for the metals—are insufficient reasons to underwrite these mining companies with U.S. Treasury money. In the first place, the industry should assume the risk of conducting business. If the risk is too high, less risky production ought to be undertaken. Secondly, the supply of the metals is no worse than many nonrenewable resources upon which we rely and no cartelization of these metals is likely.

As I have pointed out in my written comments, the bills under consideration give no more than a passing nod to the protection of the marine environment. Much has to be learned before it is safe to assume that deep seabed mining does not present costs to mankind far in excess of its benefits. The bills make no provision for adequate information gathering or Government inspection of mining operations. The bills do not permit the Government to stop seabed production in emergency situations, nor do they permit sufficient public disclosure of information to permit the public to fully evaluate any proposed deep sea mining.

In conclusion, it is clear to me that this is no time for a deep sea mining bill to be enacted due to the critical posture of the international negotiations, the likelihood that unilateral action would increase the risk of deep sea mining; the fact that the environmental risk of deep sea mining is virtually unexplored and the fact that the bills propose to have the U.S. taxpayer provide an unlimited subsidy to major corporations.

Mr. MURPHY. Thank you, Mr. Charney.

On page 2 of your testimony you state that "no domestic legislation can achieve" a stable investment climate.

Yet, all of the industry representatives who have testified before this committee have expressed a desire for enactment of domestic legislation specifically for the purpose of establishing a stable investment climate.

In fact, many felt that there was a good chance of the Law of the Sea negotiations culminating in a treaty which did not establish a climate conducive to investment.

How do you reconcile these differences of opinion?

Mr. CHARNEY. In the first instance, if the industry was given the insurance that you propose, the risk to it would be significantly lessened such that it might be willing to take the chances that it is not presently willing to take. Second, we do not agree on what the reaction to United States unilateral action will be.

My opinion, as expressed in my statement and in my article, is that the reaction of the world community will be severe and adverse, and that this will result in such an unstable situation that the industry would not be able to successfully exploit the deep seabed.

I would also like to suggest that in today's world there is a great amount of interdependence. There is a need for cooperative action in many areas of international relations, and this is one area where it is needed on all sides.

Mr. MURPHY. Well, do you think there is any parallel between deep ocean mining and the space exploration?

I did not see any great adverse reaction to the United States going to outer space with the technology and the ability to do that from undeveloped countries.

Mr. CHARNEY. I think that the situation is different. Outer space exploration began well before the developing countries organized and saw themselves as a political power in the world.

Second, at the time outer space law originated there were no expressed views of any nations of the world as to what the legal regime in space should be.

In the case of the deep seabed we have had for many years much talk about what ought to be done on the deep seabed. This has occurred before the commencement of deep sea exploration.

There is the generally accepted view that the resources of the deep seabed are the common heritage of mankind and in my opinion, it is accepted among the community of nations that the exploitation of the deep seabed ought not take place absent the agreement of nations as to how this should be conducted.

That difference in history makes a dramatic difference as to how we ought to proceed in the deep seabed as contrasted with outer space.

Mr. MURPHY. On page 2 of your statement, you assert that the Geneva session of the conference made "substantial progress towards a Law of the Sea Convention."

You state that the production of the Committee I text represented a large step toward conclusion of a satisfactory treaty on the deep seabed.

From what point of view are these texts seen as "progress" and "satisfactory"?

Mr. CHARNEY. That was the subject of my article in the "Harvard International Law Journal," and it is elaborated there.

Let me capsulize it for you.

Mr. MURPHY. The U.S. delegation called that session an unmitigated disaster.

Mr. CHARNEY. Yes, and that would be a very wise tactic to at tain the goals it seeks. I'm not criticizing that tactic. What I am saying is, that despite the many problems with the text, there is an indication of substantial agreement on many aspects of the deep sea mining regime.

In particular, and as I pointed out in the article, the United States did not criticize the Pinto II Text as strongly.

If you look at both of those texts, you will see that there is virtually complete agreement on the organs of the deep seabed regime, that there is an assembly, a council, commission, secretariat, enterprise, tribunal. Many of the technical provisions that are identical in both texts are acceptable to the United States, many of the articles which deal with the jurisdiction of the organs of the authority, the basic principles and procedures as to how the regime should be conducted, are acceptable to the United States. Yet there are significant economic issues still to be negotiated.

I am not underestimating the importance of that issue. However, that is what the United States was addressing when it criticized the text, not the entire text.

As I see it the nine articles that Mr. Ratiner gave to you last week show that there is movement through amendment of the single text. They are not rewriting it wholesale, rather they are amending it to reflect positions that are in conformity with the United States position. Thus we do have a working document that can be negotiated.

Before this time there had been no such working document and everything was unsettled.

That is the reason I have concluded that there has been significant movement and that the end of the negotiations is near.

Mr. MURPHY. What is your basis for saying, at the bottom of page 3, that at the very worst unilateral action could disrupt the Law of the Sea negotiations in time?

Mr. CHARNEY. Throughout the history of the negotiations the work of all three committees, Committees I, II and III as well as the disputes' settlement issue has been viewed as a package deal.

Mr. Chairman, it is interrelated. Movement on one issue has and will affect the others, alinements in one committee has and will affect alinements in other committees.

As an example, we saw in Caracas some failure of movement in Committee I. It held back the movement in the rest of the committees in Geneva. The same situation might occur in New York this spring if there is not movement in one committee. If we take unilateral action, and if the United States disrupts Committee I negotiations in the other areas will be disrupted; we may lose such vital negotiating objectives as transit through and over international straits, or limitations on the economic zone.

They are all tied together.

Mr. MURPHY. Mr. Downing?

Mr. DOWNING. Thank you very much, Mr. Chairman.

Professor, I happen to disagree with you. However, you have well expressed your point of view.

I disagree with you when you say substantial progress is being made by the Law of the Sea Conference.

I was at Geneva and I agree with the chairman that that was an unmitigated disaster. And although I did not attend Caracas, I saw nothing there that would give me any hope.

I also tend to think that if we took this unilateral action, it would serve as a catalyst more than a deterrent to get these nations together.

I know at Geneva we had just introduced the 200-mile fishing limit bill, and one of the members on the floor during the debate made reference to the fact that the United States had already introduced legislation and, that if the law of the sea did not get going and come to some resolution, the States would take unilateral action.

To that extent I would think it would be a catalyst.

I take it that you disagree with me on that.

Mr. CHARNEY. I agree in part and disagree in part.

I agree with your statement, and particularly with Mr. Levering's statement this morning, that the fact that this legislation is pending may act as a catalyst to cause the developing nations and other nations with whom we are negotiating to fear that we will take unilateral action and be more interested in reaching a compromise.

The problem is overkill. If we actually take this unilateral action, we may go too far and cause too great a reaction within the negotiations, the reaction will not be, and this is what I fear more accommodation, rather there would be radicalization of the negotiations.

At this point my reading of the new text that Mr. Ratiner disclosed last week indicates that the radicals are not in control, that there is movement toward accommodation, and that both sides have indicated the willingness to negotiate and not to negotiate on the basis of rhetoric.

Mr. DOWNING. Are you including the Group of 77?

Mr. CHARNEY. In what?

Mr. DOWNING. In this rationalization.

Mr. CHARNEY. Yes, I think the Group of 77 is not a monolithic organization that is only controlled by Algeria and some other radical nations.

Its leadership changes, its policies change, and I think we are seeing that in Committee I.

For instance, let me give you an example. In Caracas article 22 was discussed by the Group of 77. The "77" made it clear that one thing that must be in this article is that it provide for "direct and effective" control of the authority over all exploitation of the deep seabed. It was. a formal decision voted on by the Group of 77. The signal was that it was nonnegotiable. If you look at the text Mr. Ratiner showed you last week, for some strange reason, despite all the rhetoric in Caracas, that language is absent.

I consider the absence of that language significant. This indicates to me that they are willing to be moderate, to remove some of the rhetoric and to consider the hard economic issues that the United States wants to negotiate.

Now, when people are backtracking one thing you do not do is up the ante too high. If you do you might blow the negotiations.

Mr. DOWNING. Thank you very much.

Mr. MURPHY. Mr. Forsythe?

Mr. FORSYTHE. Thank you, Mr. Chairman.

It has been said and I think there seems to be some feeling that the last chance to really pull this together will occur this year; that is, this spring, and this summer, as far as the Law of the Sea.

My question is: Do you agree with that assessment?

Mr. CHARNEY. I believe that would be true, but I will not state it that categorically.

I believe that, yes, the will to negotiate, the willingness of all nations—particularly the developing nations that do not have much money to spend on this—to continually send delegates to conferences on the law of the sea is about to be exhausted, and that this summer may be the last opportunity. However, I cannot predict that with complete certainty.

Mr. FORSYTHE. I guess prediction in any of this area is not with complete certainty.

Do you suppose in this very session ending May 15, or thereabouts, that we really should get a pretty strong signal as to which way this is going, whether negotiations are going to be fruitful, or whether we are still at ground zero?

Mr. CHARNEY. You have two levels.

I would fully expect in the beginning, and maybe throughout New York, the rhetoric may still be there. There will be criticism of the single text. As you know, nations have to make a record.

There will be behind that in the backrooms real negotiation. The real test is whether there will be a summer session. If a summer session is planned it will be an indication that there has been significant progress and that the negotiations are well on the road to success.

We are not going to get a single text at the end of the conference accompanied by the Conference President's statement that we are at the threshold of agreement, that everybody is very happy, and that we are going to go to Geneva and wrap it up. The signal is not likely to be that clear.

If there is no summer session scheduled, I guess I would agree with you that we are in deep trouble, but if there is going to be a summer session, that is a good signal we are getting very close.

Mr. FORSYTHE. One way or another we are going to have a far better idea by May 15 than we do today.

Mr. CHARNEY. Definitely.

Mr. FORSYTHE. As you say, if there is no further session this year a pretty normal indication is that the game is pretty much up so far as this current conference.

Mr. CHARNEY. You're probably right.

Mr. FORSYTHE. On page 11 of your statement at the bottom of the page you refer to the deep sea mining bills under consideration, that they insure private risk inherent in commercial operations.

Can you expand on that, the type of risk, and be more specific?

This is a question I had for one of the industry witnesses and they assured me that definitely was not what they sought nor what they intended.

Mr. CHARNEY. One of the risks that is being insured in these bills is interference by other people or nations that would cause a loss of investment which cannot be recovered in the courts. I am certain that uninsured losses occur all the time to industry. Why should we insure these companies in the ocean when they are not insured in even domestic situations?

Radicals can and do cause damage to domestic corporations. The fact that it might occur on the high seas is also a business risk.

Mr. FORSYTHE. I am not sure that I fully agree nor feel that fully discloses the difference in the risk.

Take so far as commercial enterprise within the protection of our laws and the Constitution and so forth, yes, there are commercial risks, obviously, but I am trying to really pinpoint what the difference is that we are talking about.

Mr. CHARNEY. Let us talk about the specific situation. It is feared that an opposition country would go to the deep sea mining ship and sabotage it.

Could this not occur in the United States or be inflicted upon other ships on the high seas?

It could.

Mr. FORSYTHE. I think it is an insurable risk in the United States.

Mr. CHARNEY. Then it should be insured.

If it is an insurable risk in the United States, it should be insurable on the high seas.

To the extent that private insurance is not willing to underwrite this, there is no reason for the industry to go out and conduct the activity.

Why should the United States underwrite this very high risk?

Mr. FORSYTHE. That comes more to it, but what this is doing is carrying on a noninsurable risk in the commercial market, and we should not protect anybody, according to you.

Mr. CHARNEY. It is noninsurable because the risk of the occurrence is high, and secondly, the amount of loss possible is extremely high.

As I pointed out, we are talking about exposing billions of dollars to insure the fact that there will be deep sea mining. The question then comes down to: do we need the metals so desperately, particularly in the short term?

That is where we have to start balancing the interests.

Does the United States need these minerals so desperately that we are willing to subsidize, that is, give preferential insurance to these corporations.

We have to look at the minerals likely to be produced. If you look at it—and we all know there are differences of opinion on this—you will find that there is substantial authority to support my view that the shortage that the industry talks about is not sufficient to demand the subsidy.

Now, we know that copper is the pacing metal in the deep sea mining activities, and if we look at the short-term situation in copper, we know that right now there is a glut on the market in copper. The price of copper has dropped.

If we look at the medium term, say 3 to 10 years, what is the situation with copper there? You have got to take a look to see what the United States imports of copper are.

The February 20 issue of *Science* magazine has a very interesting series of articles that is relevant to this question. It shows that our dependency on foreign copper sources is 18 percent. We therefore produce domestically 82 percent of our copper.

What are our sources?

Our major sources are Canada, Peru, Chile, and South Africa.

Two or three of those are, shall we say, friendly countries. Are we afraid we might be cut off in the medium term period? The answer is very unlikely. What about the long term? Do we need to do this to protect long term interests? It is said that we have got to get deep sea mining on line right now, to avoid a shortage that is coming. In fact, the issue there is not that we are going to run out of copper. We are not going to run out of copper, rather at most, copper is going to get very expensive. If so, we could even switch to alternative metals, if necessary.

Let us look at the statistics on the United States reserves of copper in 1974. Based on 1974 production rates these reserves will last 57 years without any new discoveries. In fact we know that new discoveries of copper occur all the time. Thus, the United States production potential is greater than that. New discoveries occur when the industry exhausts present reserves and needs to find others in order to continue to mine. Thus, we have a long time to wait until the situation gets critical.

What I have tried to demonstrate here is that the need for copper is not so severe that we do not have to go out and risk exposing the American taxpayer to large amounts of liability.

Mr. FORSYTHE. The same situation does not pertain in exactly the same way, at least to cobalt and nickel.

Our dependence is far greater on those two metals.

Mr. CHARNEY. Our dependency is greater in cobalt and nickel, I agree.

In case of cobalt, the studies showed that just a small amount of production in the deep seabed will not only supply all our needs, but probably disrupt the international commodity of cobalt drastically because cobalt will be produced at such a great rate.

With respect to nickel, apparently the United States nickel reserves are not even in the process of being developed right now. I am referring to the February 20th edition of *Science* magazine, page 713. In an aticle by Mr. Ralph Kirby of the U.S. Bureau of Mines it is said that there are nickel reserves that are not even being developed.

In my view, if we are in such desperate need for nickel maybe we should first develop our own nickel reserves, before we start going out and developing the deep seabed and disrupting the Law of the Sea negotiations and upsetting international relations.

Mr. FORSYTHE. Should we not be proceeding, though, with planning, so that in the medium or long-term we are not in position of having a cartel to go back and discuss the reserves. I think probably on copper, which are substantial, but to just not move, it seems to me, we would have a great risk, because if this were to move the time frame is out probably 5 to 10 years if they are either moving under unilateral action where feasible, or if it were to happen in the Law of the Sea, if it would prove acceptable coupled with the statement that I think you agree generally that at least the existence of these bills, the existence of these hearings, is having probably a salutary effect in keeping our feet to the fire, so to speak, so far as the Law of the Sea is concerned.

With all of those considerations, is it not really important that we do not look forward to keep movement going in this field, both as to procedures on these bills and looking forward to what might be fitting even if there is a Law of the Sea adopted?

Mr. CHARNEY. I fully agree, we should be planning for all eventualities and we need to consider legislation for two reasons; first, to conduct mining if an international convention does not come into being and we decide that it is worthwhile to go forward. Secondly, even if there is an international regime, perhaps there will be a need for domestic legislation to regulate the deep sea mining that is conducted under our sponsorship. Mr. Frank spoke of the environmental problems that should be taken into consideration.

With respect to the international cartel, I take the position that international cartelization of these metals is very unlikely. Studies that have been conducted and statements that have been made by many people indicate that oil is relatively unique and it is not likely that we will see international cartelization of these metals. I refer you to a number of statements and in particular one by Edward R. Fried, "International Trade and Raw Materials Myths and Realities." Mr. Fried is a senior fellow at Brookings Institution. His article on page 644 of the February edition of *Science* magazine shows that cartelization of these metals is not likely to occur. In addition, in my "Harvard International Law Journal" article on page 48 I cite the statement of Frank Zarb, of the Federal Energy Office, stating cartelization of these metals is unlikely. I also cite a statement of Simon D. Strauss in Business Week of June 1975, all indicating cartelization of these metals is a bogeyman.

Mr. OBERSTAR [presiding]. Well, Mr. Charney, I hope the bogeyman does not come back to haunt you are me or anyone else on this committee, or on the negotiating team.

Coming back to a question Mr. Forsythe raised and which you responding to relating to insurance, I think there is a substantial difference in what happens to a company dealing in the continent of the United States and one that is conducting its affairs on the high seas.

Now, a substantial difference between the highly hypothetical question you raised that would be realistic only in time of way that sabotage by a foreign government against the company doing business in the United States, I think there is a substantial difference between an operation at sea and an operation in the United States.

And the rationale, it would seem to me, for any U.S. insurance for at-sea operation would be that this activity is in the national interest.

Mr. CHARNEY. Rather than insuring them why do we not guarantee that our naval forces will protect them?

Mr. OBERSTAR. Insurance or guarantees of naval protection or military protection of whatever kind it may be, but some activity on the part of the United States.

Furthermore, there is a parallel of sorts to this kind of activity in the Water Pollution Control Act, where we do limit liability to the amount that is insurable.

We could, for instance, provide in the legislation that Federal insurance be available only if private insurance is not capable of responding or is not available on reasonable terms or if it is not in the normal course of business to insure this kind of activity.

What would your reaction be to that?

Mr. CHARNEY. I just wonder how far this ought to go?

Should the government be in the business of covering uninsurable risks across the board?

Mr. OBERSTAR. As far as national interest goes, I think so.

Mr. CHARNEY. Then, we get back to the question of what is the need for these metals. Is the need so great and the risk of cartelization so great that we have got to break from tradition? Our tradition is free enterprise.

Mr. OBERSTAR. Where we have only one firm in the United States, that is, in the continental United States, producing only 25 million pounds of nickel a year, less than 20 percent of our consumption, it seems to me we do have a substantial overriding national interest.

Mr. CHARNEY. It is relevant to consider what our alternative sources are and how they can be insured. The question is, why do we have to go to the seabed at this point in time when we might risk critical negotiations? I am saying, before we do that let us explore the alternatives.

Mr. OBERSTAR. Well, let us explore the alternatives on page 2 of your statement where you say the Convention will provide the secure political and legal framework for U.S. investors.

At the bottom of page 2 you state that the Committee I text shows that Committee I does have agreement on the general structure of a regime for the deep seabed.

Is there a general agreement?

Mr. CHARNEY. I said, as the quote indicates, there is general agreement on the general structure of the regime for the deep seabed. On that the answer is yes. We have the organs established. We have the general jurisdiction of the organs established and not subject to significant negotiation.

The crux of the difference is the control of the authority over the actual exploration of the deep seabed and the right of private enterprise to go out there and exploit it.

Now, that is being negotiated at the present time.

Those matters can be negotiated. I suspect with very few wording changes, this could be negotiated. We do have, as I said, agreement on the general structure of the regime, but not on the economic issues. As I indicated in my statement, that will be the last to be resolved.

Mr. OBERSTAR. Those are the essential issues, though?

Mr. CHARNEY. Definitely.

Mr. OBERSTAR. So the structural understanding really will fall apart if you do not have agreement on these substantive issues?

Mr. CHARNEY. True, but you could not wrap up the negotiations until you had agreement on the general structure. At this point we are left with one basic issue to resolve. It is foreseeable that within the time frame we are talking about, this can be negotiated. If we did not have the single text, we would have a lot of negotiating to do before we could get to that economic issue. Now, we are there.

Mr. OBERSTAR. You and many of the witnesses have said passage of legislation at this time would seriously jeopardize the negotiations.

What about the congressional action on legislation in some stage, either committee action or possible scheduling for action with the realistic likelihood of House passage, or even going to that point of House passage?

Does that not put a little pressure on those foreign nations we are negotiating with to come to terms?

Mr. CHARNEY. As I indicated earlier, yes. If it is actually within Congress it will put pressure on the negotiations.

The question is, will we put on too much pressure. At this stage when the negotiations are at a crucial stage, too much pressure may be disastrous.

I fear that if you start moving this bill forward it would upset the course of the negotiations.

Mr. OBERSTAR. And how long is a reasonable time to wait for some resolution on an international basis?

Mr. CHARNEY. I think at the present time you should develop this legislation, get the flaws out of it, and get prepared to move. When the New York session is over, determine whether there is going to be a summer session.

If not, we will then have to take our chances. I will be back here, perhaps, and state my views then.

But if there is going to be a summer session, I would hope that you would wait until the end of the summer session before moving forward.

Mr. OBERSTAR. Do you think there is a climate among the negotiators now that would lead to a settlement on the economic issues in the forthcoming session?

Mr. CHARNEY. Now, the person who knows this better is Mr. Ratiner. He is the negotiator. I am an observer.

Mr. OBERSTAR.. He did not hold too much hope.

Mr. CHARNEY. Reading his text, it gave me hope.

I have received the articles that he put forward, and have had some discussion with him. I have concluded that there has been very significant movement which indicates to me that there is the climate of accommodation.

There has been movement in Committees II and III. The nations are interested in wrapping it up and as a result there is movement in Committee I. If we can keep this seesaw going at a good rate we might come to a level at the end of summer.

Mr. OBERSTAR. Well, we will all be watching and seeing how things go along.

On page 7 and preceding pages, you discuss the United Nations voted moratorium on commercial exploitation and development and you sort of gave us evidence that moratorium is a principle of international law because no nation, as you say, has engaged in commercial exploitation during this period, but is that not due more to the fact that no country other than the United States has the technological capability to engage in this activity?

Mr. CHARNEY. I think we have to understand that it is not the United States, but U.S. corporations that have that technological capability.

Mr. OBERSTAR. They are companies.

The United States has not allowed them to go ahead with this activity.

Mr. CHARNEY. And no other nation has allowed them.

I would assume if another nation thought it was prudent to go forward on deep sea mining and it was a worthwhile investment, it would invite one of these corporations to that country to operate off its shores.

Mr. OBERSTAR. No one needs to invite U.S. Steel and the others.

They can do it on their own, if the United States decides to let them go ahead.

Mr. CHARNEY. If the United States is not of a mind to go ahead, U.S. Steel would find a country that would be of a mind to do so, but apparently neither the corporations nor the countries have a mind to do so.

Mr. OBERSTAR. I do not believe that observation has a real substantial basis in reality.

I do not think that your associate makes it a principle of international law.

Mr. CHARNEY. Let me elaborate on international law.

What I mean is that we should not violate what I say is the principle that we should not go forward with deep sea mining without the consent of nations, particularly during the pendency of the negotiations. That principle, I think, has been shown through the historical facts that I have listed in my statement.

The fact that it is international law or an international opinion really comes from the fact that I expect adverse reaction to the United States unilateral action.

In my opinion, if this unilateral action takes place, we will see the traditional reaction of nations to a traditional violation of international law, and that will be a loss of good will, statements by nations denouncing the actions, perhaps suits in the International

Court of Justice against us; perhaps some adverse action by nations in other areas of international relations to penalize us for breaking this expectation. Perhaps, although of course I do not know whether it actually will occur, there may be the use of force against us. These are the traditional reactions to violations of international law and I think it is reasonable to expect some or one of these would occur.

Mr. OBERSTAR. Chairman Murphy has asked that I submit to you several questions that you may respond to later in writing.

[The questions of Chairman Murphy to Mr. Charney and the answers thereto follow:]

Question. Do you think a legislative body comprised of over 100 less developed, and frequently hostile, countries in addition to the handful of industrialized countries would really be a "secure political and legal framework?"

Answer. It is extremely unlikely that there ever would be a legislative body comprised of over 100 less developed nations that would control the resources of the deep seabed. Under the Pinto II Text and the text that Mr. Ratiner disclosed to you it is clear that the council of the authority exercise control over seabed development within constraints set out in the Convention. That council would be comprised of 36 states and would be balanced in order to assure that there was proper representation of both developed and developing countries. The exact make-up of this council and the voting procedures are to be negotiated in the next sessions of the Conference. I addressed myself to the importance of the voting procedures in the council in my *Harvard International Law Journal* article. With the proper balance of representatives in the council and voting procedures the body that would have jurisdiction over deep seabed resources would present a secure political and legal framework for deep sea mining.

Question. Wouldn't there be a chance of that legislative body taking irrational actions, or actions directed at protecting the land-based producers of minerals at the expense of the industrialized nations which have developed the technology for seabed mining?

Answer. Under the treaty text that Mr. Ratiner disclosed to you there is no chance that the council would be able to take measures that would improperly protect land-based producers. However, it is in the interests of all nations that no nation's economy is unduly disrupted. Procedures should be adopted to make sure that this does not occur through the development of deep sea mining. I believe that a properly balanced regime can be negotiated.

Question. You say that on page 3 "it is clear that the passage of any deep sea mining act now is likely to upset and significantly set back these negotiations." I am not sure that that is "clear".

Answer. From my observations of the Law of the Sea Conference I believe that it is clear although not a certainty.

Question. Isn't it possible that since we have the technology to exploit the minerals of the sea bed, we are actually in a position of great strength at the negotiations and can make greater demands rather than constant concessions, and that by showing a strong position in the Congress, we might actually improve our chances of reaching an acceptable settlement?

Answer. We are only in a position of great strength to the extent that other nations have a strong desire to see seabed development occur at an early stage. Although, many nations agree that deep sea mining has to occur at some time, except for the United States, no nation has taken the position that deep sea mining has to occur very soon. Thus, if we continue to make more and more demands on the negotiations, we are more likely to cause a further hardening of positions on the other side causing delay in the conclusion of a treaty. Such a delay would be at the cost of deep sea mining and perhaps at the interests of the United States. In my opinion the United States has not made any real concession at this Conference up to this time. That is perhaps one reason why the negotiations have not moved as far as they might have moved. In fact, the present United States position is much more conservative than the position it took in 1970.

Question. What is your basis for saying at the bottom of page 3 that "at the very worst, unilateral action could disrupt the Law of the Sea negotiations entirely?"

Answer. I believe that I answered this question already. In summary the negotiations are interrelated. It is accepted that there will be no Law of the Sea agreement unless there is agreement on all major issues in the Conference. The deep seabed is one of the major issues. Unless there is forward movement in that area there will be no movement in the other areas. In my opinion unilateral action by the United States would encourage other nations to condemn the United States and to make greater demands for concessions by the United States. Extended negotiations would be required in order to attempt to bring the negotiations back to the stage at which they are at present. I am recommending that the Committee wait until the end of the next session in New York to see whether a further session is planned this summer. If no session is planned this summer, then serious thought should be given to passage of the legislation. If a summer session is planned, this Committee should wait until the conclusion of that session to review the situation. My belief and hope is that a treaty would be completed by the end of summer session and be signed shortly thereafter. If that does occur, I see no reason why the particular legislation under consideration by this Committee should be passed.

Question. You say on page 4 that you see "little cost in waiting until the conclusion of these negotiations." Are you recommending waiting until a treaty is signed or just until the end of this next session in New York?

Answer. See answer to question 5.

Question. Would you consider the erosion of our current technological lead a "cost" of waiting for a settlement?

Answer. Yes, it is a cost but a relatively minor one, particularly if you would consider the possible adverse impact of passage this legislation would have on the negotiations, and the fact that even with passage of the legislation the United States may not be able to take advantage of this technological lead.

Question. You mention that "the stabilizing effect of such a convention would produce very valuable political and economic benefits to the United States."

Could you explain what these economic benefits might be? I see only benefits to the land-based producers who could curtail production, and to the less-developed countries who could share in the profits of our technology.

Answer. In my opinion efficient seabed production will not occur without a convention on the Law of the Sea that includes a regime for the deep seabed. Only in that situation would it be unlikely that other nations would disrupt deep seabed mining. Thus, only adoption of a convention would assure that the United States would be able to obtain the fruits of deep seabed mining. Most of the developing countries are consumers of the metals to be produced from the deep seabed, thus, they will ultimately favor and encourage deep sea mining in order to obtain the metals from the deep seabed at reasonable cost. As a consequence, there would not be this over-protection of the land-based producers of which you speak.

Question. You state your opinion on page 4, that the "negotiations will produce a convention that will include a deep sea regime which would provide the secure economic environment the industry seeks."

What indications have led you to this opinion?

Answer. The most clear indication that this is likely is found in the treaty text that Mr. Ratiner disclosed to you. In addition to that, I have observed the conduct of the negotiations. It is my opinion that many nations recognize that deep sea mining would not occur without a system that would encourage private enterprise to engage in the mining. Even in the Engo Text, there is a role for private enterprise to engage in deep sea mining.

Question. You say on page 5 that passage of the legislation before this Committee would "necessarily result in a harder and more extreme posture by the Group of 77."

How could their position be any harder or extreme than it is now?

Answer. It would be possible for them to take a position that there is no role for private enterprise and that all activities in the deep seabed must be conducted either by the authority itself or only by developing countries. It is clear from the texts that this is not their position. In fact, their position is far more reasonable than I think the Committee is willing to believe.

Question. You refer on pages 6 and 7 to "universally recognized principle of international law that the deep sea bed and its resources are the common heritage of mankind," and to the U.N. General Assembly's Moratorium Resolution of 1969.

Isn't this resolution just a recommendation because of the nature of the U.N. General Assembly, and now, in fact, a principle of international law?

Answer. I did not state that the General Assembly resolution makes international law. Of course, the General Assembly does not have that power. However, the resolution is some evidence of international law which can be cummulated with other facts to establish an international obligation that we call law. If one would consider the many relevant facts a prima facie case can be made to support a conclusion that this moratorium resolution is an accurate statement of international law.

Question. On page 7 you give as evidence that the U.N. moratorium is a principle of international law the fact that "no nation has engaged in commercial exploitation during this period."

Isn't this due more to the fact that the technology has not existed, than to any "universal recognition" of the Moratorium as a principle of international law?

Answer. I have no doubt that if deep sea mining was permissible under international law, the technology would exist now and would have existed years ago. The reason why the technology has not developed any faster is due to the fact that international law has not permitted deep sea mining either because deep sea mining is forbidden or international relations is in such a state that deep sea mining could not be concluded without great risks to the investor.

Question. Do you know what percentage of marine life is found at water depths of 12–15,000 feet or in the water column above the deep sea?

Answer. No.

Question. Do you know if the Commerce Department's Deep Ocean Mining Environmental Study (DOMES project) has looked into these environmental questions you have brought up?

Answer. I am sure that the DOMES project has looked into many matters. However, the information available to me indicates that they have not conducted adequate and complete studies of the environmental questions necessary to arrive at conclusions on which one can reliably predict that deep sea mining does not present environmental costs far exceeding the value of the resources likely to be produced.

Question. On page 12 of your statement, you seem concerned that the insurance provisions of the bills "basically entail a direct United States subsidy of deep sea mining."

Is this any different from what other governments are doing for their ocean mining industries (UK or Japan), or from what the United States does for other industries (such as shipbuilding)?

Answer. First of all, government subsidies to shipbuilding are distinguishable from the legislation proposed here: most maritime nations subsidize their merchant fleets because of their historically proven national importance. Ocean mining, however, is still a speculative venture, or uncertain economic importance to this country. I refer you to Kominers, Federal Government Aids to Merchant Shipping, 47 Tulane L. Rev. 691 (1973).

I know of no insurance provisions that either the U.K. or Japan have adopted to support their ocean mining industries. The report of the Secretary General on the international economic implications of seabed mining, prepared for the Caracas session of the Conference (A/conf. 62/25), indicates that both the United Kingdom and Japan have given only minimal financial support to their deep sea mining industries. The United Kingdom has offered loans of up to $1.8 million, and Japan has contributed $106,000 for construction of a test plant. However, there may be additional subsidies of which I am unaware. I believe, that subsidy of a private corporation is a bad practice. It should be reserved for use only in cases of severe and vital national needs. As I have shown in my testimony, the need for this resource is not severe and not vital particularly during the time frame in which we are speaking. Even putting aside the resource scarcity issue, the Congress would need to know far more about the economics of the industry before making such a subsidy. Up to this point the industry has produced no detailed information to prove that it actually needs the financial support it seeks for this new venture. There has been no government study of the economics of this industry to verify the industry's claims that are based on allegedly privileged trade secrets. Although the Congress has supported some industries from time to time, I suspect that the record was far more complete than it is in this situation.

Mr. OBERSTAR. Well, realistically, I do not see, given the legislative process, that the Congress is going to enact legislation within the time frame of this Congress.

I think that the purpose of these hearings is to let a signal go forth to the U.S. delegation, and to the other negotiating countries, that the appropriate committees of Congress are deeply concerned with the direction the negotiations have taken, the lack of action on substantive issues, the lack of response to what we consider to be vital to the U.S. interests, and that we are going to proceed with the shaping and the fashioning of legislation that we feel will adequately protect those United States interests, and we are going to move along in the fashion that we feel is most expeditious.

That is the message that we want to convey to our negotiating team, and I think and hope in the course of these hearings we have done so.

We have a vote on the House floor, and if the gentleman from New Jersey, Mr. Forsythe, has no further questions, the meeting will stand adjourned until 10 a.m., Monday morning.

[The following material was supplied for inclusion in the record:]

STATEMENT BY C. THOMAS HOUSEMAN, VICE PRESIDENT, THE CHASE MANHATTAN BANK, N.A.

Mr. Chairman and Members of the Committee, my name is C. Thomas Houseman. I am a Vice President and Technical Director Mining of the Chase Manhattan Bank. My responsibilities include the assessment of Technical and business risks associated with financing of the mining industry. I am a member of the following Professional Associations: American Institute of Mining, Metallurgical and Petroleum Engineers; Mining and Metallurgical Society of America.

I am also a member of the American Mining Congress Committee on Undersea Mineral Resources.

My objective in presenting this statement is to discuss the possible future of undersea mining ventures and the relevance to this financing of proposed U.S. legislation or international agreement. I would like to focus my statement on three key related points. These are:

1. The increasing reliance of mining companies on external debt financing for the development of major projects.

2. The increasing willingness of banks and other financial institutions to provide financing for such projects.

3. The need to eliminate, insofar as possible, speculative elements of risk and to replace them with predictable ranges of variables that can affect the economics of a project.

It is apparent that the timely development of seabed mineral resources can be of considerable importance to the United States. If developed by United States companies, they offer a secure source of metals necessary for our economic prosperity and accompanying benefits to our balance of payments position. There is a degree of urgency in establishing a stable, secure and fair investment climate for American companies to develop these resources. U.S. companies have taken the initiative in prospecting and developing recovery and processing technology. They currently have a technological lead over other countries that have shown an interest in deep sea mining. Public reports indicate that more than one hundred million dollars have been expended by these American companies so far in deep sea mining research. The incentive to sustain a research effort of this financial magnitude can dissipate as the opportunity to put it to productive use recedes into the indefinite future. If these companies are prevented or discouraged from proceeding with a mining program for lack of a secure and stable investment climate, their technological lead and an initial marketing advantage could well be lost.

To help meet investment capital requirements, financial institutions are being called upon more and more to assist mining companies with their financial needs. Recognizing the vital role that minerals play in the economy a number of banks have developed an understanding of the mining industry's business risks and problems. This working relationship between the mining and banking communities is a relatively recent development. It was accepted for many years that mining had a higher degree of risk associated with it than most businesses and could not normally qualify for external debt financing.

This situation has changed noticeably in the last few years, especially with regard to the large, multinational companies and projects with capital costs in the tens and hundreds of millions of dollars. Much of the speculative element has been removed. Obviously, there is still risk, but its nature has changed, and it can be more accurately assessed. Technology has improved to the point where more confidence can be placed in the estimates of ore reserves and production risks. The companies involved have proven qualities of operating and management capability and financial strength. In fact, the element of greatest risk that has arisen in some recent situations has been the uncertainty of future actions of the host country government and the unpredictable financial impact of a change in government policy.

Another change that has come about is that projects of this type now entail capital expenditures beyond the means of individual mining companies to finance out of retained earnings, depreciation, and depletion. Consequently, reliance of these companies on external debt has been increasing markedly over the past several years. To meet this need, a number of commercial banks and other financial institutions have developed special capabilities including their own engineering staffs, and have estabilshed acceptable risk criteria for mineral industry financing.

From the reports of the research effort that has been put into recovery and processing of deep sea manganese nodules, it appears to be a reasonable assumption that one or more projects will be brought to the stage of investment decision in the near future. The minimum capital investment for each project will probably be upwards of three hundred million dollars. In order for a financial institutions to consider participating in such a venture, it will have to stand up under a critical evaluation of risk factors.

The operating company or companies should have proven management and technological capabilities. Based on a complete economic and engineering feasibility study, the project will have to demonstrate a projected cash flow adequate to retire the debt within a reasonable period and provide a sufficient margin for contingencies. The recoverable ore reserves will have to be available in sufficient quantity to cover the payout period with a reasonable cushion of surplus. The technical soundness of the recovery system and metallurgical processing must have been demonstrated by satisfactory pilot operations. The marketability of the products must be assured. Because of the natural hazards involved in ocean operations, major items of equipment will have to be covered by disaster insurance. There will also have to be assurance that the mining operation is compatible with the ocean environment.

The security of the investment must be free from any uncertainties related to the legal status of the venture. If operated under an interim regime, whether national or international in character, the financial and economic viability of the project must be protected against expropriation or changes that may be imposed upon transfer to a permanent regime prior to payback of the project financing. Among the changes that could threaten the financial security of an investment would be reductions in term of permit and size of permit area, reduction in permitted production levels, or increases in taxes or royalty payments.

I am aware that, under existing international law, there is no apparent restriction on any nation, individual, or company undertaking deep seabed mining in their exercise of freedom of the seas. However, in view of the demonstrated desire of the international community to establish control over such activity, the present absence of political sponsorship and security of tenure, in my opinion, constitutes an unacceptable business risk to a financial institution. I would also question the prudence of a Board of Directors of a publicly held company who authorized a major investment in a deepsea mining project at this time.

To sum up, it is my opinion that uncertainty as to the legal and political status of an ocean mining venture will affect its financial security, and that we are at a point in time that this status should be unmistakably defined.

———

LOUISIANA STATE UNIVERSITY,
AGRICULTURAL AND MECHANICAL COLLEGE,
Baton Rouge, La., March 12, 1976.

Hon. JOHN M. MURPHY,
Chairman, Subcommittee on Oceanography, Committee on Merchant Marine and Fisheries, U.S. House of Representatives, Washington, D.C.

DEAR MR. MURPHY: I appreciate your invitation of February 26th for me to testify on March 9 before your Subcommittee on the subject of deep seabed mining. Unfortunately, the press of other commitments made it impossible for me to submit a formal statement and to testify in support of it. However, I do have several views on this important piece of legislation and I would like to submit those views to you in this letter which I request be included in the record of the Subcommittee's hearings.

I have been involved with law of the sea on a nearly full-time professional basis since the seabed question was first raised in 1967 at the United Nations. I have during that period closely followed all developments in the law of the sea negotiations, particularly the legal aspects. Since 1972 I have been a member of the Advisory Committee on the Law of the Sea which serves and advises the National Security Council's Inter-Agency Law of the Sea Task Force. In June–August, 1974, I served as an expert attached to the United States delegation to the Third United Nations Conference on the Law of the Sea in Caracas, and I maintained close contact with the delegates and advisors during the 1975 session of the Conference in Geneva, though not present there.

It is my considered opinion that the Law of the Sea Conference cannot and will not produce a timely, comprehensive, and widely accepted international agreement on the law of the sea in the foreseeable future. It is conceivable that late in 1976 or sometime during 1977 limited agreements will be reached, but it is my view that these accords will not deal with the question of deep seabed mining. The ideological gap between developed and underdeveloped nations on the seabed mining issue is simply too great to be spanned in less than three to five years.

I am also of the opinion that the proper legal characterization of mineral resources lying on the bed of the ocean beyond the limit of a nation's continental shelf jurisdiction is *resnullius.* That is, though the property of no one in their natural state, such resources are subject to ownership vesting in him who first reduces them to his possession. Accordingly, United States citizens and companies are free to mine manganese nodules beyond the limits of legal continental shelf jurisdiction at the present time without regulation save that imposed by their country of nationality.

I am also of the opinion that United Nations General Assembly Resolution 2749, which declared the mineral resources of the deep seabed to be the "common heritage of mankind," is without legal effect. It is common knowledge among international law scholars that U.N. General Assembly Resolutions are not legally binding. It is often asserted, however, that they do create expectations of behavior which it is imprudent to abruptly alter. In view of the 108–0–14 vote in support of Resolution 2749, it is often alleged that this represents an emerging customary international law and that the United States cannot therefore treat the resources as *res nullius,* but rather must await the elaboration of an international regime. I disagree with this formulation. As noted, General Assembly Resolutions are not binding law. Further, Resolution 2749 was supported by the developed nations, including the United States, principally to move the negotiations forward from an impasse. The underdeveloped countries insisted upon adoption of a declaration of principles before they would move to the negotiation of specific treaty articles. The United States and other developed countries attempted to ensure that the wording of Resolution 2749 was sufficiently innocuous that their vote for it would not impair their policy positions or their ability to negotiate a treaty which would serve their national interests. The affirmative votes of the developed countries were, therefore, aimed at moving the negotiations forward, not at declaring a new legal regime for the deep seabed.

Finally, I am of the opinion, contrary to the assertions maintained by the claim of Deepsea Ventures, Inc., that no *exclusive* rights may be obtained under existing international law to mineral deposits beyond the limits of national continental shelf jurisdiction. These resources, as noted above, are *res nullius*, subject to ownership vesting in him who first reduces them to his possession. The mining industry has made it clear, however, that it is important to their willingness to commit large amounts of risk capital for deep seabed mining that some security of tenure over some area of mineral deposits be accorded to them. If for no other reason, then, it seems to me appropriate to enact a deep seabed mining bill in order to ensure that there is no conflict among seabed mining claims made by United States citizens or companies. Further, I think the legislation should be farsighted enough to play a role in the amelioration of conflict between United States mining companies and companies of other nations. In this regard, I believe the legislation enacted should contain a reciprocity clause by which the United States would agree to recognize other nations' citizens' deep seabed mining claims of a particular size and character, provided that the claiming nation enacts deep seabed mining legislation similar to that of the United States. Without further international bureaucracy this could ensure for the foreseeable future the absence of claims leading to conflict.

It is also my view that the United States Government, ought to begin negotiating a multilateral treaty with the dozen or so nations presently possessing deep seabed mining technology or likely to possess it in the near future. There is no reason why such a treaty needs to have Botswana, Bangladesh, or Bolivia as a party. One of the problems with the current law of the sea negotiations is that a wide variety of issues—sometimes involving only two nations, often involving no more than a dozen—are bein negotiated in a forum which requires the assent of 150 nations. This is utter nonsense in my view. Our first and only objective must be to protect United States only two nations, often involving no more than a dozen—are being negotiated with those states directly affected by those interests. This certainly does not include the Group of 77 on the deep seabed mining issue.

I appreciate your consideration of these views. I am at your disposal for consultation or further elaboration should you wish it.

Respectfully submitted,

H. GARY KNIGHT,
Campanile Charities Professor of Marine Resources Law.

(Whereupon, at 3:17 p.m., the Subcommittee recessed, to recon vene at 10 a.m., Monday, March 15, 1976.)

CPSIA information can be obtained at www.ICGtesting.com
Printed in the USA
BVOW05s0756271115

428507BV00010B/26/P